1981

The Gold and the GARBAGE
in MANAGEMENT
THEORIES and
PRESCRIPTIONS

The Gold and the GARBAGE in MANAGEMENT THEORIES and PRESCRIPTIONS

JAMES A. LEE
Ohio University

Ohio University Press
Athens, Ohio

Library of Congress Cataloging in Publication Data

Lee, James A   1922-
The gold and the garbage in management theories and prescriptions.

Includes bibliographical references and indexes.
1. Management.   2.   Organization.   I.   Title.
HD31.L3724   658'.001   80-12758
ISBN 0-8214-0436-9
ISBN 0-8214-0578-0 pbk.

To those managers and students of management who will not accept "Because it's so," "It's written in a book," or "There's scientific proof for it!" for a final answer.

AND

To Meg Greenfield who wrote, "Sooner or later, I have no doubt of it, we are all going to die of terminal social science; and, though the range of possibilities is vast, I suspect it will be as a result of some horrendously wrongheaded government policy that is premised on one of those 'models' . . . which the social scientists turn out like pancakes."*

* *Newsweek*, December 18, 1978, p. 112.

Contents

Preface

THIS book is for anyone who would rather see the pros *and* cons rather than just the pros of management theories, principles and techniques. Most books on management, whether texts or otherwise, are primarily descriptive and prescriptive. They describe, usually in favorable terms, scientific-appearing theories and principles, then explain how one should manage in a manner consistent with these theories. Seldom is the reader given any evidence to suggest that a theory has little to support it, nor is it carefully pointed up that many very successful managers violate various "principles" without penalty.

Any teacher of management knows that many university students (and managers, for that matter) can be sold personally plausible theories as laws. As a matter of fact, the majority of the popular theories in management are particularly attractive to university students and instructors alike (your author included). And therefore, any apparent note of skepticism or agnosticism on the part of the instructor will be considered by many students as "putting down" the textbook and will tend to demotivate the class. A book that offers management theories, principles and techniques along with research results which test or help to assess them would seem to be one way of avoiding putting down the textbook. This book is intended as such a text.

Managers and administrators curious about the evidence supporting or negating the many popular theories should find the book useful. Other managers need to evaluate advice—from inside or outside their organizations—offered to help them solve problems. This advice is almost invariably based upon theory, or purported applicable laws, and such managers need to examine the soundness of these theories or the universality of these underlying principles. These managers should find the assessments of the theories and principles in this book useful for this purpose.

The general plan of the book is to give the reasons why a state of the art-science inventory is needed (Part I), to review the recent historical-scientific foundations of management theory (Part II), to analyze the evidence supporting the most popular of the modern management theories (Parts III and IV), to assess the effectiveness of the more popular programs and prescriptions (Part V), to provide some cases which illustrate companies' attempts to apply various theories and prescriptions (Part VI), and to project the nature of the practice of management in the reasonably foreseeable future (Part VII).

This volume has been made possible primarily through the efforts of researchers who undertook theory validation and reported their results, people such as Fritz Roethlisberger, David McClelland, and E. E. Lawler, to name only a few, and management theorists and philosophers such as Douglas McGregor and Warren Bennis who have continually re-evaluated and reported changes in their theories and philosophies. And, of course, no such book would have been possible without the agnostics and others who were willing to put forth the effort to analyze theory, replicate experiments or painstakingly re-analyze old data for new insights. Such would include Orlando Behling, Alex Carey, Charles Wrege and Amadeo Perroni.

If the material in this book appears particularly critical, it is possibly due to my accumulated reactions over the years to the advocative style with which most books and articles on management theory have been written. Or it could simply be the contrasting nature of this text when set alongside a typical book on management. However, the sources of the support—negative and positive—for the various theories, principles, and techniques have been footnoted so the reader can go to the original material to check on reporting objectivity.

Of all those who helped during the preparation of this book, there are four whose contribution should be explicitly noted: first, my wife Fran, who kept most of the manuscript grammatical and within reasonable readability bounds, second and third, my son Mark and his wife Glynis, who chased all over the Chicago area locating, reproducing and rush-mailing library research materials to me in Saudi Arabia, where I wrote first drafts of the first nine chapters, and finally, Katy Baird, who did much of the final typing as well as a great deal of the tedious work involved in getting the manuscript in final form.

The Gold and the GARBAGE in MANAGEMENT THEORIES and PRESCRIPTIONS

PART I

INTRODUCTION

Management, as it is practiced throughout the world, is not yet a profession. It is not likely to become one until a common body of knowledge and skills is agreed upon as prerequisite to success in the profession.

The "knowledge" available to the student and practitioner appears to be mostly in the form of widely varying prescriptions for appropriate managerial behavior. These prescriptions, in turn, are based on an equal variety of relatively culture-bound theories. The essential problem is simply that ignorance of these theories does not prevent success in management.

This suggests, at the very least, that these theories and prescriptions need to be carefully examined to find out why. Chapter 1 addresses in detail the signs suggesting the need for a stock-taking.

Chapter 1

The Need For Stock-Taking

AN inventory of the effectiveness of the applications of the sciences in the management of organizations is overdue. The sins are unmistakable. Applied behavioral science departments (Organizational Development, etc.) have been dissolved or thinned out and behavioral consultants' billings have been declining. Since this waning movement began before any oil embargo or the inflation-recession conditions of the mid-1970's, it cannot be attributed to economic cutbacks.

Governments have become disgruntled with the lack of agreement among social science advisors such as economists and sociologists on the causes of the ills governments are expected to cure. Some social scientists have begun to shy away from offering bold solutions for social problems since experience with programs based upon cherished theories has become available.

Management Science—the collective quantitative applications—has fared little better. The revolution in decision-making based upon sophisticated quantitative techniques never materialized. Managers, after 25 years, pay little attention to management science. A few organizations such as the U.S. Defense Department suffered severe criticism, partly because of its alleged overdependence on quantitative analyses at the expense of ignoring qualitative analyses. Some critics of the U.S. involvement in Viet Nam, for example, believed that the Ho Chi Minh "spirit" should have been seriously considered, even though it apparently could not be quantified, punched onto IBM cards and treated with operations research techniques.

Signs of the Shortfall in the Literature

Articles and books have been marking the failures of the applications of the social and quantitative sciences in management with greater frequency, even though an organization rarely issues news releases on the gradual abandonment of its formerly highly touted MBO, job enrichment, MIS

5

(Management Information System), laboratory training, OR (Operations Research), and Grid Management programs. Here is a representative sample from the literature:

"Leadership Training—Has it Flopped?" (Fiedler)
"The Hawthorne Studies—A Radical Criticism" (Carey)
Social Sciences as Sorcery (Andreski)
"The Short and Glorious History of Organizational Theory" (Perrow)
"Where It Didn't Pay Off to Be Nice to People" (Time Magazine)
"Have We Lost Our Way in the Management Theory Jungle?" (Urwick)
"Nudeless Disencounter Groups to Promote Insensitivity" (La Fave)
"The Performance Gap in Management Science" (Drucker)
"General Systems Theory—The Promise That Could Not Be Kept" (Thayer)
"Sensitivity Training: Caveat Emptor" (Rogers)

The knowledgeable reader will note among these authors a number of well-known and highly respected writers and researchers in the management field. The signs pointing to the need for stock-taking, however, are by no means limited to the formal management literature.

Unheralded Cases of Failures

Case studies describing failures of behavioral science based on organizational changes, programs, and projects are few for at least two reasons. One, obviously, is simply that companies and consultants are wont to advertise failures. The second, more important for the development of the social sciences, is the reluctance of scientists to seek the knowledge that can be gained from such studies. The literature, scholarly and otherwise, busily documents the launchings of various forms of "humanistic" management approaches. Who in management has not read of program announcements at TRW (Thompson-Ramo-Woolridge) Systems (career development program), Volvo (job enrichment), Union Carbide (Organizational development department and Management by objectives), and the Non-Linear Systems "experiment"? Who has read follow-up accounts of these efforts with enough data for careful analyses of the results? Almost no one. And yet some of these programs were abandoned completely. One almost bankrupted the corporation, and others fell far short of achieving stated goals.

No scientific discipline can afford to ignore the opportunity to learn from its critics and its failures—especially from its failures—least of all fledgling sciences such as psychology, sociology, and anthropology, or if one prefers— the behavioral sciences. The track record of psychology in dealing with individual behavior problems hardly warrants resting on laurels. Sociologists' government based welfare, uplift, and rehabilitation program results certainly suggest more rigorous research work is needed. And the U.S. failures in dealing with the American Indian problem with the best anthropological advice available ought to urge us back to the laboratory and to more field research.

The Growing Twits and Ridicule

Many such programs, and their social science trained proponents, are being increasingly ridiculed, both within the organizations and in print. MBO (Management by Objectives) is referred to by some line managers as "More Bureaucratic Overhead" or "Management by Ozone"—evidently because ozone is powerfully bleaching, poisonous, has an irritating odor, and is used to purify, deodorize, and sterilize. Other humorous forms of criticism are more elaborate. Some, hearteningly, are beginning to come from within the social sciences. Here is a humorous gouge at MBO:

Mr. Grossbucket, manager of the Aces professional basketball team, is talking with Coach Fasbrake of West State U.:

G: I need a new forward, who is your best man?

F: Well, Harry Short gets my highest rating!

G: But he's only 5 feet 2 inches, and weighs 205 pounds—what kind of a basketball player is that?

Achieved His Goal

F: Well, his goal in his three years of eligibility was to be able to run the length of the court without stopping to catch his breath. He reached this goal by the middle of his junior year, and then set a new goal of being able to dribble the ball without fumbling it while running the length of the court. As a senior, he has now achieved this goal. On the basis of his having done all that he set out to do, I have to give him the highest rating.

G: But what about Jim Long? He's 6 feet, 7 inches, runs the hundred in 10 seconds, and has averaged 25 points and 20 rebounds a game. That looks pretty good to me!

F: Negative! Long is way down on the list. He has achieved almost no objective in his entire college playing career. He wanted to average 30 points to a game; he wanted to average 20 rebounds—he's reached neither of these goals. Furthermore, he plays the game just the way the coaching staff tells him it should be played. He has developed skills exactly as the coaches have described them to him. This tolerance for the we-shall-oversee-attitude promoted by the coaches is clearly undesirable. He has to get a low-rating.

G: But Long was picked on the All-Conference and first team and received a number of nominations for All-American—how does this stack up with your rating?

No Common Criterion

F: How can you compare two players on that kind of data? Long played because he
     wanted to acquire some old-fashioned basketball skills; Baachbord played
     because it gave him social status on the campus. How can you compare these two
     players—there's no relevant common criterion for comparison, how can you say
     one man does better than the other? There's so much error in shooting a
     basketball that you can't say a 25-point average is really higher than a 21-point
     average.
        No, if you really want a good man for your pro team you'll pick Harry Short.
     He's the only one who has shown that he can do it all, just like he set out to do.
G: Thanks, I think I'll look elsewhere for help.[1]

Punch magazine, in a piece for Australians called "Let's Not Be Beastly to
the English," offers a fairly widespread view of social science training in this
suggestion.

Many young Englishmen and Englishwomen are trained at universities in so-called
social sciences, which unfit them for making their way in the real world. DO try to
understand their quaint defensive jargon and see if you can help to get them jobs in
coffee bars.[2]

Dr. Lawrence La Fave, in suggesting the need for *In*sensitivity Training
which would "advise encounter groups to criticize each other freely and
remain unperturbed" explained that our sick society needs this protection:
"An employee too sensitive to criticism by his superiors may well develop
ulcers, heart trouble, high blood pressure, drug addiction or alcoholism."
According to the UPI reporter covering the "Science and Humor" section of
the annual meeting of the American Association for the Advancement of
Science, some of the listeners were not at all sure he was kidding.[3]
   One observer, a sociologist apparently quite disgruntled with social science
and its practitioners, went well beyond the noting of failures and suggests that
social scientists *cause* a considerable number of society's ills. Stanislav Andreski asked specifically what benefits are produced by sociology and psychology. He assumed, from reviewing textbooks and training programs, the main
usefulness of psychology was to help people adjust to society with a minimum
of pain and to live in harmony with their companions. He reasoned that
countries or regions where the services of psychologists are widely used, the
relationships between humans should be much better than where such services
are not used or are not available. He further reasoned that in such places
which use the services of psychologists, criminals, drug addicts, and vandals
should be far fewer. The following is his reasoned conclusion: "On this basis
we could infer that the blessed country of harmony and peace is, of course, the
United States; and that it ought to have been becoming more and more so

during the last quarter of a century in step with the growth in numbers of sociologists, psychologists, and political scientists.

It may be objected that this is no argument, that the causation went the other way round, with the increases in drug addiction, crime, divorce, race riots, and other social ills creating the demand for more healers. Maybe; but, even accepting this view, it would still appear that the flood of therapists has produced no improvement. What, however, suggests that they have been stimulating rather than curing the sickness is that the acceleration in the growth of their numbers began before the upturn in the curves of crime and drug addiction."[4]

Andreski's conclusion of causation ignores the possibility of other factors causing both the increase in social scientists and society's ills. It is a perfectly plausible conjecture, using psychological theory, that since psychologists (and surgeons) are merely types of voyeurs—societally acceptable ones, of course—these other causal factors have merely increased the production of *all* types of voyeurs.

More plausible conjectures, however, are not what is needed in the social sciences. Given the rumblings evident in the literature and management circles, social science practitioners need to examine more thoroughly the results of their applications. And, of course, where these results have gone counter to cherished theories or so-called principle, every effort should be made to find out why. Coincidental with such investigations should be an analysis of the origins of these theories and principles. It is just possible that such investigations may reveal that the term "myth" better describes them.

The Viewpoint of Practicing Managers

A 1969 survey of opinions of 302 North American member companies by the National Industrial Conference Board revealed considerable distrust of the behavioral sciences on the part of many "companies." Below is a table from the report showing the frequency with which certain statements were checked in order to determine company views of behavioral science in general:

Almost a third of the responses were clearly negative "comments", and by far the most severe criticism was of behavioral science *research*—180 responses representing 55% of all the negative responses. In describing the "other" responses, the report quotes remarks from companies so responding. Two of these were essentially negative and the third, a mixed response, was by a company's own behavioral scientist. These three comments are given below:

1.   "Personnel manager in a large communications company: "I really do not understand what the term means or includes as it relates to business. And with no compelling need to know, I am not terribly interested."

2.   Canadian firm in the lumber industry: "Behavioral scientists can do useful work in industry, but they need to deal with specific problems of individual enterprises. There

What Respondents Say About The Behavioral Sciences
(Number of times statement is checked)[5]

	Pos.	Neg.
Brings new and valuable insights to management	245	
Is a fad that will pass		1
Is a waste of time and money		3
Needs more developmental research		*180*
Is much ado about nothing		0
Helps management to predict performance	140	
Helps me understand and perform my job better	141	
Is a self-perpetuating pseudoscience		2
Uses too much jargon		69
Is justification for weak or soft management		5
Is often concerned with insignificant problems		42
Adds to productivity and profitability	164	
Should be viewed with a "wait and see" attitude		28
Provides a conceptual framework for practical managing	81	
Applies to some, but not all, work situations	(92)	(92)
Other	(22)	(22)

	Pos.	Neg.
Totals (excluding numbers in parentheses)	771	330
Percentages	70%	30%

(Italics, parentheses, sums, and percentages not in original)

should be less of the attitude that industry is a laboratory for social science experiments. The behavioral scientists also need to use language which industry management can understand. They should be less involved with technical jargon and what too often appear to be lengthy elaborations of the obvious."

3. "Behavioral scientist in a petroleum company: "I am personally convinced that the broad area of the behavioral sciences has much to offer in regard to the practical problems of industry. The industrial psychologist and the human relations specialists have only 'scratched the surface.' During the years to come the quality of the human resources available to industry will set the pace for progress and profits. Managers and supervisors must come to see themselves not only as developers of finished marketable end products, but also as developers of human resources.

It is incumbent on the practitioners in the behavioral sciences to provide effective technology for use in developing human resources. All too often these practitioners have been remiss in that regard. The 'credibility gap' between behavioral theory and practice is a prime responsibility of the behavioral scientists. As a group we have failed to take the steps necessary to implement our theories and research findings in application to the practical problems of day-to-day business. In a very real and literal sense, few behavioral scientists speak the language of business and industry. I see my own role largely as one of an interpreter. I must take tested theory and research findings and interpret them so that they may be understood and appreciated by management. I find that, as rational people, management may be counted on to make appropriate decisions once they have the necessary information in a form they can understand."[6]

Unfortunately, the study report does not tell us *who* in each company completed the questionnaire. The subject quotes "presidents", "insurance executives", "personnel managers", "behavioral scientists", and such sources as "an automobile company states", "one large multinational consumer product firm says", and "according to an office machine firm". The reader is left to assume that if the chief executive did actually receive the form first, he probably passed it on to someone in his organization responsible for personnel administration, organization development, or industrial relations. If this was how the questionnaire got completed, the social or behavioral sciences are in serious trouble in these companies. It is unreasonable to expect people in these companies responsible for the applications of behavioral science to offer many serious criticisms of the field which is the primary basis for their existence.

Apropos to the jargon-mongering complaint of practitioners, at least one social scientist agrees with them. In his latest book, Andreski devotes an entire chapter to "The Smoke Screen of Jargon." In this chapter he offers a formula which expresses the relationship between the character of a jargon-monger and the amount of his verbiage—partly as a spoof on all the pseudo-mathematical models used by social scientists, and partly to offer his opinion of jargon-mongers. His equation is:

$$\frac{A \; (Ambition)}{K \quad (Knowledge)} - 1 = V \; (Verbiage)[7]$$

Anyone interested in a venomous approach to criticizing the social sciences should read other of his chapters, some of which are entitled as follows:

Manipulation Through Description
The Uses of Absurdity
Evasion in the Guise of Objectivity
Hiding Behind Methodology
Quantification as Camouflage
Ideology Underneath Terminology[8]

Western Exports of Dubious Value

Another reason stock-taking is needed is that the West—primarily North America and Western Europe—is exporting behavioral science theories and principles at a very rapid rate. Most of the management textbooks in the new universities of the so-called third world are Western. They contain all the prescriptions now beginning to be partially suspect. Since business and industrial management have been subjects of higher education longer in the U.S. than in other Western countries, U.S. texts are naturally preferred choices in most such countries. Since the U.S. is also in a better position to export professors of management than other countries, their influence in textbook choice is heavy, if for no other reason than that they have vested interests in "pet" texts they have used in the U.S.

These professors are advocating sensitivity training, TA, (Transactional Analysis) MBO, grid management, etc., as partial cures for management problems in developing countries when the evidence supporting such applications in the U.S. is, at best, mixed (see Part V.) Even if it could one day be proven that American managers needed sensitivity training, it does not follow that Ethiopian, Pakistani, or Chilean managers need such training. In countries where a key industrial problem is that supervisors and managers are *too* sensitive to individual requests, complaints, and grievances, sensitivity training can hardly be useful. A professional manager in an oil company in Bangladesh authorized so many one-by-one leaves of absence as to severely cripple his section's performance. He was replaced. It hardly seems possible that sensitivity training would have helped him save his job.

As these countries' managers and administrators gain experience, they will discover what many Western managers are beginning to find. They will wonder how so many attractive theories came to be considered principles. They will also wonder about American professors with U.S. Ph.D. degrees and years of teaching behind them. They will likely also wonder about textbook and journal authors, editors, and consultants. Another American supremacy bubble will burst.

There is no opportunity to prevent this unfortunate, revealing experience. Too many books and too many professors are already involved. There is no reason, however, why Western applied social scientists can't begin a stock-taking. This book is intended as a headlong start in that direction.

The Goals, Assumptions, Methods, and Roles of Science

Before reviewing management's scientific foundations (Part II) and before analyzing the scientific support for popular management theories (Parts III and IV), several definitions and explanations are in order. What is meant by the term *scientific* in this book can be explained in terms of the goals, assumptions, methods, and rules of science.[9]

The Goals of Science

The goals of science are simply *understanding, predicting, and influencing.* Understanding and prediction permit the establishment of expectations which are logical and confirmable. The third goal—influencing—is the essence of *applied science.*

Behavioral science, as it is used in this book and in most management literature, is mainly concerned with research and applications of psychology, sociology, and anthropology in organizational settings.

The Assumptions of Science

The *first* assumption necessary if one is to apply the scientific method is that events and things can be ordered or classified into groups or kinds. This is sometimes referred to as the *assumption of natural kinds.*

The *second* assumption is simply that there is enough stability—absolute or relative—to warrant efforts at predicting. This is the *assumption of permanence.* Since human behavior is one of the least stable appearing events in nature, behavioral science research is one of the more difficult of the research disciplines.

The *third* assumption is that of *determinism*, i.e., that events and objects have causes for their happenings or existence. Most scientific theory is concerned with explaining these causes and how they operate.

The *last* assumption of science is that *humans (scientists, primarily) can be trusted to be reasonably reliable in perceiving, remembering, recording, and reasoning.* Unlike physics or geology, much social science suffers from one of its own principles: perception is functionally selective. If a sociologist and a production manager both view the behavior of an assembly line worker because their descriptions of the worker's behavior are necessary observations to a piece of research, careful account must be taken of their own natural biases. By the same token, examples of problems in operations research texts are often so "sanitized" as to bear little relation to reality. The textbook authors are not particularly interested in the barriers in the real world to the application of their matrices, models or formulae, so they don't see them. Their primary focus is on technique.

Methods of Science

The *first* of the methods of science is labeling or *symbolizing* with words, numbers, etc. Unlike many scientific disciplines, social science labeling spills over into the *second* of the scientific methods: *description*. Description involves the ordering of symbols to make them correspond closely with the actual events themselves. It is easy enough to *label* a behavioral pattern of a foreman, say, as paternalistic or democratic supervision. It is quite another matter to *describe* such behavior using agreed-upon labels or symbols. If a 54 year-old foreman walks up to a young machine operator whose brow is unusually furrowed and asks "What seems to be the trouble, son?" is he using a paternalistic style of supervision? The only reasonable answer to this question is "It all depends."

The *third* of science's methods is *explanation*. Only when *all* the facts relevant to the phenomenon can be logically fitted together, do we have the makings of a theory. An extremely heavy burden is placed upon the scientist here. The scientist must determine all the facts which would be relevant. Suppose a social scientist conducts a paper and pencil "morale" survey in a factory. The survey scoring system yields high morale and low morale scores. So far, the scientist has both symbolized and described employees' responses on pieces of paper. If the employees' morale scores were found to be positively correlated with supervisors' ratings of employee productivity, the scientist is likely to move towards explaining this relationship. If the explanation is stated as theory, the scientist is presumed to have examined *all* possible causes of this relationship. Unfortunately, the scientist all too often stops here and offers a theory that low morale *causes* low productivity. If this theory is popular enough, i.e., espoused—not checked—by others of influence, the scientist or others might begin to label it a *principle* or *law*.

As efforts at "morale raising" bring mixed results, doubts arise in the minds of some social scientists and practitioners. Later research suggests that the causes of high or low productivity or morale are more complex and varied than originally thought; it is suggested that a third or fourth or fifth factor heretofore unconsidered, could be working together causing both the high morale and the high productivity. (See Chapter 7 for detailed discussion of research in this area.)

In development economics, massive error has resulted from economists' failure to consider anything other than quantitative models. Gunnar Myrdal, whose theories guided much post-World War II economic aid to developing countries, spent 10 years in Asia trying to find out why the development models apparently failed. His three-volume book *The Asian Drama*[10] begins with a massive apology for having failed to consider enough variables in developing his economic development models. In *The Asian Drama*, he treats seriously, for the first time, such uninteresting subjects (to an economic modeler) as bribery, religion, education, caste systems, etc. His initial problem was simply that economic development theory was stated before all the facts relevant to the phenomenon of economic development were fitted together.

Rules of Science

Following the rules of science in research in the social sciences is extremely difficult. For example, the *paramount rule* is that *all terms and concepts be clearly defined* in terms of procedures involved in their measurement. If "high morale" is defined as a constellation of answers on a specific questionnaire, the rule is being followed even if the reader may not agree with such a definition. The effect of this disagreement is that the reader will likely reject the researchers' conclusions and generalizations drawn from the study.

A *second rule* requires that *definitive statements must be such that generalizations can be made to other comparable groups*. It does not necessarily follow that the results of research on a New England university freshman psychology class are generalizable to a Mexican-American railroad track repair gang in southern Arizona.

The third rule is that *variables which could possibly contaminate* interpretations of causation *must be controlled*. In the Hawthorne studies the experimental assembly group was put on a special incentive system at the same time working conditions (social and physical) were experimentally manipulated. Conclusions that the causes of increased output were the experimental working conditions were rendered scientifically impossible— even though the researchers reached such conclusions. (Chapter 3 carries an analysis of this historic piece of research in considerable detail.)

It is not unlikely that this rule of science—controlling extraneous variables—is the major obstacle to definitive research in the social sciences. In their eagerness to overcome this serious scientific disadvantage, as compared with the hard sciences, some social scientists either ignore many possible contaminating variables, or they draw their conclusions loudly and add their reservations *sotto voce*. Worse still, the second and third hand versions of such studies rarely carry any of the reservations at all.

The *fourth rule* requires *adequate sampling*. Professor Herzberg's original research sample was made up of accountants and engineers in his initial study of motivation. Considerable criticism was aimed at his generalizations regarding motivation to work of non-engineers and non-accountants. (More details of his research on motivation are given in Chapter 6.)

The *fifth rule* is that the *experiment must be repeatable*. It must be described so that it permits empirical confirmation. In social science it is very unlikely that *any* experiment could be reproduced *exactly* as it was originally performed. For the same reason that controlling all relevant variables (rule 3) is nearly impossible, the establishment of identical human or social conditions is remote. This handicap, more than any other, has led to the "clinical" or "case study" approach among behavioral scientists. Unfortunately, this approach tells us a great deal about the studied person, group or organization, but makes generalizations quite tenous. An example of theory growing out of the clinical approach would be Sigmund Freud's "unconscious mind." To the scientist, however, Freud only contributed a theory based upon insights gained from his extensive clinical experience, personal objectivity, and admitted brilliance. The existence of the unconscious mind as a construct for explaining motives "unknown" to the individual was not really accepted in wide scientific circles until rigorous research verified these phenomena. A parallel in the physical sciences would be Einstein's theories, which, when checked by atomic clocks, etc., led to rewriting physics textbooks and the advent of modern physics. Again, it was a rare, tenacious genius at work adding brilliant insight to insight which led to his theories of relativity. As hardware became available for verifying them, the movement from theory to law began.

In summary, the essential rules of science are the following:

1. Terms and concepts must be clearly defined.
2. Statements of definitions must permit generalizations to other comparable groups.
3. Contaminating variables must be controlled.
4. Sampling must be scientifically adequate.
5. The experiment must be repeatable.

Because much of the remainder of this book involves evaluation of scientific research which purports to support management theory, principles and techniques, a working understanding of these rules of science will be helpful in following these evaluations.

Interpreting Research Results

Every reader has no doubt heard of books with titles such as *How to Lie with Statistics* or *The Numbers Game.* Without suggesting that an interpreter of research studies needs the full protection of material contained in such books, there are a few concepts and techniques which, if understood, would help in evaluating various types of research findings. The material on this and the next few pages is written for the nonsophisticate in statistics and research design to enable him or her to follow various evaluative statements and statistics to be found throughout Parts II, III and IV. Most of this material will be an effort to verbalize the meanings of statistical data, ratios, coefficients, etc. No calculations of these will be included—only what they mean in as plain English as is possible in a discipline fraught with technical terms and Greek symbols. In what follows are some of the more important concepts and techniques:

MEAN. A plain old arithmetic average.

MEDIAN. The middle score or measure in an array. 69 is the median in the following distribution: 74, 72, 71.3, 70, *69*, 67, 66.5, 65, and 64.

CONFIDENCE LEVELS (STATISTICAL SIGNIFICANCE). Special statistical techniques are used to help us decide how much we can trust a given measure or statistic. If we take measures from a control group and from an experimental group, how much confidence have we that the measured differences are real and not chance? Or, if we find a correlation between two sets of variables, what is the likelihood that such a correlation would occur on a chance basis? Convention (arbitrary) in traditional statistics suggests that if such a correlation (or difference) would happen on a chance basis more than five times in a hundred, we shouldn't put too much faith in the relationship (or difference). Another part of the convention is that if such a correlation (or difference) would occur less than once in a hundred times, we can pretty well accept that the two variables do actually co-vary (or are really different). *The confidence level or statistical significance tells us nothing directly about the strength of a relationship or the size of the difference*—only the likelihood of its being real or chance. Researchers use the following various ways to describe confidence levels of their statistics: $(p = < .05)$; $(p = < .01)$; "significant at the 1% or .01 level." Occasionally researchers will report levels of less confidence than these such as $(p = < .10)$ or $(p = < .15)$. Take each of these with a grain of salt because they are saying that their results have a 10-15% chance of being accidental.

STATISTICAL MAGNITUDES. If the differences between two averages can be theoretically shown likely to occur less than once in a hundred comparisons, this tells us nothing about how much the *actual* difference is. In the case of two averages, we are forced to use some common sense. If the average I.Q. difference between a group of foremen and their bosses is six I.Q. points, and it is found to be a statistically significant difference, it means simply this: the differences in I.Q. are *slight, but real and not very likely chance* differences. Another example: If a salesman over a 36-day period averages $650 sales per day and, after sensitivity training, averages $663 sales per day for 36 days, did the training improve his sales? If a researcher claims that this difference is significant at the 5% level, he means only that he has determined that such a difference would occur less than 5% of the time if the experiment were repeated over and over. He is saying nothing about the magnitude of the difference in sales for the two periods—$13 per day additional sales after training. Your common sense is just as good as his in determining that $13 represents a 2%

increase in average daily sales. If you believe that the researcher has controlled all possible other variables affecting sales, you can ascribe this small increase to the training.

MEASURES OF VARIABILITY.   If we know the average I.Q. of the foremen in the example above is, say 105, it tells us nothing about the I.Q. of the dumbest or smartest in the group. For certain research reasons, we sometimes need to know the extent to which these scores varied. The simplest statistic to answer the "dumbest and brightest" question is the *range*. Suppose it is given as 89–134. We know a little more now about the distribution: Low 89, Mean 105 and High 134. If we are still curious about the distribution, we either have to see all the scores or resort to statistical short hand.

One of these short-hand symbols is simply the *average deviation from the mean*. This is figured by finding the difference between each foreman's score and the average score of 105, adding all the differences together, and dividing by the number of foremen. Suppose this is 5.5. We can infer very little from this number. At most we can infer *very roughly* that about half of the scores are within the range of 105 ± 5.5.

There are two other short-hand measures of variability used frequently by researchers, sometimes more because they lend themselves to further statistical treatment than for direct interpretation purposes. The first of these is the *variance:* the average of the *squared* differences from the mean. This is done by finding the difference between each foreman's score and the average score (as above), then squaring each one, adding these together, and dividing by the number of foremen. The second, and far more important, is called the *standard deviation* which is simply the square root of the variance.

This may seem a lot of useless work, squaring and "unsquaring," but there are sound mathematical reasons for such manipulations. When dealing with so-called normal (or similar) distributions, the standard deviation is a very important symbol in statistical short-hand.

THE NORMAL DISTRIBUTION CURVE.   The famous bell-shaped curve represents the distributions of many biological phenomena and events which are functions of human behavior. Many characteristics of this curve are important to researchers. The most important are various measures along the base-line outward from the center or mean. The standard deviation, described above, is one of these dimensions, and the most often used to describe variations in the measures used. The area under the curve from the mean to one standard deviation (either way) encompasses about one-third of a total curve area. From the mean to a vertical line two standard deviations away (either direction) encompasses about 48% of the area. Assuming that a given foreman's I.Q. in the example was measured as 96 or 9 points below the mean of 105, and that the standard deviation was calculated as 9, his score would be one standard deviation below the mean. Without examining the scores one by one and ranking them, we can tell that his score was higher than about 16% of those who took the test and lower than 84% (50% − 34% = 16%; and 50% + 34% = 84%). As you have probably guessed, if a distribution can be assumed to be "normal", we need only the mean and standard deviation to determine its exact nature. This only requires that we know the characteristics of the curve, which can be found in any statistical textbook.

OTHER DISTRIBUTIONS.   There are a number of other distributions (curves) which, for a variety of reasons, are more appropriate for certain statistical uses. Their usefulness is, of course, that their characteristics are mathematically known and measures can be manipulated and related to their particular model dimensions for testing and interpreting data. If you choose, think of them as master patterns to which samples will be compared to see how closely they match or where they fit. The names of some of these other distribution models are as follows: Binomial and related models; Poisson and exponential models; chi-square (X^2); and F - distribution.

NONPARAMETRIC MODELS.   These distribution models, unlike those described above, are designed for data distributions whose boundaries or shapes are unknown or about which no inferences need be made. It is not necessary to make assumptions about the nature of a sample distribution in order to use these methods of testing research findings. In general, nonparametric tests of significances are less powerful than parametric tests, although the amount of the loss depends a great deal upon sample sizes and other sample characteristics.[11]

CORRELATION COEFFICIENT.   This is an index of the intensity of the relationship between two or more variables. The *two-variable* relationship index is usually designated by the term "r." The term "R" is usually used to designate a *multiple correlation* where the relationship between one variable and a weighted mixture of several other variables is examined. A linear relationship is the most often assumed and examined but curvilinear relationships can be examined. An example of a *positive* linear correlational relationship would be the weight in pounds of incoming mail in a post office and the man-hours required to sort it. An example of a high *negative* linear relationship was found between U.S. auto thefts between 1948–1955 and the per capita consumption of chewing tobacco. An example of an obvious *curvilinear* relationship would be the ability to lift (weights) and age over the full life span. An example of a *multiple* correlation might be college grades and a combination of high school grades, scholastic aptitude, and father's income.

CORRELATIONAL STRENGTH OR INTENSITY.   As usually presented in research journals, the correlation coefficient is uninterpretable! The only way to make any sense out of a correlation coefficient is to square it. This will give the percentage of common variance between the two sets of variables. Suppose a statistically significant correlation of + .40 is found between I.Q. and college grades. This means that 16% (.40 squared) of the variance in grades and I.Q. is common. Although it is not strictly accurate, it is sometimes useful for the layman to conceptualize the strength of such a correlation like this: If I know the I.Q.'s of a similar group of students, I can predict their grades 16% better than chance.[12]

REGRESSION ANALYSIS.   In a very general way, regression can be thought of as the use of correlation for prediction purposes. It not only indicates *whether* a relationship exists, but the regression equation estimates how the variables move together. In much research, however, the distinction between the correlation and regression models is more artificial than real.

COMMON SENSE AND RESEARCH INTERPRETATION.   While non-statistical in nature, common sense coupled with a little arithmetic and logic can be very useful in reviewing research data. For example, if you see some figures that don't appear to add up, don't hesitate to check them. W. A. Wallace decided to check some suspicious figures in the famous Kinsey Report on male sexual behavior. He found on one page of the report a reference to the sample size as 12,214 men. On the sample geographic distribution map he counted 427 dots, each of which was noted to represent 50 men sampled. Unfortunately, 427 × 50 equals 21,350—not 12,214! Further, Mr. Wallace found on one page the 30-year-and-under sample given as 11,467 while the next page noted it as 11,985.

Beware of shifting bases for percentage comparisons. In the famous Hawthorne studies (discussed in detail in Chapter 3), the base average output of a group of workers was compared to the average of each worker's *peak* output week during the experiment period. Other faulty comparisons, although rare in research literature today, are prevalent in the journalistic reporting of research results or statistical data. We have all heard that we are safer at work, or in the Navy, Army, or an airplane, than we are at home. Unfortunately the samples from which these statistics were all drawn are not the same as the "general population at home." For example, the annual U.S. *naval* death rate during the Spanish-American War was 9 per 1000 compared to *New York's* 16 per 1000. No one can say, however, that New York is populated by young men who passed a naval physical exam.

Occasionally, research reports will not carry enough data from which conclusions can be drawn. If your common sense tells you that the conclusions are from incomplete or oversimplified data, remain agnostic. *Time* magazine quoted some "sober statistics compiled in recent months by various state authorities" concerning the safety of driving large cars versus small cars. Later in their account, *Time* mentioned that the report also showed that small cars do not get into as many accidents as large cars, making the risks about the same for both.

It is not suggested here that a psychic set of suspicion should be assumed when reviewing research results and conclusions. What is suggested is that we should, as accurately as possible, catalog our incoming knowledge carefully— as incoming opinions, theories, hypotheses, principles, or techniques. When the evidence and reason moves an hypothesis from theory to principle, its category and our actions based on it can be changed.

NOTES

1. Appeared originally in *The Chronicle of Higher Education*, April 10, 1972. Reprinted with permission. Copyright 1972 by Editorial Projects for Education, Inc.
2. *Punch*, March 20–26, 1974, p. 31.
3. *Indianapolis Star*, December 28, 1971, p. 4, col. 1.
4. Stanislav Andreski, *Social Sciences as Sorcery*, (New York, N.Y.: St. Martin's Press, 1972), p. 26.
5. Harold Rush, *Behavioral Science, Concepts and Applications*. Personnel Policy Study No. 216 (New York, N.Y.: The National Industrial Conference Board, Inc., 1969), pp. 59–70.
6. *Ibid.*, pp. 69–70.
7. Andreski, p. 82.
8. *Ibid.*, pp. 32–42; 89–93; 94–107; 108–122; 123–143; 155–173.
9. The general format for these definitions was patterned after portions of a chapter on the nature of science in the following: John B. Miner, *Management Theory*, (New York, N.Y.: The Macmillan Company, 1971), pp. 108–112.
10. Gunnar Myrdal, *The Asian Drama*, I–III (New York, N.Y.: The Twentieth Century Fund, 1968).
11. See the following if interested in more detailed estimates of relative powers of parametric and nonparametric tests: S. Siegel, *Nonparametric Statistics for the Behavioral Sciences*, (New York, N.Y.: McGraw-Hill, 1956).
12. No apology is offered for this less than accurate advice. The reason is simple: The vast majority of students who have had a statistical course in which correlational techniques were taught either have no idea of how to interpret the strength of a correlation or they convert it *directly* to some kind of percentage which is meaningless! While the advice is not an accurate interpretation, it is far, far, more accurate than allowing the gross misconception—usually resulting in gross

overestimation of correlational intensity—to continue. Further, I do not feel it absolutely necessary for all who may read management research reports to be statistical sophisticates.

PART II

SCIENTIFIC FOUNDATIONS

There is no clear beginning of the applications of the sciences to management. One can assume, however, that a crude form of the scientific method has been used since the beginning of recorded management history. Such techniques as man-specifications and job specifications (Varro in 50 B.C.) and assembly line with interchangeable parts (1440 A.D. at the Arsenal of Venice) were no doubt arrived at by some form of experimentation. Other concepts such as delegation (Jethro and Moses) and the use of staff (the Chinese Emperor Yao 2300 B.C.) were likely the result of fairly careful observations of performance under various conditions, although not likely deliberately controlled as in experiments.

Each of the two chapters in this section is focused on the best known modern origins of the applications of the scientific method leading to discoveries in the field of management. In Chapter 2, a brief history will be given of the more significant contributions to what is labeled today "management science." The bulk of the chapter, however, will be concentrated on Frederick Taylor's alleged and actual contributions to management science. Taylor is the best known of the contributors to this stream of management theory, principles and techniques. He is called the father of scientific management both on his tombstone and in virtually all the introductory textbooks. His most popular and influential contributions were therefore selected for a foundation chapter.

For the foundation chapter on applications of social science, the Hawthorne Studies were chosen for analysis. Most of the chapter will be devoted to the very popular portion of these studies carried in almost all introductory management texts—the productivity increases of the relay assemblers.

This chapter will also contain, at the beginning, a pre-Hawthorne history of the significant contributions to the behavioral science stream of management theory, principles, and techniques.

The contributions of both Taylor and Elton Mayo—the latter the guiding social scientist behind the Hawthorne Studies—have come under somewhat severe criticism at various times. These two chapters explore the merits of their work in light of these criticisms. On balance, both emerge more as management philosophers—not scientists. They seem to have been identified with rather unscientific researches which appear to have helped them legitimize and promote their philosophies—philosophies which significantly influenced thinking and subsequent research in both streams of contributions to management thought.

Chapter 2

Taylor and Management Science Foundations

BEFORE Frederick Taylor's period of contribution (1890–1915), much of what is considered basic to modern management education had either been suggested or applied. By 400 B.C. Cyrus had applied the basics of motion study, layout and materials handling.[1] Plato enunciated the principle of work specialization and Cato and Varro, around Caesar's time, were using job descriptions and job specifications.[2] The 14th and 15th centuries saw the introduction of applications of cost accounting, work in process accounts, interchangeability of parts and assembly line techniques. By the mid-nineteenth century, the calculus was well developed and a variety of probability distributions were available. Before the beginning of the 20th century, correlational statistics had been developed. By 1832, Charles Babbage had provided the basic design for the computer which had a memory device, an arithmetic unit, a punch card input system, an external memory storage, and conditional transfer.[3] The work system had evolved from the domestic to "putting out" to the factory system,[4] and the challenges of designing and organizing the work in the factory held Frederick Taylor's interest for most of his career.

FREDERICK W. TAYLOR (1856—1915)

Since Frederick Taylor failed in most of his efforts to apply his "principles of scientific management," it should be instructive to look first at the man himself. This is especially important if one wonders why his principles became an institution and yet he ultimately failed in three of his four management positions.

Taylor was born in 1856 in Philadelphia, Pennsylvania. His mother was an

25

intelligent, outspoken taskmaster, and she provided much of his early education.[5] Taylor's father was wealthy enough to avoid pursuing his law profession. Taylor once described him as a soft and mild mannered gentleman with a "gentleness which is almost that of a woman."[6] After preparation at Exeter and passing Harvard's entrance examinations, Taylor failed to pursue his planned law studies. Instead, at 18, he went home to recuperate from eye troubles and headaches.

Taylor is described by various people who knew him as a child as somewhat peculiar, compulsive about order and efficiency, and tense and withdrawn. He was known as an extremely hard worker, and resented those who were not. The following abbreviated excerpts from biographical descriptions and accounts should serve to characterize the parts of Taylor's personality useful in interpreting the results of his efforts to "install" scientific management in various organizations.

One of his childhood friends is said to have remarked that many quarrels were caused by Frederick's insistence on playing games by strict and elaborate rules.

In cross country walks he constantly experimented with his legs in an endeavor to discover the step which would cover the greatest distance with the least expenditure of energy. Before going to a dance, he would systematically list the attractive and unattractive girls with the object of dividing his time equally between them.

One of the games popular with the children of his day was "beanbag." The beanbag was tossed from one group of players to another standing in a line. As the bag passed down the line it became necessary to wait one's turn to receive the beanbag. Taylor, realizing the idle time imposed upon the participants, devised a new set of rules by which the waiting time could be reduced. He suggested using two beanbags and having them start at each end of the line.

Taylor, while at Exeter, was considered as a bit of a crank in the opinion of his friends there. In the game of croquet he would carefully work out the angles of the various strokes, the force of impact, and the advantages and disadvantages of the various strokes before he started to play.

Taylor is said to have turned white at the mere mention of sickness or death. He had nightmares often and was a chronic sufferer from insomnia and indigestion. He believed his nightmares were due to sleeping on his back. He designed an elaborate harness whose sharp wooden points would wake him when he turned onto his back.[7]

After a few restless months upon leaving Exeter, Taylor, at 18, joined a small Philadelphia pump manufacturing firm owned by friends of his family. He successfully completed an apprenticeship as a pattern-maker. In 1878, at age 22, Taylor went to work for Midvale Steel Works as a laborer. One of the principal owners of Midvale was a family friend and neighbor.

During the next twelve years Taylor held jobs as gang boss, assistant foreman, machine shop foreman, master mechanic, chief draftsman, and finally as chief engineer. During his early years there he earned, by special arrangement, a mechanical engineering degree at Stevens Institute of Technology. The degree was granted in 1883.

While Taylor was gang boss in the machine shop, he began a three-year struggle to install some of the approaches later referred to as basic principles of scientific management. Most notably during this period Taylor was concerned with the first and third of the following principles:

FIRST: Develop a science for each element of a man's work, which replaces the old rule-of-thumb method.

SECOND: Scientifically select and then train, teach, and develop the workman, whereas in the past he chose his own work and trained himself as best he could.

THIRD: Heartily cooperate with the men so as to insure all of the work being done in accordance with the principles of the science which has been developed.

FOURTH: There is an almost equal division of the work and the responsibility between the management and the workmen. The management take over all work for which they are better fitted than the workmen, while in the past almost all of the work and the greater part of the responsibility were thrown upon the men.[8]

His major biographers, Copeley and Kakar,[9] consistently agree that Taylor appeared to be determined to find a way to eliminate "soldiering." From various accounts of these efforts, this term could mean anything from "goofing off" to planned, coordinated work output restrictions. Taylor tried every conceivable approach to control soldiering. In the beginning of this period, Taylor would direct a worker to increase his output on a lathe, for example. When this failed, he would demonstrate personally that the higher output was possible. This failed. Taylor would then bring in some better-than-average laborers, teach them how to run a lathe efficiently. Each would promise to turn out a "fair day's work" but all would soon join the older workers in output restrictions. The workers are reported to have planned ingenious accidents and attributed them to Taylor's driving the men and machines beyond their limits. Taylor would respond by charging the men a portion of the machine repair costs. In one case he began by fining a worker two dollars, doubling the fine for each succeeding breakdown until it reached sixty-four dollars, or about two months' wages. Another worker was fined for having a scratch on his machine. When he protested to Taylor that he was not responsible for the scratch, Taylor fined him for not reporting it.

Eventually, according to his biographers, Taylor's relentless efforts in the machine shop paid off and his men were doing a "fair day's work."

In 1882, Taylor, with permission of his superiors, began experimenting on various jobs to determine how quickly different kinds of work ought to be done. Essentially, this work appears to be the beginning, in the U.S., at least,[10] of time and motion study. Many years later, Taylor described these studies as follows:

1. Divide the work . . . into simple elementary movements.
2. Discard the useless movements.
3. Study various skilled workers performing the job and, using a stop watch, select the quickest and best method of making each elementary movement.
4. Describe, record, and index each movement with its proper time.
5. Determine the necessary time which must be added for unavoidable delays, interruptions, and minor accidents.
6. Determine the time to be added for new workers.
7. Study and record the percentage of time that must be allowed for rest, and the intervals at which rest must be taken in order to offset physical fatigue.
8. Add together into various groups such combinations of elementary movements as are frequently used in the same trade.
9. From these several records, select the proper series of motions which should be used by a workman in making any particular article.[11]

Incidental to these time and motion studies, Taylor began to work in the area now referred to as methods engineering and tool design. He began studying cutting tool shapes, feeds and speeds, and other variables naturally relating to time and motion studies. Eventually this work led, in association with J. Maunsel White, to an improved heat treatment process for high speed cutting tools.

According to his biographers, Taylor's management methods were fairly well adopted at Midvale Steel Works before he left them in 1890. Taylor then joined the Manufacturing and Investment Company, a new paper-making venture owned by President Cleveland and some of his friends. He failed in this job, primarily due to conflicts with the owners.

From 1893 until 1896 Taylor worked off and on as an independent consultant on shop management. Although he was not too successful as a consultant, his professional reputation continued to grow due primarily to his publications and speaking engagements.

In late 1896 Taylor was offered complete control of the Simonds Company of Fitchburg, Pennsylvania. Although he began his new job with great enthusiasm and energy, his approach failed to bring about the desired results. In 1898, when a shut-down was necessary because Simonds was unable to meet competition, Taylor had a "nervous breakdown."

While recovering, Taylor was invited to join Bethlehem Steel Company. Russell Davenport, now at Bethlehem Steel Company and one of the owners of Midvale when Taylor was employed there, asked Taylor to establish a piece-rate system in their machine shop. Taylor is reported to have begun work in the foundry yard before tackling the machine shop. It was here that the famous classic example of scientific management using pig-iron loading was supposed to have occurred. The example of the "Story of Schmidt" and a detailed description of Taylor's Pig-Iron Loading Experiments have been carried in most primer texts in industrial psychology, industrial engineering, and management, and in all management history texts.

Unfortunately, Taylor's various accounts of these famous "studies" were mostly fabricated. I offer the most common account of Taylor's conversation with the famous "Schmidt." Following this is a review showing that this story and most of Taylor's account of the entire pig-iron loading experiment are more fiction than fact.[12]

"Schmidt, are you a high-priced man?"

"Vell, I don't know vat you mean."

"Oh yes you do. What I want to know is whether you are a high-priced man or not."

"Vell, I don't know vat you mean."

"Oh, come now, you answer my questions. What I want to find out is whether you are a high-priced man or one of these cheap fellows here. What I want to find out is whether you want to earn $1.85 a day or whether you are satisfied with $1.15, just the same as all those cheap fellows are getting."

"Did I vant $1.85 a day? Vas dot a high-priced man? Vel, yes, I vas a high-priced man."

"Oh, you're aggravating me. Of course you want $1.85 a day—every one wants it! You know perfectly well that that has very little to do with your being a high-priced man. For goodness sake answer my questions, and don't waste any more of my time. Now come over here. You see that pile of pig iron?"

"Yes."

"You see that car?"

"Yes."

"Well, if you are a high-priced man, you will load that pig-iron on that car tomorrow for $1.85. Now do wake up and answer my question. Tell me whether you are a high-priced man or not."

"Vell—did I got $1.85 for loading dot pig-iron on dot car tomorrow?"

"Yes, of course you do, and you get $1.85 for loading a pile like that every day right through the year. That is what a high-priced man does, and you know it just as well as I do."

"Vell, dot's all right. I could load dot pig-iron on the car tomorrow for $1.85, and I get it every day, don't I?"

"Certainly you do—certainly you do."

"Vell, den, I vas a high-priced man."

"Now, hold on, hold on. You know just as well as I do that a high-priced man has to do exactly as he's told from morning until night. You have seen this man here before, haven't you?"

"No, I never saw him."

"Well, if you are a high-priced man, you will do exactly as this man tell you tomorrow, from morning till night. When he tells you to pick up a pig and walk, you pick it up and you walk, and when he tells you to sit down and rest, you sit down. You do that right straight through the day. And what's more, no back talk. Now a high-priced man does just what he's told to do, and no back talk. Do you understand that? When this man tells you to walk, you walk; when he tells you to sit down; you sit down, and you don't talk back at him. Now you come on to work here tomorrow morning and I'll know before night whether you are really a high-priced man or not.[13]

Taylor's Several Versions of the Study

The best documentary evidence reveals that the "Story of Schmidt" and the accompanying pig-iron loading study varied to suit Taylor's purpose of the moment. The earliest documented version was presented on December 5, 1901, at a meeting of the American Society of Mechanical Engineers. This version stressed the importance of:

1. The physical ability of pig-iron handlers.
2. The economic value of using workers with the right physique. "Our average pig-iron gang had loaded 12 tons to the man and were paid $1.15 per day. So that it cost . . . 9 cents per ton to load pig-iron. Our man who loaded 45 tons earned $1.85 per day (costing about 4 cents per ton)."[14]

A second version of the pig-iron experiments delivered by Taylor at the ASME convention held on June 24, 1903 can be characterized by the following:

1. Stress on the physical build of the worker was omitted.
2. Stressed the scientific determination of task elements before selecting workers or making any observations.
3. In the unedited version for the ASME proceedings, Taylor said that the pig-iron study was planned as an object lesson for Bethlehem workers and not as a demonstration of how to solve problems scientifically.[15]
4. Introduced the "fact" that Schmidt was building his own house before and after work and suggested that this was an important factor in Schmidt's willingness to be a "high-priced" man. Explained that he kept other workers 200 feet away and used 5 men to protect his worker.[16]
5. Gave 5–20 as the pig-iron loading gang size.[17]

The 1911 version, contained in Taylor's book on Scientific Management, of course, was more elaborate than all the others. Essentially, it was an edited version of one of his speeches taken in short-hand in 1907 by a court reporter. The pertinent characteristics of the 1911 version are summarized below:

1. The total tonnage to be loaded was given as 80,000.

2. The price increase of pig-iron due to the start of the Spanish-American War was the reason the company decided to sell its inventory in 1898.
3. The pig-iron loading gang was made up of 75 *men* who were carefully watched and studied.
4. The recruitment and selection of these men was done scientifically with concentration on motivation—not physical build as in the 1901 version (hence the addition of the account of Schmidt's house-building as a relevant worker selection characteristic).
5. The loading procedure was described as a simple plank ramp to the rail car.
6. Formal rest periods are given as an integral part of the work procedure.[18]

THE EXTENT OF TAYLOR'S FABRICATIONS

The previous section focused on how Taylor varied his description of the study from time to time. There is new evidence that much of each version was pure *fabrication*. This new evidence has been provided by two extremely diligent researchers, Charles D. Wrege and Amadeo G. Perroni. Their primary source of information on the study as it was actually performed is in the form of recently discovered documents. These documents contain the actual report of the study as it was performed by Harvey C. Wolle and James Gillespie. Other evidence of Taylor's fabrications provided by Wrege and Perroni came from public records and preserved correspondence.

The following is an abbreviated comparison of the Taylor versions of the pig-iron experiments accompanied by the actual events as they are contained in the recent Wrege and Perroni article revealing what they call "Taylor's Pig-Tale":

ON PIG-IRON LOADER SELECTION

Taylor's Version

1901 version: ". . . a man properly built for that work could load forty-five tons a day."[19]

1911 version: "Now one of the very first requirements for a man who is fit to handle pig-iron as a regular occupation is that he shall be so stupid and so phlegmatic that he more nearly resembles in his mental make-up the ox than any other type. . . . He is so stupid that the word percentage has no meaning to him, and he must consequently be trained by a man more intelligent than himself into the habit of working in accordance with the laws of this science before he can be successful."[20] Also in his 1911 version Taylor reported that four men were selected who were physically able to load 47 tons a day and that these men were studied carefully to discover the ". . . character, habits and ambitions of each of them."[21]

As It Actually Happened

On March 15, 1899, ten men were told that they would begin loading pig-iron the next day for $.0375 per ton. Before the actual pig-iron researchers Gillespie and Wolle arrived the next day, the workers had refused to work on piece rate and their foreman put them on day rate. On instructions from superiors they were fired on March 17th. Pig-iron was loaded on day rate during the next nine days. A gang of seven men was recruited from a different Bethlehem mill stockyard and began on piece-rate on March 29th. On March 30th only five showed up for work, among them Henry Noll, who has been identified as Taylor's "Schmidt" by researchers Wrege and Perroni. The following day only three workers reported to work on piece rate, again including Noll. From then on the loading gang varied from 1–4 men—always including Noll.

The three best loaders out of the many observed in the study had the following physical specifications which hardly seem to fit any conceivable scientifically determined set of physical characteristics:

(1)   Simon Conrad, height: five feet ten inches; weight: 180 pounds.
(2)   E. Auer, height: five feet nine inches; weight: 190 pounds.
(3)   Henry Noll (Schmidt), height: *five feet seven inches*; weight: *135 pounds.*[22]

ON RECRUITMENT OF WORKERS WILLING TO WORK ON PIECE-RATE

Taylor's Version

Taylor claimed that successful loaders had spread the word of Bethlehem's need for "high-priced" men to load pig-iron. He said that local newspapers published articles critical of his methods, but that the actual effect was to enhance Bethlehem's recruitment efforts.[23]

As It Actually Happened

The *South Bethlehem Globe* or *Bethlehem Star* carried no mention of Taylor's work on pig-iron handling during the period from February 1898 to January 1901. The pig-iron loading studies began in March 1899 by Gillespie and Wolle. The last study using "two extraordinary laborers" began in March, 1900.[24]

ON THE REASONS FOR THE NEED TO LOAD PIG-IRON AND THE AMOUNT STOCKPILED AND SOLD

Taylor's Version

Taylor claimed that depressed prices caused Bethlehem to stockpile 80,000 tons and that the start of the Spanish American War caused pig-iron prices to rise motivating Bethlehem to sell its stockpile.

As It Actually Happened

Records from *Iron Age* and *Engineering News* show that pig-iron prices *declined* steadily until the Spanish American War was ended.[25] Wolle reported that the actual amount sold was approximately 10,000 tons.[26]

ON THE METHOD OF LOADING AND THE WORK LAYOUT

Taylor's Version

"An inclined plank was placed against the side of a car and each man picked up from his pile a pig of iron weighing about 92 pounds, walked up the inclined plank and dropped it on the end of the car."[27]

As It Actually Happened

The previous standard loading procedure at the outset was to have gangs of from 8 to 12 men load a car with two of these men in the car placing the pigs carried up inclined planks by the remainder of the crew. Because the crews varied so much in size due to the resistance to piece-rates, this procedure was not followed.

Shortly after the study began Gillespie and Wolle had fabricated easily relocated metal hangers made to hook onto the side of a car. One end of each plank was placed on these hangers and the other end on a pig-iron pile. The loading car end of the planks was two feet below the car floor level, thus reducing the carry elevation and the bending over for dropping the pigs.[28]

ON THE REASONS FOR THE LESSENING OPPOSITION TO PIECEWORK

Taylor's Version

Taylor reported that a special force of men was recruited and selected from outside the company for the pig-iron loading job. They were given protection from interference by workers who were hostile to piece-rates. Regarding

"Schmidt's" protection, Taylor's 1903 version is as follows: ". . . I put him to work . . . by himself, no man being nearer to him than 200 feet. I then put five men around to watch him and keep other men off, and to see that he had a decent fair chance."[29]

As It Likely Happened

The loaders studied by Gillespie and Wolle were given easier work until they could return to pig-iron loading if they were injured or too tired. In addition to not fearing time loss, the loading method with the hangers made it easier to load enough tonnage to earn substantially more than a daily rate and with less effort.[30]

ON THE SCIENTIFICALLY DETERMINED REST PERIODS

Taylor's Version

With " . . . almost any type of manual labor, rest pauses are necessary." It was further claimed that his pig-iron studies were " . . . the first and one of the best controlled studies on the problem."[31] These formal rest periods are in further evidence in an unidentified author's version in the description of the supervision of Schmidt: "Now pick up a pig and walk. Now sit down and rest. Now walk. . . ."[32]

How It Actually Happened

No rest pauses were ever scheduled during the study and no such instructions were given to any of the workers. Whatever resting was done was during the empty-handed walk back to the pile for another pig. This constituted about 57 percent of the working day.[33]

SOME CONCLUSIONS FROM THE COMPARISONS

Leaving aside for the moment that Taylor himself did not perform the research or experiments he claimed to have carried out personally, his *versions* of the study are almost totally a set of fabrications. Certainly the most important parts, from a scientific standpoint, were falsified in one way or another. Critical to any experiment from which generalizations are to be drawn such as Taylor's "Law of Heavy Laboring" (pertaining to scheduled rest periods) would at least be objectivity in selection of the workers, controlled work procedures, gang size and gang make-up. It is not difficult to conclude, therefore, that generations of managers and students have been fooled into thinking that scientific management was invented and almost solely pioneered by Frederick W. Taylor.

TAYLOR'S REMAINING YEARS

Taylor's career at Bethlehem was to end not unlike most of his other company careers. Shortly over two years after joining them, he and the associates he persuaded to join him there were fired. Among them were H. L. Gantt of Gantt-Chart fame and Carl G. Barth, inventor of the Barth slide rule for machine set-up. Bethlehem was to be Taylor's last employer.

From 1901 until his death 14 years later, Taylor spent his time primarily in promoting scientific management. He was elected president of the American Society of Mechanical Engineers in 1906 and he later helped to organize the Society to Promote the Science of Management which was renamed the Taylor Society after his death.

Some of Taylor's Other Contributions

Almost every managerial technique associated with "order" was at least improved upon by Taylor and his associates. The available biographies of Taylor and Gantt, for example, do not permit very clear identification of the "owners" or origins of the many such techniques evolving out of this period.

Taylor's biographers tend to give him more credit for managerial inventions than can be substantiated historically. Given a man who could fabricate and then popularize a study in several versions such as the pig-iron experiments, one would have to remain very agnostic about much of his own claims and documents. How much of the work claimed in his name could have been H. L. Gantt's, for example? Gantt was certainly innovative and capable of devising such techniques as standardized repair procedures, systematized purchasing and inventory control, cost accounting systems, and the use of printed job instruction cards, which are all attributed to Taylor.

Biographers do point out that Gantt and Taylor went their separate ideological ways in 1901. One can conjecture that Gantt got tired of pulling Taylor's (labor relations) chestnuts out of the fire, since he evidently spent a great deal of his time when he worked with Taylor persuading him to see the workers' viewpoints, as well as dealing with Taylor-produced grievances. Barth, too, should probably be given considerable credit for certain of the Taylor era contributions. According to some, "Many of the standardized tools on which the Taylor system depended were the fruit of Barth's ingenuity."[34] Taylor's first biographer attempts to summarize the two men's relative contributions as follows:

> If they became known as Taylor's tools, they were so only in the sense that Taylor had inspired and directed the course of the experiments. If he avoided singling out Barth for special attention, it was for the good of the movement *just as he subordinated his own part*. But he came to recognize that this operated to do Barth not a little injustice.[35] (Italics not in original.)

To this I could only add that Taylor's claiming to have performed the pig-iron experiments when in actual fact he did not, is a peculiar form of role subordination. "Taylorism," in the minds of the labor unions of the period, was such an apparent threat to the American worker that the U.S. Congress was persuaded to establish a commission to study "The Taylor and Other Systems of Shop Management." Taylor's formal testimony denied that scientific management was sweatshop management, pointing out only that it did require both labor and management to think in new ways for the betterment of all. At the end of his formal presentation at the commission hearings, however, he lost self control under the hostile labor leaders' questioning. This portion of the testimony was stricken from the record.[36]

On March 10, 1915, Taylor entered a hospital with pneumonia. He died nine days later. Copeley, his official biographer, reported his death as consistent with the way Taylor lived and worked. Every morning Taylor would systematically wind his watch at the same hour. On the ninth day, he was heard to wind his watch at half-past four in the morning—not his usual time. He was found dead a half hour later.

Conclusions Regarding Taylor's Foundation for Management Science

The so-called founder of scientific management was clearly an intelligent, arrogant, innovative, and energetic obsessive compulsive (about work, order and efficiency) manager. Unfortunately, he was also a prevaricator, if the Wolle report can be believed. He and/or his colleagues improved upon most production management techniques in vogue in his day. He may even have actually invented some new techniques, but the historical evidence on this point is too obscure, in my opinion.

Taylor tirelessly promoted a set of principles of production efficiency. He called attention to the various parties responsible for efficiency and admonished each for violating the principles. History seems to show him most critical of workers' violations, however.

Taylor principles are, in general, no better followed today than they were at Bethlehem Steel. We have standard times (and standard costs) today and we have workers who can and do add to them at their will.

We have numerous incentive systems—both group and individual. Most are considered "demoralized" and are in the expensive process of being removed or updated. One reason they are demoralized is simply that their installers—and Taylor, it seems—never realized how complicated it would become to maintain fair rates as the production process became more complicated. Certainly Taylor did not seem to appreciate the simple fact that many factors would soon complicate the assessment of the workers' net contribution, and thereby add considerable cost to the maintenance of the incentive system.

In their excellent expose, Wrege and Perroni make the point that heroes *will* not be destroyed—least of all by any hard evidence that they were not heroes. They point out that Richard III was not the murderer of the "Princes in the Tower" and yet school children are still generally taught to abhor the villain Richard.

I prefer the simple example of Baltimore's annual celebration of its attack by the British which never took place. The mayor of Baltimore, when this was brought to his attention, merely insisted that it *could* have happened, and then proceeded to help promote the event's celebration.

POST-TAYLOR DEVELOPMENTS IN MANAGEMENT SCIENCE

Since Taylor, developments contributing to the management science field have been growing steadily. Below are a few of the benchmarks:[37]

MODERN MANAGEMENT SCIENCE TECHNIQUES

Most of the techniques available today are refinements of earlier approaches. The computer has stimulated further development of many "theoretical" tools which were rarely used simply because of the manpower required. Anyone who has done many Wherry-Doolittle multiple correlations without modern equipment can attest to this. Some of the modern techniques being taught in business courses are given below, although it does not follow that they are in widespread use:

Decision theory	Queuing theory
Information theory	Sampling theory
Game theory	Statistical decision theory
Inventory control	Simulation theory
Probability theory	Replacement theory
Linear Programming	Symbolic logic

In summary, then, management science could have gotten its start by scientific applications to management problems. It likely did not, however. Most of the management science techniques available over the years were rarely put to use when they became available. Most of the techniques listed above are rarely used, for a wide variety of reasons. One important point is, of course, whether, with so unpalatable a start, management science is better serving management in general today because of this start. At least a partial answer to that question should be provided in various of the chapters which follow.

Approximate Year	Contributor(s)	Contributions
1910	Harrington Emerson	Efficiency engineering; principles of efficiency.
1911	Hugo Diemer	Pioneering text in factory administration.
	Harlan S. Person	Initiated first scientific management conference in United States; gave academic recognition to scientific management.
1915	Horace B. Drury	Criticism of scientific management— reaffirmed initial ideas.
	F. W. Harris	Economic lot size model.
	Thomas A. Edison	Devised war game to evade and destroy enemy submarines.
1916	A. K. Erlang	Anticipated waiting-line theory.
1917	William H. Leffingwell	Applied scientific management to office.
1919	Morris L. Cooke	Diverse applications of scientific management.
1924	H. G. Dodge H. G. Romig W. A. Shewhart	Use of statistical inference and probability theory in sampling inspection and in quality control by statistical means.
1925	Ronald A. Fisher	Various modern statistical methods including chi-square test, Bayesian statistics, sampling theory, and design of experiments.
1928	T. C. Fry	Statistical foundations of queuing theory.
1938	P. M. S. Blackett, et al.	Operations research.
1949	Norbert Wiener Claude Shannon	Emphasized systems analysis and information theory in management.

NOTES

1. All historical references in this paragraph except the mentions about mathematics and Babbage's computer were taken from Claude S. George, Jr., *The History of Management Thought*, (Englewood Cliffs, New Jersey: Prentice-Hall, Inc., 1972), pp. vii–xiii.

2. Today such functions are usually part of the personnel administration apparatus but since Taylor was active in the area of man-specifications and work analysis, it is included here.

3. Daniel A. Wren. *The Evolution of Management Thought*, (New York, N.Y.: The Ronald Press, 1972), pp. 69–70.

4. Refers to the practice of the entrepreneur's provision of raw materials, designs, etc. to a variety of producers, then collecting the finished goods. Similar to the so-called "cottage industries" in developing countries today.

5. Frank B. Copeley, *Frederick W. Taylor: Father of Scientific Management*, Vol. I, (New York, N.Y.: Harper & Bros., 1923), p. 62.

6. Ibid., p. 52.

7. Samuel Haber. *Efficiency and Uplift*, (Chicago, Illinois: University of Chicago Press, 1964), pp. 3–8.

8. Frederick W. Taylor, *Principles of Scientific Management*, (New York, N.Y.: Harper & Bros., 1911), copyright 1911 by Frederick W. Taylor, copyright 1939 by Louise M.S. Taylor, copyright 1947 by Harper & Row, Publishers, Inc., reprinted by permission of the publisher; as quoted in Claude S. George, Jr., *The History of Management Thought, op. cit.* (Englewood Cliffs, New Jersey: Prentice Hall, Inc., 1972), p. 93.

9. Copeley, Vols. I & II, and Sudhir Kakar, *Frederick Taylor, A Study in Personality and Innovation*, Vols. I & II, (Cambridge, Mass.: The Massachusetts Institute of Technology Press, 1970).

10. Since the Soho Foundry in London had installed piece-rates for drilling by hole diameter as early as 1800, it is reasonable to assume that time study experiments were used to determine these rates. For details on how much of Taylor's work was pre-dated by up to a century, see George, pp. 59–62; John Hoaglund, "Management Before Frederick Taylor," *Proceedings of the Academy of Management*, December, 1955, pp. 15–24; and Daniel A. Wren, *The Evolution of Management Thought*, (New York, N.Y.: The Ronald Press, 1972), pp. 68–73 and 76–78.

11. Frederick W. Taylor, *Shop Management*, (New York, N.Y.: Harper and Row, 1903), pp. 149–150.

12. The main refutation sources are to be found in documents discovered at the former farm of Henry C. Wolle plus public records and library sources as analyzed by researchers Charles D. Wrege and Amadeo G. Perroni, "Taylor's Pig-Tale: A Historical Analysis of Frederick W. Taylor's Pig Iron Experiments," *Academy of Management Journal*, May, 1974, pp. 6–27.

13. Taylor, *Principles*, pp. 44–47.

14. Milton L. Blum, *Industrial Psychology and Its Social Foundations*, rev. ed., (New York, N.Y.: Harper and Bros., 1956), as given in Charles D. Wrege and Amadeo G. Perroni, "Taylor's Pig-Tale: A Historical Analysis of Frederick W. Taylor's Pig Iron Experiments," *Academy of Management Journal*, May, 1974, p. 8.

15. Edited and unedited versions of *The American Society of Mechanical Engineering Transactions*, 1903, as given in Wrege and Perroni, p. 9.

16. Unpublished transcript of conversation of F. W. Taylor and Hawkins at ASME

Convention, June 24, 1903, pp. 86–87, Taylor Collection, under "Shop Management" as given by Wrege and Perroni, p. 10.

17. Frederick W. Taylor, *Shop Management*, (New York, N.Y.: Harper & Bros., 1911), as given in Wrege and Perroni, p. 13.

18. *Ibid.*, p. 11 & 13.

19. Blum, as given in Wrege and Perroni, p. 8.

20. Taylor, *Shop Management*, as quoted in Wrege and Perroni, p. 17.

21. *Ibid.*, p. 14.

22. Original pig-iron study report by Harvey C. Wolle owned by Charles D. Wrege. A duplicate of the report is preserved in Taylor's papers at Stevens Institute of Technology, summarized by the author from portions of the study report given in Wrege and Perroni, pp. 13–16.

23. *Engineering Views*, Vol. 42, No. 16, (October 19, 1899), p. 257, as given in Wrege and Perroni, p. 18.

24. Wrege and Perroni, p. 18.

25. Various public records containing U.S. pig-iron prices as given in Wrege and Perroni, p. 13.

26. Wolle report as quoted in Wrege and Perroni, p. 12.

27. Taylor, *Shop Management*, as quoted in Wrege and Perroni, p. 13.

28. Wolle report as quoted in Wrege and Perroni, p. 13–14.

29. Unpublished transcript of conversation of F. W. Taylor and Hawkins at ASME Convention, June 24, 1903, pp. 86–87, Taylor Collection, under "Shop Management" as given in Wrege and Perroni, p. 10.

30. Wolle pig-iron study report as given in Wrege and Perroni, p. 18.

31. *Iron Age*, January 26, 1899, p. 24, as given in Wrege and Perroni, p. 21.

32. Taylor, *Principles*, p. 37.

33. From analysis of graphs prepared by Carl G. Barth for Taylor by Wrege and Perroni, pp. 19–23.

34. L. Urwick, ed., *The Golden Book of Management*, (London, England: Newman Neame Ltd., 1956), p. 81.

35. Copeley, Vol. II, p. 253.

36. Kakar, pp. 185–186.

37. George, Jr., pp. xi–xii.

Chapter 3

Mayo and Modern Behavioral Science Foundations

ALTHOUGH the origins of modern behavioral science date from the period 1910–1930, most of what we associate with modern human resource management theory and principles has its roots in much earlier periods. Maslow's Need Hierarchy model is essentially a dynamic version of a need hierarchy model stated by Aristotle some 2300 years ago.[1] Our efforts to train foremen in grievance handling by teaching them to listen attentively and to appreciate the psychological concept of "catharsis" spring from a "principle" stated about 4700 years ago by a vizier of King Issi of Egypt:

> If thou are one to whom petition is made, be calm as thou listenest to what the petitioner has to say. Do not rebutt him before he has swept out his body or before he has said that for which he came . . . It is not [necessary] that everything about which he has petitioned should come to pass [but] a good hearing is soothing to the heart.[2]

Most modern human relations concepts began with the industrial revolution and the factory system. An early pioneer, Robert Owen, is considered the father of "personnel management." In an essay to factory superintendents in about 1812, he set forth the rationale for his human resource management as follows:

> . . . you will find that from the commencement of my management I viewed the population [workforce] . . . as a system composed of many parts, and which it was my duty and interest so to combine, as that every hand, as well as every spring, lever, and wheel, should effectually cooperate to produce the greatest . . . gain to the proprietors . . . Experience has also shown you the difference of the results between a mechanism which is neat, clean, well arranged, and always in a high state of repair; and which is allowed to be dirty, in disorder, without the means of preventing unnecessary friction, and which therefore becomes, and works much out of repair . . . If, then, due care as to the state of your inanimate machines can produce such beneficial results, what may not be expected if you devote equal attention to your vital machines . . . ?"[3]

41

In addition to Owens' "people maintenance" concept, most of the fundamentals of behavioral science and organizational theory taught today in introductory management courses (and in many management training programs) were noted before 1910. The need for careful planning, organizing and controlling, the advantages and disadvantages of decentralization, and the use of staff were noted by the Egyptians between 4000–1600 B.C. By 35 A.D. the so-called "principles" of unity of command, delegation of authority commensurate with responsibility and a hierarchy of needs had been noted. Also around this time job descriptions, man-specifications, wage incentives, and rudimentary production control techniques were in use. By 1910, job standards and psychological tests for selection of personnel were standard techniques in a few organizations.[4]

By the time the Hawthorne studies had begun in the late 1920's, most of the basic research techniques and statistical tools such as correlational and probability techniques were available. The era of sociological and social psychological research on humans at the workplace was fully launched in these Hawthorne studies at Western Electric in Chicago under the direction of Professor Elton Mayo of Harvard University.

ELTON MAYO (1880–1949)

Because Professor Mayo's career did not see him attempting to apply his "theories" as did Taylor's, his biographical details[5] are less relevant to the study of the origins of modern behavioral science. Mayo, born a generation after Taylor in Adelaide, Australia, initially took a degree in Logic and Philosophy at Queensland University, after which he studied medicine in Scotland. From 1911–19 he was Lecturer in Logic, Ethics, and Philosophy at Queensland. During the first World War he undertook in his spare time the psycho-therapeutic treatment of "shell shocked" soldiers, the first man in Australia to use this treatment. Although he was at various times briefly in the printing business, a newspaperman, and a laborer, Mayo continued to gravitate towards the social sciences through his interest in clinical psychology. In 1919, Mayo was appointed to a newly established chair of philosophy at Queensland.

Mayo migrated to the U.S. in 1922. In 1923, he undertook industrial research for the Rockefeller Foundation, as a Research Associate at Pennsylvania University. At Pennsylvania, while under Rockefeller auspices, he began research on the causes of high labor turnover in a local textile mill.

The most productive period in his life, according to his biographies, began in 1926 when he joined the Harvard Graduate School of Business Administration. With Lawrence J. Henderson, an eminent biological chemist who was also a devotee of Pareto[6], he began a study of psychological and social problems of industrial workers. A year later, in 1927, he began work on the Western Electric Hawthorne plant experiments. Mayo served as academic director of the research project in association with F. J. Roethlisberger of Harvard, William J. Dickson, research officer at Western Electric, and T. N. Whitehead, whose interest was primarily in data analysis.

The Hawthorne Works, in collaboration with the National Research Council, had been engaged in research primarily in a study on the effects of illumination intensity on worker output. This project failed mainly because of the difficulty of isolating other variables affecting output.[7] In 1927, the research was extended into the study of a wider variety of factors in the work environment such as rest periods, snacks, reduced workdays, and altered work weeks. This phase of the extensive research going on at Western Electric was to become the main foundation for much work in the area of "human relations"—later behavioral science—in industry and academe. Although the research involved several different kinds of investigations over a period of years, it was the relay assembly "experiments" (1927–1932) which held the attention of psychologists, sociologists, personnel administrators, and others concerned with the human-relations-in-industry movement.

THE HAWTHORNE RELAY ASSEMBLY RESEARCH—AN EVALUATION

"The most exciting and important study of factory workers ever made has been going on for 16 years in the Western Electric Company's Hawthorne plant, near Chicago. If managers of other factories, large and small the country over, were aware of things which this huge experiment in industrial relations has found out, American industry could be made over." So wrote Stuart Chase in 1940,[8] launching the evangelism of the Hawthorne Studies. Between his and other lay accounts and those of the advocative social scientists, these studies became a near-miracle.

Even a casual review of the original research report and its conclusions, however, will reveal flaws so serious as to render the results useless except for the lessons to be learned in avoiding shoddy science and the need to eliminate scientific illiteracy in drawing conclusions. We can also learn just how difficult it is to tease out the variables involved in research on human motivation if we are not already aware of such problems.

So that the slippage to a kind of evangelism on the part of personnel people and lay authors and the slippage toward advocative social science on the part of academics is made clear, the presentation of the relay assembly research project flaws will be as follows:

1. A complete popular version of the entire experiment will be recreated as it appeared piecemeal in psychology, personnel administration, organizational behavior, and introductory management textbooks, as well as in various journal and lay accounts.[9]
2. The various aspects of the experiment which were seriously flawed will be discussed. Where pertinent, variations of accounts of the research by George C. Homans[10] and Elton Mayo[11] plus excerpts from the Roethlisberger and Dickson[12] original account will be given. Many of the negative criticisms follow those of Alex Carey,[13] H. M. Parsons[14] and Richard Herbert Franke with James D. Kaul.[15]

The Standard Version

In 1927 at the huge tension-ridden Hawthorne plant of the Western Electric Company, six relay assemblers were selected from a main 100-employee relay assembly department and placed in a separate experimental room. The researchers, led by project director Elton Mayo of Harvard University, wanted to find out the effect on productivity of a variety of changes in work scheduling such as rest pauses, lunch breaks, and overall hours per day and week. The research was divided into 13 different experimental periods. The first period was the two week period in the main department before they were moved to the experimental room and before they knew they were to be selected.

The second period constituted another "base" period in that, although the girls were moved to the experimental room, no other changes were made. Output for these periods was about 2,400 relays per girl per week. For period three the girls were put on a special group piecework payment basis, but as with periods 1 and 2, no other changes were made. In period 4 the researchers introduced two five-minute rest breaks and output went up. In period 5 these were increased to two ten-minute breaks and output increased more than in period 4. For period 6, the researchers tried six five-minute rest breaks, but the girls complained of this procedure and their output dropped slightly. In period 7 these breaks were reduced to only two and the girls were given a hot snack provided by the company. Again output increased. For period 8, the breaks and the snack remained but, in addition, the company reduced their work-day by a half hour. As before, output went up. The only change for period 9 was to cut another half hour off their scheduled work day. This did not seem to affect output one way or the other. In period 10, the breaks and the snacks remained, but the work-day was increased by an hour back to the original schedule. The girls responded with a very sharp output increase. The researchers were becoming more puzzled with each succeeding output increase. For period 11, the originally scheduled Saturday morning shift was eliminated resulting in no appreciable change in weekly output. For period 12, all the work schedule arrangements were returned to the original conditions. The girls worked Saturday mornings and had no rest breaks and the company-provided hot snacks were eliminated. To the astonishment of the researchers and company personnel people, output climbed to an all-time high of 3,000 relays per week per operator! What caused this steady increase in production from 2,400 relays per week to 3,000? With the final period having the same control conditions as the beginning, the rest pauses and changes in work schedules could not be the causal factors. The explanation of these increases could only be the psychological and sociological climate changes. The girls liked the relaxed supervision and the opportunity to enjoy conversation in the main assembly room which had not existed under previous supervision. The key, then, was a set of *social* factors which had nothing to do with money, rest pauses, or hot snacks.

What Really Took Place at Hawthorne

First, Stuart Chase's description of the plant as "tension-ridden" hardly agreed with the facts. Professor Homans offered quite a different view of the Western Electric Company as an employer at the time of the studies: "The efforts of the company (in good personnel administration, benefits, etc.) have been rewarded in good industrial relations; there has been no strike or other severe symptom of discontent for over 20 years. (Since this was written in 1941, the period from 1929–1941 is a reasonable interpretation.) In short, there is no reason to doubt that while these researches were being carried out the morale of the company was high and that the employees, as a body, had confidence in the abilities and motives of the company management."[16] (Parenthetical phrases added.) Professor Homan's assessment is essentially correct. During the period of the Hawthorne Studies the company did have a union, but it was what would have been called a "company" union, and did not engage in strikes, boycotts, etc.

Selection of the Girls for the Experiment

The six assemblers were certainly not selected scientifically from the main assembly room. Two assemblers, known to be friends, were told to pick four others to work in the experiment. Professor Homans ignored the social aspects of the selection process: "Six girls were selected from a large shop department . . . They were chosen as average workers, neither inexperienced or expert."[17] Research Director Mayo pointedly ignored the selection process: "I shall not discuss the method of choosing these operatives, except to say that all were experienced workers."[18] Both of these accounts are clearly inaccurate and misleading from a scientific reporting standpoint. Yet accurate reporting would seem especially important since the two originally selected girls were actually dismissed from the experiment for "behavior approaching gross insubordination."[19] (More on this later in the chapter.)

As an aside, it is interesting to note one possible reason why industry was not "made over" as Stuart Chase suggested in his account. If a company decided to apply the special supervisory approach involved in the test room, severe changes in span of control—and therefore overhead—are involved. Assuming a span of 1/24 in the main assembly room, the test room's foreman-observer and "several assistants"[20] (assume only two) would alter the span to 12/24, or one indirect employee (overhead) to two direct employees working on the product. Assuming that the girls earned sixty cents an hour each (reasonable for Western Electric assemblers at the time) and a supervisor earned $1.20 (behavioral science trained supervisors were hardly cheap), break-even output would require an 85% increase, considerably more than the 25% increase claimed for the experiment over the five year span.

The Special Incentive System for the Girls in the Experiment

The reader may have noted that the third period was omitted from the standard version. This is the period in which no changes were made in scheduling or other conditions except that the experimental assemblers were put on a special incentive system. The actual wage incentive changes made during period three were twofold: (a) the group was to be the six girls in the experiment as contrasted with much larger groups in the main assembly room, and (b) the basis for the piece rate was altered (we are not told exactly how by the original researchers)—evidently to the advantage of the operators in the experiment, since it was preferred by the girls in the main assembly room. Both Professors Homans and Mayo ignore the short-term output increase results evident during this 8–week period.

Three months later someone must have had doubts about the interpreted negligible effects of the new piece rate system. In order to test the effect of the new (and evidently preferred by the operators) incentive system outside the experimental environment, a group of 5 assemblers in the main assembly room were put on the new system, after a 5 week base output had been established. Almost at once these girls' output increased by 12.6% but because this caused so much discontent among the other girls in the main assembly room who wanted in on it also, it was discontinued after only 9 weeks. The output of the five girls promptly dropped by 16 percent.[21]

Neither Homans' account nor Mayo's mentioned this part of the research. Homans pointedly ignored the role of money incentive in his conclusions: "In brief, the increase in the output rate of the girls in the Relay Assembly Test

Room could not be related to any changes in their physical conditions of work, whether experimentally induced or not. It could, however, be related to what can only be spoken of as the development of an *organized social group in a peculiar and effective relation with its supervisors.*"[22] (Italics added.)

In order to settle the matter of the effect of the incentive system versus the friendly supervision, still another side experiment was performed. In the experiment, ". . . the test room situation was to be duplicated in all respects except for the change in pay incentive . . . if output showed a trend similar to that noted (in the relay assembly experiment), it would suggest that the wage incentive was not the dominant factor in the situation."[23] The original research reports show that the output of these five girls increased 15.6% during the 14 month study. Carey's analysis points up that the researchers had to do some fancy juggling of the figures to be able to claim such an increase: ". . . the output rate for each girl shows continuous and marked fluctuations over the whole (period) of the study. To obtain the percentage increase to be attributed to each girl, the investigators chose for each girl a "peak" output period within the study period and measured her increase as the difference between this peak and her output rate at the outset of the study. These peaks occur at different dates for different girls. There is *no one period* over which the group achieved the 15 percent average increase claimed."[24]

If the effect of the incentive system as a motivator was overlooked by the researchers in their conclusions, it certainly was not overlooked by the assemblers. As an integral part of the research activities, each girl was interviewed regularly. In her October 2, 1931 interview, the parts runner responded to the interviewer's questions concerning what she liked about the experimental room as follows:[25]

E.   "Well, and of course, the money part is nice. You know we have a separate gang and we have our own percentage. We get more money, you see, because there are just a few to divide it among, that's why."
I: "What difference does that make?"
E: "Well, it means you get more money because there are few people to divide it among."
I: "I don't see just how that makes you get more money. How is that?"
E: "Well, you see, out in the big department there are a lot of people in one gang . . . and in the Test Room there are just a few. Well, if you have to divide it among just a few, it means that you get more money. It's no more than right that it should be that way. You just get what you're earning there. You're not working for anyone else so why should you give them some of your money. You're working for yourself. The way it used to be, one person would turn out a whole lot and then another girl would just take advantage and take it easy. That's the way it is in the big department."

I: "Oh, it's *that* that makes you get more money, is it?"
E: "Yes, because everybody *works* in our gang. It's pretty hard to take advantage there, you see. For a while they had some other girls there, but then they had to put Mary and Jenny in their place. I guess they had to take the other girls out because they didn't care to cooperate."

Misleading and Confusing "Output" Terms

The term "output went up" found throughout the original account of the research and in all the lay and brokers' accounts can have several possible meanings. Alex Carey's attempt to clear up the meaning of the term led him to the following remarks:

> Two measures of the workers' performance are used: total output per week, and hourly rate of output by weeks. It is not clear from Roethlisberger and Dickson's report (of the Relay Assembly Room experimental periods 1-13) whether the increase is in total output or rate of output. It is described only as "increase in output," and "output rose . . . roughly 30 percent," which would ordinarily be taken to mean an increase in total output. But the investigators make it clear in passing that throughout the studies they used rate of output per hour as "the most common arrangement of output data" by which to "portray the general trend in efficiency of each operator and of the group." Whitehead, who produced a two-volume statistical study (of the Relay Assembly study) as companion volumes to Roethlisberger and Dickson's standard report, is very clear on this point: "All output will be expressed in the form of a *rate* . . . as so many relays per hour."
>
> However, Whitehead employs throughout his study the description "*weekly rate of output*" when he means *rate of output per hour by weeks*. This practice, coupled with his habit of not labelling the ordinates of his charts dealing with changes in output, and added to by Roethlisberger and Dickson's use of phrases such as "increase in output" to mean both *increase in rate of output per hour* and *increase in total output*, has led to widespread misinterpretation of the Hawthorne results, and textbook accounts which are seriously in error.[26]

Work Method Advantages in the Experimental Room

Omitted in the interpretation of most accounts of the experiment is that the number of different relays to be assembled was drastically reduced for the girls when they moved to the experimental room. Also omitted in these accounts were other significant differences unrelated to "social" or "psychological" differences between the main and experimental assembly set-ups. The girls in the experimental room did little house-keeping, did not have to stack their finished assemblies in boxes, worked on much longer "runs" per type of relay, and had exceptionally good parts-runner service. Below are more heretofore unpublished excerpts from the interview notes of various operators and others connected with the experiment which point up the considerable non-social differences between the main room and the experimental room (The interviewer here has attempted several times without success to get the assembly inspector to characterize the difference between the Test Room and Main Assembly room. Finally, the inspector, identified only as "E," began to respond in her interview for June 18, 1931):

E: "Well, for one thing they have the chute. They don't have to put the relays in boxes like they do in the department."
I: "How is this systematical?"
E: "Well, because they have the chute."
I: "Yes, I have seen those chutes, but I don't understand why they are more systematical?"
E: "Well, because they can save time, that's why!" (Girls in the main assembly room had to put finished relays in boxes kept near their benches.)
       In her interview for July 9, 1931, the interviewer is again asking about differences between the main room and the test room:
E: ". . . I can't see any difference between the test room and other places except their orders."
I: "How do you mean?"
E: "Well, they don't work on so many different kinds of relays. They've got larger orders in the test room. They may have lots of different kinds—they may have twenty-five different kinds in the big department—and in there (Test room) maybe they'll only have two or three kinds. That makes a difference because you don't have to change so often. Every time you have to change a set-up it takes time, but in the Test Room you'll work for a whole week or a couple of weeks on one set-up."

       Interviews with the parts runner/layout operator revealed further variables not considered in any of the published accounts. In response to the interviewer's request for suggestions for improvements in the Test Room, the parts runner offers the following in her June 17, 1931 interview:

E: "There aren't any improvements that I could suggest for the Test Room. In the big place (main department) I think they could—well, I don't know— but I should think they could work it out some way. I don't know if they could give everyone the attention they do there or not."
I: "How do you mean?"
E: "Oh, like seeing that their tools are as good as they can be, and things like that. You know sometimes in the big place they're not fixed the way they should be, but if there's anything the matter with them there (in the Test Room) I have to chase around until they're just so, and in the Test Room the girls always have their work in time. They don't have to wait for it."

In her October 2, 1931 interview, this parts runner complains of "many extra trips for handfuls of parts to tide the girls over."

Following are some additional brief quotes from interviews with the assembly operators further pointing up contaminants: Operator 2: "They have had those insulators (thick, more difficult) out in the department for a long time, and we have had the thin ones . . . and we hardly ever have to wait for parts in the Test Room." A different operator said, "You ought to be glad you're not out in the department. They have to go home when they run out of parts." When the Test Room operators were out of parts, they were paid their average earnings. Operator 4 remarked in one of her interviews that "In the Test Room we never have to pick up anything (referring to housekeeping at the workplace)." Operator 5A, referring to the side experiment in which five operators in the main department were temporarily put on the preferred incentive system, said, "You know they had a small gang working together in the main department when I came back and they almost made as much as they make in the Test Room."

The key reasons for examining these differences between the test room and the main room are as follows: Since the girls' main room period 1 was considered as a base, were there reasons for output there to be abnormally depressed? We can see from the interview notes that there would be motives to stretch out the work if there were dangers of running out of parts and being sent home. And from these notes it is clear that the test room offered a number of other advantages unrelated to human relations factors, such as longer runs, better set-up coverage, easier-to-assemble relay models, relief from housekeeping and stacking their relays in boxes. Add to these the preferred small group incentive plan and the policy of not sending the experimental operators home when they ran out of parts (which was less often than in the main room), and we can expect a significant difference between the two locations quite unrelated to social factors and friendly supervision. Unfortunately, we are told nothing of any consequence by the researchers of most of these non-social advantages. It is likely that the methods improvements developed over time and could have had an effect extending over most of the life of the experiment.

The Effects of Replacing Two of the Assemblers

One of the most significant events of the entire experiment took place at the end of period seven. The original two operators, who had chosen the other four operators, were dismissed from the experiment primarily for low output, excessive talking, and for ignoring reprimands regarding this behavior. After twelve weeks in the experimental room, four of the five girls were brought before the foreman and reprimanded for too much talking. Their general response was that they had understood that they were to work naturally as they felt like doing. Three months later, because the girls had shown no improvement in their behavior, talking was prohibited and the supervisors were asked to suggest to the girls that if they didn't improve, they might lose their free lunches. Neither such hints nor daily reprimands regarding excessive talking seemed to produce the "wholehearted cooperation" desired by management and the researchers, so operators 1A and 2A were dismissed from the experiment.[27]

There are several puzzling aspects to the decision to dismiss these two girls from the experiment. First, they were told to behave naturally when they started the experiment. Second, one of the duties of the test room observer was to create ". . . a friendly relation with the operators which would ensure their cooperation. He was anxious to dispel any apprehensions they might have about the test and, in order to do this, he began to converse informally with them each day. Sometimes the topics he brought up pertained to their work, sometimes to personal matters, and occasionally they took the form of a general inquiry as to the attitude of the operators toward the test."[28] Third, Professor Homans wrote that the girls liked to work in the test room because "it was fun," and because the absence of the old supervisory control made it possible for them to work freely without anxiety. He did note that ". . . an effort was made in the beginning to discourage conversation, though it was soon abandoned. The observer in charge of the experiment was afraid of losing the cooperation of the girls if he insisted too strongly on this point. Talk became common and loud. Indeed, the conversation of the operators came to occupy an important place in the log. T. N. Whitehead had pointed out that the girls in the test room were far more thoroughly supervised than they ever had been in the regular department. They were watched by an observer of their own, an interested management, and outside experts."[29]

One might wonder how the two dismissed operators felt after learning that efforts to discourage conversation had been abandoned, and instead, conversation was encouraged after they left. And how might they have felt when learning that, as Homans wrote, the removal of the old supervisory control "made it possible for them to work freely without anxiety."

For whatever reasons they got rid of operators 1A and 2A, their replacements hardly performed as though they were garden variety. *These two girls, chosen by the foreman, immediately produced more—hourly or weekly—than any of the girls who had had the benefit of the friendly supervision for many months and the opportunity to be an integral part of a well-knit social group! The two new operators continued to outproduce the rest of the group throughout the remaining 18 months of the study.*

The clearly superior performance of these two girls for the rest of the study offers at least one alternative interpretation for the output increases over most of the study. Prior to their joining the group, the average hourly output had increased by 13% and weekly output by 9% over the average for these indexes for Periods 1 and 2. Since the preferred incentive plan produced among an uncontaminated group an output increase of at least this magnitude, perhaps this increase thus far could be attributed to the incentive system. And since there is no statistically significant difference between the average hourly output for the first period with the new girls (Period 8) and the average of the remaining 5 periods, it is just possible that these two high producing pacers made the difference. One thing is clear from the data: the largest single increase in average hourly output was $+11\%$ from period 7 to period 8. The average hourly output variation for all other pairs of sequential periods was less than $+2\%$.[30]

Franke and Kaul conclude, from their exhaustive regressional analysis, that these two pacers were part of the "managerial discipline" applied. Their study revealed that 56% of the output variation can be accounted for by managerial discipline.[31]

Summary of the Flaws in the Research Design and Execution

Below is a summary list of the flaws rendering the research of little use for generalizing or establishing behavioral science laws or principles:

1. Subjects were not chosen randomly from the main relay assembly room. Instead, two were chosen and allowed to pick three others. Two of the criteria for choosing and approving the choices were cooperativeness and experience.
2. After 8 months, two operators were moved from the experimental room for low productivity, excessive talking, and insubordination.
3. These two were replaced by two operators whose performance immediately and for the remainder of the experiment exceeded that of the other three girls in spite of the fact that they had not experienced the claimed motivating effects of the warm and friendly supervision for eight months as had the other girls.
4. The output base performance (control) was established while the five assemblers were in the main assembly department which did not offer the same non-social advantages given the girls in the experimental room. For example, the girls in the main assembly room worked under a less preferred incentive system. Items 5-12 describe more such differences.
5. There was motivation to stretch out the work due to being sent home when out of parts during the base period in the main assembly room, whereas in the experimental room the assemblers were given busy work or were paid for waiting.
6. There was a wider variety of relays to be assembled by each worker (up to 25) in the main room as compared to from 2 to 5 in the experimental room.

7. Assembly job runs were much longer in the experimental room thereby reducing set-up time for any given period of production.

8. In the main room, the girls had housekeeping chores around their benches whereas this was not true in the experimental room.

9. In the main room the operators had to stack their finished relays in boxes near their benches as compared to pushing each relay off their benches into a chute in the experimental room.

10. The span of parts and set-up service was 1/7 in the main room compared to 1/5 in the experimental room.

11. In the main room the girls assembled more relays with the more difficult-to-assemble thicker insulators compared to the more easily assembled thin insulators used in the experimental room.

12. In one of the side experiments in order to establish the possible effect of the incentive system, five girls were put on the preferred incentive system (5-girl base) in the main assembly room. Their production went up 12.5% almost immediately. When the other girls in the main room wanted in on it, it was removed for these five girls whose output dropped 16%.

13. In another side experiment to determine any effects of the incentive system, the test room situation was duplicated except for the change in the incentive system. The original research report showed a 15.6% increase during the study. This gain was possible, because the researchers compared an average of each girl's peak week during the experimental period with the average of their output rate at the beginning of the study.

14. All of the shorter hour variations (Periods 8, 9, and 11) in the operator's work day provided no economic penalty. In addition to their piece rate, they received pay for these hours removed from their scheduled work-day.

15. Threats (to remove free lunches) were used to motivate for higher output, although one of the hypotheses was that friendly and permissive supervision would cause higher output.

Conclusions Reached by the Researchers and Various Observers

We can now look at the various conclusions reached by the different parties regarding the causes of the output increases which occurred during the 30 month experiment.

Roethlisberger and Dickson discussed five possible hypotheses as being considered causes of the output increases:

1. Improved material conditions and methods of work introduced in the

test room. Conclusion: None of the analyses showed any conclusive evidence in favor of this hypothesis.[32]

2. The rest pauses and shorter hours provided relief from cumulative fatigue. Conclusion: No evidence in support of this hypothesis.

3. The rest pauses and shorter hours provided relief from monotony. Conclusion: No definite conclusion could be drawn.[33]

4. The increased wage incentive introduced in Period 3. Conclusions: (a) No evidence that the increase could be attributed to the wage factor alone, and (b) The effect of a wage incentive was so dependent on its relation to other factors that it was impossible to consider it as having an independent effect.[34]

5. Changes in the method of supervision. Conclusion: "The chief result of the first two years of experimentation in the Relay Assembly Test Room, then, had been to demonstrate the importance of employee attitudes and preoccupations. The importance of employee attitudes had been apparent in the "Apprehension of authority" which had been common to all the operators, although in different degrees, in the early stages of the test room and which could be "lit up" at the slightest provocation. It had been evident in the effects of the experimentally introduced changes in working conditions which had proven to be carriers of social meaning rather than mere changes in physical circumstances . . . Over and above this, the results from a research point of view were negative."[35]

Homan's conclusions were as given earlier, that the output increase could not be related to any changes in their physical conditions of work, but that it could be related to the ". . . development of an organized social group in a peculiar and effective relation with its supervisors."[36]

Mayo's account, for the most part, offers quotes from interim unpublished reports by Western Electric Research Division officers. These closely parallel the Roethlisberger and Dickson report. His major interpretation of the results is that in bringing the girls into the test room and altering a number of conditions, they were forced to adjust themselves to a new industrial "milieu," ". . . in which their own self-determination and their social well-being ranked first and the work was incidental."[37]

In spite of a number of careful reviews of the data since 1939, the above conclusions have prevailed in psychology textbooks, sociology textbooks, management textbooks, and numerous materials for management training courses all over the world. The first of the analyses of the data refuting the claims for social causes of the output increases came in 1953 from Michael Argyle, who concluded that there was "no quantitative evidence for the conclusion for which this experiment is famous—that the increase of output was due to a changed relation with supervision."[38] Alex Carey's 1967 review of the data was similar: ". . . it is clear that the objective evidence obtained . . . does not support any of the conclusions derived by the Hawthorne investigators. The results of these studies, far from supporting the various components of the "human relations approach," are surprisingly consistent with a rather old-world view about the value of monetary incentives, driving leadership, and discipline. It is only by massive and relentless re-interpretation that the evidence is made to yield contrary conclusions."[39] By "massive and relentless reinterpretation," Carey referred to the scientifically illiterate procedure of ignoring unpopular explanations simply because the researchers could find no conclusive evidence in favor of them and assuming that since no single non-preferred explanation accounted for all the increased output, *none* of these was valid. He further pointed out that such procedures were not, of course, applied to the interpretation of the data regarding their obviously preferred hypothesis.

H. M. Parsons' study of the data led him to conclude that the key factors producing the majority of the output increases were the incentive system coupled with rapid feedback of output information to the assemblers. His conclusion is simply that operant conditioning principles prevailed.[40] (See Chapter 15 for a detailed discussion of operant conditioning principles.)

In October, 1978, still another set of conclusions differing from those of the original experimenters was published. Franke and Kaul concluded that 97% of the output variance can be explained by such variables as work hours per week (24%), managerial discipline (56%), the depression (8%), rest time (8%), and the small group incentive (1%).[41]

CONCLUSIONS

Any but a casual analysis of the original research report can lead only to the conclusion that the Hawthorne "experiment" more resembles a clinical style *case study* in an institutional setting than a *scientific experiment*. Even though elaborate apparatus for recording output were employed, even though the report included charts, tables, and graphs and even though the researchers had academic status, the Hawthorne studies were not scientific *experiments*. It doesn't follow that nothing can be learned from them, however. Below are some of the more important elements of this instruction:

1. It is extremely difficult if not impossible to tease out scientifically for examination all the significant factors involved in employee work motivation in a socio-industrial subculture.

2. The study provided a reaffirmation of the already well-known fact that money incentives alone are, for many workers, dependent upon many factors for their motivational success. At least one of these is a group of social factors. In 1898, some 30 years earlier, a close knit group of Hungarians at Bethlehem Steel blocked Frederick Taylor's monetary incentives on a very straightforward ethnic group basis.

3. Considerable evidence was made available to suggest that under nearly ideal working conditions—physical, social, and monetary—significant output increases may result. A casual review of these conditions reveals that they are most likely not economical. To have duplicated them at Western Electric for the entire relay assembly department, for example, would have at least doubled the cost of the relays.
4. We learned that the principle "perception is functionally selective" is universal enough to include behavioral science researchers, academic followers, and many practitioners. All seem to have rejected out of hand any interpretation of the results that was not dominantly or exclusively social in nature.
5. We learned, too, that a profound management philosopher with a respectable academic base, whose philosophy is consonant with the feelings and beliefs of academia and whose philosophy is supported by scientific trappings, will get a lot of mileage out of his "research."

The reader may wish to question the viewpoint that the diagnostic and clinical approaches can offer valuable instruction for scientists. This should not provide any serious problem for the reader if he or she is aware of the successes and failures of this approach for developing general principles (laws) in such fields as clinical psychology, sociology, and medicine. While such studies are extremely instructive, their usual role is to suggest directions for rigorous research upon which generalizations, based upon scientific *experiments*, can be drawn. Shortening this tedious process only brings on the setbacks obvious in the field of behavioral science. After 50 years we still know precious little about the causes of worker productivity variations.

MAYO'S REAL INFLUENCE

If his name is associated with a severely criticized scientific research effort and interpretations therefrom, what contribution did the man Mayo make to the development of social science in management? Is there a role for a philosopher who is somewhat in the *avant garde* of an ongoing cultural change? The evidence of his impact, of course, is in the hundreds of accounts of the Hawthorne Studies in the literature in over 10 languages. If we leave aside for the moment the relatively unnoticed besmirchment of social science, what have we left? Fritz Roethlisberger, who worked with Mayo for over 2 decades, wrote the following in his introduction to the 1960 republishing of Mayo's 1933 *The Human Problems of an Industrial Civilization:*

> For me, Mayo—the living reality I knew—was a man of imagination, a stimulator of thought, a promoter of clinical research, and the discoverer of a useful way of thinking about organizational behavior that could be developed fruitfully in the directions of both knowledge and practice. This last is for me by far his greatest con-

tribution . . . Mayo was not a systematic thinker. Although he stated his ideas vigorously, he never stated them rigorously. His accomplishments are best seen in the context of face-to-face relationships. His chief products were the people that he influenced and helped to develop. Even the ideas that he developed in books were more often in the nature of seeds to be cultivated in the field rather than of rigorous hypotheses to be tested in the laboratory.

To the scientist who is primarily interested in the hypothesis-testing end of the scientific enterprise continuum, Mayo has little to say. But to the scientist who is also interested in the hypothesis-generating end of this continuum, he has plenty to contribute. Mayo, it might be said, was the enemy of the sterile hypothesis and of the meaningless correlation of high statistical significance.

Although Mayo was for the opportunity for growth for everyone everywhere, he recognized the possibility of lopsided growth. He saw that many things, both desirable ones and undesirable ones, can be both functional and dysfunctional (sic). Restriction of output among workers, for instance, although functional for the solidarity of the group and the emotional security of its members, is dysfunctional for the group's identification with the economic objectives of the enterprise.

But frozen states of equilibrium are not inevitable; they are man-made, and new ways of thinking can liquidate them . . . What Mayo is saying is: Let's study organizations as natural organic wholes or systems striving to survive and maintain their equilibrium in different environments. Let's see if this way of looking at them will allow us to specify better the many factors in a complex situation and "wherever the general effect is unsatisfactory to the worker and to industry, to discover the nature of the disequilibrium and the source of the interference."

Let's note that this conceptual scheme is essentially a model for clinical and diagnostic inquiry with significant overtones for the practitioner . . . but let's not underestimate this accomplishment. What Copernicus, Galileo, and Newton did to Aristotle, Mayo's way of thinking also did to the dogmas of his day about organizational behavior. It reduced them to the status of empirical questions, that is, questions to be settled by observation and judgment and not by argument and debate.[42]

One thing is clear from my review of the Hawthorne Studies. The five-year "observation and judgment" effort under the direction of Professor Mayo settled no "empirical questions" about worker motivation.

NOTES

1. Richard McKeon, ed., *The Basic Works of Aristotle*, (New York, N.Y.: Random House, 1941), p. 596.
2. John A. Wilson, *The Culture of Ancient Egypt*, (Chicago, Ill.: University of Chicago Press, 1951), as quoted in Claude S. George, Jr., *The History of Management Thought*, (Englewood Cliffs, N.J.: Prentice-Hall, 1972), p. 66.
3. Robert Owen, *The Life of Robert Owen*, (London, England: Effingham Wilson, 1857), as quoted in Daniel A. Wren, *The Evolution of Management Thought*, (New York, N.Y.: The Ronald Press Co., 1972), p. 66.

4. Claude S. George, *The History of Management Thought*, (Englewood Cliffs, N.J.: Prentice-Hall, 1972), pp. vi–xi.

5. Details of Mayo's biography condensed from "Elton Mayo," *The International Encyclopedia of the Social Sciences*, (1968), 10, pp. 82–83.

6. Vilfedo Pareto, an Italian, one of the first sociologists to deal with the sociology of administration and bureaucracy.

7. George C. Homans, *Fatigue of Workers*, (New York, N.Y.: Reinhold Publishing Corp., 1941), as reproduced in Walter Nord, ed., *Concepts and Controversy in Organizational Behavior*, (Pacific Palisades, Calif.: Goodyear Publishing Co., Inc., 1972), p. 242.

8. This is the beginning of the most popular account of the Hawthorne studies: Stuart Chase, "What Makes Workers Like to Work," *Reader's Digest*, February, 1941, pp. 15–20.

9. The specific references used to construct this version are the following: Henry Clay Lindgren and Donn Byrne, *Psychology: An Introduction to the Study of Human Behavior*, (New York, N.Y.: John Wiley & Sons, 1961), pp. 404–406; Committee on Work in Industry, National Research Council, *Fatigue of Workers: Its Relation to Industrial Production*, (New York, N.Y.: Reinhold Publishing Corp., 1941), pp. 56–66 (This portion of the Committee's report was written by George C. Homans, secretary to the Committee): Justin G. Longnecker, *Principles of Management and Organizational Behavior*, (Columbus, Ohio: Charles E. Merrill Publishing Company, 1973), pp. 316–317; and Stuart Chase, *op. cit.*

10. Homans was one of the more influential of the early behavioral science academics whose writings frequently carried accounts of various phases of the Hawthorne Studies. His account of the Relay Assembly Experiment, which will be referred to, is from George C. Homans, *Fatigue*, as in Nord, *op. cit.*, pp. 242–262.

11. Mayo's account from which several subsequent quotes will be drawn, is from Elton Mayo, *The Human Problems of an Industrial Civilization*, (New York, N.Y.: MacMillan Co., 1933), as republished, (New York, N.Y.: The Viking Press, 1960), pp. 53–73, copyright 1933 by The Macmillan Company, copyright assigned to The President and Fellows of Harvard College 1946.

12. Fritz J. Roethlisberger and William J. Dickson, *Management and the Worker*, (Cambridge, Mass.: Harvard University Press, 1939).

13. Alex Carey, "The Hawthorne Studies: A Radical Criticism," *American Sociological Review*, 32 (1967), pp. 403–16, as abridged in Nord, *op. cit.*, pp. 262–80.

14. H. M. Parsons, "What Happened at Hawthorne?" *Science*, Vol. 183 (March 1974), pp. 922–933.

15. Richard Herbert Franke and James D. Kaul, "The Hawthorne Experiments: First Statistical Interpretation," *American Sociological Review*, Vol. 43, No. 5 (October 1978), pp. 623–643.

16. Homans, *Fatigue*, as in Nord, p. 242.

17. *Ibid.*, p. 243.

18. Mayo, p. 56.

19. Roethlisberger and Dickson, p. 54.

20. Homans, *Fatigue*, as in Nord, p. 244.
21. Roethlisberger and Dickson, *Management*, as quoted by Carey, "Hawthorne," as abridged in Nord, p. 267.
22. Homans, *Fatigue*, as in Nord, p. 248.
23. Roethlisberger and Dickson, *Management*, as quoted by Carey, "Hawthorne," as abridged in Nord, p. 267.
24. Carey, "Hawthorne," as in Nord, p. 268.
25. Unpublished interview notes of interviews with the relay assemblers made available with permission by the Baker Library Archives of the Harvard Business School.
26. Carey, "Hawthorne," as in Nord, pp. 268–269.
27. *Ibid.*, pp. 272–274.
28. Roethlisberger and Dickson, p. 37.
29. Homans, *Fatigue*, as in Nord, p. 247.
30. Calculated from data in Roethlisberger and Dickson, pp. 76–78.
31. Franke and Kaul, p. 632.
32. Roethlisberger and Dickson, p. 89.
33. *Ibid.*, p. 127.
34. *Ibid.*, p. 160.
35. *Ibid.*, p. 184.
36. Homans, *Fatigue*, as in Nord, p. 248.
37. Mayo, *op. cit.*, pp. 70–71.
38. Michael Argyle, "The Relay Assembly Test Room in Retrospect," *Occupational Psychology*, Vol. 27 (1953), p. 103.
39. Carey, "Hawthorne," as in Nord, p. 280.
40. Parsons, p. 929.
41. Franke and Kaul, p. 632.
42. Reprinted with permission of Viking Penguin Inc., from Elton Mayo *The Human Problems of an Industrial Civilization*, (New York, N.Y.: The Macmillan Co., 1933) as republished by Viking Press, 1967, pp. ix-xiv. Copyright 1933 by The Macmillan Co., Copyright assigned to The President and Fellows of Harvard College, 1946.

PART III

MAJOR THEORIES
OF MOTIVATION

Easily the most often researched subject in behavioral science is the subject of motivation. Behavioral science's ancestors and cousins—philosophy, sociology, anthropology, psychology, and political science—have all been heavily occupied with many aspects of the "why?" of human behavior. A review of the evolution of the many theories of motivation reveals the extreme complexity of the subject and many theories which do little justice to these complexities. And theories, not laws or principles, seem to be about all we have on the subject. (The one thing we seem to have more of than theories is a large number of prescriptions telling us how to motivate people.) Most of these theories have been around for some time in one form or another, but serious and sustained scientific efforts to gather evidence for their support have been underway for only about 30 years.

Because one of the major objectives of this book is to bring into focus the degree to which there is appropriate support for the more popular theories, the basic organization of Part III will be around these theories.

Theoretical Approaches

Although various academic writers have attempted to classify theories of motivation, this requires considerable distortion of most of them unless it is considered only a classification of the major components or general thrusts of various theories. Below is a list intended only to point up the variety of approaches to the subject evident in the more popular theories discussed in Part III:

1. Needs list analyses, models, and hierarchies. *Major theorists: Abraham H. Maslow, David C. McClelland, and John Atkinson.*
2. Work environment and work characteristics. *These theorists study the work specifications and organizational climates to determine what "makes" people perform or what they want out of their jobs. A major theorist in this arena is Frederick Herzberg.*
3. Path-goal theorists. *These theorists examine the motivational processes of the effects of human desires in terms of their strengths and the perceptions of the degree to which they may be satisfied by various behaviors. Victor Vroom is a major theorist in this area.*
4. The role of money. *Although considered fairly passé in the literature, evidence is insufficient to reject money as a fruitful motivational approach. Major theorists no longer exist in this area, although the Lawler-Porter model, essentially a path-goal variant, is often researched under this label. And, of course, many managers whose careers depend heavily upon motivation in their organizations still believe that economic incentives can contribute to performance improvement.*

Other theories, sometimes only implied or embedded in their proponents' prescriptions for leaders or managers, are based on sociological and psychological viewpoints. Because their contributions concern human relationships and their results, these contributors are discussed in Part IV.

Chapter 4

Maslow's Need Hierarchy Theory

IT is not likely that many human relations courses for supervisors over the last 20 years excluded any mention of Maslow's need hierarchy theory. In most such courses, it is also unlikely that the presentation was billed as untested "theory." Most supervisors and managers have probably heard only of Maslow's "Need Hierarchy." Maslow's name was the fifth most often named in a National Industrial Conference Board study which asked "companies" which behavioral scientists had influenced them. His 54 mentions ranked behind McGregor, Herzberg, Likert, and Argyris and ahead of such names as Bennis, Drucker, Odiorne, Rogers, and 194 others. The study did not ask in what way these different behavioral scientists had influenced the respondents![1]

Maslow's Need Hierarchy Theory has appeared in texts in Urdu, Hindi, Amharic, Swahili, and Arabic, not to mention all the major European languages. Unfortunately, as is the case with most second and third hand versions of theories, these versions were selectively abridged and usually carried nothing of the evidence (or lack of it) which supported the theory. One reason for the lack of supportive evidence is simply that there isn't much. In Maslow's own words, as late as 1970, "[the theory] seems, for most people to have a direct personal, subjective plausibility. And yet it still lacks experimental verification and support. I have not yet been able to think of a good way to put it to the test . . . "[2] This does not mean that there have not been a few attempts to validate his theory. The results of these will be considered later in the chapter. What this does mean, given the disappointing results of these few studies, is simply that any present evaluation of Maslow's theory must necessarily be based mostly upon logic, common sense, personal observation, and experience.

Before looking at the theory in this light and in some detail, here is a typical description of the theory as it appears in management textbooks and management seminar handouts.[3]

The Need Hierarchy

Abraham Maslow's theory states that the motivation to work comes from attempts to satisfy certain basic needs. These needs are ranked in a hierarchy. Lower level needs must be satisfied before higher level needs emerge as motivators. Thus the theoretical framework of his theory stresses (1) that humans are wanting animals whose motivation will stem from unsatisfied needs, which means that satisfied needs are not motivators; and (2) that these needs are arranged in a hierarchy of importance, which results in shifts in motivation to the next higher level of needs as lower levels are satisfied. The theory contains five categories of needs. These are given below in order of importance:

1. PHYSIOLOGICAL NEEDS. This category refers to the basic needs of the human. Included here are such needs as those for food, water, sex, protection from the elements, etc. The higher level needs described below are not operative if the physiological needs are in a state of deprivation.
2. SAFETY OR SECURITY NEEDS. This level of needs assumes importance after the physiological needs are satisfied. These needs are the protection against danger and for personal security. Satisfaction of these needs in industrialized societies is represented by the many job security demands of unions, from contractural protection against layoff to the elaborate order in which these may be processed and their recall provisions. Included here would also be the unions' lobbying efforts for stricter safety laws and for safe working conditions in union contracts.
3. BELONGINGNESS AND LOVE NEEDS. Once the first two levels of needs above are satisfied, the motivators become the person's need for positive relationships with others. Frustration in attempts at the satisfaction of these needs can lead to impaired mental health of employees. The activities at this level involve efforts to gain acceptance by other people. They also involve giving and receiving affection, and, in general, satisfying the many forms of affiliation needs.
4. ESTEEM NEEDS. At this level, the behavior is aimed toward the gaining of recognition, status and appreciation by others. The acquiring of an appropriate level of self-respect represents the satisfaction of some of the needs in this level of the hierarchy.
5. SELF-ACTUALIZATION. The capstone on the hierarchy is the set of needs which can only be fulfilled by satisfying all the lower needs and by becoming what one is capable of becoming. These are the needs which require that one's own potential is realized. Also included in these needs is

the desire for continued self-development. (Some descriptions of the theory carry many of the original details given by Maslow in his discussion of this level of needs.) Below is a summary of the characteristics of self-actualizing persons:

a. Spontaneous
b. Problem-centered
c. Detached
d. Autonomous
e. Not given to stereotyping
f. Identify with mankind

g. Have a non-hostile sense of humor
h. Creative
i. Realistic
j. Unprejudiced
k. Resist conformity
l. Have intimate relationship with a special few.

The typical account of the theory carries advice to managements who would provide an environment which achieves maximum motivation. This advice varies in its focus, but usually emphasizes the importance of managements' efforts at facilitating need-fulfillment of the top three need levels—belongingness, esteem, and self-actualization. Some versions advocate employee participation in decision-making and planning as a good way to assist employees to fulfill esteem and self-actualization needs. Others point out that close supervision will likely frustrate the fulfillment of the top two needs—esteem and self-actualization. Still others insist that managers who have had sensitivity training are more likely to be able to facilitate the fulfillment of these two needs in their subordinates.

Efforts at Validation

No significant research evidence is presented in the typical description of the theory. Most such presentations are clearly advocative and the accounts usually make it clear that the authors find the theory, at the very least, quite likely to be valid.

Even though Maslow could not suggest ways of gathering empirical evidence in favor of his theory, there have been several scattered attempts to check the model. None is reported as an effort to test the entire model directly. Most were side analyses of research data whose original purpose was the exploration of other dimensions of motivation. There are several nearly insurmountable problems connected with attempting to validate the complete theory. Without suggesting that any research is useless unless it meets these, below are some of the more important specifications of an appropriate research design for testing the need hierarchy model:

1. THE RESEARCH MUST BE LONGITUDINAL—NOT CROSS-SECTIONAL—since it must test the successive prepotency among the five levels of needs.

According to the theory, for any given person, one class of needs will be more motivating than others. As these needs become satisfied, the next higher level needs emerge as stronger. In a sense, Maslow contended that the satisfaction of one level "causes" the next level to emerge as the most important. This can only be tested over time. Since Maslow's original definition of a self-actualizing person is akin to a human perfection model, many specifications of which are likely to take years of "growth," a longitudinal research design is clearly indicated. Moreover, in his preface to the second edition of *Motivation and Personality*, he ". . . removed one source of confusion (about self-actualizing people) by *confining the concept* very definitely to *older people*." (Italics added.)[4] In giving his reasons for this decision, Maslow almost appears to be retaliating for the "over thirty" stereotype of the generation gap style of the late 1960's and early 1970's.

By the criteria I used, self-actualization does not occur in young people. In our culture at least, youngsters have not yet achieved identity, or autonomy, nor have they had time enough to experience an enduring, loyal, post-romantic love relationship, nor have they generally found their calling, the altar upon which to offer themselves. Nor have they worked out their own system of values; nor have they had experience enough (responsibility for others, tragedy, failure, achievement, success) to shed perfectionistic illusions and become realistic; nor have they generally made their peace with death; nor have they learned how to be patient; nor have they learned enough about evil in themselves and others to be compassionate; nor have they had time to become post-ambivalent about parents and elders, power and authority; nor have they generally become knowledgeable and educated enough to open the possibility of becoming wise; nor have they generally acquired enough courage to be unpopular, to be unashamed about being openly virtuous, etc.[5]

Now that we have two dimensions of the self-actualizing person—the far-from-it youth and the original list of characteristics (realistic, accepting of self, detached, autonomous, etc.)—it would appear that a straight longitudinal verification research model would require a study of nearly a lifetime. A cross-sectional study could be done using five samples, but it is clear that for the sample whose salient need level is autonomy/esteem, considerable time would be required for them to move into self-actualizing. Even a cross-sectional study would have to be longitudinal enough to see significant portions of all samples through at least one need level change cycle.

2. THE RESEARCH DESIGN MUST MEASURE THE RELATIVE STRENGTH OF EACH CLASS OF NEEDS for the sample subjects. This is necessary to determine the successive prepotency among the five levels.

3. THE SAMPLE MUST BE LARGE ENOUGH TO YIELD ADEQUATE SUBSAMPLE SIZES BY DOMINANT NEED FOR EACH OF THE FIVE LEVELS OF NEEDS. This is necessary to permit inference from changes in needs as satisfaction at a

given level for various members of subsamples is achieved. Furthermore, since Maslow does not claim a predicted or constant *rate* of "growth" through the various levels, the subsamples must be large enough to permit inferences about unknown portions of each, as their members' needs are fulfilled at different levels at different rates. Every time a subsample member gets fixated regardless of reason, he or she reduces the subsample size of "growing humans" by one.

4. NEEDS MUST BE IDENTIFIED BY LEVEL AND MEASURED BOTH THROUGH TECHNIQUES CAPABLE OF DETERMINING "CONATIVE" (CONSCIOUS STRIVING) AND UNCONSCIOUS MOTIVES. Any conscious or conative source of need measures must be validated against the unconscious measures. These specifications are necessary because Maslow contended that the basic needs in his hierarchy are ". . . on the whole, . . . in the average person . . . more often unconscious" and that ". . . unconscious motivations, on the whole, (are) rather more important than the conscious motivations. What we have called the basic needs are very often largely unconscious . . ."[6] He further points out that dealing only with conscious motivation will not only neglect much of the important motivation, but may be misleading: "Indeed the relationship (between conscious and unconscious motives) may actually be a negative one . . ."[7]

The kinds of techniques required, then, to overcome this obstacle, if they could be validated for this purpose and found reliable, would be clinical projective tests, such as the Rorschach Ink Blot Test, hypnosis, and sodium amytal.[8] Maslow, however, although he used the Rorschach in his personal and unscientific search for self-actualizing people, rejects its basic usefulness on the grounds that it merely helped in determining who was *not* self-actualizing—not who *was*.[9] This can't be too surprising to a professional psychologist, since the Rorschach was well known to have been designed as a clinical tool for the diagnosis of various forms of *abnormal* behavior.

5. EACH SUBJECT'S ENVIRONMENT MUST BE EXAMINED IN RELATION TO HIS SALIENT needs to determine if there is a realistic "possibility of attainment" of the next higher level of needs. Maslow points up the requirement for this research specification in his statement "Attention to this factor of possibility of attainment is *crucial* for understanding the differences in motivations . . ." (Italics added)[10] Earlier in his section headed "POSSIBILITY OF ATTAINMENT" he remarked that, ". . . on the whole, we yearn consciously for that which might conceivably be attained."[11] The information on environmental need-fulfillment possibilities would be used to account for subjects' failure to grow. Evidently, Maslow recognizes two somewhat indistinct constraints

on growth: (a) failure to fulfill needs due to environmental opportunity and (b) non-current reasons such as neuroses in the ". . . basic-need-gratification-bent impulses . . . that have somehow got stymied or misdirected or confused with other needs or fixated on the wrong means."[12]

6. OPERATIONAL DEFINITIONS OF TERMS FOR CLASSIFYING AND MEASURING NEEDS ACCORDING TO THE HIERARCHY MUST BE AGREED UPON AS APPROXIMATING THOSE USED IN THE MODEL. Since each need level is described by a number of different need examples, determining if needs have been met at a given level will require dealing with unlike—for research purposes—variables at each level. Some means will be required for determining the *satiation level mix* of such needs as hunger, sex, relief from pain, and shelter, for example. If all these needs in a given subject are found to be fulfilled, except sex, for example, is the next level of needs supposed to emerge as dominant? Or what of the case of safety needs which consist of needs for order, law, security, stability, dependency and protection from fear, anxiety, and chaos, etc.? An adequate fulfillment mix must be determined, else we will have to consider that there could be few people, if any, beyond this stage of need-fulfillment in all the turbulent areas in Europe and America, not to mention Solzhenitsyn's Russia or other oppressively insecurity-producing environments.

Bearing in mind what an ideal need hierarchy research verification study would require, let's examine what has been done since the theory was first stated in 1943. The simple fact that only a few studies have been attempted suggests that while research-oriented behavioral scientists may have found the theory "personally plausible," they appear to have generally recognized, as did Maslow, the insurmountable obstacles in testing or proving the theory. It is obvious from Maslow's presentation in his book that his theory attempts to include, if not integrate, almost all other theories and facts available about human behavior. It attempts to incorporate clinical theories from Freud to chemical therapy, theories from child psychology, industrial psychology, cultural anthropology, and sociology, to name a few.

The most ambitious research effort at testing his theory was a longitudinal study of five years by Douglas T. Hall and Khalil E. Nougaim.[13] Their sample was 49 young managerial-level employees of an American Telephone and Telegraph Company operating division who remained with the company for at least 5 years. Their assessment of needs data gathering was five annual three-hour interviews by consulting psychologists. The interviews produced data regarding job attitudes, superior, peer, and subordinate relationships, sources of satisfaction and dissatisfaction, career aspirations and strategies, and major occurences during each year. The following nine need category yields from the interviews, coded by two psychology doctoral candidates, were collapsed into Maslow's top four need levels.

1. Meaning and sense of purpose: the need to serve some higher cause.
2. Personal development: the need for integration and development of personal skills.
3. Stimulation: the need for stimulating activity and excitement.
4. Achievement and challenge: the need to compete for challenging standards.
5. Power and responsibility: the need for accountability and control.
6. Support and approval: the concern over acts of notice, praise, or blame.
7. Affiliation: developing and maintaining affective relationships.
8. Structure: the need for predictable and ordered environment.
9. Safety: the need to feel safe and prepared; to avoid threat.[14]

The statistical analysis of their data—correlations between need satisfaction and need strength—revealed that need strength was more often correlated with need satisfaction, not the next higher level of needs. Correlations between changes of lower need satisfactions and higher need strength on a year to year basis ranged between .05 to .22. Statistical significance tests were not possible (or warranted with such low relationships) due to the necessary method of pooling need codes.

When the data were analyzed by need intensity and satisfaction from first to fifth year by more/less successful (salary), a few interesting relationships are suggested. The term "suggested" is used because only statistical significances, not meaningful magnitudes, are given. Although the two groups did not differ in need strength at year five, the successful group showed a (statistically) "significant" increase in Affiliation need strength, and the less successful group showed a reduction in Achievement and Esteem satisfaction. Although no differences were evident at the outset, by the fifth year the more successful group appeared to be more satisfied on the job than the less successful group, as anyone could probably predict without research data.

The authors concluded their report by saying that ". . . no strong relationships were found to support the hierarchy of needs we hypothesized. Furthermore, none of the correlations between need and satisfaction levels was high enough to support the existence of a hierarchial order different from the one we tested."[15] It should be noted here that their hypotheses represented the nearest approximation to Maslow's model of all the studies reviewed. They further concluded that the ". . . success analysis . . . yielded disconfirming results" and that "an analysis of the changing need and satisfaction patterns of both groups (more and less successful) provides further group-level disconfirmation of the hierarchy."[16]

As in the Hall and Nougaim study, all the other studies gathered "conscious" data—the others usually using paper and pencil questionnaires for measuring need strength and satisfaction. Some used inferences for need fulfillment or frustration by the nature of the jobs being performed and statistical data such as absenteeism, turnover, and productivity for need satisfactions.

J. V. Clark's study used data from studies undertaken for purposes other than testing Maslow's model. His reframing of the data to provide information on need satisfaction was used to try to predict indices such as absenteeism, turnover, and productivity. The conclusions were more hypotheses-generating than validation of the need hierarchy theory.[17]

Beer, in a study of supervisory leadership style and its effect on need satisfaction among a sample of female clerks, concluded that the Maslow model is lacking as a useful theory for industrial motivation. However, since his subjects, on a forced ranking system, tended to rank needs somewhat similarly to the model, he believed that the model provided a fairly reliable ranking of the *a priori* needs of workers in industry. He found no relationship between leadership style and motivation, nor between need satisfaction and motivation.[18]

In an earlier international study, Porter, using a paper-pencil data gathering instrument, gathered information from managers in 14 countries. He found that only the U.S. and British managers' need satisfactions tended to follow Maslow's model, although the physiological needs were ignored in his study. The other 12 countries' sampled managers' responses did not follow the model, and the needs emerging as most important to them seemed to be the least satisfied.[19] This is quite different from the findings of Hall and Nougaim who found that "With the exception of Affiliation, the strength of each need correlated more strongly with its own satisfaction than with the satisfaction of any other need."[20]

The researchers in another study offer the following conclusions from their studies on needs and need satisfaction: ". . . the failure to find support for Maslow's need categories in organizational settings is due to: (1) an inadequate conceptualization which does not readily facilitate the development of operational indicators, and (2) the initial orientation of Maslow's theory which was not specifically aimed toward organizational settings."[21]

Summary of Validation Efforts

The most that can be gained from a review of research efforts to support Maslow's need hierarchy theory is that while it is a "personally plausible theory," it is not likely to benefit from scientific verification. (We must be mindful of the simple observation that, for most of the people in the world today, it is still personally plausible that the world is flat.) But are there alternative personally plausible need hierarchies? Can the observations of men like Maslow be organized in acceptably different forms? Without pretending that alternatives could be verified—it didn't seem to seriously hinder Maslow—are there any other theoretical constructs which agree with his basic observations?

A number of behavioral scientists have suggested alternatives. All of them end up either telescoping or combining several of his need levels. All seem to ignore the physiological level, perhaps because they have little interest in a universal theory, since the concerned behavioral scientists in the literature do not seem to live and work in India, Ethiopia or Northern Nigeria. The levels most often combined are the middle three—safety/security, belongingness/social/love, and autonomy/esteem—perhaps for sound personally plausible reasons.

If we can be persuaded to back away from the theory enough to alter our scope and perspective, say to the point of view of a biologist or zoologist, what might be a reasonable alternative theory? If we hypothesize that survival and perpetuation of the species is the *paramount motive*, how many of Maslow's need levels could be seen as direct extensions of this need? If we look to the roots or embryonic versions of Maslow's three middle levels—safety/security, belongingness/social/love, and autonomy/esteem, is it plausible that they all began and grew in the service of the human organisms' need for survival and for species perpetuation? Our earliest behavior patterns exhibiting needs for safety and security begin as infants. Our first assurances (fulfillment?) of safety and security needs likely came about from being picked up, held and/or fed when we cried. If being picked up and held provides any basis for further gratification of Maslow's security/safety level, and his belongingness/social/love level, our amalgamation begins to be plausible.

If autonomy can be seen as an improved form of security due to dependency reduction, a portion of Maslow's third level can be grouped with level two. If being esteemed means, among many other related things, that one can call his banker on the phone and be granted an informal over-draft, is it not reasonable that another major dimension of Maslow's level three could be related to security? The point of these conjectures is simply to suggest that with a concept so iceberg-like as human motivation, there are a number of ways to rationalize on a personally plausible basis the underwater shape of the unknown mass.

One of the main reasons managers dare not eliminate money as a reward system is likely their intuitive recognition that, although it may be used to buy a non-edible boat or patio, money may well symbolize, however elaborately for many people, the fulfillment of the fundamental need for survival and perpetuation.

Conclusions

Maslow's need hierarchy, an up-to-date "dynamicized" version of Aristotle's hierarchy of the soul, which included a "nutritive" (physiological) soul at the lower end and the noetic (self-actualization) soul at the top[22], remains unverified, yet personally plausible to many.

Knowledge of Maslow's theory is likely of little real operational value to most managers, for reasons mostly unrelated to the validity of the theory. The reasons are simply that most managers, like most of us, do not change very much as a result of having learned a new personally plausible theory. Although the ascription is more appropriate to Douglas McGregor's prescriptions for managers, it could be easily hypothesized that Maslow's influence was merely evolutionary, in the sense that he was only a harbinger of inevitable Western cultural change—a change of motivation focus away from the physiological due to increasing affluence and education, which was taking place with or without his and McGregor's implied or direct prescriptions.

In summary, it can be said that science seems to have no quarrel with Maslow's physiological need level. This seems to be the most personally plausible of the five levels, because, although everyone does not necessarily know if he self-actualizes, he knows that he eats, wants sex and goes to the bathroom. Maslow's highest need level—self-actualization—seems to be not much of a problem, either, but mainly because most people are somewhat unsure of what it means. In between these, his model appears sufficiently ambiguous and therefore difficult to refute or support, thus permitting individual interpretations with sufficiently wide margins to allow everyone to be right. Chapter 14, which discusses Douglas McGregor's Theory Y, will deal more directly with the managerial usefulness of behavioral prescriptions based mainly upon Maslow's need hierarchy model.

NOTES

1. Harold Rusy, *Behavioral Science, Concepts and Applications*, Personnel Policy Study No. 216, (New York, N.Y.: The National Industrial Conference Board, Inc., 1969), p. 10.

2. Abraham H. Maslow, *Motivation and Personality*, 2nd ed., (New York, N.Y.: Harper & Row, 1970 Revision), p. xii.

3. This typical description was developed from the following: Don Hellriegel and John W. Slocum, Jr., *Management: Contingency Approaches*, 2nd ed., (Reading, Mass.: Addison-Wesley Publishing Company, 1978), pp. 336–340; Edward Lawless, *Effective Management*, (Englewood Cliffs, N.J.: Prentice-Hall, 1972), pp. 84–88; and Paul Pigors and Charles A. Myers, *Personnel Administration*, 8th edition, (New York, N.Y.: McGraw-Hill Book Company, 1977), pp. 99–101.

4. Maslow, p. xx.

5. *Ibid.*
6. *Ibid.*, p. 54.
7. *Ibid.*, p. 22.
8. The Rorschach Ink Blot is the test in which the subject tells what he sees in a series of cards containing ambiguous figures originally devised by pouring ink on the center of a piece of paper and folding it in the middle. The underlying assumption of this measuring instrument is that whatever the subject sees, when interpreted by experts, gives clues to his personality structure. Sodium amytal is like what is popularly known as "truth serum" and can produce subject responses similar to somnambulistic hypnotic states.
9. Maslow, p. 150.
10. *Ibid.*, p. 31.
11. *Ibid.*
12. *Ibid.*, p. 30.
13. Douglas T. Hall and Khalil E. Nougaim "An Examination of Maslow's Need Hierarchy in an Organizational Setting," *Organizational Behavior and Human Performance*, III (1963), pp. 12–35.
14. *Ibid.*, p. 17.
15. *Ibid.*, p. 23.
16. *Ibid.*, p. 20.
17. J. V. Clark, "Motivation in Work Groups: A Tentative View," *Human Organization*, 19 (1960), pp. 199–208.
18. M. Beer, "Leadership, Employee Needs, and Motivation," Monograph No. 129, (Columbus, Ohio: Bureau of Business Research, Ohio State University, 1966).
19. L. W. Porter, *Organizational Patterns of Managerial Job Attitudes,* (New York, N.Y.: American Foundation for Management Research, 1964).
20. Hall and Nougaim, p. 19.
21. Benjamin Schneider and Clayton P. Alderfer, "Three Studies of Need Satisfaction in Organizations," *Administrative Science Quarterly*, December, 1973, p. 489.
22. Richard McKeon, ed., *The Basic Works of Aristotle,* (New York, N.Y.: Random House, 1941), p. 596.

Chapter 5

McClelland's Need For Achievement Theory

IT is likely that more respectable research effort has gone into the study of achievement motivation than all other theories of motivation combined. And yet McClelland, its founder, is not even mentioned among the 18 behavioral "scientists" with 10 or more mentions by companies in the National Conference Board's survey of sources of behavioral scientist influence.[1] And McGregor, who headed the mentions list, was *not* a behavioral scientist. He was a management philosopher. (See Chapter 14.)

McClelland appears to be less interested in promoting a theory than in adding to the fund of knowledge about the motive to achieve. This is not to suggest that the need for achievement "school" is completely disinterested in theory, or that it does not research other needs such as the need for power and for affiliation, for example. It would appear, however, that they have discovered more motivational phenomena by turning the need for achievement inside out.

The formal statement of a viable-appearing motivation (to achieve) theory came long after much research had been done on the functional significance of individual differences in achievement motivation. Much of the theoretical work appears to have been the work of early McClelland associates John W. Atkinson and N. T. Feather.

Because a great deal of pioneer work on achievement motivation came before formal theory statements, this work will be discussed first in this chapter, followed by Atkinson's statement of the theory in 1966 and reprinted in his 1974 book (with co-editor Joel O. Raynor).

Motivation and Achievement: Developing the Motive Measuring Instrument.

In late 1948 McClelland and his colleagues began studying the effects of

74

hunger on the content of imaginative behavior, followed by the effects of experimentally induced motives to achieve on imagination. The term "thematic apperception" was given to this imaginative behavior early in their research activities. The first development to come out of this work was the Thematic Apperception Test, a companion diagnostic clinical tool to the Rorschach Ink Blot Test. As did the Rorschach, the TAT, as the test is referred to by clinicians, suffered from the problem of scoring reliability and measurement validity. Much of McClelland's and his associates' work for the next five years was in the development of the means of measuring the motive to achieve.

The rationale behind the instrument is quite simple. If a group of people, all exposed to the same somewhat ambiguous picture, make up stories about what is going on in the picture, the differences between their stories represent differences between these people. Development of a valid and reliable measure of individual differences in these "projected" needs turned out to be a sizeable problem. Selection of an appropriate set of pictures, for example, which would elicit a rich range of stories for most subjects required much trial and error. In selecting the pictures for testing a national sample (N = 1619), the researchers finally decided that a separate set of pictures would be necessary for women. Their final choices for male and female forms are briefly described below:

1. Two men (inventors) in a shop at machine.
2. Four men seated at a table with coffee cups. One man is writing on a sheaf of papers.
3. Man (father) and children seated at breakfast table.
4. Man seated at drafting board.
5. Conference group. Seven men variously grouped around a conference table.
6. Woman in foreground with man standing behind and to the left.

Female Form of the Test

1. Two women standing by a table and one woman working with test tubes.
2. Woman (mother) seated by girl reclining in chair.
3. Group of four women. One standing, the others seated facing each other.
4. Woman kneeling and applying a cover to a chair.
5. Two women preparing food in the kitchen.
6. Same as item 6 above.[2]

These pictures, the researchers were satisfied, resulted in a reasonably balanced proportion of imagery for the needs for affiliation, achievement, and power for each sex.

A second major problem, of course, was to develop a scheme for meaningful quantification of the differences in the stories by different people for the same pictures. The final approach was to develop a method for analyzing the behavior of the central character in each story in terms of needs he or she seemed to be expressing or fulfilling. The procedure thus developed was naturally complex and required considerable training. Trained coder-produced story analyses, however, which correlated about .9 (81% common variance),[3] suggest a reliability considerably better than other need assessment instruments such as the Porter Satisfaction scale, for which a reliability coefficient was found to be around .7 (49% common variance).[4]

Because other projective tests, such as the word-association test, were found to produce different results when the stimuli (words) were presented in different order, a preliminary study using controlled variations of picture order was carried out to determine if this contamination was present with their selected pictures. The study revealed that picture presentation order was irrelevant.

Other problems involved in the nation-wide study were never fully resolved. For a variety of reasons—educational, rejection of the procedure, intelligence, etc.—about 15% of the sets of responses were discarded as inadequate for a full motivational needs range. Another unresolved problem was what to do about minorities of different racial or ethnic characteristics who might not be able to identify fully with the whites in the pictures. No special sets of pictures were provided for different races or ethnic groups in the sample. Although this was less than desirable, the problem of the need for separate sets of pictures remained. This problem is commented upon by the researchers in the national survey as follows:

> We realize, however, that the pictures finally selected undoubtedly still have differential cue values for some respondents. Negroes, for example, have to respond to situations depicting white people. Very old and very young people have to make up stories about figures that are obviously not so old nor so young as they are. The work scenes do not include farming, surgery, ditch digging, sales, and countless other occupations, although both blue-collar and white-collar work situations are included. Despite these differences, our working assumptions are that the situations portrayed in the pictures finally selected are not altogether foreign to most of the people with whom we are dealing, and that, by and large, the pictures will be as suggestive of the three motivational content areas to a person of one social stratum as to a person in another. We had finally to recognize that only through intensive study of the motivational cue value of these pictures for different social groups would we sharpen our insight and discover criteria that might enable us to construct a better set and to evaluate the over-all merits of the present set of pictures.[5]

A correction, statistically determined for verbal fluency, was used to eliminate the high raw scores on all needs due simply to the length of the stories. An analysis of possible interviewer effect was also undertaken, and it was discovered that, although certain interviewers did appear to affect the results, the major effect was on the length of the stories, and was therefore taken care of by the correction above.

Early Need-to-Achieve Theoretical Thrust

Most motivational theorists today relate or claim to relate their models to Kurt Lewin's 1938 model: Behavior = f (personality × environment). The achievement-motivation theorists are no exception. Unlike many theorists, however, their initial and fairly sustained focus was on studying the P (personality) in Lewin's model. The basic idea of psychogenic needs and their behavioral effects no doubt was one of McClelland's early interests. For this reason, much of the research activity for the first 10–15 years was in *relating personality needs to behavior and to their psychogenic origins.* This relating of needs to behavior can be seen simply as efforts to validate the needs measurement instrument—the pictures plus their interpretations. Additional validation support is also available somewhat peripherally from the many studies which attempt to discover the *origins* of the need-for-achievement personality. On the following pages, a sample of the findings relating the need-to-achieve to a variety of phenomena are given as presented by McClelland *et al.* Before presenting them, however, two cautionary points should be made: (1) In most of the research findings, it is impossible to determine if the need-to-achieve differences reported are due to early influences on personality dispositions or to temporary situational pressures which are overcoming underlying need dispositions, and (2) controls have rarely been possible to permit clear-cut causal relationships with apparent "origin" variables.[6]

Miscellaneous Findings Relating Need-to-Achieve and Other Variables[7]

1. "The percentage of college-educated (subjects), whether men or women with high *n* Achievement scores is substantially higher than the percentage of (subjects) who have had only a grade school education. Among women, the same result appears in connection with affiliation scores and power scores."

2. "Achievement motivation scores are much more frequently high among persons in higher status occupations (professionals, managers and proprietors, etc.)."

3. ". . . the highest achievement motivation is found among the youngest men (21–24) and the next highest among a middle-aged group, (35–44), while the lowest achievement motivation scores appear in the older groups."

4. "For both men and women there is a greater concentration of high achievement motivation scores in small towns and rural areas than in larger communities. High affiliation motivation seems to be more prevalent among men from smaller communities, but highest in women living in metropolitan areas."

5. ". . . parental divorce seems to have had effect on achievement motivation—lowering it for males and raising it for females. Death in

the family lowers affiliation motivation in males, but not in females, and either death or divorce raises power motivation in males and lowers it in females."

6. Students with high need for achievement get better grades even when the sample is controlled for socio-economic class.

7. ". . . subjects with high n Achievement scores, while they start at about the same level of performance as the subjects with low n Achievement scores, do progressively better as they proceed with the rather complex task of unscrambling words. They do not ordinarily do better at routine tasks like canceling the number of "e's" and "o's" in a long string of unrelated letters. . ."

8. "American males with high n Achievement . . . have better memory for incompleted tasks, are more apt to volunteer as subjects for psychological experiments, are more active in college and community activities, choose experts over friends as working partners, are more resistant to social pressure. . ."

9. ". . . summarize(d) evidence . . . (leaves) very little doubt that the average n Achievement among Jews is higher than for the general population in the United States at the present time."

10. ". . . social class is a much more important determinant of n Achievement score than is ethnicity (or religion plus ethnicity)."

11. Those reared in polygamous or "serial monogamy" households are more likely to have low need for achievement.

12. Mothers in Germany and Japan who have high need for achievement are more likely to have sons with lower need for achievement.

13. College students with high need for achievement are more likely to engage (later) in entrepreneural work than those with low need for achievement.

(Parenthetical material added in No's. 9 and 10 above)

Need for Achievement and Economic Development

The reader will no doubt appreciate, from the above small sample, how wide-ranging the researches on need-to-achieve have been. Part of this is due to the initial investigators' maturing interests. McClelland, although participating in motivational theory development, became more interested in determinants of economic development of which the need to achieve was theorized to be an important one. Atkinson, *et al.*, however, have pursued research to support an Expectancy $\times$ Value type of motivational model (more on this later in the chapter).

McClelland's research work, beginning in the late 1950's, has had two economic development dimensions: (1) to prove that achievement motivation was an important prerequisite for economic development and (2) to develop successful programs for increasing the need to achieve in various groups of people, primarily in developing countries. The brilliant and painstaking work by McClelland and his associates succeeded, with very ingenious inter-disciplinary research approaches, in demonstrating the relationship between need for achievement and economic development. Early in this period, for example, David Berlew, using the need-to-achieve story scoring system on randomly sampled Greek literature from 900–362 B.C., demonstrated that high achievement motivation preceded the rise of the Empire and that declining achievement motivation preceded its fall. The quantitative measures used for the rise and fall was the Empire's trade area as measured by the number and location of typical trade goods containers (large earthenware jars) by their century of manufacture.[8]

McClelland's and others' major work leading to the relationship between economic development and need for achievement was concerned with more recent data and was wide-ranging in approach. It was demonstrated by de Charms and Moeller, for example, that the frequency of achievement imagery in sampled U.S. children's stories has had a preceding relationship with patents issued per million population from 1810–1950.[9] Another study, by Bradford and Berlew, demonstrated a similar relationship between achieve-ment motivation in random samples of English literature and an index of London coal imports between the years 1550–1800.[10]

The clinching research project, however, demonstrated a lagging statistically significant relationship between national electricity output and achievement motivation as measured by imagery in a nation's children's stories. The study involved 23 countries and 1300 selected children's stories for the periods 1920–1929 and 1946–55. As with the other studies, increases in achievement motivation in the children's literature preceded economic development, and decreases in achievement motivation preceded economic decline.[11]

Efforts to Stimulate the Need-to-Achieve Motive

McClelland and his associates, interested in using social science findings to help with some of the world's economic development problems, did not begin their efforts to see if need achievement could be artificially produced or stimulated without knowledge of the likelihood of failure. Here is how McClelland saw the prospect in 1961 in the final chapter of his book *The Achieving Society:*

Any country or agency concerned with speeding economic development should be interested in raising n Achievement levels, unless its level is already high (e.g., as in Israel). But how can it be done? Unfortunately, all of the large body of evidence summarized in Chapter 9 goes to show how embedded n Achievement level is in the total culture—in its religion, life style or more particularly in the way its parents raise their children. Changing child-rearing practices on a large scale is not likely to be done easily. The family is the social nucleus of the society, the main carrier of the basic motives and values of the culture. And it may be as hard to alter it intentionally as it was to crack the nucleus of the atom.[12]

Before describing some of the studies used to evaluate need-to-achieve training, a comment or two about McClelland's objectives are necessary. Note first that he used the term "raising achievement levels" above. After stating, at the beginning of his detailed report of the studies done in India, that the "research plan requires that achievement motivation *be developed* in adult businessmen" (Italics added), he goes on to discuss the "dominant view among psychologists . . . that it was highly unlikely that motives *could be acquired* in adulthood." (Italics added.)[13] Still further, he is back to discussing the "prevailing psychological theories (which) argue against the possibility of developing n Achievement in adulthood." (Italics added)[14] Ordinarily one should probably not quibble over the difference between "acquiring," a fairly precise term, and "developing." However, since most of his research has been done using entrepreneurs and salesmen who, according to his own research and that of others, have the *highest n Achievement scores to start with*, the notion of running training courses for them *to acquire* what they already have in abundance would seem peculiar. In fact, some of the studies in the literature were attempting to raise n Achievement from a very low level (high-school drop-outs) and others to raise n Achievement of already high n Achievement businessmen. In no case has an experimental group been described with zero achievement at the outset of training.

The ideal research approach, though nearly impossible to use, would be to compare before and after objectively determined achievement behavior of a control and a trained sample in an environment with equal opportunities for exhibiting achievement behavior. It is clear from their writings that McClelland's researchers were aware of these requirements, but for many very practical reasons could never get them all together in the same study. The most common means of evaluating behavior after training seems to have been a coding system to quantify achievement activities. This involved an investigator's evaluation, usually beginning with a questionnaire of each subject's business improvements or expansion, increased activity with business organizations such as Rotary Clubs, unusual improvements in business procedures, increase in family or community activities at the expense of business improvements (a negative score), etc.[15] In spite of the elaborate and necessary pains taken to develop a high reliability for the coding of the original n Achievement measuring instrument, no comparable work seems to have been done on the achievement activity coding reliability.

The typical content of the short-course training (a few days to 3 weeks) was a mixture of the following:[16]

1. Subjects were taught how to think and act like high need achievers. This included practice in the production of high n Achievement fantasies and playing business games while being taught to evaluate their own behavior.
2. Subjects were helped to relate improvement in need for achievement to themselves—to their careers, their images, their values, their families, etc.
3. Subjects were urged toward and trained in goal setting, and commitment to these goals.

Several studies—a few quite extensive—attempting to prove the effectiveness of the training have been reported. Below are some of these briefly described followed by evaluative comments on each.

1. ". . . a group of high potential school drop-outs or failures, 16 to 17 years of age, were taken to a country retreat for a five day course. . . . Half of the boys dropped out of the motivation course, following the same pattern they had been showing in school; but among those who stayed, the changes in behavior a year and a half later were quite marked. Seven out of nine, as contrasted with three out of nine of their matched controls, showed a marked improvement in grades. Furthermore, all of them reported thinking very seriously about their vocational plans, as contrasted with practically none of the control boys, who reported that their chief concerns at the moment were sports, cars, and girls. The results are not conclusive because the numbers are small and because of the number who dropped out.[17]

   Comment: If a comparison is to be made between the behavior of those remaining in the experimental group and that of control group subjects, the control group must be trimmed by eliminating theoretical drop-outs. There is no scientifically acceptable way to do this. As McClelland noted, the results are not conclusive.
2. A group of 19 adult males (16 black members of a "fathers" club plus three whites) were given the achievement training in a retreat setting outside Boston. Follow-up evaluations were made using an activity coding system similar to the one described above. The mean follow-up activity score was 1.31 with eight scoring 2.0[18]

   Comment: Since 2.0 represents the highest possible activity score, the instrument or its coding system (including coder) seems ill-fitted for this group. Conclusion: encouraging but inconclusive.
3. A group of 41 businessmen were given n Achievement training in McAlester, Oklahoma, and evaluated on the achievement activity scale

three or six months later.[19] Untrained matched controls were less "active" than those trained—24% vs. 61%.

Comments: In view of the inherent difficulties in finding subjects for matched control groups exhibited in other such studies, and since McClelland and Winter do not describe this process in their book, any final evaluation will have to be withheld. The results reported are quite encouraging, however. (The study source appears to be an "in-house" report of the Sterling Institute.)

4. In Barcelona, Spain, three n Achievement training courses were given to a total of 34 subjects, of which 26 were used for evaluation 15 months later. Faculty and students were removed as non-business. Activity scores showed an increase but not very significant ($p < .10$). No control groups were used.[20]

    Comment: inconclusive.

5. A group of nine Japanese management consultants were given a need achievement course and a five year follow-up revealed that five of the nine had reached a maximum activity ($+2$) level from two to three years after completing the course, although the mean post-course activity level was 1.1. The 5/9 gain is highlighted in the McClelland and Winters book by converting this fraction to "56 percent!"[21]

    Comment: Encouraging.

6. The major study reported in their book *Motivating Economic Achievement* was done in India. Two cities of approximately 125,000 population, Kakinada and Rajahmundry, were selected for the study. The intention was to train a group in Kakinada and compare the subsequent achievement related behavior of this group with two matched control groups—one in each of the two cities. Criteria for participant selection included English proficiency, preferred age of 30–45 (a high n Achievement age group), being a businessman or potential businessman, strong desire to take the training, and willingness to pay for transportation, room and board. The Kakinada trained group totaled 52 participants. The Kakinada control sample was made up of 11 leftovers ("waiting list") from the volunteers plus 11 who had not applied to go for reported personal or otherwise compelling reasons unrelated to their attitudes toward the course. The control sample in Rajahmundry (N–35) was selected to match the participant group as nearly as possible. Some differences in the experimental and control groups remained, if small; e.g. educational level and personal capital invested were higher among the trained group. In addition to the achievement activity index, the groups' behavioral changes were compared on such indexes as working longer hours, entrepreneurs' gross income increases, unsuccessful and successful attempts to start new businesses, and changes in capital investment (for entrepreneurs). The majority of these data were from self reports.[22]

Although there were attempts to verify some of the business or career status changes, the researchers were frank about difficulties in doing this. They had originally planned to give detailed follow-up questionnaires to the participants every six months for two years. This was to assess changes on several psychological and business-activity dimensions. One of their problems was that they could not get enough of the participants to complete the questionnaires often enough to yield meaningful results. McClelland noted that ". . . there was sometimes a spurious objectivity about the figures they reported. A man might state that he had been given a double jump in promotion . . . whereas a talk with his superior . . . or even with some of his friends would show that actually he had been "kicked upstairs" into a position of lesser responsibility."[23] The researchers also failed to probe carefully to determine the nature of the outcomes of attempts to start new ventures for the period before the experiment began. Therefore only such data for the period after completion of the course were used.[24]

The research plan called for the subjects to fill out a questionnaire and be interviewed in depth after each six month period beyond the course completion. This was to determine changes in job activities and the nature of salary increases. These data were to be verified by interviews with friends or associates. As reported by McClelland, "Sometimes one or more of these sources of information was either unavailable or unnecessary."[25]

The before and after results of the trained and control groups were therefore not very clear cut. The researchers, in noting intra-sample variations, reordered part of their data to discover, among other things, that the major changes occurred among trained participants who were "in charge" (entrepreneurial). Since the researchers' own conclusions very accurately reflect their findings, they are offered below:

Perhaps more than anything else (the results) serve to correct any simple-minded notion that teaching n Achievement is sufficient to increase levels of entrepreneurial activity. The comparative yields of various training courses do not support this conclusion. Other training inputs are demonstrably important, and teaching n Achievement alone is not sufficient. Nor do the personality change data support such a simple-minded hypothesis. The men who became active after the course on the whole do not retain better command of the n Achievement associative network than those who are inactive. Above all, opportunity plays a major role in determining whether increased n Achievement leads to greater activity. For men who were not in charge of their business, the n Ach increase had no significant effect, at least within the time period of the evaluations reported here. Furthermore, there is even a suggestion in the data, as the theoretical model predicts, that increasing n Ach when no opportunities exist will actually lead to less activity.

. . . What seems to differentiate the Changers and the Inactives is that the former start out more dissatisfied with the level of their activity and learn to think more efficaciously. In other words, the effect of the training depends on the initial goals of the participant . . . Achievement motivation worked best by strengthening the sense of efficacy among those men who already wanted it, by giving them concrete information as to the means by which they could overcome their felt discrepancy between real and ideal selves. And it worked at all only among those men who had some opportunities to display these new characteristics.[26]

And on summarizing the results as they relate to psychological theory:

In short, our theoretical account of what we were doing and what happened is too limited. It was biased by our psychological background in the direction of neglecting the system requirements of putting on the course and maintaining their effects afterwards.[27]

Comments: This major research project in India, given the selection of high need achievement subjects (businessmen between 30–45) could never have proven anything about "acquiring" the need as was mentioned in connection with an early discussion of their objectives. Their work could only show what can be done with *high n* Ach people. And, of course, they demonstrate very forcefully that this in itself is a very complex endeavor. There is little doubt that the total training system, from the attention and recruitment by prestige people, to the course content work, to the attention and jogger nature of the follow-up, to the formation of new relationships, had a significant effect upon those in the training who had the entrepreneural opportunities to respond behaviorally to the total course system stimuli.

Implications for Management

What can this mean in terms of motivation theory for management? First, it illustrates on a social system basis, the very complexity of the problem of motivating any person or group towards specific behavioral change. In their very interesting single case studies, the number of one-of-a-kind circumstances (and luck?) involved defy most attempts to order the elements in the process of increasing achievement activity. This work certainly suggests a posture of wariness when confronted with simple-dimensional motivational models. Since the researchers spent much time in the field wallowing in their data, they, fortunately for social science, could not sanitize their experiments in the image of a freshman psychology class questionnaire or laboratory game or puzzle. It is likely that this experience gave them an infinite advantage in the ability to describe a complex social system such as exists in an organization (prior to model design for change) over the social scientist without this experience. Hopefully, this will continue to pay off for social science and management in their future work.

Second, the finding that lack of "opportunity" seems to keep high need achievement personalities from increasing their activities relating to career achievement suggests, for institutional managers, that the traditional urgings from social scientists for more delegation on the part of managers have some validity. It has never been clearly established that their advice to managers to delegate more was born of their research findings or their own strong personal needs for autonomy *per se*, but the *n* Achievement training case histories do offer peripheral support for increasing opportunity for the high *n* Achievement personality. There is no evidence here, however, that increased opportunity stimulates achievement behavior increases across the range of *n* Ach levels.

Thirdly, the suggestion in the data that need achievement training could lead to lower performance levels where opportunity is missing, warns against such wholesale training where nothing is to be or can be done about opportunity. Parallels of this phenomenon are found in foremen-only human relations training history in which the foreman was prevented from trying out something new by the static environment represented primarily by his untrained superior. Personnel department inspired employee opinion polls can go sour, too, if the opportunity to act on significant findings is not available.

THE NEED ACHIEVEMENT MOTIVATION MODEL BUILDERS

For reasons to be given shortly, the achievement motivational theories of Atkinson, *et al*, will not be discussed in great detail. As was mentioned earlier, the Atkinson splinter group from the original need-for-achievement researchers appears to have been more engaged in theoretical model building, beginning with the model B = f(P,E) (Behavior is a function of the combined effect of the given personality and environment). Without discussing here the research supporting their development of this model (more on this later), what follows are some of the evolutionary stages of this line of achievement motivation models:[28]

$$B = f (P,E)$$

(Behavior is a function of the interaction of personality and environment).

$$T_s = M_s \times P_s \times I_s$$

(*Tendency* to achieve *Success* = *Motive* to achieve *Success* × the subjectively determined *Probability* that the performance of a task will be followed by *Success* × the *Incentive* value of *Success*.) Where $I^s \times 1 = P^s$ or where (the *Incentive* value of *Success* – 1 = the *Probability* that the performance of a task will be followed by *Success*).

Adding the effects of the "tendency to avoid failure" factor and the concept of the summation of component tendencies to achieve, the model becomes, in the theorists' notion of algebraic statements, the following:[29]

$$T_s + T_{-f} = (M_s - M_{AF}) \sum_{n=1}^{N} (P_{1sn} \times 1_{sn})$$

Where M_{AF} = the motive to avoid failure.

No effort will be made to verbalize here this last algebraic-like statement, although the interested reader can likely do so from what has been given. It is beyond the scope of this book to carry its readers through theory building exercises, even though verbalization would likely make "personally plausible" sense. Common sense tells us that the fear of failure likely affects our motivations, and so does the probability of success. But such algebraic statements do not automatically make the variables quantitatively and reliably measureable.

In reviewing Atkinson's and Raynor's book *Motivation and Achievement* searching for research evidence of the mathematical relationships between the quantifiably measured values in the various models, two quick discoveries are apparent: (1) Considerable license has been taken regarding the *mathematical* nature of the relationships, and (2) the models will, if satisfactorily verified, likely be of little value except in predicting a very narrow range of institutional behavior of male university students in introductory psychology classes. The subject sample total for the 25 different studies whose findings were reported in tabular form in Atkinson's and Raynor's book was 2,792 of which *43% were male introductory psychology students!*[30] The sum of all college subjects in the 25 studies was 2103 or 75% with all but 3% of the remainder being accounted for by samples from junior and senior high schools. Males accounted for 87% of the total of all samples. Table 1 gives more details on the 25 studies in terms of subject samples used.

Unfortunately, the majority of the relationships in the achievement motivation models (equations) provided by Atkinson and Raynor are based upon research using student samples. The research based relationships, moreover, are almost all weak, albeit statistically significant, suggesting only threadlike connections. The modelers are not unaware of this problem, however; Atkinson pointed up Freud's "eloquent defense of the importance of small signs in the inferential work of a psychologist; the detective does not expect to find an autographed photograph of the murderer pinned to the shirt of his victim!"[31]

Commenting generally on his analysis—primarily of findings on the effect of motivation strength on performance efficiency—Atkinson concludes that:

. . . no work situation is optimal for everyone, no type of personality is most productive in all situations, (and) no single generalization about the effects of strength of motivation will apply to all tasks. It means, more specifically, that for every

TABLE 6-1

**Research Samples By Subject Descriptions In All Tables
In Motivation And Achievement By Atkinson And Raynor[32]**

Number of Studies	Description of Subjects	Sum of Sample Sizes	% of Total All Samples
Male Subject Studies (plus half of the "mixed" samples)			
7	Male introductory psychology students	1190	43%
4	Mixed introductory psychology students ÷ 2	173	6
5	College males	408	15
3	Junior High, High School males	384	14
2	Mixed Junior High, High School students ÷ 2	66	2
1	Male college juniors in management course	105	4
1	Air Force personnel (assumed male)	92	3
	Total males	2418	87%
Female Subject Studies (plus half of the "mixed" samples)			
1	College females	53	2%
1	Jun. H., H. S. females	80	3
4	Mixed introductory psychology students ÷ 2	174	6
2	Mixed Jun. H., H. S. ÷ 2	67	2
	Total females	374	13%
Sample Subjects by Institutional Identity			
18	College or Univ. Stud.	2103	75%
5	Jun. H., H.S. Students	597	21
1	Air Force personnel	92	3
	Total of all samples	2792	

particular occupational role (a combination of task and work situation), there is a different kind of *most productive* personality. And for every personality, . . . there is a particular role which offers an opportunity for *relatively* greater productivity and greater contribution than others as a solid foundation for the individual's self esteem. (Italics added.)[33]

For the achievement motivation behavior "detective," such conclusions can be meaningful. For the manager, of course, who is always looking for something he can *use now*, there is little in these conclusions of real value. The measureable connections between occupational roles and productive personalities are so weak that they cannot be used as operational tools for selection of personnel. This same problem prevents the redesigning of combinations of tasks and work situations with any degree of confidence.

Conclusions

Both McClelland's wide ranging measurements of the motive to achieve and his attempt to alter it offer further support that the personality is a fairly stable structure. Such needs as the need for achievement, need for power, and need for affiliation appear more clearly rooted in childhood than before McClelland's work began in the late 1940's. The development of these needs, moreover, depends upon socio-economic, ethnic, and child-rearing factors. Although many of those with high needs for achievement may respond to specialized training, this response will largely be a function of opportunities for expansion of entrepreneurial-like behavior.

The achievement motivation theorists are moving in the same direction most motivational theorists have been moving—the adding of more variables. The Atkinson-Raynor models suggest far more precise relationships between their variables than the supporting research warrants. And this research is, for the most part, a large group of studies done on school or college populations, the majority of which are introductory psychology students. Nearly all this research suffers from the obvious defects of small or opportunistic samples, and from the generalization barriers presented by samples dominated by people from 18–20 years of age, most of whose institutional attachment more resembles a womb than a steel mill, a retirement village, or a Madison Avenue advertising agency not to mention a mine in Iran or Zambia, a cattle ranch in Venezuela, or an Indonesian sugar plantation.

Skeptical old-line managers who have resisted behavioral model-building on an intuitive basis as being oversimplified and restrictive can take heart. All the behavior model-builders seem to be adding dimensions in the contingency style of "it (almost) all depends."

NOTES

1. Harold Rush, *Behavioral Science, Concepts and Applications*, Personnel Policy Study No. 216, (New York, N.Y.: The National Industrial Conference Board Inc., 1969), p. 10.
2. John Veroff, John W. Atkinson, Sheila C. Feld, and Gerald Gurin, "The Use of Thematic Apperception to Assess Motivation in a Nationwide Interview Study," *Psychological Monographs*, American Psychological Association, 1960, as reprinted and abridged in John W. Atkinson and Joel O. Raynor, *Motivation and Achievement*, (New York, N.Y.: John Wiley & Sons and Washington, D.C., V. H. Winston & Sons, 1974), pp. 45–46.
3. *Ibid.* p. 51.
4. Marc J. Wallace, Jr., and Phillip K. Berger, "The Reliability of Difference Scores: A Preliminary Investigation of a Need Deficiency Satisfaction Scale," *Proceedings of the Thirty-Third Annual Academy of Management Meeting*, edited by Thad B. Green and Dennis F. Ray, Boston, Mass., 1973.
5. Veroff, *et al.*, p. 46.
6. Veroff, *et al.*, p. 64, made cautionary point (1) in more detail than is given here, and throughout McClelland's writings one will find cautionary point (2) made in a variety of ways.
7. Findings 1–5 are from John Veroff, *et al.*, pp. 65–70; finding 6 is from John Atkinson, *Learning and the Educational Process*, D. Krumbolt, editor, (Chicago, Ill.: Rand McNally, 1965), as reprinted with minor abridgement in John W. Atkinson and Joel O. Raynor, *Motivation and Achievement*, (New York, N.Y.: John Wiley & Sons and Washington, D.C., V.H. Winston & Sons, 1974), p. 23; and findings 7–13 are from David C. McClelland, *The Achieving Society* (New York, N.Y.: The Free Press, 1961), pp. 44, 365, 365, 374, 349, and 246 respectively. The reader can safely assume statistical significance for all relationships and differences reported in these findings, although as one might expect, given the many other variables operating in such studies, the relationships were not particularly strong nor the differences particularly wide.
8. David C. McClelland, "The Use of Measures of Human Motivation in the Study of Society," John W. Atkinson, ed., *Motives in Fantasy, Action and Society*, (Princeton, N.J.: D. Van Nostrand, 1958), Ch. 37.
9. R. deCharms and G. H. Moeller, "Values Expressed in American Children's Readers: 1800–1950," *Journal of Abnormal and Social Psychology*, 1962, 64, pp. 136–42, as reported in David C. McClelland, *The Achieving Society*, pp. 150–51.
10. N.M. Bradburn and D. E. Berlew, "Need Achievement and English Economic Growth," *Economic Development and Cultural Change*, X (1968), pp. 8–20.
11. McClelland, *The Achieving Society*, pp. 82–103.
12. *Ibid.*, pp. 403–4.
13. David C. McClelland and David G. Winter, *Motivating Economic Achievement*, (New York, N.Y.: The Free Press, 1969) p. 39.
14. *Ibid.*, p. 41.
15. *Ibid.*, pp. 81–6.
16. *Ibid.*, pp. 39–92.

17. *Ibid.*, p. 351.
18. *Ibid.*, p. 352.
19. *Ibid.*, p. 354. The reason for the "three or six months" is that McClelland and Winter report the follow-up at six months and cite its source as Behavioral Science Center, "Business Leadership Training: a *three month* Evaluation" (Italics added), (Boston, Sterling Institute, 1968).
20. *Ibid.*, pp. 315–16.
21. *Ibid.*, p. 89.
22. *Ibid.*, Chapters 3–11.
23. *Ibid.*, p. 80.
24. *Ibid.*, p. 216.
25. *Ibid.*, p. 82.
26. *Ibid.*, pp. 334–35.
27. *Ibid.*, p. 361.
28. John W. Atkinson and Joel O. Raynor, *Motivation and Achievement*, (New York, N.Y.: John Wiley & Sons and Washington, D.C., V. H. Winston & Sons, 1974), pp. 13–15.
29. *Ibid.*, p. 127.
30. Most of these studies were cited as supporting various relationships in the achievement motivation models appearing in the Atkinson and Raynor book.
31. Atkinson, *Motivation and Achievement, op. cit.* The tables or descriptions from which the sample sizes and descriptions were obtained appear on the following pages: 21, 23, 24, 25, 36, 84, 93, 94, 112, 145, 157, 174, 176, 182, 195, 196, 209, 222, 227, 240, 261, 335, 350, and 360.
32. *Ibid.*, p. 217.
33. *Ibid.*

Chapter 6

Herzberg's Dual-Factor Theory

WHEN a child learns to ride a bicycle, he is becoming more competent, increasing the repertory of his behavior, expanding his skills—psychologically growing. In the process of the child's learning to master the bicycle, the parents can love him with all the zeal and compassion of the most devoted mother and father. They can safeguard the child from injury by providing the safest and most hygienic area in which to practice; they can offer all kinds of incentives and rewards; and they can provide the most expert instructors. But the child will never, never learn to ride the bicycle—unless he is given a bicycle![1]

Leaving aside that "never, never" are very strong words, especially in view of the simple fact that many of us learn to ride bicycles on someone else's bike, Frederick Herzberg, with this account of the child's dependence upon the parents for the opportunity for "psychological growth," attempts to explain why ". . . hygiene factors are not a valid contributor to psychological growth." He goes on to tell us that ". . . you cannot love an engineer into creativity, although by this approach, you can avoid his dissatisfactions with the way you treat him. Creativity will require a potentially creative task to do."[2]

Although Herzberg exhibits unjustifiable certainty regarding the motivational origins of creativity, what he is attempting to do is to rationalize various of his research findings which have led to his dual-factor theory of motivation. The well publicized dual-factor theory holds that job satisfaction consists of two separate dimensions: job satisfaction and job dissatisfaction. The theory further contains the notion that these two dimensions are not opposite ends of the same continuum, but are separate continua. Also, according to his theory, satisfaction is not usually the result of a reduction in dissatisfaction. Although his theory notes that a few job characteristics do function as simple continua from satisfiers to dissatisfiers, in the main, the characteristics of the satisfiers are different in kind from the dissatisfiers.

Before providing a critical evaluation of the dual-factor theory, an account of the theory as it typically appears in publications for management and student consumption is given below.[3]

91

Typical Popular Version of Herzberg's Two Factor Theory

After surveying the somewhat disappointing literature on motivation up to 1959, Herzberg designed a research study to learn of the need satisfaction of 200 engineers and accountants from eleven firms in the Pittsburgh, Pennsylvania area. In this study Herzberg and his colleagues asked their subjects about events which made them feel especially good about their jobs and about events which made them feel especially bad. Each subject was asked to describe the conditions which led to these events. Herzberg found that these employees described different kinds of things which made them feel good about their jobs than those things which made them feel bad. For example, if a participant described an event in which he received especial recognition for something he did on the job, the lack of recognition was rarely given as the cause of bad feelings. Analysis of these responses resulted in Herzberg reaching the following conclusions:

A.   Some job conditions mainly result in causing dissatisfaction with the work or the job. If these dissatisfaction-causing factors are removed, however, this does not result in high motivation on the job. These factors he named "maintenance" or "hygiene" factors since they operate to keep employees reasonably free from dissatisfaction. He also suggested that for some time, managers had been mistakenly thinking of these factors as primary causes of job motivation. From his analyses of these interviews, Herzberg extracted ten maintenance factors as follows:

1. Company policy and admini-
    stration
2. Technical supervision
3. Interpersonal relations with
    supervisor
4. Interpersonal relations with
    peers

5. Interpersonal relations with
    subordinates
6. Salary
7. Job security
8. Personal life
9. Work conditions
10. Status

B.   The factors which Herzberg found to be highly motivating did not seem to produce dissatisfaction if they were not present. These six motivational factors are as follows:

1. Achievement
2. Recognition
3. Advancement

4. The work itself
5. The possibility of personal
    growth
6. Responsibility

In general, Herzberg decided that the opposite of job satisfaction is not job dissatisfaction. It is simply the lack of job satisfaction. And the opposite of dissatisfaction with the job is not job satisfaction. Instead, it is only a lack of job dissatisfaction.

Herzberg's theory, then, points up the fallacy of thinking that job satisfaction and job dissatisfaction represent opposite ends of a continuum. Instead, they must be considered as distinctly separate scales. Herzberg sees these results as supporting a philosophy of the dual nature of man—the Adam-Abraham duality[4] which underlies the Judeo-Christian tradition. The animal or Adam nature avoids pain and unpleasantness. When they cannot be avoided, they (the maintenance factors given above) produce dissatisfaction. The human or Abraham nature of man is motivated by the six motivational factors given above.

Herzberg's model is generally consistent with Maslow's Need Hierarchy. The self-actualization level of needs will only be satisfied by Herzberg's motivational factors and the physiological security, social and esteem needs will be satisfied by the maintenance or hygiene factors.

The hygiene factors are considered preventive in that if the company provides them, employees will not be dissatisfied with their jobs. But if the company expects its employees to do creative work, to extend themselves beyond the routine requirements of the job, they must be willing to provide the motivators.

From this point on the typical account goes directly into prescriptions for management, exhorting them to provide an appropriate balance of hygiene and motivators. It is suggested that hygiene factors have usually been over-provided and that motivators have too often been ignored by most organizations.

Before analyzing the theory and relevant research, it should be noted that most of the popular accounts mention little of the evidence which does not support the theory. Occasionally, mention will be made that the theory has aroused a good deal of comment, support and some controversy. Most references to research on the model are Herzberg's and most are supportive. Typical current introductory management *textbook* accounts describe the theory and Herzberg's research methodology in some detail. Most add that there are detractors and either give specific criticisms[5] or refer to critics. The National Industrial Conference Board Report on Behavior Science concluded their report on Herzberg's theory by pointing out that ". . . while among the most controversial of all behavioral research theories, (Herzberg's theories) are gaining steadily in favor among managers."[6]

Since the motivators appear to some to be more closely related to Maslow's higher order needs, i.e., esteem and self-actualization, and the hygiene factors to Maslow's lower order needs for safety and belonging, the dual factor theory gains some "ride-on" support without reference to validation research. In one introductory management text, for example, the "transition" between the two theories became a link and was begun as follows:

Specifically relating needs and motivation to the job context, the two-factor theory roughly divides Maslow's hierarchy into two parts: needs that motivate effective behavior on the job and needs that merely prevent dissatisfaction. Needs that tend to motivate are at the top of the hierarchy: esteem and self-fulfillment. Satisfaction of the lower-level needs—physiological, safety, and social—prevents dissatisfaction on the job, but, according to the theory, these needs will not motivate effective task behavior.

In searching for what satisfies esteem and self-fulfillment needs, Frederick Herzberg . . . initially questioned 200 accountants and engineers. . ."[7]

Nowhere in the original account of this research[8] is there a hint that the researchers were specifically searching for "what satisfies esteem and self-fulfillment needs." The researchers would likely deny that they were specifically searching for anything except the answers to their questions about what people felt about their jobs.

Still other non-research support for the dual-factor theory comes from people who use the self-referenced criterion for judging theory. This is illustrated by the following highlighted stimulus question to the reader in a popular introductory management text: "Have you ever *felt* the two factor theory applying to your job?"[9] (Italics added.) If the reader can answer "yes" to this question, for whatever reason, he is naturally likely to be less inclined to accept scientific evidence negating or casting doubt on the theory.

Previous Findings and the Dual-Factor Theory

A natural first step in evaluating any motivation theory would be to determine how consistent it is with research findings available on work motivation. Since the theory predicts that highly satisfied workers would be more productive, reviews of studies relating job satisfaction and productivity are appropriate for this first step. It should be pointed out, however, that the primary focus of the dual-factor theory and much of its research support is not on productivity or performance. The theory is stated in terms of employee motivation and dissatisfaction. The job performance dimension, however, is clearly implied in the following statement from the book in which the theory is stated:

> The fulfillment of the needs of the second group (hygiene factors) does not motivate the individual to high levels of job satisfaction and to extra performance on the job. All we can expect from satisfying the needs for hygiene is the prevention of dissatisfaction and poor job performance.[10]

The first comprehensive literature review of significance of the satisfaction-productivity relationship was done by A. H. Brayfield and W. H. Crockett in 1955.[11] Their exhaustive study of previous research efforts began with what is very likely the first formal attempt to quantify the relationship between job satisfaction and job performance. Reported in 1932, the results of this early study did not show a significant relationship. Over 30 studies later, as reviewed by Brayfield and Crockett, the yield was much the same. Judging from the response in the literature, these findings seemed to have come as somewhat of a shock to behavioral scientists, although it did not appear to slow the perpetuation of the myth among many professionals in the field of personnel administration and management training. The key conclusion that resulted from this search, was that ". . . there is little evidence in the available literature that employee attitudes bear any simple—or, for that matter, appreciable—relationship to performance on the job." Absenteeism and turnover, however, *were* found by the reviewers to be related to job satisfaction.

Two years later, Herzberg *et al.*, reviewed the literature for a similar purpose. Of the 27 studies analyzed in which a quantitative relationship between job performance and job attitudes was reported, only 14 revealed a positive relationship. Although the reviewers pointed out that ". . . the correlations obtained in many of the positive studies were low," their conclusions were unaccountably optimistic: ". . . there is frequent evidence for the often suggested opinion that positive job attitudes are favorable to increased productivity. The relationship is not absolute, but there are enough data to justify attention to attitudes as a factor in improving the workers' output."[12] In addition to the unwarranted optimism, it should be noted here that Herzberg is not only assuming a *causal* relationship, i.e., that certain *attitudes cause higher productivity*, but implying that they likely can be produced or altered by management. While this was hardly a new notion within the "human relation" movement, it would seem to have added momentum to the unsubstantiated idea that job attitudes in some fairly simple and direct manner can be manipulated within the organizational environment. This notion goes counter to Brayfield and Crockett's conclusion that productivity is likely only *peripherally* related to employee motivation which includes many goals not directly related to his workplace.[13]

Research on work as a CLI (central life interest) has been considerable since the early 1950's. In 1954, Robert Dubin found that only 24 percent of a sample of industrial workers considered work as a central life interest. Subsequent research has revealed that this figure can go as low as 12 percent for truck drivers and as high as 76 percent for Amana Society clerks. For supervisory-managerial samples the variation is similar. Only 26 percent of sampled first line supervisors in aircraft manufacturing gave work as a CLI. Similar statistics on other groups were 32, 40, 43, 54, 82, and 84 percent. And among the supervisory-managerial samples, there was little relationship between job "level" and percentage reporting work as a CLI.[14]

Seven years after the Crockett and Brayfield review, with the relationship between job performance and satisfaction apparently yet unclear and five years after Herzberg presented his theory, still another comprehensive review of the relevant research was undertaken by Victor H. Vroom. Twenty studies resulting in 23 quantitative relationships were reviewed of which 20 were positive.[15] The median correlation, however, was only .14. When squared, this co-efficient tells us that slightly over *two percent* of the variance in productivity could be accounted for by job satisfaction measures! While it is true that 20 such positive correlations out of 23 would occur less than once in a hundred times on a chance basis, it is equally true that the 23 researches reveal only the *very faintest* of relationships.

Because they were mindful of the *strengths* of relationships in their review, as compared to whether the relationships were statistically significant, Brayfield and Crockett's conclusions were the least optimistic of the three research reviews.

Vroom's review did confirm one of the findings of both previous reviewers—namely that both absenteeism and turnover, which had been known for years to have been fairly highly correlated themselves, are quite consistently found correlated with the various measures used to assess job attitudes.

What can be concluded from that which has been discovered about the motivation to work from researches undertaken for purposes other than to test Herzberg's dual-factor theory? One simple conclusion is that the results of these research efforts offer precious little encouragement for anyone whose theory depends upon a clear-cut relationship between satisfaction and performance. In view of the fact that his theory *does* assume such a relationship, support for his theory will have to come from elsewhere, *and* be substantial enough to refute most of the hundred-odd studies which have demonstrated faint or no relationships between job satisfaction and job performance.

Herzberg's Research Methodology

To build a research foundation for a new theory—a theory which is inconsistent with or unsupported by most of the relevant previous research findings—usually necessitates a new or different methodology. Herzberg's methodology was hardly new. It was, however, a departure from traditional paper-pencil questionnaires most often used to measure satisfaction. His approach was to conduct individual semi-structured interviews asking for incidents relating to feelings about the subjects' jobs. They were asked to respond to this question: "Think of a time when you felt exceptionally good or exceptionally bad about your job or any other job you have had. . . . Tell me what happened."[16] In addition to being a fairly common technique in clinical psychology and psychiatry, the technique was used at least as early as 1929 to study worker motivations. Henri DeMan asked 78 subjects (salaried and non-salaried employees in various parts of Germany) to make a statement ". . . concerning their own feelings about their daily work." DeMan's conclusion, based upon non-quantitative data, was that there was a natural instinct in man to find "joy in work." In this drive, positive motives were instincts for "activity," "self-assertion," to be "constructive," and a longing for "mastery" (power). The negative factors which inhibited this natural impulse for joy in work were found: (1) in the job itself in factors such as detailed work, monotony, reduction of worker initiative, fatigue, and poor working conditions: and (2) in "social hindrances" such as the dependent position of the worker, unjust wage systems, speed-ups, insecurity of livelihood, and lack of social solidarity.[17]

Both Herzberg's and DeMan's approaches fall prey to the criticism of contamination of the results by the interpreter of the interviewees' responses. Someone must convert an unrehearsed response, which may be a series of descriptions of a supervisor's behavior, to "supervisor competent," "incompetent," "shows favoritism," etc. This conversion technique, usually referred to as "coding" in social science research, typically requires a great deal of supervised practice by trained coders or judges. A number of clinical techniques such as the Rorschach Ink Blot Test and the Thematic Apperception Test require such skilled coders. Studies of coding reliabilities on the latter test, for example, indicate that the median interjudge correlation coefficient hovers around .9 with only about 25% falling below .85.[18] This means that one coder's judgments on a set of responses would have 81% ($.9^2$) of variance common with judgments obtained by other experts in the method.[19] Herzberg paid far too little attention to this problem, especially in his early research, according to his critics. Robert J. House and Lawrence A. Wigdor describe two such criticisms in their excellent evaluation of Herzberg's theory:

> The necessity for interpretations of the data by a rater may lead to contamination of the dimensions so derived. Employing one of Herzberg's own incidents to illustrate the dimension of recognition, Vroom (1964) pointed out the way in which the dual-factor theory may contaminate the coding procedure. The dimensions in the situation can quite possibly reflect more the rater's hypothesis concerning the compositions and inter-relations of dimensions than the respondent's own perceptions. A more objective approach, to minimize the possibility of learning more about the perceptions of raters than those of interviewees, would be to have the respondents do the rating and perform the necessary evaluations. (Graen, 1966)[20]

Empirical Evidence and Herzberg's Theory

Two kinds of evidence are available for evaluation in assessing Herzberg's dual-factor theory: (1) Evidence from research using Herzberg's critical-incident approach of which the principle criticisms have been given earlier, and (2) evidence based on non-critical-incident methods. Regarding the former, House and Wigdor, in their comprehensive review of the literature, point up a fundamental flaw in Herzberg's own report of supportive studies in his 1966 book *Work and the Nature of Man*. They examine carefully his assertion that 97 percent of the "cases" support his theory. Herzberg's presentation shows that theoretical predictions, when made for each separate *study*, were valid in 97 percent of the *cases*. House and Wigdor's review, however, contained a more logical arrangement of the data—a compilation of the *number of people* mentioning one of Herzberg's ten factors as a satisfier or dissatisfier. From this re-ordering of his data, House and Wigdor offer the following:

> Achievement is seen by *most respondents* as more of a dissatisfier than relations with supervisors or working conditions. In fact, Achievement can be considered the third major dissatisfier. Recognition is also found to be more of a dissatisfier than both Working conditions and Relations with superiors.[21]

They emphasize that their secondary analysis of the data ". . . yields conclusions contradictory to the proposition of the two-factor theory that satisfiers and dissatisfiers are unidimensional and independent."[22]

The other evidence available for evaluating Herzberg's theory comes from studies using methods other than the critical-incident approach. In their review, House and Wigdor summarize 31 such studies—all supposedly avoiding the critical-incident methodology. However, of the 31 studies, 8 appear to have been erroneously included by House and Wigdor since their descriptions of the research procedure for them clearly does not remove them from the critical-incident methodology classification:

1. Fantz (1962). Subjects: Three hospital rehabilitation patients. Procedure: ". . . six events described by the patients."
2. Friedlander and Walton (1964). Subjects: 82 scientists and engineers. Procedure: Semistructured interviews in which respondents gave the most important reasons keeping them in the organization and factors that might cause them to leave . . ."
3. Hahn (1959). Subjects: 800 officers in the U.S. Air Force. Procedure: "Content analysis of questionnaire on relating satisfying and non-satisfying experience."
4. Hinrichs and Mischkind (1967). Subjects: 613 engineering technicians. Procedure: "Content analysis of open-end responses . . ."
5. Myers (1964). Subjects: 282 male scientists, engineers, manufacturing supervisors and technicians, and 52 female hourly assemblers. Procedure: "Content analysis of Herzberg-type interviews."
6. Saleh (1964). Subjects: 85 managerial level male employees, ages ranged from 60 to 65. Procedure: "interview with a 16-item job attitude scale."
7. Schwartz (1959). Subjects: 373 third-level supervisors. Procedure: "Analyses of responses to questionnaire in part, asking questions similar to Herzberg in his critical-incident studies."
8. Wernimont (1966). Subjects: 50 accountants and 82 engineers. Procedure: "Self-description of past satisfying and dissatisfying job situations, using both free-choice and forced choice items . . ."[23]

The findings from research studies 1, 2, 3 and 7 above tended to support

Herzberg's theory, while the results from the remaining four were either negative or mixed. Some of these findings suggest that a number of factors not included in the theory may account for unpredicted (varying from the model) responses. Among these are the following:

1. Sex differences.
2. Age differences.
3. Intrinsic job factors are more important to both satisfying and dissatisfying job events.
4. These conclusions lead us to agree with the criticism advanced by Dunnette, Campbell, Hakel (1967) that the Two Factor theory is an oversimplification of the relationships between motivation and satisfaction, and the sources of job satisfaction and dissatisfaction.[24]

Another study by Charles L. Hulin and Patricia A. Smith[25] approached the testing of the duality theory from a different standpoint. They reasoned that if duality existed, there would be no relationship between the degree of contentment with motivators and overall job satisfaction, nor between degree of dissatisfaction with hygiene factors and overall job satisfaction. The results of their research on a group of office workers was not clear-cut but tended to offer less support for separate dual factors than for a single factor scale.

Ignoring the issue of duality, other critics have wondered aloud how is it that Lincoln Electric, et al., can continue to produce outstanding work performance by using pay, a non-motivating hygiene factor. Anticipating this possible criticism, Herzberg and co-authors claim that both the Lincoln Electric[26] and George A. Hormel employee reward systems are far more than simple bonus pay systems. They explain that many of the motivators are combined in their reward systems, and insist that these companies are actively increasing "job content and job responsibility by giving workers knowledge of, and responsibility for, operations and improvements."[27] Herzberg explains that the pay in these organizations is not just hygiene as in across-the-board increases. Instead, pay is a reinforcement of the motivators such as recognition and achievement. The point is an important one. If, in an effort to improve output, an employee participates in the design of an improved production tool or fixture, which of his needs is being fulfilled? If the design does increase production, he will get more money (hygiene factor). But he is also likely to gain in feelings of achievement and overt recognition for his contribution (motivating factor). Which of these caused the improved productive performance? So far, the literature contains no successful efforts to tease out these causal factors in a work environment such as exists at Lincoln Electric. Herzberg's quotation from Mr. Lincoln himself suggests that management there recognizes, intuitively, if not from empirical evidence, that high level performance is not a function of pay alone:

The most insistent incentive is the development of self-respect and respect of others. Earnings that are the reward for outstanding performance, progress, and responsibility are signs that he is a man among men. The worker must feel that he is part of a worthwhile project and that the project succeeded because his ability was needed in it. Money alone will not do the job.[28]

Herzberg's response to the many studies failing to support his theory using data-gathering techniques other than the open ended critical incident method is based upon the "fakeability" problem with questionnaires:

The general practice of psychologists of giving lists of factors for employees to rate with respect to their job satisfactions by now should be recognized as one of the most misleading approaches to the study of work feelings.[29]

Behling, Labovitz and Kosmo, authors of a critical appraisal of the Dual-Factor Theory, point up that the protagonists and observers in this issue may be missing an important lesson to be learned from the controversy. They suggest that the real value of the finding that work motivation research results depend upon the approach used is that "job satisfaction" as a single attitudinal entity is only a theoretical construct. They point to the simple fact that "there is no evidence that any single, unitary, overall attitude toward an individual's employment exists,"[30] but there is considerable evidence that the relationship of a person to his job is quite complex and not fully understood. They believe that much work must be done, including the development of better measuring approaches, before the components of a "total (job) attitudinal complex" will be fully understood. Then, and only then, can these components be ordered in terms of job satisfaction, job environment and job behavior.

Conclusions Regarding Herzberg's Dual-Factor Theory

Although all of them are not necessarily new, below are some conclusions which could be reached after reviewing the Herzberg's Dual-Factor Theory and efforts to validate it:

1. Any theory which is launched with support from a single study using a "clinical" methodology, will invite traditional researchers (using non-clinical methodologies) in large numbers to test the theory.
2. Any work motivation theory which depends heavily upon a clear relationship between job satisfaction and job performance is likely doomed, given research results to date attempting to correlate these two variables.
3. The notion is reaffirmed that work motivation is extremely difficult, if not impossible, to define and measure to the satisfaction of most of the researchers in the field.

4. The evidence to date clearly eliminates Herzberg's theory as a general or universal theory of work motivation. Far too many findings fail to support the Dual-Factor model.

It is possible that a multi-factor contingency approach considering variables such as types of jobs, hierarchical levels, age, sex, education, etc. might find some research support. This approach, however, would merely underscore what critics have claimed—that total attitudinal job relationships are quite complex, and at present, rather poorly understood.

More disturbing than the research support shortfall is the speed with which the theory gained popular and non-researcher academic acceptance, especially during the first ten years after its original statement. The history of science contains many examples of new theories not being accepted by peer scientists, the laity, and authorities. The Pope and other authorities, for example, lent their offices to the rejection of the notion of the axial rotation of the earth as proposed by Jean Foucault, *et al.* Einstein's and Freud's theories faced rejection and even ridicule by peer scientists and the public. But in the case of Maslow's and Herzberg's theories, we had a rapid initial acceptance by many practitioners and academics with inadequate supporting evidence and a growing following subscribing to them in the face of a steady stream of negative research findings. What this phenomenon means may be answered by Andreski in his book *Social Sciences as Sorcery:*

There is an asymmetry between the expertise in the natural and in the social sciences. Someone unacquainted with an exact science is completely dumbfounded in any discussion about it; but, being reduced to silence, he is saved from any possible temptation to spout nonsense. On matters pertaining to the social sciences, on the other hand, the opposite is the case: everybody feels entitled to express strong views, and there are no solid signposts to warn against the pitfalls of ignorance, sophistry, or even folly; while the lack of knowledge regularly breeds a conviction that things are simple and require no deep study . . . The contrast between exactness and certitude (relative but sufficient for most practical purposes) on the one hand, and vagueness and tentativeness on the other, entails a further assymmetry between the natural and the social sciences. A mediocre natural scientist, albeit unable to think of anything new, or even to keep fully abreast of current progress, remains nonetheless a repository of useful . . . knowledge, whereas a mediocre social scientist, unable to distinguish between worthwhile ideas and the half-truths . . . which flourish in his controversial field, will be an easy victim . . . and will act as an agent of mental pollution.[31]

A less pessimistic view would be that the social sciences are fortunate in that the products of research and rational thought are cumulative, whereas fads and fashions not only do not sum, but often cancel each other out. In the case of Maslow's and Herzberg's theories, perhaps we have not waited long enough.

NOTES

1. F. Herzberg, *Work and the Nature of Man*, (Cleveland, Ohio; World Publishing Company, 1966), p. 75.
2. *Ibid.*
3. This account was developed from the following sources: David J. Lawless, *Effective Management*, (Englewood Cliffs, N.J.: Prentice-Hall, Inc., 1972), pp. 96–97; James H. Donnelly, Jr., James L. Gibson and John M. Ivancevick; *Fundamentals of Management*, (Dallas, Texas: Business Publications, Inc., 1975), pp. 150–157; and Paul Hersey and Kenneth H. Blanchard, *Management of Organizational Behavior*, (Englewood Cliffs, N.J.: Prentice-Hall, Inc., 1972), pp. 54–58.
4. The Adam-Abraham analogy is carried in considerable detail in Lawless, but is rarely found in typical college texts.
5. By far the most common criticism is that Herzberg's sample of engineers and accountants are not representative of the general workforce.
6. Harold Ruch, *Behavioral Science, Concepts and Applications*, Personnel Policy Study No. 216 (New York, N.Y.: The National Industrial Conference Board, Inc., 1969), p. 25.
7. Earl F. Lungren, *Organizational Management: Systems and Processes*, (San Francisco, Calif.: Canfield Press, A Dept. of Harper and Row, 1974), p. 285.
8. Frederick Herzberg, B. Mausner, and Barbara Snyderman, *The Motivation to Work*, (New York, N.Y.: Wiley, 1959).
9. Joseph L. Massie and John Douglas, *Managing, A Contemporary Introduction*, (Englewood Cliffs, N.J.: Prentice Hall, Inc., 1973), p. 55.
10. Frederick Herzberg, *et al.*, *The Motivation to Work*, p. 113.
11. A.H. Brayfield and W.H. Crockett, "Employee Attitudes and Employee Performance," *Psychological Bulletin*, LII (1955), p. 423.
12. Frederick Herzberg, Bernard Mausner, R. O. Peterson, and D. F. Capwell, *Job Attitudes: Review of Research and Opinion* (Pittsburg, Pa.: Psychological Services of Pittsburg, 1957).
13. A. H. Brayfield and W.H. Crockett, p. 424.
14. Robert Dubin, Joseph E. Champoux and Hyman Porter, "Central Life Interests and Organizational Committment of Blue Collar and Clerical Workers," *Administrative Science Quarterly*, September, 1975, p. 411.
15. Victor H. Vroom, *Work and Motivation* (New York, N.Y.: Wiley, 1964), pp. 183–85.
16. Frederick Herzberg, Bernard Mausner, and Barbara B. Snyderman, *The Motivation to Work*, Appendix I, p. 141.
17. Henri DeMan, *Joy in Work*, translation by Eden Paul (New York, N.Y.: Holt, Rhinehart and Winston, 1929), p. 9 as quoted in Daniel A. Wren, *The Evolution of Management Thought* (New York, N.Y.: The Ronald Press Co., 1972), p. 206.
18. The problem of reliability of measures of "satisfaction" (and like measures) is not limited to interview results coding. Paper-pencil data gathering instruments such as the Porter Need Satisfaction Questionnaire, *et al.*, have become targets of criticism for generalizations from results without due regard to reliability standards. (See Chapter 7 for further discussion on this problem.)

19. John Atkinson and Joel O. Raynor, *Motivation and Achievement* (Washington, D.C.: V. H. Winston & Sons, 1974), p. 191.

20. Robert J. House and Lawrence A. Wigdor, "Herzberg's Dual-Factor Theory of Job Satisfaction and Motivation: A Review of Evidence and a Criticism," *Personnel Psychology*, XX (1967), pp. 369–89, as reprinted by permission in William K. Graham and Karlene H. Roberts, *Comparative Studies in Organizational Behavior* (New York, N.Y.: Holt, Rhinehart and Winston, Inc., 1972) p. 232.

21. *Ibid.*, p. 236.

22. *Ibid.*, p. 237.

23. *Ibid.*, pp. 237–45.

24. *Ibid.*, p. 246.

25. Charles L. Hulin and Patricia Smith, "An Empirical Investigation of Two Implications of the Two-Factor Theory of Job Satisfaction," *Journal of Applied Psychology*, LI (1967), pp. 396–402.

26. Workers at Lincoln Electric, a major manufacturer of welding and related equipment, have for years earned large annual bonuses, many greater than the average annual wage in the industry itself.

27. Frederick Herzberg, et al., *The Motivation to Work*, p. 115.

28. *Ibid.*

29. *Ibid.*

30. Orlando Behling, George Labovitz, and Richard Kosmo, "The Herzberg Controversy: A Critical Reappraisal," *The Academy of Management Journal* (1968), p. 108.

31. Stanislav Andreski, *Social Sciences as Sorcery* (New York, N.Y.: St. Martin's Press, 1972), pp. 201–2. Reprinted by permission of St. Martin's Press © 1972.

Chapter 7

Vroom's Expectancy Theory

THE general path-goal theory of work motivation discussed in this chapter has arrived at its current stage by painstaking processes. Primarily these involved theorists' continued efforts to reconcile the wide variety of research findings about the relationship between job satisfaction and work performance, with a fundamental psychological theory. The psychological theory was that the motivation to work depended upon how hard one had to work to get a goal or reward and upon the worker's perception of the likelihood that if he worked hard, the reward would be his or hers.

Until the early 1960's it was evidently widely accepted that there was a simple and direct relationship between job satisfaction and performance. Furthermore, job satisfaction levels were generally thought to *cause* job performance levels, although there appears to have been almost no evidence to support this. Some observers, not to mention a number of researchers and theorists, were caught in one of the oldest traps in scientific interpretation— that since two things (apparently) happen together, one caused the other. In choosing which caused which, many probably used a "personally plausible" test, since the research designs rarely yielded even a hint of causality. And evidently it didn't seem plausible that good job performance would *cause* job satisfaction.

The Brayfield and Crockett inventory of research findings on the subject in 1955 mentioned earlier seems to have started a slow awakening that something was wrong, not only with the assumed relationship but with the causality notion. The gradual change in selective perception of a few observers began to uncover indirectly related findings which seemed to go counter to the assumed causal relationship. From animal research, for example, there came the contaminating finding that *insufficient* reward and its consequent *frustration* can lead to greater effort and persistence[1]. In another experiment in which subjects had endured embarrassment to gain admission to a group, the subjects thought more highly of the group than subjects who gained easy access to it.[2] These two findings do not support the idea that satisfaction *causes* performance. In the first case the frustration appeared to lead to greater effort and in the second the frustration made the goal appear more attractive.

Other observers of the human motivation scene were never enticed into the satisfaction-causes-performance blind canyon. Saul Gellerman, for example, had maintained a motivation-is-an-extremely-complex-phenomenon posture for years while attempts were being made to prove a simple and direct relationship between job satisfaction and performance: "The first and most important thing to be said about motives is that everybody has quite a lot of them and that nobody has quite the same mixture as anyone else. We have to deal with human diversity . . . regardless of whether we find it administratively convenient or conceptually easy to grasp. And it is neither."[3]

And George C. Homans, who has studied work behavior in small groups extensively, tells his students today that ". . . there is no general relationship between productivity and satisfaction."[4]

The original impetus pressing for research evidence that job satisfaction caused variations in job performance was likely the Hawthorne studies. The popular conclusion, although inaccurate, perpetuated by the inordinate publicity of these studies, was that a change in mental attitude brought about by a friendly relationship with supervisors caused job satisfaction which, in turn, caused the reported improved job performance. The satisfaction-causes-performance notion was perpetuated for years in the face of (1) continuously recorded low or negative correlations between the two variables, (2) employees' and unions' continued demands, not for "tender loving care," but for wage and fringe benefits, and (3) failures in human relations training of supervisors to replicate the alleged advantages of the Hawthorne experimental supervisory style.

The re-examination movement gained more momentum from Victor Vroom's inventory of findings in the early 1960's. The median correlation of these studies (discussed in the previous chapter) of .14 ($.14^2 =$ only 2% better than chance prediction from one variable to the other), with 20 of them positive, had various effects on observers. Edward H. Lawler III and J. L. Suttle were encouraged: "The consistency of the direction of the correlation was quite impressive."[5] To a manager, of course, such faint relationships are useless. To researchers it would seem that any statistically significant relationship, however tiny, is important if it can be used for model building or theory validation. The manager or student of management has only to worry that such a finding is never extracted and trimmed for management consumption to read: "87% of the studies of the relationship between job satisfaction and job performance showed a significant positive relationship."

Since shortly after Vroom's book was published in 1964, path-goal theory, or expectancy theory as it is sometimes called, has dominated the research on work motivation. On the following pages, Vroom's model will be described in detail. Following this, a critical evaluation of the model will be provided, including criticisms by other researchers and theorists.

The Vroom Path-Goal Model

Since at least 1932, a number of psychological theorists have proposed variations on a path-goal theory of motivation. Most were concerned with a *general* motivation theory, based essentially on *hedonism*, the philosophy which holds that *behavior is guided to seek pleasure and avoid pain*. Except for alterations of the models to avoid defining goals on a pleasure-pain continuum, and elaborations on the "seeking" (choosing, weighing, etc.), most modern expectancy theories are still based on hedonism. Most are also "ahistorical" to use Vroom's term for the models' ignoring all causes of behavior not directly related to "events occuring contemporaneously with the behavior."[6]

Because Atkinson's model, an expectancy theory variation, began as part of an approach to the psychological origins of needs—primarily the need for achievement—it was discussed in Chapter 5 along with McClelland's achievement need work. Lawler and Porter have proposed a model similar to Vroom's, but since most of their research validation efforts have been concerned with the relationship of pay and work performance, it will be discussed briefly in Chapter 8 on economic motivation. Other variations on the basic expectancy model have been presented or researched by a number of people.[7] The Vroom model is chosen here for detailed discussion primarily because it began the movement to use expectancy theory on work motivation. It also appears to be the most popular of the model variants.

In its simplest form the Vroom model is the 40-year-old Motive Force = Valence $\times$ Expectancy ($MF = V \times E$). Simply stated, a highly motivated producer would desire the reward (valence) he or she sees as the result of hard work and would be confident (expectancy) that if one worked hard to produce, the perceived reward would be won. The Motive Force can be seen as lower if one desires the rewards, but doesn't believe that working hard will get them. Conversely, a strong Motive Force to restrict output could be due to a strong desire to be accepted by the work group and the belief that if one does so he or she will be rewarded by their acceptance. The Vroom model, unlike a number of similar models such as the Lawler-Porter model, does not differentiate between extrinsic rewards (pay, security, benefits, etc.) and intrinsic rewards (private rewards self-administered for achieving growth or fulfilling some inner need).

The actual Vroom model is very sophisticated and formidable-appearing to the non-behavioral scientist. Like the Atkinson model, it is also offered in algebraic equation form. The hazards of such nonsense have already been pointed out by Andreski in his book, *Social Sciences as Sorcery*. After reviewing H. A. Simon's elaborate mathematical model of Homans' theory of human interaction, Andreski wrote that a better physical equivalent to Simon's formalization of Homans' theories would have been a sentence like "the wind bloweth where it listeth," which he suggests could also be written in the mathematical symbolism of vector calculus as $V_b = V_L$.[8]

Vroom's first equation is for determining the desirability of a goal. This desirability is defined very fancifully as "affective orientations toward particular out-comes." Thus goal desirability values can vary between positive ("pleasure") and negative ("pain") numbers. A zero value would represent indifference. Expectancy is defined by Vroom as ". . . the degree to which (a person) believes (certain) outcomes to be probable." Expectancy, when quantified, is like a probability value and can only vary between 0 and 1.0. An expectancy value of zero indicates that a person just doesn't believe that a certain effort will be followed by a reward. A value of 1 represents the belief that the effort *will* be followed by the reward. *Instrumentality* refers to the amount of hard work seen as leading to the attainment of a goal—say of a pay increase or promotion. In Vroom's model, instrumentality can vary between −1 and +1. The extreme of −1 indicates the belief that the pay or promotion will be sure to come without working hard and that hard work will guarantee that the promotion will not come. A value of +1 indicates the belief that hard work is all that is necessary to get the promotion. At this point Vroom's description becomes incomprehensible to the majority of behavioral scientists who haven't followed the literature, ludicrous to a few who have, and profound to many others. For the few readers who might wish to understand in detail the ridiculousness engaged in by modern motivation theorists, Vroom's model is described in his terms and analyzed according to scientists' use of logic and evidence. Other readers should browse the jargon-laden phrases and definitions for the next few pages and write the theory off as virtually untestable in their lifetimes.

Vroom's verbal and algebraic equations for the Valence value of a given outcome are as follows:

The valence of an outcome to a person is a monotonically increasing function of the algebraic sum of the products of the valences of all other outcomes and his conceptions of it's instrumentality for the attainment of these other outcomes.

$$V_j = f_j \left[\sum_{k=1}^{n} (V_k I_{jk}) \right] (j = 1 \ldots n)$$

$$f_j' > O;\ i\ I_{jj} = O$$

where V_j = the valence of outcome j

I_{jk} = the cognized instrumentality
($-1 \leq I_{jk} \leq 1$) of outcome
j for the attainment of outcome k

The above constitutes Vroom's model for the term Valence in the original Expectancy Theory equation MF = V × E.

The verbal equation for (motive) *Force* in Vroom's model is given as follows:

The force on a person to perform an act is a monotonically increasing function of the algebraic sum of the products of the valences of all outcomes and the strength of his expectancies that the act will be followed by the attainment of these outcomes:

$$F_i = f_i \left[\sum_{j=1}^{n} (E_{ij} V_j) \right] (i = n + 1 \ldots m)$$

$$f_i' > O;\ i \cap j = \phi,\ \phi \text{ is the null set}$$

where F_i = the force to perform act i

E_{ij} = the strength of the expectancy ($O \leq E_{ij} \leq 1$)
that act i will be followed by outcome j

V_j = the valence of outcome j

In explaining the reasons for expressing Force as a monotonically increasing function of (Valence × Expectancy), Vroom offers the following:

An outcome with high positive or negative valence will have no effect on the generation of a force unless there is some expectancy (i.e., some subjective probability greater than zero) that the outcome will be attained by some act. As the strength of an expectancy that an act will lead to an outcome increases, the effect of variations in the valence of the outcome on the force to perform the act will also increase. Similarly, if the valence of an outcome is zero (i.e., the person is indifferent to the outcome), neither the absolute value nor variations in the strength of expectancies of attaining it will have any effect on (motive) forces.

Along with his original statement of the model, Vroom himself pointed out that it is untestable until the concepts embodied have been related to observable events. In suggesting possible means of scientifically measuring and of manipulating the variables valence and expectancy, Vroom points to an occasional problem:

Analysis of Vroom's Suggestions for Measuring Valences

1. VERBAL REPORTS. After summarily dismissing the "unconscious

motivation" proponents by explaining that such motivation "is not available to direct verbal report," and that "behaviorists . . . have seriously questioned the use of introspective data," Vroom suggests that "faking" is the most convincing argument against self reports. This, too, he sets aside fairly easily by explaining that researchers are aware of this problem and that "they try to minimize or eliminate (it) by structuring the testing situation in such a way that the subject believes his responses are confidential or anonymous."

Even though Vroom dismisses unconscious motivation because he does not believe it "available," it does not follow that unconscious motives which mislead their owners in completing questionnaires do not exist. The existence of a variety of unconsciously operating defense mechanisms is well documented. After reviewing a summary of the literature on unconscious motivation, Berelson and Steiner, in their inventory of scientific findings on human behavior, point out that while simple human motives such as hunger are usually accompanied by a conscious sense of striving,

. . . with the more complex social motives, however, this direct and consistent relationship between purposive behavior and subjective experience does not always hold. People often act in consistent ways that produce consistent results—and under conditions where they seem to have a choice in the matter. Thus their behavior bears all the external signs of being purposive and goal-directed. Yet they themselves often vehemently deny the motive that would be inferred, or even report the opposite motivation.[9]

Berelson and Steiner's literature review also resulted in the following specific conclusions pertinent to the validity of *verbal reports* for measuring valences:

The goal sought, and the means employed, can be so habitual or automatic as to *escape awareness*. Some motives are so unacceptable, threatening, or repugnant that they are unrecognized or unacknowledged; conscience or the need to maintain self-esteem act as internal barriers that block direct expression and awareness. As in such cases, people may express the motive in any number of devious or disguised ways, i.e., in indirect expressions that do not seem to be related to it. (In summary) the goals and motives inferred from consistent, purposive behavior do not always match the goals and the motives experienced or reported by the actor, and the discrepancy is not necessarily a matter of intentional misstatement. In short, motives can operate and find expression outside of awareness . . .[10] (Italics and parenthetical phrases added)

Kubie, in his review of psychoanalytic validation problems and techniques, points out that the findings summarized above had ". . . been reproduced in experimental hypnosis to the satisfaction of the most exacting skeptic."[11]

In their efforts to relate "job performance" to "effort" or to "satisfaction," expectancy theory researchers often use verbal questionnaire reports of peers and/or superiors for measures of performance. The research findings on the mechanism "projection" warns that these reports can also be contaminated by unconscious motivation. Berelson and Steiner, after reviewing research on this mechanism, conclude that "Repressed motives or other unacceptable and unrecognized aspects of one's own personality may be attributed to others."[12]

2. ANALYSIS OF FANTASY (using the Thematic Apperception Test as used by McClelland, Atkinson, *et al.*) This approach to the measurement of valences is considered by Vroom to be ". . . restricted by the gross nature of the motivational variables which are employed." Vroom explains that his model is concerned with information regarding *single* outcomes, not broad classes of outcomes. However, many expectancy theory researchers who identify their work with Vroom's model are themselves attempting to predict very broad outcomes such as job performance.

3. CHANGES IN BEHAVIORAL RESPONSE PROBABILITY. Vroom suggests that "if an outcome strengthens a response tendency, it could be assumed to be positively valent" and vice versa. The measure of valence would be ". . . the amount or rate of change in response probability when the outcome is made contingent on the response." Vroom is likely thinking of laboratory experiments for this approach, although examples of specific uses are not suggested. Experimenting with alternate outcomes in work situations while controlling other variables may not be impossible, but it is difficult to foresee its likelihood. Furthermore, as Vroom points out, such comparative measures would only indicate *whether* an outcome is positively or negatively valent, with little if any indication of the magnitudes of valences.

4. INFER VALENCES FROM CHOICES MADE AMONG ALTERNATIVE COURSES OF ACTION. A person choosing alternative x over y when attainment expectances are both equal (certain), would be indicating that x is more positively valent than y. Although not mentioned by Vroom, this approach assumes that there is no relationship between a person's valence of an outcome and his assessment of the likelihood that it will follow with a given effort level. The evidence from decision making research does not seem to support this. The theory's assumption of the independence of these two variables is discussed in more detail later in the chapter as part of a review of all the assumptions upon which Vroom's model is dependent.

5. CONSUMMATORY BEHAVIOR. "We might assume that the hungrier a person is, i.e., the greater the valence of food, the more food he will eat. Thus measures of amount of rate of eating, drinking, or copulation would be used to indicate the extent to which the consumed outcomes were positively valent. . . ." Leaving aside the problems in measuring copulation rate while attainment expectancies are held equal or certain, the research on

unconscious motivation discussed earlier suggests that models for physiological need satisfaction behavior are not necessarily applicable to more complex social behavior. Further, such an approach to valence measurement appears to assume a linear relationship yet to be demonstrated between the degree of physiological need deprivation and satiation activity rate. In studies of adult rats, food deprivation behavior depended upon whether they had been deprived during infancy.[13] More comprehensive forms of deprivation such as the raising of monkeys in separate cages have not demonstrated an enhancement of the valences of deprived outcomes: "(Monkeys in) total isolation for two years resulted in failure to display social or sexual behavior in the next two years, spent in a joint living cage."[14] No relevant research on humans appears to be available.

6. DECISION TIME. This approach as described by Vroom would lead only to the measurement of differences in outcome valences. The quicker outcome x is chosen over y the greater the difference in their valences. Again, we are faced with an assumption of a linear relationship, this time between choice rate and outcome valence. If research is available supporting such a relationship, it is not in the mainstream of the literature. Peripherally related to this situation might be the interpretation of the results of a clinical word association test. This test is one in which the researcher speaks a word and the subject responds with the first word which comes "to mind." In scoring the results, clinicians have validated two characteristics of the responses—the actual words (content) and the length of time required for responses. However, in interpreting the meaning of response delays, deviations from the mean response time, *whether shorter or longer*, are indicative of emotional loadedness of the stimulus word. In other words, if a subject responds very quickly or with an unusual delay, the stimulus word is said to have higher valence than normal (for that subject). Unfortunately, there is no valid indication of whether the valence of the stimulus word is positive or negative. Even though these findings are not directly comparable to the choice rate of one variable over another, it suggests that before such a linear relationship is assumed for research purposes, it ought to be verified.

Vroom's Suggestions for Experimental Manipulation of Valence

1. COMMUNICATED INFORMATION CONCERNING THEIR DESIRABILITY. This approach assumes that valences can be varied or induced by suggestion especially where the subjects have little or no prior experience with the outcomes. As Vroom suggests, this approach has been demonstrated to be possible on low emotionally loaded motives where the subjects are inexperienced, or had no previous psychic sets. Motives that spring from

highly valenced values, however, cannot be so easily manipulated. One would assume, for example, that the general motive to work hard or little is not a lightly loaded value to be influenced significantly by overt suggestion. Otherwise, foremen would have stumbled across the magic words long ago, since they have likely tried far more varieties of such suggestions than psychologists could ever think up.

2. AROUSING APPROPRIATE MOTIVES. Assuming that individual desires and motives can be varied predictably by stimulation, Vroom suggests that outcome valences can be increased by arousing certain motives. "The valence of food can be increased by depriving an experimental subject of food for an extended period of time or even by subjecting him to the sight or smell of food. The valence of sexual intercourse can be increased by showing him photographs of unclothed members of the opposite sex; and the valence of doing well on a task can be increased by telling him that it is a measure of his intelligence." The assumptions necessary for this approach are identical to those discussed above in number 5 regarding the measurement of valences, except that a few additional assumptions would be necessary to measure sex valence variations by flashing pictures of naked people around. Although legitimate research is conspicuously absent on the percentage of women who respond to buttocks or front view thighs, it is well known that male arousal varies with both the dimensions and view of "unclothed members of the opposite sex." Studies would be necessary to determine some quantifiable relationship between arousal valence values and a standardized set of photographs by sex. If universality were important to the researcher, cultural and racial response patterns would be necessary.

3. VARY OUTCOME VALENCES BY ASSOCIATION WITH REWARDS AND PUNISHMENTS. This approach is properly considered questionable by Vroom since it is yet to be shown that long term changes in valences are due to any form of classical conditioning.

Vroom's Suggestions for Experimental Measurement of Expectancies

1. VERBAL REPORTS. Vroom suggests that "if a person states that an outcome is certain to follow an act, we assume an expectancy value of 1.00, whereas if he states that an outcome has a 50-50 chance of following that act, we assume an expectancy value of .50." Vroom notes that decision theorists criticize this data gathering approach for the same reasons that verbal reports of outcome valences are suspect. The same criticism regarding the ignoring of unconscious motivation applies here as was given under Vroom's suggestions for measurement of valences. (See number 1 under "Suggestions for Measuring Valences" above.)

2. ACTUAL CHOICES OF DECISIONS MADE.   The amounts subjects are willing to wager in relation to a known prize value could be used to assess outcome valences. Vroom notes the problem with this approach would be to disentangle the roles of expectancies from preferences.

Vroom's Suggestions for Experimentally Manipulating Expectancy.

1. COMPARISON WITH OBJECTIVE PROBABILITIES.   This approach assumes that expectancies correspond perfectly with objective probabilities. Vroom notes that this approach might be viable only with subjects with considerable experience who have had accurate feedbacks with a specific class of outcomes. The same problems are associated with this approach as were discussed in number 4 above.

2. COMPARISON WITH COMMUNICATED PROBABILITIES.   This approach assumes that ". . . expectancies are completely determined by communicated probabilities" and is considered by Vroom tenable only "when subjects have little additional basis for judging probabilities and when they have not previously been deceived in experimentation."

3. EXPECTANCIES DETERMINED FROM KNOWN (CONTRIVED) OUTCOME EXPERIENCE.   Vroom suggests that "If, in previous exposures to a situation, a person has received an outcome each time he has performed an act, his expectancy is assumed to be 1.00; if he has received the outcome only 50 percent of the time, he is assumed to have an expectancy of .50 . . ." This may appear sound, except for the mountainous evidence that the reward pattern (spacing) must be clearly specified. If there is any learning principle which could be called a law by virtue of its consistent verification, it would be the learning rate and relative permanency as it relates to the timing pattern of rewards.[15]

Fifty percent reward is meaningless until reward spacing characteristics, i.e., random or regular, are known, since wide differences in learning and forgetting are evident between random and scheduled reward patterns of different types.

ASSUMPTIONS OF VROOM'S MODEL REVIEWED

Before discussing actual research efforts on work motivation aimed at testing Vroom's variant of the expectancy theory, a review of a few of the more critical assumptions upon which the theory is based will be presented. Orlando Behling and Frederick A. Starke have provided a summary of these assumptions, and considerable evidence—primarily from decision theory research—that many of them cannot be met. They describe seven postulates which must be satisfied and two that "are logical extensions of current expectancy formulations, but deal with areas where expectancy theorists are silent."[16] Four of these postulates are presented below.

Their first postulate: the assumption of comparability.

Behling and Starke rightly point out that the model assumes that any two products of expectancies and valences are directly comparable. They indicate that the model assumes that an "individual can and does develop functions that permit him to . . . trade off, say, 19 units of salary increase for 14 units of acceptance by his peers, or 20 units of promotion for 30 units of recognition." They cite a study by Soelberg which appears to support the idea that individuals make crucial personal decisions (job choices) without clear valence dimensions or weightings of them. They conclude that the assumption of unidimensionality is open to question.

Postulate two: "Transitivity".

Behling and Starke point to the evidence indicating that this assumption cannot be met since intransitivities are always evident, if at varying rates. They conclude that ". . . the bulk of the existing evidence indicates that individuals in laboratory situations do not consistently order alternatives, but make their decisions in sequential fashion." They summarize their contention that the transitivity assumption cannot be met with a quotation from decision theory researcher Tversky:

Thus, having chosen y over x and then z over y, one is typically committed to z and may not even compare it with x, which has already been eliminated. Furthermore, in many choice situations the eliminated alternative is no longer available, so there is no way of finding out whether our preferences are transitive or not. These considerations suggest that in actual decisions, as well as in laboratory experiments, people are likely to overlook their own intransitivities. Transitivity, however, is one of the basic and most compelling principles of rational behavior.[17]

Postulate three: "Independence."

The model assumes that there is no relationship between how much an outcome is desired and the estimate of the likelihood that it will be attained from a certain effort level. Behling and Stark cite a dozen studies on behavior which have demonstrated the connection between expectancy and desirability, and conclude that the two must be considered interrelated to varying degrees.

Postulate four: "Optimization."

Although it is related to postulate two (transitivity), Behling and Starke argue that this assumption cannot be met, primarily because of the limitations of the human brain in dealing with multi-dimension, multi-alternative decision problems. They cite evidence from the literature in support of their doubts indicating that, although the human memory is extraordinary in terms of strong capacity, its input, output, and data manipulation are handled by a short-term system limited to

. . . seven or so bits of information. Data are processed serially rather than in parallel and at a relatively slow speed. Obviously, in even a simple problem in which the individual might conceive of perhaps three levels of effort and ten relevant outcomes, the likelihood of system overload is great.

They suggest that a satisfying model[18] would be more realistic than the optimizing model inherent in Vroom's theory. Lawler, Porter and Hackman agree:

If man truly attempted to optimize his behavior, he probably would be so heavily involved in search and evaluation activities and in constant "operating" activities aimed at meeting the test for optimal performance that he would never do anything."[19]

In spite of the problems in meeting the assumptions inherent in the model, research efforts to validate the theory have proceeded.

Research Designed to Test Vroom's Model

On the subject of testing Vroom's model there are clearly two views: observers such as J.G. Hunt and J.W. Hill, in their popular article "The New Look in Motivational Theory"[20] present the view that the model is testable and that the theory holds "great promise." Their article describes four studies under the heading "Empirical Tests of Vroom's Model" (more on these and other such studies later). On the other hand, there are those who hold that the model is untestable. One base for this position is simply that all the variables cannot be operationalized at once. In their conclusions to an article describing their efforts to compare Vroom's model with another behavioral model, Mawhinney and Behling suggest that "the task is even greater than would appear on the surface."[21]

Some Empirical Studies on the Model

One of the studies described by Hunt and Hill under their heading "Empirical Tests of Vroom's Model" involved the prediction of the choices of organizations of graduating graduate students.[22] Vroom developed an index from students' ratings of 15 goals and the extent to which they thought these goals could be gained by joining each of three organizations. The correlation between these two measures was converted to be used as the instrumentality-goal index. Recall that instrumentality is defined by Vroom as the degree to which the first level outcome (joining a given company in this case) is viewed as leading to a second level outcome (achieving desired goals). The expectancy variable in the model can vary between 0 and 1.0 and is the degree to which a person believes a certain outcome is probable. Instead of using measures of these perceived expectancies, Vroom simply waited and picked expectancies for his subjects which were primarily, if not exclusively, determined by the organizations themselves. If a student received an offer, his expectancy was considered high, and if not, low. The valence variable as given in the model has a value between 0 and 1.0 representing "orientations toward particular outcomes." In this study no effort was made to determine this value. Instead, alternate goals were ranked, and *relative* goal importance was used in developing the instrumentality goal index. It should be noted here that Vroom's hypotheses to be tested in this particular study were not stated in terms of testing a total model. Only one hypothesis—the attractiveness of an organization will be related to the belief that joining it will lead to goal attainment—can be considered expectancy model oriented. Seventy-six percent of the students' choices among those companies from which an offer was received were for organizations corresponding to the highest instrumentality-goal index. Consistent with the model assumptions, this research design treats goals and goal strength as independent of any influence by interviews, plant visits, and job offers. As mentioned earlier, neither evidence nor common sense supports this assumption. In this experiment, this flaw in the model appeared to have helped to generate support for other portions of the model.

In a similar study by John Sheridan, Max Richards, and John Slocum,[23] using job choice behavior (of graduating nurses) to compare Vroom's expectancy model and Soelberg's decision process model,[24] the findings tended to support the descriptive power of Vroom's model. Soelberg's contention was that such choices would be based upon two or less primary outcomes as criteria. Soelberg also found, as did Herzberg, that after the decisions were made, distortions in favor of the choices occurred. The Sheridan, *et al.*, study supported neither of these findings. Their summary of their results is as follows:

(1) Many nurses could not identify necessary and sufficient conditions for accepting a job. (2) The significant difference in the motivational force between the accepted and rejected job alternatives did not emanate solely from a small group of highly important job outcomes, but was cumulative over all available outcomes. (3) There was no significant perceptual distortion in motivational force after the nurses implicitly made their job decisions.[25]

It should be noted here that the internal reliability correlation coefficient for valence measures used in this study was .8 ($r^2 = 64\%$) and the test-retest correlation of the instrumentality measures was only .55 ($r^2 = 30\%$). The former coefficient is more a measure of internal consistency and tends to overestimate stability of measures over time. The latter coefficient clearly suggests that certain of their results may be spurious. Since behavioral science research results, although statistically significant, are typically of weak relationships and small real differences, contradictions in findings are to be expected. Many could be the result of data gathering instruments of low reliability such as that used to measure instrumentality in this study.

The second study cited by Hunt and Hill as supportive of Vroom's model in their review of motivational theory was one which operationalized and tested the interactive effects between valence and instrumentality on job performance.[26] The goal variables considered were high performance itself (intrinsic motive), money, fringes, promotion, supervisors' supportive behavior, and work group acceptance. Company output records were used for productivity measures and valences, instrumentality, and ego involvement (intrinsic motive) were measured by questionnaires. Reliability coefficients in r^2 values of these questionnaires on a test-retest one month apart on university personnel were 25% (valence), 64% (instrumentality), and 66% (ego involvement). It should be noted that the valence measures were taken with an instrument which showed only 25% common variance from one questionnaire administration to another a month apart. In order to use analysis of variance to test the effects of variables and interaction, measures of valence, instrumentality, and work "ability" were dichotomized into "high" and "low" measures. Since supervisors' ratings of worker ability did not correlate with output measures, it was decided that a worker with more than six months on the job would be considered to have "high ability." Under six months job experience constituted "low ability." The sample was 32 voluntary operatives in a mid-west heavy equipment factory. They were selected as having considerable control over their workpace.

A multiple regression analysis indicated that output was related to instrumentality-goal interactions for pay and supervisor's support. The multiple correlation of .57 between the significant motivational variables and output means that about a third ($.57^2$) of worker productivity could be explained by the model. Adding the ability (experience) variable resulted in a multiple correlation of .68, meaning that about 46% of output variance could be accounted for by the expanded model. The researcher's conclusions were cautious:

> The present study also offers support for the Vroom (1964) model of the interactive effects of valence and instrumentality in determining motivation for a particular performance outcome. Data collected across a larger sample (and across samples composed of differing occupational and skill groups) are needed before statements concerning the generality of the relationship can be made.[27]

Further caution is warranted here because of the possible spurious nature of the findings due to the very low reliability of one of the critical measures—valence. It is very doubtful that a replication would yield these same results.

Another study in the Hunt and Hill review found a 5% level statistically significant correlation of .26 ($r^2 = 7\%$) between worker job bidding behavior and subjective expected outcome indexes. These indexes were developed from perceived ratings of consequences of bidding and of probability of success. The faint though significant relationship offers less support for a portion of the Vroom model than does the final study by Lawler and Porter[28] reviewed by Hunt and Hill below:

> Finally, Lawler and Porter report a study that attempts to relate managerial attitudes to job performance rankings by superiors and peers. In it, 145 managers from five different organizations completed questionnaires concerning seven kinds of rewards, and their expectations that different kinds of behavior would lead to these rewards. The expectations and the ratings of the importance of instrumentality and valence, respectively, were combined multiplicatively to yield multiple correlations which were significantly related to supervisor and peer rankings of the manager's effort to perform his job well. The correlations were higher with effort to perform the job than with the rankings of job performance. Lawler and Porter predicted this result because they reasoned that job performance is influenced by variables other than motivation, e.g., by ability and role perceptions.[29]

Conclusions and Summary

Hunt and Hill conclude that "taken together, the four studies discussed . . . seem to show that Vroom's model holds great promise for predicting behavior in organizations."[30] They do point to a number of unanswered questions, however, such as our lack of knowledge of all the goals which have positive valence in work situations, and the unknown of how much difference in force leads to a choice of one goal over another. They also point up the problem of determining appropriate combinations of measures for prediction in different situations.

Later reviews of the research on expectancy indicate that the "great promise" has not been fulfilled. Heneman and Schwab in their article on the evaluation of performance prediction research using Expectancy Theory conclude that, "the predictive power of the total (expectancy) theory is thus essentially unknown."[31]

The choice of research examples discussed in this chapter was based primarily upon the need to illustrate the complexities of the problem of validating a popular theory of work motivation and the variety of research approaches and problems. Secondarily, they were chosen to show how reviewers interpret and report research results.

The consequences of ignoring many of the assumptions of the model as pointed out by theoreticians Behling and Starke are clearer when the mixed research results continue to be generated. A variety of motivational and other variables and interactions have been found related to job performance. These co-relationships have generally been of low strength. Such results are reasonable, given at least (1) the questionable reliability of many of the paper-pencil measuring instruments, (2) the virtual elimination of unconscious motivation, (3) the minor role work plays in the lives of many people and (4) the lack of accurate descriptions of human motivational systems. Until these and other barriers are considered seriously by the majority of the researchers in this area, significant progress on work motivation theory will be confined to a plateau of uninspiring validation findings. Dubin, in his book *Theory Building*, sums up a large part of the problem: "How is it possible to predict an outcome in the form of social behavior without knowing how this outcome is produced?"[32]

NOTES

1. E. G. Aiken, "The Effort Variable in the Acquisition, Extinction and Spontaneous Recovery of an Instrumental Response," Journal of Experimental Psychology, LIII (1957), pp. 47–51; and Leon Festinger, "The Psychological Effects of Insufficient Rewards," American Psychologist, XVI (1961), pp. 1–11.

2. Elliot Aronson and Judson Mills, "The Effect of Severity of Initiation on Liking for a Group," Journal of Abnormal Social Psychology, LIX (1959), pp. 177–81.

3. Saul Gellerman, Motivation and Productivity, (New York, N.Y.: American Management Association, 1963), p. 175.

4. George C. Homans, "Conversation—an Interview with George Homans," Organizational Dynamics, Autumn, 1975, p. 40.

5. Edward E. Lawler, III, and J. L. Suttle, "The Effect of Performance on Job Satisfaction," Organizational Behavior and Human Performance, VII (1972), p. 266.

6. All quotes on the following pages descriptive of Vroom's model and research approaches for validating it were taken from his book in which the model was described in detail: Victor H. Vroom, Work and Motivation, (New York, N.Y.: John Wiley and Sons, Inc., 1964), pp. 14–28.

7. See E. C. Tolman, Purposive Behavior in Animals and Man, (New York, N.Y.: Century, 1932); Kurt Lewin, A Dynamic Theory of Personality, (New York, N.Y.: McGraw-Hill, 1935); J. B. Rotter, "The Role of the Psychological Situation in Determining the Direction of Human Behavior," in M.R. Jones, ed., Nebraska Symposium on Motivation, (Lincoln, Nebraska: University of Nebraska Press, 1955), pp. 245–68, and in the same Proceedings, see Helen Peak, "Attitudes and Motivation," pp. 149–88; D. Davidson, P. Suppes, and S. Siegel, Decision Making: An Experimental Approach, (Stanford, California: Stanford University Press, 1957); B. S. Georgopoulas, G. M. Mahoney, and N. W. Jones, "A Path-Goal Theory Approach to Productivity," Journal of Applied Psychology, XXXXI (1957), pp. 345–53.

8. Stanislav Andreski, *Social Sciences as Sorcery*, (New York, N.Y.: St. Martin's Press, 1972), p. 129.

9. Bernard Berelson and Gary A. Steiner, *Human Behavior*, (New York, N.Y.: Harcourt, Brace & World, Inc., 1964), p. 279.

10. *Ibid.*, p. 280.

11. Lawrence S. Kubie, "Problems and Techniques of Psychoanalytic Validation and Progress," in E. Pumpian-Mindlin, ed., *Psychoanalysis as Science*, (Stanford, Calif.: Stanford University Press, 1952), pp. 46–124, as quoted in Bernard Berelson and Gary A. Steiner, p. 280.

12. Berelson and Steiner, p. 282.

13. *Ibid.*, p. 76.

14. Harry F. Harlow and Margaret K. Harlow, "The Effect of Rearing Conditions on Behavior," *Bulletin of the Menninger Clinic*, XXVI (1962), p. 224.

15. Berelson and Steiner, pp. 150–55.

16. All quotes on this and the following pages referring to these postulates are from Orlando Behling and Frederick A. Starke, "The Postulates of Expectancy Theory," *Academy of Management Journal*, XVI, No. 3 (September, 1973), pp. 376–81.

17. A. Tversky, "Intransitivity of Preferences," *Psychological Review*, LXXVI (1969), pp. 31–48, as quoted in Orlando Behling and Frederick A. Starke, p. 378.

18. Variously defined in the literature on motivation as choices or decisions which are "adequate," "good enough," or "satisfactory."

19. Lyman W. Porter, Edward E. Lawler, III, and J. Richard Hackman, *Behavior in Organizations*, (New York, N.Y.: McGraw-Hill, 1975), p. 60.

20. J. G. Hunt and J. W. Hill, "The New Look in Motivational Theory," *Human Organization*, XXVIII, No. 2 (1969), pp. 100–109 as reproduced in Harold J. Leavitt and Louis R. Pondy, eds., *Readings in Managerial Psychology*, 2nd ed., (Chicago, Ill.: The University of Chicago Press, 1973), pp. 43–59.

21. Thomas C. Mawhinney and Orlando Behling, "Differences in Predictions of Work Behavior from Expectancy and Operant Models of Individual Motivation," *Thirty-third Annual Proceedings of the Academy of Management*, Thad Green, ed., (Boston Mass., August, 1973), p. 388.

22. Victor H. Vroom, "Organizational Choice: A Study of Pre- and Postdecision Processes," *Organizational Behavior and Human Performance*, I (1966), pp. 212–25.

23. John E. Sheridan, Max D. Richards and John W. Slocum, "The Descriptive Power of Vroom's Expectancy Model of Motivation," *Proceedings of the Thirty-third Annual Meeting of the Academy of Management*, Thad Green, ed., (Boston, Mass., August, 1973), pp. 414–20.

24. P. Soelberg, "A Study of Decision Making: Job Choice," (Ph.D. dissertation, Carnegie Mellon University, 1967.)

25. John E. Sheridan, *et al.*, "The Descriptive Power . . .", p. 415.

26. J. Galbraith and L. L. Cummings, "An Empirical Investigation of the Motivational Determinants of Task Performance: Interactive Effects between Instrumentality-Valence and Motivation-Ability," *Organizational Behavior and Human Performance*, II (1967), pp. 237–57.

27. *Ibid.*, p. 255.
28. E. E. Lawler and L. W. Porter, "Antecedent Attitudes of Effective Managerial Performance," *Organizational Behavior and Human Performance*, II (1967), pp. 122–42.
29. J. G. Hunt and J. W. Hill, "The New Look . . .", *op. cit.*, as reproduced in Leavitt and Pondy, eds., *Readings* . . . , p. 58.
30. *Ibid.*
31. H. G. Heneman and D. B. Schwab, "Evaluation of Research on Expectancy Theory Predictors of Employee Performance," *Psychological Bulletin*, LXXVIII (1972), p. 8.
32. Robert Dubin, *Theory Building*, (New York, N.Y.: Free Press, 1969), p. 14.

Chapter 8

Theories of Economic Motivation

THEORIES of economic motivation are based upon a variety of viewpoints. Broadly viewed, economic motivation includes the "carrot" of the "carrot and stick" approach. The carrot represents any kind of *material* award. Management philosopher-observers such as Peter Drucker clearly see such incentives as very much alive and operational today. Drucker insists that the carrot of material rewards has not, like the stick of fear, lost its potency.

On the contrary, (the carrot) has become so potent that it must be used with great caution. It has become too potent to be a dependable tool. . . . The Sunday issue of every newspaper these days contains an article by a learned sociologist or philosopher reporting that people are turning away from material satisfaction. On the front page of the same paper, Sundays *and* weekdays, there is then always a story that this or that group of workers—teachers or electricians, newspaper reporters or firemen, salesclerks or stevedores—have presented the biggest wage demand ever or have obtained the biggest wage raise ever.[1] (Parenthetical phrase added.)

He concludes his argument by asserting that "there is not one shred of evidence for the alleged turning away from material rewards. . . . Anti-materialism is a myth, no matter how much it is extolled."[2]

At the other end of the theoretical continuum are the Neo-Hawthorneists still clinging to the faulty conclusions pointed out in chapter three that since the Hawthorne researchers could not isolate economic incentives as causing *all* the productivity improvements, they had *no* significant effect on output.

The vast array of literature covering the subject in between these two viewpoints only succeeds in clouding the issue. A review of over 100 articles published in the last 20 years whose titles purported to deal with the subject of economic incentives in one form or another, revealed several distinct types of approaches to the subject. They fell into the following general categories:

1. Inventories of theories and findings from research and labor statistics (10 articles).

2. Research experiments on various forms of monetary incentives in laboratory or field settings (39 articles).
3. Case studies of single incentive plan experiences (20 articles).
4. Normative (prescriptive) articles on how to make economic incentives work (40 articles).

The types of monetary incentives researched, installed, and promoted in the above articles vary from tax-free or deferred compensation plans for top executives to bonuses for absent-free months or labor cost reductions to piece-rates for typists.

BRIEF HISTORY OF MONETARY INCENTIVES

Monetary incentives go back in history at least to 3000 B.C. Clay tablets from the ruins of Sumer indicate that merit pay was used to reward good work.[3] During Nebuchadnezzar's reign in Babylonia, which began in 604 B.C., women engaged in spinning and weaving work were paid incentives in the form of food, the amount paid depending upon output.[4] Xenophon, one of Socrates' disciples, urged estate owners to permit workers to share in the success of the estate because this would improve their motivation for the improvement of the estate.[5]

As barter systems gave way to money systems, the concept of wage incentives was carried over. By the time Frederick Taylor began his work, the work technology for some jobs was increasing in complexity, requiring considerable study before establishing incentive standards. The further development of piece-rate systems went hand in hand with the growth of motion and time study and with what we know today as methods and process engineering. And, as we shall see in reviewing the evidence pointing to money as a motivator, this parallel growth has rather consistently caused much contamination of the research to the point of almost eliminating the possibility of singling out incentives as causing the substantial output increases claimed for them.

Recent Trends in the Use of Incentives

According to a 1945–46 study by the Wage Analysis Branch of the Bureau of Labor Statistics about 7 million American employees worked under some kind of incentive plan, 5.5 million in manufacturing industries and 1.5 in non-manufacturing industries. The 5.5 million workers in manufacturing represented about 30% of the total plant employees.[6]

In 1958 a similar study found that about 27% of production employees in the manufacturing industries worked under incentives.[7] The researchers accounted for a part of the 3% difference from 1945–46 by pointing out that certain major, low-incentive industries such as airframe, printing, and sawmilling were not included in the earlier survey. By 1963, according to a study by the Bureau of Labor Statistics, 26% of production workers in manufacturing industries were on incentives of some kind.[8]

The percentage of workers on incentives varies with the age and the geographic location of the industrial units. In such cities as Hartford, Milwaukee, and Pittsburgh, over a third of the production employees are on incentives whereas the figure is only about 10% for comparable workers in Dallas, Houston, Los Angeles, San Francisco, and Portland, Oregon.[9]

In certain industries, the percentage of employees on incentives does not seem to have changed over time. For example, in cotton textiles, leather tanning, men's apparel industry, and farm machinery there has been no significant change in this percentage. In other manufacturing industries, such as office and computing machines, cigars, industrial machinery, and service industry machines, the percentage of production employees on incentives showed a drop between 1957 and 1966.[10]

The causes of the declines in the percentage of workers on incentives in certain industries is difficult to pinpoint. In some cases, the ratio of white to blue collar reflecting greater automation and mechanization may be involved. In others it may simply be the result of the movement of plants into American sub-cultures (such as from Eastern Seaboard to the West and Southwest) where hourly pay systems dominate and the workers, self-selected migrants, are motivatable without money incentives. Although no recent survey is available on the changes in the extent of white collar workers on incentives, the literature suggests that installation of such plans is on the increase in the banking, insurance, and finance industries.

INVENTORIES OF THEORIES AND FINDINGS

There are two distinctly different approaches to inventorying the literature on the effects of money as an incentive. One is to be found in the journals covering labor economics and the other in the journals reporting research in the behavioral sciences, mostly psychology journals. The reviewers using labor economics data invariably find incentives quite effective in reducing costs, increasing earnings, and reducing turnover. The behavioral science reviews typically find the evidence wanting and claim that we know little of the effects of money as a motivator.

Labor Economics Reviewers' Findings

Typical of the reviewers using labor economics data and articles by consultants whose main business is design and the installation of incentive systems is that of Leon Megginson's coverage of financial rewards for his personnel management textbook. Below are some relevant quotations:

Studies conducted immediately after World War II in hundreds of plants in a great variety of industries showed that labor productivity under the straight hourly rate form of compensation seldom exceeded 60% of the performance obtained with good wage incentive methods. (Megginson cited a reference authored by a consultant to back up this conclusion.) It was found that with the introduction of incentive wages of 25 percent over and above the regular basic hourly wage scale were paid. . . . One of the more comprehensive studies of the effects of incentive plans on productivity was conducted in 1959. The sample for this study included 29 industries and 305 plans, most of which had been installed during the 1950's; the study showed that productivity increased an average of 63 percent.

In summary, with a properly developed and administered wage incentive plan, the output per man-hour should increase by 20 to 50 percent over what it was before the installation of the scheme. It has been proved that the output of the individuals in any group of employees on incentives will distribute itself in a pattern which follows the normal distribution curve about the midpoint. This midpoint is generally found at about 130 percent of the standard, or at the 30 percent bonus level.[11] (Parenthetical phrases added)

On the effects on employee earnings, Megginson concluded from his view that ". . . incentive earnings of employees are generally 20 percent higher than hourly earnings."[12] Among other effects of using incentive wages Megginson concluded that companies will experience a smaller number of employees on the payroll, better control of costs, better scheduling and the pointing up of bad management practices.[13]

Behavioral Science Reviewers' Findings

The authors of a typical inventory of the behavioral science literature on monetary incentives found the evidence in favor of money as a motivator wanting. The various theories discussed in one review were as follows:[14]

1. *Money as a generalized conditioned reinforcer.* Most evidence in favor of this theory was from animal studies with little generalization potential for humans.
2. *Money as a conditioned incentive.* According to this theory, repetitive pairings of money with primary incentives would establish a new learned drive for money. The only research cited in favor of this theory was one using poker chips and chimpanzees.
3. *Money as an anxiety reminder.* This theory is simply stating that an empty wallet or a stack of unpaid bills produces anxiety. No research is cited supporting or negating the theory.
4. *Money as a hygiene factor.* This is part of the Herzberg theory (discussed

in Chapter 6) which holds that money may serve as a potential dissatisfier if not present in appropriate amounts, but not as a potential satisfier or positive motivator. The authors found no substantial support for the differential role of money in leading to job satisfaction or dissatisfaction.
5. *Money as an instrument for gaining desired outcomes.* This theory category refers primarily to Vroom's model discussed in Chapter 7. The authors note that the evidence in support of the theory was largely anecdotal although they found it somewhat convincing. Typical of the conclusions of the authors of such articles, regardless of the dates of the inventories, follow those of Opsahl and Dunnette:

> Strangely, in spite of the large amounts of money spent and the obvious relevance of behavioral theory for industrial compensation practices, there is probably less solid research in this area than in any other field related to worker performance. We know amazingly little about how money either interacts with other factors or how it acts individually to affect job behavior. Although the relevant literature is voluminous, much more has been written about the subject than is actually known. Speculation, accompanied by compensation fads and fashions, abounds. . .[15]

RESEARCH ON MONETARY INCENTIVES IN LABORATORY AND FIELD SETTINGS

The majority of the research experiments reviewed dealt with the testing of different aspects of one of the various expectancy theories, usually the Vroom or the Lawler and Porter model. The Lawler and Porter Model indicates that the motivation to perform at a given level is mainly determined by (1) a person's belief, based upon his self-esteem and previous experience, about the probability that if he exerts effort to perform at that level, he can actually perform at that level, and (2) a combination of his beliefs about what will actually be the result if he performs at that level along with his desire for these outcomes. The model is one of several variations on the Vroom model described earlier in Chapter 7.[16] Another category of researches included those experiments designed to test the differential effects of "continuous (like piecework) and variable ratio (random) reward systems" using pay as a reward. Still another category contained researches on worker satisfaction as it related to performance and pay.

Laboratory Research on Monetary Incentives

These research efforts offer adequate if sometimes ludicrous support for Opsahl's and Dunnette's conclusions. Typical of the laboratory research studies is one performed by George Graen whose jargon-laden hypotheses to be tested included the following:

Hypothesis I. If a role outcome is attained following the attainment of the role of job incumbent, higher perceived instrumentality of that role for the attainment of like outcomes will result.

Hypothesis II. Satisfaction with the role of job incumbent is a monotonically increasing function of the products of the attraction of each role outcome and the perceived instrumentality of that work role for the attainment of like role outcomes summed over all role outcomes.[17]

The reader may recognize these hypotheses as partial statements of a modified version of Victor Vroom's motivational model described in Chapter 7.

Graen claimed to have conducted his study in a "realistic" environment by ". . . performing the experiment in a business setting with many of the usual props (e.g., personnel manager, selection testing, company offices, etc.)" and by ". . . hiring female applicants from the local market. . ."[18] These "employees" were also, according to Graen, given realistic tasks and provided with an organizational purpose for the work.

The pity is that the actual description of the conduct of the experiment revealed the following: (1) the majority of the "female applicants hired from the local labor market" were between 15 and 18 years old, high school students and single, (2) the "realistic" business setting was a rented conference room in a downtown hotel, (3) the "employment" was for parts of the three days, about half of which was spent in orientations, reading instructions, and completing questionnaires, and the other half was having subjects check and round off six decimal correlation coefficients to two decimals, and (4) explaining that this work would help the "company" improve its future contract bidding.

Also in these three partial days, the researcher was miraculously able to provide three different organizational climates: "a reciprocating climate" (reward depending upon effective performance), "a prompting climate" (reward as motivation to effective performance), and "control climate" (reward neither depending upon effective performance nor as inducement to effective performance). And with various paper and pencil instruments whose validities and reliabilities went unmentioned, Graen was able to divide his "employees" into four groups: (1) high ability—prefer achievement, (2) high ability—prefer salary, (3) low ability—prefer achievement, and (4) low ability—prefer salary.

Two experimental groups received different "feedback" treatments. The "achievement feedback" group members were told that their performance was among the best of the groups and that the company was very happy with their work. The "money feedback" group members were told that their performance was average but that the company was going to increase their pay from $1.50 to $1.75 in the hopes that they would improve. The control group members were told that their performance was about average and that they would stay on the $1.50 rate. As one would suspect, nothing of consequence was learned about the role of money incentives. The researcher notes that ". . . in the money treatment, this contingency was undermined by presenting a raise in pay not contingent upon previous performance."[19]

It is interesting to note that Graen credits much to his "mentor," Marvin D. Dunnette, co-author of the previously covered literature review in which self-report data gathering techniques such as those used by Graen were severely criticized. Mr. Graen further credits the National Science Foundation, the University of Illinois and the General Electric Foundation for grant support for the study. One can only speculate as to why it took three grantees for such a study, and, of course, what their motives were in supporting such a study. The findings were guaranteed to forbid generalizing to employee motivation in real organizations. High school students spending parts of three days in a hotel conference room rounding off decimals are hardly representative of *any* group of permanent workers in business, industry, or government.

Another type of research found in the laboratory settings is characterized by a study of the effectiveness of pay incentives under variable ratio (random rewarding) and continuous reinforcement (rewarding for each unit of work) schedules by Gary Yukl, Kenneth N. Wexley, and James D. Seymore.[20] Their research was conducted in what they referred to as a "simulated job situation." Very few, if any, real-life work situations use a variable ratio schedule of reinforcement except for the informal forms of praise passed out by bosses. Most employees are monetarily rewarded on a fixed interval (hourly, weekly or monthly), or, in the case of piece rates, on a continuous schedule (so much for each unit produced). Research in laboratory settings with animals and humans has shown that the variable ratio reward system is very powerful. In real life, the slot machine provides an excellent example of the effectiveness of the variable ratio schedule of reinforcement for certain people.

Unfortunately, the Yukl, Wexley, and Seymore research work situation and reward system was so far removed from real life work situations as to render their results useless from a managerial standpoint. Their subjects were 15 females from ages 18 to 23 hired through a university placement office to work an hour a day for two weeks. Their task was to score multiple choice exam answer sheets. The first week they completed questionnaires (Monday) and worked for $1.50 per hour scoring the answer sheets (Tuesday-Friday). The second week they were divided into three groups and assigned to different experimental conditions. One group was told that they would have a 50–50 chance to get a 25 ¢ bonus for each completed sheet by calling a coin flipped by the "boss" upon completion of each sheet. The third group was simply told that they would get 25¢ for every sheet completed. All of these rewards were in addition to their $1.50 per hour pay. The greatest hourly output gain was made by the group given the 50¢ on a 50–50 chance basis. Their gain was from 250 units per hour to 362 which was found to be statistically significantly greater than the gain in output of either of the other two groups. The gains made by the 50–50 chance of getting an additional 25¢ per sheet scored was about the same as the gain made by the group whose members received 25¢ for each completed sheet scored.

If the effects of the schedule of rewarding were ignored, one would expect the continuous reinforcement schedule (25¢ for each sheet scored) to have about the same output effect as the 50¢ variable ratio schedule. This was not the case. One would also expect that the continuously rewarded group would have outperformed the 25¢ variable ratio group since the former would be earning about twice as much bonus money. Instead their performance was about the same.

The results certainly suggest that a variable ratio schedule of reward has more power to motivate than a continuous reinforcement schedule in this laboratory experiment. But, as the authors admit, "It is doubtful that such schedules (bosses flipping coins for bonus rewards) would be readily accepted by employees . . ."[21] One can only ponder at the concept of real job situations held by such researchers as these who describe their experiment as having been conducted in ". . . a simulated job situation."

Other studies reviewed which described the testing of a variety of incentive pay related hypotheses were also flawed by the fleeting nature of the task and opportunistic (student) samples. Examples of such studies are given in summary form below. Note the rather global nature of the titles compared with the actual research effort:

1. "A Comparison of Group and Individual Incentive Plans"[22] Subjects: 70 male students enrolled in an introductory course in organizational behavior.
   Groups: Pairs of students who did not know each other and were not allowed to meet or see each other during the experiment. In the jargon of the psychologist, these are called "co-acting groups."
   Task: Sorting IBM cards by hole patterns. Duration of work involved in the complete experiments: 25 minutes (5 periods of 5 minutes each).
   Incentive plan variations: (1) groups (pairs) paid according to lower performers' output. (2) paid according to higher performers' output, and (3) paid according to average output of the pair.
2. "Effects of Varying Goal Types and Incentive Systems on Performance and Satisfaction."[23]
   Subjects: 180 students enrolled in an introductory course in organizational behavior.
   Tasks: Sorting IBM cards by hole patterns.
   Duration of work involved in the complete experiment: 21 minutes.
   Variations in type of goals: After a no-incentive trial (to establish output rates), subjects were asked to set goals of 10%, 25%, and 40% above trial rate and minimum targets of 5% and 25% below trial rates.

3. "An Analysis of Changes in Performance Quality with Operant Conditioning Procedures."[24]
   Subjects: 160 male junior and senior level undergraduate students.
   Task: Collating six punched and interpreted data processing cards wherein approximately 4% of the cards were error cards.
   Duration of complete experiment: 3 hours.
4. "Effects of Varying Performance-Pay Instrumentalities on the Relationship between Performance and Satisfaction: A Test of the Lawler and Porter Model."[25]
   Subjects: 60 male and female high school and college students who "were hired for what they thought was a real job . . ."
   Task: "A clerical task . . . which eliminated variation in quality of performance . . ."
   Duration of complete experiment: 2 hours.

Differences between Simulations and Real-Life Situations

A number of potentially important differences exist between such simulations as described above and real life work situations. Generalizations to the real world of work motivation are next to impossible for the following reasons:

1. Little or no informal social systems associated with the work situation exist in the simulations.
2. Relationships with leaders or bosses is fleeting and distant.
3. Money earned for an hour or two has a different meaning than money earned for basic livelihood needs. It is likely to be treated as a windfall and the opportunity to earn it responded to differently.
4. Working at a high output rate carries no potential threat of job retiming nor to job security for any of the "employees."
5. Potential for promotion or discharge as a possible outcome of output variations is non-existent in such simulations.
6. The "employees" are usually students—young and considerably more dependent on others for their livelihood than real life workers. Students' attitudes toward work, money, wages, authority, profits, and capital are considerably different from average real-life workers performing unskilled tasks in business and industry. The I.Q. range and average of college students are not the same as for the general work population.
7. The organizational structure (system of policies, procedures, relationships between many work units, etc.) is so simplified in these simulations as to be almost non-existent.

The authors of many of these studies do note briefly, after elaborate discussions of their methods and results in terms of correlations, F-ratios,

Chi-squares, t-tests, etc., that there are barriers to generalizing from their findings to the real world. Typically, they call for additional research, referring to their studies as only exploratory.

One of the more unusual laboratory research approaches reported in the literature was the use of computer simulation to test the impact of different pay policies and constraints on 100 hypothetical employees over a 20-year period. The usefulness of such research would naturally depend upon how accurately the motivational aspects of the simulation model reflected reality. The author pointed out that ". . . our understanding of (the relationship between pay and performance) is deficient, despite the magnitude of expenditures on financial compensation and the recent intensity of research activity in the area of work motivation."[26] He then explains that the best way to study the phenomenon would be *in situ* but that this is nearly impossible for several reasons: (1) companies won't manipulate pay policies for research, (2) employee performance measurement is difficult in non-piece-work jobs, and (3) organizations' complex systems influence the (short) time-frame typical of possible research studies. He concludes that computer simulation solves these problems quite effectively.

Even though noting that our understanding of the relationship between pay and performance is deficient, he proceeded with a model which assumed that "effort" bears a positive curvilinear relationship to performance and that "effort" responses would get smaller in overpayment situations. This portion of the model follows Adams' equitable theory. This theory holds that the motivation to work is a function of the relationship between the employee's inputs and rewards and of the employee's perceived ratio of inputs to outputs of other employees. This model simply reflects the motivational aspects of the implementation and violations of the old policy of "A fair day's work for a fair day's pay" *for everybody.*[27]

The pay policy decision rules used in the simulation were (1) random increments, (2) pay raises proportional to performance changes, (3) pay based upon seniority, and (4) pay based on experience and performance. Decision rules reflecting administrative constraints on pay changes were (1) no constraint, (2) decreases in pay prohibited, (3) raises limited from 4% to 10%, and (4) both (2) and (3).

The author concluded from his results that if pay *efficiency* is important, a company ". . . is ill-advised to provide pay increments randomly, . . ." and that "Costs had a larger impact on pay efficiency than did performance."[28] He further suggests that if this is not due to his restrictions on the rate of the performance variable in the model, it could reflect reality, and if this is the case, ". . . the cost-conscious payroll practices of many employers may be considerably less short-sighted than they are frequently characterized as being."[29] Unfortunately, until a money motivational model is developed which can be shown to reflect reality, such simulation approaches as Mr. Demick's will be of no real value in developing pay policies for maximizing pay efficiency.

Research on Monetary Incentives in Field Settings

Field Setting experiments in the literature vary widely in the hypotheses tested and the methodology employed. Three of the studies reviewed attempted to determine the effectiveness of continuous and variable ratio schedules of reward as did Yukl, *et al.* in a laboratory research described early in this chapter. Two of these[30] even employed the coin-tossing approach used in the lab experiment. The third used a variation on the coin toss as follows: Employees would have a chance to get $8 every time they had planted 1,000 trees by guessing the color of a marble held in the supervisor's hand two consecutive times.[31] It is hardly surprising that the researchers reported that ". . . the workers so disliked this schedule that a compromise was reached by substituting a VR–2 schedule. In this condition a $4 bonus was made contingent upon planting 1,000 trees and correctly guessing the color of only *one* marble."[32] The subjects in the two Yukl, *et al.* experiments were temporary employees. The subjects in the third experiment were South African black factory workers. The durations of the three experiments were a few weeks in each case.

Under these research circumstances it was not surprising to find that one of the results of all three studies was that their variable ratio schedule appeared less effective for improving performance than their continuous reinforcement schedule. One author noted the obvious—that no administratively feasible procedure had been found for using a VR schedule which is predetermined for each employee when the reinforcement is money.[33] The attraction of the slot machine for some people notwithstanding, it is not likely that such a reward system will be found which will not be rejected out of hand by workers, if for no other reason than that it will clearly be seen as manipulative as though they were chimpanzees from the zoo performing for the psychologist.

Using paper and pencil questionnaires the South African researcher found that, for his sample, there appeared to be no inherent relationship between satisfaction and performance (output). He concluded that what relationship does exist depended heavily on the particular reward contingencies in force: "If the rewards are made contingent upon good performance, there will be a positive relationship between performance and satisfaction; if the rewards are not, there will be a negligible relationship between performance and satisfaction."[34]

Field Research on On-Going Incentive Plans

One reported study, using mainly historical data for 12 years on a group of shipping department employees, set out to document the effectiveness of the incentive plan as it related to employee attitudes. Based upon attitude measures taken from interviews and paper and pencil instruments, the researchers found reason to conclude that in this "successful" plan, the employees trusted management, understood the plan, and saw a close relationship between their earnings and their performance.[35] The records they gathered clearly showed what might be called fantastic increases in output as measured by dozens of pajamas shipped per man-hour. Their data showed that this index was about 23 for two years prior to starting the plan and rose fairly steadily over the next 11 years, except for a plateau for 2 years, to about 42 dozens per man-hour. Their records revealed that the plateau was due to restriction of output in order to get overtime. When the company altered the plan to provide an additional incentive to reduce overtime, output started to climb steadily and continued to do so for the next three years (the last three years of the study data). Unfortunately, we are not told anything which might indicate that the base output was or was not artificially low or anything about changes in work methods, packing box design, equipment additions, or layout which could have caused or contributed to the almost doubling of output per man-hour.

Conclusions from Field and Laboratory Experiments

Again, opportunistic sampling—mostly handy students or temporary workers—rendered many of the experimental results useless. Their only value might be in the development of a motivational model to guide university officials who would hire students in social science classes to work an hour or so a day grading tests or doing silly work such as hand sorting IBM cards by hole-patterns.

The existence of the somewhat powerful motivational force of random reward for some people—there are many who refuse to gamble or play slot-machines—is supported by some of the experiments. Another dubious contribution of some of the experiments might be to reveal to some readers the ignorance of some researchers regarding the gross differences between their "realistic" simulated job situations and *real* job situations.

In longitudinal studies of output for a group of employees in one company such as the pajama packing study, the results are beclouded by the reporters' tendencies to ignore other possible causes of increased production such as capital equipment additions and methods engineering. It can be inferred from the data that the incentive systems probably had an impact, and in some cases this may have been the major cause. However, the output increase results from global labor statistics analyses must be discounted by some unknown proportion simply because no information on possible other causes is considered. The story of the American increases in productivity over the last 50 years hardly has as its hero the ever harder working factory worker. Most economic analyses point to engineering and capital as the primary cause.

CASE STUDIES OF SINGLE INCENTIVE PLAN EXPERIENCES

The majority of the articles in this category are written about small-to-medium sized manufacturing companies' incentive programs. These programs are all tailored to a greater or lesser degree to suit the nature of the work and workforce and to suit the companies' managements' philosophies and their goals for the programs. A typical example would be Richard I. Henderson's article "Money is, too, an Incentive; One Company's Experience."[36]

The Conley Mill Works

The description of the program is prefaced by the usual "the-theorists-say-money-doesn't-motivate-any-more-but-they're-wrong" followed by a brief history and description of the company at the time of the introduction of the program. The Conley Mill Works, a small wood products manufacturer near Atlanta, Georgia, had sales in 1972 of $360,000 and backorders were increasing. They had 22 production and 5 white collar employees. The production employees' average age was 47, their tenure 14 years, and their average earnings $700 per month.

In 1973 these workers told the management that they needed a 5% cost-of-living raise. The company responded with a bonus system based upon a monthly shipment standard of $30,000 (the previous 18 month average) and a 5% bonus for each 10% increase in monthly shipments up to a 20% bonus limit. Bonus earnings above the $42,000 shipment level would be placed in a future pool to be paid when less than 20% bonus was earned. The bonus was paid monthly by separate check. The base would shift at the rate of $1400 per worker ($30,000/22 workers).

The results were almost immediate with the first program month reaching $33,970 in shipments, an all-time monthly record. The average shipment value for the first seven months of the program was $40,000 and after about 4 months, the figure did not fall below the 20% bonus limit at $42,000 shipment level. Direct labor costs dropped from a pre-program 1972 average of 21% to 17%. By-products of the program were reported to be a greater eagerness to seek supervisory help with difficult jobs, a greater willingness to help others and to look for work when a job was finished. The author points out that the success of the program is partially owed to the able operations manager who visited each worker daily at his workplace to help, counsel, or listen to complaints or suggestions.

These results are consistent with Megginson's conclusions given earlier that output should increase by 20–50%. The $42,000 shipment level represents an increase of 40% ($12,000/$30,000). Employee earnings jumped approximately 20% which was Megginson's estimate for incentive plans in general.

The conclusion is difficult to avoid that incentives, properly tailored and administered, are effective, if one can generalize from such case studies. However, this particular incentive system clearly depended upon a build-up in back-orders and continually expanding sales. A company with stable (or falling) sales could not even consider this type of program. Such companies must opt for some form of bonus on cost reductions and this requires policy attention to the problem of such reductions requiring the elimination of certain jobs. Three other case histories are illustrative in dealing with this problem and in demonstrating the effects of their tailored programs. All are somewhat famous in the literature: The Midlands-Ross Tennessee plant, the Lincoln Electric, and Donnelly Mirrors Companies.

The Midland-Ross Plant's Scanlon Plan

To demonstrate how slowly managements adopt successful schemes for improving productivity, it might be instructive to note a remark by an executive at Midland-Ross' plant in Tennessee in 1976: Several companies ". . . have decided that it makes sense to treat this management breakthrough in the same manner as a research and development breakthrough. It has given them a definite competitive edge, and they see no good reason to make it an item of public attention."[37] The breakthrough was about 45 years old at the time of his remarks in 1976. By 1950, at least 50 Scanlon plans were in operation.[38] Joseph Scanlon's approach first received widespread publicity in 1946 due to an article in *Life*[39] magazine which gave an account of the first plan he introduced while a trade union official. Shortly thereafter Scanlon was asked to help install his plan at Lapointe Machine Tool Company. The success of this plan was written up in *Fortune* magazine[40] in 1950, long after many companies had installed his plan.

The Scanlon Plan is more than a plan or program. It represents the forerunner of the management philosophies which, when turned into policy, permitted employees to share in overall cost reductions. Furthermore, employees share the opportunities for determining the means of these cost reductions under a Scanlon Plan. The primary aim of a Scanlon Plan is to increase productivity by changing work practices and methods, not by simply increasing work effort or pace. The two main characteristics of a typical Scanlon Plan are (1) a base productivity norm, usually a representative year's performance and (2) a works committee system usually formed on departmental bases whose recommendations for improvements are evaluated by an overall screening committee. These committees function to consider all suggestions—from employees and management—on means to improve efficiency and productivity, to reduce costs, and to see that accepted suggestions are implemented.[41]

The typical Scanlon plan uses a norm which represents the ratio of the total wage bill to the sale value of production (SVOP), including inventories. Improvements on this norm determine the overall bonus to be distributed to the company and employees, a ratio determined at the outset but usually about 30% for the company and 70% for the workforce. For example, if the base year SVOP is $1 million and the total wage bill $350,000, the ratio norm would be 35%. In a month for which the SVOP was $95,000 and the wage bill $25,250, the total bonus to be distributed between the company and employees would be (95,000 × .35) − $25,250 or $8,000. The plan usually calls for holding back a certain percentage (usually about 25%) of the bonus for protection against negative bonuses for months during which the wage bill is greater than the allowable wage bill for the value of production. Anything remaining in this pool at the end of the year is distributed to the employees.

After industrial relations executives had sold the idea of a Scanlon type incentive plan to top management at Midland-Ross, their Athens, Tennessee Electrical Products plant was chosen for the launch. The primary reason for this particular choice was the attitudes of Ellis Perry, the plant manager, towards his employees. Midland-Ross' Vice-President for Industrial Relations believed that "The absolutely vital ingredient to a successful Scanlon concept installation is a location where the top executive or other key executives have a genuine respect for every individual and the potential contribution each can make."[42]

According to various reports in the literature, the results at Midland-Ross' Athens, Tennessee plant have been worth the effort, both for the company and for the employees. The average bonus per employee for 1976 was about $1,500 plus a locally competitive hourly rate. Bonuses were earned in all but 6 of the first 27 months under the plan. During the last half of 1976 the bonus was averaging about 15% of hourly wages.[43]

Other results indexes offer possible explanations for the general successes of the Scanlon approach. At Midlands-Ross, according to George Sherman, the following improvements are attributable to the plan:

Direct labor efficiency has improved 10 percent in one major area of the plant and 8.5 percent in the other. There has been a substantial increase in our utilization of indirect labor. Using the same equipment, there has been a 16 percent increase in productivity. An immediate and further direct result of this plan has been a savings of $250,000 which had been set aside to expand the plant and add another line to get additional productive capacity. This means we have not only saved the quarter-million dollars for expansion but we have not had to add workforce. We can document savings of 30 people and believe the savings in additional personnel will more closely approach 60. This is a plant of 500, so the people savings could amount to 12 percent of the workforce. Bear in mind also that we not only saved up to 60 salaries but also fringes and another 25 to 30 percent savings in payroll costs.

Grievances have been cut in half, absenteeism has dropped from 5.6 percent to 2.8 percent and the turnover rate which formerly was quite high, also has dropped dramatically—from a 1973 high of 35.8 percent to a 1975 low of 2.6 percent.[44]

Lincoln Electric Company

In 1934 the Lincoln Electric Company started its famous bonus system. The system was simple: deduct from the profit the money needed for reinvestment and a "fair return" dividend for stockholders. Share the remainder with all employees based on their performance evaluation and salary. Lincoln employees' base wages and salaries have been kept competitive with comparable jobs in the Cleveland, Ohio area. In 1973 the company distributed $21,137,705 to its 2,256 employees for an average of $9,370 per worker.[45] In 1975, a blue-collar worker earning $14,000 in wages at Lincoln Electric would earn nearly $30,000 for the year including his bonus. Lincoln's board chairman, William Irrgang, summarized their philosophy as follows:

> The worker must feel that he actually wants to work more efficiently and produce more. He must be convinced that he will be rewarded fairly. The worker must also feel that greater efficiency will not endanger his employment. At Lincoln Electric we have found the most potent incentives, if accepted and believed by the worker are: (1) Money in proportion to production; (2) Status as a reward for achievement; (3) Publicity of the worker's contribution and the reward that is given for it; (4) Continuity of employment through Lincoln's guaranteed employment plan; (5) The worker's satisfaction in knowing that he is making an above average contribution to the company and, through the company, to society.[46]

By policy, Lincoln limits its activities to stable products that it can handle well. Wages today are about five times what they were in 1934, and their raw materials costs have increased from three times (for steel) to seven times (for copper), yet their 300-amp welder costs about the same as it did in 1934.

Lincoln employees work in a no-frills environment since expenditures for non-productive assets reduce the bonuses. Employees are guaranteed 75% of their weekly earnings as protection against producing themselves out of jobs, but no such terminations have occurred for the last 20 years. Advancement at Lincoln is based upon merit, not seniority, and this is determined by supervisory ratings. In addition to the bonus, piecerate incentives are used where the job so lends itself to adequate worker influence. The company has a firm policy of not altering standards once they are set by time-study regardless of earnings, unless additional equipment or different methods are introduced.

The psychological environment as seen by an MBA student who worked at Lincoln one summer may offer the reader some insights into this unusually successful program:

> Having worked at the Lincoln Electric Company for one summer, I would like to express my views of the system. The results that are obtained are truly remarkable. The efficiency of the operation is a tribute to the workers and management working towards a common goal. Scrap loss was extremely low and there was very little "goofing off" by the workers.
>
> While the operations of Lincoln Electric are very successful, there are drawbacks to the system in regards to human relations. The overall relationship between the workers is far from ideal. In some cases, workers on assembly lines are told by the other workers not to come in to work if they feel sick. The workers do not want one person to hold back their earning power. In many cases, there is very little communication between workers on the jobs because many of the workers are so intent on working. I believe that it takes a special type of person to work in this atmosphere.[47]

This student pointed out in his description of the work environment that the employee suggestion system is richly rewarding to the contributor in award money (he cited an example of a $50,000 award) and recognition and that much of the traditional methods engineering work was performed through this system with appropriate publicity within the company for adopted ideas.

There is naturally no union at Lincoln Electric. Instead, an advisory board consisting of elected representatives from each department, an elected foreman, the plant superintendent and the president meet weekly to discuss all matters that affect the organization. One measure of the system's effectiveness: Lincoln Electric has never suffered a labor-caused work stoppage. As would be expected, labor turnover after a self-sorting first year is extremely low, as is absenteeism. And Lincoln's applicant back-log numbers in the thousands, suggesting that there are large numbers of people who believe that they are the "special type of person" referred to by the student above.[48]

Donnelly Mirrors Company

This company is the largest producer of automobile mirrors in the U.S. with about 60% of the market. Prices of its products in 1975 were lower than they were in 1952. Absenteeism is about a third (1.5%) of the typical U.S. rate as is tardiness at less than one percent. Donnelly employees are the highest paid in their Holland, Michigan, U.S. area and their fringe benefits equal the United Auto Workers Detroit contracts.

Their incentive system is often described by observers as characterized more by participation than by money incentives. Donnelly Mirrors' approach is typically contrasted with Lincoln Electric as people-oriented while the latter is considered money-oriented. This is likely the result of serious over-simplification as we shall see later in the discussion.

Some years ago, Donnelly considered placing all employees on a straight salary thus eliminating deductions for time-clock absences. The estimated cost of these expected paid-for absences at the time was $60,000 per year. In return for this arrangement, the employees accepted the challenge of finding ways to save this amount in costs. According to one report, cost savings suggestions after one month on straight salary exceeded $250,000.[49]

Donnelly, like Lincoln, has dealt effectively with the threat of job loss through suggested improvements in cost savings. They have an elaborate set of procedures which virtually protects employees from technological unemployment. The Donnelly approach also includes the use of work teams which assume responsibility for product quality, absenteeism, tardiness, and decisions regarding general salary increases. Representatives from these teams serve on a company-wide committee which decides next year's general salary increase to be based upon cost reduction plans to which the committee will commit the workforce, after consultation with members of each team and after collating the cost savings suggestions.

Below is one observer's comparison of the Lincoln and Donnelly plans:

Lincoln Electric compared to Donnelly Mirrors

It is an oversimplification to say that Lincoln Electric's system is competitive and Donnelly Mirrors' is cooperative, yet one gets that feeling when studying the companies in depth.

Lincoln Electric appeals to the individual's money motivation, selects those individuals who are attracted to that percept and then allows a variation of Adam Smith's "Invisible Hand" theory to operate the system. If all members of the organization are highly motivated by money, they will produce more, produce better and *apply pressure* on everyone else to do the same.

Donnelly Mirrors says we are all in this together; let's pull together as a team and we will all win. They provide the incentive and the protection, but they *require commitment* by all organization members.[50] (Italics not in original)

From the popular descriptions of Donnelly's approach there is little to suggest that "require commitment" is significantly different from "apply pressure." And Lincoln employees are well aware that they ". . . are all in this together" through the shared-by-everyone company profit bonuses. Just because a work team at Donnelly, as described by the above authors, takes responsibility for product quality, absenteeism, and tardiness, there is no evidence that this never results in "pressure" applications any more than Lincoln's employees' willingness to show up for work and work hard while there is not due to a "required commitment." And the remarkable Lincoln record for output efficiency cannot conceivably have been achieved with all employees working selfishly for themselves and ignoring the need for teamwork and cooperation.

In both companies, many employees are fulfilling needs for recognition and esteem through both companies' recognition systems for improvement suggestions. If there is a significant difference, it may be that Donnelly employees' recognition needs fulfillment may come more from peer notice than these same need fulfillments in Lincoln employees. However, in both cases, the employees' monetary benefits come from the entire workforce's general commitment to efficiency. At Donnelly, this commitment results in bigger salary increases and excellent fringe benefits, and at Lincoln, it results in bigger bonuses.

The reader should note that neither approach is likely to succeed in any industry characterized by ups and downs in work-force levels, or by rapid changes in the work technologies requiring rapid response in the form of equipment changes and rapid changes in standards and expense patterns. Because of somewhat radical results produced by Lincoln Electric in their performance on military contracts, James Lincoln was brought to Washington to be questioned by the House Naval Affairs Committee on the charges that Lincoln Electric Company was cheating the government out of taxes by paying such large bonuses. Lincoln won his case by proving that his company saved the government much more than the amount of the taxes claimed over what they would have been charged by a typical contractor. Here we see conventional ratios and indexes attempting to thwart innovative approaches to motivation.

In the late 1950's Sperry Rand's new Aeronautic Equipment Division in Phoenix cut so much off gyroscope assembly standard times originally developed in its New York facility on Long Island that both military and headquarter accountants descended on the plant to search out the error or banditry. What had actually happened was simply that standard process times developed under union pressure to make them longer were not available to the supervisors or employees at the new facility which had non-union easier-to-motivate employees. At the time, both operations worked on hourly rates with no piecework rates in gyroscope manufacture.

The great positive characteristic of both Lincoln Electric's and Donnelly's approaches is simply that they have remained successful over a considerable range of time. They cannot be said to have succeeded because they were very inefficient at the outset and once the operation became efficient, the motivation system lost its power. One possible partial cause of their successes over time could simply be that their competitors continue to remain so far behind them in efficiency that they cannot fail to be extra-profitable year after year.

Aetna Life & Casualty

The literature on case histories contains two articles on Aetna's approach to incentives for portions of their clerical workforce. Although almost ten years apart (1967–1976) the reports describe essentially the same incentive systems, an office version of traditional piecerate incentive systems. Aetna's version has five steps: (1) Establish work standards; (2) Record items of production; (3) Evaluate the time allowed to process work; (4) Record time actually taken to process work; and (5) Evaluate performance.[51] Sample individual performance report forms are given in both articles, and except for slight changes in the percent of standard required to start bonus earnings, the programs seem the same.

One significant difference reported is the number of Aetna employees under the plan for 1967 and for 1976. The earlier plan had only 2000 employees covered by incentives whereas by 1976 the number had grown to 7500 employees. Another difference in the reports was the ratio of savings to expenditures on the plans. The earlier plan paid $1,300,000 for the operation of their plan for the year 1965 of which $300,000 was non-bonus costs of the Expense Controls Department. In return, the company received increased production or reductions in staff amounting to $2,400,000 or a return of $2 for each $1 spent. The later report showed net benefits of $25 million compared to a cost of $8 million, or $3 for every $1 spent.

Unfortunately, both descriptions contain information on non-incentive system changes which eliminate any clear conclusions about the role of the bonus itself in producing the savings or increased output. The two main contaminants were the industrial engineering contributions in the form of work methods improvements and the detailed performance information provided to supervisors which resulted in pressures to supervise more closely, plan better, and do a better job of training of their low producers. The plan produced for supervisors detailed information on the amount of time each clerical employee was on loan to other units. It recorded the exact amount of time employees were waiting for work, and it recorded precisely errors and necessary re-work time. These could no longer be ignored or taken lightly by the supervisors. As an example of industrial engineering contaminants, their standards determination activities often resulted in redesign of forms for more efficient typing and checking.

Unlike many of the case histories reported in the literature, both of these articles carried enough information to identify many of the elements in the complex of changes which took place. In the article by Devlin, examples of organizational units which failed to respond were given. The audit of one unit showed that a staff of ten employees were doing the work that could have been done by six. When the unit management was confronted by the audit report, they decided to discontinue the incentive plan for their unit. Devlin's comment: "This exemplifies a situation where management was not committed to the program and was not willing to make the hard decisions necessary to achieve high productivity. Instead, when the news was bad, they decided to kill the messenger!"[52]

Conclusions from Reviews of Case Studies

It is clear that the case studies are all reports of very complex phenomena. Not all of the authors are willing to elaborate on the many factors which could be contributing to the reported increases in efficiency. In the Aetna reports, the authors believe that where the plans fail, it is due mainly to a kind of global "lack of management support." A close reading of their reports will reveal that they really mean that the failures are due to *bad management*. A manager who refuses to admit he or she is overstaffed or one who refuses to cut his or her staff from 15 to 10 is not giving "proper support" to the incentive system. Similarly, a manager who fails to heed the performance indexes indicating poor training, or unqualified employees, is withholding "management support."

From the other case studies reviewed (Conley, Lincoln, and Donnelly), it is clear that for each of their particular programs, a special set of circumstances is required. In all three, the production technologies were comparatively stable. The Conley Mill Works depended heavily upon an increasing backlog of work. The 30 employees increased shipments from $30,000 per month to the maximum bonus level of $42,000 and leveled off there. If orders dropped and potential shipments were reduced to a significant level below the $42,000, management would have to respond rapidly with layoffs, in order to keep the 20% potential bonus available. Given the average tenure of 17 years and average age of 47, this might be difficult or an undesirable solution.

The Lincoln Electric and Donnelly Mirrors companies, both being very desirable places to work, have no doubt attracted and kept a very selective workforce—certainly not the garden variety of American factory workers. In addition to the economic advantages of working for these companies, the opportunity to participate in the overall success of the enterprise is more available than in other places of work. Their suggestions are heeded and carefully analyzed and rewarded either by clear management recognition or direct money awards or both. In both cases the employees are awarded extra money. At Lincoln Electric this is in the form of an annual bonus and at Donnelly, it is in the form of generous salary increases.

From these cases, however, it is difficult to tease out the precise effects of money as a motivator. The superior industrial engineering environments where everyone can be a methods or process engineer offers some forms of need fulfillment other than money alone. The pride in working for extremely successful enterprises cannot be sorted out nor can the exact effects of atypical employees, who aside from being willing to work hard, are likely more intelligent and with a greater general aptitude for improving their performance year after year. The major lesson to be learned from these case studies is simply that under the right conditions, industrial organizations should be able to increase their overall performance by a great deal. The problem, of course, is simply that these "right conditions" can require everything from a founder with a philosophy like that of a dedicated James Lincoln to a particular work technology under stable or expanding market conditions.

Normative Articles on How to Make Incentives Work

The normative articles in the literature cover a wide variety of how-to-do-it prescriptions—from incentive plans for credit managers to the requirements for setting up a group incentive plan for assemblers to plans for an incentive system for first line supervisors to how to rehabilitate outdated and demoralized incentive plans. Below is a partial list of representative article titles in this literature category:

1. "Productivity: Can 'New Carrot' Be an Old One—Money?"
2. "Is Motivation by Money Still Fashionable?"
3. "The Scanlon Concept: Its Capabilities for Productivity Improvement"
4. "Reevaluation of the Scanlon Plan as a Motivational Technique"
5. "Productivity from Scanlon-type Plans"
6. "Restoring the Incentive to Wage Incentive Plans"
7. "Putting Incentive Back Into Wage Incentives"
8. "Selecting and Designing a Group Incentive Plan"
9. "Increasing Productivity Through Incentive Compensation"
10. "Incentive Pay For Line Supervisors"
11. "The Higher The Branch, The Sweeter The Fruit"

The general category of articles on how to design incentive plans usually contained most of the same ingredients. Below is a typical list of questions which should be answered before an organization seriously considers any kind of money incentive system:

1. Are money incentives consistent with the management philosophy? For example, management philosophy should be consistent with high employee earnings of around 20 percent beyond straight time workers.
2. What are the collective work force predilections? Will incentives be unalterably opposed by a union? Do employees really believe that they can increase their productivity? Will employees respond only to some

form of group incentive and reject the competitiveness they forecast for piece-rate plans?

3. What is the company's forecast for the future in terms of the lifespan predicted for an incentive plan? What is the company future in terms of growth, stability, decline cycles?
4. Is the work reasonably standardized and working conditions uniform?
5. Is the volume of work to be the subject of incentives reasonably ascertainable? Can the units of production be clearly and accurately measured?
6. Can the work be so organized that there is no division of labor within the process for which incentives are to be paid?
7. What protection can be offered when increased output creates redundancies?

If the above questions can be answered in the affirmative or in terms favorable to an incentive plan of some kind, the advice of most of the authors on the subject is to see that professionals are involved in the design and installation of the plan. Inaccurate standards will destroy the program at the outset. Methods engineering should be done before standards are set, not after.

A good example of the need for an "expert" is demonstrated by the article by Ken J. Forshee describing how to design an incentive program for credit executives. Since the likely objective for the credit manager in most companies is a vague "maximum sales and minimum losses," considerable analysis is required to tailor the incentive payment ratios based upon sales, collections and account liquidity levels. Someone must convert management's objective of increasing sales, keeping the customers happy while staying out of the finance business as much as possible, to incentive pay schedules. [53,54]

All the experts agree that jobs must be evaluated accurately before any incentive standards are established so that the *base* pay is reasonable and equitable. Although methods improvements should be an on-going activity, care should be taken to reduce the need for methods improvement during the early stages of the installation of an incentive plan. If the company does not have effective methods engineering, they must acquire these services, either by establishing them in-house or through consultants.

Effective communication of the detail of the plan is considered by most authors as critical to its success. If management, foremen and each worker under the plan do not understand the plan thoroughly, it has little chance for success. Plans for explaining the program in detail to first line supervisors and employees and for answering any and all questions about it must be integral with the design of the plan.

Finally, most experts agree that companies should be prepared to make adjustments in their plans as they gain experience with them. The several articles on how to rehabilitate demoralized plans point up that had the companies been willing to make the necessary adjustments as the needs arose, the plans would not need rehabilitating.

Conclusion Regarding Economic Based Motivation

Although the evidence is clear that money has *some* rather significant effect on output, the research and field evidence is not clear enough to tell us *how much* the effect of money alone is. It is clear enough to allow us to conclude that, on the average, the installation of incentive programs, with their natural concommitants, usually reduces the unit cost of direct labor significantly and provides greater earnings for employees. Below is a list of the non-incentive contaminants which are usually involved in the installation of incentive programs:

1. More accurate standards are established through job study.
2. Tooling and equipment are usually improved also.
3. Work layout, methods and work processes are usually improved.
4. Supervisors are given better performance information on their units and are given more detailed responsibilities for correcting output and cost deficiencies.
5. Management is made more aware of the need for better communication and organization as well as of the need for reductions in personnel.
6. The employee receives more accurate and detailed performance feedback information such as scrap rates, output rates, down-time, etc.
7. On most group incentive systems or profit or cost-savings sharing programs, all involved employees receive more training and other help— especially from fellow employees looking to increase total earnings.
8. Low producers in group plans are more often removed or improved either by management or group measures.

The restriction-of-output phenomenon under incentives noted by Frederick Taylor in the 1900's and described as a social phenomenon by the Hawthorne researchers in the 1930's seems to be less operative today. This may be because the original interpretation of its origin as social has given way to a more reasonable interpretation of the phenomenon as economic in origin expressed in the social terms of group norms and group sanctions. Many modern and some older incentive programs contain some policy protections against workers working themselves out of a job.

The evidence does *not* indicate that just any company can install an incentive program and expect the average gains reported in the labor economics literature given earlier. Certain special conditions must be met and the nature of many of these would depend upon features unique to a given *company*, not industry. For example, unions may be generally anti-incentive, but the attitude of the local members and their leadership would be more important in determining whether a plan is possible at all, as well as who would be covered. They would also partially determine many other details of the plan from who evaluates the jobs and who times them to the penalty for bad pieces to the thresholds for going on hourly rates when equipment is down. Add to these conditions the variations in suitableness for incentives of the different tasks, the attitudes of management, the objectives of the company, and the list of contingencies can grow to sizeable proportions.

The total company or plant profit or cost reduction sharing plans may eliminate a number of these types of contingencies, but often add other ones such as the degree to which employees will be able to participate in decisions they feel will affect their bonuses or the determination of conditions upon which cost or profit level bases may be changed.

In sum, the only viable economic motivation theory would be a contingency theory since the question of the likelihood of success would have to be answered "It all depends!"

NOTES

1. Peter F. Drucker, *Management: Tasks, Responsibilities, Practices* (New York, N.Y.: Harper & Rowe, 1974), p. 238.
2. *Ibid.*, p. 239.
3. Samuel N. Kramer, *History Begins at Sumer*, (Garden City, N.Y.: Doubleday & Company, Inc., 1959), p. 53.
4. L. P. Alford, *Laws of Management*, (New York, N.Y.: The Ronald Press), p. 37.
5. Xenophon, *Memorabilia and Oeconomicus*, Translated by E. C. Marchant, The Loeb Classical Library ed. (Cambridge, Mass.: Harvard University Press, not dated), pp. 186-7.
6. Joseph M. Sherman, "Incentive Pay in American Industry, 1945-56," *Monthly Labor Review*, Vol. 65, No. 5 (November, 1947), pp. 535-37.
7. Earl Lewis, "Extent of Incentive Pay in Manufacturing," *Monthly Labor Review*, Vol. 83, No. 5 (May, 1960), pp. 460-63.
8. John H. Cox, "Wage Payment Plans in Metropolitan Areas," *Monthly Labor Review*, Vol. 87, No. 7 (July, 1964), pp. 794-96.
9. Wage Structure: *Machinery Manufacturing* (Winter 1957-58), Bureau of Labor Statistics, Report No. 139, p. 17.
10. George L. Stelluto, "*Report on Incentive Pay in Manufacturing Industries,*" *Monthly Labor Review*, Vol. 92, No. 7 (July, 1969), p. 52.
11. Leon Megginson, *Personnel: A Behavioral Approach to Administration*, (Homewood, Illinois: Richard D. Irwin, Inc. 1972), pp. 454-55.
12. *Ibid.*
13. *Ibid.*, p. 456.
14. Robert L. Opsahl and Marvin D. Dunnette, "The Role of Financial Compensation in Industrial Motivation," *Psychological Bulletin*, No. 2 (1966), pp. 95-97.

15. *Ibid.*, p. 94.
16. Lyman W. Porter and Edward E. Lawler, III, *Managerial Attitudes and Performance*, (Homewood, Illinois: Richard D. Irwin, Inc., 1968), p. 165.
17. George Graen, "Instrumentality Theory of Work, Motivation: Some Experimental Results and Suggested Modifications," *Journal of Applied Psychology Monograph*, Vol. 53, No. 2, Part 2 (April 1969) p. 7.
18. *Ibid.*, pp. 5–6.
19. *Ibid.*, p. 19.
20. Gary Yukl, Kenneth N. Wexley, and James D. Seymore, "Effectiveness of Pay Incentives Under Variable Ratio and Continuous Reinforcement Schedules," *Journal of Applied Psychology*, Vol. 56, No. 1 (1972), pp. 19–23.
21. *Ibid.*, p. 22.
22. Manuel London and Greg R. Oldham, "A Comparison of Group and Individual Incentive Plans," *Academy of Management Journal*, Vol. 20, No. 1, pp. 34–41.
23. Manuel London and Greg R. Oldham, "Effects of Varying Goal Types and Incentive Systems on Performance and Satisfaction," *Academy of Management Journal*, Vol. 19, No. 4 (1976), pp. 537–546.
24. Everett E. Adam, Jr., "An Analysis of Changes in Performance Quality with Operant Conditioning Procedures," *Journal of Applied Psychology*, No. 6 (1972), pp. 480–486.
25. Robert D. Pritchard, "Effects of Varying Performance-Pay Instrumentalities on the Relationship between Performance and Satisfaction: A Test of the Lawler and Porter Model," *Journal of Applied Psychology*, Vol. 58, No. 1, pp. 122–215.
26. David E. Demick, "Some Effects of Pay Policy on Pay Efficiency," *Proceedings of the Thirty-third Annual Meeting* of the Academy of Management, Thad Green, ed. (Boston, Mass.: August, 1973), p. 409.
27. Since the theory's major support comes from two of Adams' own studies (with co-researchers) and since the results of other studies on his model have been equivocal, it will not be discussed further here. The Adams studies are described in the following: J. S. Adams and W. B. Rosenbaum, "The Relationship of Worker Productivity to Cognitive Dissonance about Wage Inequities," *Journal of Applied Psychology*, Vol. 46 (1962), pp. 161–164, and J. S. Adams and P. R. Jacobsen, "Effects of Wage Inequities on Work Quality," *Journal of Abnormal and Social Psychology*, Vol. 69 (1964), pp. 19–25.
28. Demick, p. 413.
29. *Ibid.*, p. 414.
30. G. A. Yukl and G. P. Latham, "Consequences of Reinforcement Schedules and Incentive Magnitudes for Employee Performance: Problems Encountered in an Industrial Setting" *Journal of Applied Psychology*, Vol. 60 (1975), pp. 294–298, and Gary A. Yukl, Gary P. Latham, and Elliott D. Pursell, "The Effectiveness of Performance Incentives under Continuous and Variable Ratio Schedules of Reinforcement," *Personnel Psychology*, Vol. 29 (1976), pp. 221–231.
31. Christopher Orpen, "The Effect of Reward Contingencies on the Job Satisfaction-Task Performance Relationship: an Industrial Experiment," *Psychology: A Journal of Human Behavior*, May, 1974, pp. 9–13.
32. Yukl, et al., "The Effectiveness . . ." p. 224.
33. *Ibid.*, p. 229.

34. Orpen, p. 13.
35. Cortlandt Cammann and Edward E. Lawler III, "Employee Reactions to a Pay Incentive Plan," *Journal of Applied Psychology*, Vol. 58, No. 2 (1973), p. 163.
36. Richard L. Henderson, "Money is, too, an Incentive: One Company's Experience," *Supervisory Management*, May, 1974, pp. 20–25.
37. *Wall Street Journal*, December 9, 1976, p. 26.
38. A. J. Geare, "Productivity From Scanlon-type Plans," *Academy of Management Review*," July, 1976, p. 100.
39. J. Chamberlain, "Every Man a Capitalist," *Life*, December 23, 1946, p. 33.
40. R. Davenport, "Enterprise for Everyman," *Fortune*, January, 1950, pp. 55–59.
41. A. J. Geare, p. 100.
42. George Sherman, "The Scanlon Concept: its Capabilities for Productivity Improvement," *The Personnel Administrator*, July, 1976, p. 19, © 1976 The American Society for Personnel Administration.
43. *Wall Street Journal, Op. cit.*
44. George Sherman, "The Scanlon . . . " p. 20.
45. William A. Ruch and James C. Hershauer, "Increasing Productivity: Two Different Approaches," *The Personnel Administrator*, September, 1975, p. 17, © 1975 The American Society for Personnel Administration.
46. *Ibid.*
47. Unpublished term paper submitted to the author for an MBA course at Ohio University by Richard Pocek, MBA, 1971.
48. *Ibid.*
49. Ruch and Hershauer, p. 18.
50. *Ibid.*, p. 19.
51. The description of Aetna's plan is taken from the following: Richard J. Morrison, "Incentives in Use at Aetna Life & Casualty," *The Office*, May, 1967, pp. 53–61, and James S. Devlin, "Improving Productivity: One Company's Wage Incentive Program," *Supervisory Management*, March, 1976, pp. 7–11.
52. *Ibid.*, p. 11.
53. Ken J. Forshee, "Increasing Productivity Through Incentive Compensation," *Credit and Financial Management*, September, 1973, pp. 29–31.
54. The reader who wishes to review in some detail the various types of plans currently in use, should consult the two-part article in *Industrial Management* (March and April, 1975) by H. Barrett Rogers entitled "Principal Wage Incentive Payment Plans." In it one will find an authoritative discussion of each of the following:

1.	Straight Piecework	7.	Rowan Variable Partial Sharing Plan
2.	Industrial Monetary Piecework		
3.	Standard Hour Plan	8.	Taylor Multiple Piecework Plan
4.	Full-Sharing Plan	9.	Gantt Task and Bonus Plan
5.	Halsey Partial Constant Sharing Plan	10.	Multiple Flat Rate Plan
		11.	Emerson Empiric Bonus Plan
6.	Bedaux Plan	12.	Multiple Factor Plans

For a thorough review of various aspects of the popular Scanlon-type plan, the reader should consult A. J. Geare, "Productivity from Scanlon-type Plans" cited earlier in the chapter.

THEORIES ABOUT HUMAN RELATIONSHIPS AND ORGANIZATIONS

The first chapter in PART IV is a discussion of the theories about the process by which human relationships are formed and through which all information is exchanged—the process of communications.

Chapter 10 on work group theory covers the ordering of findings about human groupings as they are believed to relate to organizational performance. The knowledge of such theories is considered essential to successful management of the efforts of others.

Organizational theory is discussed in Chapter 11 and deals with the manner in which the resources available to management (mainly the human resources) are fitted together so the organization may best achieve its objectives.

Chapter 12 on leadership traces the history of the extensive writings on this phenomenon and offers an assessment of the current state of leadership theory.

Chapter 13 on the management of change and creativity deals with relatively new subjects. Managing change is certainly not new, but theoretical considerations of it are. And the management of the efforts of creative people is primarily a phenomenon of this century.

Communications Theory

The Gap Between the Art and the Science

HISTORY confirms that progress in the art of human communications has been badly out-distanced by the rapid and spectacular scientific advances in communications technology. The space satellites, enabling almost instant visual and oral communications between almost any two points on earth climaxed more than a century of almost incredible progress in communications technology. With the beginning of the telegraph in 1844, a communications revolution was begun which has given birth to the telephone, motion pictures, radio, television, computer, and satellite relay.

This scientific progress in the communications field has tended to obscure the fact that the art of human communications has failed to keep pace with it. This is especially true in the important facet of man's ability to communicate effectively his intentions, his ideas and his opinions. The application of information theory and models from science and engineering to human communication has pointed up the human as an extremely inadequate information processor:

> The most glaring result has been to highlight man's inadequacy as a communication channel. As the amount of input information is increased, for example, by increasing the size of the set of alternative stimuli, the amount of information that a man transmits increases at first but then runs into a ceiling, an upper limit that corresponds roughly to his channel capacity. This ceiling is always very low. Indeed, it is an act of charity to call man a channel at all. Compared to telephone or television channels, man is better characterized as a bottleneck.[1]

Far more serious than man's technical inadequacy as a channel, however, are the apparent barriers to effective communications which appear to be due to psychological and cultural reasons. In business and industrial management, evidence of problems related to communications failures are abundant. Three general types of such problems stand out:

153

1. The continuing misconceptions of the general public and employees regarding the profit rates and the roles that profits, capital, and corporations play in serving society and producing jobs.
2. The numerous operational problems traceable to what are diagnosed as communications problems. These are usually found to be someone's failure to recognize someone else's "need to know." The needed information was late, incomplete, or never arrived.
3. The failure of managerial leaders to stimulate productivity, innovation, cooperation somewhere near man's theoretical potential to produce, innovate, and cooperate. Such problems are usually traced to low motivation, inappropriate psychological climate in the organization, interpersonal and group conflict, etc. Some theorists consider "good communications" to be the solution for these problems.

Initial Management Concerns about Communications

Management and social scientists both became interested in communications at about the same time but from quite different viewpoints. In general, the early management focus was on more effective communications downward and laterally in their organizations. Their orientation was mainly from the point of view of becoming more effective *senders* of information and directives, and more effective shapers of attitudes. The social scientists' early primary interests were in the influence of mass communications (newspapers, radio, etc.) and in barriers to interpersonal communications, mainly from the point of view of the receiver.

Management concerns with the subject grew out of a few research efforts which studied employee attitudes—especially economic attitudes—which appeared to management to be due to faulty information. For example, in 1951, the median public poll estimate of corporations' after tax profits as a percent of sales was 21%, up 3% over the same poll figure for 1945. Actual profit figures from the Federal Trade Commission showed these to be 5.1% (1951) and 5.2% (1945). Many managements, alarmed by this 400% public overestimate, polled their employees and found the same. Consistent with these findings was another poll finding that over half the public believed that most companies in the U.S. could raise wages ten cents per hour without raising prices.

Almost immediately, the U.S. Steel Corporation, Kennecott Copper Corporation and others began comprehensive economic education programs involving classroom discussions, pamphlet handout racks, bulletin board and house journal features on such subjects as "The Role of Profits," "Where Jobs Come From," etc. General Electric and a number of other companies with militant unions vastly increased and improved the communications directly with their employees, most of whom were union members, to ensure that they got accurate accounts of their companies' positions on controversial issues of collective bargaining positions. A number of companies created a new job for a "Director of Communications" or equivalent. There is no real scientific evidence of the effectiveness of these programs. Managements of the day seemed to believe them helpful, however. After eleven years, the public's estimate of after-tax profits on sales was 20%, or about the same as it was in 1951, compared with actual after-tax profits on sales of 4.5%.

It is interesting to note that the American public's misconceptions have gotten significantly worse since 1962. While after-tax profits have varied between 4.0% and 5.6% between 1962 and 1971, the public's estimate has steadily climbed to 28%, or about 700% more than actual profit rates.[2]

Much of the early support for company communications programs came from research done by Opinion Research Corporation of Princeton, New Jersey. Their promotional booklet entitled *Ten Myths that Limit Management's Ability to Communicate* grew out of some of this research. The communications myths contained in it are as follows:

1. Most employees aren't interested in their company—only in trivia or news about themselves and their friends.
2. When it comes to communicating with employees, unions have the inside track.
3. If you want people to read your message, you have to keep it short.
4. Management should avoid controversial issues.
5. All you need for a good company magazine is plenty of money for staff and production.
6. You can judge the effectiveness of a piece of reading matter by the number of people who are willing to pick it up and carry it away.
7. "Gimmicks," such as trick headlines or elaborate analogies, are needed to build readership for serious material.
8. A picture is worth a thousand words.
9. Simple, understandable treatment of serious material is 'talking down,' and therefore is offensive.
10. We don't need to talk about that subject, we covered it last month.[3]

These research-based myths were used by many personnel managers in the early 1950's to gain support for initiation of or improvements in their employee newspapers or magazines, bulletin board system, handout rack giveaway programs and for increased letters to employees' homes on economic concepts and company positions on controversial issues.

One can only speculate regarding the worsening of the public's accuracy of profit rate estimates from 1962–1971. It is true that most of the downward communications programs on economic attitudes had lost their momenta by

1962. It is also true, however, that many of the wide-ranging anti-establishment forces which helped to produce student uprisings and racial riots were under way and growing by this time. It is not unlikely that many of the worker-boss, union-management, and employee-company problems today are either partly caused or worsened by the deep-seated attitudes towards corporations which give rise to such profit estimate distortions. That these distortions are clearly irrational was illustrated by an unpublished study of mine in 1974. One hundred twenty-three business administration majors (who had all taken two courses each in accounting and economics) attending a required course in a state university's business college completed a questionnaire in which the following question was asked: "What do you estimate the average annual after-tax return on investment in the U.S. manufacturing industry: 1%, 5%, 10%, 25%, or 50%?" The median answer was 25% with 23 or 19% of the students answering 50%! After collecting the questionnaires in two class sections (N = 61), the students were asked to recall the last time the had seen a bank savings account or building and loan association television advertisement inviting savers to deposit their savings with them. They were then asked to write down to the best of their memory, the interest rate promised by the advertisers. The median of these numbers was 9%. Straightforward savings accounts were offering about 6% at the time. A rational approach would have required an answer to the question of why anyone would put his money in a savings account for a 9% return while shares of corporations which made 25% after taxes return on investment were for sale. Showing these students corporation annual reports or Securities and Exchange Commission reports produced fairly accurate estimates by the end of the semester, but there is no evidence available that the cluster of attitudes which produced the severe distortion in the first place was significantly altered.

Initial Social Science Interests in Communication

Beginning social scientists' interest in mass communications focused on the communications themselves and the communications environment as well as the characteristics of the "sender" and the "audience." Below are some of the major findings on mass communications as summarized by Berelson and Steiner in their comprehensive inventory of scientific findings on human behavior:[4]

1. People tend to see and hear communications that are favorable or congenial to their predispositions . . .[5]
2. Self-selection of communication exposure in line with predispositions is far from complete, even in extreme cases, so that there is usually a sizable

minority of people who read and listen to material against or indifferent to their prior position . . .[6]

3. Since audience attention is self-selective, exposure to communications in different media tends to be supplementary, not complementary; that is, those who read about a topic also tend to listen, and those who pay attention at one time also tend to pay attention at another.[7]

4. The use, and perhaps the effectiveness, of different media varies with the educational level of the audience—the higher the education, the greater the reliance on print; the lower the education, the greater the reliance on aural and picture media. The better educated are more likely than others to pay attention to serious communications dealing with aesthetic or moral or educational issues.[8]

5. People tend to misperceive and misinterpret persuasive communications in accordance with their own predispositions, by evading the message or by distorting it in a favorable direction.[9]

6. The more trustworthy, credible, or prestigious the communicator is perceived to be, the less manipulative his intent is considered to be and the greater the immediate tendency to accept his conclusions.[10]

7. The attribution of a position to "majority opinion" is itself effective in changing attitudes when the audience respects the group from which the majority is taken. Furthermore, such "majority opinion" is typically more effective than "expert opinion."[11]

8. In cases of clear incompatibility between what a speaker says and the approval he receives from trusted associates, people tend to misperceive the actual content and distort it in a direction favorable to their own prior position.[12]

9. The communication of facts is typically ineffective in changing opinions in desired directions against the force of audience predispositions; the stronger the predispositions, the less effective the communication of facts.[13]

10. People with low self-esteem (i.e., those persons high in measures of social inadequacy, inhibition of aggression, and depressive tendencies) are more likely to be influenced by persuasive communications than are those with high self-esteem; but those with acute neurotic symptoms (i.e., neurotic anxiety or obsessional reactions) are more likely to be resistant.[14]

The reader should note carefully the qualifications "more likely" and "tends" in the above summaries of findings. This simply means that the relationships and differences in the research support for these summarized findings were statistically significant, but the relationships were not strong nor were the differences particularly wide.

Interpersonal Communications

The social scientists' early interest in interpersonal communications began to produce theory and models in the 1950's and early 1960's. These early efforts frequently focused on the barriers to interpersonal communications produced by the sender. The sender in these models was usually thought of as the manager, boss, or supervisor—or some other form of authority. The focus on communications barriers is justified in the management textbooks because research had shown that managers spend a majority of their time—from 50–90 percent according to one study—in communications activities.[15] In many such texts the illustrations of barriers lead to numerous descriptions of managers as child-like, egocentric, unsympathetic bumblers. In the introduction to a 27-page chapter on interpersonal communications, one author, after quoting a fictitious manager of a semi-automated plant as wishing that he could get rid of *all* his employees so he would have *no* problems, analyzes this manager's hypothetical behavior and his motives as follows:

> This wishful thought of the technocratic manager reflected several conditions: a looming power confrontation with the union, the unpredictability of humans as compared with machines, and the difficulties that he was experiencing in his interpersonal relations. Like the autistic child, he wishes for a world where *he* was the only person; the only person whose time was valuable, whose thoughts were correct, and whose plans should be fulfilled.[16]

In spite of the simple fact that almost half a manager's communication activity is "receiving," (see below) the majority of the illustrations of models and discussions of the communications process is concentrated on the barriers produced by the *sender*-managers in most treatments of the subject.

In one study the following mean weekly distribution of managerial communications was observed: *Incoming*: initiated *by* superiors — 2.5 hours; initiated *by* subordinates — 6.7 hours; initiated *by* other inside sources — 5.4 hours; and from extraorganizational sources — 2.9 hours for a sub-total of 17.5 hours weekly. *Outgoing*: initiated *to* superiors — 2.1 hours; initiated *to* subordinates — 7.1 hours; initiated *to* other inside sources — 6.3 hours; and initiated *to* extraorganizational people — 3.6 hours for a sub-total of 19.1 hours weekly. As can be seen the subordinate/superior initiation indexes are .84 (2.1/2.5) for the manager/superior level and .94 (6.7/7.1) for the subordinate/manager level, indicating by inference that the receiving process is just about as important to a manager as the sending process. However, most of the discussions seem to be concerned with the incorrect, inappropriate, or faulty activities on the left side of the simplified model below:[17]

Thinking—Encoding—Transmitting— —Perceiving—Decoding—Understanding

There are articles in the literature on "listening"—the right half of the model above—but they are relatively scarce. Several such articles illustrate the point in their titles: "Active Listening: A Forgotten Key to Effective Communications,"[18] and "But . . . Is Anybody Listening?"[19]

The various possible barriers to effective operation of the total model are discussed at length in the literature. One discussion covers the "four images . . . crucial to the communications process:"[20]

1. Self-image of the sender.
2. The sender's image of the receiver.
3. The receiver's image of the sender.
4. The receiver's image of the sender's self-image.

According to Cribbin, the less accurate these four images, the poorer the communications quality. Omitted from this author's discussion are at least a couple of more important images:

5. The sender's image of the receiver's self-image, and
6. The self-image of the receiver.

Other psychology-based analyses of the barriers to effective interpersonal communication may focus on "assumptions" senders and receivers hold about themselves and each other. One such discussion refers directly only to the sender's faulty assumptions and the behavioral consequences as they hinder communications. Following are a few examples which, incidentally, also illustrate the author's preoccupation with the manager's faults: The sender is logical. He only wants to do what is best for the company. This is shown to result in the sender's failing to note an awareness of the meaning of events for others; he is often tactless and discourteous, gives arbitrary orders and holds back information. The sender's faulty assumptions about the receiver's responses, the nature of the environment, and the process of communication itself produces the following barriers: ". . . he fails to indicate an awareness of the meaning of events for others . . . he fails to provide opportunities for the expression of feelings by subordinates . . . he jumps to conclusions about problems . . . he does not provide structured opportunities for personnel to express their point of view and participate in planning. . ."[21] The above assumptions are said to affect the *thinking-encoding* activities in the model.

Faulty transmission—the last sender activity in the model—is also seen to affect the communication process. Considerable research has shown that much of the meaning attributed to an individual interpersonal communication is possibly transmitted non-verbally. Most non-verbal messages received come through one of the following message systems: 1) environment, 2) appearance, 3) face, 4) touch, 5) voice, and 6) motion.[22]

1. Research has shown that the effect of environmental factors in the interpersonal communications—distance, space, furnishings, color, time and temperature is considerable. The interpreted confidentiality level of a message, for example, is a function of the distance between the sender and receiver. The size and furnishings—including their arrangements and color—of an office and the distance from the occupant's office to his parking space, etc. has led one researcher to conclude that those with more status control space and those with less respect it.[23] Colors have been shown to affect moods (reds—exciting, stimulating, greens and blues—calm, peaceful, etc.) and therefore thought to affect perceptions in communications situations.[24] Temperature has been shown related to irritability (the higher, the more irritable) and therefore considered related to perceptions affecting communications.[25]

2. *Appearance* related messages include dress and personal adornments, such as glasses, emblems, etc., as well as hair styles. Glasses-wearers have been found to reflect perceived intelligence and beards suggest wisdom and other positive qualities. Unfortunately, most of the research on the effect of appearance has used college students. With the rapidly changing tastes in appearance in modern societies such as the U.S., such research results, even for generalizing to college students, can become quickly out-of-date. An ancient Arab proverb warns against stereotyping people with beards: "Every man with a beard is not your father."

3. *Facial expressions* are considered to provide more information than other non-verbal clues. The eyes—the so-called windows of the soul—are said to provide most of the facial messages. Unfortunately, little research has been undertaken to determine eye behavior as it relates to communication. Most all of eye behavior research has focused on its relation to personality, mood states of the sender, etc. Only by inference can we relate eye behavior to the communication process. The notions that the steady eye is related to integrity and that one who doesn't look us in the eye is suspect have never been tested.

4. From the friendly handshake and the appropriate pat-on-the-back, we can infer that *touch behavior* communicates. As with much of the research, however, generalizations must be suspect, since the subjects of most research in this area have been children and young adults. One study found that verbal-only interactions were characterized by the subjects as "distant, artificial, insensitive;" "visual-only as childish, comic, artificial;" and "touch-only as trustful, sensitive, and warm."[26] We must bear in mind, however, that such responses are very likely a function of

age, personality structure, and the nature of the communication objective. The effect of such variables have so far not been sorted out by research.

5. Non-verbal *vocal* characteristics refer to the *way* something is said (labeled "paralanguage" by researchers) rather than *what* is said. Except for identifying, classifying, and measuring the various characteristics such as pitch, rate, volume, pauses, "ah's", and throat-clearings, little research is available to show precisely how their variations actually affect interpersonal communications. However, one study by Mehrabian and Weiner showed that when exposed to an inconsistent message, the impact of facial expression was greatest, vocal expression second, and verbal expression had the lowest impact.[27]

6. Although accepted on a common-sense basis as affecting communications, movements, gestures, and postures have not been researched to the extent necessary for generalizing. These are the obvious gestures whose verbal messages are clear to almost everyone such as a hitch-hiker's thumb, a Rockefeller finger, etc. More subtle are those such as the dropping of a pencil by a stenographer who may be trying to slow down the dictation pace or a person's apparent effort to stifle a yawn.

Many of the findings on the nature of non-verbal communications would have to be considered academic, as far as managers are concerned. The obstacles to using such findings come from the simple fact that we have very little control over non-verbal communications behavior. One study found that many subjects were unable to produce sarcastic messages for audio recording. They could not produce a sarcastic tone of voice. They tried to do so, but ended up attempting this with facial cues.[28] As one author put it: ". . . the fact that non-verbal communication is less controllable by the sender will serve to reinforce its validity in the mind of the receiver. An individual (may) mentally edit his message before he speaks, (but) . . . there is no such option available in non-verbal communication . . . A person thus transmits non-verbal information regardless of the intensity of his desires . . . not to do so."[29]

Listening

On the receiving end of the model—perceiving, decoding, understanding—perceiving probably produces a sizeable set of barriers to effective communications. Of the inventory of 10 research findings presented earlier, numbers 1, 5, and 8 specifically point to perceptions as a cause of message distortion and ignoring. These failures are sometimes a function of sender-receiver images of each other and sometimes due to the receiver's motives, predispositions or preoccupations. An early experience of mine will illustrate these barriers: An applicant for a lathe operator's job was told that there were no current vacancies but that the company was bidding on a contract, and if successful, would probably have one or two such openings. He was further told that if he would check back in three weeks we would know if we had been awarded the contract, and that if we had, we would consider his application at that time. Three weeks to the day he showed up with his tool and lunch boxes, ready to go to work. His selective perception causing the message fragmentation and distortion was likely due, in part at least, to his being unemployed for several months with a family to provide for.

Problems of "decoding" and "understanding" are often difficult to separate from problems of perception. In the above example, the message was only partly decoded and understood, likely due to faulty perception.

Occasionally, vocabulary differences alone between the sender and receiver can cause lack of understanding. But more often than not there is more to the sender's using words not understood by the receiver than an accidental vocabulary mismatch. Social scientists, for example, are usually quite able to use plain words to explain something to a layman or manager. For reasons best known to them they are generally loath to say that "people tend to see and hear what they want to" even when talking to non-social scientists. Instead, it comes out "perception is functionally selective." And of course, most non-scientists could probably figure out what his latter phrase means, but, if their image of the sender is negative in the first place or if they become negative at what they perceive as being "talked down to," they may refuse to make the effort. In such cases, the intended communication did not take place at all. Another one did take place, however, and that was in creating or reinforcing distrustful views of each other.

Most of the scarce material on listening in communications textbooks is prescriptive in the form of "guidelines to effective listening." The reader is usually advised to become aware of the barriers to effective listening, be motivated or get motivated to listen, concentrate on what is being said, be empathic toward the sender, ask questions, and listen objectively. Unfortunately, there is no evidence in the literature that knowledge of this advice alters listening habits.

The main conclusion to be reached from the research on interpersonal communications is that embodied in the ancient proverb: "What you *are* speaks so loud that I cannot hear what you are saying!" Another obvious conclusion is that focusing on the processes of communication will do little to alter the actual relationships between people. If two managers dislike each other, analysis of their communications processes is not very likely to lead them into friendship—and therefore to effective communication.

From the above discussion on various aspects of interpersonal communications, a more general conclusion may be drawn: Our ability to describe and measure various conditions and behaviors affecting interpersonal communications has little, if anything, to do with our ability to alter the actual relationships between the communicators, and yet these *relationships* remain fairly clearly the causes of the barriers to their effective communication.

Communications Modeling

As one might expect, there are numerous models of the communications process. They go from the very ridiculous to the highly complex models which can never be fully tested, but which do point up most of the kinds of variables involved in communications. An example of the ridiculous is Frank Dance's model simply in the form of an unlabeled helix. In explaining Dance's model, one author offers the following nonsense: "Dance's model includes feedback in a dynamic model of communication that also emphasizes the effect of past experience on communication . . . its geometrical shape demonstrates that communication, while moving forward and adding new experiences, is also dependent on its past. The helix turns back on itself yet moves onward as well . . . It can correct itself through the intervention of feedback, an essential element of communication . . ."[30]

Barnlund's model includes most of the variables involved in interpersonal communication previously discussed in this chapter. His model has two communicators interpreting cues—public, private, and non-verbal behavioral—before verbal messages happen. His model assumes that meaning grows as each new cue of whatever type is detected and assigned some sort of valence. Verbal cues are considered different only because they are finite in number, and are presented in a "linear sequence."[31] Still other models are fancier using exotic labels for types of messages such as "paralinguistic," "kinesic," and "proxemic."

The major difference between the 30–odd models of the communication process in the literature is that the model elements are packaged differently. Modeling over the years (since the Korzybski model of the later 1940's given earlier) has served to add variables to the processes of thinking, encoding, transmitting, perceiving, decoding, and understanding. And all modern models are dynamic to the extent that feed-back is considered an integral part of the process. *There is no evidence, however, that intimate knowledge of all the models enables one to communicate better.* One has only to have several acquaintances and friends who are professors of communication to confirm this. (The same naturally holds true for abilities to manage among professors of management.)

Communications Sins

Some thirty years ago, the American Management Association offered a frameable version of their "Ten Commandments of Good Communications." I converted these "Thou-shalt-nots" into Communications Sins and used them in a questionnaire to find out what sins managers and supervisors felt were most often committed against them. Table 12-1 below gives the rankings by 260 American supervisors and middle managers from 45 different companies of the communications "sins" committed against them.

TABLE 12.1

Rankings by 260 U.S. supervisors (from 45 different companies) of communications "sins" committed against them.*

Order of Presentation	Description of Sin	Composite Group Rank
1	Talking over my head (language, terms, too technical words, etc.).	8
2.	Sarcastic, hostile, or emotionally loaded communications.	7
3.	Failure to notify me of something I should have known.	1
4.	Using wrong method (oral when it should have been written, etc.).	4
5.	Bypassing me in the chain of command.	5
6.	Criticizing me in front of others.	9
7.	Telling me about something too late.	3
8.	Giving me incomplete information.	2
9.	Giving me wrong information.	6
10.	Actions failed to support communications I received.	10

* After the AMA "Ten Commandments of Good Communications" Source: Unpublished study conducted by James Lee at the Management Institute, University of Wisconsin, 1961.

Since the original study (unpublished) was done in 1961, the questionnaire has been used on a variety of managerial groups in seminars and workshops. The number one sin in these early studies—"Failure to notify me of something I should have known"—has remained number one over the years. The second and third most frequently committed sins—"Giving me incomplete information" and "Telling me about something too late"—have traded rank positions in a few groups but neither has ranked other than second or third. It can readily be seen that these three sins—"didn't tell me," "didn't tell me everything," and "told me too late"—are all various forms of *sins of omission*. From these studies I concluded that the first commandment of communications must be some form of "Thou shalt communicate!" It is carried as a "principle"[32] in my list of basic principles of managerial communications below.

Principles of Communication for Managers

1. *The fundamental principle of communication is to recognize and respond to the "need to know" of others in the organization. All other principles are secondary.* The major causes of our violations of this principle are very likely various forms of egocentricism coupled with time pressures, and lack of knowledge of the information needed by those with different tasks from ours in the organization. There is no easy way to remove these obstacles. In a few cases, cross-training assignments can help, but the opportunities for managements to take advantage of this approach are few. Significant reduction in egocentricism is naturally out of the question, the grand claims of sensitivity trainers notwithstanding, since it involves changing a very stable structure—the personality. Information systems are helpful, but are limited for at least two reasons: 1) they are usually out-of-date and 2) they cannot economically be used on the one- or few-of-a-kind information need. Thus, until we produce significant break-throughs to overcome these problems, one aspect of the art of communication will grow slowly.

2. *Recognize your own "need to know" and respond to it by scanning your environment for listening opportunities.* Be reminded that a major tool of management is information and that lack of adequate information can be due to poor listening. Side conversations in staff meetings may be useful but they can be postponed easier than the meeting. Following the subject of the meeting, even if it is not on the subject of your immediate problem areas, is generally a better course to follow. Note also that you *need* information from people you dislike about as often as from your friends. Never mind trying to learn to like someone—just focus on effective information gathering. When the focus is on the depersonalized information, effective listening is not likely to be such a burden.

3. *The primary responsibility for each communication rests with the sender or communicator.* The main reason for the inclusion of this principle is simply to thwart the flank-coverer who thinks a copy of his memo to maintenance is enough to keep him out of trouble when they fail to come to fix the machine. This is not to suggest that maintenance is off the hook

for their failure "to listen." But their responsibility is secondary to that of the production foremen whose job is to move the products out the door.

4. *Every administrative, managerial, executive, or supervisory action must include planning and execution of the necessary communications related to the action.* This principle is included as a reinforcement to principle number one above. Another reason is simply that on occasion, the thinking through of the communications approach related to the action or decision may alter the decision itself. One company planning to close down a sizeable operation unit within its plant decided, after discussing the news release announcing the move, to shut down the unit in stages. The primary reason for changing the decision was the discussion of the impact on the economics of the community which grew out of their news release planning meeting.

5. *Every important communication, to be most effective, must be planned, and every communication plan, to be most effective, must contain the answer to the following questions:*
   a. *Who* is going to communicate?
   b. *To whom* will it be directed?
   c. *What*, specifically, is to be communicated?
   d. *How* will it be conveyed?
   e. *Where* will the communication take place?
   f. *When* is the most appropriate time for the communication?

   Suppose a company's employees, because of demand for its products, have been averaging 50 hours per week for over 8 months. The company foresees a reduction in demand and must cut back most employees to 40 hours per week, four weeks from now. What will be its plan for communicating this unpleasant news?

   In formulating a plan, Question a. above requires consideration of several points. Certainly credibility of the communicator would be important. Should the communicator be the general manager, the industrial relations director, or the marketing manager, etc.? Should the public relations director deal with the local community, the industrial relations director with the union, and the general manager with the employees, etc.? Question b. above is naturally related to Question a. in the sense that different communicators have varying degrees of rapport, depending upon the audience. For example, is the message going to go into the home of the employee to reach spouses? Will it be directed only to those in the plant directly affected or will it go to all employees? Question c. asks if the message will go into great detail regarding the market circumstances requiring the reduction of overtime or if it will be confined to generalities. Question d. asks if it is to be written, verbal, or both. Will it be by a mailed letter or stuffed in the pay envelope or a notice on the bulletin board? Question e. asks if it will be carried in a meeting on the factory floor, or conveyed by each foreman in a standup meeting, etc. And finally, Question f. refers to the timing of the communication. In the case of the reduction of overtime message, of course, the sooner the better, since some employees may be buying household goods and cars on credit depending upon the overtime earnings for the payments. However, within a workday, there are choices: at the beginning of the shift, before lunch, or at quitting time. If management wants opportunities for clarification questions to be handled after the message is delivered, there must be some time remaining in the day after delivery.

6. *All communications, to be most effective, must be designed in a way which produces adequate "feed-back," and the need for and nature of post-communication follow-up must be integral with the communications plan.* If it is critical that the message be clearly understood, some means of ascertaining this must be built into the communication plan. In the above example of reducing overtime, it would be advisable to have an opportunity for employees to ask questions about the change. Old-fashioned correspondence suspense files are a means of conforming to this principle, just as the printed memo forms with space for answers and extra carbon copies help to avoid violation of the principle.

In summary the successfully communicating manager will recognize his own and others' *need to know* and do his best to fill these needs by effective listening and through well-planned and well-executed communications to others.

Managements' Communications with Their Various Publics

Earlier in the chapter some measures of public and employee misconceptions were discussed along with some managements' responses to these misconceptions held by their employees. In addition to employees and their families, business and industrial institutions must communicate with a number of other "audiences"—stockholders, the financial community, the local community, suppliers, customers, and government—to name some of the more traditional audiences. Events in the 1960's and 1970's have added other groups to this list—consumer institutions, ecologists, minorities and women in general— and to a considerable extent have begun to force the term "audience" out of the management terminology. Most of these "audiences" have begun to make it clear that they don't want only to be talked to. They want to know of company plans and to ask detailed questions whose answers are often not contained in the firms carefully planned news releases or conferences.

Many managements' early responses to these changes were inadequate.

Some may have seen some of these new groups as fads which would go away. Others responded with tokenism of one form or another. At least one professional in the field of business communications, Robert Carlson, saw these early responses as contributing to the loss of public confidence in business and industry. "In retrospect, it is clear that top business management frequently did not recognize the magnitude of the social and political changes that were taking place. They did not realize how these new forces would affect the bottom line of their financial reports as well as the profile of public attitudes toward them."[33]

This writer further points out, however, that other major institutions of our society—organized religion, our universities, and government on all levels—are also suffering from a similar crisis of confidence, and that this may be due to the emergence of an "adversary culture." And, of course, it is obvious that most major institutions are under fire from a widely ranging number of quarters. Mr. Carlson's advice for business organizations which would improve communications with their publics contains the following:

1. Establish some form of early warning network to anticipate political and social movements before they pose a threat to business operations.
2. Organize to respond appropriately to these social changes. He points to the new job of vice president for corporate social responsibility as one such response.
3. Managements should overcome their reluctance to tell the public about the good things resulting from their efforts.
4. Top management people should seek a higher visibility with the publics they serve in order to certify to these publics management's continuing interest in their views, and to give top management an unfiltered appreciation of these views.
5. Coordinate the communications activities of all in the organization who may deal with the various publics but do not centralize all such communications.
6. Top management should foster the concept within the organization that these publics are not necessarily hostile, simply because they ask detailed questions about company plans and operations.
7. Managements must retain a sense of balance in viewing the relations problems facing them. Outraged indignation is not an appropriate response to incisive questions asked by various publics.
8. Establish realistic goals which take into account the time necessary for changing public attitudes.
9. Recognize, at the outset, that accurate measure of the effectiveness of communications programs dealing with the various publics are not available and are not likely to be in the near future.

The reader is invited to note that, although Mr. Carlson's article is entitled "Is Business Really Facing a 'Communications Crisis?'" most of the attention is on *relations* crises. "Communications" happens to be the medium through which these relations are formed or misformed, but there is little evidence in his article which argues that changes in communications techniques, programs, or approaches will have a significant effect on the relations problems. He warns, and correctly so, in my opinion, that little should be expected from such programs or different techniques as long as the basic attitudes and behaviors of the managements do not undergo significant changes. Again, as mentioned earlier, the ancient proverb that "What you *are* speaks so loud that I cannot hear what you are saying" seems appropriate here.

Summary and Conclusions

Communications—the process by which all information is exchanged and through which all human relations are formed or changed has been examined from several standpoints. Modern communications models seem to make sense but are so complex that operationalizing and measuring all elements in the model for validation is virtually impossible. Barriers to effective communications are shown more often to be basic failures to communicate accurately and on time than lack of knowledge of the communications process. Most of these real barriers are a function of value and attitudinal differences between communicators or lack of time to communicate effectively. The problem of the need for business and industry to improve their public images was shown to be mainly a function of the relationship between managements and their increasingly complicated constellation of publics. Managements are warned to begin to take more serious note of the signs of future social and political change likely to affect their operations and to organize and plan the communications necessarily involved in adapting to these changes.

NOTES

1. A. Miller, *The Psychology of Communication*, (Baltimore, Md.: Penguin Books, 1967), p. 48.
2. All figures on public estimates of profit rates were taken from the following publication of the Opinion Research Corporation: *ORC Public Opinion Index, Report to Management*, Volume XXXIX, No. 21, pp. 2–6.
3. *Ten Myths that Limit Management's Ability to Communicate*, Opinion

Research Corporation booklet, (Princeton, New Jersey, not dated, but text clues suggest between 1949–1951).

4. Bernard Berelson and Gary A. Steiner, *Human Behavior: An Inventory of Scientific Findings*, (New York, N.Y.: Harcourt Brace and World, 1964), pp. 529–553.

5. For an example of one of the studies supporting this summarized finding, see Paul F. Lazarsfeld, Bernard Berelson, and Hazel Gaudet, *The People's Choice*, (New York, N.Y.: Columbia University Press, 1948).

6. For an example of a supporting study, see Melvin L. De Fleur and Otto N. Larsen, *The Flow of Information: An Experiment in Mass Communication*, (New York, N.Y.: Harper and Row, 1958).

7. See Paul F. Lazarsfeld, *et al.*

8. Paul F. Lazarsfeld and Patricia L. Kendall, "The Communications Behavior of the Average American," in *Radio Listening in America*, (Englewood Cliffs, N.J.: Prentice Hall, 1948), pp. 1–17.

9. For sample support see Carl I. Hovland and Muzafer Sherif, "Assimilation and Contrast Effects in Reactions to Communication and Attitude Change," *Journal of Abnormal and Social Psychology*, Vol. 55, pp. 244–52.

10. For sample research support, see Carl I. Hovland, Irving L. Janis, and Harold H. Kelley, *Communication and Persuasion: Psychological Studies of Opinion Change*, (New Haven, Conn.: Yale University Press, 1953).

11. For sample research support see Charles E. Osgood and Percy H. Tannenbaum, "The Principle of Congruity in Prediction of Attitude Change," *Psychological Review*, Vol. 62, pp. 42–45.

12. For sample research support see Harold H. Kelley and Christine L. Woodruff, "Members' Reaction to Apparent Group Approval of Counternorm Communication," *Journal of Abnormal Social Psychology*, Vol. 52, pp. 74–76.

13. Edward A. Suchman, *et al.*, *Desegregation: Some Propositions and Research Suggestions*, (New York, N.Y.: Anti-Defamation League of B'nai B'rith, 1958).

14. For a summary of studies of responses to pressures for conformity, see Robert R. Blake and Jane S. Mouton, "The Experimental Investigation of Interpersonal Influence," in Albert D. Biderman and Herbert Zimmer, editors, *The Manipulation of Human Behavior*, (New York, N.Y.: John Wiley and Sons, 1961), pp. 216–76.

15. J. H. Horne and T. Lupton, "The Work Activities of Middle Managers," *Journal of Management Studies*, Vol. 1 (1965), pp. 14–33.

16. David R. Hampton, Charles E. Summer, and Ross A. Webber, *Organizational Behavior and the Practice of Management* [revised], (Glenview, Ill.: Scott Foresman and Company, 1973), p. 66.

17. Based upon an early model in A. Korzybski, *Science and Sanity: An Introduction to Non-Aristotelian Systems and General Semantics*, 4th edition, (Institute of General Semantics, 1962) as it appeared in David R. Hampton, *et al.*, p. 67.

18. N. H. Deunk, "Active Listening: A Forgotten Key to Effective Communications," *Hospital Administration*, Spring 1967, pp. 34–45.

19. W. Guthrie, "But . . . Is Anybody Listening," Talk at the 13th Tecnifax Seminar-Workshop in Visual Communications, April 22, 1958, as noted in David R. Hampton, *et al.*, p. 90.

20. James J. Cribbin, *Effective Managerial Leadership*, (New York, N.Y.: American Management Association, 1972), pp. 169–70.
21. David R. Hampton, *et al.*, pp. 68–9.
22. Edward T. Hall, *The Silent Language*, (New York, N.Y.: Doubleday, 1959).
23. A. Mehrabian, "Significance of Posture and Position in the Communication of Attitude and Status Relationships," *Psychological Bulletin*, Vol. 71 (1969), p. 363.
24. L. B. Wexner, "The Degree to Which Colors (Hues) Are Associated with Mood-Tones," *Journal of Applied Psychology*, Vol 38 (1954), pp. 432–35.
25. W. Griffit and R. Veitch, "Hot and Crowded: Influences of Population Density and Temperature on Interpersonal Affective Behavior," *Journal of Personality and Social Psychology*, Vol. 17 (1971), pp. 92–98.
26. J. P. Bardeen, "Interpersonal Perception Through the Tactile, Verbal and Visual Modes," (Unpublished paper presented to International Communication Association, Phoenix, Arizona, 1971).
27. A. Mehrabian and M. Weiner, "Decoding of Inconsistent Communications," *Journal of Personality and Social Psychology*, Vol. 6 (1967), pp. 109–14.
28. A. Mehrabian, "When Are Feelings Communicated Inconsistently?" *Journal of Experimental Research in Personality*, Vol. 4 (1970), pp. 198–212.
29. Richard C. Huseman, James M. Lahiff, and John D. Hatfield, *Interpersonal Communication in Organizations*, (Boston, Mass.: Holbrook Press, Inc., 1976), p. 83.
30. *Ibid.*, p. 15.
31. Dean C. Barnlund, "A Transactional Model of Communication," in Kenneth K. Sereno and C. David Mortensen, eds., *Foundations of Communication Theory*, (New York, N.Y.: Harper & Row, 1970), p. 18.
32. The term "principle" here is used in the popular academic sense, not as a law. These principles are offered more as rules which, if violated, usually cause managerial problems.
33. Robert O. Carlson, "Is Business Really Facing a Communications Crisis?" *Organizational Dynamics*, Spring 1973, pp. 35–52.

Chapter 10

Work Group Theory

THE theory surrounding social motivation, especially that which is directly related to groups, is voluminous. It is so detailed that a completely detached observer might suspect that social scientists themselves suffer from some form of affiliation deprivation syndrome. Although there are useful insights here and there in the literature on the subject, the majority of the literature is either fraught with social values or redundant. Many of the value orientations in social scientists' writings are clearly advocative social "science." For example, one author in a not-too-subtle fashion advocates that groups themselves are morally good: ". . . the hungry person may refrain from eating until he can share with his starving fellows; the politician may spurn an advantageous political bargain out of loyalty to his supporters; the member of a group struggling for equal opportunity and freedom from fear may undergo great deprivation and bodily injury to secure recognition of his group."[1]

Another author writing on the need for informal groups in a work situation advocates the following ideological values: the boss is commanding and the organization demanding and together they threaten, bore, impoverish emotionally, and frustrate. Here is the exact quotation:

The individual, not isolated, and subjected to the demands of the organization through the commands of his boss, finds that he must create with his fellow employees informal groups, not shown on any table of organization, in order to protect himself from arbitrary control of his life, from the boredom produced by the endless repetition of mechanically sanitary and routine operations and from the impoverishment of his emotional and social life brought about by the frustration of his basic needs for social interaction, participation, and acceptance in a stable group.[2]

The same author insists that groups are omnipotent: "To begin with the most general proposition, we may state that the behavior, attitudes, beliefs, and values of the individual are *all firmly grounded in groups to which he belongs* . . . Attempts to change them must be concerned with the dynamics of groups."[3] (Italics added)

172

Redundancies are almost as frequent as advocated values. Consider the following: "interaction and communication are not distinctive to group formation but are essential to any kind of human association of consequence."[4] In the following quotation, describing the characteristics of the final phase in group growth, we have in a single sentence, a prescription, a value judgment (to me at least) and a redundancy: "Each individual has a personality of his own which is different from that of other group members and *is not to be judged as either good or bad*. The nature of this personality determines the efficiency and ease with which individuals will be able to play different roles in the group."[5] (Values in added italics) Dorwin Cartwright, who provided one of the value orientations above, offers a dictionary definition as a principle: "Principle No. 4. The greater the prestige of a group member in the eyes of the other members, the greater the influence he can exert."[6] *Webster's Handy College Dictionary* gives as the *meaning* of prestige, "influence arising from reputation or esteem."

In an article casting doubt on some widely-held social science theories, Tom Alexander notes the social scientists' value orientation:

> While short on knowledge and proof, social science has generally been long on ideology. One long time observer of the species is Moynihan who was an advisor to presidents Kennedy, Johnson, and Nixon. The American social scientist, he observes, has a "dual nature. He is an objective seeker after truth. But he is also likely to be a passionate partisan of social justice and social change to bring it about." One difficulty is that the consumer (of social scientists' theories or services) can rarely be sure which part of the dual role the social scientist is playing at any particular time, the truth-seeker or the ideologist. One characteristic of the ideologist is to distort or oversimplify. Sociologist Walter Miller has analyzed the semantic confusion behind recent social legislation. He contends that concepts such as "the poor," "poverty," "deprivation," and "the power structure," were spun forth by a "Movement" (Miller's term) of ideological social scientists to provide simple, emotionally potent and utterly myth-filled theories that defined social problems primarily as the oppression of some people by others.[7] (Parenthetical phrases added.)

In addition to redundancies and ideological biases, the social science literature surrounding work groups and role theory is full of unnecessary jargon and pompous and misleading phraseology. For example, the terms "in-group" and "out-group" suggest, erroneously, that outsiders are members of one group. Following this convention, a German bus driver, the Japanese emperor and I are *members* of the Club of Rome's *out-group*.

Thus warned, the reader of social scientists' work on the group should watch for ideological bias, skip over complex restatements of the obvious and be wary of theories which, in order to be understood, require an entirely new vocabulary.

Because there is a tendency for theory and research on different kinds of groups to find their way into management literature undifferentiated, different types of groups should be clearly defined and understood.

Group Types

The vast majority of groups researched are small, face-to-face groups varying in size from two or three to about fifteen members. Larger aggregates lose what are known as group characteristics because they begin to break up into sub-groups. The varieties of small groups are generally categorized as follows: (1) the *institutionalized group*, of which the family would be an example; (2) the *autonomous group*, which includes a circle of close friends voluntarily associated, or a small bridge club; (3) the *small group within a large organization* such as a group of buddies in an Army unit or a work group in an office or factory; and (4) the *problem-solving group* such as a committee with a particular task to perform.

Common Sense Research About Groups

The verification of common sense about small groups has occupied considerable attention of the social scientist. In brief form below are summaries of all the relevant general findings in Berelson and Steiner's inventory of scientific research on human behavior:[8]

1. The more people associate with each other, the more they share values and norms and the more they like one another.
2. People tend to gravitate into groups which maximize their shared values.
3. Cross-pressures caused by norms of different groups cause emotional strain which is reduced by moving in the direction of the strongest group ties.
4. Resistance to the assimilation of new group members is a function of the proportion of new members joining an established group.
5. New personal relations tend to follow established relations. Thus if X and Y are friends and Y is unfriendly toward Z, then X will tend to be unfriendly toward Z also.
6. New members tend to feel inferior to established members.
7. The more stable a group's membership, the higher its morale will be.
8. The more an individual wants to join a small group, the more he will conform to its norms.
9. The more contact there is between related groups, the more similar they tend to become in their norms and values.

10. The amount of conflict between groups is a function of the amount of communication or interaction between these groups.

11. Free-forming groups tend to be numerous and influential in modern, advanced societies that are liberal in their social and political organization.

12. Small groups set and enforce norms, thus influencing the behavior of their members.

13. The more stable and cohesive a group is, the more it influences the behavior of its members.

14. Group deviants are more likely to change their behavior to meet the standards of model members than vice versa.

15. The more confused a group is about the right standards, the less control it can exercise over its members.

16. The less definite standards outside the group are, the more control the group can exercise, and if its own standards are definite and clear, the more control it will exercise.

17. Intra-group interaction increases and judgments tend to be unstable when there is neither a clear objective nor definite group basis for judgment.

18. A single group member tends to give in if he is the only hold-out, even on matters on which the group is clearly wrong.

19. The norms of a group are more likely to be limited when the group's activities are largely determined from outside.

20. Members typically believe the group's opinions to be closer to their own than they actually are.

21. Members can better judge the opinion of the group when there is frequent interaction among the members.

22. People in a group tend to agree with the people they like, and tend to think that the latter agree with them more than those they dislike.

23. The group strongly influences its members by providing them with support, reinforcement, security, encouragement, protection, and rationales for proper behavior, and punishes them for deviations by using ridicule, dislike, shame, and threat of expulsion.

24. Within a group there is a tendency for one's friends to reward conformity, and one's enemies are punished for deviations from group norms.

25. The order of a group's response to deviations from its norms is as follows: first, discussion; second, disapproval; third, lowering their ranks; and fourth, expulsion.

26. Small groups tend toward uniform attitudes, actions, values, and norms under the following conditions: (a) the greater the group attractiveness is

to its members, (b) the more pressures for uniform behavior there are in the group, (c) the more the perceived importance of the issue at hand, (d) the more homogeneous the group, (e) the more available the members' opinions or actions are to the group, (f) the more frequent the personal interaction among the members is, (g) the more this interaction is based upon equality with no one exercising much authority, and the less competition there is within the group, (h) the greater the participation in setting group standards, and (i) the more favorably the members regard one another.

27. Groups in socially mobile strata tend to be less tolerant of deviations from norms than groups in established elite strata.

28. The more an individual conforms to group norms, the better liked he will be; and the better he is liked, the more he conforms.

29. The more vague and social a group's objectives are, the more members rank each other on personal characteristics, i.e. charm, good-naturedness, "personality," etc.

30. The ranking of members becomes less clear as the group's norms become poorly defined.

31. The more secure and the higher ranked a group member is, the more freely he will disagree with the group.

32. The lowest ranked tend to disagree privately, but conform anyway, and the average members tend to agree privately and publicly.

33. The higher ranked a member, the more central to the group's action he will be and the more influential he will be.

34. The more cohesive a group becomes, the greater the amount of interaction among its members.

35. Interaction decreases in a group of high emotional attachment as internal dissension rises.

36. As members of a group with little emotional attachment perceive a disagreement within the group, interaction increases.

37. The more relevant the subject or the sharper the disagreement, the more the interaction.

38. When majority members believe there is a chance to change opinions into harmony, their communications will be addressed to these deviants.

39. When the majority no longer believes there is a chance for harmony, communications to the deviants drop off sharply.

40. The rise and fall of such communications to deviants are sharper in comparatively cohesive groups.

41. A group will, given time, establish formalized working lines of communication.

42. Within task-oriented groups in which no member possesses special competence, communication is most nearly equal among its members.

43. Intra-group communications are more likely directed from equal to equal and from higher ranking members to lower ranking members, than from the lower ranking to the higher ranking members.

The above "findings" are primarily from research on small voluntary groups or contrived laboratory groups usually from school or college populations. The reader is asked at this point to stop and consider the research methodology necessary to produce such findings. Acceptable definitions and the means of *quantitatively measuring* had to be found for the following variables: *internal dissension, cohesiveness, deviations from norms, group attractiveness to members, pressures for uniform behavior, vagueness of group objectives, stability of judgments*, etc. Researcher-observer bias had to be held in check. In some of the research, the researcher-observer was an active member of the group, making it difficult to remain objective. Such is the nature of this kind of research. The obstacles could account for the low magnitudes of differences and correlations typically found in such research. And the opportunities for ideological intrusions—whether conscious or unconscious—are endless. Unfortunately, many of the above findings have found their way into management literature as "principles of group dynamics" or social science "laws." While it may be true that some work groups behave somewhat like voluntary student and school laboratory groups, the research upon which many of the above findings were based has not been repeated with work groups, some of which have leaders who are both their informal leader and their foremen or supervisors. Organizational formal authority is ignored by most of the small group researchers.

Sociologists' biases regarding authority and business have been observed often. Following are a few examples: "We can take it for granted that the majority of sociologists . . . will have an ideological bias against business."[9] "Sociologists usually focus their attention on those they see as underdogs—men and women in the production process."[10] And in a research effort in which behavioral scientists' analyses of business case problems were compared with managers' analyses of the same problems, the results clearly revealed the scientists' anti-authoritarian bias to the extent that the researchers referred to the two groups as being from two different cultures.[11]

The Study of Work Groups

As far as management literature is concerned, the history of managerial interest in work groups began with the writings of Mary Parker Follett, and includes at least those of Elton Mayo, George C. Homans and Rensis Likert. Their writings roughly cover the period from 1920 to the middle 1960's. Yet none of these names appears in the list of references for an article on groups prepared for the International Encyclopedia of the Social Sciences by Muzafer Sherif. (Eight of the 33 references are writings of Muzafer Sherif and his is the only name appearing more than once.)[12] One reason for their absence could be that none of them operated in the main stream of academic sociology or social psychology. Worse yet, they were all "friendly" with business and industry. This could hardly endear them to most sociologists whose anti-profit and anti-capital values are clear from their writings and research designs.

Mary Parker Follett, a broadly educated philosopher, was a friend and informal advisor to a number of corporate chief executives. Elton Mayo and George Homans' influence came partly through their associations with the Harvard Business School, and Rensis Likert has worked as a consultant to businessmen for many years. From slightly different viewpoints, they have all pointed out social factors, including many of those associated with work groups, as important considerations for management. With the exception of Likert, none is considered to have contributed to significant research in the field. None is considered to have provided formal theory, except possibly Likert, whose "newer theory" and "System 4" more resemble prescriptions than theories. Follett provided philosophy and advice, Mayo generated hypotheses, Homans provided propositions for ordering empirical findings, and Likert provides extensive prescriptions and consulting services.

Mary Parker Follett, as a philosopher, was concerned with the psychological factors underlying *consent* in democratic groups. She saw consent not as static but as a continuous process. From this base she reasoned that intragroup conflict could be constructive in the service of the group. She believed that conflict resolution should come about not by compromise or domination but by *integration* in which the members concerned examined together various means of achieving their desires. She believed that authority should be replaced by the "law of the situation." The leader should be the person most able to secure penetration of the group with the best ideas available among the group members.[13]

Elton Mayo,[14] borrowing sociologist Emile Durkheim's concept *anomie* as the basis for his view of the industrial worker, concluded that the loss of social bonds due to migrations and industrial work organization caused much of society's and industry's problems:

Human collaboration in work, in primitive and developed societies, has always depended for its perpetuation upon the evolution of nonlogical social code which regulates the relations between persons and their attitudes to one another. Insistence upon a merely economic logic of production . . . interferes with the development of such a code and consequently gives rise in the group to a sense of human defeat. This human defeat results in the formation of a social code at a lower level and in opposition to the economic logic. One of its symptoms is "restriction" of output.[15]

George C. Homans did not set out to provide theory for management application. When asked recently what were the most important lessons for operating managers in his two major books *Social Behavior* and *The Human Group* he answered, "That is very difficult to say. I am older and less optimistic now than when I wrote that (sic)." He added that knowledge of his work served more to ". . . alert people to what may go wrong than it does in telling them what they can do about it."[16]

Homans' major work provided a scheme for analyzing small group behavior. In *The Human Group* he used his analytic system on a variety of groups from primitives to a streetcorner gang to an industrial work-group in an effort to demonstrate its universality. Homans identified both "internal" and "external" behaviorally integrated subsystems which make up the total social system of a group. The internal system contained the elements within the group's social life. The external system referred to the behaviors of the group and its members regarding the group's interdependence with its environment—policies, procedures, job definitions, organization structure, etc. Homans' approach to group analysis called for the group to be examined for its three main behavioral elements: (1) *activity*, what members do as its members, (2) *interaction*, the relationship between activities, and (3) *sentiment*, the feelings and emotions of group members about what the group and its members do. His scheme also called for analysis of the group's norms or code of behavior adopted by the group as "proper" or ideal, and the means (sanctions) of meeting these standards. Bernard De Voto in the foreward to *The Human Group* summarized the result of such an approach to small group study:

> What the small group reveals when thus studied is a social system reacting with its environment as a self-adjusting organization of response whose parts are mutually interdependent. What acts, and what reacts, is not any single part or function of the social system, nor any combination of parts or functions, but the system as a whole, a totality whose mutual interdependence *is* the system. Cause and effect disappear; what must be looked for is the resultants of complexes of interacting forces. The group is a dynamic social equilibrium. It sets up its own responses organically, determines its own measures of control, derives its own possibilities of adaptation, elaboration, and change. To state just one of Mr. Homans' conclusions . . . direction or leadership can be imposed on it only so far as the group as such is willing to accept either. If it will accept either, it will accept them only as they fit its own pattern of group necessity and only to the degree that fulfills its own conception of what is proper *in its own terms*. This is a startling illumination of the thesis familiar to us as "government rests on the consent of the governed."[17]

Homans' "rules of leadership" point up the precariousness of this role in small informal groups:

1. The leader will maintain his own position. If . . . a leader is to

originate interaction for a group, he must establish and maintain his rank.

2. The leader will live up to the norms of his group.
3. The leader will lead . . . any failure on his part to originate interaction, to take the initiative, will make him that much less a leader.
4. The leader will not give orders that will not be obeyed. When he gives orders that are not obeyed, he has by that fact undermined his rank and the presumption on the part of the members of his group that his future orders are to be obeyed. Nothing . . . will create more confusion in the minds of his followers, and nothing so quickly lead them to doubt his competence.
5. In giving orders, the leader will use established channels.
6. The leader will not thrust himself upon his followers on social occasions. By thrusting himself socially upon his followers, the leader will lower his own rank or embarrass his followers, or both. If, moreover, he associates frequently with the followers, he is putting himself in a position in which they can bring organizational demands to bear upon him without first going to his lieutenants, and he needs to protect himself from such demands.
7. The leader will neither blame nor, in general, praise a member of his group before other members. (The rule regarding blame may be obvious, but Homans' rationale for the praise aspect of the rule is worth noting.) Occasional public praise of a man is admirable, but frequent praise may embarrass him, because it may show that the leader is giving him an evaluation that the rest of the group is not ready to accept. So praise by all means. Nothing is more important. But praise in private.
8. The leader will take into consideration the total situation. In the effort to maintain a moving equilibrium, the leader will have to remember that, since they are mutually dependent, change in any one of these elements (the environment, the materials, tools, and techniques, the external system, the internal system, and the norms), will bring about changes in all the others, changes for which he may have to allow and compensate.
9. In maintaining discipline, the leader will be less concerned with inflicting punishment than with creating the conditions in which the group will discipline itself.
10. The leader will listen. It would seem obvious that if the leader is to be kept fully informed by the members of his group, he must allow them to inform him, which means that he must keep quiet himself, but no rule of leadership is more often violated, partly because leaders are apt to be active and energetic men and like to talk.
11. The leader will know himself. He must know the passions in him that, unchecked, will destroy him as a leader. (Homans points out that his last

rule did not follow from his analysis of groups, but felt it to be good advice.)[18] (Parenthetical phrases added.)

Homans never believed that all the concepts or variables in his analytical system could be quantified and tested as in a mathematical model. His primary concern has been to develop concepts and methods by which group functioning could be better understood.

Homans was one of the early minority of social scientists to study groups whose writings did not contain the ideological value that all groups are right, good, true, and more or less sacred and that their normal functioning must be supported at all costs. William Dowling in his interview with Homans noted that in his book *Social Behavior*, Homans had "described bomber crews in which there were very good human relations and very high congruence, and yet these very happy groups were also remarkably ineffective." Homans answered, "Well, there were no social tensions in the sense that there were people with high skill but low status, or vice versa. That's what we mean by status congruence." When Dowling asked if there were not a reverse relationship between high status congruence and effectiveness, Homans replied, "I'll bet you cannot prove that. But it was fascinating in this particular case. Actually, the relationship was curvilinear: Very high congruence was associated with low effectiveness, middle-level congruence was associated with high effectiveness, and very low congruence was associated with ineffectiveness." Dowling then remarked that they were still left with the unanswered question of why very high congruence was associated with ineffectiveness, to which Homans replied, "We don't know the answer . . . Maybe everyone related so well to one another that they relaxed as far as their efforts to bomb were concerned."[19] It should be noted that *formal* leadership could have "caused" this degree of relaxation to exist.

Rensis Likert, building upon social science research findings on work and other groups, formulated a management approach combining the formal and informal organizations. He suggested that a formal unit head should deal with his employees collectively. He postulated that the formal leader should view responsibility and accountability in terms of the whole work group. His "linking pin" idea was his view of the whole organization as a mosaic of overlapping and interacting groups. Both the group's effectiveness and its internal relationships were seen as dependent upon the quality of communication within the work group. Like others before him such as Follett and Chester Barnard, Likert viewed the real authority of the official leader as a function of how much authority his subordinates allowed him to exert over them. Recall that one of Homans' rules for leaders was that "the leader will not give orders that will not be obeyed." Likert's elaboration on this upward authority flow concept was his "action-influence" principle—the amount of influence exerted over subordinates is determined by how much he allows them to influence him. Likert contended that the extent to which his group is consulted on matters affecting them determines, to a large extent, their commitment in carrying out the leader's decision. Another facet of his interaction-influence concept involves the relationship between a formal leader's *upward influence* (with his own superiors) and his influence with his own group. Likert cited several research findings to support not only that upward influence affects morale and motivation, but also productivity and other work performance variables.[20]

Likert is known in management circles mainly for the advocation of his "System 4" or "participative-group management" style. Although he describes three other styles—System 1 ("exploitative-authoritarian"), System 2 ("benevolent-authoritive"), and System 3 ("consultative")—he believes System 4 is the ideal, at least for people-oriented business organizations. Much of his consulting work concerns the analyses of management styles and training in his System 4 management approach.

Group Cohesiveness

As in the cases of other group researches, the study of the work group has tended to have as a primary focus not productivity, but group characteristics such as cohesiveness, sanction systems, norms development, etc. Stanley Seashore, in a major study of 228 industrial work groups, considered productivity standards as a dependent variable affected by cohesiveness, his independent variable. Other dependent variables were member similarity, member prestige, anxiety levels, and interaction opportunity.[21] His sample work groups were not selected from any social interaction analysis, but were formally designated work sections in a machinery factory. They varied in size from 5 to over 50 members with a mean size of about 26 members. All data were collected via a single questionnaire filled out by 5,871 employees. Below are summary statements of his findings based upon statistically significant, though not large, correlations between group cohesiveness and the dependent variables mentioned above:

1. Members of high cohesive groups exhibit less anxiety than members of low cohesive groups, using as measures of anxiety: (a) feeling "jumpy or 'nervous' " (b) feeling under pressure to achieve higher productivity (actual productivity held constant), and (c) feeling of lack of support for the company.
2. High cohesive groups have less variation in productivity among members than do the low cohesiveness groups.
3. High cohesive groups differ more frequently and in greater amount than low cohesive groups from the plant norm of productivity. These deviations are toward both higher and lower productivity.

4. The direction of deviation of group productivity (i.e., towards higher or lower productivity) is a function of the degree to which the larger organization (the company) is perceived by group members to provide a supportive setting for the group.

5. (No relationship was found between group cohesiveness and similarity among members, using as measures, similarity in age and educational level.)

6. Group cohesiveness is positively related to the degree of prestige attributed by the group members to their own jobs.

7. Group cohesiveness is positively related to opportunity for interaction as measured by (a) size of group, and (b) duration of shared membership on the job.[22] (Parenthetical phrases not direct quotes.)

Seashore concluded from this study that managerial actions ought to be designed so as to (a) enhance group members' prestige, (b) organize the work so that work groups are relatively small in size, and (c) facilitate the maintenance of group membership continuity. He warned against striving for cohesiveness for cohesiveness' sake without ". . . developing among the employees a feeling of confidence and security in the management of the organization" since this is one factor determining whether productivity will be high or low in cohesive groups.[23]

The Formal Versus the Informal Organization

Ever since the Hawthorne Studies, the informal organization has been considered by most behavioral scientists to have a greater influence on employee motivation and therefore on organizational effectiveness, than the formal organization. Barnard singled out the informal organization as vital as a means of communication, cohesion, and protecting the individual.[24] He viewed the maintenance of the informal organization an important management responsibility. From this point onward, behavioral science has followed the lead with little real research for support. For most behavioral scientists, the assumption that the informal organization is more potent in influencing employees than the formal never needed testing. A further widely held and largely untested assumption is that the employee values the informal organization more than he does the formal. These assumptions may be valid. But supporting evidence comparing the formal with the informal organization in this regard is conspicuously absent.

One fairly respectable study, flawed only by its subject sample and therefore by the researchers' conclusions, attempted to test the comparative potency of the two organizations. The study further compared employees' judgments of the relative value of the two organizations. William Reif, Robert Monczka, and John Newstrom set about to test "the critical assumption . . . that the informal organization plays a more important role than the formal organization in determining motivational climate and hence organizational effectiveness."[25] Using a "Semantic Differential Technique," a term guaranteed to frighten away the uninitiated, they were able to measure employee perceptions of the informal and formal organizations on two separate dimensions: potency (strength of influence) and value (good or bad in relation to employees' need fulfillment). In choosing the component concepts of each organization, over a hundred concepts were boiled down to sixteen—eight formal organization concepts and eight informal organization concepts as follows:

Formal Organizational Concepts	Informal Organizational Concepts
Authority	Voluntary teamwork
Job description	Clique
Performance appraisal	Personal influence
Chain of command	Co-worker evaluation
Policies	Social interaction
Controls	Group cohesion
Organizational objectives	Social group membership
Supervisor	Grapevine

These were selected as those concepts separated into formal and informal organizational concepts by a pilot subject sample. All these concepts had a minimum pilot sample subject agreement of 90 percent or more.

The questionnaire asked the research sample subject to rate each of these components on a 7 point scale. For example, the *value* of each of the formal organizational concepts was rated on a 7–point scale with fair-unfair, good-bad, hazy-clear, etc. at each end of the continua. *Potency* scales had as continua extremes such adjectives as strong-weak, and hard-soft. The researchers took pains to minimize internal measurement contamination by alternating potency and value items and by reversing the order of every other scale.

Their sample, unfortunately, severely reduced the possibility that their findings would test the cherished assumption that the informal organization is good and omnipotent. Recall that the core definition of work group is the joining together of oppressed, bored, harrassed, factory workers (see the first few pages of this chapter). The sample chosen by Reif, Monczka, and Newstrom consisted of 341 *managerial and white-collar employees who were attending a management training program.* It is hardly reasonable to assume that their orientations to the formal and informal organizations could be considered the same as those of the blue collar worker.

Their findings, therefore, are not very illuminating. The formal organization was found to be perceived as both better and more potent than the informal organization. Significance tests of paired measures between formal and informal organizations showed that the rated differences were likely to occur less than once in a thousand times on a chance basis.

In their conclusions, the researchers ignore the obvious orientation differences between managerial (and white collar employees in training for management) and blue-collar workers. In their eagerness to refute the widely held assumption that the informal organization is more influential and more highly valued, they missed their mark.

After pointing out that classical organizational theory holds that the formal organization is to be designed for efficiency and that the policies and controls are designed for effectiveness, they characterize behavioral scientists as emphasizing that worker needs are only fulfilled through the psychosocial organization. They point to the contrasting strategy advocated by behavioral scientists of teamwork, social interaction. The heart of their conclusions is given below:

> . . . this study provides new insight into these discordant views. Along the potency dimension, the data show that the formal organization is perceived to be significantly stronger and more influential than the informal. It is more pervasive and more dominant. Along the evaluative dimension, managerial and white collar perceptions of the formal organization are significantly more positive than for the informal organization. Respondents perceived that the formal organization is more valuable in satisfying their needs . . . This study indicates that unless we are more careful in testing the "obvious" for its validity, we may find ourselves blindly accepting and applying incomplete, if not totally inaccurate, concepts of organization.[26]

Unfortunately, the researchers themselves missed the "obvious"—that managerial and blue-collar employees are not necessarily alike—and blindly applied their findings to a non-issue. Social scientists never have seriously addressed the managerial employees' need-fulfillment as a function of their memberships in work groups. The researchers are to be commended for their contribution on two counts, however. First, they addressed the problem of untested assumptions, many likely springing from the values held by social science researchers. Second, their methodology represents about the best means of researching the subject matter using paper and pencil questionnaires.[27]

Groups Versus Individuals

Another dimension of the study of groups involves comparisons between groups and individuals on problem-solving and decision-making. As early as 1932, M. E. Shaw compared problem-solving of individuals and groups. His samples were individual students and groups of 4 students controlled for sex and intelligence. He found that groups were more likely to find correct solutions than individuals and that they took less time. On many of the problems, however, the best individual performance was as good as the groups' on both accuracy and speed.[28]

Another early study showed the superiority of groups over individuals in solving cross-word puzzles. The problem with this type of research is simply that it demonstrates the obvious. The group members contributed solutions to different parts of the puzzle. Four people can normally produce a wider variety of human hairs or unload a cement truck faster than an individual. A continuation of the same experiment compared the groups and individuals on the task of *constructing* a crossword puzzle. Here, the individuals proved superior, a finding which should not be especially surprising to anyone who has tried to coordinate a variety of ideas into a total pattern in a small group.

Other variables have been found related to the relative effectiveness of groups and individuals in problem-solving. R. A. Webber, using a vocabulary exercise, found that 5-person groups took 50 percent longer than the average time of individuals working alone.[29] J. Hall, using a "lost on the moon" problem, found results similar to Webber's—individuals superior—but the comparative advantage of individuals was reversed in a follow-on experiment in which the groups were given a one-page handout on developing group consensus.[30]

The ages of subjects and/or factors relating to their occupation or occupation levels appear to be related to the comparative performance of groups versus individuals, at least on Webber's vocabulary research exercise mentioned above. Using samples of executives (mean age 47), middle managers (40), young managers (32), MBA students (25), and undergraduate students (20), Webber found individuals superior in all comparisons except among the undergraduate students. Recalling that the task used was a *problem-solving* task consider the following conclusion drawn from this experiment in a popular text on organizational behavior:

> So younger people seem to be more effective in utilizing groups for *decision-making* than older and higher level managers. Time and age seem to weaken the ability to work jointly with others—or perhaps the younger students came through an educational system that placed greater emphasis on group activity. The reasons why might also include less sensitivity to status, more personal flexibility, greater willingness to express opinions, and more "team spirit."[31] (Italics added.)

Since occupation (professional problem-solvers and decision-makers in this case) was not separated from age, any generalizations such as "younger people" versus "older people" are unwarranted. Who knows but that 35–50 year-old labor union bargaining committee members might be superior in group problem-solving to the undergraduates? The authors' interpretation implicitly assumes that this finding also applies to institutional work groups who work together over time, since this necessary qualification is omitted. What the researchers may have measured were variations, by age, in the ability to work with relative strangers in a laboratory problem-solving exercise.

Considering the results of the numerous studies of which the above are examples, the answer to the question of whether groups or individuals are superior must be "It all depends." This is simply because only a few of the interactions of all the combinations of tasks and group constellations have been researched. The findings thus far, however, do suggest a few cautious conclusions: (1) A task will probably be better performed by a group if it permits the group to take advantage of the heterogeneity of its members. But the group will likely be somewhat slower. (2) If the task requires work specialization but does not require that the group work to the pace of its slowest member, a group will likely outperform an individual. (3) On the other hand, simple, straightforward tasks are likely to be better performed by individuals. (4) Tasks requiring sustained, coordinated effort will also usually be better performed by individuals. (5) And naturally, one does not expect a group to produce superior paintings, concertos, poems, or inventions.

Group Decisions and Risk

As decision theory became a popular research area in the early 1970's, a number of studies were undertaken to compare groups and individuals on the risk level of decisions. Most of such studies used a technique for measuring decision riskiness developed sometime earlier by N. Kogan and M. A. Wallach called "dilemmas-of-choice task." The subject is exposed to two courses of action for each possible real-life dilemma described. One course of action is more risky—and rewarding—than the other as judged by the test designers. The subject is asked what success probability he would require before opting for the more rewarding (and risky) of the two courses of action. Most studies using this technique found that group decisions generally were more risky than the average decisions of individual group members.[32]

The literature contains a number of attempts to explain this phenomenon. One observer, after having reviewed five literature reviews, summarized these explanations from the literature as follows:

1. Making a decision in a group allows for diffusion of responsibility in the event of a wrong decision.
2. Risky people are more influential in group discussions than conservative people, and so are more likely to bring others to their point of view.
3. Group discussion leads to deeper consideration of, and greater familiarization with, the possible pros and cons of a particular decision.

In turn, greater familiarization and consideration lead to higher levels of risk.

4. Risk taking is socially desirable in our culture, and socially desirable qualities are more likely to be expressed in a group rather than alone.

5. According to a modification of the fourth explanation, a moderate risk is valued in our culture on certain kinds of issues, while on other kinds of issues, moderate caution is valued.[33]

To these the authors added a sixth: The choice shift to more risky decisions by the group than its member risk average is possibly due to the effects of group pressure.

The vast majority of research concerned with verifying explanations of the shift by groups to more risky decisions has been concerned with the various effects related to group pressure (explanations 2 and 6 above). The findings of several promising-appearing studies have been subsequently disregarded due either to replication attempt failures or questionable methodology.[34] One approach using reordered data from earlier research suggests that the procedure of ignoring variations in risk by individuals on an issue-by-issue basis has led to faulty conclusions regarding shift choice causality.[35]

From these studies and common sense, it would be safe to conclude that (1) it is interesting to see the results of laboratory experiments in low involvement risk situations, but no generalizations from these findings are applicable to decisions found in management such as new market ventures, capital investment, and adventurous new policy; and (2) a number of factors likely affect the degree of riskiness of decisions of groups and individuals, among which should be included are (a) the issues themselves, (b) the cultural norms for risk-taking in general, (c) the personalities, education, experience, and knowledge of the issues and group consensus techniques, and (d) group composition.

Since laboratory experiments on group decisions relating to risk can rarely produce such phenomena as group cohesiveness found in "old" work groups, this dimension has not been researched except on a case study basis. One of the better known of these studies was done by Irving L. Janis, a psychologist who has studied persuasability in and out of groups for years. Janis analyzed a number of poor (and good) decisions of high risk, notably the Bay of Pigs invasion, the Vietnam escalation under President Johnson, and the ignoring of Pearl Harbor invasion warnings by Admiral Kimmel and his staff. He identified a set of characteristics of groups which tend to lead them to poorly evaluated risky decisions. He refers to this set of characteristics as symptoms of "groupthink." Although all of them do not directly influence the group to more risky decisions than would be made by its members individually, most do. They are all described briefly below with some of Janis' illustrations:[36]

1. "Invulnerability": Janis found that this characteristic of cohesive groups caused them to be over-optimistic. The tendency of such groups to ignore clear dangers contributed to their taking unwarranted risks even in the face of obvious dangers ahead. Janis cites the Kennedy group responsible for the Bay of Pigs disaster as having uncritically accepted the CIA plan and that U.S. involvement could be kept secret, in spite of the enormous risk of leakage which was obvious at various times during the planning sessions to individual group members. Both President Johnson's "Tuesday Cabinet" and Admiral Kimmel's group, according to Janis' analysis, appeared to take decisions from a psychic stance of invincibility.

2. "Rationale": Janis believes that these groups are able to maintain their invulnerability partly because they are quite able to construct elaborate rationalizations to minimize their need to respond to danger signals and possible negative criticism of their plans or decisions. This also minimizes the possibilities of reconsidering previous courses of action taken by the group. Janis points out that President Johnson's group repeatedly rationalized away the clear evidence that the escalation course of action was failing. And Kimmel's group was convinced that Japan's leaders would never dare such an assault since they would know full well that the U.S. would surely win in a war.

3. "Morality": Groupthink victims rarely seriously question the morality of their group or its decisions. This makes it possible for the group to ignore ethics and morals in their deliberations which might thwart their efforts. Cited as examples are minority members of President Kennedy's group who suppressed doubts about the morality of the Bay of Pigs involvement. Arthur Schlesinger, Jr., for example, expressed strong objections to the plan in a memo to Kennedy, but suppressed them in the group meetings.

4. "Stereotypes": The habit of using disparaging stereotypes of opponent groups and their leaders seems to facilitate groupthink members' strategy development. Earnest efforts at negotiating with such groups would be hopeless because they are so immoral and wicked, or else too dumb. As evidence of this symptom Janis points to the Kennedy group's belief that Castro's air force was ineffectual, that his army was too weak to halt a small Cuban exile brigade, and that he would not be able to put down possible internal uprisings. The Johnson group's stereotyped view of the world-wide "Communist Apparatus" prevented them from noting Vietnam's previous powerful nationalistic strivings against the Chinese.

5. "Pressure": Members of such groups are quick to use direct pressure on anyone inside or outside the group who might question the course of action under positive consideration by the group. The main purpose of

the pressure is to protect the perception of unanimity. Janis cites Kennedy's failure to call on Arthur Schlesinger, Jr., the one member known to have doubts about the plan, when he called on all others one by one for their vote; and he recounts President Johnson's greeting to Bill Moyers when Moyers arrived at a meeting as "Well, here comes Mr. Stop-the-bombing."

6. "Self-censorship": With or without direct pressure, members of such groups are given to remaining silent about their doubts concerning a course of deliberation under way to a decision by a majority. Their tendency is to find ways to doubt their doubts. Janis quotes Schlesinger as being very regretful for having kept so quiet during cabinet room discussions of the plan. He further cites Schlesinger's later admission that the "circumstances of the discussion" prevented him from doing more than raising a few timid questions.

7. "Unanimity": Members who remain silent in group discussions are considered to be in favor of the direction the group appears to be going. This is partly an overlap characteristic with the self-censorship characteristic above. The ultimate result is a sharing of the illusion of unanimity. Janis points out that later evidence indicates that Kennedy, Rusk and McNamara, all key members of the group, held quite different assumptions about the Bay of Pigs invasion plan.

8. "Mindguards": Members most susceptible to the groupthink syndrome often appoint themselves as protectors of the majority view. These self-appointments lead further to the protection of the group from contrary views which might threaten the group's high opinion of itself regarding past decisions. Janis reports that Robert F. Kennedy took Schlesinger aside at a party and advised him not to push his objections any further and that he should get behind the President now that the decision had been taken. Janis further notes Rusk's failure to transmit to the group the strong objections of his own chief of intelligence, Undersecretary of State Chester Bowles, and USIA Director Edward R. Murrow. Janis argues that their view plus Schlesinger's might have caused the group or the President to take a second look at the plan.

Janis claims that the products of these groupthink symptoms severely limit alternative considerations, prevent re-evaluation of preferred alternatives after new evidence is introduced, limit the use of outside experts, suppress efforts to reduce prohibitive costs of rejected alternatives, concentrate on supportive arguments, and ignore implementation obstacles.

At least one observer-practitioner of management believes Janis' groupthink syndrome is found in business management as well as the government and the military. In his article "Is this Group Necessary?" Robert Cushman,

President of Norton Company,[37] sees the corporate planning group likely to develop groupthink:

Sometimes, the dangerously enervating effects of "groupthink" can even assure that the best minds in the company will produce the worst possible results. The best brains tend to become reluctant to be too harsh on their colleague's judgments, avoid confrontation and seemingly agree through silence. . . .[38]

Conclusions

The collective research on work groups has resulted in few laws beyond those which can be considered common sense. Managers must note carefully the existence of informal groupings and attempt to ensure that their functioning is not having a detrimental effect on organizational performance. The manager who is unaware of the workings of such groups in his unit is not likely to manage as well as one who is able to analyze group functioning.

As we have seen, it does not follow automatically that happy, cohesive groups always perform well. Groups do not necessarily solve problems better nor do they make better decisions than do individuals. Although non-groups are not studied as such by behavioral scientists, we can suspect that they exist here and there in well-performing organizational units. Just as David Mechanic pointed out in his research which showed that work is not the central life interest for many people, social need fulfillment need not always be found at the workplace. It is quite plausible that workers who are identified as "isolates" or "non-members" by small group researchers, are members of need fulfilling groups outside the workplace.

The manager who must decide to use a group or individual to solve a problem or arrive at a decision is faced with a complex problem of behavior prediction. Because the variables involved in his prediction task are many and because they have not all been identified or related by research, no law or principle is available to him. To the findings in this chapter, the practitioner must add a great deal of common sense and knowledge of his subordinates and their work if he is to see that work group functioning is enhancing his unit's overall performance.

NOTES

1. Muzafer Sherif, "Group Formation" from David Sills, ed., *The International Encyclopedia of the Social Sciences*, (New York, N.Y.: Crowell and Macmillan, 1960), VI, 280.
2. Dorwin Cartwright, "Achieving Change in People: Some Applications of Group Dynamics Theory," *Human Relations*, IV, No. 4, as reproduced in Alvar O.

Elbing, ed., *Behavioral Decisions in Organizations*, (Glenview, Ill.: Scott, Foresman, 1970), p. 542.

3. *Ibid.*, p. 544.

4. Sherif, p. 517.

5. Herbert Thelen and Watson Dickerman, "The Growth of Groups," in *Educational Leadership*, (Association for Supervision and Curriculum Development, 1949), as reproduced in Elbing, ed., 535.

6. Cartwright, p. 546.

7. Tom Alexander, "The Social Engineers Retreat Under Fire," *Fortune Magazine*, October 1972, pp. 133–34. Reprinted by permission from Fortune Magazine; © 1972 Time, Inc.

8. Bernard Berelson and Gary A. Steiner, *Human Behavior: An Inventory of Scientific Findings*, (New York, N.Y.: Harcourt, Brace & World, 1964), pp. 327–60.

9. Robert A. Dahl, Mason Haire, and Paul F. Lazarsfeld, *Social Science Research on Business*, (New York, N.Y.: Columbia University Press, 1951), p. 101.

10. William Gomberg, "The Use of Psychology: A Trade Union Point of View," *Management Science*, July 1957, pp. 348–70.

11. Peter P. Gill and Warren Bennis, "Science and Management: Two Cultures," *Journal of Applied Behavioral Science*, IV, No. 1 (1968).

12. Sherif, pp. 276–83.

13. L. Urwick, ed., *The Goldon Book of Management*, (London, England: Newman Neame, 1956), pp. 132–34.

14. For biographical details and more on Mayo's philosophy, see chapter 3.

15. Elton Mayo, *The Human Problems of an Industrial Civilization*, (New York, New York: Macmillan Co., 1933), as republished, (New York, New York: The Viking Press, 1960), pp. 120–21.

16. "Conversation: An Interview with George C. Homans," *Organizational Dynamics*, IV, No. 2 (Autumn, 1975), p. 36.

17. George C. Homans, *The Human Group* (New York, N.Y.: Harcourt, Brace, 1950), pp. xv-xvi. Adapted from THE HUMAN GROUP by George C. Homans, copyright 1950 by Harcourt Brace Jovanovich, Inc.; renewed 1978 by George C. Homans. Reprinted by permission of Harcourt, Brace Jovanovich, Inc.

18. *Ibid.*, pp. 425–40.

19. "Conversation. . . ," *Organizational Dynamics*, p. 39.

20. Rensis Likert, *New Patterns of Management*, (New York, N.Y.: McGraw-Hill 1961), p. 114.

21. The independent variable is the factor affecting or causing changes in the dependent variable.

22. Stanley E. Seashore, "Group Cohesiveness in the Industrial Work Group: Summary and Conclusions," (Ann Arbor, Michigan: University of Michigan Press, 1954) as reproduced in Robert A. Sutermeister, ed., *People and Productivity*, (New York, N.Y.: McGraw-Hill, 1969), p. 352.

23. *Ibid.*, p. 356.

24. Chester Barnard, *The Functions of the Executive*, (Cambridge, Mass.: Harvard University Press, 1938).

25. William E. Reif, Robert M. Monczka, and John W. Newstrom, "Perceptions of the Formal and the Informal Organizations: Objective Measurement Through the Semantic Differential Technique," *Academy of Management Journal*, XVI, No. 3 (September, 1973), p. 391.

26. *Ibid.*, p. 401.

27. The origination of the Semantic Differential techniques with accompanying D statistic is credited to Charles E. Osgood. For a complete description of the method, see Charles E. Osgood, George J. Suci, and Percy H. Tannenbaum, *The Measurement of Meaning*, (Urbana, Ill.: University of Illinois Press, 1957).

28. M. E. Shaw, "A Comparison of Individuals and Small Groups in the Rational Solution of Complex Problems," *American Journal of Psychology*, XXXIV, pp. 491–504.

29. R. A. Webber, *Time and Management*, (New York, N.Y.: Van Nostrand, Reinhold, 1972), as reported in David R. Hampton, Charles E. Summer, and Ross A. Webber, *Organizational Behavior and the Practice of Management*, (Glenview, Illinois: Scott, Foresman, and Co., 1973), pp. 285–86.

30. J. Hall, "Decisions," *Psychology Today*, November, 1971, p. 551ff.

31. David Hampton, et al., p. 286.

32. D. G. Pruitt, "Choice Shifts in Group Discussion: An Introductory Review," *Journal of Personality and Social Psychology*, XX (1971), pp. 339–60.

33. Earl A. Cecil, Larry L. Cummings, and Jerome M. Chertkoff, "Group Composition and Choice Shift: Implications for Administration," *Academy of Management Journal*, Sept., 1973, pp. 413–14.

34. *Ibid.*, pp. 414–15, for a detailed discussion of these efforts.

35. A. Vinokur, "Cognitive and Affective Processes Influencing Risk Taking in Groups: An Expected Utility Approach," *Journal of Personality and Social Psychology*, XX (1971), pp. 472–86.

36. Irving L. Janis, "Groupthink," *Psychology Today*, November, 1971, pp. 75–86.

37. A multinational company with 1974 annual sales in excess of $550 million which has paid dividends every year since 1922.

38. Robert Cushman, "Is This Group Necessary?" *The MBA*, May, 1973, p. 36.

Chapter 11

Organization Theory

WHAT is the most dignified retreat a theorist can make when he discovers his subject is far more complicated than it was originally thought to be? For one, he can come up with a "contingency" theory, meaning that under certain conditions this might apply, under other conditions, that might apply, and so on. Another would be to apply a "systems" concept, where the primary focus is on the behavior of *some* of the system elements rather than the identification of all of them. Both of these represent the situation in modern organization theory. It is instructive, however, to trace the path of organization theory to this point. For our purpose here organization theory is about how organizations operate and how their parts fit together in achieving their objectives. It naturally draws from academic disciplines such as the behavioral sciences, economics, engineering, and history.

THE RISE, FALL, AND RISE OF BUREAUCRACY

Pre-Weberian Organization Theory

The first human groupings of any size were likely chieftaincies or kingdoms. The first organizational hierarchies, processes, and structures were probably concerned primarily with control and perpetuation of these units. One early model of such an organization can be found in the constitution of Chow (circa 1100 B.C.):

Eight regulations (the king) holds to govern the different departments of government. The first pertains to their organization so that the government of the state may be established. The second pertains to their functions so that the government . . . may be clarified. The third pertains to their relationships so that the government . . . may be cooperative. The fourth pertains to their procedure so that the government may be efficient. The fifth pertains to their formalities so that the government . . . may appear permanent. The sixth pertains to their control so that the government . . . may be complete. The seventh pertains to their punishments so that the government . . . may be corrected. The eighth pertains to their reckoning so that the government . . . may be audited.[1]

From this point forward until modern times, organization theory existed mainly in bureaucratic forms similar to the above.[2] Theoretical analyses of bureaucracy as organization theory began in the political arena. The early 19th century philosopher Hegel saw bureaucracy as necessary and valuable to both the state and its subjects. Karl Marx viewed bureaucracy as an instrument controlled by the power elite for the purpose of domination of the non-elite. His outline of some of the features of a bureaucracy included the following: strict hierarchy, enhancement of authority, incompetent administrators, lack of initiative and imagination, and fear of responsibility. This view of bureaucracy is similar to one of the standard modern dictionary definitions of the term. From *Webster's New Collegiate Dictionary* we find "a system of administration marked by officialism, red tape, and proliferation." Another meaning from the same source is "government characterized by specialization of function, adherence to fixed rules, and a hierarchy of authority."[3]

Henri Fayol's Contributions

The first sophisticated analyses of the bureaucratic model in modern times came from two sources almost at the same time. Henri Fayol, a brilliant French engineer-industrialist and professional manager, included in his papers on administration many observations on organizations. In his writings on the "principles of management" he discussed in considerable detail the following aspects of organization theory:[4]

1. Division of work and specialization (a reiteration of earlier statements beginning at least as early as Plato).
2. Authority must be commensurate with responsibility.
3. Discipline is necessary, but it is what leaders make it.
4. Unity of command. Employees should receive orders from only one superior.
5. Unity of direction. Fayol referred to "one head and one plan . . . for a group of activities having the same objective."
6. Subordination of individual interest to the general interest.
7. Adequate remuneration of personnel.
8. Centralization and decentralization and appropriate conditions for each.

9. Scalar Chain. Fayol discussed here the acceptable procedure of two foremen, say, in different command chains dealing directly with each other, provided their superiors agreed on this procedure rather than each going up the chain to the top and back down again to the other foreman. He analyzed the reasons governments seemed unable to operate in this manner, causing much inefficiency.

10. Order: material and social. His discussion of social order referred to "the right man in the right place."

11. Equity. Fayol emphasized that he did not mean justice, which is "putting into execution established conventions." He meant that "conventions cannot foresee everything (and that) they need to be interpreted or their inadequacy supplemented" suggesting that managements must be agents of social change where necessary.

12. Initiative. Fayol emphasized in his discussion of initiative that an organization performs better if the "freedom to propose and to execute" prevails at "all levels of the organization."

13. Fayol warned against unnecessary disturbance of the relationship between individuals or groups. He also pointed out that face-to-face communications are often superior in avoiding dissension to written communications which tend to crystallize differences and increase bitterness. (This principle is being rediscovered today in grievance handling: grievances initiated verbally have a better chance for resolution than written ones, everything else equal.)

Fayol ended his discussion of the above "principles" by warning against their blind application by the inexperienced:

Without principles one is in darkness and chaos; interest, experience and proportion are still very handicapped, even with the best principles. The principle is the lighthouse fixing the bearings but it can only serve those who already know the way into port.[5]

Sprinkled through his discussion of the "elements of management," Fayol covered two areas in organizational theory. He provided roles or general *job descriptions* for 9 groups of members of the "body corporate"—from shareholders to operatives. Included here is a description of the role of staff, as opposed to line, and organizational structures for large multi-function, multi-location organizations. Using a simple geometrical progression Fayol showed that with a *span of control* of 15 (fifteen operatives reporting to one foreman) there need not be excessive layers of management in large organizations. Noted here also is the concept that the nature of the organization— commercial, industrial, religious—will necessarily shape its internal organizational structure.

Fayol's treatment of his element "co-ordination" emphasized the importance of the availability of accurate and timely information throughout the organization. In discussing the element "control" Fayol warned against overcontrol, and applied the immediacy of reward (or punishment) principle (established much later in experimental psychology) by stating that "for control to be effective it must be done within reasonable time and be followed up by sanctions."

Fayol rarely appears in a prominent place in books on organization theory. Even when he does, his work is considered peripheral. One possible exception is to be found in William G. Scott and Terence R. Mitchell's book *Organization Theory*. They concede that "Fayol covers all the bureaucratic bases identified by Weber. These authors had essentially similar views of organization. Such similarities occurred because the authors either observed or participated in organizations having similar characteristics."[7] Their interpretation of the reasons for this similarity are possibly in error. Fayol's first two papers were presented in 1900 and 1908 and his famous work, *Administration industrielle et Generale* appeared in 1916. Weber's first publication on the subject did not appear until 1922.[8]

One reason given why Fayol tends to be ignored is that ". . . his views are not integrated into a model for organizational analysis. Rather, Fayol is mostly concerned with offering advice about the best way to organize an enterprise."[9]

Max Weber's Ideal Bureaucracy

Weber recognized Karl Marx' concept of a power conflict—the masses versus the elite—but took the straightforward view, as did Fayol, that bureaucracy was necessary for establishing a rational foundation for the administration of large-scale undertakings. It is important to note that until the industrial revolution produced the factory and the railroad, the major large-scale undertakings were the running of monarchies, their armies and their churches. It is unfortunate that so many social scientists seem to see bureaucracy's birth as (1) an historical bench mark beginning after the 12th century in Europe and (2) as a syndrome of social change.[10] The reasons for this blindness to the historical evidence that elaborate bureaucracies existed as early as 5000 years ago are probably to be found in the social scientist's value system. The beginning of bureaucracy for the typical social scientist could be when it was first attacked as an instrument of oppression.

It is interesting to note that while Scott and Mitchell insist that Weber produced a model, Rolf E. Rogers in his book *Organization Theory* claims that he did not. ". . . it was not Weber's intention to create a model, but rather to identify the administrative characteristics typical of a certain kind of organization."[11]

Whatever Weber produced in his Ideal Type of Bureaucracy—model or non-model—is summarized below in the form of a list of ideal characteristics of bureaucratic organizations.[12]

1. Limited areas of command and responsibility attached to each position within the organization.
2. Hierarchical authority structure with control and responsibility concentrated at the top of the hierarchy.
3. Central system of file collections summarizing the activities of the organization.
4. High degree of specialization based on expert training.
5. Activity demands the full working capacity of the member, that is, full-time staff and the job as a "career."
6. Definite outlined rules of procedure for rational coordination of activities.
7. Impersonality of relationships between the organizational members.
8. Recruitment of officials on the bases of ability and technical knowledge.
9. Distinct separation of private and public lives and positions of members.
10. Promotion by seniority.

Weber's insistence on objective selection of members of bureaucracies was seen to be a new and desirable dimension by some social scientists since personnel selection by class, caste, race, etc. was thought to be the selection method in all non-modern bureaucracies. David Wren, in his review of Weber's bureaucracy, saw it as an "attack on tradition and the use of political control in the economy, which was to be replaced by administration by knowledge and technical competence . . . Bureaucracy was conceived as a blueprint for efficiency which would emphasize rules rather than men, and competence rather than favoritism."[13] Such writers ignore the simple historical fact that as early as 120 B.C. Chinese Prime Minister Kung-Sun Hung established a system of examinations for selecting applicants for civil service posts.[14]

As can be seen from Fayol's and Weber's writings, there is little significant difference between their views. Both approaches contained the basic concepts of specialization, hierarchy, and qualification (of members). Two of these—specialization and hierarchy—came under attack by the new wave of behavioral scientists which followed the post-Hawthorne humanist "awakening."

The Fall of Bureaucracy

Two movements within academia maintained a sustained attack on the bureaucratic organizational model up until the late 1960's. One, the organizational behavior school, née the human relations movement, attacked bureaucracy on all fronts. Centralization of authority was undemocratic and their research revealed that democratic participation was what workers wanted;[15] specialization led to boredom, and assembly line workers' comments and questionnaire results proved it.[16] The extensive attention on the small informal group pointed up the conflict between the formal organization and the informal organization which was unaccounted for in the bureaucratic model. Except for Rensis Likert, most theorists saw no role for the foreman beyond the possibility that he could thwart group development or functioning. The social processes were studied with great zeal with only an occasional reference or research orientation to organizational performance in relation to its primary reason for being—to manufacture goods, provide specific services, etc. The organization during this period was seen to exist primarily to provide a habitat for important social behavior, and it was seen to have failed.

The other attack came from those who observed changes in tasks to be performed. Citing as examples space projects, R & D work, and other complex undertakings requiring highly qualified personnel, they saw bureaucracy as an unfit design for these kinds of activities.

In 1965, Warren Bennis, in what became a very popular article, summarized the views of both groups of attackers and predicted the "coming death of bureaucracy."[17] He appeared to use the self-referenced criteria approach and reading audience appeal in setting up his argument for bureaucracy's forthcoming demise. He explained that the flaws ought to be obvious to all since everyone has been bureaucracy's victim. He pointed out that bureaucracy's bosses were without technical competence and that bureaucracy's rules were arbitrary and crazy. This resulted, according to Bennis, in "cruel treatment" of employees and that this was based upon inhumanity and other irrational grounds. Bennis' catalogue of criticisms of bureaucracy contained numerous entries of which the following should suffice to characterize his harangue:

1. Does not allow for the development of mature personalities.[18]
2. Its members are victims of conformity and "groupthink."
3. Bureaucracy ignores the informal organization.
4. Control systems and authority systems are antique.
5. It changes its members into "dull, gray, organizational types."
6. Creativity and communication are frustrated.
7. It prevents the adoption of the use of new technologies.
8. Bureaucracy prevents the resolution of organizational conflicts.
9. Because of a climate of distrust and fear, employees are subutilized.
10. It contains no provisions for administrative legal processes.[19]

Bennis, admittedly "on thin empirical ice," set forth predictions of organizational life of the future through a description of conditions he believed would dictate organizational life 25 to 50 years ahead (from 1964).

He saw the future organizational environment as turbulent and characterized by interdependent large scale undertakings. His future population was highly educated, affluent, and had strong needs for autonomy and holding jobs requiring greater responsibility and discretion. He foresaw the tasks of the firm as more technical, complicated, and unprogrammed, and with greater diversity of standards of organizational effectiveness. The firm would be concerned with "meta-goals" or "supra-goals" which would determine goal structure. He saw bureaucracy as unable to adapt to the motivational needs of numerous professional, well-educated employees and predicted that the organizational structure would have to be "organic-adaptive": "People will be differentiated not vertically, according to rank and role, but flexibly and functionally according to skill and professional training."[20]

Bureaucracy's Resurrection

Some five years later, in 1969, Bennis presented a paper on these predictions entitled "A Funny Thing Happened on the Way to the Future" in which he "started criticizing and re-evaluating (the) original temporary-systems, democracy-is-inevitable hypotheses."[21] In 1974, he candidly admitted, to his credit, that he (and others) had overlooked several factors in predicting bureaucracy's demise. He pointed out that the anti-technological bias of youth and all the aspects of the counter-culture had been ignored. Second, the sizes and membership diversity of future organizations in which consensus decision-making would be impossible were ignored.

By 1970, criticisms of Bennis' prediction of bureaucracy's death were pock-marking the literature. Robert D. Miewald, in an article "The Greatly Exaggerated Death of Bureaucracy" asserted "that the forces of bureaucratization were never in finer fettle and, indeed, that the very same theorists who are singing the dirge have had much to do with the rejuvenation of bureaucracy."[22]

John N. Yanouzas presented a paper about the same time offering research results which suggested that many of the assumptions underlying the criticisms of traditional organization theory were faulty. *The assumptions which could not pass the test of empirical investigation, based upon research cited by Yanouzas, are as follows:* (1) authority cannot be decentralized in tall organizations' structures, (2) expertness of employees and a narrow span of control cannot go together, (3) the value systems of professionals of an orientation toward service and science cannot be reconciled with the bureaucratic values of economy, order, and efficiency, (4) the line-staff concept is inherently conflict-laden, and (5) the bureaucratic model cannot be adapted to meet the needs of advancing technology.[23] Yanouzas further cited comments by James E. Webb, former NASA administrator, which support the view that such organizations can operate successfully by adapting the bureaucratic form to the nature of the task. Using flexible systems of control, coupled with real-time feedback plus what Webb called "over-the-shoulder supervision," NASA was able to achieve its highly complex task of spacecraft launchings and orbiting.[24]

Modern Organization Theory

There is no clearly defined body of knowledge of organization theory. Just as some second generation proponents of operations research appeared to claim in the name of OR almost all management techniques which used numbers, some organization theorists have claimed every aspect of organizations as their turf. Most books on organization theory cite research on individual or group values, motivation or human behavior as organizational theory territory. The primary connection is that these individuals held their values, motivations, and behaved while "members" of organizations. It is one thing to use a few findings from psychology, sociology, anthropology, and political science in developing organization theory. It is quite another to carve out a large piece of each and rename it organization theory. Thus a group of theorists concerned with orchard layout would claim under its orchard organization theory umbrella the disciplines of botany, zoology, (including entomology), meteorology, and irrigation engineering.

There is no suggestion here that the nature or design of the organization does not affect such things as individual or group behavior. The suggestion here is that the organization is one of many factors affecting the behavior of the people in the organization. In many, if not most cases, the organization's impact on the behavior of its members is minor compared to other behavior origins. For this reason most of the material on motivation, groups, etc. has been grouped in other chapters in this book. For our purpose here, the term organization will be used to mean the *combining of resources* available for achieving objectives.

Organization theory then is theory about combining resources. Thus if four scaffold painters, two tall and two short, can be paired into two pairs of short-tall teams to produce better, that is organization. If the two tall must be paired because of irreconcilable personality differences (which will reduce team performance below that of tall-short teams), that, too, is organization. But these considerations are not the concern of this book since they are operational organization decisions based upon specific local information and *common sense*. If an OR study reveals that a national marketing corporation ought to relocate two of its warehouses to reduce stock-outs and inventory costs, that is organization, but not organization theory. This, too, is common sense using specific local information and sophisticated technique. If a new bauxite smelter is located near a navigable river *and* near a rural labor pool of vigorous hill people because they work better alone (50 feet apart) than do third generation urban workers, that, too, is organization. But it is more engineering, economics and applied anthropology. The only general principle to be drawn from these three examples is that management ought to do the smart thing and use common sense and an interdisciplinary approach to organizing its resources where this approach is appropriate.

THE BASICS OF ORGANIZATION THEORY

Bearing in mind the definition of organization as the combining of resources for goal attainment, the traditional organization theory subjects directly related to this endeavor are as follows:

1. Specialization, division of labor and departmentation.
2. Span of control.
3. Unity of command.
4. Line and staff relationships.
5. Organization and technology.

Each of these areas will be discussed below to the extent that useful generalizations or universal warnings are indicated.

Specialization, Division of Labor, and Departmentation

Many of the sub-functions which evolved out of the original basic three functions of production, sales and accounting are no longer directly connected organizationally. They are listed below under these headings, however, to indicate their parent functions. Some modern organizational units were born of the necessity of meeting new organizational needs and are not directly related to any of the three original basic subdivisions. Others are transfunctional service units serving a number of organizational functions. For example, computer units today serve all three. The organizational units chosen to be listed below are fairly typical of a medium-sized modern electronic division of a major international corporation whose $80 million annual sales are divided about equally between government (principally military) and civilian markets. This listing is simply to show historical function origins and evolutionary development.

Production (now sometimes called manufacturing)

Research and development. Today usually independent of the production and function.

Product engineering. Now usually elsewhere in the organization.
Production planning and scheduling. Sometimes independent.
Plant layout. Now usually elsewhere.
Tooling engineering. Usually elsewhere.
Quality control, including inspection. Almost always independent.
Product testing and statistical reliability. Almost always elsewhere.
Maintenance. Often elsewhere or independent.
Raw materials warehousing. Now usually elsewhere.
Labor-management relations. Now elsewhere as a staff function.
Fabrication. Remains.
Assembly. Remains.

The reader will note that at the plant or division level, the production or manufacturing "department" no longer contains many of the functions which were born out of this activity. Some of the sub-functions were moved for control purposes, i.e. inspection and testing. Others were moved or started up elsewhere because they were more closely related to skills and knowledge available in other units in the organization. As tool design, for example, beginning with simple jigs and fixtures, grew in complexity it was seen as an engineering sub-function. As the engineering unit grew, it often absorbed tool design. These changes took place over a period of a couple hundred years, although most of them have occured since 1900.

Accounting

Accounts receivable. Remains in the accounting unit.
Accounts payable. Remains.
Payroll. Remains, except that salary and wage administration is now elsewhere.
Cost accounting. Remains.
Finished goods inventory. Now usually elsewhere.
Electronic data processing. Sometimes elsewhere.
Finance. Sometimes separated; sometimes performed by a committee; sometimes performed principally at corporate headquarters.
Internal auditing. Remains.
Tax accounting. Remains.
General accounting. Remains.
Budgeting. Budgeting procedures control remains but the actual budgeting is usually done by departments or other budget centers.
Accounting systems. Remains.

Accounting has retained a greater proportion of the functions it has spawned than has production. Although the accounting unit still "accounts for" inventories on paper, they once supervised the warehouses. The first major uses of electronic data processing were in the accounting unit, although this technological service function is now used by most other functional units from engineering, marketing, production planning and control to personnel units. As late as the 1950's in off-the-road industries such as mining, some accounting departments still retained the salary and wage administration function. With the development of personnel administration units, this function was transferred out of accounting.

Sales (now usually called marketing, a broader term)

Advertising. Almost always a part of the marketing or sales units.
Market research. Remains.
Sales and sales management. Remains.
Contract administration (government contracts). Usually part of marketing but sometimes elsewhere.
Public relations. Often still part of marketing, but sometimes independent or attached elsewhere.
Sales forecasting, planning, budgeting. Usually part of marketing.

A hundred years ago, most firms were production oriented. Salesmen were hired to sell the items produced. As production became more routinized in some firms, they went through a period of focusing on intensive selling, selecting or developing channels or outlets. As they faced greater competition and as the communication media developed, many organizations needed to research their markets, develop products to fit them and advertise to remain competitive. In a few companies, the chief sales executive resisted these new functions. They were sometimes located outside his department as temporary adjustment, but later returned under the broader functional unit marketing.

The reader can quickly see that the above departmentation listing is not typical of a large mail order organization or retail company such as Sears Roebuck or Woolworth's. These are essentially trading companies in which the buying and selling are the key functions. Nor is the functional organization typical of a mining company which is likely to own and operate whole townships, a hospital and possibly a small railroad of its own. The essential point here is that the industry *activity* and its *environment* (copper ore bodies are rarely located downtown), its development and production technology, its markets, and its personnel requirements more or less *determine* much of its organization. In a mining company, the industrial relations department may operate a multimillion dollar housing unit. No such organizational unit would exist in the industrial relations department of an urban pharmaceutical factory.

The above discussion should make it readily evident that no straightforward principles of departmentation are possible. Add the need to adapt to local situational variables—local history, personnel strengths and weaknesses, politics, etc.—and the odds against the development of principles or laws governing departmentation are quite high.

Because the organizing activity is a major method companies must use to adapt to ever-changing markets, competition, technologies, and personnel, it is an on-going process. In the preface to their report on organizational changes in major corporations during the 1960's, the National Industrial Conference Board's report contains the following warning: "Organization charts are current only as of the date on the chart. And possibly, because of a time lag in preparing the organization chart, even that is questionable."[25]

Span of Control

The term span of control refers to the number of employees reporting to one superior. A few early organization researchers sought optimum spans, but for obvious reasons were unable to provide more than a few very general common sense guide-lines. A span of control "principle" was often carried among lists of organization principles in the texts of the 1950's and 1960's. It was simply a statement of the obvious: There is a limit to the number of subordinates that can be supervised by one superior.[26] It is not suggested here that the concept is useless—only that no valid principle or law has been derived for its use. The concept is important, however, in several ways. First, in large organizations, it is the major determinant of the number of levels in the hierarchy, given a certain number of employees. The more employees reporting to each supervisor, the fewer layers from bottom to top. Secondly, span of control is an important consideration in any reorganization encompassing new functions or shifting of managers. Optimum spans of control require consideration of a combination of at least six situational factors:

1. The work technology and its physical layout.
2. Individual differences in supervisory ability.
3. The nature of formal operational controls and their effectiveness which in turn determine the need for supervisory personal controls.
4. The nature and effectiveness of organizational communications and the subordinates' continuous need for information.
5. The abilities of subordinates in relation to their tasks.
6. The amount and quality of staff assistance provided to supervisors.

Below are a few operational units which illustrate the wide variations on many of the above dimensions:

1. A group of international airline pilots and their superior.
2. A short machine-paced assembly line crew and foreman.
3. A typist pool in an open room with supervisor.
4. The president and vice-presidents of a conglomerate corporation (one whose business interests are highly varied).

It becomes immediately obvious why the early considerable research found few if any relationships between spans of control and organizational performance variables. Organizational theorists of the omniscient variety described earlier in this chapter have attacked classic span of control presuppositions on the basis that "close supervision" (small span) is bad.[27] Consider the following:

A narrow span of control *permits* the manager to exercise very close control over his people. He *can* make most of their decisions for them. Those who favor rigid control tend to utilize a narrow span. On the other hand a wide span of supervision requires that the employees make more of their own decisions. They are given more freedom and latitude. A wide span of control encourages general supervision.[28] (Italics added)

Unfortunately, the notion that classical organization theory (bureaucratic) specifies small spans is nonsense. Further, there is no evidence that small spans necessarily result in reductions of "freedom and latitude" or "close control." Some of the smallest spans in industry are at the top—president and a half-dozen vice-presidents—and there is no evidence that these relationships are characterized by close control. Another area where small spans are often found is in R & D laboratories. In these situations the small spans often help to beget a teamwork approach rather than a boss-subordinate system. In setting up and knocking down the straw man—classical organization theory calls for small spans, these are oppressive, and therefore bad—the behavioral science oriented organization theorist appears more guided by his own value system than by science or reason.

Unity of Command

This "principle" is simply that each employee should receive orders from one superior only. It is unlikely that the principle had not been stated before 1900, but earlier discussions of it are not readily evident in the literature. The alternatives to this arrangement are not numerous: (1) an employee can have more than one boss, possibly through functional authority, or (2) an employee can work independently with no boss.

As mentioned earlier Frederick Taylor introduced the concept of functional foremen. In his approach, the individual workman would be supervised by a gang boss, a speed boss, a repair boss, an inspector, an order of work route clerk, a time and cost clerk, an instruction card clerk, and a disciplinarian. If we can equate "take instruction from" with "is supervised by," most of Taylor's system is alive and well today. Many factory workers work on an assembly line whose moving rate is often set by industrial engineers (speed bosses), and many are told by an inspector that an assembly or part must be re-worked to pass inspection (inspection boss). Production scheduling clerks pass out work orders, time/cost clerks require many workers to fill out job cards, and maintenance personnel often tell workers to shut down machines for repair or preventive maintenance. However, the modern worker, although he or she communicates with many other line and staff people, generally has only one *boss*.

Alternative (2) above—no boss—is fundamentally unacceptable to management and owners of companies for the simple reason that they insist that accountability not be diffused—that it have a focus. If the work performance of a functional unit is substandard, disciplining or firing everyone in the unit is not considered necessary or economic. This is not to suggest that a team approach cannot be used in a work unit if the work technology so lends itself. But teams have captains or leaders who accept or assume responsibility for varying degrees of the team's performance. An assumption underlying alternative (2) above, of course, is that the work can better be done without a boss or leader than with one. While it may be true, as Charles Perrow says, that ". . . we have learned that beyond a threshold level of adequacy it is extremely difficult to know what good leadership is," there is no evidence that leaderless units are better than "adequately" led groups. One company, Non-Linear Systems, Inc., in Southern California, experimented with what could be called leaderless assembly groups with somewhat disastrous results. (See Chapter 20 for more details of this bold experiment.)

The unity of command alternative—each employee has only one boss—is the system used in most military, government, and industrial organizational units today, if for no other reason than that employees insist on it. Any consultant or personnel employee who has not heard numerous complaints about the misery of being caught in the cross-fire of instructions from two or more sources of authority is not a very good listener. In many such cases this problem is really a line-staff conflict which appears to the worker as a violation of the unity of command principle. In other cases this problem may be caused by the worker's supervisor's superior. Not too infrequently in such circumstances, the circumvention will be partly welcomed by the worker since it offers access to higher authority levels. But sooner or later the usurpation of his supervisor's authority will contaminate all three relationships and undermine the performance of the three units involved.

One obvious task for any supervisor, given the above, is to supervise in such manner that his or her subordinates feel no particular need to go to the next level. This is not an easy task. The kinds of reasons for which a subordinate will go around the boss are several. Employees will seek information they think they need or have a right to; they will go after decisions which have not been forthcoming; or they want supplies, equipment, or authority to get something done which they feel ought to get done. Two other reasons exist, although they are quite rare: (1) a particular subordinate dislikes his or her boss intensely and hopes to get him or her into trouble or (2) a supervisor's superior has no respect for the unity of command principle and encourages circumvention from below. It does not follow, however, that this superior will tolerate any such circumvention when he or she is in the middle.

Line-Staff Relationships

The term staff as used in this section refers to organizational units (and their personnel) which perform auxiliary functions to help the line units which are engaged in the major activities of the business relating to its purposes or objectives. Staff people analyze, record, report, counsel, monitor, and recommend. They are the helpers. Some are professionals with special expertise and others are merely helping to relieve line management of detail such as time-keeping, etc.

Most treatments of the concepts of staff and line organizations in organization theory literature are focused either directly or indirectly on staff-line conflict. The headings for treatment of these two concepts are either staff-line relationships or staff-line conflict. If the former is used, the author very quickly gets around to discussing the latter. One will not find in the literature a single detailed discussion described as line-line or staff-staff conflict. The student is therefore incorrectly led to believe that only staff and line personnel conflict with each other.

It is not unnatural that the social science oriented organization theorists have found that staff personnel are the oppressed and the "good guys," and the line personnel the "bad guys." One such theorist, Robert T. Golembiewski has labeled the staff organization as the NII for Neutral and Inferior Instrument and the line as an ACI for Active and Competent Initiator.[29]

The effective use of staff has been with us long enough not to allow us to toss it aside simply because such personnel are involved in some conflict with the line organization. One management historian has noted that the use of staff is as old as war itself.[30] Its use in church and government-military combinations is fairly well accepted by inference as beginning with Sumer and early Egypt (5000–2400 B.C.) and in China through the legends about the Emperor Yao (around 2300 B.C.), and by direct documentation from at least 2000 B.C. forward from Egyptian instruction books and literature on the Shang Dynasty beginning with its founder T'and's rule in 1776 B.C. The use of staff is thought to have played an important role in the successes of Alexander the

Great (336–323 B.C.) and other military conquests down to the powerful Prussian Army in the 19th century.[31] The compulsory staff service—regulations *requiring* consultation—in the Catholic Church was noted by Mooney and Riley.[32] The wide use of staff in industry, however, likely flowered primarily as a result of increases in organizational size and complexity during the industrial revolution, although such staff specializations as accountancy and inventory recorders had no doubt existed since the Sumerian period.

Considerable attention was focused on the role of staff services in industry in writings of the 19th and early 20th centuries by such men as Fayol and Taylor. Fayol, in addition to advocating the need for staff as management assistants for information gathering, analyzing and reporting, liaison and control, added the need for staff in long range planning and methods research.[33] Taylor's functional foremen concept discussed earlier gave line authority to specialists connected with the operative's work. Perhaps Taylor's staff concepts as well as others' were simply extensions of the application of the ancient division of labor-specialization principle suggested at least as early as Plato's time and practiced in China about 400 years later in rice bowl making. Taylor's specializations "speed boss" and "disciplinarian," however, may have partly been influenced by his own personal difficulties with discipline and work rate supervision.

The staff concept today is very much akin to Fayol's description, although the continued increase in organizational size and technological explosion during the last 60 years produced a far greater variety of staff specialities since Fayol's observations were first published.

General Evolutionary Pattern of Staff Functions

Today, staff functions can be seen as falling into two broad general types: (1) extensions of traditional management functions; examples would be accounting, budgeting, purchasing, employment, salary and wage administration, production planning, and finance, and (2) those mainly based on new technologies, new bodies of knowledge or the need for new function launch primarily for the purpose of emphasis and attention-getting; examples would be operations research and electronic data processing.

From a functional evolution point of view, however, most staff areas have undergone similar changes. The most typical pattern for this evolution, especially for category (1) above, has been as follows:

STAGE I.   Top management was convinced that the extraction of the function from the line organization would make it more effective or that the completely new techniques or bodies of knowledge were best utilized through a staff function. The reasons for these extractions or additions for functional staff type (1) above were generally one or more of the following:

A.   Relief for line management from detail. Examples would be routine purchasing, time-keeping, and employee recordkeeping.

B.   To utilize knowledge or skills not present in the line organization. Examples would be employment aptitude testing and statistical quality control.

C.   The function to be added demanded considerable time and effort and a transfunctional viewpoint or organizational position which was not currently available in any one line unit. Examples would be long range planning and employee benefits and services.

The reasons for adding the completely new type of staff function (type 1 above) are various. Below are a few of them:

A.   The staff function was vital for remaining competitive. An example would be a company that received a government contract requiring for the first time that its multiple component products meet clearly specified reliabilities in probability values. It established a statistical reliability unit within its quality control department and manned it with newly hired experts.

B.   Top management was convinced that its overall performance in the future would improve through the acquisition of a new staff group. An example would be an operations research unit manned by newly hired experts.

C.   Top management believed that it was necessary to change all management behavior to incorporate new behavior based on new theory or research findings. Examples would be the establishment of a separate MBO (Management by Objectives) or OD (Organizational Development) staff unit to help focus attention on the new behavior and to show the extent to which top management supported this new behavior.

STAGE II.   The new staff function was established.

STAGE III.   Parts or all of the original staff functional activities were transferred back to the line organization. This took place for a variety of reasons. Below are a few of them:

A.   Management discovered that all or part of a particular staff function was better performed by the line organization. In the case of the employment function, for example, management began to reason that, where feasible, it was better for the supervisors to have a stake in the hire choice decision for their units, since they would be more likely to train and motivate their new hires and otherwise perform to protect their decisions rather than blame the employment function out of hand. The failure of psychological tests to deal accurately with the human chemistry component of the choice further suggested this partial transfer. Today, the *avant garde* companies tend to give their supervisors a greater role in selection than they did in the 1940's and 1950's although applicant screening is still performed by the employment function. Training for foremen in interviewing and the overall increased sophistication in first line supervision have helped to further this evolutionary direction.

B.   The placing of many line managers' performance on a profit or cost center basis called attention to their need for greater control over factors affecting profits or costs. Increasing lower line involvement in budgeting was one example of the transfer of a portion of a staff function which, at one time, was almost exclusively performed by staff personnel (accounting) for top management.

C.   Work simplification training for foremen represented a transfer of portions of methods engineering and tool design to the line organization. Foremen were trained and rewarded for doing the kind of work previously done only by methods engineers. Although not designed as a transfer of staff function, the really successful employee suggestion systems accomplished a great deal through the expansion and shifting of the traditional staff function work to employees themselves. New procedures, forms, methods, tools and equipment, formerly conceived and designed by staff departments, were provided by employees from all over the organization.

D.   In many non-union companies, much of what was once a salary and wage advisory function to top management had been transferred to lower line levels. At divisions of Sperry Rand, as early as 1955, low level line units were given an hourly increment total to distribute as merit raises. The role of the salary and wage unit was reduced to monitoring the decisions in terms of wage grade minima and maxima and reporting unusual patterns. This is not to suggest that such evolutionary patterns have developed evenly across all industry or even within a single industry. As late as 1965, for example, a branch manager in a small New England banking system had no knowledge of, and naturally no role in, deciding what merit raises would be given to his or her own subordinates.

STAGE IV.   The staff function is occasionally dissolved, but most often it becomes engaged in further developments of the usefulness of its function. Increased complexity in the functional area is usually more than enough to warrant the continuation of the staff function.

Examples of this stage in which the function is dissolved would be General Electric's corporate staff communications unit of the early 1950's and Union

Carbide's OD department at corporate level. Because G.E.'s Com-munications department was an integral part of the company's Boulwarism[34] approach to labor relations, it would naturally lose its support as this approach was used less and less to guide G.E.'s labor relations activities. Its usefulness in demonstrating to line managers waned, too, as the latter began to internalize the philosophy and adopt good communications techniques. In the case of Union Carbide's corporate level OD department, established in the late 1950's and dissolved in 1968, it was evidently considered to have served its purpose in helping further the goal of the integration of corporate units. (See Chapter 18 for a detailed discussion of this project.)

The more common consequence of Stage IV is that the staff unit becomes engaged in applying new approaches in its own functional field. Safety administration staffs, after transferring much responsibility to the line, for example, have been lately busily engaged in helping their organizations to adapt to new legislation, primarily the Occupational Safety and Health Act. A similar task, dealing with equal opportunity regulations, has absorbed a great deal of the time of personnel and industrial relations staff units.

It must be noted carefully that the evolutionary process is not necessarily synchronized, even within the same industry. Across industry, the evolutionary process stages vary widely. For example, in the mid-1950's, the U.S. mining industry, like many off-the-road heavy industries, was just awakening to the importance of good communications, with an occasional unconvinced division general manager. One such division manager of a major copper mining company, after withholding support for a program to improve communications, was able to point to General Electric's elimination of its director of communications position and their apparent de-emphasis of the importance of communications as a reason for continuing to withhold his support.

Equally a problem for those managers who look to industry leaders to take the initiative incorporating new bodies of knowledge through the establish-ment of new staff units are the companies which take short cuts. ARAMCO (Arabian American Oil Company), a very successful oil producer for years has never had an operations research *unit* or *department*. This fact is noted and interpreted by somewhat obsolete managers—even within some ARAMCO non-operating departments—as negation of the value of OR. Yet ARAMCO's use of OR techniques is probably one of the most effective. The OR function there has not been sanitized and encapsulated in a think-tank type of staff unit. Instead, OR techniques have been gradually integrated as managerial tools in operating departments as required for their functional needs.

Another hazard would face the manager who notes the abandonment of an

MBO program by an industry leader and fails to note that the by-products of having launched the MBO program, thereby forcing objectives determination, forcing the discovery of perceptual differences in objectives between superiors and subordinates, were likely well worth the launch effort in spite of the program "failure."

By far the most serious consequences of a failure to note the evolutionary characteristics of staff units is top management's crystallization of their activities by too precise policy statements regarding their functions. This can come about through tight job descriptions of staff department heads or too strict boundaries for staff department charters.

Careful recognition of this evolutionary characteristic of staff functions can open the door for more rapid adaptation to the inevitable. Computer units often initially installed as parts of accounting departments were, by this organizational placement alone, stunted in their early growth in these organizations. Failure to recognize early the usefulness of this tool for many functional departments led to this stunting. The electronic data processing staff unit, partly because it was one of the later of the technologically based staff operations, has traveled through the evolutionary states very rapidly. Only 20 years ago, systems analysts and programmers were in exotic, *avant garde* occupations. Five years ago, a number of universities in the U.S. had well used terminals, not just key punch machines, in dormitory basements. Today in Saudi Arabia, a relatively backward country, there are terminals in the corridors of classroom buildings in the University of Petroleum and Minerals. The electronic data processing personnel in these university units have made rapid adaptations to their new evolutionary stage roles. They are now in the process of training in their use and spreading soft-ware library materials, and many have abandoned the somewhat covetous nature of their earlier staff function posture. This has been aided partly by the hardware sales people who are well aware of the need to prevent the stalling of evolutionary changes if they are to sell more units. But likely more important was the early forced recognition of the transfunctional nature of the tool—for research in various disciplines, in addition to its uses for administration.

In summary, this discussion of staff function evolution has shown that parts or all of initial staff functions are directly transferred or otherwise gravitate (in some cases, back) toward the line organizations. This evolutionary process is natural and normally sensible and advantageous. Most worthwhile staff functions shed these portions of their functions intelligently by facilitating this process and by directing their attention toward the forefront of the states of their arts. If the states of their arts are growing adequately, if they keep up with them, and if they share their arts gracefully, they will remain healthy, useful, growing staff units.

Technology and Organization

Prior to the late 1950's the study of the role of technology was mostly confined to its relationship to individuals and small groups. The Joan Woodward, *et al.* study of 1958 of organizational variations among a variety of companies in southeastern England began a series of studies searching for organization-technology relationships.[35] The Woodward study is reported to have found certain organizational variations relating to whether the firm was a *unit or small batch* technology, *large batch or mass production* technology or *flow-process* technology. She found, for example, that the unit or small batch production technology had the shortest command chain from bottom to top. The longest chain was in the process firms and the large batch or mass production fell somewhere in between. Another of her findings was that the manager/employee ratio was lowest in unit technology, highest in process technology, and in between these two ratios in mass production technology. Further findings included a span of control relationship: the widest spans were in mass production (46 operatives per first-line supervisor), next widest in unit or small batch (22) and narrowest in process industries (14).

The Woodward study slowly sparked an interest in the study of various other aspects of technology as they might relate to organization. Although the Woodward study report noted that the above relationships held regardless of the size of the organization, later attempts to verify her group's findings have not been very successful.[36]

Subsequent studies, carefully controlling for company size, have confirmed only one of the Woodward findings—that the first level span of control is largest in large batch or mass production technologies. Other later findings showed what common sense would have revealed—that the proportion of employees in maintenance and inspection work is greatest in the large batch or mass technologies. Further common sense findings were that the proportion of production control employees was highest in unit production and lowest in process technology with this ratio in between these two for mass production technology.

Much theoretical work has been done attempting to develop more precise technological dimensions and definitions. Woodward did not specify how small her "small batches" were, for example. One effort to develop a classification scheme includes measurements of (work) operations technology, materials technology, and knowledge technology. Operations technology is defined as the equipping and sequencing of activities in the work-flow. Materials technology involves the characteristics of the material used in the work. Knowledge technology is simply the knowledge used in the work. One scheme further breaks down the operations technology into subconcepts as follows:

Equipment used in terms of its level of automation.
Operations sequencing in terms of workflow rigidity.
Specificity of assessment of operations performance.
Continuity of units of throughput—the Woodward dimensions of unit, mass or
process technologies.

There are more technology classification attempts in the literature, but since no significant findings have accompanied them, they are omitted here. After their review of research efforts of the relationship of technology to organization, including their own efforts to corroborate the Woodward findings, Hickson, *et al.* conclude the following:

> . . . the sweeping "technological imperative" hypothesis on organizational level technology and structure is not supported. Broadly speaking, operations technology did not relate to structure or did so only secondarily to other variables. This was true in successive tests on the sample of diverse organizations and on the subset of manufacturing organizations. On these results, a general "technology-causes-structure" hypothesis could only be sustained by the argument that technology also assumes size, and that to operate a given technology, an organization must be of the requisite size. This implies that size is a component of the technology concept . . . Comparison with the apparently contradictory findings by Woodward, linking technology with a wide variety of structural characteristics, leads to a final hypothesis which, concisely stated, is that variables of operations technology will be related only to those structural variables that are centered on the workflow. The smaller the organization, the wider the structural effects of technology; the larger the organization, the more such effects are confined to particular variables, and size and dependence and similar factors make the greater overall impact.[37]

One contingency, consistently ignored, is the possibility that a third factor—the characteristics of the work-force attracted to the technology—influences the organization structure or design. It would seem reasonable that organizations are not only psychosocio-technical systems, but that there is a great deal of self-selection in the psycho-socio elements. One does not see many orthodox Jews in mining engineering (as compared to electronics engineering, for example), but one does find many Anglo rural background Westerners and Southerners in this field. It would further seem reasonable that mining companies' organizations would reflect certain characteristics which would be consistent with the organization's members' values and personality structures. Control systems, for example, which look too closely over the shoulder of the kinds of people who go into mining engineering would almost surely fail for the simple reason that they would not be tolerated by the employees, regardless of the requirements thought necessary for the technology. It is not suggested here that these two forces—personality and employee values and apparent technology organizational requirements—can be easily teased apart for measurement. The suggestion here is simply that another factor which certainly has some effect on various aspects of organization structure and organizational processes—the organizational *members*—has been ignored by the organizational technology theorists.

In summary, the research thus far on the effect of technology on organization has been a surface-scratching activity. Elaborate descriptive models have been produced and a few crude relationships discovered. Analyses of the relationships have been simplistic. About all that is confirmed is that a few organization variables *centered in the production workplace* have been found related to—not necessarily caused by—the work technology.

Summary of the State of Organization Theory

Bureaucracy, with its key characteristics of specialization, hierarchy, and qualification (of members) is still the dominant organizational form in industry, government, church, and military. It has been altered here and there to adapt to modern enterprises, but its fundamental form remains relatively unchanged. It is not the dominant form in a few specialized endeavors, but most of these are temporary. Product development "teams" made up of a mixture of functional specialists are usually disbanded once the product is launched; and operations research groups without heads are small, rare, and relatively encapsulated. The vast majority of organizational members throughout the world have one boss who also has one boss, and have been determined minimally qualified for their present jobs according to some set of standards. Further, they are usually engaged in specialized work which has become more narrowly defined over the last few decades.

The only predictions that bureaucracy's demise was imminent came from social science oriented theorists, not organizational practitioners. Their predictions were based more on their anti-bureaucracy value systems than upon hard evidence. A combination of wish-fulfillment and selective perception stalled their research for at least two decades, thus leaving them even with practitioners until about 1970. Research on the role of technology was likely delayed due to the narrow social-only focus of most organization theorists. Beginning in the late 1950's interest in this dimension was sparked by a study later discovered to have produced equivocal findings. Theoretical and research effort in this area promises a limited yield since the effects of technology are being sought without accounting for the intervening human variable which is partly a function of the technology, but likely a direct cause of some organizational variations currently thought to be due solely to the technology or size of the firm.

NOTES

1. Kuo-Cheng Wu, *Ancient Chinese Political Theories*, (Shanghai, China: The Commercial Press, Ltd, 1928), pp. 40–41 as it appeared in Claude S. George, Jr., *The History of Management Thought*, (Englewood Cliffs, N.J.: Prentice-Hall, 1972), pp. 11–12.

2. One exception would be Kautilya's principal work, *Arthasastra*, written about 321 B.C., which describes in detail the proper administration of an empire. See: R. Shamasastru, trans., *Kautilya's Arthasastra*, (Mysore, India: Sri Raghuveer Printing Press, 1956).

3. The term as we know it was coined by French economist Gournay (1712–59) from the French word "bureau" and Greek words meaning "power" and "rule."

4. Henri Fayol, *General and Industrial Management*, trans. Constance Storrs (London, England: Pitman & Sons, 1949), pp. 19–41.

5. *Ibid.*, p. 42.

6. *Ibid.*, p. 108.

7. William G. Scott and Terence R. Mitchell, *Organization Theory: A Structural and Behavioral Analysis*, rev. ed., (Homewood, Illinois: Richard D. Irwin, 1972), p. 13.

8. All of Weber's publications save one (on law) were published posthumously. The publication which established his reputation as "the father of organization theory" was Wirtschaft und Gesellschaft (The Theory of Social and Economic Organization) published in 1922. It was first translated into English in 1947. Fayol's famous work (1916) was first published in English in Great Britain in 1929 and another translation was published in the U.S. in 1937.

9. Scott, p. 13.

10. Reinhard Bendix, "Bureaucracy," in David L. Sills, ed., *The International Encyclopedia of Social Sciences*, II, (New York, N.Y.: The Free Press, 1968), p. 206.

11. Rolf E. Rogers, *Organizational Theory*, (Boston, Mass.: Allyn and Bacon, 1975), p. 6.

12. As summarized in *Ibid.*, p. 5.

13. Daniel A. Wren, *The Evolution of Management Thought*, (New York, N.Y.: Ronald Press, 1972), p. 233.

14. George, p. 14. It should be noted here that political scientists seem to exhibit no such naivete. In his book *Man and his Government*, Carl Joachim Friedrich not only details the early Chinese approach to selection of civil servants based upon competitive examinations, but points to "similar developments (which) may be traced in the bureaucracies of India, Egypt and other large governmental organizations." For his detailed discussion see Carl Joachim Friedrich, *Man and His Government*, (New York, N.Y.: McGraw-Hill, 1963), pp. 468–70.

15. For examples, see John R. P. French, Jr., I.C. Ross, S. Kirby, J. R. Nelson, and P. Smyth, "Employee Participation in a Program of Industrial Change," *Personnel*, XXXV, No. 3 (November-December, 1958), pp. 16–29 and F. P.

Wickert, "Turnover and Employees' Feelings of Ego-Involvement in the Day-to-Day Operation of a Company," *Personnel Psychology*, IV (1951), pp. 185–97.

16. Charles R. Walker and Robert Guest, *The Man on the Assembly Line*, (Cambridge, Mass.: Harvard University Press, 1952).

17. Warren Bennis, "Beyond Bureaucracy," *Trans-action*, II (1965), pp. 31–35.

18. *Ibid.*, p. 32. (Entries 1–9 are found here)

19. *Ibid.*, p. 33.

20. *Ibid.*, p. 34.

21. "Conversation with Warren Bennis," *Organizational Dynamics*, Winter, 1974, p. 52.

22. Robert D. Miewald, "The Greatly Exaggerated Death of Bureaucracy," *California Management Review*, XIII, No. 2 (Winter, 1970), pp. 65–69.

23. John N. Yanouzas, "Crosscurrents of Organization Theory: Some Comments on Recent Research," *Proceedings of the 7th Annual Conference of the Eastern Academy of Management*, ed. M. William Frey (Amherst, Mass.: Eastern Academy of Management, April, 1970), pp. 38–50.

24. James E. Webb, *Space Age Management*, (New York, N.Y.: McGraw-Hill, 1969), p. 142, as reported in John N. Yanouzas, pp. 38–39.

25. Harold Steiglitz and C. David Wilderson, *Corporate Organization Structures*, (New York, N.Y.: National Industrial Conference Board, 1968), p. 3.

26. For a sample list of 12 such principles including a span-of-control principle, see "Corporate Organizational Structures," *Studies in Personnel Policy No. 183*, (New York, N.Y.: National Industrial Conference Board, 1961), pp. 3–8.

27. Scott, p. 49.

28. Dale S. Beach, *Personnel: The Management of People at Work*, 2nd ed., (New York, N.Y.: Macmillan, 1970), p. 173.

29. The NII label is to be found in Robert T. Golembiewski, "Toward the New Organization Theories: Some Notes on 'Staff' ", *Midwest Journal of Political Science*, Vol. V (1961), pp. 237–59, and the ACI is described in Philip J. Brown and Robert T. Golembiewski, "The Line-Staff Concept Revisited: An Empirical Study of Organization Images," *Academy of Management Journal*, XVII, No. 3 (September, 1974), p. 414.

30. George, p. 22.

31. *Ibid.*, pp. 3–22.

32. Wren, p. 22.

33. *Ibid.*, p. 224.

34. This approach required intensive communications with employees.

35. Joan Woodward, *Management and Technology*, (London, England: Her Majesty's Stationery Office, 1958).

36. For comprehensive reviews of these efforts, see the following: David J. Hickson, D. S. Pugh, and Diana C. Pheysey, "Operations Technology and Organization Structure: An Empirical Reappraisal," *Administrative Science Quarterly*, XIV, No. 3 (September, 1969), pp. 16–29 copyright © by Cornell University; and D. S. Pugh, "The Measurement of Organization Structures," *Organizational Dynamics*, (Spring, 1973), pp. 19–34.

37. Hickson, et al., p. 395.

Chapter 12

Leadership and Leadership Modelers

IN order to set the stage for a study of leadership and leadership models, the observations of a few who might wonder why the subject is studied at all should be noted. The first sentence in Eugene E. Jennings' 1960 book on leadership asserts that there can be no such study: "Ours is a society without leaders."[1]

When Harry Truman was asked what Eisenhower would learn if elected president, he said "He'll sit here, (tapping his desk) and he'll say, 'Do this! Do that!', and nothing will happen!"[2]

More recently Harlan Cleveland predicted that "What sets off the future executive from all previous generations is that he (and she) will be living in a society of which nobody can effectively be in charge."[3] Alexander Butterfield, after 18 months as director of the U.S. Federal Aviation Authority, explained why he was having difficulty dealing with the agency's slow response to the need to exercise closer control over flight safety: "We're very institutionalized . . . The cliques are fantastic. So much could be done but you need a free hand. I thought as an agency head you'd have clout. But you don't."[4]

The above views notwithstanding, leadership has remained one of the most popular research interests among behavioral scientists for some time. The focus of this research shifts from time to time, but the findings continue to fall short of producing laws or principles of leadership. At various times in the history of the study of leadership, observers and researchers have felt that they were getting close to some truths, only to see their results refuted by later replications or applications of their models. For this reason, a brief history of the study of leadership will be presented before discussing the current state of this subject.

THE HISTORY OF LEADERSHIP STUDY

The conceptual center of leadership study has moved, in spite of oscillations and overlaps, from the study of great power leaders to the study of leadership personality and other traits to the study of leadership-followership systems in their organizational contexts.

The Study of Great Power Leaders

The earliest "studies" of leadership were in the form of advice to would-be princes and conquerers. In addition to the advice on handling grievances (see Chapter 3) the early Egyptians describe an ideal leader through a variety of suggestions for appropriate leader behavior. These would appear to conform to the more recent trait theories of leadership. For example, they called for the leader to be impartial, honest, and a good listener. About a thousand years later (circa 1100 B.C.), the constitution of Chow contained the essence of much of Machiavelli's advice in the form of policy. It described the powers of the prime minister as follows:

> Eight methods he holds to govern the country. The first is ritual and worship, so as to control its spirit. The second is statutes and regulations, so as to control its great officers. The third is removal and appointment, so as to control its petty officers. The fourth is emolument and rank, so as to control its resources. The sixth is ceremonies and customs, so as to control its strength. The seventh is removal that controls their failings. The eighth is farming and other employments, so as to control its multitude.[5]

In about 321 B.C., Kautilya's major work *Arthasastra* contained one of the earliest recorded list of leader traits in the form of man-specifications for a ministerial officer:

> Native born of high family, influential, well trained in arts, possessed of foresight, wise, of strong memory, bold, eloquent, skillful, intelligent, possessed of enthusiasm, dignity, and endurance, pure in character, affable, firm in loyal devotion, endowed with excellent conduct, strength, health, and free from such qualities as excite hatred and enmity. . . .[6]

Machiavelli, the most famous of the early leader analysts, provided a set of strategies for taking over and governing a city state in Renaissance Italy. Because military power came from political power, Machiavelli candidly described the power acquisition methods which were successful at this time. These included treachery, deception, and fraud. His advice was quite different from the traditional literature on advice to leaders. His observations led him to believe that a leader had to be able to be cruel on occasion, instill fear, and manipulate those around himself by whatever means was necessary. As parts of the rationales for his strategies Machiavelli pointed up the consent of the governed as an important power source, as well as the need for cohesiveness in his staff circle. Machiavelli's prince's leader style—understand people in order to dominate them—was to be seen in many subsequent leaders, from Elizabeth and Cromwell to Louis XIV, to Mussolini and Hitler.

Through a combination of force and manipulation, leaders of all kinds of institutions have been successful. Jennings gives as example of those whose styles went more to manipulation than force, Julius Caesar, Jay Gould and Jim Fisk, Henry Ford, and Franklin Roosevelt.[7]

The Study of Leadership Traits

As the fledgling science of psychology began its long time concern with the measurement of individual differences, the possible differences between leaders and followers were bound to attract its attention. For the first 50 years of the twentieth century almost every trait one can name was examined as possibly separating leaders from followers. The hope was that if a series of traits or trait strengths could be identified as unique to leadership, prediction of future leaders would be possible.

Since intelligence was one of the earliest mental characteristics for which fairly reliable measuring instruments had been devised, much early research sought to correlate it with leadership. A review of the literature by Ralph Stogdill in 1948 revealed support for the view that leadership and intelligence were probably correlated but that the relationship was not strong.[8] Further work on the subject resulted in the finding that too great a gap between leader intelligence and follower intelligence militated against leadership.[9] The reader is warned, however, that none of these studies was concerned with intellectual leadership of the kind provided by such people as Albert Einstein or William James, since the vast majority of the hundreds of studies of leadership were concerned with small face-to-face groups.

In addition to intelligence (and height and weight), various other traits have been found at one time or another associated with leadership. One summary of the studies reported in the literature attempting to relate leadership with various traits listed seventy-nine relationships. Fifty-one of these traits were found related in only single studies. Other early reviews of the literature have resulted in similar results.[10]

In summarizing his discussion on the many efforts to relate leadership with various traits, Jennings notes that while the waters were finally muddied by disagreements between literature reviewers themselves, Stodgill's review offered the best summary of the trait research:

> (Stodgill's) fruitful attempt to classify these studies under a few general headings resulted in the following traits being associated with leadership: capacity (intelligence,

alertness, verbal facility, originality, judgment), achievement (scholarship, knowledge, athletic accomplishments), responsibility (dependability, initiative, persistence, aggressiveness, self-confidence, desire to excel), participation (activity, social ability, cooperation, adaptability, humor), and status (socio-economic position, popularity).

Jennings offered several reasons for trait theory research failing to turn up more relationships. First, he pointed out that most such studies used school population samples. Because of this these studies would likely be biased more in favor of intellectual and social traits and against power traits. Second, he pointed out that the quality of the research studies varied widely. Third, the studies were based upon the researchers' prevailing concepts of leaders, thereby introducing a possible bias in the research designs. His final criticism, closely related to this flaw, is simply that "undesirable" (Machiavellian) traits were never investigated as possibly related to leadership.[11]

The Study of Leader Styles

From about 1940 onward the main approach in studying leadership focused on leadership styles. A "classic" experiment, as it is referred to in psychology textbooks, set the stage for a decade or more of comparing democratic, *laissez faire*, and autocratic leader styles. The Lewin, Lippitt, and White experiment[12] was a study of boys clubs with leaders of each of the above styles rotated every six weeks. The fact that the leaders changed their styles for the experiment was both an advantage—it was considered by the researchers to rule out the effects of leader personality—and a flaw, since there is no guarantee that these leaders were good enough actors to play all three roles accurately. At any rate, the results generally indicated the superiority of the democratic style on a variety of club member behavior dimensions.

By the mid-1950's, other research began to emerge which indicated that these three variables oversimplified the phenomenon,[13] and that the task itself as well as the leader-follower specifications played roles in determining effective leader styles. Some observers interpret the leader style research era as merely an extension of trait clusters (styles). Others probably saw the apparent superiority of the democratic leader style as confirming the American heritage.

Soon researchers began to find that considerate, employee-centered leaders had more satisfied followers.[14] It should be noted here that much of the research work on leadership effectiveness, especially until the late 1960's, ignored worker productivity. Instead, various measures of follower satisfaction and social relationships were evidently considered adequate criteria for validating leader styles. It is not clear whether this was due to the (faulty) assumption of a high general correlation between worker satisfaction and productivity or the self-referenced criteria born of the personality needs of the researchers themselves.

The other major thrust in the leader style research era resulted from the findings in another "classic" piece of research—the "Ohio State Studies." Using factor analysis, Stogdill's associates isolated two factors—*consideration* (showing concern for subordinates) and *initiating structure* (assigning and monitoring work performance) as accounting for the majority of leader behavior.[15]

As these two factors—consideration and initiating structure—were studied under a variety of leader-follower environments, other moderating variables began to contaminate the rather neat popular conclusion that consideration was "the way to go."

CONTEMPORARY LEADERSHIP THEORY

The Situationalist or Contingency Model

The contingency model pioneer, Fred E. Fiedler, began the extensive use in leadership research of a now famous questionnaire (infamous, if one looks at its track record for reliability) known as the Least Preferred Coworker (LPC). This questionnaire asks the respondent to think of the one person with whom he had the most difficulty in getting a job done, then rate that person on eight-point bipolar adjective scales. Some examples on this scale are "pleasant—unpleasant," "friendly—unfriendly," and "open—guarded."[16] The reader may rightly wonder what an LPC score means since the nature of the measure itself does not suggest meaningful interpretations. Chemers and Rice, in their account of contingency theory development offer disturbing comments on the subject:

Although the LPC scale has played a central role in a large body of empirical research, it has been a difficult measure to interpret. The interpretation of the LPC has varied over the years and is at times referred to as an index of task versus interpersonal orientation, motivational priorities, or cognitive complexity. The most enduring and widely used interpretation of LPC is as a measure of the relative task versus interpersonal orientation of a group leader.

A low LPC score indicates that the rater has evaluated his least preferred coworker negatively on most items of the LPC scale. Thus, the low LPC rater is effectively saying that "If I cannot work with you, you are a bad or unworthy person." It *appears* that the low LPC person is using task accomplishment as a key parameter in the evaluation of other people. Such an attitude *is thought* to reflect a strong orientation toward successful task accomplishment.

On the other hand, a high LPC score *indicates* that the rater has evaluated his least preferred co-worker positively on many of the items on the LPC scale. Thus, the high LPC rater is effectively saying "Although I cannot work with you, you are a good person in many respects." Such an attitude *would seem* to reflect a considerably lower emphasis on task accomplishment for the high LPC person. He *would appear*, then to be orienting toward other aspects of group activity, most probably interpersonal relationships.[17] (Italics added)

Fiedler, using the LPC as representing measures of task orientation (low score) and relations orientation (high score), developed a model which related LPC scores and three variables of situational favorableness for the leader. He reasoned that leader-follower relationships, degree of task structure, and leader power to reward or punish should be used in a 4:2:1 ratio, respectively. (The literature contains no explicit experimentally supported rationale for this ratio.) The verbal form of the hypothetical model was that leadership will be easier to implement when the leader is accepted, when his task is clear, specified, and unambiguous, and when the leader has the power to entice or coerce his followers into action. In testing the model, mostly by the restructuring of old data, Fiedler dichotomized these variables into the following:

leader-member relations: good—moderately poor
task structure: high—low
leader position power: strong—weak[18]

The model, therefore, assumes eight leader situations, four under good leader relations and four under poor leader-member relations. Numerous studies have been undertaken to validate the model, both by Fiedler and his associates, and by others. The data available from Fiedler's own inventory[19] of both field and laboratory experiments on the model are quite discouraging. For example, taking the field and laboratory experiments findings together, the range of the correlations between LPC scores and work group performance for several of the leader situations strongly suggests lack of validity. For the situation of good leader-member relations, high task structure and weak position power, the range of correlations was from -.46 to +.50. The range for the correlations for the leader situation in which leader-member relations were good, task structure low and position power weak was -.80 to +.60. The range for the leader situation of poor relations, low task structure, and strong position power was from -.30 to +.62.

His summary table reveals only two leader situations out of the eight in which all the correlations are in the predicted direction of his model: (1) Leader-member relations: good, high task structure, and strong position power, with a correlation range of from -.51 to -.77; and (2) Leader-member relations poor, high task structure, and strong position power with a correlation range of from +.03 to +.21. *However, none of the correlations between LPC scores and group performance was statistically significant.* Supporters of the model claim for its validity the fact that of the 45 correlations for all leader situations, 34 were in the predicted direction, even though only two of these 54 correlations were statistically significant. The faintest hint of support for the model lies only in the fact the 34 out of 45 *ratio* is statistically significant at the 1% level.

In addition to using nonsignificant directional results as support for the model, Fiedler had been criticized for including studies with wide variations in the specification of situational favorableness.[20]

The literature on the model reached the criticism-rebuttal level which almost equals literature from the earlier controversy in psychology over the effects of heredity vs. environment on I.Q. Subsequent research on the Fiedler model has tended to lead to modifications on the contingency concept to include more situational variables and different research methodologies. For example, Fiedler and others have studied an additional variable, the situational variable, leader training and experience, but the results have been equivocal.[21] The most devastating evidence against almost all the research on Fiedler's model and variations of it, however, came about many years after most of the research was performed. Since the model validity as researched had been almost invariably dependent upon the LPC questionnaire as the measure of leader orientation—task vs. relations—its reliability as a measuring instrument should have been thoroughly proven long ago. Chemers and Rice would seem to have believed so since their thorough examination of the model included the following: "The very fact that LPC is a reliable predictor of leadership effectiveness demands that we not discard, but make renewed efforts to understand and possibly improve upon the measure."[22] Steven Kerr, a discussant at the symposium at which Chemers and Rice presented their paper, pointed out, however, that not only had Fiedler himself warned that the LPC stability was considerably dependent upon intervening experience, but that Stinson and Tracy had found LPC scores to be fairly unstable.[23] Their test-retest correlations on two samples of students eight weeks apart were .23 and .49, suggesting common variances of only 5% and 24%. Their test-retest results of only three weeks apart were .73 and .80, suggesting that the LPC measures some fairly fleeting variable.[24] Thus the study of the most researched leadership model can be likened to the study of the correlations between heights and weights of many samples of people, using a rubber ruler for measuring the heights.

Path Goal Leadership Theory

Research has been undertaken to study the leader's role in enhancing the psychological states of subordinates as this role is moderated by situational variables. Although path-goal research has been concentrated more on the effects of task characteristics than on other variables, the results appear inconclusive. In a study using industrial workers, some support was found for the hypothesis that the simpler the task, the more effective the leader in terms of subordinate satisfaction, and expectancies that effort would lead to performance resulting in rewards. In the same study, some support was evidenced that the simpler the task, the weaker the relationship between supportive leader behavior and satisfaction, expectancies, and satisfaction with co-workers.[25]

John Stinson and Thomas Johnson,[26] using non-industrial samples, found two task characteristics related to leader initiating structure and to subordinate satisfaction, but *in the opposite direction* from the House and Dessler finding above. The contradictions were interpreted by Stinson and Johnson as functions of the differences in sample characteristics. They reasoned that their better educated sample subjects (government and military) held greater autonomy needs and, therefore, would respond less to "path-goal" help from their leaders. Their finding would seem to suggest that leader power to influence may be a function of subordinate expertise and possibly affluence. Their suggested alternations in path-goal theory included the possibility that under conditions of high task repetitiveness and structure where path-goal relationships may be more obvious, leader initiating structure would be seen by subordinates as unnecessary close control and its resentment result in lower satisfaction levels. Recall that Fiedler's original model included the notion that the *more* structured the task, the better the leader's situational favorableness. None of the contingency models considers it relevant *who* structured the task, however. It would seem reasonable that if its structuring were outside the leader's sphere of influence, i.e. designed by an industrial engineering staff group, his ability to influence his subordinates would be less than if he controlled its structuring.

The Expanding List of Situational Variables

R. N. Osborn and J. G. Hunt, noting the weak validation support for contingency theory, have responded with new theory.[27] They have suggested a separation of situational variables affecting leadership into those altering leader behavior and those altering leader impact. They hope to provide a deeper understanding of the influence of certain situational variables such as the organization, its size, technology, and formal structure. They found, in their study of 60 chapters of a business fraternity, that environmental complexity, as measured by chapter president's perceptions, was related to initiating structure and consideration. Although the interactions of leader behavior and environmental complexity were unrelated to performance or satisfaction and chapter size irrelevant for all measures, the researchers were encouraged. They note that a beginning is needed to point up the influence of what they refer to as "macro" variables affecting the leader-follower system.

The Merging of Authority-Power Theory and Leadership Theory

Except for Machiavelli's often overlooked references to power coming from the consent of the masses, the command concept generally prevailed until the beginning of the twentieth century. This view clearly separated the acts of deciding and commanding (leader) from executing (subordinate). Chester Barnard's refutation of the downward power flow theory[28] summed up much of the thinking surrounding the Hawthorne and other studies of work groups during the period from 1920–1950. A recent review of power-flow theory points out several changes which have taken place in this theoretical field since Barnard: (1) the subject-matter has been discovered to be more complex than traditionalists and Barnard had thought, (2) researchers have found it increasingly difficult to devise operational definitions for important concepts and (3) scholars have pretty much abandoned authority-flow theory and turned to power flow analysis.[29]

David Mechanic's definitive article on power at lower levels called attention to several relevant power sources not usually considered by traditional power or leadership theorists. He described the following overlooked power sources: (1) Expertise power and power accruing to difficult-to-replace personnel. (2) Collective power due to informal, formal, or coalitional groupings. (3) Power assumed by subordinates where superiors leave a vacuum. (4) Power derived from subordinate proximity to the social and physical center of the organization.

Unfortunately, his analysis had little immediate impact on power theorists or leadership theorists. Power and Authority theorists have remained focused on an oversimplified leader-follower sub-system. They have produced a variety of rationales for compliance and non-compliance on the part of the subordinate, but have ignored most other power sources affecting this sub-system.

Frank Heller's research offered the first truly fresh approach to the study of power sharing and leadership.[30] Using an influence-power continuum scale, he sampled 260 American executives' decision-making styles. One of his findings was that about half their decisions were taken *without* any subordinate participation or influence. Heller rightly points out that traditional research on power sharing was focused on *group* behavior, and his finding suggests that the frequently used non-participation styles are best understood in terms of *non-group* behavior. His findings that the greater the subordinates' experience, the less likely their superiors will use centralized decision styles supports Mechanic's concept of subordinate expertise power as likely to affect their superior's behavior. Another of his findings was that the greater the skill difference between the senior manager and his subordinates, the more likely the former will use a centralized decision style.

The Manager-Subordinate Systems Approach

Forty years ago if a manager were asked what he would do under a given set of circumstances, he would probably have answered, "It all depends."

Researchers at the forefront of the state of the art in leadership research now appear to be willing to interpret his answer as other than flippant. The number of variables believed to influence leader-follower systems have been growing by leaps and bounds. One of the more elaborate models attempting to incorporate many of these variables in a systems approach contains as system inputs five organizational variables, three work group variables, five task variables, and four subordinate personality variables. In addition to these, the model contains four "within-system relations" organizational variables and four "within system relations" work group variables. Also included as "within systems" variables are five assessments of managerial styles. The three system outputs are measured by performance effectiveness, worker job satisfaction and supervisor satisfaction.[31]

Although such models appear to be the only recourse to the study of the extremely complex phenomenon, leadership, the number of variables considered relevant have over-run researchers' ability to measure them and relate them. When one considers the additional elements suggested by the discussants at the symposium at which Bass and Valenzi presented their model, the task becomes mind-boggling. Erich P. Prien, for example, suggested that their model ignored the complexities of the *functions* that supervisors or managers perform. He also reiterated the often heard criticism of the research methodology of accepting as a measure of the effectiveness of a system the judgments of subjects within the system. Another discussant, Robert J. House, believed the model overlooked the importance of the impact of a variety of technological characteristics on the leadership style. And Koeman's remarks indicated his concern that the "separate kinds of mechanisms by which technology can operate have been neglected . . ."[32]

Charismatic Leadership

For decades charisma has not been a fit leadership subject for study. This may have been because social scientists simply were not interested in charisma much as the economic development modelers were not interested in religion and bribery so omitted them from their models. Still it may have been because a list of charismatic leaders would usually have to include such people as Adolf Hitler and Benito Mussolini. Another possible reason could have been that the basic notion of charismatic leadership seemed inconsistent with ideologies of meritocracy or egalitarianism. Regardless of the reason or reasons, except for an occasional theoretical discussion in the literature, the subject has been almost ignored. And none of the theories discussed has been the subject of empirical studies.

The idea that charisma ought to be studied was introduced by Robert J. House at the 1976 Leadership Symposium held at Southern Illinois

University. Although he called his paper "A 1976 Theory of Charismatic Leadership,"[33] it was dominated by a discussion of the characteristics and behavior of charismatic leaders and of some social determinants of charismatic leadership. From these discussions, House extracted seven propositions which supposedly make up his 1976 theory of charismatic leadership. To verify these propositions might be of interest to researchers just beginning to study the subject, but such verifications would be of no practical use to managers. For example, his proposition number 6 is that "Leaders who have charismatic effects are more likely to engage in behaviors that arouse motives relevant to the accomplishment of the mission than are leaders who do not have charismatic effects."[34] In testing this proposition, a manager who regularly used memoranda containing threats to fire employees who desperately needed their jobs could be found to have more charisma than one who did not.

House's summary of the 1976 theory represents a fairly accurate common definition of a charismatic leader. Such leaders are different from others because they are dominant, self-confident, have strong needs to influence others, and appear convinced of the moral righteousness of their beliefs. They articulate goals, set examples by their own behavior, engage in personal image-building and motive-arousal behaviors, and appear to have great confidence and high expectations for their followers. As House points out, testing the propositions would require that new data-gathering instruments would have to be developed. Should this come to pass, managers might find use for some of them in prediction of the behaviors of candidates for jobs in which charisma had been proven to enhance performance of the organizational unit. Unfortunately, in the two years since House stated the propositions, I have been unable to locate any research attempting to test any of them.

SUMMARY AND CONCLUSIONS

The student of managerial leadership can only note carefully the rich complexity of the phenomenon leadership and attempt to build his or her own flexible model element by element while mindful of the many variables identified as possibly affecting leadership and work unit performance. The research data on leadership contain a number of interesting piece-meal correlations between model elements but almost all are low and not statistically significant. And the narrow samplings in most of these studies calls for extremely limited generalizations where statistically significant relationships of adequate strengths have been found.

Managers who have resisted attempts to "style" their behavior toward some ideal can note that they are probably much like the vast majority of managers.

In surveying the opinions of 124 subordinates who were asked to characterize their managers' behaviors, Bass and Valenzi found that 117 out of 124 of them indicated that their bosses exhibited a multi-styled approach since they characterized their bosses' behaviors as using three or more different styles, depending upon the situation.[35]

Practicing managers who have read this chapter can take heart that when they resist the question of what they would do under certain circumstances by saying "It all depends," they aren't far off the mark. Comprehensive models such as the one supplied by Bass and Valenzi can possibly help them organize and refine their contingency thinking which is likely based mostly upon their multi-dimensional scattergram of experiences, some of which may have been forgotten or repressed.

Further discussion of leadership is to be found in Chapter 13 where the management of change is considered in detail. Leader power in particular, as it influences the leader's ability to manage change, will receive extensive coverage there.

NOTES

1. Eugene E. Jennings, *An Anatomy of Leadership* (New York, N.Y.: McGraw-Hill, 1960), p. xv.
2. Richard E. Neustadt, *Presidential Power* (New York, N.Y.: Wiley, 1964), p. 22.
3. Harlan Cleveland, "Systems, Purposes, and Watergate," *Operations Research* (September-October, 1973), p. 1021.
4. "A Need to Get 'Tough as Hell,' " *Time* (December 23, 1974, p. 31–32.
5. Claude S. George, Jr., *The History of Management Thought* (Englewood Cliffs, New Jersey, 1972), p. 12.
6. *Ibid.*, p. 19.
7. Jennings, *An Anatomy of Leadership*, p. 52–69.
8. Ralph M. Stogdill, "Personal Factors Associated with Leadership," *Journal of General Psychology*, XXV, (1948) p. 40.
9. Cecil A. Gibb, "Leadership," in Gardner Lindzey, ed. *Handbook of Social Psychology* (Reading, Mass.: Addison-Wesley, 1954), II, 886.
10. Jennings, *An Anatomy of Leadership*, p. 161–62.
11. Ibid., p. 164–65. More recently attempts have been made to measure Machiavellian dimensions of modern leaders, but with little success.
12. K. Lewin, R. Lippitt, and R. K. White, "Patterns of Aggressive Behavior in Experimentally Created Social Climates," *Journal of Social Psychology*, X, (1939), 271–79.
13. For an example see W. Haythorn, A. Couch, D. Haefner, P. Langhan, and L. Carter, "The Effects of Varying Combinations of Authoritarian and Equalitarian Leaders and Followers" *Journal of Abnormal and Social Psychology*, LIII, (1956), 210–19.

14. E. A. Fleishman, E. F. Harris, and H. E. Burtt, *Leadership and Supervision in Industry* (Columbus, Ohio: Bureau of Educational Research, 1955), No. 33.

15. A. W. Halpin and B. J. Winer, "A Factorial Study of Leader Behavior Descriptions" in *Leader Behavior: Its Description and Measurement*, R. M. Stogdill and E. Coons, eds. (Columbus, Ohio: Ohio State Bureau of Business Research, Monograph No. 88, 1957), pp. 39–51.

16. There are several versions of the LPC. For a description of one of the more popular versions, see Fred E. Fiedler, *A Theory of Leadership Effectiveness* (New York, N.Y.: McGraw-Hill, 1967), p. 41.

17. Martin M. Chemers and Robert W. Rice, "A Theoretical and Empirical Examination of Fiedler's Contingency Model of Leadership Effectiveness" as Chapter 4 in James G. Hunt and Lars L. Larson, eds., *Contingency Approaches to Leadership* (Carbondale, Ill.: Southern Illinois University Press, 1973), p. 95.

18. *Ibid.*, p. 96.

19. Fred E. Fiedler, "Validation and Extension of the Contingency Model of Leadership Effectiveness: A Review of Empirical Findings," *Psychological Bulletin*, LXXVI, (1971), 128–148.

20. G. Graen, D. Alvares, J. B. Orris, and J. Martella, "The Contingency Model of Leadership Effectiveness: Antecedent and Evidential Results," *Psychological Bulletin*, LXXIV, (1970) 285–95.

21. See a review of these studies in Martin M. Chemers and Robert W. Rice, "A Theoretical and Empirical Examination of Fiedler's Contingency Model of Leadership Effectiveness", *op. cit.*, pp. 108–115.

22. *Ibid.*, p. 115.

23. *Ibid.*, pp. 124–129.

24. The Stinson and Tracy study of the stability of the LPC score was carried in the Hunt and Larson list of references as having been presented at the Thirty-Second Annual Meeting of the Academy of Management in Vancouver in 1973. Their paper can be correctly located in the *Proceedings* of this meeting which was held, however, in Minneapolis, Minnesota, in 1972 as follows: John E. Stinson and Lane Tracy, "The Stability and Interpretation of the LPC Score," *Proceedings of the Thirty-Second Annual Meeting of the Academy of Management* (Minneapolis, Minn., August, 1972), pp. 182–84.

25. R. J. House and G. Dessler, "The Path-Goal Theory of Leadership: Some Post Hoc and A Priori Tests," eds. J. G. Hunt and Lars L. Larson, *Contingency Approaches to Leadership*, pp. 29–56.

26. John E. Stinson and Thomas W. Johnson, "The Path-Goal Theory of Leadership: A Partial Test and Suggested Refinement," *Academy of Management Journal*, XVIII, No. 2 (1975), 247–48.

27. R. N. Osborn and J. G. Hunt, "An Adaptive-Reactive Theory of Leadership: The Role of Macro Variables in Leadership Research," a chapter in J. G. Hunt and L. L. Larson, *Leadership Frontiers* (Kent, Ohio: Kent State University Press, 1976), pp. 27–44.

28. Chester I. Barnard, *The Functions of the Executive* (Cambridge, Mass.: Harvard University Press, 1947) p. 163.

29. James A. Gazell, "Authority Flow Theory and The Impact of Chester Barnard," *California Management Review*, XIII, (Fall, 1970), 73-74.

30. Frank A. Heller, *Managerial Decision-Making* (London, England, Tavistock Publications, Ltd., 1971).

31. Bernard M. Bass and Enzo R. Valenzi, "Contingent Aspects of Effective Management Styles," as Chapter 5 in *Contingency*, eds. James G. Hunt and Lars L. Larson, pp. 130-155.

32. *Ibid.*, pp. 153-157.

33. Robert J. House, "A 1976 Theory of Charismatic Leadership," as Chapter 12 in *Leadership: The Cutting Edge*, eds. James G. Hunt and Lars L. Larson, (Carbondale, Illinois,: Southern Illinois University Press, 1977), pp. 189-207.

34. *Ibid.*, p. 203.

35. Bass and Valenzi, p. 144.

Chapter 13

Managing Change and Managing Creativity

WHEN behavioral science researchers and consultants finally figured out what leaders have been doing since the beginnings of organizations, they gave it a name of their own—"managing change." Unfortunately, this discovery took place in the middle of this century many hundreds of years after such change management accomplishments as those of Alexander the Great or Ghengis Khan. Social scientists would likely argue that, while these leaders no doubt managed change, they did it by force and without the benefits of modern behavioral science knowledge or assistance. They would further argue that today's environment will not permit a Ghengis Khan style of change management by beheading, exiling and enslaving.

Most behavioral scientists seem unable to grasp or countenance the modern versions of such change management approaches even though they are in wide use, effective, and well publicized. Henry Ford II has fired most presidents who have served under him. Howard Hughes used surgery as a change strategy very effectively, and examples of such approaches can be found almost daily in the Wall Street Journal. Exiling is also effectively used today in all types of organizations. Corporations transfer managers to less desirable jobs in outlying divisions and they "promote" executives to jobs with little power or authority. Governments, democratic and otherwise, transfer administrators to the hinterlands, and unwanted military officer behavior is dealt with by relieving of command and assigning to a "desk job," usually a staff position requiring much writing of unread reports.

These change management techniques are also often used today to help the organization recover from damage inflicted by consultants, behavioral science oriented or otherwise. The president of the Dutch firm Kinetics Technology International B.V. fired his executive vice-president and temporarily exiled another vice-president, to effect the recovery from the

233

internal political aftermath of ministrations by an organization development consultant who was working with their top echelon. The president, Mr. Jake Voogd, believed the company lost several hundred thousand Guilder through poorly overseen major foreign projects due to the executives' failure to leave headquarters to supervise them properly. The fear of leaving headquarters was due to their concern for preserving their positions in the headquarters hierarchy which had become very political as a result of the consultant's activities. Needless to say, the $300 dollar-per-day British consultant who had been working there for several months was also fired.[1]

After reorganizing the company with the assistance of two consulting companies, Tonka Corporation's board chairman fired two vice-presidents and the president was forced to resign. After this, the company hurried to go back to the way they were organized before their profits plummeted from $2.7 million a year in 1968 to $1.8 million in 1969. Pointing to the reorganization and increased delegation as primary causes of Tonka's problems, the Chairman, Russel L. Wenkstern, was quoted as saying, ". . . we didn't know the effect the system (reorganization) would have. For example, our divisional manager, who's always done a great job with the tooling, last year kicked the responsibility for dealing with subcontractors down the line a couple of levels."[2] This resulted in unprecedented delays in tool and die deliveries, stalling the introduction of new products and forcing Tonka to run up excessive labor costs to fill orders on time.

Although surgery is occasionally mentioned in passing as a possible strategy for managing change, it benefits from no research as a change strategy. As we shall see in reviewing the literature, the vast majority of the articles on managing change cover some kind of effort to alter managerial values, attitudes, and behavior. The ignoring of other alternatives simply reflects the value systems of behavioral scientists. Benjamin Tregoe speaks to this point when he points out that "Too often the value systems that underlie OD (Organization Development) efforts remain implicit and are not confronted openly. Besides being inherently dishonest, if these values are not shared values, line managers will come to feel they are being manipulated. As they sense these implicit values, they may reject the whole OD program out of hand as being a missionary effort serving objectives unrelated to those of their organization."[3] (Parenthetical phrase added)

Because of their value systems and their training, behavioral scientists have focussed almost exclusively on methods and processes of social relationship changes and communications often referred to as OD. Their preoccupation with the *processes* of change and their lack of interest in the objectives of results of change was documented by a survey of 200 professional training and development managers from business and government. Tregoe, who reported the results of the survey, concluded that "There is a definite tendency to define

OD more in terms of its methods and techniques than in terms of organizational objectives."[4] Tregoe also surveyed 320 line managers from business and government and concluded that for them (as well as the surveyed trainers) OD had a very wide variety of meanings, from MBO to reorganization to systems and procedures overhaul to sensitivity training. His survey also revealed that one organization in five did nothing to evaluate the results of OD activities, nine percent tried to measure effectiveness in terms of profits or costs, and six percent attempted to measure changes in productivity. Most of the remainder used various forms of surveys of opinions and perceptions of the participants to ascertain the value of OD in their organizations.

From the change-management literature in general, it is clear that most behavioral scientists and trainers do not believe that much change will be managed without OD, whatever it is. Tregoe believes that if trainers do not focus on objectives of the changes it is impossible to determine whether what is being done is OD or not! This is as close as he comes to telling us what OD is in an article entitled "What is OD?" This is primarily because his survey revealed that just about anything done by a professional trainer or consultant can be labeled OD if the trainer wants to call it that.

Classification of Approaches to Managing Change

One of the earliest classifications of change approaches was given by Harold Leavitt in 1964. He noted three approaches: *structure*, *technology*, and *people*. Changing through structure manipulation included changes in procedures, organization, budgets, and regulations. Technological approaches involved changes in work flow through changes in layouts, methods, standards, and equipment. People approaches required alterations in motivation, attitudes, and therefore behavior. The people changes come about through training, selection, and the effects of performance review procedures, according to Leavitt's classification.[5]

A later classification scheme provided by Larry E. Greiner in 1967 focussed on change processes as they relate to the use of power. Under his "Unilateral Power" classification he described the decree, replacement, and organizational structural approaches. These approaches are typically associated with very directive management and naturally deemed inappropriate. His other two approaches of "shared power" and "delegated power" have naturally received the bulk of attention. The former involves group problem identification and solving as well as group decision-making. The delegated power approach includes a "data discussion approach" which requires a change catalyst (usually a consultant) or an internal "change agent." The change agent's job is to encourage company participants to gather

and analyze data relating to problems they identify. The other approach
under Greiner's delegated power process, and one which for the last two
decades has received most of the attention of professionals, is the sensitivity
training approach. This approach requires that managers be trained through
sensitivity sessions to be more attentive to the underlying processes of human
behavior and relationships. The assumption is that attitudes will change
causing interpersonal relationships to change thus changing performance for
the better.[6]

A few years later, Greiner and Barnes decided that "Although both
Leavitt's and Greiner's conceptions are useful, they can be taken too
simplistically."[7] They offered a classification involving the *decisions required
in planning for change*. Their new scheme was concerned with the choices to
be made along the following continua:

1.   The change process plan—from structured to unstructured.
2.   The use of power—from unilateral to delegated.
3.   The involvement of relationships—from impersonal to personal.
4.   The tempo or timing—from revolutionary to evolutionary.

Suggesting moderation in the choices from these alternatives, the authors
conclude:

> At the risk of sounding "middle-of-the-roadish," our own experience suggests that
> orthodox adherence to extremes on any one of these dimensions is not likely to be very
> effective. Rather, the intriguing challenge, we believe, is to find new and
> complementary combinations of these extremes—such as a structured plan that
> permits unstructured actions to emerge! For example, certain degrees of structure may
> be essential for bringing together appropriate people and focusing their attention on
> specific problems. Bechard's article on "The Confrontation Meeting" (Harvard
> Business Review, March-April 1967) illustrates how key managers can be required to
> attend a meeting and discuss change-related issues in a planned sequence. At the same
> time, solutions to the problems identified by these managers are not planned in
> advance. Rather they design and "tailor-make" their own solutions as they interact
> within a structured problem-solving atmosphere.[8] (Parenthetical material was foot-
> noted in the quote)

Without the benefit of emotionally-loaded meeting titling, managers have
been "structuring" such meeting situations for years before Bechard's
discovery of the "Confrontation Meeting." An example from the many such
meetings I witnessed in the 1940's and 1950's would be the division manager's
directive instructing the manufacturing superintendent, the controller and his
cost accounting supervisor, and the marketing manager to get together and
thrash out their differences over the pricing of a forthcoming new model. He
had also, on several occasions, instructed principals to meet to effect new

organizational relationships. The only possible difference would be that the participants probably did not know that they were having "confrontation" meetings as the result of their boss using "structure" on them.

Most of the theory regarding the *processes* of change are variations on the old social change model of Kurt Lewin whose main elements are *unfreezing, changing,* and *refreezing.*[9] The unfreezing represents the process during which the forces acting on an individual are rearranged so that he sees the need for change. The changing process occurs after the readiness for changing has been established by the unfreezing and ideally should result in the internalization of the need for the new behavior. The refreezing stage represents the process by which the newly acquired behavior is integrated as patterned behavior representing the "new" personality characteristics which are consistent with the new behavior.

Following this model social scientists grew the myth that to produce behavioral change, attitude change must take place first. While the evidence may be somewhat muddied by the simple fact that one cannot hold up an attitude and look it over carefully, (attitudes are essentially clusters of marks made on survey questionnaires) what evidence we have suggests that behavioral change produces attitudinal change and not the other way around. Consider the following conclusion reached by Raymond and Alice Bauer in 1960:

A considerable body of common sense observation, clinical data, and, more recently, experimental findings indicate that in many instances attitude change follows after behavioral change. Such common phrases as "rationalization," "sour grapes," etc., are adequate labels for the process at work . . . Research under the direction of Leon Festinger has shown that precisely this sort of attitude change follows after a commitment to action . . . Kelman, working independently of Festinger, has affected children's attitudes toward comic books by "bribing" them to make statements in favor of one or another type of comic. Kelman's findings make it possible to specify conditions under which a private change of opinion will and will not accompany the coerced change of public position.[10]

After reviewing the management development literature, in 1970 Wallace Wohlking noted the persistence of the implicit assumption in most management development programs that attitudes should be changed first and then behavioral changes would follow. He cites numerous research efforts which strongly suggest that a more effective strategy would be to attempt to alter the behavior and forget about changing attitudes. One of his concerns was that ". . . the apparent consequences of (attempting attitude change first) has been to give line managers the impression that *the appropriate way* to achieve behavior change is through the attitude change/behavioral change sequence, and that therefore, line managers should manage changes in a similar fashion."[11] (Parenthetical phrase added.) Wohlking suggests two possible causes for the persistence of this strategy: (1) The management development personnel are not empowered to create structural changes and so have no other alternatives but to use what he calls a psychological approach and (2) most of the research evidence showing the more appropriate sequence of behavioral change through structure comes from the sociological literature. He left unsaid the old problem of one social science discipline ignoring the other social science discipline's findings.

Most of the management-of-change literature is concerned with the "changing" stage in Lewin's model through the use of a variety of approaches which usually fit into one or another of the following:

1. *Survey Feedback.* This approach begins with a survey of perceptions about the organization. The survey is followed by group discussions which catalog their implications after which the groups become committed to solutions to problems identified in their discussions. These discussions are usually led or guided by a "resource person," either an inside or outside consultant.

2. *Interpersonal Process Consultation.* The consultant or change-agent attempts to establish rapport with individuals and groups in order to bring about a catalyzing process of surfacing data in areas usually not sought in work organizations such as attitudes, feelings, individual needs, reasons for conflict, etc. After such probing, the consultant feeds back his or her findings and attempts to get individuals or groups to begin activities designed to alter the dysfunctional relations revealed in these probes.

3. *Task Process Consultation.* With this approach the change agent usually begins by analyzing a client's work situation privately through interviews designed to identify the client's objectives and organizational forces blocking progress. Through various forms of counseling, the change agent will attempt to get his or her client committed to courses of action designed to remove the roadblocks. This counseling may include many techniques, from role-playing to nondirective counseling techniques to guide the discussion toward commitment to the desired courses of action.

4. *Laboratory Training.* Sometimes referred to as T-Group or sensitivity training, this approach is one which attempts to focus on inter-personal and group processes but not on task problems. Some of the more common objectives are to get the participants to "level" with each other, and open communications channels to the extent that feelings, attitudes and

sentiments are revealed in such a way that work relations and work related communications will not suffer because of relationship conflicts.

One of the earliest attempts to measure the results of such change-management approaches beyond the case studies of single companies was done by the University of Michigan's Institute for Social Research.[12] The study involved more than 14,000 respondents in 23 organizations in a wide array of industries. Their study tried to answer the following question: What was the comparative effectiveness of the above "treatments" (Survey Feedback, Lab Training, etc.) as measured by the Survey of Organizations? This Survey of Organizations validating criterion measure is a paper and pencil instrument which purports to measure "organizational climate" from the perceptions of respondents in the organization. In addition to the four change management treatments described above, the researchers noted two additional sets of circumstances—"Data Handback" in which survey data were given to the appropriate supervisory and management personnel but nothing further was attempted, and "No Treatment" in which the survey feedback material was tabulated and returned to the top manager who did nothing more with it.

The major portion of the results were reported in a table of 188 correlation coefficients, each one representing the association between the use of each treatment and the 16 "measures" of changes in organizational climate taken over one year apart. In all there were only six correlation coefficients of over +.30 which were significant at the 5% level. The *highest* of these was +.39 which, when squared, represents a common variance of the two variables of only 15%. There were also only six statistically significant *negative* correlations of over –.30 indicating that about as many treatments appeared to be (faintly) associated with deteriorating organizational climates as with improving climates. The median correlation among the 188 coefficients was +.01 and their distribution was not significantly different from a normal distribution suggesting a bunch of random numbers on each side of a .00 mean which can be summarized by saying that there was no relationship between their measures of organizational climate and the OD treatments taken together. The table of correlations contained two sets of correlations for each treatment, one for changes in climate for *groups* receiving the treatments and one for changes in the climate for all the *individuals* in all groups receiving the treatments. Because the organizational climate instrument used 16 different measures, there were 16 correlations for groups receiving a treatment and 16 for members of all groups receiving the treatment. Table 13–1 gives a summary of the correlations between climate measures taken one year apart for groups and individuals by OD treatments. Comparing these summary figures and indexes it is extremely difficult to understand some of the researchers' conclusions given below:

TABLE 13-1

Summary of Correlations Between Climate Measures Taken One Year Apart For Groups and Individuals By Organization Development Treatments*

	Lab Training		Interpers. Proc. Cons.		Task Proc. Cons.		Survey Feedback		Data Handback		No Treatment	
	Group	Ind.	Group	Ind.	Group	Ind.	Group	Ind.	Group	Ind.	Group	Ind.
Number of Significant Correlation Coefficients	6/16	10/16	0/16	7/16	2/16	5/16	12/16	11/16	4/16	9/16	5/14	9/14**
Range of r's	-.42 to +.20	-.18 to +.27	-.25 to +.31	-.07 to +.21	-.24 to +.32	-.19 to +.03	.00 to +.39	+.01 to +.36	-.33 to +.33	-.21 to +.20	-.59 to +.21	-.61 to .00
Median r among 16 r's	-.02	+.07	-.07	+.08	+.08	-.06	+.26	+.15	+.08	.00	-.09	-.14
Median r among all 32 r's	-.05		+.02		-.03		+.18		+.05		-.11	

* These entries were derived by your author from the original table in Bowers' article which contained 188 individual correlations between changes in 16 measures contributing to the overall organizational climate as measured by the Survey of Organizations.

** Two cells in each column of correlations for "No Treatment" were N/A reducing the total number of correlations for Groups and Individuals to 14 each.

The results indicate that *Survey Feedback* was associated with statistically significant improvement on a majority of measures (Comment: This statement is technically correct, since from the table 13–1 we can see that 12 of the 16 correlations for groups and 11 of the 16 for individuals were statistically significant at the 5% level. Please note carefully, however, the strength of these relationships. The median r for groups was +.26 representing a thread-like relationship of only 7% common variance. The median r for individuals was only +.15 representing only 2% common variance and the median r for all 32 correlations was only +.18 representing a common variance of only 3%.) . . . *Interpersonal Process Consultation* was associated with improvement on a majority of measures . . . (This conclusion is hardly warranted since *none* of the group correlations was significant and only 7 out of 16 of the individual correlations were significant. Worse yet, the median r's were –.07 and +.08 or less than 1% common variance for each.) . . . *Laboratory Training* and *No Treatment* were associated with declines. (As can be seen from the table these conclusions were reached on the basis of choosing the individual r's/ 16 since the statistically significant group r's/ 16 were less than 8 in each case. And note the range for all these median r's: –.02 to +.08!)[13] (parenthetical remarks added)

The author draws a number of other conclusions which can be supported no better than those given above. From this study, which no doubt required considerable time and effort, we can conclude simply that the variety of OD activities examined had no measurable effect of any consequence on organizational climate as measured by the Survey of Organizations questionnaire.

In 1978, Jerry I. Porras and P. O. Berg managed to locate only 35 articles describing OD interventions which ". . . were done in reasonably representative samples of real-life organizations; measured as a minimum, organizationally relevant process variables; and used empirical techniques."[14] The authors sorted the 308 different variables measured in these studies into what they referred to as *process* and *outcome* variables. The process variables were such variables as measures of peer support, leader approachability, decision making processes, and self-actualization. In all, 48 such variables were assessed in the 35 studies. Only 21 outcome variables were measured in these studies. The authors defined this category of variables as ". . . impact on organizational outputs, typically performance types of variables such as profits, costs, productivity and efficiency and other outcome measures such as absenteeism and turnover, employee satisfaction, individual job effectiveness and quality of group meetings."[15] Of the 21 such variables measured in these studies, *only four were economic performance variables*, and the authors claimed that ". . . overall economic performance variables substantially changed in *65 percent of nine studies*."[16] (Italics added) There are no clues given which would suggest that the authors did not mean that in 5.85 (65% of 9) studies (out of the 35 studies) performance variables changed as a result of OD activities! For the remainder of the interpretations of OD effects on outcome variables, they mixed the four economic variables in with 17 such outcome variables as satisfaction with supervisor, number and length of meetings, and quality of meetings. They report an *average change rate* for all these *combined outcome variables* of 51 percent and an average change rate for all process variables of 46 percent. No details of the amounts of any of the changes were reported. Their over-all conclusion was that "Organizational Development, still an embryonic field, has produced relatively little systematic evidence about its efficacy."[17] Regarding such OD activities as T-Groups, Encounter Groups, and Sensitivity Training Groups, they further conclude that they do not have a strong impact on either the processes or the outcomes of organizations and that these techniques had the least reported change among the various change techniques.

This finding is interesting especially since the majority of OD related articles in the literature are on some aspects of Sensitivity Training. The behavioral scientist's love affair with sensitivity training did not last as long as his affair with the small work group, but it was as intense while it lasted. Most of the literature on OD activities from 1960 until about 1975 were articles concerned with some aspect of sensitivity training. And no possible dimension of this process seems to have been ignored, although there are precious few studies on its effect on economic performance variables. Below is a *partial* list of some of the titles from one journal from 1968–72 whose subjects suggest the beating to death of sensitivity or laboratory training through research[18]:

1. "Accelerating Laboratory Learning Through a Phase Progression Model for Trainer Intervention."
2. "Impact of Laboratory Training on Sociopolitical Ideology."
3. "Sensitivity Training for Staff in an Institution for Adolescent Offenders."
4. "Mutually Perceived Therapeutic Relationships in T-Groups: The Co-Trainer Puzzle."
5. "Laboratory Training Stress Compared with College Examination Stress."
6. "Touch Me, Like Me: Testing an Encounter Group Assumption."
7. "Effects of Feedback on Interpersonal Sensitivity in Laboratory Training Groups."

From the period 1960 to 1975 one could locate over a thousand such articles in the professional and trade journals. The few reviews of the effectiveness of sensitivity training have been generally negative. One of the most comprehensive reviews reported by Dunnette and Campbell, seemed to have little effect on the growth of sensitivity training. Their conclusion is given below:

Laboratory education has not been shown to bring about any marked change in one's standing on objective measures of attitudes, values, outlooks, interpersonal perceptions, self-awareness, or interpersonal sensitivity. In spite of these essentially negative results on objective measures, individuals who have been trained by laboratory education methods are more likely to be seen as changing their job behavior than are individuals in similar job settings who have not been trained.[19]

Other reviews whose results were essentially negative were done by John H. DeMichele, William J. Kearney and Desmond D. Martin, and Rolf E. Rogers.[20] Rogers' article, "Sensitivity Training: Caveat Emptor," represents one of the few reviews which seriously considered the ethical aspects of an organization's sponsoring such training. As early as 1965 a few social scientists were sounding faint warnings regarding ethical considerations. Robert J. House's warnings were in the form of questions which managers should ask before deciding to use sensitivity training as a management development approach. Several of these questions pointing to the ethics involved are as follows: "Question 3. Can the candidate tolerate the anxiety involved in the T Group process? Question 4. What are the credentials of the T Group leaders? Question 5. Is it within management's prerogatives to direct an employee to attend a T Group?"[21] Needless to say very few managements of various organizations from business, government, churches, or education paid any serious attention to these considerations. Thousands upon thousands of people were trained in the U.S. and Europe with little consideration for the possible damages which could be done to some of the participants. And if we consider the T-Group to be a first cousin of the clinical technique of group therapy, the preparation of the trainer falls far short of any reasonable professional minimum standard. Although they do not become the subjects of journal articles, reports of occasional post T-Group suicides and psychotic breaks continue to surface.

As an aside, it is worth noting here that managements also persist in using clinical psychological evaluations for candidates for middle and upper level executive positions ignoring any possible ethical considerations. Such instruments in combination (the Thematic Apperception Test, the Rorschach test, etc.) purport to be able to identify such personality characteristics as latent homosexuality, phobias, manias, and a host of pre-psychotic leanings. The executives who order such tests and the psychologists who administer and interpret them do not seem to be concerned about the ethics of scratching around inside the candidate's psyche with no intention of explaining to the candidate what has been discovered about him. This is akin to a surgeon, after having performed exploratory surgery, refusing to tell his patient what he discovered. And if one considers the lack of validity studies showing that these clinical psychological instruments, which have been normed mostly on abnormal or neurotic patients, are valid instruments for assessing normal personalities, there is reason enough to discontinue their use. But both sensitivity training and clinical psychological testing continues, albeit the former practice is waning. It is being replaced by other fads or fashions.

Transactional analysis started to take over for sensitivity training in the early 1970's. Thousands of companies' employees have had transactional analysis training either through programs sponsored by the American Management Association or in-house programs such as those sponsored by American Airlines, Bank of America, and Westinghouse Corporation.[22] The movement did not seem to have the staying power of sensitivity training, however, perhaps because the author of one of its founding books *I'm OK— You're OK*, Thomas Harris, was reported to have committed suicide at the peak of the movement.

The newest fashion on the scene at this writing is "Assertiveness Training." Between October 24, 1977 and April 26, 1978, a manager could choose two different Assertiveness Training programs in Chicago, three in New York, or one in Los Angeles all sponsored by the American Management Association or any number of programs sponsored by Universities and consulting companies. The typical huckster appeal was used in the AMA brochure selling the program:

Can assertiveness training really make a difference back on the job? Yes! Because you'll learn not only how to build on your own strengths—but also how to use the strengths of others. For greater productivity . . . higher morale . . . and more commitment to the goals of both your department and your organization. And that's not all. You'll learn how and why a strong leader can give in on one issue without losing the whole battle. And when raising the roof can get you better results—and more respect—than holding your peace ever could.
Assert yourself today. Register for this practical course.
Who should attend. All managers who want to exercise a greater influence on others, get their proposals and directives across more effectively, and resolve conflict situations decisively yet diplomatically.

Why are Management Fads So Successful?

The answer to this question is at once both simple and complex. First, most managers with difficult decisions to make or heavy responsibilities to fulfill want all the help they can get. Second, successful managers often have had good training in either the hard sciences where evidence, controls, and conclusions can be fairly clear-cut, or training in the applications thereof such as in engineering. Or they have been trained in one or the other of the business disciplines which are applications of mathematics such as finance or accounting whose contaminants such as time and taxes are generally knowable. They are, from their training and professional practice, unaccustomed to the intangibles and ambiguities involved in managing the efforts of other humans. Once their major responsibilities shift to performing primarily through the efforts of their subordinates, many seek panaceas with a passion. For example, during the height of the 1950's competition for electrical engineering talent, a chief engineer of a major electronics company agreed to purchase $1,000 worth of questionnaire materials which were "guaranteed" to predict creativity in new electrical engineering graduates! He bought this packet on an airline flight without so much as asking pointed questions about the test's validity or checking with his personnel director. I noted this emerging syndrome of "when-engineers-discover-affect" in an in-house publication some 23 years ago.[23]

The third cause for the panacea approach to problem-solving or managing change in the human resource management area may be the vaguely noticed but poorly identified loss of power or ability to influence of today's managerial leaders. Our literature in sociology, political science, and management is sprinkled with various classifications of the powers of leaders. Most are variations on a *classical list of leader powers*. They are the *position powers*, the *coercive powers*, the *reward powers*, the *expertise powers* and the *charismatic or referent powers* of the leader.[24] For reasons best known to social scientists, non-leader sources of powers generally went unexplored except for David Mechanic's descriptions of employees' collective and expertise powers and various powers they derive by being near the social or physical center of the organization.[25] However, careful observation of any organization today will reveal the existence of power systems whose elements include many power sources beyond those of the leader and those identified by David Mechanic. Examples of powers other than leader power are observed and often lamented in many organizations today. Consider the following:

1. A new president of a large U.S. chemical company wanted to integrate what had been for years a group of semi-autonomous operating divisions. His background was in corporate finance and law. In considering his power to bring about change, he should have taken into account his lack of adequate power to effectively decree integrative policy changes. His influence shortage was due largely to a) the collective power of the division managers; b) their expertise in the chemical production technology and marketing; c) the legal powers resulting from their autonomous nature; and d) the physical distance between him and the various division headquarters. Since he did not deal first with his power shortage, his attempts at integration led to failure.

2. A university medical school dean whose medical school attracts 8000 candidates annually has a difficult time controlling admission criteria due to extraneous (to his power system) sources of power. The medical school

can accommodate only 120 new students, but their selection decisions naturally affect all 8000. According to the university president, such numbers attract considerable attention from outside his university:

"The state legislators get in the act, and they say, "Let's look at how many students U.C.'s medical school is taking. What percentage of them are Ohio residents?" We're not fully state supported, but we get some state support. "How many of them are Cincinnati residents?" asked a city councilman. "Why in the world should the city be paying the University of Cincinnati any money for its medical school if they just take in . . . 40 percent of the total from the city of Cincinnati?" Regents get into the act, too; then they start calling the shots for admissions . . . It's more than pressure . . . it may be legislation, or it may be the board of regents' handing down some policy.[26]

3. A general manager of a Kennecott Copper Corporation mining division oversaw an underground and an open pit mining operation, a primary crusher, a 27-mile company-owned railroad and a mill at the other end of the railroad. He was constantly plagued by a slow change rate at the mill. (His office was at the mine site.) Part of his lack of power over the mill management was a simple matter of lack of physical proximity to the mill. A further reduction in his power was due to subordinate expertise since his background was mining engineering, not chemical engineering. And their collective power at the mill—he said "they always stick up for each other over there"—further reduced his influence.

4. Picture any foreman over a work group on a machine-paced assembly line where his subordinates are represented by a militant industrial union. All rewards and personnel policies of any consequence are determined by union and management negotiators, and the collective and legal powers of his workers are awesome. About all he has left in his power kit is his personality. The odds against his power to "initiate structure" to produce change of any magnitude are astronomical.

In the above examples there are several other non-leader general sources of power affecting the leader-follower-technology systems. Managements have reached for OD and any other device they think will help them make changes needed in their organizations. Dale Carnegie courses are in a revival period and they offer the possibility of "influencing people." The assertiveness training described earlier offers the possibility of converting some of the subordinates' powers which can reduce leader powers to support changes needed. What is needed is a framework for analyzing all the powers in a leader's subsystem. One approach would be a power system as follows: The *total power equals the leader powers, subordinate powers, work design powers, plus extraneous powers.* Solving for leader power we find that he has that power which is left after subtracting all subordinate power, the power removed from his grasp by the nature of the task, and that removed by power sources outside his subsystem.

Subordinate Powers

Below are some of the more important sources of subordinate powers:

1. COLLECTIVE POWER: This power derives from subordinate membership in a union or an informal association of workers which can collectively prevent the leader or the organization from reaching desired objectives.
2. LEGAL POWERS: These emanate from laws governing the treatment of employees or their associations regarding their selection, hours, pay, race, sex, national origin, religion, and working conditions such as health and safety at the workplace.
3. AFFLUENCE POWER: This power derives from the reduction of subordinate dependence upon their employing organizations for economic reasons. This power is often seen exercised through subordinates' inclinations to resist change, to quit their jobs, absenteeism, tardiness, and threats to violate leaders' rules or company policy.
4. EXPERT POWER: This derives from the leader's and the organization's dependence upon subordinates' expertise, special skills, or knowledge.

Work Design Power

Most change management theorists tend to ignore the effects of the nature of the task and its design on the leader's ability to influence his subordinates. Below are some of the more important categories of leader power loss due to these factors:

1. ENGINEERED TASK POWER: This power derives from the governance of subordinate behavior through the work design over which neither the subordinate nor his leader has much control. Examples are machine-paced assembly lines, engineered assembly sequences, and production schedules. Since such jobs are usually routine and their components obvious to many workers, the opportunities for leader power through special knowledge or skill are considerably reduced. Machine pacing and tight scheduling (by non-leaders) limit the contact time available for the application and exercise of referent power.
2. DISPERSED SUBORDINATES' WORK DESIGN POWER: This power derives from the limitations of leader-follower interaction because of "distality"

(lack of proximity) to each other. Some examples are dispersed division and plant managers, field geologists, international airline captains, territorial sales representatives, shovel runners in a large open pit, and bauxite smelter workers. Also included here would be shift foremen reporting to a general foreman who worked a different shift.

3. OVER-THE-LEADER'S-HEAD TASK POWER: This power derives from tasks whose approaches for accomplishments and possible outcomes are not fully understood by the leader. An example of such a task would be exploratory R & D projects at the forefront of the state of a particular interdisciplinary art where each subordinate is an expert in one of the disciplines.

Extraneous Powers

The last source of power which robs the leader of some of his or her power might be called, for want of a better term, extraneous (to the immediate leader-follower-technology sub-system) power. Extraneous powers are derived from a wide variety of sources. Below are a few of them:

1. POLICY POWER: This power derives from the organization's policies and procedures that prescribe what leaders *must* do in given situations. Policy powers continue to increase and seriously diminish the leader's power to assign, direct, decide, reward, or punish.

2. THE LEADER'S BOSS'S USURPATION POWER: This emanates from the leader's boss's power to withhold delegation of power to the leader and from bypassing of the leader (to and from subordinates) by the leader's superiors.

3. PUBLIC SENTIMENT POWERS: These result from the threatened unofficial censure of leader behavior from sources completely outside his organization. These influences or pressures may come from such groups as environmentalists or other special interest groups with no formal connection to the organization. An example would be the public citizen pressure group which tried to force the board of directors of an Athens, Ohio hospital to take back the personnel director they had fired. There was no legal action (nor grounds for it) involved at all—only "pressure."

Power and Managing Change

The primary usefulness of the power system model is simply to offer a more analytical approach to leaders who would improve their management of change. We have seen from the literature that OD activities which are psychologically based on the notion that attitudes must be changed before behavior can be changed offer little chance for success. Structural changes including surgery, reorganizations, etc. are fairly well-known to produce behavioral change. But these approaches require power. A leader interested in managing change successfully should take a power inventory before attempting the change to see if he or she has enough to succeed. If the leader faces a considerable loss of power due to collective powers of subordinates, he or she either must find a way to get some control over these powers or go upstairs and get more position or reward-coercion powers. Certain kinds of needed changes can benefit from subordinate participation in varying degrees. This might reduce the subordinate powers which could frustrate the change effort. But if some of the changes needed require layoffs or undesired transfers or demotions, it is unreasonable to expect subordinate groups to preside over their own demise. To what degree participation can be used in a given situation needing changing will depend upon so many factors unique to the situation that a universal principle simply cannot be established.

Conclusions about Managing Change

Managing change theory and research in the literature offer little hope for improving the management of change. Most of these theories are value-oriented to the behavioral scientists whose descriptions of organizational systems are generally inaccurate and whose change models reflect their orientations. Their "advocate" social science stance attempts to get managers to abdicate through "power-sharing" and other forms of delegation and subordinate participation. Their approach to change management theory is clearly a university-referenced collegial style in which the professors ought to be able to fire their dean. (At Ohio University, 51 percent of any college faculty can fire their dean but it takes two thirds to fire a lowly department chairman since he is one of them—faculty, and often tenured.)

While it is clear that employees do hold more powers than they did even a few years ago, it does not follow that a diffusion of power is helpful to managing change. Power is a little like capital in that large undertakings require a collection of it.

Modern organization systems have tended to ignore the complexities of power and this failure has permitted behavioral science modelers to offer change management models which, when applied, do not work. This probably accounts for much of the faddism and failures in the field. It is suggested here, however, that once the complexities of the power system are taken into account, the choice of change models is not critical, because the ability to produce change is more a function of power—the ability to influence—than of technique.

THE MANAGEMENT OF CREATIVITY

The most striking aspect of the advice given in the literature about how to manage creativity is the extremely wide diversity of opinions on the origins and processes of creativity coupled with a monorail-mindedness about how to manage it. We are told that a tranquil hot-house environment free of inhibiting management policies and behaviors is the only appropriate approach. For examples see the following: "Creativity . . . prospers most in a friendly atmosphere of cooperation. This atmosphere frees individuals from pressure for uniformity . . ."[27] "Almost all the studies of scientists agree that the need for autonomy, for independence of action, is something that seems to be particularly strong in this group."[28] "In order for creative thought to occur, it is essential that the individual have some degree of freedom in mental activity. He must be free to manipulate his perceptions and past experiences and to recognize and use his emotional and artistic responses. This capacity is termed "spontaneity," and its opposed function is called "conformity."[29] "The creative atmosphere should be free from external pressure. A person is not likely to be creative if too much hangs on the successful outcome of his research activities, for he will have a strong tendency to accept the first satisfactory solution whether or not it seems novel or the best possible. Thus, he needs indulgence in time and resources, and particularly in organizational evaluations of his activities. He needs freedom to innovate. He also needs considerable, but not complete, autonomy and self-direction and a large voice in deciding at what he will work."[30] "Independent thought, freedom to experiment, freedom to err, and freedom to initiate change are characteristic of the climate necessary for invention."[31]

None of the above advice was accompanied by research showing comparative creative *performance* under various degrees of freedom or other inhibiting dimensions of the work climate. One study was located which is somewhat relevant in that the performance of research and development laboratories was examined in relation to perceived pressures for quality performance and pressures for financial responsibility.[32] The researchers, studying a sample of 22 development labs, found a positive statistically significant correlation of .44 ($r^2 = .19$) between a composite index of lab *performance* and *pressure for quality* output. The composite lab performance index included the following: (1) net change in research and development budget during the last year, (2) number of new outside contracts, (3) number of new internally funded projects, (4) percentage of projects meeting time schedules, (5) number of contracts renewed, (6) percentage of projects meeting cost budgets, and (7) research director's rating of the comparative global technical performance of the development group. They also found a significant correlation of .54 ($r^2 = .29$) between perceptions of *financial pressures* and the *global ratings of the laboratories*. The authors concluded that ". . . the overall performance of a research and development organization and perhaps other types of systems as well, is related to the degree of pressure and responsibility for total system effectiveness felt by the research professionals. In an effective system, each member is aware of the total system as it relates to its environment and knows how his job ties in with the total goals of the organization."[33]

By far the most fascinating aspect of a search for appropriate management-of-creativity theory is the wide-ranging theories of the origins or conditions which produce creative people. The theorists who have studied history and the biographies of eminent people lean to various forms of early trauma, adversity, and psychopathology as playing roles in *producing* creativity. The depth psychologists (neo-Freudian, Jungian, etc.) lean to sexual fixations, Oedipus complexes, and strong feelings of repressed guilt as causal. Other theorists see creativity as societally acceptable forms of rebellion and the need to prove superiority. Most all see the characteristics of tenacity and driving hard work as having begun early in the lives of creative people.[34]

None of those who recommended the hot-house environment as ideal bother to deal with the possibility that a true hothouse and tranquil environment may *reduce* creativity of its occupants. If the rebellion theory has any merit, removal of all possible obstacles against which to rebel could prove disastrous. Another facet of creativity which seems to be overlooked is simply that genuine creativity has required intense training or practice, has come about only after a number of failures, and is extremely strenuous work. Another researcher in the area of creativity and a skeptic as far as the hothouse environment theory is concerned puts it this way: "What I am skeptical about is that the persons who needed such felicitous environment would ever be able to manage creativity in the real world of varying and uncontrollable environments."[35] Maddi's argument is based on observations to the effect that ". . . virtually all those we remember as having been creative were so despite enormous social forces arrayed against them. Galileo, Marx, Darwin, Freud, Dante, Byron, Yeats, Christ, Michelangelo, Zapata—the list is very long indeed of those whose creative endeavors involved socio-political risks and punishments. Once again, I must point out that garden-variety imaginativeness is not the same as creativity."[36]

To illustrate the point that turbulence is common in the early lives of eminent people, the reader is invited to speculate on the adult outcomes of the three childhood summaries below:

Case 1. Girl, age sixteen, orphaned, willed to custody of grandmother by her mother, who was separated from alcoholic husband, now deceased. Swallowed penny to attract attention at five. Father was fond of child. Child lived in fantasy as the mistress of father's household for years. Four young uncles and aunts in household cannot be managed by the grandmother, who is widowed. Young uncle drinks; has left home without telling the grandmother his destination. Aunt, emotional over love affair, locks self in room. Grandmother resolves to be more strict with granddaughter since she fears she has failed with her own children. Dresses granddaughter oddly. Refused to let her have playmates, put her in braces to keep back straight. Did not send her to grade school. Aunt on paternal side of family crippled; uncle asthmatic.

Case 2. Boy, senior year secondary school, has obtained certificate from a physician stating that nervous breakdown makes it necessary for him to leave school for six months. Boy not a good all-around student; has no friends—teachers find him a problem—poor adjustment to school—has odd mannerisms, makes up own religion, spoke late—father ashamed of son's lack of athletic ability—chants hymns to himself—parents regard him as "different."

Case 3. Boy, age six; head large at birth. Thought to have had brain fever. Three siblings died before his birth. Mother does not agree with relatives and neighbors that child is probably abnormal. Child sent to school—diagnosed as mentally ill by teacher. Mother is angry—withdraws child from school, says she will teach him herself.

Outside this context the typical reader of these caselet histories never sees these people growing up to be Eleanor Roosevelt, Albert Einstein, and Thomas Alva Edison.[37] The point is simply that our notions of the origins of genuine creativity must not eliminate early life turbulence as a possible condition facilitating its emergence.

Based upon biographies and statistical studies of scientists, one can conclude that their backgrounds were less turbulent than those of poets, writers, and painters. They seemed to decide early in their lives to be scientists, usually mentioning the encouragement of a teacher in high school or early college and/or a relative (usually father or brother) who was a scientist. They spent more time alone than did their classmates and acquired much more knowledge and considerable skill in their fields than did their contemporaries.[38]

With only personal observation of several R and D labs and the university scene plus scientist recruitment experience, it is my opinion that many of the recommendations for the hothouse environment for creative people are based on the self-referenced values and personality needs of the social scientist. There is some support for this view in the differences between the backgrounds of social and other scientists. Anne Roe noted in her studies of the early lives of scientists that social scientists differed from all the other scientists in their early lives in several ways. They did not develop a pattern of living that did not necessitate close personal relationships as did the other scientists: "The social scientist differed most in this regard, showing early and continued interest in personal relations. *Relations with parents were difficult*, however, for this group. For about three-fourths of them, social status was of conscious importance during childhood. Their vocational interest would thus seem to follow from the *tremendous emotional investment in interpersonal relations* and the technique of handling a problem by generalizing it in order to make it less painful."[39] (Italics added)

From my own experience in recruiting engineers and scientists three factors seem to be more important to candidates than the characteristics of the environment of no-constraints and tranquility: (1) The more creative among the younger candidates seem quite interested in the opportunity to work with or around reputable scientists known to them through their contributions in their fields, (2) They are interested in the nature of the projects on which they will likely be assigned, and (3) They are interested in the facilities and equipment which would be available to them. The best recruitment device a recruiter can have is a brilliant scientist or two already on the payroll and identified with his company. The early pattern of mentor stimulus evidently prevails as a motivational device beyond the college professor. Scientists appear to be very interested in their own technical growth and if the histories of Edison's lab and Watson's IBM lab are of any value, scientists want challenging assignments and good facilities and are very forgiving of superiors' behaviors which might cause a social scientist's hair to stand on end. Their primary sources of recognition come from in-house peers, mentors, and outside peers through their research articles. Unlike many employees whose main recognition needs are fulfilled by a paycheck and an occasional compliment by a supervisor or peer employee, scientists and engineers have a wider community of other scientists and engineers for sources of recognition.

Conclusions Regarding Managing Creativity

Without better understandings of the origins and impetus for creative behavior, little certainty can be established about the appropriate organizational structure or climate. The no-constraints, tranquil hothouse environment approach to managing creativity does not fit with the known facts about creative people. While it is true that scientists tend to be more independent and desire a great deal of autonomy it has yet to be demonstrated that fulfilling their autonomy needs by a no-constraints environment will enhance their output. There is some reason to believe that the opportunity to oppose the established order and be recognized for successful oppositions may be an important ingredient in developing and facilitating creativity. An absence of quality standards or high expectations, financial responsibilities, and time constraints is not likely to be shown to improve organization research and development laboratory performance any more than such conditions can be expected to improve the performance of manufacturing or marketing departments.

NOTES

1. From a conversation with the President in The Hague in February, 1977.
2. *Business Week*, August 1, 1970, p. 38.
3. Benjamin B. Tregoe, "What is OD?" *Training and Development Journal*, March, 1974, pp. 16–23.

4. *Ibid.*
5. H. J. Leavitt, "Applied Organization Change in Industry: Structural, Techno-logical, and Human Approaches," in W. W. Cooper, H. J. Leavitt and M. W. Shelly II, eds, *New Perspectives in Organization Research*, (New York, N.Y.: John Wiley and Sons, Inc., 1964), pp. 55–56.
6. L. E. Greiner, "Patterns of Organization Change," *Harvard Business Review*, May-June, 1967, pp. 120–126.
7. Larry E. Greiner and Louis B. Barnes, "Organization Change and Develop-ment," in Gene W. Dalton, Paul R. Lawrence, and Larry E. Greiner, Eds., *Organizational Change and Development*, (Homewood, Illinois: Richard D. Irwin, Inc. and The Dorsey Press, 1970), pp. 4–5.
8. *Ibid.*, pp. 5–6.
9. For a popular description of the complete model see Paul Hersey and Kenneth Blanchard, *Management of Organizational Behavior*, (Englewood Cliffs, N.J.: 1972), pp. 162–63.
10. Raymond A. Bauer and Alice H. Bauer, "America, Mass Society and Mass Media," *Journal of Social Issues*, Vol. 16 (1960), pp. 3–66.
11. Wallace Wohlking, "Attitude Change, Behavior Change," *California Manage-ment Review*, Winter, 1970, p. 48.
12. David G. Bowers, "OD Techniques and Their Results in 23 Organizations: The Michigan ICL Study," *Journal of Applied Behavioral Science*, Vol. 9, no. 1 (January-February, 1973), pp. 21–43.
13. *Ibid.*
14. Jerry I. Porras and P. O. Berg, "The Impact of Organization Development," *Academy of Management Review*, April, 1978, p. 251.
15. *Ibid.*
16. *Ibid.*, p. 255.
17. *Ibid.*, p. 263.
18. All these articles are from various issues of the *Journal of Applied Behavioral Science*, from Volume 4 through Volume 8.
19. Marvin D. Dunnette and John P. Campbell, "Laboratory Education: Impact on People and Organizations," *Industrial Relations*, October, 1968, p. 23.
20. John H. DeMichele, "Measuring the Effectiveness of Laboratory Training in Organizational Development," *Academy of Management Proceedings*, 1972, pp. 47–8; William J. Kearney and Desmond D. Martin, "Sensitivity Training: An Established Management Development Tool?" *Academy of Management Journal*, December, 1974, pp. 755–760; and Rolf E. Rogers, "Sensitivity Training: Caveat Emptor," *The Journal of Nursing Administration*, Vol. 2, No. 6 (November-December, 1972), pp. 48–54.
21. Robert J. House, "T Group Training: Some Important Considerations for the Practicing Manager," *Bulletin of the New York Personnel Management Association*, Vol. XXII, No. 9 (May, 1965), pp. 4 ff.
22. *Business Week*, January 12, 1974, p. 74.
23. I was the personnel director. An in-house memo from me to my division manager, Robert Roe of Sperry-Rand's Aeronautical Equipment Division in Phoenix, Arizona.

24. John P. French and Bertram H. Raven, "The Bases of Social Power," in Darwin Cartwright, *Studies in Social Power*, (Ann Arbor, Michigan: Institute for Social Research, University of Michigan, 1959), pp. 150–167.
25. David Mechanic, "Sources of Power of Lower Participants in Complex Organizations," *Administrative Science Quarterly*, Vol. 7, No. 3 (December, 1962), pp. 349–364.
26. "Conversation: An Interview with Warren Bennis," *Organizational Dynamics*, Vol. 2, No. 3, Winter, 1974, p. 55.
27. Ross A. Webber, "Innovation and Conflict in Industrial Engineering," *The Journal of Industrial Engineering*, as reproduced in David R. Hampton, Charles E. Summer, and Ross A. Webber, *Organizational Behavior and The Practice of Management*, (Glenview, Illinois: Scott, Foresman and Company, 1968), p. 421.
28. Anne Roe, unpublished manuscript, as quoted in Bernard Berelson and Gary A. Steiner, *Human Behavior: An Inventory of Scientific Findings*, (New York, N.Y.: Harcourt, Brace & World, Inc., 1964), p. 234.
29. W. E. Vinacke, *The Psychology of Thinking*, (New York, N.Y.: McGraw-Hill, Inc., 1952), p. 258.
30. Victor A. Thompson, "Bureaucracy and Innovation," *Administrative Science Quarterly*, June, 1965, p. 12.
31. Norman R. F. Maier and John J. Hayes, *Creative Management*, (New York, N.Y.: John Wiley & Sons, Inc., 1962), p. 28.
32. Douglas T. Hall and Edward E. Lawler, "Job Characteristics and Pressures and the Organizational Integration of Professionals," *Administrative Science Quarterly*, Vol. 15, No. 3 (September, 1970), pp. 271–81.
33. *Ibid.*, p. 280.
34. For over 300 abstracts of articles on creativity see Morris L. Stein and Shirley J. Heinze, *Creativity and the Individual*, (Glencoe, Illinois: Glencoe Free Press, 1960).
35. Salvatore R. Maddi, "Creativity Is Strenuous," *The University of Chicago Magazine*, September-October, 1973, p. 18.
36. *Ibid.*, p. 22.
37. Such an exercise was used many times by Victor Goertzel and Mildred George in their speaking engagements on their studies of eminent people. These and many other case histories are contained in their book as follows: Victor Goertzel and Mildred George, *Cradles of Eminence*, (Boston, Mass.: Little, Brown & Co., 1962).
38. See Morris I. Stein and Shirley J. Heinze, *Creativity, op. cit.*, pp. 361–400, for 22 various statistical studies of different groups of creative people—mostly scientists.
39. Anne Roe, *The Making of a Scientist*, (New York, N.Y.: Dodd Mead, 1952) as summarized in Stein and Heinze, *Creativity*, p. 276.

PRESCRIPTIONS AND ANTIDOTES

I no longer believe that articles on home repair or how to fix one's car are contenders for the most numerous "How to do it" articles. Not only are there thousands upon thousands of articles on how to manage, but there are many articles on how managers should feel about people, what they should believe in, how they should decide, and how to be aggressive, assertive, sensitive, compassionate and how to be understood.

PART V deals with only a few of the more popular prescriptions found in textbooks, management training program contents, and the management literature in general.

Chapter 14 covers the ever-popular Theory Y of Douglas McGregor and a few of the hitchhikers—namely Chris Argyris' Theory YB, X-Y Systems, and two theories named "Z." These theories are essentially philosophical prescriptions to guide managers in how to feel about their fellow humans, especially their subordinates. Chapter 15 describes a trio of "programs" which, when "installed," should lead to much better organizational performance.

The final chapter in PART V covers some of the more popular advice and prescriptions for managers in the matter of making decisions. The prescriptions here are typically in the form of specific quantitative techniques which are supposed to vastly improve the quality (if not the timeliness) of managerial decisions. This chapter also includes the prescriptions for developing, processing, and utilizing information in the decision-making process.

Chapter 14

Theories X, Y, YB, X-Y Systems, Z, and Z'

CLEARLY heading the list of behavioral scientists whose "writings, theories and teachings" are reported to have influenced American managers is Douglas McGregor.[1] His theory Y has been common fare in management training programs since it was first introduced in his book in 1960. His major contribution, however, was not theory, as he called it, but philosophy. Most descriptions of his contributions are oversimplified to the point of almost inviting misinterpretation. McGregor himself presented various brief versions of his philosophy in tailored forms for different audiences, thus contributing to possible oversimplifications.[2]

The most popular versions of his philosophy focus almost exclusively on his descriptions of Theory X and Theory Y, and how Theory Y is consistent with Maslow's Need Hierarchy. His Theory X assumptions billed as "The Traditional View of Direction and Control" are given below:

1. The average human being has an inherent dislike of work and will avoid it if he can.
2. Because of this human characteristic of dislike of work, most people must be coerced, controlled, directed, threatened with punishment to get them to put forth adequate effort toward the achievement of organizational objectives.
3. The average human being prefers to be directed, wishes to avoid responsibility, has relatively little ambition, wants security above all.[3]

McGregor's arguments that these assumptions prevailed as the guiding view of employees by managers included no cited research into the matter at all. He *stated* that they were *implicit* in the literature and "in much current managerial policy and practice." To illustrate deep roots for such assumptions, McGregor cited the banishment of Adam and Eve to a "world where they had to work for a living."[4] He alluded to assumption Number 3

259

above as the assumption of the "mediocrity of the masses" and insisted that managers thought "the dislike of work (is) so strong that even the promise of rewards is not generally enough to overcome it. . . . Only threat of punishment will do the trick."[5] As a practicing manager for nine years prior to the publication of his book, your author found the assertions in his 1960 book as simply further evidence of how removed academics were from the actual workplace. It was surprising to learn that with his academic association with a university unit involved in industrial relations, he had not noticed that the effective threat of punishment as a motivating device had all but disappeared in American industry, especially in unionized operations. The collective powers, expertise powers, and affluence powers of the employee in most organizations at that time simply would not permit Theory X management as he described it. McGregor, however, insisted that he was not raising a "straw man for the purposes of demolition." Others would disagree: "(McGregor) did not name individuals nor delve into past management thought very deeply; if he had, he would have found that Theory X was not quite as prevalent as he assumed."[6]

Theory Y was offered by McGregor as a "modest beginning for new theory." Its heart was a new set of assumptions:

1. The expenditure of physical and mental effort in work is as natural as play or rest.
2. External control and the threat of punishment are not the only means for bringing about effort toward organizational objectives. Man will exercise self-direction and self-control in the service of objectives to which he is committed.
3. Commitment to objectives is a function of the rewards associated with their achievement.
4. The average human being learns, under proper conditions, not only to accept but to seek responsibility.
5. The capacity to exercise a relatively high degree of imagination, ingenuity, and creativity in the solution of organizational problems is widely, not narrowly, distributed in the population.
6. Under the conditions of modern industrial life, the intellectual potentialities of the average human being are only partially utilized.

In his discussion of Theory Y, McGregor contrasts the two sets of assumptions:

Theory X offers management an easy rationalization for ineffective organizational performance: "It is due to the nature of the human resources with which we must work. Theory Y, on the other hand, places the problems squarely in the lap of management. If employees are lazy, indifferent, unwilling to take responsibility, intransigent, uncreative, uncooperative, Theory Y implies that the *causes lie in management's methods of organization and control.*" (Italics added)[7]

The above indictment of management methods as the *causes* of "intransigent" and "uncooperative" behavior seems strange from several viewpoints, not the least of which involves the following quote from an earlier McGregor article " . . . since no important decision ever pleases everyone in the organization, (the boss) *must . . . absorb the displeasure, and sometimes severe hostility,* of those who would have taken a different course."[8] McGregor wrote these words upon the eve of his retirement from the presidency of Antioch College. In this essay, to his great credit, McGregor quite candidly described the impact of experiencing management on some of his previous views which were based on observations only:

It will require time to think back over the many events that have been crowded into these few years and to draw a proper meaning from them. However, two related convictions have developed slowly but steadily out of this experience.

The Boss Must Boss

The first conviction—has been derived from my personal struggle with the role of college president. Before coming to Antioch I had observed and worked with top executives as an advisor in a number of organizations. I thought I knew how they felt about their responsibilities and what led them to behave as they did. I even thought that I could create a role for myself that would enable me to avoid some of the difficulties they encountered. I was wrong! *It took the direct experience of becoming a line executive and meeting personally the problems involved to teach me what no amount of observation of other people could have taught.*

I believed, for example, that a leader could operate successfully as a kind of adviser to his organization. I thought I could avoid being a "boss." Unconsciously, I suspect, I hoped to duck the unpleasant necessity of making difficult decisions, of taking the responsibility for one course of action among many uncertain alternatives, of making mistakes and taking the consequences. I thought that maybe I could operate so that everyone would like me—that "good human relations" would eliminate all discord and disagreement.

I could not have been more wrong. It took a couple of years, but I finally began to realize that a leader cannot avoid the exercise of authority any more than he can avoid responsibility for what happens to his organization. In fact, it is a major function of the top executive to take on his own shoulders the responsibility for resolving the uncertainties that are always involved in important decisions.[9] (Italics added)

Four years after this candid observation that a leader cannot succeed as "a kind of advisor to his organization," McGregor, in his chapter on "Management by Integration and Self-Control," apparently changed his mind or forgot some of the lessons learned while a line executive. McGregor, in this chapter, gave an ideal example of Theory Y in practice, a dialogue between an executive (Evans) and one of his subordinate managers (Harrison) which included the following: "So try to think of me as a colleague whose experience and knowledge are at your disposal—not as your boss."[10] A little further on in the chapter McGregor analyzed the results of this approach in this example: "The critically significant factor in these discussions . . . was the redefinition of the roles which took place. Evans succeeded, by his manner more than specific words, in conveying to Harrison the essential point that *he did not want to occupy the conventional role of boss*, but rather, to the fullest extent possible, the role of a consultant . . ."[11] (Italics added)

McGregor is reported to have complained that his theory had later been widely misunderstood and misinterpreted.[12] Perhaps the vacillations evident in the above could account for some of what appeared to him as misunderstandings and misinterpretations. McGregor is reported to have ". . . continually pointed out that both theories (X and Y) embodied assumptions about the nature of man—but assumptions *only*, and not a 'cookbook' on how to manage. Although they are normative, they were not intended to be prescriptive."[13] But even these remarks are confusing since any dictionary definition of "normative" will offer as a meaning the *prescribing* of norms, and norms refer to typical or standard patterns of behavior. If there is anything normative, therefore, about McGregor's theory, it would be Theory X, not Y, since this is the behavior he describes as typical of managers. Later in his unfinished second book, *The Professional Manager*, he explains that "it was not (his) intention to suggest more than that these were examples of two among many managerial cosmologies. . . ."[14] Anyone who has read his original description of Theory X and Theory Y cannot mistake McGregor's intention. It was clearly to describe Theory X as typical and bad and to describe Theory Y as new and good.

From 1957, from his writings, McGregor seems to have gone through three position stages arriving at a fourth:

1. The boss shouldn't be a boss in the traditional sense. The boss should be a kind of consultant or advisor to his organization.
2. The boss must boss. The boss cannot operate only as a kind of advisor to his or her organization.
3. The boss shouldn't be a boss in the traditional sense. The boss should be a kind of consultant or advisor to his or her organization.
4. It all depends upon the characteristics of the manager and upon the particular situation.

Another dimension of the interpretations of McGregor's theories would be the hard-soft dichotomy sometimes ascribed to X and Y. He was unmistakably clear on this point from the beginning. He pointed out early that these descriptions were irrelevant to his theories. He also insisted that the application of Theory Y did not involve any abdication of management, mandatory participation, or the lowering of standards.

Aside from the emotional appeal carefully exploited by McGregor to "sell" Theory Y, he based its rationale on two other factors. He argued that Theory Y was consistent with Maslow's motiviation theory of a need hierarchy. He insisted that conventional organizations and management approaches thwarted social and ego need-fulfillment, and offered few opportunities for self-development needs to emerge.[15] Another anchor in his rationale was his observation of the following changes: (1) the explosive growth of science, (2) the rapidly changing industry-society relationships, and (3) the changing composition of the industrial work force (from blue-collar to white).[16] These sound remarkably like the trends noted by Warren Bennis as reasons for his erroneous prediction of the coming death of bureaucracy. McGregor predicted in 1961 that "we will witness during the next couple of decades some profound, far-reaching changes in the strategy utilized to manage the human resources of enterprise."[17] The above trends he saw as forcing these changes to come about, just as Bennis saw them as forcing bureaucracy's demise. Neither viewed management as only one element in an integrated system, however. Neither appeared to see management's behavior as largely dependent upon the behavior of the other elements in the system.

At this point we may ask if McGregor was offering extrapolations of behavioral changes in managers (which were already well underway in 1960) or predictions of *changes in systems* of which managers were only one element. From his writings, one clearly gets the idea that he felt that managers were lagging behind in their adaptions to these trends, and that this was producing sub-optimal performance. Yet it is inconceivable that he was unaware of the multi-million dollar expenditures on human relations training for foremen in the 1950's which went down the drain as their behavior reverted as they re-entered their work environments.

At least two views of McGregor's role are possible. One is that he was recording what was already happening and predicting that it was going to happen on a grander scale rather quickly. The other would be that he was making it happen by his analyses and urgings. I prefer the first view. McGregor himself seemed to be alternately doing both at times. It was as though he was saying "These trends in the socio-industrial culture are forcing Theory Y on you whether you like it or not, so why not take my advice and get on with it now." The only problem, as he pointed out in his later writings, is simply that the ability and opportunity to "get on with it" depends upon a great many factors over which the manager sometimes has little or no control.

From the point of view of a psychologist, the most disturbing of McGregor's views would be his naive notion that managers and their organizations   *cause*   whatever   laziness,   uncreativeness,   and   uncooperativeness are to be found in their work forces. Even conceding that McGregor was an *advocative* social scientist and that he used such techniques in selling his theories, such assertions are clearly irresponsible. The omission of crime from the list is a puzzle. If crime were added to his list, the manager and his organization could then be held to account for almost all of modern society's ills; and their obvious development in the home, the school and the wider (non-workplace) culture could be ignored as irrelevant.

Defense of Theory Y

Edgar H. Schein, a colleague of McGregor's at M.I.T. and co-editor of a book of McGregor's essays, has responded to what he saw as Theory Y critics. Their criticisms, according to Schein, were mainly because the Theory was misunderstood:

> Many authors have interpreted the group behavior of workers as evidence against McGregor's Theory Y. To be specific, they have argued that because workers are often alienated from work and/or are often fundamentally in conflict with the organization that employs them, it is not possible to apply participative theories in many kinds of situations. Therefore, by implication, Theory Y is inadequate or wrong.[18]

Schein's argument is based upon what he saw as four fallacies:

> (1) The Theory is one of motivation, not on how to manage, (2) No claim is made in Theory Y that organizational and human needs can always be integrated, (3) The Theory does not imply participative management. Instead it is a statement about human behavior fundamentals and how people would behave under appropriate organizational conditions, and (4) The Theory is not without research support. He asserts that most pertinent research is supportive of Theory Y assumptions about human behavior.[19]

Schein supports his points by arguing that research findings on workgroup output restrictions (specifically the Hawthorne Bank Wiring Room) are proof of the accuracy of Theory Y assumptions about human nature.[20] The energies directed toward thwarting management's production goals are proof to him that Theory X assumptions were incorrect. He implied that if management had held Theory Y assumptions such production restrictions would not have existed.

Much of Schein's elaboration of Theory Y appeared to be late McGregor. Many of the harsh indictments of management in earlier McGregor writings were softened by Schein. For example, he claims that "When workers fail to exhibit behavior consistent with Theory Y assumptions at their place of work, it is *likely* (not certain) that past management practices, organizational traditions, and control systems have conditioned them. . . ."[21]

Schein appears to be the only author, however, to pointedly separate

McGregor's assumptions about human nature (Theory Y) from certain of McGregor's value positions. Referring to "sources of confusion" about McGregor's theories, Schein said that he believed "that McGregor himself muddied the conceptual waters when he linked to his analysis of managerial assumptions about human behavior a value position that it was management's obligation to create opportunities for self-actualization."[22] Schein pointedly disagreed that it was management's responsibility to arrange the organizational environment so as to facilitate the integration of individual and organizational objectives.

In addition to supporting a vaguely defined contingency approach to managerial leadership, Schein emphasized the point that a manager who holds Theory Y assumptions is more likely to be a better manager than one holding Theory X assumptions, mainly because he will, on the whole, be more flexible.

From Theory XB to Theory YB

Chris Argyris, an organizational development and laboratory training proponent and practitioner, has used McGregor's Theory X and Theory Y as foundations for analyzing certain managerial behavior patterns, especially those he sees as critical to managing change. In his book[23] describing three organizations' efforts to effect fundamental changes toward Theory Y management, Argyris initially used the A and B designations for organizational behavior patterns which he saw as functions of Theory X and Theory Y management assumptions respectively. Pattern A represents Argyris' findings from his case studies and laboratory training research regarding the interpersonal behavior, group dynamics, and organizational norms which tend to go with Theory X assumptions. Pattern B represents his findings regarding these dimensions which are associated with Theory Y. Pattern (X)A characteristics were described by Argyris as follows:[24]

Behavior tending to be more frequent	Behavior tending to be less frequent
Owning up to ideas	Owning up to feelings
Conforming to ideas	Individuality of ideas
Concern for ideas	
Openness to ideas	
Not helping others to express ideas and feelings	Helping others to express ideas
Inconsistent behavior	Consistent behavior

Rarely observed behavior

Experimenting with ideas or feelings
Concern for feelings
Trust of ideas or feelings
Helping others to express their feelings

The reader must bear in mind that the above behavior patterns were those observed in organizational development training sessions such as sensitivity training or some other form of laboratory training. They were *not* scientifically validated against behavior on the job. Other references to XA behavior patterns appear throughout Argyris' book as bald statements such as the following:

The XA world emphasizes achieving the goals, with little attention to the human beings, and thus a high cost is paid in terms of the interpersonal and group factors. The executives who tend to be attracted to, become successful in, and are gatekeepers for the new entrants are those whose leadership style tends to be oriented toward getting the job done and ignoring interpersonal issues. . . . XA produces subordinates who are dependent, oriented toward the superior, fear risk taking, and rarely level about interpersonal issues.[25]

(To follow this view of Argyris the reader will have to ignore the largest Theory X organization known—the military—whose members are quite risk-taking.)

Argyris' description of behavior pattern YB was given in an earlier publication of his as "pattern B."[26] It requires that managers have ". . . more trust, concern for feelings, and internal commitment; more openness to and experimenting with, new ideas and feelings *in such a way that others could do the same. . . .*"[27] The YB adherent is essentially one whose laboratory or sensitivity training has been successful. Throughout the book, the implication is clear that one is not likely to be a YB type manager without OD training. Consider the following:

Another quality which the overwhelming number of executives who had no laboratory experiences manifested was little predisposition to look "inward" to ascertain the extent to which they might be important causes of the human problems within their system. . . . Our findings (were) that executives who have had successful laboratory experiences tend to become more self-responsible. The YB adherents in organization B, for example, were constantly concerned about their personal responsibility and about changing the system.[28]

What Argyris did essentially was to hypothesize that managers with Theory Y assumptions were like managers who have had OD training. By implication, therefore, if a company wants to change from XA to YB managerial patterns, it must have a sustained OD program, and if one follows

Argyris, must have an outside consultant-change agent-interventionist. He cautioned, however, that such a change is slow, painful and turbulent, since it involves altering many peoples' viewpoints and their thinking and behavioral patterns.

Theory Y and Task-Organizational Fit

Using primarily a case study approach and a fairly vague and somewhat misleading reporting style, John J. Morse and Jay W. Lorsch, in their article "Beyond Theory Y,"[29] introduce the variables of organization and task as important considerations in assessing managerial approaches such as Theory X or Theory Y. They reported on their study of four organizations, two of which were judged by corporate managers as low performers and two as high performers. Each performance category contained one research and development operation and one manufacturing operation with a "relatively certain manufacturing task." They found that the two high performing organizations fitted "their respective tasks much better than did their less successful counterparts."[30] Below is their description of the formal organizational characteristics of the two high-performing operations:[31]

Characteristics	Akron	Stockton
1. Pattern of formal relationships and duties as signified by organization charts and job manuals.	Highly structured, precisely defined	Low degree of structure, less well defined
2. Pattern of formal roles, procedures, control and measurement systems	Pervasive, specific, uniform, comprehensive	Minimal, loose, flexible
3. Time dimensions incorporated in formal practices	Short term	Long term
4. Goal dimensions incorporated in formal practices	Manufacturing	Scientific

In addition to the formal characteristics, the researchers attempted to assess what they referred to as organizational climate characteristics. This was done by interviews and questionnaires with "about forty managers" in each unit. They also measured the feelings of competence of the people with a questionnaire in each organization in order to compare organizational characteristics with feelings of competence. One problem in interpreting their findings results from the vagueness of their participant identification. Below are the identifying descriptions of the participants whose responses apparently contributed to their findings:

The *people* at the Akron plant perceived a great deal of structure . . .
In contrast, the *scientists* (assume worker-scientist or boss-scientists?) in the Stockton laboratory perceived very little structure.
Scientists in the less structured Carmel laboratory perceived much more structure . . .
Akron *personnel* (assume both managers and workers?) felt that they had much less influence . . .
Therefore there was less need for *individuals* (?) to have a say in decisions concerning the work process.
Akron's *members* perceived themselves to have a low degree of freedom vis-a-vis superiors . . .
Stockton's *scientists*, on the other hand, felt that they had a great deal of freedom vis-a-vis their superiors. . . . They described supervision in the laboratory as being very participatory.
The *people* at Akron perceived . . .
By contrast, Stockton's *scientists* perceived . . .
Akron's *individuals* were highly oriented toward a relatively short time span and manufacturing goals.
Stockton's *researchers* were highly oriented toward a longer time span . . .
Finally, the *individuals* in both Akron and Stockton perceived their chief executive to have a "managerial style" that expressed more of a concern for the task than for people or relationships . . .[32] (Italics and parenthetical material added)

On the one hand, the researchers tell us that their data came from *managers* in each operation and on the other hand we are told how "personnel," "members," "scientists," "people," "individuals," and "researchers," perceive various aspects of their organizations. Did the authors actually include non-supervisory researchers and scientists from one plant and not hourly workers at the other? If so they are comparing apples with nails, since there is little evidence offered that managers can speak for the perceptions of manufacturing workers.

Citing that the Akron managers were highly motivated in their formalized setting and that managers at Hartford, the low performing manufacturing operation studied, were not as highly motivated in their less formalized setting, the authors pointed to the need for a contingency theory. Demonstrating what Schein and McGregor called a misinterpretation of Theory Y, they pointed out that "the managers at Akron worked in a setting with relatively little *participation* in decision making. To deal with this paradox they offered the following "Contingency Theory," which they believed explained the findings at all four operations:

1. Human beings bring varying patterns of needs and motives into the work organization, but one central need is to achieve a sense of competence.
2. The sense of competence motive, while it exists in all human beings, may be fulfilled in different ways by different people depending on how this need interacts with the strengths of the individuals' other needs—such as those for power, independence, structure, achievement, and affiliation.
3. Competence motivation is most likely to be fulfilled when there is a fit between task and organization.
4. Sense of competence continues to motivate even when a competence goal is achieved; once the goal is reached, a new higher one is set.[33]

Morse and Lorsch conclude that McGregor's Theories X and Y are inadequate because neither the nature of the task or the organization (including its climate) are accounted for by these models.

Theories X and Y as Systems

LeRoy Johnson, as a result of his observations of a company attempting to move toward a Y approach to management, has concluded that organizations are made up of sub-units whose patterns of activities can best be described as systems. He designated X and Y *systems* as ends of a continuum and far more than comprising just a set of assumptions about human nature by managers. He described these systems in terms of the characteristics of their elements. A summary of these descriptions is given below:[34]

X System Elements

The X System end of the continuum contains short job cycles, predetermined work methods, machine paced, tiresome jobs requiring little mental attention. Leaders in an X System are mainly involved in planning, organizing, controlling the work, and motivating workers for output. The workers in the System X end of the continuum are typically unionized and do as little work as possible. The policies of the X organization are mainly aimed at keeping the employees from taking advantage of the company.

Y System Elements

The Y System end of the continuum contains challenging work which stretches the workers abilities and offers a chance to develop and grow and thus provides each worker with opportunities for individual recognition. The leaders in the Y System are mainly facilitative, performing more as coordinators and advisers than as bosses. They are strongly supportive of worker attempts at innovation for work improvement. Employee attitudes in the Y System are such that they work because it is a satisfying activity and their output is limited only by their abilities. Work groups do not tolerate abuses of privileges. The organizational policies under the Y System are designed mainly to facilitate work accomplishment, provide information to workers about how they are doing, provide recognition, benefits and promotions based on performance.

Johnson's concern was primarily the task of moving a company toward a Y system. He insists that careful analysis of each subunit must be undertaken to determine where it is on the continuum (from X system to Y system) before any change activity be begun. He believes that the traditional approaches— mass communications, development courses introducing concepts, and new corporate policy programs with directives—do not work because of these subunit variations.

Johnson appears to have rediscovered, through his research, the phenomenon discovered in the 1950's—after training foremen in "human relations" those who came from Theory X type systems would slip back into their old ways:

> A single specific course of action cannot be prescribed for accomplishment of such a shift. Nor can change be made by focusing on effective teaching methods. This approach assumes that the proper set of concepts generates a Y situation. Our findings were the reverse—that a given situation determines the feelings and point of view of supervisors as well as workers. Behavior arises from these feelings. *A supervisor becomes locked into X systems by the job tasks, individual and group attitudes, and company policies.* He cannot break out of these systems by his own determination.[35] (Italics added.)

Leaving aside the wasted effort a knowledge of history might have saved, one serious problem with Mr. Johnson's approach remains. If these systems are made up of interacting and interdependent elements of work tasks, leader assumptions, worker attitudes and company policies and practices, then *all* elements must undergo change for a system to be moved along his X-Y continuum. But it may not be reasonable to make changes in all these elements. For example, a critical element—and one which may actually determine many characteristics of certain of the other elements—is the nature of the work task. For an X system unit to be moved to a Y system unit, its tasks would have to be changed from those which are "short, machine paced with predetermined tools and motions requiring surface mental attention" to — strangely enough—"stretch ability and offer chance to develop and grow, give opportunity to apply skill and experience, and allow seeing the results of actions." Another way of viewing this proposed change, although not mentioned in his article, is that job enlargement and job enrichment are essential to theory Y management. The mixed results of such experimental ventures are discussed in detail in Chapter 20.

Theory Z Management

Laurence Foss, responding to what he saw as the radically different values of those born after 1950, has postulated a "Theory Z management." He views the concerns for the well-being of society of this new generation as requiring a management approach which recognizes their new values. The U.S. is considered bicultural by Foss: those with "frontier cowboy" concerns and those with "spaceship husbandry" concerns. The former are associated with the "open earth" profit and economic growth view of their environment and the latter with the "closed earth" socio-ecological view. To better understand Foss' theory, it is important to see his view of today's organizational environment as established and managed by the open earth, frontier cowboys:

> If we look to "depth factors" in the corporate environment—conventions pertaining to color, sound, space, dress, language, hair style, and so on—what do we see? We see muted colors, we hear the preceding environment strains of Muzak, we encounter semi-military, coat-and-tie dress codes; smells are virtually eliminated; a complete break between formal and informal speech is made regarding four-letter words; and meaningless quarter-inch increments of sideburns and hair are observed—after the fact.[36]

Foss' description of corporate environment makes it clear that he does not view a corporation's steel mill, copper mine, or factory as part of the corporate environment. It is further clear that he sees short sideburns as "meaningless," thus demonstrating that he cannot keep his personal prejudices out of his descriptive reporting.

Foss saw this corporate environment, however narrowly he viewed it, as quite inappropriate for husbandry oriented space-agers. They are described as taking relative abundance for granted. They are evidently not particularly concerned with finding good jobs, but with what kind of social citizen the employer is. They are concerned with how the company ministers to the quality of life on earth. Inflation and unemployment problems do not appear to interest them, probably because Foss published his article 6 months before the oil embargo and 9 months before the first oil price increase and before U.S. unemployment had peaked to record highs.

The Z management proposed by Foss is one which accounts for these different values—husbandry, and the quality of life concerns. Foss never specifies, however, any particular management behavior for Theory Z. He only insists that whatever behavior managers do exhibit should be consistent with these new values as they are manifested in the husbandry-spaceship employees' self-actualization needs. He sprinkles the fashionable managerial leadership modelers' names throughout his Theory Z presentation but leaves the reader much room for guessing about actual Theory Z management. Below are illustrative examples of this vagueness:

How does this development affect management training? From its perspective, what might Argyris' concept of job enlargement look like, the ideal point on the Mouton-Blake managerial grid, Likert's System 4, or Herzberg's motivators? This defines the Theory Z question.[37] Categories of motivation, achievement, and so on (Herzberg's "satisfiers") need to be reviewed in the light of today's controlling concepts, particularly among the young; relevance, co-control, legitimacy, community . . . How this wedges into management development concepts is a problem that defines the target area of Theory Z Management[38] . . . Moreover, it underlines "depth factors" in Herzberg's hygiene factors toward which even Theory Y managers tend to be selectively inattentive, undercutting managerial strategies for improving worker motivation.[39]

Foss suggests that Maslow's concept of a need which has been satisfied should contain the notion of "culture variant" needs to which managements must respond. He contends that many of the so-called "motivators" are antiquated and must be revised to incorporate the view that a company is a sub-system in the total world system, and that the company's response to these culture-variant needs is necessary to promote "social equilibrium."[40] Foss explained that his Theory Z "stresses relations between organizational life and individual motivation . . . through the medium of the social field as it now affects the organization itself and on the individual as a socio-ecologically concerned citizen."[41]

Foss prefaced all but one of the above ideas with "Before giving on-the-job applications to Theory Z management . . ."[42] Unfortunately, he never gets around to discussing "on-the-job applications." However inarticulate he may have been on this point, he did make the point well that value differences are important in understanding motivation of many younger employees, especially those who graduated from universities and colleges in the late 1960's and early 1970's. He never suggested that he had examined the husbandry values of the blue-collar or red-neck workers except to refer to the shut-down of the General Motors Lordstown plant by a group of workers whose mean age was 25 and who were described by the Detroit Free Press as ". . . a young hip, often bearded and bell-bottomed group of UAW (United Auto Workers) workers."[43] (parenthetical phrase added) None of the voluminous reports of this strike, however, noted any serious demands by these workers for more attention to earth husbandry or ecological factors. Foss' focus on culture in analyzing worker behavior could possibly help in understanding the Lordstown strike, however. The culture in which these workers grew up was quite different from that of the open-earth cowboys, or for that matter, the modern Taiwanese or Japanese worker. Most of these Orientals, when they were growing up, could not easily avoid learning to tolerate boredom by switching channels, hunting a new FM station, or shifting to their cassette hi-fi when bored. And Foss is correct, too, in pointing to the technical and economic origins of some of the generation differences. Where he erred, however, was in assuming for the husbandry values, the same *strength* of the values of the earlier generations. He did not foresee that when the job market for college graduates seriously declined with the 1980's inflation and relative joblessness, these values would be fairly easily backgrounded. This is not to suggest that all such values were cancelled out by the economics of the period—only that the real development of these values in the U.S. and parts of Western Europe would turn out to be a gradual change as with most other value evolutions observed by anthropologists. Anyone who has witnessed the husbandry-oriented university students' outrage over corporations' lack of concern for ecological problems to which they are major contributors must have also noticed the student apathy for beer can clean-up campaigns in college towns. And of course, as the job market got tighter, the ecological concerns were relegated to a residual level, which, although a higher value concern level than that of previous generations, was not the over-riding concern seen by Foss as requiring a radical change in management style for its accommodation.

Foss' Theory Z simply suggests that a third "concern" dimension be added to the Blake and Mouton two dimensional grid. Their ideal manager was a 9,9 manager on a 9 × 9 point grid which simply meant that he should have a maximum concern for both task and people (as compared to a 1,1 manager who was seriously concerned with neither). Foss' ideal Theory Z manager is a 9,9,9 manager with concerns on three dimensions: concern for people, concern for task, and concern for "the company as a subsystem in a total system."

Theory Z, as a managerial normative notion, appears to be nothing more than advice to the over-30 managers that they should note the husbandry values of the space-age generation and somehow accommodate them. With or without Foss' theory, managers, naturally responding to the urgencies of corporate objectives, whether they be Foss' outdated profits or corporate contribution to the quality of life now and in the future, will evolve managerial behavior for the motivation, direction and control of their subordinates necessary to the achievement of these goals. If history is of any value, this evolution will take place gradually and largely without the assistance or guidance of academicians.

Theory Z' Management

Another "Theory Z Management" was offered in the early 1970's by Edward Lawless. This Theory Z Management was described even more vaguely by its proponent than Foss'. It was referred to in Chapter 4, but the essence of Lawless' one paragraph description of it is repeated below:

As the organization changes, evolves, shifts its purposes, takes on new personnel, matures, the management function will change . . . Theory Z management calls for the recognition that management style must adjust to the needs of the organization at whatever state of evolution it has reached . . . Suspicion of absolutes is the key to Theory Z management.[44]

Summary

The non-theory Theory Y of McGregor summarized, in somewhat advocative journalistic style, the post human relations period sentiments of behavioral scientists. It became instantly popular with university students and academics as well as with training directors concerned with management development. It was popular partly because it offered an easy identification of the bad guys (X). Other similar management diagnostic approaches followed. Blake and Mouton's 9,9 managers and Likert's System 4 management are examples of "good guy" styles. Theory Y has never benefited from rigorous research for support, and for good reason. Scientific measurement of a manager's "assumptions about the nature of man" could be rather tricky. Instead, its popularity has been due to the simple reason that it is personally appealing. It makes legitimate the criticisms of authority and provides easy labels for them: Theory X, 9, 1, etc.

The problem with Theory Y, et al. is the same as that produced by most zealots. For wide-spread emotional appeal, the zealot's arguments must be very simple, polarized and emotionally loaded. McGregor's popular presentation of Theory Y allows no room for a manager to behave as a Theory Y manager with all of his or her 15 subordinates but 3. The manager is either X or Y just as Americans who were one-eighth black were all black in parts of the U.S. not too many years ago. The practical side of the matter is simply that very few managers are all X or all Y. More tended toward Theory Y assumptions in 1960 than McGregor was aware of, however. And more are doing so today, perhaps. There are many successful managers, however, who make no generalized assumptions about man. They take "man" one by one, and if this "one" justifies peicemeal Theory Y assumptions, this one is often managed differently than if he or she justifies Theory X assumptions. Few managers would accept responsibility on behalf of their managerial forebears, for all the employees who, to them, justify Theory X assumptions. Although they are not social psychiatrists, few managers are willing to believe that all the laziness, indifference, irresponsibility, intransigence and unco-operativeness is their own or their managerial forebears' doing. After all, some of them (and professors and machinists) even have children who clearly manifest some of these characteristics. And most of these children never spent any time being so shaped in a corporate organization by its Theory X managers and their control systems.

Leaving the above behavior patterns aside, even if Theory Y management assumptions could be magically "installed" in all managers, there is no evidence that all nonmanagers would want the responsibility which necessarily accompanies Theory Y management. As McGregor has pointed out, Theory Y management is not an easy road—either for the manager or his subordinates. Many of us, due to deepseated cultural patterns, are too uncomfortable maintaining the necessary self-direction and self-control required under Theory Y. For such people, the loss of the Theory X-like direction to which they have successfully adapted during most of their lives, can produce serious anxieties.

The leader-follower system must be made up of human elements which fit the task and work environment and which fit in terms of assumptions about each other and their behaviors toward each other. This system cannot be effectively altered by admonishing only one element in it—managers—to change their ways.

NOTES

1. In the Poll of American and Canadian managers by the National Industrial Conference Board referred to in Chapters 4 and 6.
2. See Douglas McGregor, "Executive Responsibilities in a Period of Exploding Technology," (a conference paper later published in:) *The Technology Review*, LXIII, No. 4 (1961), 2–4 and "A Philosophy of Management," a talk presented at E. I. du Pont de Nemours Co. in 1954 and later published in *Leadership and Motivation, Essays of Douglas McGregor*, eds. Warren G. Bennis and Edgar H. Schein, with the collaboration of Caroline McGregor, (Cambridge, Mass.: The M.I.T. Press, 1966) pp. 30–45.
3. Douglas McGregor, *The Human Side of Enterprise*, (New York, N.Y.: McGraw Hill, 1960) pp. 33–34.
4. *Ibid.*, p. 33.
5. *Ibid.*, p. 34.
6. Wren, *The Evolution of Management Thought*, (New York, N.Y.: The Ronald Press, 1972) pp. 449–50.
7. McGregor, *The Human Side of Enterprise*, p. 48.
8. From an essay "On Leadership" which appeared in *Antioch Notes*, XXXI, No. 9 (May 1, 1954).
9. *Ibid.*
10. McGregor, *The Human Side of Enterprise*, p. 64.
11. *Ibid.*, p. 65.
12. Caroline McGregor and Warren G. Bennis, Eds., *The Professional Manager*, (New York, N.Y.: McGraw-Hill, 1967) p. 8.

13. Harold M. G. Rush, *Behavioral Science Concepts and Management Application*, (New York, N.Y.: National Industrial Conference Board, 1969) p. 13.
14. McGregor, Ed., *The Professional Manager*, p. 79.
15. Douglas McGregor, *The Human Side of Enterprise*, pp. 6–12.
16. *Ibid.*, pp. 21–22.
17. Bennis, *et al.*, Ed., *Leadership and Motivation, Essays of Douglas McGregor*, p. 21.
18. Edgar H. Schein, "In Defense of Theory Y," *Organizational Dynamics*, IV, No. 1 (Spring, 1975), p. 17, © 1975 by AMACOM, a division of American Management Associations. All rights reserved.
19. *Ibid.*, pp. 18–19.
20. In particular, Schein referred to workers undermining management control systems and not responding logically to management's incentive system. Although Frederick W. Taylor clearly documented such behavior many years earlier, Schein refers to them in relation to the Hawthorne Studies as "the first of their kind." *Ibid.*, p. 20.
21. *Ibid.*, p. 19.
22. *Ibid.*, p. 23.
23. Chris Argyris, *Management and Organizational Development, The Path from XA to YB*, (New York, N.Y.: McGraw-Hill, 1971).
24. *Ibid.*, p. 133.
25. *Ibid.*, p. 138.
26. Chris Argyris, *Interpersonal Competence and Organizational Effectiveness*, (Homewood, Illinois: The Dorsey Press and Richard D. Irwin, Inc., 1962).
27. Argyris, *Management and Organizational Development, The Path from XA to YB*, p. 18.
28. *Ibid.*, p. 134.
29. John J. Morse and Jay W. Lorsch, "Beyond Theory Y," *Harvard Business Review*, (May-June, 1970), p. 63., Copyright © 1970 by the President and Fellows of Harvard College; all rights reserved.
30. *Ibid.*
31. *Ibid.*
32. *Ibid.*, p. 67.
33. *Ibid.*
34. LeRoy Johnson, "Toward a Theory Y System", *California Management Review*, (Fall, 1972), p. 23.
35. *Ibid.*, p. 28.
36. Laurence Foss, "Managerial Strategy for the Future: Theory Z Management," *California Management Review*, (Spring, 1973), p. 74.
37. *Ibid.*
38. *Ibid.*, p. 68.
39. *Ibid.*, p. 78.
40. *Ibid.*, pp. 78–79.
41. *Ibid.*, p. 79.
42. *Ibid.*, p. 78.

43. *Ibid.*, p. 80.
44. Edward Lawless, *Effective Management* (Englewood Cliffs, N.J.: Prentice Hall, 1972), pp. 361–62.

Chapter 15

Management By Objectives, Operant Conditioning And Job Enrichment

"PETER Drucker didn't invent MBO . . . Henri Fayol (1916) and Ralph Davis (1928) pushed goal-setting . . . participation and involvement were discussed by Lillian Gilbreth (1914), H. Dubreuil (1932) and Alfred Morrow/Kurt Lewin (1940's) . . . and Frederick W. Taylor (1911) noted the importance of feedback and performance evaluation . . . so the elements of MBO aren't new . . . but putting them all together into a total management system is new."[1] As a matter of fact much earlier accounts of management approaches using most or all the elements of the standard MBO foremat can be found as far back as Caesar's time. *Roman Farm Management* contains translations of works by Marcus Cato (234–149 B.C.) (*De Re Rustica*), and by Marcus Varro (116–23 B.C.) (*Rerum Rusticarum Libri Tres*) which carry descriptions of their management systems calling for *objective-setting with participation and evaluation of performance against objectives.* And it is unreasonable to suggest that this approach is not much older, especially in earlier *military* organizations in Europe, the Middle East and in Asia, especially China.

Drucker's contribution in 1954 was to offer a "philosophy" of management embodying the above characteristics in the modern idiom. He related various elements of the philosophy to organizational needs and ascending theories of management such as participation and performance review approaches which were beginning to use objectives instead of personality traits and behaviors which may or may not have been found related to achievement of goals.

The slippage from *philosophy* to (MBO) *program* was unfortunate. The subsequent rash of "installations" of these programs naturally produced a number of failures simply because a particular philosophy cannot be implanted by announcements accompanied by a set of forms and procedures and a few training sessions by staff personnel or consultants. Once viewed as a *program* or technique it became a fashion to be followed. Imagine four Fortune 500 corporation presidents who planned lunch together one day in 1965 at the Yale Club in New York. The three who arrived on time began discussing their MBO programs. Since the late president did not know what MBO stood for he ate in relative silence, but upon returning to his office he summoned his vice-president for Employee Relations and asked what MBO meant. The vice-president told him it referred to a program called Management By Objectives whereupon the president asked if they had such a program. When the vice-president told him that they did not, the president told him to hurry up and get one going or he would become the laughing stock among his friends.

Most major corporations in the U.S. have, since 1960, undertaken to "install" some version of MBO. Many carry labels adopted by the organization either to identify modifications necessary for their own applications or to distinguish theirs from the commonness of the term MBO. Examples would be "Work Planning and Review (WPR)" at General Electric and "Goals and Controls" at Purex Oil Company.

The equivocal results of researchers on the global effects of MBO programs have naturally led researchers to concentrate on the elemental *processes* of such programs. Below are the two elements most often studied:

1. The establishment of goals or objectives
2. The reviews of performance in relation to these goals

One researcher revealed four different processes generally used in the establishment of goals:[2]

1. The highest level of mutual involvement in goal setting was the situation in which the superior would hold a department meeting during which the unit goals and projects for the coming operating period were discussed. The subordinate would then, using information from the meeting, prepare a set of personal goals. At the same time, the boss would independently prepare a set of goals and targets for the subordinate. Later they would meet to discuss these and arrive at some mutual agreement on the subordinate's goals. Their research showed that 28 percent of the managers used this approach.
2. This goal-setting process began with an informational meeting as in the first process. Then the subordinate prepared a set of goals and target dates which the boss edited and altered. A meeting was then held to discuss the goals, the basis of which was the subordinate's edited and revised goal statement. About 21 percent of the managers used this method.

3. Another 21 percent used still another variant of the goal-setting process. In this process, the boss called a meeting to discuss departmental objectives. From this, subordinates prepared individual goal statements which they sent to the boss. These were accepted without any meeting or discussion; the subordinate had no opportunity to determine whether the goals were acceptable to his boss. His manager's silence left him to assume so.
4. The most "boss-centered" approach was process 4. The subordinate was simply informed about the objectives program. The boss and subordinate met, at which time the subordinate was given a set of goals the boss had prepared. The subordinate had little to say about the goals or target dates. The remaining 30 percent of the managers used this approach.

The fairly even spread of managerial approaches along this goal setting process continuum (from employee, to mutual setting, to boss sets) points to some basic *philosophical* differences among these managers. It should be obvious that any "program" which sets out to make this process uniform is either doomed to failure if it is a short term effort or will take quite a number of years and cause considerable turbulence. And some of these years will be needed to wait for retirements, deaths, and discharges since the origins of such philosophies are related to deep-seated personality characteristics and long-term reinforced values.

Research on the goal setting process is voluminous. A recent review of the literature on this aspect of MBO alone turned up 27 reports of field research, mostly done in industrial organizations.[3]

Research on the Effects of Varying Degrees of Participation in Goal Setting

In their review Latham and Yukl found five studies in organizations providing data on the *effects of participation* in goal setting. Their conclusions:

> With respect to the . . . applied question of whether participative goal setting results in higher performance than assigned goals, the results are not consistent. Although most of the studies found some evidence supporting the superiority of participative goal setting, a significant difference is found only under certain conditions or with certain types of employees. The most satisfactory way of explaining these discrepancies probably is in terms of a contingency model, but further research is needed to clarify the nature of the limiting conditions and the manner in which the moderating variables operate.[4]

One of the major flaws of most of these studies was that the degrees of participation were usually determined through the perceptions of the subordinates. As the researchers point out, "the leadership literature suggests that subordinate judgments about their influence in decision making are of questionable accuracy."[5]

Research on the Setting of Goals Vs. No Setting of Goals

It should not be surprising that 10 of the 11 studies reviewed by Latham and Yukl comparing results of performance under a no-goal-setting situation with a goal-setting situation found a goal-setting situation superior. The most convincing study in this category was one which showed that truck drivers who had been hauling only 60 percent of the legal limit began almost immediately to haul 94 percent of the legal maximum. The goal given them was a firm 94 percent. This improvement lasted for the nine months of the study and according to the researchers resulted in a cost savings of over a quarter of a million dollars.[6]

The Effects on Performance of Goal Difficulty

The reviewers interpret the results they found of the seven studies on the effects of goal difficulty on performance in terms of E. A. Locke's theory on goal setting which includes the proposition that hard goals lead to greater performance than do easy goals as long as the goals are accepted.[7] Six of the studies generally support Locke's theory although most of the researches were flawed because the goal difficulty level was not experimentally manipulated.[8] Locke's laboratory studies and subsequent laboratory studies continue to support the proposition, although most leave unanswered the question of how one measures employees' genuine acceptance of hard-to-achieve goals versus tolerance of them.

From a study done by Carroll and Tosi, there is evidence that certain functional area managers have more discretion in setting their own goals than do other functional area managers. They report that from most discretion to least are the following: marketing, finance and administration, manufacturing, and engineering. Perpetuating the low-constraint myth for engineering organizations, they note that it would seem that the engineering group would have high influence over their work goals. Their study also discovered that the higher the level in the organization, the more discretion the manager had over the setting of his own goals! The following of their findings offer further confirmation of common sense predictions:[9]

1. As goals increased in perceived clarity, importance, and relevance, subordinate managers a) were more positive toward the program, and   b) reported they had improved relations with their boss.
2. When priorities were established for goals, subordinate managers a) were more positive toward the MBO program and b) improved their relations with their bosses.
3. Neither the amount of subordinate influence in establishing goals nor the number of goals established was related to any of the four measures of MBO program success criteria. These were established by the researchers

as follows: a) increased effort over previous years, b) general orientation toward the program, c) success in accomplishing performance and self-improvement goals, and d) changes in relations with the superior.

4. The manner in which the boss of the superior carried out the MBO process with her or *his boss* was related to how the superior carried out the process with his or her subordinates: a) clearer goals for the superior were associated with clearer goals for the subordinate, b) frequent review of the superior's performance by his or her boss was related to the superior's more frequent review of his or her subordinates' performance, c) establishment of priorities among the superior's goals for the subordinates of that superior, and d) higher amounts of participation by the superior in setting his or her goals were related to greater subordinate participation in setting goals.

From the 27 studies reviewed by Latham and Yukl we had confirmation of managerial common sense—that performance is better if some kind of goals have been set than if they have not. From Carroll and Tosi, we learn that, as far as behavior regarding the MBO program is concerned, "like boss, like subordinate" is a fair generalization. Beyond these findings, we know little more about the effects of various forms of goal setting and types of goals without learning more about the other variables which are beginning to indicate that the subject matter is considerably more complicated than originally thought to be. As with leadership, motivation and organization theory, goal setting theory is headed towards contingency theory. Latham and Yukl recognized this inevitable outcome in their conclusions about all aspects of goal-setting research in the literature. They warn that ". . . much still remains to be learned, and several lines of research are essential for further validation and elaboration of the theory (Locke's). *Such research is likely to result eventually in the formulation of a contingency model of goal setting effectiveness.*[10] (Parenthetical word and italics added)

Research on Feedback, and Performance Evaluation in MBO Programs

The laboratory and the factory floor studies have rather consistently shown that feedback improves performance more than no feedback. These studies further show that the more timely and relevant the feedback the better the performance results.[11] The findings on the effects of feedback in MBO programs are similar. Higher feedback frequencies have been found associated with a) higher satisfaction with the program, b) higher reported goal accomplishments, c) improved relations with the boss, d) higher amounts of perceived organizational support for the program, e) perceptions of greater decisiveness for the superior, and f) perceptions of greater job satisfaction for the superior. While most of the relationships were small, the message is fairly clear that many benefits result from appropriate and timely feedback of performance.[12]

Organizational Climate and MBO Program Performance

Because so many findings seem to point to particular behaviors of managers at all levels as affecting the outcome of the installation of MBO programs, some researchers have begun to attempt assessments of what they refer to as "organizational climate" in relation to MBO program performance. One such study by Robert W. Hollmann suggested that such a relationship does exist. Using a questionnaire designed to measure the "supportiveness" of the climate and which also asked for perceptions of MBO effectiveness, he found several statistically significant but low correlations between these two variables. The climate assessment portion of his questionnaire completed by 111 managers in a large utility company attempted to measure the levels of trust and confidence between superiors and subordinates, multidirectional communications, cooperative teamwork among workgroup members, the degree of subordinate involvement in decision making and general goal setting, and the degree of self-control as compared to superior-imposed control. This portion of the instrument was a shortened version of Likert's organizational characteristics questionnaire. Perceptions about the MBO program effectiveness were measured by questions about "(1) planning and organizing work, (2) objective method of evaluating work performance, (3) motivation of the best performance, (4) coordination of individual and work group objectives, (5) improvement in superior-subordinate cooperation, and (6) over-all satisfaction with MBO . . ."[13] When each of these was correlated with overall measures of organizational climate, the correlations ranged from .42 to .27 or with coefficients of determination (r^2) of from .17 to .07. Five r^2's were above .13 suggesting that ". . . supportiveness of the climate accounted for more than 13 percent of the variation in managers' assessment of MBO effectiveness for five of the seven effectiveness dimensions."[14]

The majority of the literature on MBO contains advice on how to install it right, how to improve the program, or on the pitfalls of installing a program without considering this factor or that. This list usually begins with the need for top management support and encouragement. Here is a list of additional typical warnings to be found in such articles:

1. The total organizational goals must be established first considering the future economic outlook, the organization's strengths and weaknesses, and major opportunities and problems facing the organization in the near and distant future. This can take up to several years and if not done, the program has little chance for success.

2. The statements or goals of objectives should be clear, concise, unambiguous, accurate, and consistent with policies, procedures and plans already applicable to the organizational unit. A few prescriptive writers very perceptively point to the need for dove-tailing the MBO objectives with such on-going systems as budgeting and performance appraisal systems. They point out that most companies have been establishing some kinds of objectives all along and have concrete goals in the form of budgets, targets, etc. They make the point that an MBO program cannot simply be grafted on to the organizational systems—that its subsystems must be integral with the other systems in operation. The early MBO programs almost all focussed on an annual cycle regardless of cycles already established to respond to the realities of their businesses. A simple example would be a company which had a performance review on the employees' anniversary basis and went to an MBO program on an annual calendar basis, with little regard for the employee who was just evaluated and who might have to be evaluated much later.

3. Be aware of the variations in limitations on goal setting discretion. Lower levels rarely have the same amount of discretion as do upper levels.

4. One observer suggests that the features worth keeping in an MBO program are the conscious emphasis on goal-setting, the frequent feedback and interaction between superior and subordinates, and the opportunities for participation. He also suggested that the following features be discarded: a) Linking MBO to the compensation system, b) insisting on only "objectively" measureable performance goals, c) most of the forms now in use, and d) pre-packaged programs and their costly consultants.[15]

5. If the program is intended to produce significant personnel development results, personal development goals should be based on actual performance deficiencies. Attention should be on a) improvement of interpersonal skills, b) improvement of technical skills, and c) preparation for advancement.[16]

Summary of Conclusions on MBO from the Literature

Below are a series of quotations representing conclusions reached by a sample of authors on the effectiveness, usefulness, and appropriateness of Management by Objectives:

1. "MBO may be effective for some members of the organization and counterproductive for other members."[17]

2. "With respect to the perceptual nature of MBO effectiveness, it is reasonable to assume that MBO will not be highly successful if managers have negative attitudes toward it. On the other hand, neither positive

attitudes toward MBO nor positive climate-MBO effectiveness relationships guarantee its success."[18]

3. "The findings in both organizations show that the effects of MBO training and implementation are both short-lived. When perceived job satisfaction of participants was examined, there were no significant differences between measures before external-change agent intervention and MBO training and measures twenty months after these events."[19]

4. "It is still difficult to gain a clear perspective on the efficacy of MBO in terms of corporate and individual performance. There is a distressing lack of well-documented and well-controlled research using a before-after measurement design. Partial field experiments, case studies and survey reports of reactions to MBO have been published, but these, together with the available case studies, are not enough to provide sufficient evidence."[20]

5. "Not long ago a new concept, management by objectives (MBO) is rapidly becoming a gospel message—what was once considered a possibility is now widely applied (or misapplied) as an infallible technique by tunnel-visioned trainers. It is a technique that does *not* work in many cases, though, because the only successful application is through custom designing, thoughtful implementation, and careful evaluation within the context of a total organization development effort."[21]

6. "Management by Objectives represents the most widely accepted approach to management. Some firms have had years—even decades—of experience with this technique. Yet, persistent difficulties still exist."[22]

7. "In sum: MBO is usually offered as a high-cost long-run package whose success is by no means guaranteed (or even likely), which generates many side effects impossible to predict or to control . . . MBO is yet another technique that requires friendly, helpful superiors, honest and mature subordinates, and high mutual trust. *It works best for those individuals who need it least* . . . MBO is best suited to those static, mechanistic environments where adequate alternatives already exist. Rapidly changing conditions and low role clarity render it worse than useless. *It works best in those situations where we need it least* . . . MBO adds nothing to our ability to reward and control. It correctly emphasizes goal-setting, feedback, interaction, and participation. These strengths should be maintained, but not at the cost of jolting the organization with massive and simultaneous changes. We must substitute a "mini-MBO" which introduces fewer variables, takes less time to work, costs less, and minimizes both employee anxiety and unpredictable side effects . . ."[23]

The above conclusions are consistent with my findings in a follow-up study of the Union Carbide Chemicals Division's MBO program launched in 1960. These findings are contained in a post script at the end of Chapter 19.

OPERANT CONDITIONING

Operant conditioning is nothing more than an accentuate-the-positive program elaboration of the old conditioned response learning principle. All of its elements have been presented elsewhere in this book. From the three step program installation procedure provided by its number one guru, Edward J. Feeney, former Vice-President of Emery Air Freight Company, its overlap with other programs already covered is obvious:

Step one: Specify the desired level or standard of performance, preferably in quantitative terms.

Step two: Provide immediate, quantitative feedback informing employees of their level of performance in relation to the standard (preferably this feedback will come directly to the employees such as through performance records which they keep themselves.)

Step three: Provide positive reinforcement in cases where the feedback indicates that performance meets the standard, and encouragement in cases where it does not meet the standard. Praise is recommended as the most practical positive reinforcer.[24]

With very little adjustment, these could be the steps for installing a piece-rate system or MBO program. In step one the "performance standard" could easily be goals or objectives as in an MBO program or the standards necessary to earn bonuses in a piece-rate system. Step two is fairly standard for piece-rate operators. Not only does the operator know how many pieces or batches he or she is turning out, but often the entire crew knows each other's output. And progress toward objectives is usually known and kept track of by MBO program participants. For piece-rate systems, the step three reinforcer is the bonus money usually received weekly but psychologically it can be considered hourly, or daily since the operator can quickly and continuously keep track of bonus increments which will go into the paycheck. MBO training typically emphasizes the need for praise when objectives are met. Many MBO programs do not tie achievement of objectives directly to compensation. Instead, they rely, as does operant conditioning, on the intrinsic rewards of accomplishment plus the praise for meeting or exceeding objectives.

Since piece rates have been with us since at least Nebuchadnezzar's reign in the sixth century B.C., operant conditioning cannot be considered very new. And MBO goes back to Ceasar's time as mentioned earlier. Varro described an approach involving the setting of standards, feeding back performance data, and positively rewarding. And as Locke pointed out, operant conditioning ". . . has been used for centuries by animal trainers, parents, diplomats, and employers."[25] So what is new or different about operant conditioning? It is simply that it now has a Messiah in B. F. Skinner and a gospeler in Feeney, who now heads his own consulting company. It is also now available in packaged form and can be *installed*, preferably by a consultant, according to Feeney.

The most interesting data on operant conditioning programs uncovered thus far in the literature is the very small percentage of employees covered by the programs in the very companies which are so highly touted for their operant conditioning programs. The W. C. Hamner and E. P. Hamner study of ten on-going programs gave the number of employees in the programs and the total number of employees in eight of the companies or units. When converted to percentages, these data revealed that the pro-operant conditioning companies seem to believe that it has very limited applications. Table 15-1 contains these data restructured from their study.

TABLE 15-1

Percentages Of Employees Covered In Eight Companies' Programs

Company	Employees covered/total employees	Percent covered
Emery Air Freight	500/2,800	18
Michigan Bell	2,220/5,500	40
Connecticut General	3,000/13,500	22
Weyerhaeuser Company	500/40,000	1
City of Detroit Garbage Collection Department	1,122/1,930	58
B. F. Goodrich Chemical	100/420	24
ACDC Electronics	350/350	100
TOTALS	7,792/70,000	11

As can be seen from the table, only one employee in nine is covered by the program. This seems strange in light of the almost unbelievable claims made for these programs. For example, at Emery alone, in their well-publicized container savings success, the company is supposed to have realized $600,000 savings in 1970 and over $2 million in 1975. At the City of Detroit garbage collection department savings amounted to $1,654,000 in 1974. Their reinforcers were bonuses, profit-sharing and praise. And the ACDC Electronics Company ". . . experienced a profit increase of 25 percent over the forecast; a $550,000 cost reduction on $10 million in sales; a return of 1,900 percent on investment including consultant fees; a reduction in turn around time on repairs from 30 days to 10 days . . ."[26] Such claims sound very much like those made by Arthur Kuriloff while he was at Non-Linear Systems, Inc. (See Chapter 20 for an account of the near demise of this company due to their experimental installations of many popular behavioral science based programs.)

What could possibly be wrong with establishing standards, providing feedback on performance and praising for good work? Considerable, according to some of the company executives who use the program and according to operant conditioning critics. Mr. Emery himself has pointed out the fundamental problem with using praise as the reinforcer on a programmed basis: "Inasmuch as praise is the most readily available no-cost reinforcer, it tends to *dull* its effect as a reinforcer through its sheer repetition, even to risk making praise an *irritant* to the receiver."[27] Reinforcers other than feedback and praise are either in use or being considered. Mr. M. W. Warren, director of organization and management development at the Questor Corporation claims that the five most effective reinforcers are as follows: (1) money, (2) recognition or praise, (3) freedom to choose one's own activity, (4) opportunity to see oneself become better, more important, or more useful, and (5) power to influence both co-workers and management.[28]

The main problem with all of the above reinforcers is that when operant conditioning is installed as a "program," there is the assumption that all the people "covered" by the program will respond to the particular reinforcers used. This assumption simply cannot be met. Sales managers searching for prize reinforcers to use in sales contests have noted cultural variables within the U.S. on what will work. Hi-Fi equipment may work well enough in Chicago but deep freezers motivate in Atlanta. A few shop employees may want to be promoted to foreman, a third of the remainder would not touch the job if offered the promotion but want all the overtime they can get, while another third might want more time off as a reward. Thus a bonus for perfect attendance may be fairly successful for a majority of employees in this shop but would, in effect, leave out (or engender hostility among) all those who want more time off. The list of preferred reinforcers on an employee-by-employee basis would be almost endless. This problem is handled by proponents of operant conditioning by simply specifying as one of the conditions which must be met for program success that ". . . reinforcers must be selected that are sufficiently powerful and durable to establish and strengthen behavior . . ."[29]

The criticisms of the operant conditioning model in the literature are growing. The main points of these criticisms are summarized below:

1. The model assumes that there will be no conflicting stimuli in the work situation—that there will not be other reinforcers which would cancel the effects of the chosen reinforcer.[30]
2. The model naively assumes that the recipient of the reinforcement will interpret the stimuli and respond precisely as intended; he will not add any other meanings to the stimuli.[31]
3. Operant conditioning will soon be seen as pure worker behavior manipulation and rejected by many who find this treatment repugnant.

Hart and Scott point to ". . . Skinner's position as an extreme expression of the image of man in the sense that the autonomous element is completely and scornfully rejected."[32]

4. The operant conditioning proponents' argument that feedback automatically reinforces the behavior which precedes it is absurd since this would mean that performance would never change—the employees would be stimulated to repeat their same previous behavior.[33]

5. Most of the studies done in industry have been evangelistically reported "case" studies reporting gains not likely to have come about only through conditioning. "In Feeney's studies, performance in the customer service offices improved 'rapidly'—in one case from 30 percent to 95 percent of standard in a single day! In the container departments, container use jumped from 45 percent to 95 percent, and in 70 percent of the cases this improvement also occurred within a day."[34]

6. Much of the improvement claimed in case studies can be accounted for by management having put pressures on managers to do what they should have been doing all along—managing their operations effectively. Once the performance standards aspects of the jobs were outlined and managers were made aware of how bad their performance had been, they began to do *many* things to improve the performance of their units, one of which may have been the use of the specified reinforcers. "Most managers genuinely think that operations in their bailiwick are doing well; a performance audit that proves they're not comes as a real and unpleasant surprise."[35]

Conclusions about Operant Conditioning

In spite of the extensive laboratory proof that certain positive reinforcements can, under narrowly specified conditions, modify human behavior, the institutional application of operant conditioning *using praise on a programmed basis* is not likely to grow. In the first place, it must be confined to tasks most of whose results can be objectively measured or quantified and where other reward systems such as piece-rates are not already in use. It cannot succeed in conflict with informal reward systems. Secondly, the "mechanical" use of praise on cue and resulting from instruction to praise from above will soon be seen by employees as unwanted manipulation. If the supervisor whose reward style was to call to his or her workers' attention their mistakes suddenly starts praising by the numbers, the principle of "what you *are* speaks so loud I can't hear what you are *saying*" will prevail. The supervisor whose style is to reward with praise but who has not seemed to find the time to do it enough will probably benefit from an operant conditioning program.

At the heart of the "successes" of most operant conditioning programs is the performance analysis and concommitant standard setting. In operations where this has not been done and where there has generally been poor management, these by-products of an operant conditioning program alone will likely improve performance. This improvement will be due to a variety of changes, one of which may be the introduction of reinforcers. Where workers have been kept in the dark about their actual performance and about what specifically is expected of them, there is obviously the possibility that their performance can improve with the introduction of this information.

The role of information *per se* of all varieties—not just feedback on performance—has been explored very little. What is to be expected if on every piece of capital equipment in a breakfast cereals plant management installed a plaque plainly visible to each operator of the equipment giving the number of boxes of cereals which must be sold just to make enough profit to buy and install the machine? Common sense about human behavior would suggest that maintenance costs would go down as would down-time. But such roles of information alone have not been studied. If the hypothesis were proven, that is, if information about equipment value alone altered behavior, our view of operant conditioning theory becomes even more critical. *All* behavior change, according to Skinner's operant conditioning model, is due to direct *reinforcements* from the environment, not from "neutral" information with no external reinforcements. If there were any significant behavior change such as maintenance cost going up *or* down, operant conditioning theory fails the test.

The literature simply does not contain reports of experiments proving operant conditioning programs effective. As with incentive system introductions, the changes in employee behavior cannot be ascribed to the reinforcements alone. Too many other variables were operative which could have altered the behavior and these were not controlled in the numerous case studies reported in the literature. It is not difficult to conclude that managements which are enticed or forced into doing what they should have been doing all along—managing—will effect improvements in their operations. Any introductory textbook on management will tell the reader that a manager should set standards, monitor and feed back performance information and reward good performance. And this advice is not found under the heading of exotic theories of motivation. It is simply distilled common sense about managing which has been with us for ages.

JOB ENRICHMENT

"There is no clear understanding of how jobs influence the level of employee motivation."[36] This is the conclusion of one reviewer of the literature on job enrichment. Another concludes "It is unfortunate that most studies (of the effectiveness of job enrichment) provide indirect evidence, at best . . . Many of these studies have been poorly controlled, and most of the authors have attempted to generalize from severely limited data."[37] The titles of other articles and books suggest similar conclusions: "Job Enrichment: Evangelist or Carpetbagger of the 70's?," "Job Enrichment: Long on Theory, Short on Practice," *Work Is Here to Stay, Alas,* and "Whatever Happened to Job Enrichment?"[38]

The idea of job enrichment is based generally on the popular notion that most blue-collar workers are bored with the repetitive natures of their jobs and would be motivated to work harder if their jobs gave them ". . . greater planning and control responsibilities in the execution of their overall assignment."[39]

The notion that most blue and white collar workers are bored with their jobs is yet to be substantiated in spite of newspaper and journal articles on the "Blue Collar Blues." After a huge survey sponsored by The U.S. Department of Health, Education, and Welfare led to erroneous conclusions by the researchers as well as by most behavioral scientists, a rash of such articles appeared depicting the American factory workers as nearly driven out of their minds by the boredom caused by repetitive tasks. The bulk of the HEW report[40] was based on a large scale survey of workers' attitudes toward their work and working conditions conducted by the University of Michigan for the U.S. Department of Labor. In journalistic style the report concluded that "Dull repetitive, seemingly meaningless tasks, offering little challenge or autonomy, are causing discontent among workers at all occupational levels."[41]

These conclusions, however unscientifically drawn as will be shown shortly, launched a rash of front page newspaper articles such as "Bucking the Assembly Line" and "Blue-collar Blues Begin to Make National Impact."[42] The "Blue-collar Blues" article by Ward Sinclair begins by illustrating the consequences of the "dead-end syndrome" with dramatic cases such as the following: "A worker in a Detroit axle plant shot three foremen, then pleaded insanity due to noise and filth at the factory. Judge and jury visited the plant, then acquitted the worker."[43] Here we see the boring assembly line being blamed by association for filth, noise and assault with a deadly weapon! Most of the remaining paragraphs of the article follow Senator Kennedy's attempts to get the government more involved in promoting job enrichment. Kennedy is quoted as saying "For what workers want, as over a hundred studies have shown, is to feel that they and the work they do is important and has meaning."[44]

The erroneous conclusions of the report which opened up these new sources of emotionally loaded human interest articles were carefully pointed out by

Mitchell Fein in an article in the *Sloan Management Review*.[45] The survey required workers of all levels to rank twenty-five characteristics of their work in order of importance to them. Interesting work was ranked first, pay was ranked fifth, and job security, seventh. But as Fein notes, "The researchers neglected . . . to indicate that these rankings averaged together the survey results for all levels of workers, from managers and professionals to low skilled workers. The researchers created a composite image that they called a "worker." The study, however, was based on a cross section of the United States work force rather than just lower-level workers. When separated into the basic occupational categories and analyzed separately, the data show that blue-collar workers rank pay and job security higher than interesting work."[46] As Fein points out, by lumping all workers together—managers, professionals, skilled and unskilled—the researchers were able to get uninteresting work to come out as the number one problem. As Fein argues, it is reasonable to assume that blue-collar workers might have different views of their jobs than professionals and managers. He cites a study covering 60,000 people in more than fifty countries which indicated that attitudes toward jobs and work was greater *between jobs* than between cultures. Unskilled employees in the study ranked physical conditions first, security second, earnings third, and benefits fourth. A cluster of factors representing "interesting work" ranked far below the employees' four top needs.[47]

Other indications that the vast majority of blue-collar workers are not alienated from their jobs by their boring nature come from employee union representatives. An officer of the United Electrical Workers complained, in a full page union newspaper article denouncing G.E.'s efforts to enrich its steam iron assembly operation, that on the old continuous assembly line the employees were able to do the jobs without thinking about them. They could talk to one another. The new system required employees to attend to the job constantly, depriving them of the relief from thinking about the job. And he claimed that the new system was just as boring. Another representative was quoted as saying, "I've finally been able to show (management) that the more repetitive or rhythmic the job, the less unhappy the worker. On jobs where the rhythm is broken and unrepetitive, the employees are unhappy and must constantly fight these jobs (rather) than do them by natural reflex."[48]

In his newspaper article "Bucking the Assembly Line," Dennis Polite, using a typical journalist's sample of interviews with four employees at G.E.'s Appliance Park plant, found two employees satisfied with their jobs and two not satisfied. One of those who was satisfied—even proud of her role in producing appliances—pointed out that production would suffer if employees were allowed to build whole units by themselves. The other satisfied employee pointed to the younger employees as the dissatisfied: "But the younger generation . . . maybe it's our fault. We gave it to them and they think they should have it easier than they got it." The other two employees who were dissatisfied pointed to the dullness of the work and the short times off for breaks to visit and smoke. They were allowed two ten-minute breaks plus lunch break per day.[49] The wide differences in cultures' tolerance for boring work was illustrated not long ago in a training session I conducted in Washington, D.C. for visiting junior administrators and managers from 15 developing countries. The session included a role playing exercise in which a foreman (role) was supposed to persuade three fuel pump assemblers (roles) who normally rotated assembly stations every few hours because of the boredom, to remain at the stations on which each was best. This would result in 18% greater output, and since they were on group piecework, this would increase their earnings. Because the participants' backgrounds were unknown, the four roles were handed out in sets of worker, worker, worker, foreman by walking around the "U" shaped table arrangement. Four groups were involved in the role plays and observers were stationed at each to record the arguments for and against the proposed change by the foreman. After only about two minutes, one of the observers came forward and said that his group had made the decision to accept the foreman's proposition. Other groups were to take twenty to thirty minutes to arrive at some kind of a compromise agreement. One glance at the group was enough to surmise what had happened, but an effort to get them into the conflict role play was made anyway. When the boredom aspect of the workers' role was pointed out to them and they were asked to make an effort to play the role as described, one of the "workers" complained, "Sir, this role is not correct, because boring work does not bore us." Because nationals typically sit together, three Taiwanese had received the worker roles and an Argentinian Army Lieutenant was the foreman!

The Scarcity of Job Enrichment Programs

From a survey of a random sample of the top 1,000 Fortune industrials, Luthans and Reif found little reason to call job enrichment a fast-growing phenomenon. Only one firm in 25 of the responding firms had *any* formal program and these programs covered only a very small percentage of their employees. The coverage was from 30 percent of the employees in one firm to a firm whose program covered only 247 employees out of 65,000. Their survey revealed that the typical company does little to evaluate the effectiveness of their programs, usually relying on impressions and anecdotal evidence rather than hard performance data. Lack of management interest and the large number of jobs which defied enrichment were the most often given reasons for not initiating or extending existing programs. Some companies also reported problems in getting employees to accept additional authority and responsibilities. The authors gave the following as a response which best summarized respondents' attitudes toward job enrichment:

As an applied concept job enrichment is probably here to stay. As a formalized program I view it as a passing fancy created by unions for purposes of disruption and featherbedding, by consultants to create more clients, and by publishers and educators as a current fad to talk and write about. If properly used, a good social improvement. But we still need to retain the ability to design, make, and sell widgets for profit or there won't be any jobs left to enrich.[50]

Case Studies on Job Enrichment

Many of the case studies included in the literature as *job enrichment* were really cases in which *job enlargement* or *job rotation* was introduced or expanded. A few include none of these. (See Monsanto's program given later.) Recall that job enrichment is defined as giving employees greater planning and control responsibilities in the execution of their overall assignments. Job enlargement is simply adding different tasks. An example would be the practice introduced at Volvo of having the same group of assemblers follow the same car body for 7 stations. Very similar to job enlargement, and an ancient technique at that, is job rotation, in which groups trade off tasks or stations every few hours or every day. This technique is also employed at Volvo. Because the insulation of the insides of car bodies was a disliked job, workers on other parts of the insulation task must take their turns at this tedious job in the cramped quarters.

Proponents of job *enrichment* have a strong tendency to include just about anything they choose to and call it job enrichment. The HEW study used a more general term—*job redesign*—which could possibly cover job enrichment, job enlargement, and job rotation. Another term used in the HEW study, the *humanization of work* has no useful denotative meaning and its connotation includes anything from the introduction of democracy at the workplace to supervisors who are warm and friendly and do not ever become uncivil. The HEW study reports' Appendix entitled "Case Studies in the Humanization of Work" gives some detail on 34 case studies considered by the researchers. They included such categories as the year initiated, the number of employees affected, the techniques (of humanization) used, etc. Below are some of the "techniques used," reported verbatim from the HEW report, which suggest that the researchers considered almost any change under the heading of humanization of work:

GENERAL FOODS: Workers were organized into relatively autonomous work groups with each group responsible for a production process. Pay is based on the total number of jobs an employee can do. (This is essentially job *enlargement*.)

POLAROID CORPORATION: Factory operators were rotated between their factory jobs and more desirable non-factory jobs. (Job *rotation*)

H. P. HOOD & SONS: On numerous occasions workers teamed with supervisors to simplify work, often using films of actual operations. *Workers with two or more years of seniority are secure against layoff.* (Whatever it is, it has been around for a long time. Supervisors, managers, generals and Cardinals have been taking counsel from their subordinates about how to solve problems facing their organizations for centuries. The inclusion of the policy of guaranteed jobs for those with more than two years seniority is a puzzle.)

NOBØ-FABRIKKER A/S (Norway): Production groups and subgroups were established and put on group bonus rates. A "contact person" (with department head) was substituted for the supervisor and was chosen by election. (In the U.S. this would represent the establishment of a group incentive plan plus the election of a union steward.)

MONSANTO: *The foremen were given responsibility for interviewing, indoctrinating, and giving skills training to new hires.* (This has been the practice of literally thousands of companies in the U.S. for decades.)

I.C.I.: Weekly staff assignments provide job rotation. Small groups (8) input "own ideas" into work process. (Here we have simple job rotation plus a verbal suggestion system. Neither is new nor unusual.)

P.P.G. INDUSTRIES: The frame cleaner job was eliminated. Since cleaning takes 15% of the time on each job, the machine operators took over the cleaning function. (A simple case of sharing the dirty work.)

MICRO-WAX DEPARTMENT—SCHELL STANLOW REFINERY (England): Operators formed group teams that provided both more flexibility within shift teams and rotation in jobs. Time clocks were also removed. (Simple job rotation within work groups plus a change in salary and wage system.)[51] (parenthetical remarks and italics added)

Most of the remainder of the techniques reported on the 34 companies appeared to be genuine job enrichment of one form or another or extensive job enlargement. In addition to including almost anything a company does which suits them, some writers are downright dishonest in reporting a company's program. One of the cases given in the HEW report was that of General Foods-Topeka. Fein has pointed out that Walton's report of this case omitted important information which would alter the interpretation of what actually occurred and why. Walton attributes the success of the Topeka plant to ". . . autonomous work groups . . . integrated support functions . . . challenging job assignments . . . job mobility and rewards for learning . . . facilitative leadership . . . managerial decision making for operations . . . self-government for the plant community . . . congruent physical and social context . . . learning and evolution . . ."[52] Fein notes that Walton does not mention that the sixty-three employees were a very special group since they had been selected from 700 applicants. This selection procedure required five interviews, the last two of which were one hour and four hours respectively. The screening process also included a two-hour personality test. Fein further characterizes the misrepresentations in Walton's case report:

General Foods-Topeka is a controlled experiment in a small plant with conditions set up to achieve desired results. The employees are not a cross section of the larger employee population, or even of Topeka. The plant and its operations are not typical of those in industry today. The results obtained are valid only for this one plant. What are other managers to do? Should they screen out nine of ten possible candidates and hire only from the select group that remains? What happens to the other nine who were not selected?

If the investigators had shown how they converted a plant bursting with labor problems into one where management and employees told glowingly of their accomplishments, the study would truly merit the praise it has received. Instead they turned their backs on the company's parent plant in Kankakee, which has many of the problems of the big city plants. Even worse, they tantalize management with the prospect that, in building a new plant with new equipment, carefully selected employees, and no union, productivity will be higher . . . Is this Walton's message to managers in his article, "How to Counter Alienation in the Plant?"[53]

A number of other "dishonest-by-omission" case reports are noted by Fein. One of these was the well-publicized Texas Instruments maintenance (janitorial) personnel case. The HEW report gives the changes made: "Workers were organized into 19 member/cleaning teams. Each member (was given a) voice in planning, problem-solving, goal-setting, and scheduling . . . Quarterly turnover dropped from 100% to 9.8%. Personnel requirements dropped from 120 to 71. Cost savings averaged $103,000 annually . . . Building cleanliness ratings increased from 65% to 85%."[54] When Texas Instruments took over the janitorial work from its outside contractor the janitors' wages were raised from $1.40 to $1.94 plus shift differentials of 10c and 20c and the Texas Instrument benefits package which amounted to about a third of their direct wages. Fein argues correctly that the additions of a 46 percent wage increase, paid vacations, sick leave, a good cafeteria, profit sharing, and good insurance programs made it possible for TI to hire much better workers. He points out that ". . . the study insists on attributing the improved performance to job enrichment. The omission of this pay data is strange, since the data appear prominently in the report from which the HEW task force obtained the case material."[55]

With such examples as these, most of the glowing reports of the effects of job enrichment may be suspect to a greater or lesser degree. In addition, the reports that employees *want* some form of job enrichment must also be questioned. In his article, "Assembly Line Workers Humbug Job Enrichment," A. A. Imberman reports on his survey of employee attitudes and opinions about job enrichment in five varied manufacturing plants:

In all cases, the employees were asked what suggestions they might have to make their job situations happier, more productive, and more satisfying. In analyzing the thousands of interview responses, most employees were found to prefer jobs with less high-quality demands, with less direct responsibility, with less troublesome variety, and with more money . . . The sharpest complaints that the assembly line worker had about his job were (1) supervisors who didn't know how to supervise, were abusive, unfeeling, dictatorial, and unhelpful; and (2) poor management that was responsible for the poor planning of material, shortage of parts, ill-maintained machinery, inefficient working conditions (lights, heat, drinking water, etc.), unbalanced inventories (trips to the tool crib wasted 15 minutes, when the foreman could maintain a small inventory of tools in the department), wrong sizes of parts, poorly machined parts that didn't fit, ignored safety regulations, arbitrary management policies, and disregard of employee sentiments.[56]

The various reports of typical behavioral scientists' views of the assembly-line may be seriously affected by this group's self-referenced criteria, just as it is in other programs and techniques they recommend. If they ever held a factory summer job, they were very likely bored themselves. And their university students report similar experiences. Given that social scientists' I.Q.'s are among the highest among university disciplines, it is unreasonable to expect that they would not be considerably more bored than the typical factory worker. Since these scientists are generally given to theories which reflect their values and needs (democratization is good for all institutions, high autonomy needs, and greater than average authority hostility), their findings in this area of investigation may be somewhat less than objective.

The research data taken together seems to indicate that employees want a variety of things changed. Some want more authority and responsibility in their work and some want less. Some want more variety and some want less. Some want to participate in decision-making which will affect them, and some do not. In addition to the variations in employee attitudes toward job enrichment, there are a host of other factors limiting the growth of this technique.

Other Limits to the Growth of Job Enrichment

The *technological constraints* to the use of job enrichment are far too numerous to discuss or even list here. In the assembly of any device, there is little discretion possible about the sequence of assembly. One simply does not install the pan or sump cover on an engine before the crankshaft has been installed. The legs of a chair cannot be assembled on the chair until the seat has been made. A ditch-digger could be told that he may swing the pick over his left shoulder or his right, but this is hardly job enrichment. Very little reflection is required to conclude that most of the job enrichment which has taken place over the last century—and a very great deal has been done—is due to engineering and capital investment. The digger operating a digging machine would certainly be considered to be in a more humanized job than swinging a pick. And tractors have certainly humanized the following of a mule behind a plow for 12 hours a day in planting season. And the vast majority of drudgery-laden farmers of 150 years ago are now in the factories, many monitoring automatic transfer machines that perform various machining tasks. And they are working only 8 hours per day. Surely there is something about a boring job which enriches a life if the boring work time is cut nearly in half.

It is likely that many if not most jobs when enriched would *increase the unit costs*. This is one of the reasons managements have been so cautious over the last 20 years in adopting job enrichment programs. In most of the companies with groups on job enrichment, hard data have not been forthcoming which would show *net* changes in costs. Luthans and Reif were unable to clearly determine from their studies of three Scandinavian enrichment projects whether the economic consequences were positive or negative.[57] A study by Louis E. Davis comparing cost differences between a machine-paced line, a line with no pacing, and a line with individuals performing all of the jobs as a "one-man line" resulted in the following: the non-paced line produced at 89 percent of the paced line and the one-man line at 94 percent. The question management must ask is would the consumer be willing to pay the additional 12.5 percent for the product off the non-paced line or 6.4 percent more for it as produced on the one-man line.[58]

Labor unions constitute a major limitation on the installation of job enrichment programs in their bargaining units. Since they consider the conditions of work subject to collective bargaining, the twenty million or so Americans represented by unions are not likely to have their jobs humanized unilaterally by the company. And the unions are likely to have so many strings attached to their acceptance of job enrichment that the managements will not be able to go along with this joint activity. And as we have seen earlier in this chapter, some union officials, in protecting the needs and desires of the workers they represent, are trying to convince managements that many of their constituents simply do not want more responsibility and authority. They want more repetition so they can take their minds off the job and visit or think about their real interests which may be gardening, bowling, model-building, their families, or the lodge. Regarding the need to democratize the workplace as the Scandinavian projects appear to many social scientists, Nat Goldfinger, Research Director of the AFL-CIO, believes that this form of industrial democracy is not needed in America. He points to the effectiveness of collective bargaining in America as performing the necessary functions the Europeans expect from democratizing their factories.

The Future of Formal Job Enrichment

The evidence is that many employees do not want it. The unions either do not want it in certain situations or want it the subject of collective bargaining in others. In the companies now using it, they are confining it to a very small proportion of their workforces. This proportion has remained small for almost 20 years. In most manufacturing operations, the nature of the technology severely limits its application. Where the technology is not a serious constraint, the additional costs in most operations would be. It is applicable today and in the foreseeable future to the small percentage of jobs not constrained by the factors described above. Its future in these limited applications partly hinges on managements' resistance to change. This resistance depends, considerably, upon their confidence in the proponents of job enrichment, whether they be in-house staff behavioral scientists' findings, or consultants peddling a program. Continued exaggerated claims as reviewed in this chapter are not likely to reduce this resistance.

NOTES

1. *Consultants News Special Report*, October 1977, p. 3, reporting on a paper presented by William R. Lafollette at the 37th Annual Meeting of the Academy of Management, August, 1977.
2. Adapted from Stephen J. Carroll, Jr. and Henry J. Tosi, Jr., *Management by Objectives: Applications and Research*, (New York, N.Y.: The MacMillan Co., 1973)
3. Gary P. Latham and Gary A. Yukl, "A Review of Research on the Application of Goal Setting in Organizations," *Academy of Management Journal*, Vol. 18, No. 4, (December 1975) pp. 824–845.
4. *Ibid.*, p. 840.
5. *Ibid.*
6. *Ibid.*, p. 828.
7. E. A. Locke, "Toward a Theory of Task Motivation and Incentives," *Organizational Behavior and Human Performance*, Vol. 3, (1968), pp. 157–189.
8. Latham and Yuki, p. 835.
9. Stephen J. Carroll, Jr. and Henry J. Tosi, Jr., pp. 29–30, 35–40.
10. Latham and Yukl, p. 843.
11. For examples see W. Schramm, *The Research on Programmed Instruction: An Annotated Bibliography*, (Washington, D.C.: U.S. Department of Health, Education and Welfare, G.P.O. 1964), J.A. Weitz, J. Antonetti, and S. R. Wallace, "The Effect of Home Office Contact on Sales Performance," *Personnel Psychology*, Vol. 7 (1954) pp. 381–384, and H. T. Leavitt and R. A. Mueller, "Some Effects of Feedback on Communication," *Human Relations*, Vol. 4 (1951), pp. 401–410.
12. Stephen J. Carroll, Jr. and Henry J. Tosi, Jr., p. 181.
13. Robert W. Hollman, "Supportive Organizational Climate and Managerial

Assessment of MBO Effectiveness," *Academy of Management Journal*, Vol. 19, No. 4, (December 1976), p. 563.

14. *Ibid.*, p. 568.
15. Steven Kerr, "Some Modifications in MBO as an OD Strategy," *Proceedings of the Thirty-second Annual Meeting of the Academy of Management*, Vance F. Mitchell, Richard T. Barth and Frances H. Mitchell, eds., (Minneapolis, Minnesota, August 1972), p. 41.
16. All the above save number 4 was adapted from the collection of advice contained in Stephen J. Carroll, Jr. and Henry J. Tosi, Jr., pp. 77–78.
17. R. J. Chesser, "The Development of Change Models of MBO Reflecting Moderator Effects of Personality Characteristics," *Proceedings of the Thirty-third Annual Meeting of the Academy of Management*, Thad Green, ed. (Boston, Mass., August 1973), p. 394.
18. Robert W. Hollman, p. 573.
19. John M. Ivancevich, "A Longitudinal Assessment of Management by Objectives," *Administrative Science Quarterly*, Vol. 17, (1972), p. 126.
20. Bruce D. Jamieson, "Behavioral Problems With Management by Objectives," *Academy of Management Journal*, Vol. 16, No. 3, (September 1973) p. 504.
21. Richard E. Byrd and John Cowan, "MBO: a Behavioral Science Approach," *Personnel*, March-April, 1974, p. 42.
22. William B. Werther, Jr. and Heinz Weihrich, "Refining MBO through Negotiations," *MSU Business Topics*, Summer 1975, p. 53.
23. Steven Kerr, p. 42.
24. Edwin A. Locke, "The Myths of Behavior Mod in Organizations," *Academy of Management Review*, October, 1977, p. 543–544.
25. Edwin A. Locke, p. 545.
26. W. Clay Hamner and Dennis W. Organ, *Organizational Behavior; an Applied Psychological Approach*, (Dallas, Texas: Business Publications, Inc., 1978) pp. 249–258.
27. *Ibid.*, p. 253.
28. *Ibid.*, p. 246.
29. *Ibid.*, p. 20.
30. For this and numerous additional criticisms by W. F. Whyte, see W. F. Whyte, "Skinnerian Theory in Organizations," *Psychology Today*, Vol. 5, No. 11 (1972) pp. 66, 68f.
31. C. Argyris, "Beyond Freedom and Dignity by B. F. Skinner, a Review Essay," *Harvard Educational Review*, Vol. 42, No. 4 (1971) p. 556.
32. D. K. Hart and W. G. Scott, "The Optimal Image of Man for Systems Theory," *Academy of Management Journal*, Vol. 15 (1972) pp. 532, 535.
33. Edwin A. Locke, p. 548.
34. *Ibid.*
35. A Feeney quote from "Emery Air Freight," as carried in Hamner and Organ, p. 244.
36. Richard M. Steers and Richard T. Mowday, "The Motivational Properties of Tasks," *Academy of Management Review*, October 1977, p. 645.
37. C. L. Hulin, "Individual Differences and Job enrichment—The Case against

General Treatments," in J. Maher, ed., *New Perspectives in Job Enrichment*. (Berkeley, California: Van Nostrand Reinhold, 1971) as quoted in Hamner and Organ, p. 276-277.

38. Frank Plasha, "Job Enrichment: Evangelist or Carpetbagger of the 70's?" *The Personnel Administrator*, July-August 1973, pp. 43-51; Fred Luthans and William E. Reif, "Job Enrichment: Long on Theory, Short on Practice," *Organizational Dynamics*, Winter 1974, pp. 30-39; S. A. Levitan and W. B. Johnston, *Work Is Here to Stay, Alas*, (n.p.: Olympus, 1973); and J. C. Baxter, "Whatever Happened to Job Enrichment?" *Iron Age*, November 8, 1973, pp. 35-36.

39. Hamner and Organ, p. 271.

40. U.S. Department of Health, Education, and Welfare, *Work in America*, Report of a Special Task Force to the Secretary of Health, Education, and Welfare. Prepared under the Auspices of the W. E. Upjohn Institute for Employment Research. (Cambridge, Mass.: MIT Press, 1973).

41. *Ibid.*, p. xv.

42. Dennis Polite, "Bucking the Assembly Line," and Ward Sinclair, "Blue-collar Blues Begin to Make National Impact," *The Louisville Times*, December 6, 1973, p. 1.

43. *Ibid.*

44. *Ibid.*

45. Mitchell Fein, "Job Enrichment: A Reevaluation," *Sloan Management Review*, Winter 1974, pp. 69-88.

46. *Ibid.*, pp. 70-71.

47. D. Sirota and J. M. Greenwood, "Understanding Your Overseas Workforce," *Harvard Business Review*, January-February 1971, pp. 53-60 as reported in Mitchell Fein, p. 71.

48. Fein, pp. 75-76.

49. Polite, op. cit.

50. Luthans and Reif, pp. 34-35.

51. U.S. Department of Health, Education, and Welfare, pp. 188-201.

52. R. E. Walton, "Work Place Alienation and the Need for Major Innovation," paper prepared for a Special Task Force to the Secretary of Health, Education, and Welfare (for *Work in America*), May, 1972. Unpublished.

53. Fein, p. 72.

54. U.S. Department of Health, Education and Welfare, p. 195.

55. Fein, p. 74.

56. A. A. Imberman, "Assembly Line Workers Humbug Job Enrichment," *The Personnel Administrator*, March-April 1973, pp. 31-32.

57. Luthans and Reif.

58. Fein, p. 76.

Chapter 16

Management Science and Information Systems

About Systems (from Lofti-Zadeh, Cooper, and Mesarovich)[1]

A system is a big black box
Of which we can't unlock the locks,
And all we can find out about
Is what goes in and what comes out.

Perceiving input-output pairs,
Related by parameters,
Permits us, sometimes, to relate
An input, output, and a state.
If this relation's good and stable
Then predict we may be able,
But if this fails us—heaven forbid!
We'll be compelled to force the lid!
(Lofti-Zadeh)

Programming sticks upon the shoals
Of incommensurate multiple goals,
And where the tops are no one knows;
When all our peaks become plateaus,
The top is anything we think,
When measuring makes the mountain shrink.

The upshot is, we cannot tailor
Policy by a single scalar,
Unless we know the priceless price
Of Honor, Justice, Pride, and Vice.

This means a crisis is arising
For simple-minded maximizing.
(Cooper)

According to Mesarovich,
A set of proper statements which
Has mastered, in well ordered schools
A set of transformation rules
Which rules in turn have rules to twist 'em
Deserves the name of general system.

All systems, it is now proposed
Are either open, or are closed,
The closed have one-to-one relations
But don't result in innovation.
The open are disturbed, adaptive,
Or Heisenberg observer-captive.
(Mesarovich)

In addition to the "systems" concept, which some management scientists do not believe managers understand, the field of management science has claimed in its name almost any technique which uses numbers and symbols beyond the level of eighth grade arithmetic. Most textbooks on the subject of management science define it as a problem-solving approach or decision-making approach whose foundations are the scientific method and the systems orientation often using mathematical models and high speed electronic computers. Its role as an academic discipline has been mostly one of gathering up techniques which have been around for some time and raising an Operations Research or Management Science flag over them.

The accounts of "Blackett's Circus" mark the beginnings of operations research for most management scientists. This was an interdisciplinary team of three physiologists, two mathematical physicists, an Army officer, a surveyor, two mathematicians, an astrophysicist, and a general physicist. Such teams have been credited with helping to win the Battle of Britain and the Battle of the North Atlantic in World War II. They worked on such problems as those associated with antisubmarine warfare, civilian defense and the optimal deployment of convoys to accompany supply ships.

Operations Research/Management Science's status today is difficult to determine from the literature. One finds accounts of the 40-year growth of OR or MS such as this: "Since 1950, OR/MS has progressed steadily, sometimes explosively. More than 20,000 people are presently involved in applying, teaching, or researching the field."[2] And this from Peter Drucker: ". . . management science has been a disappointment. It has not lived up, so far, to its promise. It certainly has not 'revolutionized' the practice of management. Few managers, indeed, pay much attention to it."[3] This view is evidently shared by Dr. David Bendel Hertz, one of Management Science's elder statesmen, according to *Organizational Dynamics'* descriptions of some of his views before their interview with him:

> He is wary in the recognition that a combination of excessive expectations on the part of some users of management science and the narrow training and perspective of many management scientists has led to widespread disillusionment with the fruits of management science. He is wary, as he looks to the future, because he foresees that a combination of the inherent limitations of management science and the lack of any new breakthroughs in methodology set distinct limits to its future contributions.[4]

The first view—describing explosive growth—is that of the authors of an introductory textbook on management science. Drucker is a management philosopher and observer. Hertz, whose views are expressed immediately above, is a former president of The Institute of Management Sciences and founding member, council member and editor for publications in operations research of the Operations Research Society of America.

Now that the discipline of "management science," "operations research," "decision sciences," "systems sciences," "systems analysis," or whatever it is called[5] has settled down enough to become a fairly standard university discipline in colleges of business and engineering, what does it contain? What techniques does it offer that do not seem to be spawning new techniques for the discipline's growth? Below are the 13 main topics covered in a textbook entitled *Management Science—A Self Correcting Approach.*[6] The proportion of the text occupied by each topic is given as a percent of total pages in the book.

1. Cost Volume Analysis (5%): These 15 pages cover variations on break-even analyses typically found in accounting courses for many years.
2. Probability Concepts (6%): This section covers elementary probability concepts up to finding the average number of spots on a die if it were thrown "over and over."
3. Decision Theory (13%): Coverage includes decision criteria, decision trees and utility theory, and marginal analysis. The final problem in the chapter is as follows: "Demand for widgets has averaged 100 units. Marginal loss is $8 and marginal profit is $2. What is the optimal stocking policy?"[7]
4. Inventory Analysis (7%): This section covers economic order quantity, reorder points, sensitivity analysis, production, backorder, and probabilistic inventory models, quantity discount models, and service level concepts. Most of these models are variations on inventory control models developed almost 50 years ago.[8]

5. Determinants and Matrices (6%): This chapter begins, "Two new mathematical concepts, determinants and matrices are introduced in this unit . . ."[9] The "newness" of matrix algebra is strange since Arthur Cayley, a British lawyer-mathematician developed it about 125 years ago.[10]

6. Linear Programming (25%): Covered here are graphic and Simplex linear programming allocation models and other related topics such as infeasibility, unbounded solutions, more than one optimal solution, etc. This management science technique, developed primarily by George Dantzig of the Rand Corporation circa 1947, is probably the most often utilized of the kit of techniques in management science. However, it owes most of its popularity to the modern high speed electronic computer, without which most of linear programming's most useful models would not be used.

7. The Transportation Problem (6%): The focus here is on various approaches to scheduling shipments from sources to destinations to minimize transportation costs.

8. The Assignment Problem (4%): The Hungarian Method is demonstrated. This method focusses on arriving at an optimal solution by avoiding opportunity losses.

9. Game Theory (7%): This section demonstrates two-person, zero-sum games.

10. Markov Analysis (3%): This section demonstrates matrix of transition and vector of states for predicting future events.

11. Waiting Lines (3%): Single and multiple channel queuing problems are demonstrated in this section. The theoretical base for material in this section was fairly well developed by A. K. Erlang about 70 years ago.

12. Simulation (4%): This section covers the Monte Carlo method, simulation of inventory analysis, and further queuing problems.

13. Network Models—PERT (10%): Simple PERT examples and critical path problems are demonstrated.

Almost every one of the above subjects has been expanded and made the subject of one or more university courses. These courses are primarily further applications of these techniques to more complex problems. The manner in which these techniques are presented both in the classroom and in the textbooks almost guarantees to select and develop a student whose major interest is the symbol manipulation required by the techniques. Probably more than any other cause, this approach has done much to alienate the manager from the management scientist. The instructors of these techniques typically begin by writing a formula or equation on the blackboard to introduce a new topic. After the student can manipulate the symbols, the instructors will describe a problem which this technique will solve. The problem is typically an oversimplification of part of a real problem which managers might face. The student leaves the school as a management scientist with a kit of techniques and little understanding of the real problems faced by managers. The typical management scientist has become a little like the boy who, when given a hammer, treated all the world as a nail. Peter Drucker describes the phenomenon this way:

> . . . the focus of much of the work in the management sciences has not been on such questions as "What is the business enterprise?" "What is managing?" "What do the two do, and what do the two need?" Rather, the focus has been "Where can I apply my beautiful gimmick?" The emphasis has been on the hammer rather than on driving in the nail, let alone on the building of the house.[11]

This technique orientation is illustrated further by the following:

In the late 1960's professor Myles Mace of the Harvard Business School and a former executive Vice President of Litton Industries, chided a well-known professor in Quantitative Methods there for not having any cases in his new book. The professor was reminded by Mace that the Harvard Business School was known for teaching by the case method and asked why no cases appeared in his book. His reply was straightforward: "I can't use cases in teaching my subject. The real world is too messy."[12]

A few years ago at Ohio University, a graduate student of management science needed one semester hour to graduate. He was given some untreated data—8 different aptitude test scores and the salaries on 76 Ethiopian bank managers—and told that if he analyzed these data, he would be given his one hour of credit for the independent study. Two days before grades were due, he brought to the professor two massive computer print-outs and asked his instructor to help him interpret his findings. Brief examination of the print-outs revealed that he had attempted, among other approaches, to analyze the relationships in the data by a statistical technique known as analysis of variance, a technique designed for different purposes. When asked why he chose analysis of variance instead of some correlational technique, he explained that at the time he had accepted the independent assignment, they were studying analysis of variance in his statistics course and that he wanted to try it out!

David Bendel Hertz has also observed and complained of similar problems with management scientists:

> . . . there exists a certain kind of pragmatic operational economics, and if a management scientist is well trained, he will be probing in that area, whereas a financial vice-president or a legal counsel or a personnel man probably would not be putting little pieces of various disciplines together. The modern buzz word for this, of course, is systems analysis, or systems science, which has no more meaning by itself than

management science. To have management science mean anything, you have to look at what management scientists have been taught and what they do on the job. Plenty of management scientists were trained very narrowly; some really don't know much more than linear programming, and they apply it to every problem they face, with generally dismal results.[13]

One of the problems involved in the training of management scientists referred to by Hertz is that the almost 100% technique-learning approach fails to give the scientist an understanding of the total environment in which his techniques are to be used. The textbook is rare which discusses in detail the need to consider impending strikes or other possible causes of shortages of the material to be ordered when teaching such techniques as economic order quantity formulae. The assumption of the human element as a constant, as in the direct labor cost as a part of the unit cost regardless of batch size, oftentimes cannot be met. Seldom are such warnings given as part of the teaching of the economic order quantity techniques. A few students themselves will point out the need for such considerations. While teaching economic order quantity approaches in a production management course at the University of Petroleum and Minerals in Saudi Arabia, I was interrupted by a Lebanese student there on a scholarship. He said simply that the formula could not work in his father's business. He went on to explain that his father had a cement block factory and that he bought most of his raw materials from his elder brother's trading firm. The student explained that when his uncle had a cash flow problem he made his father buy more raw materials than any such formula would suggest.

A classical example of the failures of management science due to its narrowness of approach was what is referred to as the Roskill Commission decision. The commission was set up to analyze possible site selections for a third London airport after the government had investigated only one site—Stansted—and selected it. The House of Lords rejected this decision because of Stansted's residential lobbying efforts and because other possible sites brought up during the debates appeared, at least superficially, to be better locations. The commission applied management science and rational decision-making procedures in evaluating four alternative sites, selecting Cublington. In reaching their decision on a "scientifically" oriented cost-benefit basis, the "cost" of having to eliminate 14th century Norman churches or abbeys was taken to be the amount the churches were insured for. The Cublington site was then rejected partly because the management scientists evidently could not conceive of any other means of assessing the value of the churches. Worse yet, the original site, Stansted, was not included in the final list for consideration. In reviewing the lessons to be learned from the Roskill decision, P. G. Moore points out that

. . . the main lesson is the need for communication between the analyst and the decision maker from the start of the problem formulation right through to its resolution. Both parties should see and accept the relative and varying roles that technique and judgment perforce play in the final decision and not see them as two distinct—and possibly opposing—methods of tackling a problem. This requires the decision maker to explore what the analyst can do to assist him and the analyst to have respect for the judgment of the decision maker.[14]

Hertz believes that such problems as the failure to do justice to the emotional or social setting of the total Roskill problem are often found even in relatively simpler industrial decision making.[15] When a decision to eliminate a product is based on careful analysis of its current and future profitability using typical management science approaches, the sentiments of its inventor are not typically plugged into the model even though he may be a valuable R & D director. Such factors are often not considered because the management scientist cannot personally see why they should be. For some reason, he probably feels that his effort would no longer be "scientific." Yet the first really successful operations research activities were the work of interdisciplinary teams primarily to make certain that such variables were not ignored. It is unreasonable to assume that heavy mathematics and quantitative techniques training given to people who equate quantification with science will equip single individuals to perform as did Blackett's Circus in World War II.

The fundamental mistake was made when the term management science was shaped to mean the use of quantitative techniques and these techniques were rounded up from systems engineering, statistics, economics, accounting and production management and a fence built around them.

Since physiologists, anthropologists, psychologists, sociologists, and many other possibly needed specialists would not typically know how to use these techniques, how could they possibly be management scientists?

Left alone, these quantitative technicians fall prey to their own interests and the narrowness of their training. They are much like the economic development economists mentioned earlier whose models for the development of underdeveloped countries omitted elements which either did not interest them or which they did not understand very well. The omission from their models of such forces as religion and bribery allowed them to sanitize the problem sufficiently to permit the use of tools they had already developed— primarily models referenced on advanced economies of the Western world. McNamara's inability to plug the Ho Chi Minh spirit into his models for the conduct of the Vietnam War, mentioned earlier, is just another example of the mistaken idea that just because something cannot be measured in traditional methods, it cannot or should not be treated scientifically.

Long before *management* science came on the scene, such problems with *science* in general were noted. From a standard dictionary of quotations we can find the following:[16]

A first rate piece of furniture for a man's upper-chamber if he has common
sense on the ground floor. (Oliver Wendell Holmes I)
Science equips man, but it does not guide him. (James Darmsteter)
The dry husks of facts. (William Osler)
A system which robs men of wisdom (Miguel de Unamuno)
A collection of successful recipes. (Paul Valery)
Only tools in a box. (Frank Lloyd Wright)
A very limited part of reality. (Werner Heisenberg)
A selective system of cognitive orientations to reality. (Talcott Parsons)

An interesting phenomenon is managements' general rejection of
management science coupled with its gullibility when it comes to the social or
behavioral sciences. However, this may simply be a matter of marketing.
Taken as a group, behavioral science consultants are much better marketers
and salesmen. And once one gets his foot in the door, he continues to sell. The
management scientist appears to be considerably more conservative in his
sales approach. And, of course, if the customer can understand little of the
nature of the service as it is typically marketed, selling is not likely to be very
easy. Behavioral scientists and consultants regularly use the general
management literature and copies of reprints of their articles by mail or in
person to sell their services. Imagine any general manager's reaction to
receiving reprints of any of the following in the mail with a letter introducing a
management scientist's services:[17]

"Stag Monotone Experimental Design Algorithm (SMEDAL)."
"Nonlinear Effluent Charges."
"Alternate Formulations for Static Multi-attribute Assignment Models."

Summary of the Status of Management Science Contributions

With the narrowing of the field of management science to the repository of
quantitative methods techniques, the growth of a much needed institution for
assisting managers has been stunted. This institution will not develop until
management scientists' training and experience is broadened to enable them
to understand what managers must do besides reduce costs and risks and
maximize profits and not until the management scientists can use this
broadened background to assist them in the enlistment of other disciplines
and in communicating with managers. This institutional growth will remain
in check until managers feel confident of their abilities to manage the
management science as it is practiced in their operations. Nothing is on the
scene at this writing to suggest that either set of conditions will be met in the
next couple decades.

This is not to suggest that more organizations will not be using techniques
such as linear programming, economic lot size formulae, and simulations.

The use of these techniques will grow about as slowly as has the use of sophisticated statistical techniques which have been with us for some time. The use of these tools will gradually be integrated with the management of the functional areas such as marketing, materials management, production, and accounting. The package now called management science will gradually shrink everywhere except in academia until truly scientific approaches by interdisciplinary teams start to work effectively with the generalist managers and vice versa.

MANAGEMENT INFORMATION SYSTEMS (MIS)

"A management information system is an organized method of providing past, present and projection information relating to internal operations and external intelligence. It supports the planning, control and operational function of an organization by furnishing uniform information in the proper time-frame to assist the decision-maker."[18] From this grandiose idea of a global system, it becomes obvious that management information systems and management science have a number of things in common. The applications of each assumes almost omniscience on the parts of the technicians who will determine the applications of their offerings. As was pointed out earlier, the management scientist with relatively narrow training in mathematics and quantitative techniques has replaced what was once an operations research team of specialists from such diverse fields as physiology, physics, and the social sciences. The omniscience of the MIS specialist is necessary to be able to understand, gather, store, treat, and deliver in time for effective use the information from external and internal sources, required in managing such diverse functions as marketing, production, finance, accounting, industrial relations, engineering, public relations, and materials management, as well as the information required by the generalist responsible for coordinating these functional activities. Assuming that the impossible or impractical can be accomplished, grand promises held out to the manager are to be expected. Here is a collection of them from different MIS sources:[19]

1. A clearer appreciation by managers of the objectives of the organization.
2. A closer relationship between the activities of the organization, and of its sub-units, and its objectives.
3. A greater appreciation by management of progress made toward achieving those objectives.
4. An ability to relate progress toward objectives to the resources used, or required, to achieve this progress.
5. A greater ability to compare the contribution of different sub-units of the organization towards the same objective.

6. Increased communication between sub-units working toward the same objective, by virtue of the standardization of terms, definitions and data formats.

7. More timely and more pertinent information being available to managers to assist in their day to day tasks of decision making.

8. Delegation of those decision-making tasks that can be considered to be routine to computer-supported systems, thus relieving managers of this routine work.

9. Discarding unneeded data and information flow and thereby confining the amount of data and information presented to managers to what they themselves find useful in their day-to-day work.

10. A greater amount of historic data being available in readily identifiable form for use in planning and other related activities.

11. Because the MIS is developed as a unified, single system, rather than as a number of separate systems, it is completely coordinated and completely consistent.

12. Information needs are determined from the top down. Hence top management will be in better control; the frequent practice of letting lower management decide what information will pass upward is eliminated.

13. The company reduces its direct information costs by eliminating systems. Also, the MIS itself is cheaper to run because it has been designed by information experts who know the most economical means for satisfying management's information needs.

14. Since one expert or group is responsible for the system, management's desire that the system be kept up-to-date can readily be satisfied.

In spite of all these promises held out to managements, why have they generally resisted efforts of inside and outside consultants to persuade them to order up the installation of a total information system? Perhaps some are able to see the fallacies pointed out by a number of experts in the field. John Deardon of the Harvard Business School faculty, and a former Ford Motor Company executive, points to some inherent assumptions in the concept of MIS which simply cannot be met, the most cogent of which is that "Management information is a subject for study and specialization (and) it is sufficiently homogeneous so that a set of principles and practices can be established for evaluating all management's information needs and satisfying them."[20] Deardon points out that just because a specialist can help a company create a good logistics system, there is no reason to believe that such specialists can similarly service the broad domain of general company activity and create a general management information system. He details several reasons for this conclusion beginning with the expertise required to develop information systems in the diverse functional areas. He suggests that ". . . the man who could master all the functional specialties—the true MIS expert—would have to be an intellectual superman . . ."[21] He dismisses the need for a "total systems approach" by illustrating that many companies have had excellent functional information systems which successfully manage the needed interface between functional areas.

Most of the proponents of MIS have erected a straw man to be knocked down. They point to the need for a *systems* approach in managing information as though it is new and more effective than the traditional static approach. This suggests that they are not very keen observers of what managers and leaders in other fields have been doing all along. Alexander the Great considered and integrated many different aspects of an intended endeavor, from the culture of the city to be taken to the terrain and weather to the condition of his troops. Able managers who successfully oversee the launching of a new product or expansion into new markets consider many relevant variables "simultaneously." They have been merely practicing good management.

The concept of the "total system" is attacked by other observers on the grounds that this approach makes no attempt to explain, predict or understand why the human members of the business system act the way they do. W.M.A.Brooker, in his article "The Total Systems Myth,"[22] insists that "If it cannot explain the way things are, the total systems approach cannot be expected to explain the way things are going to be. Insofar as the total systems approach is weak analytically with regard to the most significant aspects of the business system (viz., the people), it must also be weak in predicting future developments with regard to people."

The weakness of the specialists in the field in understanding how top managers acquire and use information partially accounts for the relative failures of information systems. In his article "The Manager's Job: Folklore and Fact," Henry Mintzberg describes the folklore/facts about managers' acquisition and use of information:

Folklore: *The senior manager needs aggregated information, which a formal management information system best provides.* Not too long ago, the words *total information system* were everywhere in the management literature. In keeping with the classical view of the manager as that individual perched on the apex of a regulated, hierarchical system, the literature's manager was to receive all his important information from a giant, comprehensive MIS.

But lately, as it has become increasingly evident that these giant MIS systems are not working—that managers are simply not using them—the enthusiasm has waned. A look at how managers actually process information makes the reason quite clear.[23]

Mintzberg's studies of how managers actually do their jobs indicate that managers much prefer the verbal media, especially telephone calls and short, unscheduled meetings. His studies show that top managers rarely pay much attention to formal reports prepared in their companies. The mail received by one sample of managers studied by Mintzberg was rarely of immediate use to the executives. He pointed out that ". . . not much of the mail provides live, current information—the action of a competitor, the mood of a government legislator, or the rating of last night's television show. Yet this is the information that drove the managers, interrupting their meetings and rescheduling their workdays."[24] The manager's emphasis on the use of verbal information is a major barrier to his adopting an MIS as a source. As Mintzberg points out, most of the timely verbal information sought by a manager is not written down and therefore cannot be stored in a computer. This makes the real data bank of the organization the *minds* of its managers.

Conclusions Regarding MIS

Two general changes must take place before Management Information Systems will become vital tools for most organizations. The first is that the information systems specialists undertake to study and include in their models, managers themselves. Until they understand the nature of managerial work as it is currently practiced, they have little to offer to assist in carrying out this work. Given the increasing narrowness of the training for management information specialists—systems and computers—this comprehension will be some time off.

The second change which must take place before MIS is a useful tool for managing must be in the behavior of the managers themselves. They will have to start recording much of the important information they receive verbally so that it can be disseminated through formal MIS channels to those who need it. If gossip that an executive of a company's major customer was seen playing golf with the company's major competitor is useful information for preventing a sales drop during the next quarter, what can the MIS do? Record all golfing partners where executives of the company's customers play? Considering Mintzberg's example of the need to know the mood of a legislator, is the MIS to record the moods of all Senators and Congressmen? Much of the information sought by top executives is information which *they intend to use* in doing their jobs, not simply some facts which ought to be spread around in other executives' in-baskets. And the political nature of all managerial or administrative jobs strongly suggests that if these managers and administrators *could* find the time to record much of the information they receive through their scanning approaches, many would probably opt not to do so.

The need for ordered information in organizations will obviously increase *ad infinitum*. The evidence is scant, however, that this need can be successfully met by a general management information system. Much of the critical information sought and used by executives is inside the minds of other executives. And the natures of these executives have been systematically ignored by most MIS specialists in their models.

NOTES

1. Publication sources, if any, unknown.
2. Thomas M. Cook and Robert A. Russell, *Introduction to Management Science*, (Englewood Cliffs, N.J.: Prentice-Hall, Inc., 1977), p. 4.
3. Peter F. Drucker, "The Performance Gap in Management Science: Reasons and Remedies," *Organizational Dynamics*, Autumn, 1973, p. 21.
4. "Conversation with David Bendel Hertz," *Organizational Dynamics*, Winter, 1973, p. 53.
5. These were all given as terms which are used interchangeably in N. Paul Loomba, *Management—A Quantitative Perspective*, (New York, N.Y.: Macmillan Publishing Co., Inc., 1978), p. 18.
6. Barry Render and Ralph M. Stair, Jr., *Management Science—A Self Correcting Approach*, (Boston, Mass: Allyn and Bacon, 1978).
7. *Ibid.*, p. 77.
8. Claude S. George, *The History of Management Thought*, (Englewood Cliffs, N.J.: Prentice-Hall, Inc., 1972), pp. 158–162.
9. Berry Render and Ralph M. Stair, p. 106.
10. *Webster's New International Dictionary*, second edition, (Springfield, Mass.: G. & C. Merriam Company, 1956), p. 3142.
11. Peter F. Drucker, p. 22.
12. I was having lunch with Mace at the faculty dining room when this exchange took place.
13. "A Conversation with David Bendel Hertz," p. 56.
14. P. G. Moore, "Technique vs. Judgment in Decision Making," *Organizational Dynamics*, Autumn, 1973, p. 78.
15. "Conversation with David Bendel Hertz", p. 61.
16. Eugene E. Brussell, ed., *Dictionary of Quotable Definitions*, (Englewood Cliffs, New Jersey: Prentice-Hall, Inc., 1970), pp. 511–512.
17. These were taken from a single issue of *Management Science*, Vol. 20, No. 2 (October, 1973).
18. From "MIS Universe," in *Data Management*, September, 1970, as quoted in John Deardon, "MIS Is a Mirage," *Harvard Business Review*, January-February, 1972, p. 91.
19. The first ten of these are from K. J. Radford, *Information Systems in Management*, (Reston, Virginia: Reston Publishing Co., Inc., 1973), pp. 138–139; the last four are from John Deardon, "MIS Is a Mirage," p. 92.
20. *Ibid.*
21. *Ibid.*, p. 94.

22. W.M.A. Brooker, "The Total Systems Myth," as reproduced in Robert H. Trent and Thomas L. Wheelan, eds., *Developments in Management Information Systems*, (Encino, California: Dickenson Publishing Company, Inc., 1974), pp. 61–62.

23. Henry Mintzberg, "The Manager's Job: Folklore and Fact," *Harvard Business Review*, July-August, 1975, pp. 51–52.

24. *Ibid.*, p. 52.

CASES ILLUSTRATING APPLICATIONS

The literature, especially trade and popular journals, is full of cases and accounts of new program launches such as MBO, job enrichment, operant conditioning, organization development, etc. Seldom, however, is the initial write-up of the new program in sufficient detail as to offer the reader an opportunity to assess its likelihood of success. And naturally one does not expect to read a sequel account describing the program's demise or gradual abandonment. The four chapters in PART VI represent an attempt to fill this need in a very small way.

Chapter 17 is about a company which was an avowed Theory Y company. The case series contains a detailed look at how the company was actually managed plus an essay by the president about his views on managing under Theory Y assumptions. Also included at the end of this series is a telling remark made by the president several years after his retirement.

Chapter 18 describes the operation of a sizeable organization development department at company headquarters of a major U.S. chemicals corporation before the unit was dissolved. The reader should be able to glean from these details fairly obvious reasons for the department's eventual doom.

Chapter 19 contains the launch and a four year later follow-up of an MBO program in a major division of the same company whose OD program is described in Chapter 18. A third section of the chapter gives some details about their MBO effort as of 1970, some ten years after the original program was started up. This excellent report by a company executive points up many of the realities affecting program success and survival.

Chapter 20 is a follow-up study of the originally highly-touted Non-Linear Systems Inc. bold attempts to apply practices consistent with many of the modern human resources management theories. In addition to other valuable lessons, this very scholarly review clearly demonstrates the problem of exaggerations of results by company executives as they contaminate evaluation efforts by outsiders.

Chapter 17

Cases On Applications
Of Theory Y

THE following series of cases[1] I wrote describe one company's successes and failures while attempting to operate under Theory Y assumptions. They were not written to illustrate either good or bad results of a Theory Y approach to management. The final case, Consultronics, Inc. (D) is an essay written by the company president at your author's request. It contains his reflections on his company's five years' experience of "living with Theory Y." This essay is followed by a post-script by your author based upon an interview with the president some years later after he had sold out all his interests in his companies and resigned his positions in each.

CONSULTRONICS, INC. (A)[2]

During the first week of July 1965, Paul Johnson, president of Consultronics, Inc. was pondering a new kind of problem. The sales forecasts and departmental budgets developed at open management meetings in March 1965, for the fiscal year April 30,1965–April 30, 1966, were so far off that Mr. Johnson felt they were useless. The company was also facing the problem of late deliveries since its backlog was building up faster than its productive capacity.

Consultronics, Inc., a midwest manufacturer of a line of radio-telephone equipment founded in October 1958, had had a somewhat turbulent history. It had lost $198,000 the year before its reorganization in April 1961, when Mr. Johnson assumed responsibility for its direction. Total losses prior to the take-over had amounted to $438,000. A summary of sales, earnings, and net equity accounts for 1959–1965 and the forecasts for the year 1966 are illustrated in the following table.

Summary of Sales, Earnings, and Net Equity Accounts

April 30, 1959-April 30, 1965

Fiscal Year Ending	Sales	Earnings*	Net Equity*
April 30, 1959		$ (96,000)	
April 30, 1960	$215,400	(144,000)	
1961	314,500	(198,000)	$(372,000)**
Reorganization			
1962	$193,600	$ 6,600	$ (69,800)
1963	422,300	39,200	(30,600)
1964	435,000	41,900 ***	11,340
1965	792,800	155,800	258,500 #
Projected 1966	$1,570,000	$267,000	$525,000

   * Negative figures in parentheses.
  ** Creditor's liabilities $295,600 transferred to equity by arrangement during
      reorganization.
*** Does not include earnings of nonconsolidated subsidiary.
   # Sale of common shares $91,500.
     Source: Company records.

In March 1961 Paul Johnson saw in the crippled company assets to weigh against the balance sheet deficit of $372,000 when, as a consultant, he was asked to review the firm's situation. His preliminary examination indicated a potentially profitable small company if expenses were cut drastically. Furthermore, he visualized a possible expansion of Consultronics' market share as well as an expanding market in the broader communications field. And most important in his final consideration, the company had a small but capable team of development engineers and other key staff members. Mr. Johnson remarked to a friend that he had never before seen a company in such bad shape that was still "alive." He told his friend that everyone who knew of Consultronics said the situation was impossible. He couldn't resist the challenge to try to save it.

The primary product, a complete line of radio-telephone equipment, had been designed and was in production for use in point-to-point marine and vehicle communications. Most of this equipment had been thoroughly field-tested and was considered by some sources to be among the best available in North America.

The engineering team was headed by a man long identified with the radio communications industry. He had held various committee memberships and other key professional posts in both government and professional organizations. Furthermore, he had had extensive experience as an engineer with a major competitor of Consultronics and was quite familiar with the market. Here is his own account of the company's situation in early 1961:

In March 1961, Consultronics had reached the point of imminent bankruptcy. In fact, for at least six months it had been at that point with production, sales, and product development ground to a halt for lack of funds.

As the company's chief engineer, I had gone to the IRE (Institute of Radio Engineers) National Convention in New York to interest any one of a number of companies in acquiring the company or, failing that, to investigate the possibility of suitable employment.

As one of the first steps taken in the attempt to save the company, Mr. Johnson offered the production superintendent, Fred Peters, the job of general manager under his direction. Mr. Johnson told Mr. Peters that the odds were heavily against success, but it might be fun to try to pull the company out of its difficulties. He also had told Mr. Peters he could learn more about business in a short time trying to save Consultronics than he could anywhere else. Mr. Peters, however, was quite skeptical about the possibility of salvaging the company. In addition to his doubts about the consultant's ability to work magic, Fred Peters knew that Consultronics faced two other main problem areas: the creditors and the potential loss of the key employees.

Bob Hansen, sales manager, in talking to Paul Johnson in 1961, described the sales history as plagued by lack of funds and poor strategy decisions. He cited the former president's recording of demonstration "on loan" sets to dealers as actual sales, his entering into an agreement to manufacture 200 sets for the private label of a company that later became a competitor, and his refusing to have equipment installed in salesmen's cars.

In spite of almost overwhelming skepticism, the key employees decided to remain to try to help save the company they had worked hard to build. Paul Johnson, in his initial proposal to the original management committee, had outlined what he considered the critical steps to be taken immediately:

1. To analyze and evaluate the economics of the situation and to plan an organization with minimum overhead which could operate immediately on a profitable basis.
2. To sell this plan to the key men who would have to be retained to ensure the continuity of the company.
3. To enter into an arrangement with the Valley Bank to reduce the quality of its claim against the assets of the company and to accept in lieu thereof an equity position of noncumulative redeemable preferred shares and/or common stock.
4. To gain the cooperation of the bank so that greater flexibility in the cash situation could be developed. In addition, someone would have to get the bank to grant the firm an extension of about $100,000 more credit.

In stating his terms of service to Consultronics, Paul Johnson's proposal memo to the managing committee contained the following:

. . . I would require a retainer from the directors and shareholders personally of $500 dollars before undertaking this activity. I would accumulate against the company's accounts an hourly fee of $25 to be paid at my option by the issuance of common shares at 10c per share (they do not now have any value) or on a deferred basis in cash or in participation in net profit before taxes. The decision with regard to this option is to be at my discretion, but let me assure you that such claim would not be exercised at any time that would unfavorably affect the company operations.

I feel that there is a remote chance that we can extract from the situation a going, profitable business which will, in the long run, return to the shareholders and creditors their investment and perhaps some profit . . .

Paul Johnson's method of operating the company after the reorganization, however, offered quite a contrast to the tone of the above-quoted letter. His pattern had been to disseminate as much information as possible about company operations throughout the ranks. His method of communication was almost always person-to-person on an *ad hoc* basis. He kept paper work to a bare minimum and held almost no *scheduled* meetings.

One of the most important communications mediums developed was a somewhat informal gathering in his office at the close of each business day. The memberships of these meetings varied from day to day on a self-selective basis. If a supervisor or department head had a problem he wanted to discuss, he was likely to show up. The subjects discussed at these gatherings varied from Douglas McGregor's "Theory Y" to quality control problems, to political discussions, to engineering specifications. In the early days the men discussed cash flow almost daily, and this subject still consumed a considerable portion of their attention at times.

Mr. Johnson's approach to these meetings was most often that of a classical case-method teacher. He asked many questions which could not be answered by yes or no. He listened a great deal, too. Another of his management techniques was to avoid appointments to specific leadership jobs until the emergence of an indigenous leader for the job was clear.

Another of Mr. Johnson's approaches to the management of Consultronics was the development of objectives by each department head. These men were given a reprint of a *Harvard Business Review* article entitled "An Uneasy Look at Performance Appraisal" by Douglas McGregor.[3] Mr. Peters said he passed around a few copies of another *Harvard Business Review* article on "A Positive Program for Performance Appraisal" by Alva Kindall and James Gatza.[4] A copy of Peter Drucker's book *The Practice of Management*[5] was a permanent part of the lab library. Also in the lab library (actually a row of bookshelves along one wall) were several reprints of an article on corporate strategy[6] from the *Harvard Business Review* and a copy of Douglas McGregor's book, *The Human Side of Enterprise.*[7]

There was no formally scheduled management-by-objectives appraisal program in the usual sense. There were no forms to be followed and no scheduled intervals for setting or evaluating performance. Mr. Johnson did not believe that formal paper-work procedure affected the *success* of management by objectives. When asked about the nature of some of the objectives set by various people in his company, he produced a copy of a work schedule developed in a meeting between the model shop foreman, the chief development engineer and the production superintendent. This schedule carried project titles and estimated completion dates for each project. Below are excerpts taken from it:

Project	Engineer	Time
RTS wiring job	Pitkos	3 months
Suplexer	Stylianos	5 months
Rural telephone adapter	Colard	5 months
Chassis XIO	Colard	4 months

Until 1965 the annual planning and forecasting, usually in the form of *pro forma* cash flows, had been done by Mr. Johnson and Mr. Peters after extensive discussions in these "bull sessions" and with each cognitive expense center head. The rationalizing of the budgetary requests was done partly by them as a two-man team.

In early March, 1965, the word was passed to all supervisory, administrative, and clerical staff that a few meetings were to be held to assess the company situation and to consider its future—for the coming year, at least. Supervisors were told to invite anyone they felt would benefit or make a contribution, but at the same time being careful in their selection not to risk crippling the current productive effort. Here is a list of those who actually attended:

Partial Attendance Roster for March 3, 1965, Open Planning Meeting

Paul Johnson	President
Fred Peters	Vice President and General Manager
Bob Hansen	Director of Sales
Bob Burnstein	Director of Engineering
Louis LeBlanc	General Manager, Consultronics Sales Company[8]
Ed O'Brien	Salesman (Sales Company)
Louis Kierstadd	Customer Service
Jack Saunders	Treasurer (also in charge of purchasing and stores)
Mal Barker	Accountant
Nick Ankos	Purchasing
Joe Lawson	Manager, Development Engineering

Partial Attendance Roster for March 3, 1965, Open Planning Meeting (continued)

Gunther Tuten	Engineer
Howie Pitkos	Engineer
Al Stylianos	Engineer
Harrison Hump	Engineer
Clem Colard	Engineer
Claude Valset	Draftsman
Pete Fields	Production Clerk
Mike Alkonis	Production Superintendent
Jacques Bergerac	Production Supervisor
Charles Kipp	Quality Control
Louis Bishop	Model Shop Supervisor
	Secretary (part-time attendance only, due to answering telephones)

There were no written memoranda covering the agenda or invitation list. It is probable that an assembler could have attended had he made an earnest effort to persuade his supervisor that it was important for him to go.

The production department was primarily of non-Anglo-Saxon stock. The largest single group (about 65%) was of Greek origin, as was the production superintendent. Many of the production workers could barely read, write, and understand English.

When asked about an organization chart, Mr. Peters said he had attempted on several occasions to draw one but finally gave up. He did not feel the absence of a chart a particular handicap, however, because of the well-known nature of the reporting relationships. Mr. Johnson's attitude toward an organization chart was that it had a tendency to "delineate equivalent status" and a chart "could never reflect the *primus inter pares* status of individuals."

At the suggestions of several key employees, the first meeting was concerned with electing or appointing a chairman for the series of meetings. The primary question was whether or not Paul Johnson should chair these meetings. Some felt that his presence in that role might dampen the expression of opinions from the junior members of the group who attended. At this time, total employment had grown to almost 100 employees. After a lengthy discussion, led primarily by engineering personnel, Paul Johnson was finally elected chairman of the committee. The results of the meetings were summarized weekly by him and distributed to those who were in the meetings. (See Exhibit 1 pp. 326-332 for the minutes of meetings held from March 3-April 1, 1965).

By the time that the five meetings were completed, most of the 30–odd employees in attendance had participated in one or more discussions and were conversant with such concepts as cash flow and gross margin, as well as the general nature of Consultronics' potential market. This had not been their first exposure to such information, however. For the year 1964–1965 a *pro forma* budget had been widely distributed inside the company. (See Exhibit 2 p. 333 for the 1964–1965 budget and Exhibit 3 p. 334 for 1965–1966 budget developed in open meetings held in March and April 1965.)

Sales for the first part of 1965 had begun to increase, partly because of a change to a bank which placed fewer limitations on its working capital and partly because of increased equity capital provided by friends outside the company. Mr. Johnson, however, felt that more important than this increase in sales was a far greater commitment to company goals which he viewed as resulting from increased employee participation in establishing objectives at all levels and especially for the company as a whole. Below are the order figures for the first six months of 1965:

Orders

January-June 1965

	Orders	Backlog		Orders	Backlog
January	$135,000	$269,000	April	$212,000	$442,000
February	168,000	331,000	May	137,000	451,000
March	165,000	368,000	June	454,000	765,000

As of July 5, 1965, Consultronics' backlog had climbed to $850,000 and the firm's salesmen were beginning to avoid field contacts for fear of getting more orders or of having to face customers for whom delivery schedules had not been met.

The impact of the somewhat sudden upsurge in orders after the last of the planning meetings was not yet being fully felt throughout the organization. Everyone was aware that the company was now "out of the woods," but the backlog increase was not yet viewed as a serious problem by many.

Mr. Johnson knew that all budgets would have to be revised and that this should be done soon. He wondered how he should go about this problem, since his last group approach had missed the 1965–1966 sales forecast (target) so far. By July 1, 1965, actual orders totaled $591,000 compared to a projected two-months' total for May-June of $290,000.

Another problem Mr. Johnson felt would have to be faced was the problem of having some "extra" money for the first time. He felt that there were usually three priorities to be considered in most companies: that which *had* to be done; that which *should* be done, but could wait; and that which one would *like* to do. He felt that he had to help his staff to realize that there was no reason to operate differently in a cash-surplus company than in a cash-deficient company. By this he meant that regular operating controls such as inventory controls, etc., should not be relaxed.

Mr. Johnson further knew that his competition could very often deliver off the shelf, and he was worried that a slow delivery reputation and possible quality drop due to rushed production could seriously threaten the company's future. He foresaw the necessity of development engineers dropping their work on the "new family" of mobile radio equipment to help out at electronic test stations. These switches, he felt, would produce a morale problem if continued for very long. He further saw a morale problem among key management people and especially those in sales if marketing activities had to be suspended.

He was beginning to hear people worry aloud about what happens when "the bubble bursts" and wondered what kind of program of action should be designed to solve these problems.

Exhibit 1
CONSULTRONICS, INC. (A)
Minutes of Meetings Held with Employees
from March 3-April 1, 1965

March 8, 1965
MEMORANDUM
FROM: Paul Johnson

The following summary is subject to review and approval at the next management-planning meeting which will be held on Thursday, March 11th, at 3:30. At the first meeting on March 3, we attempted to discuss and define the objectives of the company and the strategy which we intend to employ to achieve these objectives.

Basically, I think it is agreed that we have competence in a number of areas. We are competent in the field of communications engineering. We have, in addition, increasing competence in the fields of administration, marketing, production, procurement and finance.

In Consultronics our prime resource is the group of people we have in the company; thus it may well be that the best long-term opportunities will lie in exploiting the combined skills of the group.

To take advantage of the skills of the group and to maximize the opportunities for each individual within the group, we should probably expand into new products, new companies, and new geographic areas. It would be reasonable to hope that within five years Consultronics will be a stronger and more stable enterprise, that we will have acquired subsidiary and associated companies, that there will be a public market for the stock and that there will be ample opportunity within the scope of these undertakings for all of the individuals in the company.

To accomplish these objectives, we must first make sure that Consultronics is both successful and profitable.

Our particular strategy for the coming year should therefore be to:

a)   Improve or replace the design of the high-power unit.
b)   To continue to expand the present line of products with particular emphasis on those products which serve the telephone company market.
c)   To increase the marketing staff and strengthen our marketing effort.
d)   To conduct a management training course in the company.
e)   To make a good profit.

In addition, it would be consistent with our present strategy to look at new companies, new geographic areas and new product lines *only* if it seems particularly advantageous to do so.

The above summary is subject to modification and improved definition at the next meeting. In addition, the agenda will include a discussion of our philosophy of management and a specific discussion of marketing plans and establishment of sales targets for the coming year.

MEMORANDUM

March 16, 1965

FROM: Paul Johnson

This memo will attempt to summarize the subjects discussed at the meeting held on March 11th.

Our basic strategy is to build up Consultronics as quickly and as effectively as possible by specializing in telephone company radio equipment so that we will be able to create or acquire other companies. In this way we will utilize to best advantage the combined skills of the group.

It is our basic assumption that people are intelligent, responsible and ambitious and that each of us has personal goals which he hopes to achieve. The essential task is to arrange organizational conditions and methods of operation so that people can best achieve their own goals by directing their efforts toward the objectives of the company.

In other words, we believe that the goals of the individual and the goals of the company complement each other. If we succeed as a company in achieving our objectives, there will be ample opportunity within the organization for the individuals to achieve their personal goals. We try to encourage each individual to plan and appraise his own contribution to the objectives of the organization. We think that most people will act responsibly and creatively in such an environment. We also believe that each person can obtain more satisfaction in his job if he has a considerable measure of freedom to plan and direct his own objectives.

Until this time the objectives for the company have been established in individual meetings and the management of the company has been responsible for making others aware of the decisions. By holding meetings at which we discuss and decide upon the objectives, we hope that all of the employees will not only understand what the objectives are but will also understand the reasons why they have been decided upon and the problems involved.

It is still the responsibility of each individual to establish the objectives for his job, for his department and to obtain concurrence.

By following this procedure we believe that the company can be operated successfully and that there will be a better chance of achieving the company goals because each person will understand his responsibility in helping to achieve them.

At the coming meetings we will complete the sales forecast for the coming year, we will look at the way in which the budget and cash flow statements are made up and we will review individual department budgets and objectives.

MEMORANDUM

March 22, 1965

FROM: Paul Johnson

At the meeting on Thursday, March 18th, sales targets and budget were reviewed and established.

Basically our sales organization is divided into *four* sections:

1.   *The Telephone Company Market.* In this case we have individual account supervisors as follows:

AB Tel	—	Fred Peters
CD Tel	—	Louis LeBlanc
EF Tel	—	Louis LeBlanc
GH Tel	—	Bob Burnstein

The day-to-day relationship with each of these telephone companies is handled by the account supervisor and he should be advised of any problems which occur. During the course of the next year we hope to get more of the telephone company market and it is the responsibility of the accounts supervisors and of Bob Hansen, Will Holden, Joe Lawson, and myself to work with new telephone companies. We may possibly also extend our activities into Canada. Bob Burnstein has, in addition to the responsibilities described above, the job of visiting all of the telephone companies across the country to find out what their problems are so that we can design and produce the equipment they need.

2. *Consultronics Sales, Inc.* is the selling organization to which the agents of the company report. These agents include Bill Walker in Territory C and Will Holden in Territory A. In addition to direct sales by our agents, it is our policy to have the local distributor report through our agent in any area in which we have established an agent. This is the only way that we can be sure that the local agent is in control of the sales in his area. During the course of the coming year we hope to add to our sales staff in the sales company. The job of Louis LeBlanc is, therefore, to recruit, train, and develop agents to supervise the distributor organizations in Territories A and C and to assist in the supervision and servicing of telephone company accounts. It is our objective in Consultronics Sales to develop a high-quality, direct selling force.

3. *The Dealer and Distributor Organization* is supervised and administered by Bob Hansen. In all areas of the country other than Territory C and A, it is Bob's job to recruit, assist and supervise dealers and distributors. The dealer and distributor organization is the device by which we must get broad-scale coverage. This is a very difficult area both from the standpoint of selection and of supervision. It is particularly important that the dealers and distributors selected should be able to do a good job of servicing our equipment in the field and should also pay their bills promptly. In addition to his specific responsibilities for the dealer and distributor organization, Bob's job is to assist in the telephone company selling and in direct selling to certain professional users.

4. *House Accounts* are those accounts for which no specific assignment of responsibility has been established. They include such things as bids to municipalities and government agencies. Each of these

The sales forecast for the coming year is as follows:

	Target* ($000)	Index**	Budget** ($000)
Telephone companies	$ 870.00	80%	$ 700.0
Consultronics sales company	450.0	75%	340.0
Distributors	160.0	90%	145.0
House accounts	100.0	55%	55.0
	$1,580.0		$1,240.0

*Mr. Johnson referred to "targets" as an internal goal to "fight for."
**The target is reduced to a budget figure by a factor which represents Mr. Johnson's assessment of the general probability of the target being achieved.

bids is treated on an individual basis and in many cases the responsibility for quotation requires the work of several people.

Our pricing policy is well established but in cases where special prices are to be fixed or unusual risks are involved in the bidding of a job, then Fred Peters or I must be consulted prior to making the quotation.

At the next meeting the department heads will be expected to review and submit budgets for the coming year. This information together with the sales forecast will enable us to establish our profit and loss budget and to determine the cash requirements of the company.

At the next meeting we will put all of the figures together into an operating statement, prepare cash flow, and each department manager will be given an opportunity to explain his plans and to answer questions concerning his budget. Details of the individual budgets will be handed out prior to the next meeting.

MEMORANDUM

March 29, 1965

FROM: Paul Johnson

This memorandum will summarize the overhead expenses budgets submitted by each of the department managers at the meeting on Thursday, March 25. The total estimated monthly expenses including changes of staff anticipated are as follows:

Administration	—	$4,200.00
Sales	—	2,630.00
Engineering	—	8,520.00
Factory	—	3,280.00
Purchasing & Stores	—	4,270.00
Distribution	—	3,600.00
		$26,500.00

In addition to the above budget of monthly overhead expenses which totals $318,000 per year, the budget for the purchase of materials, including warranty expenses, is expected to be 50% of the net value of sales, i.e., $620,000, and the anticipated value of the direct labor budget, including overtime expenses, is 1/4 of the value of the materials used, i.e., $155,000.

The statement of departmental overhead has been increased by an amount of $1,000 per month to provide for expenses as follows:

Provision for Bad Debts	—	$ 500.00 per month
Consultronics employees' trust	—	$ 250.00 per month
Write-off of shop improvements	—	$ 250.00 per month

$1,000.00 per month

In reviewing the actual operating statements, we have discovered that no previous provision for these items has been made.

As a matter of principle it should be clearly understood that the purpose of preparing these budgets is to define as accurately as possible our anticipated level of expenditures. Each department manager should realize that it is better to operate on a tight budget and to come back for more money later on, if necessary, than it is to have a cushion in his budget. Prior to preparing his budget, each department manager has to decide upon and establish objectives for his department.

MEMORANDUM

April 8, 1965

FROM: Fred Peters

On Thursday, April 1st, a cash flow budget was developed. First each month's shipments were estimated and listed. From this we prepared a budget of operating statement for each individual month as shown in the example.

Net sales	$100,000	
Direct material	50,000	(50% of net sales)
Direct labor	12,400	(12% of net sales)
Total direct	62,400	
Direct margin	37,600	
Overhead expense	26,600	
Profit	11,000	

From these figures, a cash flow was developed making the following assumptions:

1. Our customers pay on the average 90 days after shipment date.
2. Material gets paid for in the month in which it is used.
3. Direct labor and all overhead expense is paid for in the month incurred.

4. Repayment of loans, payment for capital equipment, payments re deferred accounts, reduction of accounts payable all require cash over and above that shown in the operating statement.

A cash-flow budget provides a great deal of information. For instance it shows how we can get into a cash squeeze if shipments fall drastically for even a short period. It shows how an incorrect decision today may not have an effect for as long as three or four months. To obtain maximum information from a cash flow, it is necessary to become experienced in its use and derivation.

This completes the preparation of the budget for the company for the coming year. During the meetings a number of additional topics have been suggested for discussion. The next meeting can be used to provide additional information and also to discuss specific problems.

P.S. FROM PAUL JOHNSON

During the past several weeks we have discussed and agreed upon long- and short-term plans and objectives for the company and have prepared a budget for the year ending April 30, 1966. We know that actual performance may be different from the budget that has been established. One reason for preparing a budget is to enable us to find out where and how we are wrong so that the next time we will be able to make a more accurate budget. The second purpose is to acquaint you with the way in which the performance of each department fits together into the over-all plan. We believe that the better you understand the objectives of the company, the more capably you will be able to operate in your own job.

CONSULTRONICS, INC. (B)

Early in July 1965, Paul Johnson, president of Consultronics, Inc., a mobile communications equipment manufacturer, with almost 100 employees, was facing an unusual problem for his company. Sales increases for the previous 12 weeks (April-June 1965) had been so rapid that the sales budget and operating plans needed drastic revision. Deliveries had fallen behind, and the backlog had climbed to almost six months' production at current production rates. (See Exhibit 1 p. 344 for Consultronics' order position as of July 1, 1965.)

When Mr. Johnson had assumed control of this small electronics company in 1961, it had been bankrupt without official pronouncement. (See Exhibit 2 p. 345 for abbreviated profit and loss statements during recovery period, 1961–1965.) With a tight cash flow control program coupled with extraordinary motivation to save the company on the part of the management and engineering nucleus, the company, over a three-year period, had become a profitable enterprise.

Exhibit 2
CONSULTRONICS, INC. (A)
Budget and Cash Flow 1964-1965
(Figures in $000)

	1964					1965			
	Aug.	Sept.	Oct.	Nov.	Dec.	Jan.	Feb.	Mar.	Apr.
Sales	$ 55.0	$ 65.0	$ 75.0	$ 85.0	$ 75.0	$ 85.0	$ 80.0	$ 90.0	$ 90.0
Direct costs	29.7	35.2	40.5	45.8	40.5	45.8	43.2	48.5	48.5
Direct margin	$ 25.3	$ 29.8	$ 34.5	$ 39.2	$ 34.5	$ 39.2	$ 36.8	$ 41.5	$ 41.5
Manufacturing overhead	10.5	10.5	11.0	11.0	11.5	11.5	12.0	12.0	12.5
Gross margin	$ 14.8	$ 19.3	$ 23.5	$ 28.2	$ 23.0	$ 27.7	$ 24.8	$ 29.5	$ 29.0
S.A. & F.*	9.1	9.7	9.7	10.0	10.0	10.5	10.5	10.5	11.0
Profit or (Loss)	$ 5.7	$ 9.6	$ 13.8	$ 18.2	$ 13.0	$ 17.2	$ 14.3	$ 19.0	$ 18.0
Collections	$ 45.0	$ 50.0	$ 55.0	$ 65.0	$ 75.0	$ 85.0	$ 75.0	$ 85.0	$ 80.0
Expenses	$ 49.3	55.4	61.5	66.8	62.0	67.8	65.7	71.0	72.0
Advances	35.0	15.0							25.0
Cash change	(39.3)	(20.4)	(6.5)	(1.8)	13.0	17.2	9.3	14.0	(17.0)
Bank 150-0	189.3	209.7	216.2	218.0	205.0	187.8	178.5	164.5	181.5

*Sales, administrative and finance charges.

Source: Taken from company records.

Exhibit 3

CONSULTRONICS, INC. (A)

1965-1966 Target Developed in Open Meetings Held in March-April 1965

(Figures in $000)

| | 1965 | | | | | | | | 1966 | | | | | |
	May	June	July	Aug.	Sept.	Oct.	Nov.	Dec.	Jan.	Feb.	Mar.	Apr.	Total	Budget
Sales (net)	$135.0	$155.0	$130.0	$130.0	$145.0	$145.0	$135.0	$115.0	$115.0	$115.0	$125.0	$125.0	$1,570.0	$1,240.0
Direct costs (total)	82.2	93.2	80.7	80.7	88.2	88.2	83.2	73.2	73.2	73.2	78.2	78.2	973.4	748.0
Direct margin	51.8	61.8	49.3	49.3	56.8	56.8	51.8	41.8	41.8	41.8	46.8	46.8	596.6	492.0
Manufacturing overhead	18.0	18.0	18.0	18.0	18.0	18.0	18.5	18.5	18.5	18.5	18.5	18.5	219.0	210.0
Gross margin	33.8	43.8	31.3	31.3	38.8	38.8	33.3	23.3	23.3	23.3	28.3	28.3	377.6	282.0
S.A. & F.*	9.0	9.0	9.0	9.0	9.0	9.0	9.5	9.5	9.5	9.5	9.5	9.5	110.0	110.0
Profit	24.8	34.8	22.3	22.3	29.8	29.8	23.8	13.8	13.8	13.8	18.8	18.8	267.6	172.0
Collections	$ 95.0	$118.0	$130.0	$135.0	$155.0	$130.0	$130.0	$145.0	$145.0	$135.0	$115.0	$115.0	$1,548.0	
Expenses	118.0	128.0	116.0	116.0	123.0	123.0	119.0	109.0	109.0	109.0	114.0	114.0	1,398.0	
Net change	(23.0)	(10.0)	14.0	19.0	32.0	7.0	11.0	36.0	36.0	26.0	1.0	1.0	150.0	
Bank 200.0	223.0	233.0	219.0	$200.0	168.0	161.0	150.0	114.0	78.0	52.0	51.0	50.0		

*Sales, administrative, and finance charges.

Source: Taken from company records.

Mr. Johnson took pride in the apparent success of his theory of management approach which afforded the opportunity for maximum participation in planning and setting objectives. In 1964, department heads in small informal discussion groups in and outside his office had set their own operating objectives and budgets. These were based upon over-all company objectives—primarily sales budgets—which were also established in these informal meetings.

Background of Present Sales Budget

In March of 1965, Mr. Johnson decided to begin broadening the decision-making base and to invite a larger group to discuss over-all company objectives and intermediate strategies, such as sales budgets, budgets, operating plans, future product line development, and expansion plans. This series of meetings was held in an area just outside Mr. Johnson's office every Thursday afternoon from March 3 to April 1, 1965. Minutes in the form of memoranda were prepared by Mr. Johnson and Mr. Peters (see Exhibit 1 in Consultronics, Inc. (A) pp. 326-332.

Early in July, Mr. Johnson became acutely aware of just how much in error the group-developed sales budgets were. After several large orders came in during the first week of July, the orders for the previous three-month period totaled $836,000 compared with the sales budget of less than $420,000. He had known in April that the group-developed forecast was somewhat too conservative and had prepared a "padded" version of the forecast to send to the bank to pave the way for greater working capital needs. His own more realistic forecast was never communicated to the group, and only Mr. Peters, vice president and general manager, was aware that it had replaced the official company plans in communicating with the bank.

After wrestling with the problem of how to go about revising the forecasts and budgets, Mr. Johnson finally decided to take the matter back to the group. A meeting was set for July 15 at 2 p.m. to be continued on the next day if necessary. During the several days prior to the meeting, Mr. Johnson discussed the sales forecast on an informal personal basis with those in charge of various large accounts. In addition, he discussed the possibilities of building up the sales force and development engineering group now that it appeared that there would be available funds.

Several days prior to the meeting, Mr. Johnson tacked up a number of freehand charts which he and Mr. Peters had made showing various aspects of Consultronics' business situation. One of these was the order position chart (Exhibit 1). Another was the sales budget for the fiscal year ending April 30, 1966. (See Exhibit 3 p. 346.) There was also a chart showing the old *pro forma* P & L with space allowed for revised figures to be based upon new sales budgets to be developed in the meeting, and a chart which summarized the company's overall strategy and current objectives.

Although the meeting had been scheduled for 2 p.m. on July 15, it did not get started until 2:40. At about 2:30 p.m. the case writer asked Mr. Peters what time the meeting was to start, and the latter said that it was probably about time it got under way. Chairs were taken from most of the adjoining offices and informally grouped just outside Mr. Johnson's office and facing one of the two walls which held the charts.

The Meeting (July 15, 1965, 2:40 p.m.)

Paul Johnson (president) opened the meeting with a few remarks about the annual financial report to be released in a few days. Then he referred to the sales objectives of 12 weeks before and suggested that since the performance was so far ahead of the budget, a change in thinking might be necessary. He referred to the budgeted sales forecast of $1,240,000 developed in these meetings and to the sales target[9] of $1,570,000 and suggested that actual performance for the first 12 weeks of this period was almost double the sales budget for this period. He mentioned that the bookings for the four-month period, March through June 1965, amounted to around two-thirds of the total budgeted sales for the 12-month period beginning in May 1965. (See Exhibit 1 for backlog, shipments, and orders for the four-month period March through June 1965.) He then suggested that the sales picture be reviewed account by account so that the budget could be revised. He mentioned that such a review should also lead to questions as to where the overhead budgets should be increased and that the possibility that the building of a new facility might be one consideration. He asked Bob Burnstein to start off with GH Tel.

Bob Burnstein (director of engineering) discussed GH's buying patterns, their stock situation, and Consultronics' competition in considerable detail, mentioning several unusual factors which could make a forecast miss the actual sales over the next 12 months. Some of his remarks crept into product line considerations.

Joe Lawson (manager, chief development engineer) broke in to ask when the group was going to discuss the product line. Someone suggested that this should come later and remarked that Joe Lawson was in a hurry to get into product line to make sure he got away early for his usual camping trip.

Paul Johnson asked Bob Burnstein what he thought should be added to the GH Tel sales budget.

Bob Burnstein said that an additional $100,000 could be the target with only $50,000 added to the budgeted figure. He referred to the latter as a somewhat pessimistic forecast. Johnson broke in, saying that they wanted a realistic budget, not a pessimistic one. Burnstein then said to make the new budget figure $200,000 and the target $250,000.

Louis LeBlanc (general manager of the sales subsidiary) said that $200,000 was too conservative considering the sales possibilities discussed earlier. Burnstein said "Let's leave it at that."

Johnson said that since Louis was "nit picking," they should take on CD Tel.

LeBlanc discussed a favorable revision in CD Tel's marketing policy and said they had pretty well accepted Consultronics' unit. He mentioned that CD Tel was understocked and would be increasing its orders. He discussed briefly its resistance to Consultronics' price increase, then suggested a target of $400,000 and a budget of $325,000.

Burnstein and LeBlanc discussed the breakdown of CD Tel mobile units by maker, the reaction of CD Tel's management to Consultronics' prices, and general product design as it pertained to CD Tel's needs.

LeBlanc mentioned that the recent delivery problem no longer existed and that CD Tel was happy with service.

Someone offered that they may be OK now but as soon as Mike Alkonis (production superintendent) went on vacation they would "go to pot" because Fred Peters (vice president), temporarily taking Mike's place, would see that his own account, AB Tel, got priority.

Johnson asked about CD Tel's purchasing policies. LeBlanc said that their purchasing director suggested that with the increases in their order quantities they should not be subject to price increases.

Paul Johnson introduced the subject of the "Buy American" policy of the telephone companies. Fred Peters (vice president and general manager), LeBlanc, and Clem Colard (engineer) discussed the official versus unofficial purchasing policies of the telephone companies.

Peters (vice president and general manager) suggested a change in his sales budget for AB Tel to $640,000 and a change in the target to $725,000. He mentioned that the 12-week bookings had already exceeded the previously budgeted figure of $320,000.

The meeting continued in this vein until all the new sales budget and target figures were plugged in. The variety of subjects discussed during this period can be seen from the partial list below.

1. Policy of customer buying locally (stated policy versus actual practice).
2. Behind-the-scene pressures exerted on a major customer by a very large competitor.
3. Investigations inside customers' shops which could lead to possible new product lines that Consultronics could supply.
4. Consultronics' product reliability under different physical conditions imposed on it by various customer uses.
5. Pricing problem in relation to competitors' product for certain market segments.

6. Pressures from customers and competitors to make more powerful transmitter equipment for competitive price.

7. Problems with distributor system.

8. Danger of major customer in one business (telephone company); problems of expanding nontelephone business.

9. Need for another tester was discussed in connection with a discussion of the realignment of duties of the former lead test technician who had been transferred to customer service (at his own request).

10. Lead time in ordering materials for increased production. This was extended to a discussion, in connection with overhead budget for purchasing, of whether to hire an extra man in accounting to relieve Jack Saunders in purchasing of some detail work. Type of man (background, education) and salary level was also discussed.

11. Question of where to charge the new tester—production or engineering? It was decided to charge his salary to production.

12. Possible changes necessary in various overhead accounts such as shop supplies, etc.

13. Need for any additional capital equipment for the production shop because of increased production. A wire cutter, compressor, riveter, benches and stools were agreed upon, and $5,500 added to the capital equipment budget.

14. Increase in model shop capacity.

After the last forecast figure was named and written on the chart by Mr. Johnson, he began to total the columns. While Mr. Burnstein was talking about forecasting details for the house account, Mr. Johnson reached a total. Several soft whistles were heard and a number of members of the group looked at each other in surprise. The figures, $1,860,000 for the budgeted figure and $2,160,000 for a targeted figure, evidently impressed the whole group, with the possible exception of Mr. Burnstein, who continued his discussion of the house account situation with a raised voice to get over the whistles and murmured remarks about the new sales figures.

After the overhead budget revision (with the exception of engineering) appeared to Mr. Johnson to be bearing little fruit (all new figures had been tentatively agreed upon), Mr. Johnson turned to Joe Lawson and said simply, "Engineering?"

Lawson answered, "$10,380."

Several said "Wow!" and "Justify!" Mr. Lawson said that two new people had already been added but that two more were needed, along with $5,100 more in capital equipment and lab materials. He then hung his own chart, on which were listed various active and inactive engineering projects.

Following the reading of the chart by Mr. Lawson, who added pertinent information such as time schedules, etc., as he went along, a lively discussion followed stemming from the forthright statement by Louis LeBlanc that communications between sales and engineering had apparently broken down. He named one of the projects on Mr. Lawson's chart and said that he had no knowledge of that development project. He named another and claimed that he was not informed that it had been suspended. Mr. Lawson said that he thought the status of those two projects was common knowledge. Mr. LeBlanc said that he had not been consulted prior to the various changes in product development projects and added that sales should have some say in such matters. After about five minutes of this discussion Mr. Johnson, noting that it was 5:30 p.m., suggested that the meeting be continued the next day at 10 a.m.

Mr. Lawson continued for a few minutes explaining that the decision was not firm to add two more engineers and raise the engineering budget to $10,380 per month. He reiterated that any increase in development activities would mean an increase in the budget. He said he added two engineers to take care of the increased engineering load related to the increased business with the possibility that some new development work could be undertaken.

At this point the meeting began to break up but Mr. LeBlanc and Mr. Lawson continued their discussion regarding their communications problem between sales and engineering. Mr. LeBlanc indicated by his excitement that he felt strongly that he was being bypassed in product line development decisions even though it was really sales who had to move the stuff out the door. The discussion almost approached an argument, and, at its apparent height, Mr. Johnson withdrew quietly to his office along with the case writer, Mr. Peters, and Mr. Burnstein. Mr. Johnson mentioned to the case writer that Mr. LeBlanc had felt this way on several occasions before and had come to see him about it. Mr. Johnson explained that his practice was to urge Mr. LeBlanc to go to Mr. Lawson and ask for the status of any product he wanted to know about. He assured him that Mr. Lawson was not trying to hide such information. Mr. Johnson said that Mr. LeBlanc's over-all attitude toward the problem had remained sincere and that there had been no serious problem resulting from these open confrontations. Both men appeared to be held in high regard by Mr. Johnson, although on one occasion he did voice some doubts to the case writer regarding Mr. LeBlanc's ability to develop and direct the over-all marketing program needed by Consultronics.

The Meeting Continuation (July 16, 10:40 a.m.)

Joe Lawson was asked by Mr. Johnson to round up everybody. He said "It's your meeting." By this remark he evidently meant that the main topic left unfinished at the meeting the afternoon before was the subject of engineering projects, present and future.

Clem Colard (engineer) asked if he could ask a question before Joe began. After Mr. Johnson nodded, Clem asked how they were to meet working capital needs if the bank was using the old forecast which was much too low.

Paul Johnson answered by explaining that he had sent to the bank a different forecast than that developed by the group. He said that since his own personal forecast differed from the group's (his was considerably higher), he sent it to the bank to give Consultronics a potential for growth during this period not possible with the old forecast.

Clem Colard said he understood what had happened but that he thought the group ought to know about these things. He then asked, "If we make the revised sales target of $2,100,000, will the credit line developed under your personal forecast be enough?"

Paul Johnson answered by explaining that he felt that if it could be made adequate by the introduction of a different delivery and, therefore, a cash-flow cycle, the old line would be sufficient. He then proceeded to explain to the entire group the essential nature of Consultronics' banking relationships. He said that they had a $200,000 line and that they owed $61,000 to the Valley Bank and $21,000 to National. He further explained that their relationships with the various banks had improved steadily and that as long as they continued to meet their obligations and carry out preplanned activities of which the banks were made fully aware, Consultronics had little to worry about in terms of working capital.

Bob Burnstein mentioned that the $10,000 owed them by a former sales agency would probably be collected during the current year. He then asked a question directed to Mr. Johnson: "What is the percentage of our receivables which are never collected?"

Mr. Johnson said that last year, on a $790,000 sales volume $4,200 had been written off as uncollectible, or a little over 1/2 of 1 percent. He added that one reason it was so low was because their credit policy was so tough. He explained that Consultronics simply could not afford the 5%–6% bad-debt rate which goes with the commercial market. He said he recognized that their credit policy hurt them in commercial competition but that, at this stage of their economic recovery, a loosening of credit policy was not advisable. He explained that this was one additional reason why the strategy of the company has been to concentrate sales and development efforts in the telephone company market. Mr. Johnson, noting that the subject had shifted from engineering to sales, called on Louis LeBlanc to discuss his overhead budget.

Louis LeBlanc said that he would need two more salesmen and two more cars, which would amount to an average for the year of an additional $900 per month.

Bob Burnstein asked, "Where will those men go? Chicago?"

Mr. LeBlanc answered, "That all depends on who you get. Their qualifications decide."

Mr. Colard asked, "Well, where would you *like* them to go?"

Louis LeBlanc said, "Dealers and distributor coverage, or for more western telephone company coverage."

After a discussion of some of the policies to be followed by the new sales subsidiary, Mr. Johnson said that he wanted the engineers to keep out of this for a few minutes. Then he turned to Louis and asked, "How much do you think we should spend on research and development in engineering? More than we do now? Less?"

Louis LeBlanc responded, "Do we sell it first or develop it first?" (It seemed to the case writer that his answer was offered somewhat sarcastically. It was not directed toward Mr. Johnson, who had asked the question, but to Clem Colard, an engineer.)

Clem Colard said, "Are we growing new products too fast or too slow?"

Bob Hansen (director of sales) said, "Too slow. How much of our present engineering budget is on future product development?"

Joe Lawson replied, "About one sixth is on major product development."

Fred Peters added, "*Most* of our engineering time is spent on future development."

Gunther Tuten (engineer)[10] said, "There are three separate kinds of work performed by the engineering group: basic, auxiliary, and services." (He continued to elaborate on the differences as they relate to product line development in the marketing sense.)

Bob Burnstein said that he felt that the Consultronics engineering group spent its money very wisely. He said that they had good men, good equipment, and good leadership (referring apparently to Joe Lawson) and that it was to their credit that every product developed had sold reasonably well. He compared their productivity favorably with that which he had observed in his experience as an engineering supervisor in a large competitor's R & D department. He went on to say that what worried him most was whether the expansion of engineering activity could be accomplished *without loss of engineering quality.*

Joe Lawson explained that Consultronics' engineering was not an "out front" group technically. He said that their pattern was to follow the technology developed in the big shops, but that when they did adapt their competitors' designs, they did a better job on both the product and the service.

Ed O'Brien (salesman in the sales subsidiary) suggested that it was pricing which got them the telephone business. Fred Peters said that it was not one thing, but a combination of service, quality of the unit, and prompt delivery which was the key to survival.

The meeting continued for a few minutes longer with a discussion of pricing policies. As a few men withdrew to make or receive phone calls, and a few to go to lunch, the meeting gradually broke up. Small group discussions continued in small clusters all over the office and engineering area. Mr. Johnson remarked to the case writer that everyone in attendance had contributed except one, even though a few contributed only in direct response to questions put to them by Mr. Johnson or some other members of management. The over-all group seemed to be quite alert and attentive and apparently following all the discussions closely whether they were about cash flow or amplifier specifications likely to be necessary in the next family of mobile communications receivers.

Concern Over the Future

Both Mr. Johnson and Mr. Burnstein openly but individually expressed to the case writer concern over the future of Consultronics' marketing activities. Mr. Johnson was interested in some market research and the possibilities of introducing a marketing manager, and Mr. Burnstein's focus was more toward the need to diversify. He was interested in seeing Consultronics branch out to nontelephone company products and into areas which would ensure a broader communications product line several years hence. Mr. Johnson was entertaining the idea of setting aside at least one full-time engineer to work full time on a product predicated to be ready no sooner than three or four years in the future.

The major concern of the engineering group, it seemed to the case writer, was somewhat different. Although they were not unconcerned with the longer range product-development aspects of Consultronics' future, their major concerns were with what would happen to the company as it grew larger. Clem Colard, for example, said that he would hate to lose the kind of atmosphere they now worked in. He said they now had what he had left the big competition for: a job which was fun. Joe Lawson's concern was along similar lines, although his focus seemed to be more involved with what would happen if Mr. Johnson "traded us in on a bigger model." He described one of Mr. Johnson's major interests as rehabilitating dying companies[11] and openly wondered what Mr. Johnson would do with a *successful* company.

Mr. Johnson was aware that a number of the engineers were concerned about what he was going to do now that Consultronics was "out of the woods," but had no intention of making any commitments to them about his future activities. He told the case writer that *they* had to learn to live with these kinds of uncertainties by themselves.

On July 20, 1965, Mr. Johnson distributed the minutes of the meetings held on July 15 and 16 in a memorandum to those who had attended the meetings. It read as follows:

July 20, 1965

MEMORANDUM

FROM: P. E. Johnson

The following is a brief report on the meetings held on Thursday and Friday, the 15th and 16th of July, 1965, to review and revise the budgets established at the earlier meetings in April and also to bring up to date the information available to employees.

At the April meetings we established a sales budget of $1,240,000 and a sales target of $1,500,000 for the fiscal year April 30, 1965–April 30, 1966. These budgets and targets were based upon anticipated sales from the telephone companies, from dealers and distributor organizations and from the Consultronics Sales Company. In the original forecast, for example, we anticipated sales of $600,000, to the three major telephone accounts. In a period of only 12 weeks, our sales to these three accounts have been $721,000. It is obvious, therefore, that we should adjust our objectives so as to obtain the most realistic forecast that it is possible to make. This is necessary so we can properly anticipate the cash needs of the Company and also to determine the employment and material requirements so as to meet the higher production levels. The new budget and target figures established are as follows:

| | Monthly Overhead Budget | |
	Original	*Revised*
Sales	$ 2,630.00	$ 2,830.00
Engineering	8,520.00	10,380.00
Factory	3,280.00	3,640.00
Purchasing & stores	4,270.00	5,100.00
Administration	4,200.00	5,000.00
Distribution	3,600.00	3,350.00
	$26,500.00	$30,300.00

It was agreed that we will create a new departmental budget for the accounting and control function and that we will have to hire an accountant to add to the existing staff.

The new sales budgets are as follows:

	Original	*Revised*
Telephone companies—major	$ 600,000	$ 1,165,000
Other	100,000	100,000
Sales subsidiary	340,000	340,000
Distributors	145,000	200,000
House accounts	55,000	55,000
	$ 1,240,000	$ 1,860,000
Target	$ 1,550,000	$ 2,160,000

Combining these figures we obtain a new profit budget of

Sales	$1,860,000		
Direct costs	1,150,000	$	710,000
Total overhead			364,000
Profit		$	346,000

Exhibit 1
CONSULTRONICS, INC. (B)*
*Order Positions** (in units)*
March-June 1965

(000 omitted)

	Backlog	*Shipments*	*Orders*
March	553	242	----
April	664	264	375
May	677	303	316
June	1,129	285	737
July 1-5			430
			1,858
VALUE		$486,100	$836,000
VALUE/UNIT		$ 447	$ 540

* Source: Chart outside president's office.

** The backlog, shipment, and order figures cannot be rationalized from these data due to the variation in the dates during the months when the figures were taken.

The engineering program was discussed in detail and it was agreed that, in view of the increased profit budget, the company should accelerate, if possible, the pace of research and development expenditures so as to diversify the line and also to bring to the market as much new equipment as possible. At the same time it was agreed that consideration should be given to undertaking a long-range development program of a project which anticipates the needs of the market. The decision as to the project which we will undertake will be reviewed and decided upon at a further meeting of the employees. Specifically, the engineering program was expanded to include personal paging equipment, a new family of transistorized transmitters, and the immediate development of a 25+ watt version of the President Two.

Exhibit 2
CONSULTRONICS, INC. (B)
Summary Profit and Loss Statement*
May 1, 1961-April 30, 1963

(000 omitted)

	12 months Ended 4/30/61	12 months Ended 4/30/62	12 months Ended 4/30/63	12 months Ended 4/30/64	12 months Ended 4/30/65
Sales	$ 314	$232	$422	$435	$793
Cost of sales	279	151	289	298	532
Gross margin	$ 35	$ 81	$133	$137	$261
Selling, administration, and finance charges	233	75	94	95	105
Profit or loss	$(198)	$ 6	$ 39	$ 42	$156

CONSULTRONICS, INC. (C)

On November 5, 1965 Paul Johnson, president of Consultronics, Inc., was seriously concerned over what to do about the attempts of the International Brotherhood of Electrical Workers (IBEW) to organize the workers in the factory. The October 22 letter from the National Labor Relations Board notifying Mr. Johnson of the IBEW petition, came as a complete surprise to everyone in the Consultronics management. It was later learned that a few

Exhibit 3
CONSULTRONICS, INC. (B)
Sales Budget, Fiscal Year April 30, 1965-April 30, 1966

(000 omitted)

Customers	Developed in March-April, 1965 Open Meetings		12-Week Bookings April-June 1965	Revised in July, 1965, in Open Meeting*	
	Budget	Target**		Budget	Target
AB Telephone	$ 320	$ 390	$386	$ 640	$ 715
CD Telephone	200	220	220	325	400
EF Telephone	80	85	115	200	240
Other telephone	100	115	----	100	100
Sales subsidiary	340	425	65	340	450
Distributors	145	210	50	200	200
House accounts	55	55	----	55	55
	$1,240	$1,500	$836	$1,860	$2,160

* These columns were added to the chart by Mr. Johnson as the objectives were estimated in the group discussions.
** Defined as a goal which could be achieved if normal breaks were in Consultronics' favor. The various customer target and sales budget figures may differ among the tabulations due to informal inputs primarily by salesmen.

shop employees had gone to the IBEW to ask for help in organizing Consultronics' shop employees. The production superintendent, Mike Alkonis, had been on an extended leave of absence to Greece for the five weeks prior to the receipt of the letter. Mr. Johnson thought that this might have accounted for management's lack of knowledge of the organizing activities.

During the period between October 22 and November 5, Consultronics' management had engaged in very little activity related to the organizing attempt. Their very first move was to make a copy of the NLRB notice and post it without comment on the shop bulletin board. Because the letter was in English it is doubtful that, without translations, all shop employees fully understood its meaning. Approximately 65% of the production work force were Greek immigrants and not very fluent in English. A few others in the work force were recently arrived immigrants from various other European countries, and some of these probably had some difficulty understanding the notice.

Consultronics' management's next step was to consult with their lawyer, who gave them a government pamphlet which contained excerpts from the labor laws applicable to company behavior in an organizing situation.

During the early afternoon of October 23, a number of employees and supervisors came to see Mr. Johnson, Mr. Peters, vice president and general manager, and others in management to ask what the notice meant and what would be the consequences of a union at Consultronics.

At 4:15 that afternoon, October 23, Mr. Johnson held an open meeting in the factory lunchroom to answer these and other possible questions he felt were on the minds of many employees. Here is a summary of the various points he covered in this meeting:

1. The meaning of the notice: that the IBEW had satisfied the NLRB officials that at least 30% of the bargaining unit had signed cards indicating an interest in having IBEW represent them in dealing with management.
2. Consultronics' management respected the employees' rights to organize and to have representation. Mr. Johnson explained that this representation could be either an outside union like the IBEW or possibly an independent union of their own.
3. He further explained that Consultronics' management would deal with any true representative of the majority of Consultronics employees and that their rights to organize under the various labor laws would be respected.
4. He explained that Consultronics would comply with all legal requests of the representatives of the NLRB.
5. Mr. Johnson assured employees that no action would be taken against any of the organizers for their part in the organizing attempt.
6. He also explained in a general way Consultronics' current business situation. He indicated that the firm's backlog would take about three months to process and that business in general looked encouraging.

At the end of his talk Mr. Johnson asked the group if they had any questions. This query was met with complete silence. He reiterated his desire to answer any questions, and again there was silence. Mr. Johnson, who was proud of his ability as a case-method teacher at a local university's annual executive development program, felt that he should be patient, and that eventually questions would start to flow. After several minutes of silence, however, he gave up and closed the meeting. Between 10 and 15 employees came up to where he stood and thanked him for his talk.

Mr. Mike Alkonis, the production superintendent, thought that one of the reasons for the workers' interest in a union was job security. He suggested to Consultronics' management that, since the key organizers were junior employees, the posting of a seniority list might be of some value. The seniority list was prepared and posted with a request that employees check it individually for the accuracy of their seniority dates. Mr. Peters suggested that the seniority list posting might be of greater value if some attention were called unobtrusively to the more junior employees. In order to achieve this, he put a small pencil mark beside the names of those who had less than three months' service and a different kind of pencil mark beside the names of those who had less than six months' service. The approximate number of names in the three-month group was 25 and in the six-month group, 38. One noteworthy aspect in the shop activities was that Frank Schmidt, a shipping clerk who was rather unpopular with the majority of the factory workers, continually argued against having a union.

On October 27, Mr. Johnson, in a conversation with the NLRB representative, agreed to an election date of November 12th.

On October 28, Consultronics' management held another meeting with all employees for the purpose of showing a film, "Zero Defects," which pointed up some aspects of quality control which had been troubling Consultronics in the past. The showing was held on company time, and afterward Mr. Johnson talked for a few minutes on the importance of quality at Consultronics. He further mentioned that he had been asked a lot of questions by employees about the union situation. He said that he thought he might be able to provide information to the entire group by answering in the meeting any other questions that they might raise. When he called for volunteer questions, none came. After a wait of a minute or two, Mr. Johnson told a joke and then asked for questions again. There still was no response.

He then explained the organizational possibilities open to Consultronics employees—outside union, independent union, or no formal organization—and asked for questions again. This time there were a few questions, some of which were in Greek. Mr. Alkonis began answering those questions, and on several occasions Mr. Johnson had to interrupt to ask for a translation in order to have an opportunity to consider those questions himself.

On November 1, Consultronics engaged the services of a personnel management consultant. In the afternoon Mr. Alkonis was asked to review for the consultant his opinions of why the work force wanted a union. He suggested that a fear of layoff might be one factor. When asked if he thought they feared a specific layoff, he said that they might be expecting one of about 18 people in December. He explained that this could possibly be surmised from his advanced schedule postings if careful interpretations were made. Mr. Johnson interrupted to note that such plans for the production force were new to him and to ask why Mr. Alkonis was considering a layoff. Mr. Alkonis explained that, since factory productivity had exceeded his expectations and since he had hired enough employees to man the short-term Tel contract without overtime, a reduction in force might be necessary in December. He further explained that he had not formulated any firm plans for a certain number to be laid off—only that at the present time it appeared that a layoff would be necessary.

The consultant also asked Mr. Alkonis if he had any additional ideas about why the workers wanted a union. Mr. Alkonis said that the outside union people, the IBEW organizers, had probably made promises of big wage increases. He further explained that Consultronics paid area rates and compared their wage scales with government figures for the industry from time to time. He admitted however, that it was not Consultronics' practice to conduct regular formal wage surveys of comparable local firms. He believed that the workers felt that a strong union would guarantee a fair policy in layoffs and would prevent the company from playing favorites.

Late that afternoon, November 1, Mr. Johnson asked the consultant, who was already somewhat familiar with Consultronics, to review a rough draft of a notice he was thinking of posting for employees. Mr. Johnson hastened to explain to the consultant that he was unhappy with the contents of the draft and said that it was far from being in final form. The consultant read the draft (below) and suggested that he would like to study it carefully before making any suggestions.

NOTICE TO EMPLOYEES

We have been asked by several employees to request that a vote be held to determine whether or not the majority of hourly-paid employees wish to join the union. We have, therefore, sent a letter to the NLRB requesting that the inspectors supervise the voting when they come to see us.

The request for a vote has been received from people who have not signed union cards and also from people who have signed union cards. Some employees have indicated that they would like to obtain additional information about the advantages and disadvantages of having an international union before they make a final decision.

The management of Consultronics recognizes and respects the rights of employees to join together in a bargaining organization. Whatever the decision of the majority of employees, we will recognize and negotiate with your representatives. This will apply whether the employees decide to have an International Union or an independent union.

I am sure you all know what an International Union is. An International Union can help to provide you with information concerning the benefits which are available at other companies within the industry and they have people who are experienced in negotiations with management. A union might be of particular advantage in a case where management of the company has acted unfairly towards its employees and was unwilling to negotiate sensibly with the representatives of employees.

An independent union has the same rights as an International Union and is recognized by the NLRB in the same way as an International Union. To form an independent union it is necessary that the employees act on their own initiative to form the organization and petition the NLRB for an election. If the management of the company is fair and cooperative, then the relationship between an independent union and the management of the company will be a good one and there is considerably more flexibility in such a contract, which might be to the advantage of the employees and management. By working together the two parties can reach an agreement without reference to someone outside the company.

It is very easy for an independent union to join an International Union if the relationship between the former and management is not satisfactory. If you, as employees, decide that you would prefer to form an independent union, then you can always change to an International Union at a later time if the majority of the members vote to do so.

A vote will be held by the NLRB representatives when they come to this plant within the next few weeks. Although we do not believe that an International Union is the best answer, if the majority of the employees vote in favor of joining the union, we will honor your decision. If the majority of the employees decide not to join the International Union you, as employees, will have to take immediate steps to organize your own independent union and we will, of course, recognize the employees that you choose to represent you.

Paul Johnson
President

The consultant then mentioned that from his casual reading of the draft he did not see detailed reasons why Consultronics did not want a union. He asked Mr. Johnson and Mr. Peters if they felt the workers needed to know in more detail how Consultronics' management felt before they were faced with a voting decision. Both these men indicated that Consultronics' employees should have this information. The consultant then said that he had assumed that Consultronics did not want a union and he believed that management believed that a union would be a net detriment to Consultronics' credit and future operational plans. He admitted that he had not heard many people in Consultronics' management express this attitude openly but he felt that it had been expressed covertly through the various activities the company had engaged in since October 22. He cited the posting of seniority dates and the efforts to get workers to "open up." The statement in the draft of Mr. Johnson's letter was the first overt statement of management's attitude.

The consultant suggested that it might be to Consultronics' advantage for them to find out what the consensus was among various members of management. He also agreed to work on a draft of the kind of communication he would recommend.

The next day, November 2, the consultant brought in a draft of a letter to be considered as a mailing to employees' homes.

STATEMENT OF CONSULTRONICS, INC. PHILOSOPHY
(Draft only)

1. We believe that our success in saving this company from bankruptcy was due to the sincere spirit of teamwork among our employees.
2. We know that our *job security* in Consultronics depends directly upon the success of the company in a very competitive business.
3. We sincerely believe that a union will disrupt that teamwork and jeopardize the success and growth of the company.
4. We also believe that a union will divide our employees against each other. We are proud to have the many different people in our company. It proves to us and to many others that different people can work well together to make a company succeed, in spite of their different education, skills, and languages.
5. We know that we in management are only human beings and that we will make mistakes. We also know that if our employees do not sincerely tell us of their suggestions and complaints, we cannot make the company succeed. We believe that the union way of submitting complaints will sooner or later replace the sincerity with hostility.
6. We believe that the destruction of this spirit of teamwork will jeopardize our ability to build quality equipment at a competitive cost and thereby jeopardize the job security of *everyone* in Consultronics. We know, therefore, that a union seniority clause cannot protect our jobs in Consultronics.
7. We believe, therefore, that our employees' only *real* job security is in the preservation of the spirit of teamwork and in their willingness to offer suggestions and complaints to help management do a better job of managing.

Because we believe you should know how the management feels about unionization at Consultronics, we have set down our beliefs on the enclosed paper. We want to reassure you that even though we are not in favor of an outside union at Consultronics, we will honor your final decision in the matter. We have, therefore, asked the NLRB to supervise a secret ballot vote here at Consultronics. We ask only that you think over your decision carefully, looking at all sides of the question.

We believe that your final choice will be to preserve the spirit of team work which has *created* and preserved all our jobs thus far in Consultronics' young life. We believe further that you will resolve to further offer your complaints and suggestions without fear of reprisal, to help management do a better job in dealing with problems of wages, promotions, and other personnel matters.

Mr. Johnson passed the draft around to a few members of the management and by 4:30 that afternoon this action had resulted in considerable discussion regarding what Consultronics' management really believed in. Mr. Lawson, manager of development engineering, was strongly opposed to a statement which showed the management to be against unions or employee associations. Louis LeBlanc, general sales manager, on the other hand, felt that the company's statement should be unambiguous and that the consultants' version was clear and to the point. Mr. Lawson referred somewhat vaguely on several occasions to management's failure to "do the right thing" in the past and that, as a consequence, they had no real right to oppose employees' choice for a corrective measure. He, however, did indicate, that he preferred that Consultronics communicate a preference for an independent union instead of an outside union like the IBEW. The consultant explained that an independent union was not likely to be on any ballot at this time and that the employees had already formed a Consultronics IBEW local and had elected its own officers.

While this discussion was underway, Mr. Johnson drafted another communication incorporating some of the ideas of his original letter, some from the consultant's draft, and some from the various discussions which had taken place during the day.

STATEMENT OF CONSULTRONICS, INC. PHILOSOPHY
(Draft only)

1. We believe that the growth and success at Consultronics has been due to a sincere spirit of teamwork among all employees.
2. We know that the security of our jobs at Consultronics depends upon the ability of the company to serve a highly competitive market.
3. We know that we must continue to work together cooperatively and effectively to provide good jobs, steady jobs, and more jobs at Consultronics.
4. We are proud to have many different people in our company. It proves to us and to others that different people can work well together to make a company succeed in spite of differences in education, skills and languages.
5. We realize that it is difficult to achieve complete understanding and close cooperation in a company which is growing very fast.
6. We know that we in management make mistakes and we rely upon our employees to tell us about them. Only by so doing can we work together to solve our problems.
7. We believe that the introduction of any outside person will make it more difficult to define and solve problems.
8. We believe that anything that hinders the free flow of information

between the employees and the management will adversely affect the competitive position of the company.

His new draft, however, did not seem to help the informal group to reach a decision. Mr. LeBlanc, for instance, suggested that the new draft had "the corners knocked off it" and that it had lost its punch. Mr. Lawson was also unhappy with this version and the informal meeting in Mr. Peters' office broke up with the understanding that further discussions would take place before any final definition of management's position would be communicated.

The next day, November 3, at 10:30 a.m. Mr. Johnson called a meeting to discuss the union problem with the supervisory staff. Below is a list of the people who attended:

Paul Johnson	President
Fred Peters	Vice President
Mike Alkonis	Production Superintendent
Hal Karonis	Production Superintendent, Assistant
Mike Gonzales	Production, Senior Lead Hand
Juan Petropoulus	Production, Senior Lead Hand
Charles Kipp	Model Shop Superintendent
Derek Dreyfus	Quality Control Superintendent
Henri Rousseau	Service Superintendent
Louis LeBlanc	General Manager, Sales

This meeting which lasted until 12:15 p.m. was primarily for the purposes of gathering information, ideas, and suggestions from those closest to the workforce. Mr. Johnson's notes from the meeting were as follows:

In essence, the first-line supervisors told us:

1. That the majority of employees have signed union cards.
2. That many of the employees do not fully understand what they hope to achieve by joining the union.
3. That the employees lack confidence in their own ability to negotiate with management.
4. That the employees feel that anyone that deals with management is likely to be corrupted by management.
5. That the employees have no one with knowledge or experience in labor relations and that, therefore, they must rely upon the union.
6. That, if we sent a statement of our opinion to employees, the employees would take this as an indication that we were afraid of a union and that this would reinforce their stand in support of the union.
7. That the union has promised that all existing benefits will be retained and that a substantial increase in benefits will result from the negotiations. The employees believe this to be the case.

8. That there is very little communication between the first-line supervisors and the employees on the subject of unionization.
9. That the employees are aware of the fact that a vote has been requested but they do not understand what will happen if they vote against the union.
10. That we must inform the employees of how they would deal with management if they do not go with the IBEW.
11. The proposal to introduce a grievance procedure with final and binding arbitration is not likely to have much appeal to the employees because they would not understand it and they would feel that the decisions would be made in favor of the company.
12. It was noted that the three members of the union committee were all working lead hands (i.e., bench leaders).
13. The first-line supervisors' firm suggestion was that all working lead hands be called into a similar meeting. My interpretation of this request was that the first-line supervisors wanted an opportunity to speak out against the union to the working lead hands. They have not had this opportunity (with solid management backing) prior to this time.
14. The first-line supervisors are well aware of the arguments against the union and of the arguments of the employees. The basic argument of the employees is characterized by a lack of self-confidence, a lack of trust in their own abilities, and the assumption that management was not interested in the well-being of the employees as such.
15. It is probable that the first-line supervisors felt that very little could be done to change these basic attitudes of the employees but they welcome an opportunity to react.
16. The trigger mechanism required to influence a vote would be a firm solution to the problem of providing the employees with some method of dealing with management with skilled and experienced outside assistance without recourse to a union.
17. The employees at this point distrust one another.

At the request of many of those who attended the morning meeting on November 3, a further meeting was held in the afternoon which included those attending the morning meeting plus the following:

Jacques Choisnel	Lead Hand and Secretary Treasurer of Union
Constantine Levis	Lead Hand and President of the Consultronics Local Union
Alexandras Ypsilanton	Lead Hand
Stephanos Manos	Lead Hand

Philippe Demey   Lead Hand and Vice President of
                                        the Consultronics Local Union
James Slaval   Lead Hand

Mr. Johnson's dictated notes of what happened in this meeting are given below:

I started off the meeting by telling everyone what we had talked about at the morning meeting, and I asked the opinion of the meeting as to what might be done to establish a good working relationship in the future.

Ypsilanton immediately attacked the company's decision to request an election. It was clear that he felt that we were accusing him and his associates of having tried to mislead the employees. We tried to explain that our decision to request a vote was based upon the fact that the employees had to be fully informed about the alternatives to a union. Ypsilanton was not convinced.

Levis then took over on behalf of the union and, throughout the balance of the meeting, apart from minor comments by Demey and Choisnel and personal grievances of Ypsilanton, presented the union point of view.

He said that the employees have a number of individual grievances and that Mike Alkonis' refusal to deal with them represented the point of view of management as a whole, i.e., when Ypsilanton asked for a raise and Mike said that they could not give him a raise, then all of the people in the shop assumed that this was company policy rather than a decision regarding an individual. They, therefore, felt that it would be useless to submit their complaints to any member of management.

Mike Alkonis jumped in to say that *he* was probably the whole cause of the trouble. It was Levis who said, "Look, it is not really necessary to get down into individual cases."

I asked why the employees as a group would assume that a decision with regard to one person would be interpreted as management policy. Levis answered, "Because we don't even know you, sir."

One of the supervisors asked, "Why did the employees feel that it would be better to deal with management through a union than by dealing directly with management?" Levis answered that these people have experience and the ability to deal with management that the employees don't have.

He also said that the employees at Consultronics had discussed, in detail, their point of view with regard to negotiations and that they were determined that the IBEW would not be used other than for advice purposes, i.e., that the demands would be formulated and presented by the employees and the demands would not be unreasonable.

Charles Kipp (model shop superintendent) asked what the purpose of having the IBEW was in that case, and Levis replied that the union would help them in their negotiations with management.

A broad discussion of the role of an International Union in negotiations with management followed, the point being made by the management group was that if the IBEW came in they would call the shots and do the talking for the employees group. My impression was that the union group was not at all convinced by this argument.

At this point Ypsilanton told his personal story of being held at the starting rate for eight months after joining the company and asked what guarantee would management give that this type of thing would not happen in the future. I said that I was surprised that this could happen but that we have probably made many mistakes. I said that we were looking forward to establishing a machinery by which such mistakes could be corrected and that, in my opinion, if the employees and management can talk directly together, they are more likely to resolve their differences than if any third party is introduced into the discussion. The union group laughed at my admission that we have made mistakes and that we are likely to continue to make mistakes.

Ypsilanton pointed out that he had been considered for a quality control job and was not selected, that the reason being given to him by Joe Lawson was that he did not have sufficient experience. He then personally attacked Derek Dreyfus (quality control superintendent), because Derek is a quality control supervisor and does not have five years' experience. Derek tried to explain about his educational background, etc.

We then talked about the policy of the company in hiring untrained personnel. Levis suggested that this policy was a wrong one because it doesn't differentiate between experienced people and inexperienced people and that people should be paid according to their capabilities, not according to the job they perform. A broad discussion followed with Levis claiming that the majority of people had some experience before coming to the company. Mike Alkonis pulled from his files a figure of 62% of people with no prior shop experience.

Levis again said, "How can we know about how you people feel when we have never talked to you?" Hal Karonis (assistant production superintendent) and Jacques Chiosnel tried to explain that the top management has never been given a chance to talk to the employees, so why should the employees assume that they couldn't talk to them.

Fred Peters stepped in and explained that the employees should know us pretty well by now after what we have done and he listed a number of the benefits, i.e., educational policy[12], special sick benefits, special payments prior to group benefits in hospital cases, and that these and many other things should give the employees a good idea of what kind of people we are.

Levis then started to tell his personal story and Fred stopped him to ask some question, i.e., how long should it take to change the capabilities of an employee; how many raises should a man expect if there is a union contract; how should these raises be given out, etc.? He also asked Levis why he thought he had gotten a raise in September. Levis said "Because the company wanted to buy me off from organizing activities."

Everyone laughed and Levis turned on the group with some hostility and said, "I don't get the joke." Charles Kipp immediately said, "I am not trying to make fun of you, Levis," and went on to explain that each person's wages are reviewed on regular anniversary dates and on change of function and that the raise which Levis received was part of the regular review program.

After this the meeting stuck pretty closely to the basic question of direct dealing between the employees and the management with pitches being made by Hal Karonis, Mike Alkonis, Louis LeBlanc, Charles Kipp, and me and basic agreement being expressed by Demey, Levis, Choisnel and Ypsilanton. Manos and Slaval (lead hands) did not talk at all. At the end of the meeting we asked the question, "What should be done?" and Levis said, "Unless the NLRB holds a vote we can tell the employees what has happened here and let them make up their own minds." We asked if it might be useful to send out a summary of opinions expressed at the meeting to all employees and we did not arrive at a decision.

The meeting adjourned at 5:20 p.m.

After the meeting, I asked Hal Karonis and Mike Alkonis about Ypsilanton, and they explained that Ypsilanton was fairly clever but, at the time he came to the company, he had the wrong work attitude and was relatively slow. At the end of the three-month starting period they had to make a decision as to whether he should be fired or retained, and, while his performance was not satisfactory, they felt that he had the intelligence and ability to do a better job, so they decided to keep him on, holding his wages at the starting rate. They said that they had explained this to him on several occasions. It is obvious that Ypsilanton does not buy this explanation.

Because he was requested by the consultant to keep a running record of happenings, relating to the union situation, Mr. Johnson dictated further notes to cover certain activities which took place on November 4. Below is the complete text of those notes:

At 11:40 on Thursday, November 4th, Jacques Choisnel and Philippe Demey came into my office with James Slaval. They explained that the plant union executive had held a meeting the previous evening and had decided that management could be trusted and that management should be given a chance to deal with the employees directly without a union.

During the course of the morning they had presented this point of view to the other employees in the shop and in particular held a discussion during the morning break period. The reaction of the employees was simple and predictable. The general opinion was that the union executive, after only one meeting with management, had been corrupted by management and that this was a further reason to have a union.

Demey and Choisnel explained this opinion to me at the meeting and I asked, "What do you think we should do?" They suggested that a meeting should be held that afternoon to tell all the employees about the meeting which had been held the previous day. At 10 minutes to 3:00, just prior to the afternoon break, all the employees were gathered together in the shop, and I made the following statement which was translated into Greek, so as to permit all people to understand. I deliberately picked the 10-minute period prior to the break so as to limit that time to 10 minutes, and to give the employees a chance to discuss things among themselves during the break period.

I said as follows: "Yesterday we had a meeting with the shop management and the lead hands. We have called all of you together to tell you exactly what was said at that meeting. We acknowledged that we have probably made many mistakes in our dealings with employees. It is quite possible that there are some mistakes about which we still do not know. If we had known about the complaints and suggestions of the employees, we would have done something about them, because we want to work together effectively and intelligently with all of the employees.

"The policy at Consultronics is to provide steady jobs and we really believe that this is important. Until you as employees started to organize, we did not have a way to talk to you and to find out what your problems are. It is likely that the reason you started to organize is because there was no way in which you could talk to us. You now have a committee with whom we can talk and the meeting yesterday is the first opportunity that we have had to discuss problems. At the meeting we said that we are not against a union, but we do not think that a union is the best way to solve our problems. The reason we do not think that the union is the best answer is because we believe that two people talking directly to each other can work together more effectively and understand each other better than if any outside third party gets in the middle.

"At the meeting we said that we do not guarantee that we won't make mistakes in the future, and we do not guarantee that we will always be able to reach agreement with the employees' committee. We do, however, guarantee to deal fairly and reasonably with your requests. We also stipulated that in the event of a dispute, we will agree to binding arbitration. If in dealing directly with you, you find that we are not fair and reasonable, then you can always join a union. In the meantime, we think that we can work better with you if there is no union. What we are asking for is a chance to work directly with your committee.

"When the government representatives come in, they will hold a vote by secret ballot. You can vote whichever way you wish whether or not you have signed a union card. If the majority vote in favor of the union, we will honor your decision. If the majority vote against the union, we will act immediately to try to prove our good faith."

The time was then about two minutes to 3:00, and I suggested that the break should start immediately. I returned to my office and started to work on some other problems. At 3:15 Louis (LeBlanc) and Mike (Alkonis) came into my office and said, "Are you coming back to answer questions?" I said no, that all I intended to do was to make a statement of position. They said, "All the guys are waiting for us to return." So I decided that I could not refuse to do so. It was a mistake.

The first question came from Ypsilanton and again he referred to the question of our request for an NLRB-supervised vote. It was clear that he believed that our request for a vote was an indication that we had dealt with the employees in bad faith.

The second question came from Demey, who asked me to explain how things would work out if the employees voted against the union. I did not have a chance to answer this question because a third employee stepped in. He spoke at some considerable length about the injustices that have existed and strongly defended the decision to have a union. He said that the only thing an association of employees is good for is to hold Christmas parties and annual picnics. This brought a cheer from the employees. Another employee stepped forward immediately to restate the opinion that the only way to deal on equal basis with management was to have a union, the main point being "How do you expect us to deal with college-trained people?"

The discussion continued at some length, the only statement on our part being that we felt that it was better to have people dealing directly with each other than through a third party. We pointed out that, if things did not work out well, the employees could always affiliate with the union. This discussion continued until closing time at 4:25 and in small groups after 4:25.

On Friday, November 5, things were in a quiet turmoil, and it was reported to us that 45% of the employees now favor dealing directly instead of through a union. On Monday, November 8, two meetings were held. The first was with Demey and

Choisnel, who asked for a copy of the applicable labor laws and for some explanation of them; and the second with Levis and Demey, who asked for a clarification of procedures and restated the employees' committee decision to support direct negotiations.

At the end of the meeting Levis said, "Whichever way the vote goes, I'm not going to serve on the committee. I never realized what I was getting into."

CONSULTRONICS, INC. (D)

Observations on Living with "Theory Y"

In January 1966, Mr. Paul Johnson, president of Consultronics, Inc., a midwestern radio-electronics manufacturing company, wrote a short report on his five years' management experience with "Theory Y." Since 1961, in addition to the Consultronics company, Mr. Johnson had also managed successfully another company. Both of these companies became more profitable enterprises by any standards after Mr. Johnson took over.

Mr. Johnson attributed these successes primarily to the people in these firms, whose efforts were managed largely under "Theory Y" assumptions. Below is an excerpt from the letter that accompanied the report mailed to a friend at the Harvard Business School:

There appear to be a lot of misconceptions about actual theory "Y" administration, and I have long felt that someone should say something to take the "it's a nice theory" curse off the subject.

Mr. Johnson's report on his five years' experience with "Theory Y" is reproduced as follows:

Observations on Living with Theory "Y"

For a period of five years we have tried to apply "Y" assumptions in the management of our Company. The experiment, if it can be called an experiment, has been interesting and instructive to people at all levels, and our success in some areas is matched by an equal lack of success in others.

Each day we find a little bit more about the art of living with theory "Y," and we become a little bit more aware of the problems and difficulties. We learn more about the applications, the concepts, and the techniques which work extremely well, which are reasonably effective, and which do not work at all.

While our record of performance is not one of unqualified success, we are, at the end of the period, firmly dedicated to the basic concept. We are at the same time more sophisticated in our approach, more realistic in our application, and a bit more skeptical in our expectations than we were at the beginning.

The reason we operate in this manner is because we believe the concept makes good common sense. We are, after all, people who must first be able to live with ourselves, and we have found the "Y" assumptions easy to live with. This does not mean that operating on a "Y" basis is easy. One must be genuinely convinced that the basic approach is sensible in order to hold fast when things are going wrong.

We have had to learn a great deal about ourselves as well as about the people in our Company. We have learned slowly and not well enough. Looking back, we can see many occasions on which we have made mistakes that we hope we would not repeat. We also know we are going to be faced with an equal number of decisions in the future upon which, if only for the reason that there are no precedents, we will make mistakes.

We will also find it difficult to correct our errors. Some of the actions we have taken in the past have created problems that will take some time to resolve. One of them is the question of communications with the hourly employees.

Theory "Y" is basically a set of assumptions about people—not a system of management. This, perhaps more than anything else, has caused us problems. Our employees will tell you that we are a "Y" Company. Our problem in this regard has been, is, and will continue to be that people hearing this statement make assumptions about us that are invalid. It is perhaps the labelling or identifying of theory "Y" as theory "Y" that has caused more difficulties and misunderstanding and more misconceptions than any other fact. Many people automatically assume we are not only soft-hearted but also soft-headed. What they fail to appreciate is that the good "Y" manager will always take action when it is necessary to do so.

The most important and least understood element of "Y" operation is the assumption that people will act responsibly and intelligently applies to the bosses as well as to the employees. Such an environment permits the individual to have substantial personal freedom and to exercise a considerable amount of discretion. Because of this, people tend to assume that the order of rule is "laissez-faire." This is not correct. The obligation of the boss to act responsibly is paramount, and the boss who fails to act when he should do so is not doing his job properly. This rule must be clearly understood by the employees and the bosses.

After five years we clearly appreciate that a Company operating with common sense and sound management can succeed whether it uses "X" or "Y" assumptions. The key to the decision on which way to operate depends first and foremost on a clear-cut knowledge of oneself. If, however, management success depends upon the effective utilization of human resources, it is our opinion that the "Y" assumptions applied intelligently and realistically will succeed better than any other. It is thus for pragmatic as well as idealistic reasons that we have adopted "Y" assumptions. Let it be understood that poor

"Y" management will destroy a Company just as quickly and just as surely as any other type of bad management.

It is unfortunate but true that there are a great many more adults in this world than there are mature people. The expectation that people will react in a completely predictable manner does not seem wholly realistic. It is our experience that any set of assumptions that fails to recognize the differences in people is impractical.

We reject the assumption that management must always act to eliminate the individuals who do not quite fit a particular mold. Good management not only recognizes individual differences, but it must accommodate these differences to the accomplishment of the goals of the Company.

The principle that people are paid for the work they perform does not permit the elimination of all negative influences on the grounds of psychological incompatibility. Without overemphasis it might be suggested that "Y" management should apply a revised version of the golden rule, i.e., "Do unto others as they would be done by." This is surely a less selfish and more realistic management attitude than the proposal that each individual within the organization should be required to conform to a particular behavior pattern.

It is the fact that the good "Y" manager will intervene when necessary which permits the employees who are somewhat less self sufficient to understand clearly where they stand and to feel secure and comfortable in the "Y" environment.

Although it may sound trite, the objective is to run a Company as well as it can be run under the circumstances which exist. Not everything can be resolved by the democratic process. The boss must still boss, and there are times when decisions must be made which will not please everyone. There is no way to duck this responsibility.

Most people are capable of acting responsibly on their own initiative, and the environment created by "Y" assumptions will allow a great many people within the organization to do so. Some people will not act responsibly under some circumstances, particularly when emotions are involved, but this does not decrease the value of these individuals to the organization.

Perhaps because of our lack of skill and understanding, we have found that "Murphy's Law" very often applies; that is, that if something can go wrong, it probably will. We simply misjudge the degree of reaction by individuals, and in most cases we underestimate or err on the conservative side.

In applying "Y" assumptions, management has a great responsibility for the education of the employees. This creates problems that concern the speed at which people of different skills, education, and psychological maturity assimilate information, and it also creates problems of misinterpretation that result therefrom. A real part of the practical application of theory "Y" is to catch misunderstandings fast, and to correct them as expeditiously as possible.

It is not at all unusual in our Company to bypass management levels in our communications. This seems to work very well and we are not aware, if it exists, of any reaction of distrust or jealousy from the levels which are bypassed in tightening up the communication links. We are careful, however, to be sure that the department manager is involved in any question or decision that will result in change.

If anything, we overcommunicate, and we have had to resolve problems resulting from overcommunication. Overcommunication can waste a lot of time. A couple of the unwritten rules we have within our Company are: first, any person identifying a problem and initiating action automatically assumes responsibility for the satisfactory solution of the problem; and, second, the initiator of such action must inform those people concerned about the problem and about the solution.

It is obvious that, if everybody gets into the communications act and feels responsible for passing along all information, one individual can be told the same thing by 20 different people (and probably in 20 different ways).

We assume in our organization that good ideas will stand on their own merit and that a person proposing a change or improvement must expose his suggestion to others concerned with the problem. If the idea has merit we believe it will stand of its own accord. We have, as a rule, found this to be true.

We have followed the principle of allowing people to find their own particular niche within the organization. We have deliberately permitted some square pegs to drift until they have found a square hole. We have found that, if there is not a square hole available, it soon becomes obvious. The people in our Company will not tolerate redundancy and quite quickly reach agreement among themselves upon the necessary course of action.

We have followed to the extent possible the policy of trying to select the natural leaders. We have found the "Y" assumption that people are ambitious is correct, and there are more volunteers than there are vacancies. As a general rule, we have found that the more mature individuals are those who rise up as the natural leaders but that this does not solve the problem created by selecting such persons over those who are less mature but equally ambitious.

We identify different types of "Y" administration. We recognize the unconscious "Y" type, i.e., the Company that basically trusts people and operates in this fashion but does so out of natural inclination rather than consciously. We identify the conscious "Y" type organization which knows what it is doing and why it operates using these assumptions. We recognize the programmed "Y" type of organization which uses "Y" assumptions and includes the establishment of personal individual objectives against which performance can be measured.

We now think, but we are not sure, we can identify a mature type of "Y" organization, which is more tolerant of individual differences in people and accepts and applies them for the benefit of the Company. We could be wrong about this.

Within our company we run into new situations almost every day. When the question of engineering attendance at conventions and conferences came up for discussion, the chief engineer asked "What should our policy be?" The answer was "Why don't you Y it." No one had to ask what was meant by this answer. The chief engineer simply said "Of course" and went back to his department to ask the engineers themselves what the policy should be. Incidentally, the engineers came up with a decision that was more logical and more favorable to the Company than any we could have established without reference to them. The decision was also more acceptable to the engineers than any decision promulgated by management.

We have faced an interesting problem in establishing objectives and corporate strategy. We use the term *objective* to mean goal and word *strategy* to mean the methods by which to achieve the goal. We now involve all salaried and some hourly paid staff in the joint establishment of objectives, budgets, and strategy.

In theory, the chief executive officer should accept the objectives thus established and submit them for ratification by the directors and the bank. We realized, however, that the submission of a somewhat overconservative budget would have cash flow implications. Accordingly, a revised cash flow was prepared for submission outside the Company. When this fact was discovered during a budget revision meeting some 12 weeks later, the employees questioned our right to submit revised budgets without their concurrence.

Why, they asked, if we see that a mistake is being made would we not take action to correct it? The answer was that we felt we had accomplished as much as we could from an educational standpoint in the budgeting and planning session; and we also realized a subsequent session would be a further educational aid. At the same time, we could not permit a budget to be released that might endanger the opportunity of the Company to realize its potential.

We have not found that we revert to "X" assumptions when we get into trouble and certainly we have been in a lot of trouble. If "Y" assumptions are to be adopted within a Company, they must start at the top and they must represent the sincere point of view of the management. We would regard it as fatal for any management to give lip service to "Y" in order to derive the benefits therefrom. People are clever and would realize and react against the dishonesty of such a management position.

The process of giving people "Hell" is one which is not often required, but basically when it is done we try to make sure that the guy dishing it out does not relieve the recipient of the responsibility for work performance. As a general rule, it takes the form of a review of the objectives of the individual in relation to the objectives of the Company and a sincere attempt by both people to establish new and realistic goals for the individual concerned.

We find in our organization that self-sufficient individuals use their own mistakes as examples to prevent others from doing so. We find also that the person making a mistake feels worse about it than anyone else. Any one can make a mistake, and, if management assumes that it has been deliberate, then they are providing an escape hatch by which the individual can avoid responsibility. Usually, the identification of the error in judgment is all that is necessary. The individual, however, must know and feel that management assistance and advice is available if he needs it.

In a relatively short period of time, we have come from being a very small Company to being a rather vigorous medium-size Company. This has required us to shift gears and to change our ideas and patterns almost continuously. Things that worked when there were only a few people around are no longer effective. Our lines of communication have become extended and at times broken. We have added almost 50% to our employment every six months, and in this process we have had our greatest failure in maintaining communications.

The process of growing quickly has involved all of us to an excessive extent in solving day-to-day problems. During this period our hourly paid work force grew very quickly, and, while we kept all new salaried employees "plugged in," we became sloppy about our communications with the hourly paid group. Had we been wise we would have maintained this line of communications and have used it to inform the newcomers. We failed in doing so, and we are now faced with an application for union certification. If we had spent as much time communicating with our hourly paid people as we have with our engineers, accountants, and sales people, this would never have happened. It has, and we now have a problem on our hands.

A second failure we have had concerns our directors. Our directors are basically people who do not work within the Company. They are, I would think, rather typical of people whom one would select for board membership. If anything, they are much better than average. At the same time, they do have conservative views about the nature of their responsibilities and of their role with respect to management. In spite of the many efforts we have made to make them aware of the differences in our approach to management, they do not wholly "buy" our ideas, and they still make the assumption it is necessary to challenge and prod in order to make management perform responsibly. They do not accord us the same measure of trust that we vest with our employees.

Perhaps one of the greatest dangers of "Y" type management is the very fact that the senior people feel a genuine dedication to the concept. Because of this, the tendency is to assume that everyone feels the same way.

When people ask us what type of a Company we are, we say jokingly that we are a $Y^2 + 2XY + A$ type Company, "A" being the built-in prejudices of the management.

The senior management recognizes that it is more difficult to operate on a theory "Y" basis than it is to operate using "X" assumptions. First of all, it requires that management be able to defend its decisions on rational grounds against all comers. This does not mean that the organization is entirely democratic. It does mean that legitimate differences of opinion have to be recognized and weighed and decisions must be made in spite of differing opinions. "Y" management has to be tough enough to lose a battle and to come back fighting just as hard on the next issue. The "Y" manager must be equally capable of winning or losing a battle without its influencing the next decision to be made.

The "Y" manager must also be capable of exercising deliberate noninvolvement in situations that would normally be resolved by directive action. At the same time, he is prepared to step in if it becomes absolutely essential that he do so. The assumption the manager makes is that people will ordinarily act responsibly and intelligently, and that if mistakes are made self-correcting action will be taken. He recognizes that this will be an excellent educational experience. The manager also assumes that he will be sufficiently aware of what is going on to be able to judge the precise time at which direct action must be taken if required.

As the technological complexity of industry increases, more better trained, better qualified, and higher skilled people will be needed. These are highly motivated people; and certainly, if they are specifically directed, the Company will not obtain the full benefit of the skill, knowledge, judgment, and experience for which it is paying. We believe this will be increasingly true in the future.

Living with theory "Y" for more than five years has been a rewarding experience. Far from giving up, we are more than ever determined to see what else we can learn.

Postscript

After several more rehabilitating dying company experiences, Paul Johnson sold all his interests in the series of companies which began with Consultronics, Inc. His main occupation at this point was in locating high risk capital and putting it in touch with companies in trouble for a fee and enjoying his hobbies. Mr. Johnson, about 50 at this time, was an excellent golfer and a ski instructor. He was also still an active pilot having begun flying as a fighter pilot in World War II.

When I asked him why he sold all his interests he said, "I got sick and tired of being a father-figure to all those dependent people."

NOTES

1. Reproduced by permission of the Harvard Case Clearing House, Soldiers Field Road, Boston, Massachusetts.
2. All names and other data that would identify the company have been disguised. Case material of the Harvard Graduate School of Business Administration is prepared as a basis for class discussion. Cases are not designed to present illustrations of either effective or ineffective handling of administrative problems.
3. Douglas McGregor, "An Uneasy Look at Performance Appraisal," *Harvard Business Review*, May-June, 1957, pp. 89–94.
4. Alva Kindall and James Gatza, "A Positive Program for Performance Appraisal," *Harvard Business Review*, November-December, 1963, pp. 153–166.
5. Peter Drucker, *The Practice of Management* (New York, N.Y.: Harper & Row, 1954).
6. Seymour Tilles, "How to Evaluate Your Corporate Strategy," *Harvard Business Review*, July-August, 1963, pp. 111–121.
7. Douglas McGregor, *The Human Side of Enterprise* (New York: McGraw-Hill, 1960).
8. A wholly owned marketing subsidiary whose main task was to develop a national sales and agent organization.
9. Somewhat vaguely defined as a reasonable goal which could possibly be achieved if all the normal breaks were in their favor. Mr. Johnson referred to it as an internal target to "fight for."
10. Tuten was considered by everyone in management to be both the most creative of the engineers and the logical replacement for Joe Lawson should he quit or if expansion required that he be moved into management or transferred.
11. Joe Lawson knew all about Mr. Johnson's half interest in another dying company purchased only a year ago, and held considerable knowledge about Mr. Johnson's experiences when he worked for a holding company.
12. Consultronics paid 100% of the tuition, books and supplies for any employee for any course. Some employees were even enrolled in premedical courses in night school at the expense of the company.

Chapter 18

Cases On Applications Of Organizational Development

THIS two-case series[1] covers the formation and some of the projects of one of the earliest sizeable organization development (OD) departments. Union Carbide's organization development department, at its peak size in 1965, contained nine full-time OD professional employees plus clerical support staff. It was dismantled a few years later and most of its staff was threaded into various personnel activities. Perhaps the reader will gather some clues from the cases which led to its demise. Although its formation was heralded with great fanfare and coverage in the management literature and by the missionary zeal of its first director, its termination was not. John Paul Jones, its first director, left the company for a conventional industrial relations position shortly after these cases were written by me. His termination coincided roughly with the elimination of the department.

As the reader may note from the exhibits at the end of the first case, the organizational development specialists in this department are mostly trained in non-social science fields such as engineering, business administration, science and mathematics. In writing the case it became obvious to me that few of them had any special training of any consequence to prepare them for their OD work. Most of them had gravitated toward various aspects of personnel work prior to their joining the organization development department. During their work days while I was writing the case, much time was spent in discussing various theories of human behavior such as motivation, leadership, and organization theory.

The extensive utterances and writings of John Paul Jones in the case are there because these are the kinds of materials given to me to help me understand what the organizational development department did and why they did it. As can be surmised from the case, Mr. Jones spent considerable time with speaking engagements describing his philosophies and the activities of the new department. At the time of the writing of the (A) case, the group did not seem to be very busy with projects for the corporation. Instead, they spent an inordinate amount of time discussing various applications of Mr. Jones' theories and those of consultants such as Chris Argyris, Douglas McGregor (Theory Y) and Abraham Maslow to their own group. Mr. Jones could not be persuaded that such applications might not be useful for generalizing to engineering or production groups within the corporation. When I suggested to him that some of the changes in managerial behavior he was seeking for Union Carbide managers might not be achieved through OD techniques, he rather forcefully brushed such notions aside. Nor did he ever consider that some of the client managers would see his group as "hatchet-men" doing the work Corporate Headquarters executives couldn't otherwise get done, as noted in Chapter 13. (It should be noted here that about the time the organization development department was eliminated at Union Carbide, other companies were getting on the band wagon.)

UNION CARBIDE'S ORGANIZATION DEVELOPMENT DEPARTMENT (A)

In early 1965, Mr. John Paul Jones, head of the organization development department in Union Carbide Corporation, was about to move on to new responsibilities in the corporation, and he was trying to decide how to choose a possible successor for his position. In making this decision, he was wondering whether he should apply some of the principles his department had been putting into practice.

Company History and Organization

The Union Carbide and Carbon Corporation was founded in 1917 by the consolidation of four companies, Linde Air Products Company, National Carbon Company, Prest-O-Lite Company, and Union Carbide Company. By 1964, Union Carbide Corporation (the "and Carbon" was dropped in 1957) was one of the largest corporations in the United States, and the second-largest chemicals producer. It had grown from the original four companies into a corporation with 15 major divisions. Principal business activities were in chemicals, consumer products (Prestone and Ever-Ready brand names), food products, nuclear materials, mining and metals, plastics, and carbon products. Carbide had a corporate staff and headquarters in its own 52–story building on Park Avenue, New York City. Sales in 1964 were nearly $2 billion. It employed nearly 74,000 people in plants operating in 500 different locations in the United States, Canada, and Puerto Rico. The international company was affiliated with about 60 overseas companies, which were serving markets in over a hundred countries.

Exhibit 1
UNION CARBIDE CORPORATION'S ORGANIZATION DEVELOPMENT DEPARTMENT (A)

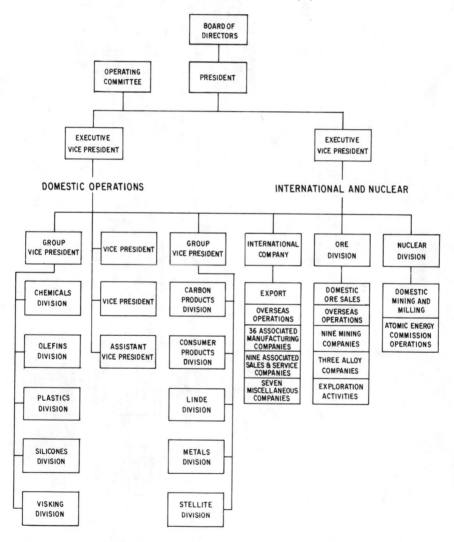

Exhibit 1 (*continued*)

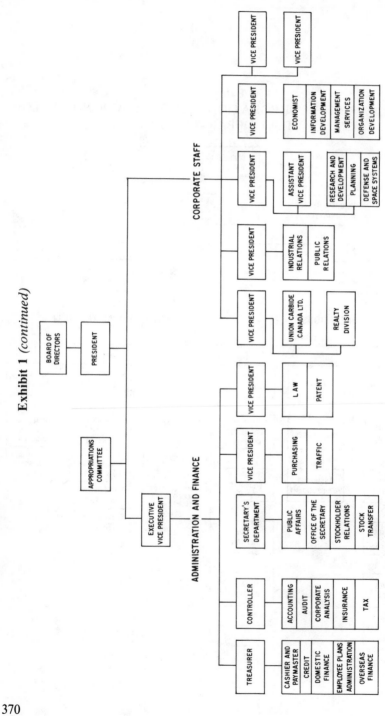

Before 1948, Union Carbide was a holding company. Its various companies were autonomous entities with their own presidents and boards of directors. An operating committee, made up largely of the presidents of the many companies, was the corporation's principal means of holding the autonomous companies together. Starting in 1949, however, to meet the pressures of competition and the corporation's plans for vast expansion in the 1950's, Carbide's top management began developing a basic long-range program to weld the independent companies into a more cohesive, centralized organization.

Mr. Morse G. Dial, president of Carbide from 1952 to 1957, actively began work on the unification of the corporation. An appropriations committee was set up in 1952, under the board of directors, to screen requests for capital and to review broad policies. The operating committee was retained and its scope broadened. Mr. Birny Mason, Jr., president since 1960, and chairman of the appropriations committee since 1962, became instrumental in bringing about changes in the management structure to further unify the corporation's complex world-wide operational and marketing efforts. In 1963, with the exception of the international division, the operating units dropped the "Company" after their names and became simply divisions of Union Carbide Corporation. (See Exhibit 1 pp. 369-70 for a chart showing the broad outlines of the management structure of the corporation in 1963.)

The Organization Development Department

In late November 1959, Union Carbide Corporation established a small group within its corporate staff whose objectives were defined at that time as follows:

To assist in evolving and implementing sound principles of motivation, management, and organization with respect to the efforts of administrative, technical, and professional people.

The new unit, first known as the "management personnel services" department (MPS)—and, later, in 1962, titled "organization development" department (OD)—was to operate on a "consulting" basis in performing its services for other units in the divisions and departments of the corporation. Their "clients" were to request its services on a completely voluntary basis. Members of MPS were to be free to refuse to provide services if asked to serve in a manner inconsistent with what they felt were sound principles. Any client, in turn, could terminate MPS services at any time.

In addition to its consulting services in the work defined above, the new group was to have three other more specific responsibilities assigned to it: exempt salary administration, training, and maintaining organization charts. During the first six months, members of MPS had only one client but were performing other more traditional services for the corporation. At this time, for instance, they undertook the development of a unified salary plan.

Mr. Mason, before becoming president, had authorized the formation of the management personnel services department, and he remained a strong supporter and critic of it.

Three of the original staff of four men of MPS had been members of the corporate industrial relations department. The fourth had joined the department at the beginning, coming from a management position in one of the divisions.

The department's head, John Paul Jones, had been with Union Carbide for 17 years. He had been in the industrial relations department of the corporation's chemicals division in 1941 and, by 1951, had become a plant industrial relations director. The following year, 1952, he was one of the chemicals division's union negotiators. In 1956, he moved to the corporate staff at headquarters as corporate labor relations coordinator, and, in the following year, became the assistant general manager of the corporate industrial relations staff.

Throughout his many years in industrial relations work, Mr. Jones became increasingly skeptical of the effectiveness of the traditional management approach to the utilization of human resources. After reviewing the diverse efforts at developing managers in Union Carbide, for instance, Mr. Jones likened them to what he referred to as the Swiss woodcarving technique: "Cut away all the wood that doesn't look like a man." (Mr. Jones's point was that when you did this through most traditional techniques nothing that remained "looked like a man.") His conclusion was that the problem of how to develop managers should be approached only after a thorough review of what was known at the time about motivation of human behavior. His search for guiding principles in the behavioral sciences led to the writings and personal acquaintances of such behavioral scientists as Professors Douglas McGregor, Rensis Likert, and Mason Haire.[2]

In the early months, members of the MPS department also began the struggle to "develop themselves" as a group by experimenting with many of the approaches emerging from certain social science research findings. Many discussions, both formal and informal, were held within the MPS group itself. They were also continuously searching for approaches that their group could use to facilitate management's further adoption of social science principles in managing the efforts of their people. Members of the department were especially interested in overcoming the obstacles to managing under Theory Y assumptions and in facilitating the development of more effective management teams. Although Mr. Jones and his group agreed with many of the principles for managing human effort developed from the behavioral sciences, they were eager to try these theories out and observe firsthand some of these obstacles to their effective application. As a consequence, they began to apply some of the principles in their own department.

One of the earliest of these experiments was the effort to develop further the "interaction mechanism" through which the activities of their own group were to be coordinated and integrated. Their interpretation of the behavioral science findings was applied to themselves to give them a chance to experience the consequences. They felt that the following conditions should be adopted:

1. Full and efficient communication of all relevant information within the department.
2. Opportunity for members to exert appropriate influence on others in ways related to their experience, knowledge, and information.
3. Decision-making processes which intelligently used all the information available in the organization and which were designed so that members of the organization were highly motivated to carry out these decisions.

In July 1959, Mr. Jones had participated in a seminar entitled "Evolving Principles of Modern Management" conducted by the Foundation for Research in Human Behavior. Mr. Jones considered this experience to have been an important influence in the evolution of his concept of organization development. The discussion leaders of this seminar were Professors McGregor, Likert, and Haire. A report on the seminar, prepared by Mr. Jones for distribution to his staff and others inside Union Carbide contained the following subtitles for the material covered:

I. On the Relationship Between Social Science and Industry.
II. On the Control of Human Behavior.
III. On the Organization of Human Effort.
IV. On Modifications of Management Theory.
V. On the Theory of Change.
VI. On Management Development.
VII. On the Size, Shape, and Function of Organizations.

The bibliography that accompanied his report contained the following references:

Cartwright, Dorwin. *Achieving Change in People.*
Drucker, Peter F. *The Practice of Management.*
Likert, Rensis. *A Motivational Approach to Management Development.*
Likert, Rensis. *A Motivational Approach to a Modified Theory of Organization and Management.*
Mann, Floyd C. *Studying and Creating Change: A Means to Understanding Social Organization.*
March, James G., and Simon, Herbert A. *Organizations.*
McGregor, Douglas M. *The Human Side of Enterprise.*

The foreword to Mr. Jones's report contained a statement which underscored the stage of his thinking at the time of the formulation of the new department:

There is no question but that human resources hold the key to the future of Union Carbide Corporation. The formal statement of the Corporation's planning program sets forth several improved techniques to be applied to planning in the use of our "non-human" resources. The same statement points out, however, that in the last analysis "our achievements must derive from the determination, judgment, and imagination of the many people who participate in the creation and operation of our business."

The challenges we face in operating a major industrial corporation are becoming more complex every day, and the rate of increase in man's knowledge of the physical universe is operating somewhere on the vertical plane of an exponential curve. If our future achievements are to match or exceed those of our past, we need to be certain that our ways of organizing and managing our human resources are adequate to the task. No such certainty can be assumed on the basis of a comfortable reliance on past performance.

It may be that our principles of organizing and managing are adequate and consistent throughout the Corporation. It is possible that our people are contributing all they can possibly contribute toward the success of the enterprise and that there are no different or better principles of organization and management which would contribute to better motivation and higher performance. It seems obvious, however, that we can't be sure of these things until we have explored the problem with the same creative vigor we devote to product research, development, and production. If this premise is acceptable, we can begin by considering the ideas that are merging from research projects in these fields, checking our own ideas against them, and communicating the results of our own thinking to each other. This report is a step toward increasing such communication.[3]

As Mr. Jones and his staff continued to search further for "ideas that are emerging from research," they became convinced that behavioral science findings suggested that many traditional management approaches were ineffective or operated to destroy motivation. Mr. Jones's own published speeches and writings provide some significant bench marks in the evolution of the philosophy of the management personnel services department.

In December 1960, Mr. Jones read a paper at a symposium conducted by the Foundation for Research on Human Behavior, which was held in Ann Arbor, Michigan. His philosophy at that time about people as the "prime movers" of organizations is reflected in the following excerpts from his paper:

. . . it is the premise of this paper that a view of people as the independent variable of organization (the "prime movers") leads to some interesting and, hopefully, productive hypotheses as to how business enterprise might be better organized to achieve a continued and profitable existence.

Let's start from scratch (e.g., a manager planning the organization of a previously nonexistent function) and tentatively accept the premise that people are the prime movers of money, materials, and equipment. This suggests that the first aim of an organization plan might be to devise both principles and "people structures" of organization which are most likely to encourage people to give generously of their talents and their innovative and creative energy toward the objectives of the organization. . . .

If we look outside the industrial enterprise for organizations in which, as McGregor says, people may seek and find "satisfaction for their egoistic and self-fulfillment needs away from the job," we find some significant differences from the assumptions which go into conventional management theory. In political groups, PTA's, volunteer charitable organizations, and voluntary, non-hierarchical church groups, we find people giving generously of their talents and their innovative energy and skills. We find them assuming responsibility, exercising leadership, and integrating their personal objectives with those of the organization. There is no coercion, no punishment, and often there is no reward other than the satisfaction of accomplishment.

Looking at such organizations through a "wide-angle lens" permits some empirical observations:

1. Voluntary organizations generally seem to be built around the interests and natural abilities of people rather than around the designation of functions.
2. Small, freely communicating, face-to-face groups under articulate and dedicated leadership appear to be important elements in such organizations.
3. There is a considerable amount of leadership displayed, but it is based on the ability to lead rather than on the power to direct or coerce.
4. The more successful of these organizations appear to have a clear and often difficult objective toward which they are working.
5. The more successful of these organizations also appear to be held together by a sense of common commitment to the objective based on a both logical and emotional involvement in the problems of achieving it.
6. The presence or lack of this "involvement" appears to be a critical factor in discriminating between vital and successful organizations on the one hand and apathetic and unsuccessful organizations on the other.

From these observations we can draw a tentative statement of organizational principles:

More effective organizations are made up of interested and able people; in small, freely communicating, face-to-face groups; under articulate and dedicated leadership; deeply committed to a clear and challenging objective; and thoroughly involved in solving the problems which stand in the way of achievement of the objective. . . .

(The hypothetical manager hopes to create the following kind of organization:)

1. An organization in which each member will participate in setting objectives and in which each member will be as free as possible to contribute what he wishes to the achievement of that objective and to assume responsibility for that achievement;
2. An organization in which the individual becomes responsible for decisions and the group becomes responsible for his support;
3. An organization in which information is freely shared and many minds are brought to bear on the problems which must be solved.[4]

On September 25, 1961, almost two years after the group's formation, Mr. Jones, in a speech before the American Management Association Fall

Personnel Conference, described the struggle of the group to develop themselves as a group by experimenting with some of the new behavioral science findings:

. . . About five years ago, some of us in Union Carbide Corporation decided to do something about our dissatisfaction with current management-development activities. As we studied the problem, we became more and more disenchanted with the gimmicks, programs, and procedures being applied in the name of management development, primarily because no positive consequences were being produced. The procedures and programs seemed artificial and unrelated to the process of management and were regarded by managers generally as an added and unwelcome burden. We then turned our attention to studying the organization and observing empirically the composition of our human resources, the behavior of managers and managed, and the effects that organization structure and managerial behavior seemed to have on the development of people. We also became aware of a consistent thread of challenge and discovery in the writings of mature behavioral scientists who were observing the industrial environment with a friendly but objective eye. Men like Argyris of Yale, Haire of California, Likert of Michigan, and McGregor of M.I.T. seemed to be challenging industry not only to use some of the findings of behavioral science, but its own common sense in modifying current management theories.

We observed that the composition of our human resource had changed dramatically since World War II, that in many areas of our corporation and others the ratio of administrative, technical, and professional people (exempt salaried people) was approaching or exceeding 50 per cent. It became apparent that many of our principles and practices in the area of organization, motivation, and management were inappropriate to the problems of today's infinitely complex corporate structure and purpose. We also concluded that if better principles and practices were to be evolved, we would need to experiment toward greater flexibility and effectiveness in organization and that such experimentation was most likely to bear fruit in our administrative, technical, and professional force simply because flexibility was already present. A militant union and a legalized collective bargaining contract leave little room to experiment in these areas.

From this point of view we also became convinced that personnel or industrial relations, while it had risen nobly to meet the challenges of collective bargaining and the problems of blue-collar employees, had not yet found a way to adequately serve management in these areas; but we felt that a responsibility to so serve was inherent in the personnel function. . . .

As General Manager of Management Personnel Services, I am consciously attempting to manage the efforts of these people by a deliberately different set of assumptions, and one of the key decisions I made in this respect was that I would follow these assumptions and principles to the furthest possible end so that we would have not only an on-going, hopefully dynamic and useful organization, but an on-going action research program.

Having gotten together a core of people, the first step in getting this process under way was to sit down together and discuss these assumptions, the same things I've been discussing with you. We didn't know as much about the problem then since we had not really examined cause and effect in our own behavior, but we did share assumptions and agree on what we would assume about each other—that we would operate this department on the assumption that everybody in it had integrity, had ability, was highly motivated, and had self-control.

The next logical decision that emerged from these discussions was that we would have no secrets from each other; that is, of course, business secrets. There are no privileged communications, and while we deal with a great amount of personal and confidential information, we treat it as part of our environment. Everyone in the department has access to the information; therefore, there is no reason for anyone to worry about secrets.

We then confirmed our long-term objective, our reason for being in business. Along with this, of course, went a great deal of discussion not embodied in the formal objective. We were certain that one of the hazards we would face would be that of being confused with the "happiness boys" although our real aim was to contribute to profit. We agreed that this impression could be overcome if the principles we evolved gave promise of contributing to a more profitable, more effective organization.

We then evolved an interesting idea which we have come to call the "50/50 ratio." We had become concerned with what appeared to us to be overfunctionalization and specialization in staff areas. We felt that the narrowness of staff jobs in many areas contributed to apathy and lack of challenge and that perhaps one way around this was to eliminate functionalism. We had brought over into the new department from Industrial Relations, three functions: Exempt Salary Administration, Training, and Organization (charting). The idea of eliminating functions completely was considered, but discarded on the grounds that each man was bringing into this organization certain special experience, training, education, and interest which was unique and valuable. We decided that this uniqueness had to be preserved, but that we also needed to "double in brass" so that we could keep our department small enough to provide great challenges and personal growth to the people in the group. The "50/50 ratio" then simply means that individuals have prime accountability in the function in which their interest, training, and ability leads them to take a leading role. Each man also has secondary accountability for assisting other people in different functions. Thus, it is not unusual in our group to find the Manager—Salary Administration working on an organizational analysis project under the leadership of the Training Consultant, and the Organization Consultant working on a salary job description project under the leadership of the Manager—Salary Administration. The point is that we have a common goal, and the pursuit of functional and individual objectives all contribute to the over-all objective.

The next very important process we went through was trying to unscramble the role of the individual from the role of the group. The behavioral sciences tend to place great emphasis on group dynamics, and there tends to be in industry an equally strong coterie of rugged individualists. We concluded that life really isn't that way in either sense. In other words, we needed to have a role for the group and a role for the individual, and we made a kind of simple decision that has proved extremely useful to us. We decided (and that was virtually the last group decision) that the group wouldn't make any decisions, that individuals would make decisions, and that, therefore, the role of the group was to communicate, to provide a forum for discussion, to provide help—a place for individuals to bounce their ideas around and get criticism or assistance. This has worked very well and in our opinion is the answer to the rather formal and futile idea of delegating decision-making to the lowest possible level. When this kind of decision is made, one is led into another interesting area. What are the implications with respect to authority and accountability? How about the decisions that involve spending money, that involve communication with other people? Who travels? Who decides who goes to professional societies or conventions? These kinds of problems plague all organizations. One might say at this point we discovered a great principle, which is: Follow the principle! If individuals are to make decisions, they must make these kinds of decisions too. On this basis, spending authority was established for each individual. By the same token, this established budget accountability for everyone in the group. The logical progression of the application of these principles is inescapable. Before anyone could say what spending authority he needed, it was necessary for him to determine his short-term objectives or projects for the forthcoming year and to estimate the cost of achieving these objectives.

Decisions to travel or not to travel, to attend a conference or not to attend it, rest with the individual. Communications are free. Everyone has a responsibility to communicate, to attempt to influence in ways appropriate to his experience and ability. He also takes accountability, of course, for that communication. We have found that this creates no problem because we spent a greal deal of time thrashing out what our role in the Corporation would be, what relationships we would have to other people, and by what principles we were going to operate. Having already decided that we would be conceptual and consultative, that we would be available but not insistent, that we would not interfere in line operations, that we would defend principles but not try to impose them, and that we would have to make the same assumptions about other people we made about ourselves, we found it unnecessary to set up a control system to make decisions and communications "safe." All of this sounds easy in the telling. It was not. It was extremely difficult.

What have been the consequences? Let me describe it in the same terms as my earlier example in the game we played:

1. No information is withheld. Confidential information is as safe with the newest member of the department as it is with me. In two years there has never been any misuse of such information. Far beyond that, even the newest members of the department are fully aware of the environment in which they are operating. If there are financial or other problems which might affect our operation, such problems are freely discussed. As a consequence, for example, when it becomes time to budget against a tight year, we have no problems. When it becomes time to reduce expenditures, to curtail programs, or to expand them or increase them, everybody is fully aware of what is going on.
2. Each man helped set the departmental objective and then set objectives for himself which, if achieved, would contribute to achieving the departmental objective. I am available to him, as is everyone else, for help, but he sets his own deadline, plans his own work, and works his own way.
3. In communicating and setting the example for free communication within the department and outside of it, I have a primary responsibility. If I don't

communicate, nobody does. If I don't insist that people communicate, communication falls off.

4. When a problem is to be tackled, it is each man's individual responsibility not to recommend a solution to me, but to help the people involved to solve their own problems. This is an important difference.

5. I have a conscious objective of seeing that, insofar as is humanly possible, everyone in the department knows what I know. No privileged communications, no playing one man off against another.

6. If someone is interested in having a member of the group work for him, he must negotiate with that man, not with me.

7. We have as a basic and fundamental objective the growth of every individual to greater performance. It's a conscious objective and it is discussed and openly pursued. We believe that only by this means can the organization grow in effectiveness.

There are many more such illustrations, but they all serve the same point. What kind of "organizational" behavior has this produced?

a) Since there aren't any secrets, nobody spends any time ferreting them out and secrets have no status value. Not a single confidence has ever been violated.

b) Everyone is reaching for new work and everyone believes he can do more.

c) Everyone is aware that there is only so much work and that adding unnecessary people only lessens the challenge and opportunity for each individual.

d) Everyone is aware of the fact that there is only so much compensation money to go around, and that adding unnecessary people (or tolerating substandard work) simply lessens the financial rewards which are available for performance and contribution.

e) Everyone has had to learn to communicate for himself, and, incidentally, to learn for himself that busy executives appreciate clarity, brevity, and honesty, and are impatient with inconsequential matters.

f) New ideas are constantly being generated and intergenerated because each man is interacting freely with others in the department and in the Corporation at large.

g) Nobody has to study me for acceptance. They are far too busy studying real problems and working with managers to help managers solve problems. (We don't solve them for them.)

In short, the organization is alive, dynamic, flexible, and vitally interested in achieving the goals that have been set.

Don't confuse this with soft management. The standards of expectation in this kind of operation are very high. Don't confuse it with abdicative management. The manager here has a very positive role. It is his job to be the principal upward influencer, to be the defender of the faith, if you will. It is his job to constantly seek new innovative ways of applying these principles, not only in his organization but in the larger organization. He must communicate and insist on communication. He must commit himself to these principles and behave by them. He must encourage openness and collaboration on complex tasks with other groups in the company. He must fight for the integrity of the total operation. He must be prepared to accept mistakes and support the principles, the people, and the objectives.

Looking at our own operation in terms of more conventional results, actual departmental expenditures were slashed 30 per cent in the first full year of operation. Expenses will move upward, of course, but only in proportion to the effort. During the first six months of operation, the department had one "customer" on a project basis. Today there are 38 projects in operation, covering compensation systems and procedures, organization studies, personnel and managerial consultation, and pilot applications of these same principles to line operations. We are told that our principles are having an effect, and we see in some line operations, both old and new, that they are having an effect; but since our role is catalytic, helping managers think through problems of motivation, organization, and management of human effort, our results can't always be measured and they can't, in the last analysis, be measured by anyone but the people we serve. We are content that it be this way.

There is no sociological goal involved here. We are profit oriented. The happiness of people is not a goal although we suspect that people are probably happier working this way. In profit-oriented terms, we are convinced that an organization operating by these principles can operate with fewer people, lower costs, far greater effectiveness, and higher individual rewards for the people who are so involved. What we can do, others can do. The steps, the procedures, the specifics will be different, but I believe the principles are sound, timeless, and universally applicable. It is a concept which can be studied and argued about for years, but I honestly believe the time is short. Only action is needed to make the concept a reality.[5]

Mr. Jones has subsequently admitted that, since this speech was delivered, he has changed his thinking about who should make decisions, groups or individuals. He now believes that groups *should* make those kinds of decisions that require a coordinated team to implement.

The following comment on John Paul Jones's work and the excerpts from an interview with Mr. Jones were taken from a special study of the American Management Association entitled *A Look at Personnel Through the President's Eye*, a study based on interviews with company presidents, chairmen of boards, and prominent personnel administrators:

. . . When executives sit down to discuss ideas of this sort, very often the name John Paul Jones occurs in their conversation. He is general manager-organization development at Union Carbide. For several years he has been moving along a route somewhat parallel with McGregor, but he has actually applied the principles in his organization development work at Union Carbide. He commented on this work as follows:

The Y assumptions are essentially a set of assumptions about the basic nature of people. I'm using Y as a "shorthand" phrase, because there's a lot more to it than we've seen in the literature.

I think it was Likert who pointed out that we've been able to get increased production, and sometimes even increased efficiency for short periods of time, by following management systems which have implicit in them the X assumptions—in other words, increased pressure, hard driving, pushing people, crowding them, using punishment as a spur. And nobody can say that we haven't done quite a production job, quite an industrial job generally, in the United States and elsewhere, by using systems based on the X assumptions. The question is: Haven't we pretty much reached the point of diminishing returns? Where do we make our breakthrough? That's where we get into the Y assumptions.

Any manager will probably tell you: "Oh, I've always managed by Y assumptions." But you find out, of course, that he hasn't. The Y assumptions are nice things to believe, and he can be perfectly sincere in telling you he believes in them. They sound good. But I can tell you that very few managers in Union Carbide buy us on the basis of X versus Y. . . . They come to us for what they need . . . help on a specific problem. We keep applying the principles, and we try to make a learning process develop in our work with organizational clients, in terms of X, Y, and that general area much broader than Y, out of the work we do for them. In other words, when we've done a piece of work that seems to satisfy them, one that energizes the organization, we point out what kinds of principles we've followed, what kinds of assumptions we have operated with . . . sometimes we're successful. . . . Then again, sometimes a guy just listens to us and says "Yeah, thanks a lot; great job" . . . or he figures it was a lousy job and says nothing. You just have to be very patient. You can't expect to revolutionize the world.

We came over here from the industrial relations group in December 1959; so this work has been going on four years. . . . I don't know if there's another corporation in the world where this kind of operation could have grown and continue to exist. Our total corporate climate has a lot of instinctive Y in it—and that includes our top officers, who are willing to back an experimental approach even when they may not understand all that is involved.

One of the methods in making the whole approach successful at the start was making group decisions regarding the "laws" by which the group would live. But no group decisions are made with respect to an individual's work or his accountability for method, deadline, and the like. The results of what John Paul Jones initiated and nurtured to its present state are profound, particularly in cost savings. As he said:

We have very few functional lines in this group. We've got people who have a unique interest in training, in education, in salary, and what have you. We have created a process of deliberately breaking down the lines between these things, and making jobs *whole*, so that *one* guy takes accountability for *one* job and enlists whatever help he needs. As a result, everybody is becoming able to handle more and more work.

Now you can well afford to pay for this because your costs are lower. Actual expenses for one year were about 20 per cent under budget—and it wasn't a fat budget, it was an honest budget. We found that people get more and more ingenious about saving money.

This works with our girls the same way. We have three girls working for seven people here. We pay them a little better. They know it. But we get results from them that you just can't get by other X assumptions. For instance, one summer our youngest girl—who's only 18 and who has been with us only six months—was the first girl scheduled to go on vacation. One of the staff men went over to her and said: "In the past, we've always brought in an office temporary to fill in for vacation relief; so we had better get her in a little ahead of time so you can break her in." And she said: "No, we've discussed this thing among ourselves, and we think it's too expensive. We're not going to have a vacation relief girl this year. We'll cover for each other."

Well, that's $500. Maybe $500 doesn't sound like a lot of money in a total corporation, but if you can get this principle operating all over the corporation . . . the money . . . just plain hard cash that can be saved, and conserved, is fantastic![6]

In February 1964, Mr. Jones read a paper titled "How Should We Manage—by Myth, Magic or Knowledge?" at the American Management Association Fall Personnel Conference, in which he discussed his experiments in applying some of the new theories in creating work groups as "building blocks" in developing effective organizations:

For the past four years, a growing number of executives, managers, supervisors, and their immediate organizations in Union Carbide have been using relevant research findings from the behavioral sciences in an attempt to build better organizations and to improve organized human effort. Not all of this effort has been successful; there has been confusion, misapplication, and much groping in the dark.

During these years, however, the body of knowledge has grown steadily, and there is no doubt in my mind that there is available today enough systematic knowledge to enable managers to build human organizations capable of productivity several hundred percent greater than we now have.

In order to do this, however, I believe managers are going to have to persuade themselves to become more professional in their management of organized human effort. I don't mean that a manager must be a behavioral scientist, but I do suggest that he should use systematic knowledge in his management of human effort; the use of systematic knowledge is, of course, the hallmark of any professional.

I have an uneasy feeling that far too many managers today are becoming buried in things and numbers and that because of this they are relatively isolated from the new knowledge which could help them handle the human side of their job.

Things and numbers have their place; but make no mistake about it, the real problem of industry today is not the manipulation of capital but the integration of special talents and skills, all of which are both products and prisoners of the human resource. *The price of specialization is interdependence*—dependence on one another—and while the good instinctive manager may have always sensed this, our problems are too severe these days to rely solely on an unreliable supply of "born managers." Interdependence among people is a fact, but recognition of this fact is not an easy thing to achieve, and, if we are to achieve it in our industrial organizations, we must rely on knowledge. We can no longer manage organized human effort, as we often have, on the basis of myth and magic. . . .

For example, take the basic myth that motivation is something the boss does to the subordinate to make him perform better. The most common piece of magic used here is the traditionally oriented performance review where the subordinate is told of his shortcomings (freely translated, that means where he differs from the boss) and exhorted to perform in ways that meet his boss's needs. The fact is, of course, that people are motivated by their own needs, not someone else's, and all the magic in the world isn't going to change that fact. This does not mean that people won't perform for the good of the organization, but we know today that traditional motivational assumptions simply will not work: the problem is infinitely more complex.

A related myth-magic sequence can be expressed in the commonly heard statement: "We may differ around here, but once the boss makes the decision, we all get behind it." Yet research experiments done time again show that differences don't automatically disappear under such circumstances and that the myth of the "good soldier" is just that. . . .

Or take the notion that is one of my three main points of concern today: the myth that a man is or can be a completely rational, nonemotional decision maker. Managers who hold this point of view are likely to wave the wand with such statements as "let's keep emotions out of this," and most of our notions about "the ideal manager" visualize him as a man whose decisions are unaffected by emotion. The fact is, however, that only on paper can man be separated into rational and emotional components; in life each of us is an inseparable blend of emotion and rationality.

Thus, all human decision making is affected by emotion, and this explains why it is often very difficult for us to accept fact, no matter how well it may be supported by data. When research contradicts our long-held assumptions, our response will almost always be primarily emotional. Because of this, it's unrealistic to expect people to readily change the premises on which they operate. . . .

On the other hand, as Rensis Likert of the University of Michigan has pointed out, the knowledge of what makes the difference between an ineffective and an effective organization has reached a state where independent investigators can repeat the research anywhere and test the validity of the findings.

The implications here for management are tremendously significant. It means that we will need more leaders in industry who are willing to lay aside traditional mythology, accept knowledge in its place, and lead in the changes that must follow. We will need to be concerned, as executives, managers, and supervisors, that change takes place. We will need to seek managerial and nonmanagerial learning processes of a nature entirely different from the past.

At the same time, we will need to rethink the nonhuman aspects of our organizations and revise our systems, methods, and procedures to be sure they support rather than impede the application of new knowledge in the human side of enterprise. . . .

I said earlier that there were three myth-magic sequences commanding most of my time and effort today. One was man, the purely rational decision maker. The other two are these: first, that the exclusive building block of organization is the individual; second, that groups can't make decisions. Up until quite recently, I believed all of these, but I don't any more. Let me try to be unmistakably clear: I still believe that rationality is important, I still believe in individual excellence, and I still believe in individual decision making. I simply no longer accept these as exclusive value determinants in organized human behavior. Or, to put it another way, to say that our decisions are unaffected by emotions, that groups do not constitute building blocks in organization, or that groups cannot and do not make decisions is to perpetuate myths.

On the basis of such myths, we have many times organized and managed our enterprises in ways that denied interdependence and suppressed differences which could have been assets to our productivity. We have often tried to live in a "never-never" world where the researcher, the developer, the engineer, the production man, the marketer, the salesman, and a host of other specialists theoretically go blithely on their separate way somehow making completely rational individual decisions without regard to each other, with everything coming out all right in the end. That is magic, indeed!

A great many scientists have contributed to the debunking of this series of assumptions, but I'd like to interrelate the work of Rensis Likert of Michigan and Douglas McGregor of M.I.T. . . .

Let's begin with Likert and I will quote very briefly from his paper, "Trends Toward a World-Wide Theory of Management," presented at the CIOS (Conseil International pour l'Organization Scientifique) XIIIth International Management Congress in September 1963:

> An organization will make full use of the potential capacities of its human resources only when each person in the organization is a member of one or more effectively functioning work groups that have a high degree of group loyalty, effective skills of interaction, and high performance goals. This means that the work group rather than the individual is the building block out of which the organization is created.

There is, of course, much more in the paper than this one statement, but it's enough to make the point. Suppose we accept this statement. What are the implications? Can groups make effective decisions? What distinguishes an effective group from a typically ineffective committee? What kind of decisions should be made by groups? If we believe in group decisions, how would we find time to build groups and find time to use groups to make effective decisions?

Here I must turn to McGregor and the kind of insight he has been providing recently in discussions with us and with some other managers and groups in Union Carbide.

Some of our myth versus knowledge problems come out when people use the term "common sense." Common sense tells us that human groups are nothing but collections of individuals (it tells us also that the sun revolves around the earth!) Acting on this common-sense knowledge, we discover that groups are frequently inefficient, conformity producing, poor tools for decision making. Without further knowledge, we are unlikely ever to believe anything but that these are inevitable characteristics of groups. Many people are so convinced today. However, this is a myth and it rests on ignorance about certain variables and their relationships which are uniquely characteristic of human *groups* as groups. . . .

Actually, research tells us that there are distinct, isolable but interdependent variables that apply *only* to groups, *never* to individuals, and that when a group has developed these variables, it can make powerful decisions which cannot possibly be made and implemented by individuals.

Not all of these "group" variables are clearly established in my own mind yet, but at least eight in my experience are absolutely indispensable and apply only to groups:

MUTUAL TRUST.   Each of us can state our views openly without fear of ridicule or reprisal and permit others to do the same. We may "fight" and we probably will disagree, but we won't seek to hurt or "destroy" each other.

MUTUAL SUPPORT.   Each of us can give help to others on the team and get help from them without being concerned about prerogatives. We don't need to protect our functions against each other.

OPEN, AUTHENTIC COMMUNICATION.   We don't have to be guarded and cautious about our communication. Because of our mutual trust and support, we can say what we feel and how we are reacting. We *listen* to and understand each other.

THE ABILITY AND WILLINGNESS TO ACCEPT AND WORK THROUGH CONFLICTS.   We accept conflicts as necessary and desirable. We don't deny them, suppress them, nor pretend they don't exist; we work them through openly, as a team.

THE UNDERSTANDING OF AND COMMITMENT TO TEAM OBJECTIVES OR PERFORMANCE GOALS.   We won't assume a team objective until it is clearly understood by all members nor until we've worked our way through our differences and can honestly say we're committed to achieving the objective.

UTILIZATION OF MEMBER RESOURCES.   Our individual abilities, knowledge and experience are fully utilized by the team. We accept and give advice, counsel and support to each other while recognizing individual accountability and specialization.

CONTROL METHODS.   We accept the responsibility for keeping discussions relevant and for the integrity of the team operation. We don't need a chairman or other devices to control us.

ORGANIZATIONAL ENVIRONMENT.   We respect individual differences. We don't push each other to conform to central ideas or ways of thinking. We work hard at keeping our "team climate" free, open and supportive of each other. . . .

We have tested this systematic knowledge within Union Carbide and I can assure you the answer to two of the questions I raised a moment ago can be contained in one statement: Groups can make effective decisions when these variables are built into the group.

Three other questions remain unanswered. What kinds of decisions should be made by groups; how do we build groups; and how do we find time to build groups to make effective group decisions. Here I'm going to make what I know to be a much oversimplified condensation of another piece of McGregor's work—one on which I hope he will publish something soon.

He points out that there is nothing inherently wrong about arbitrary or unilateral decisions. Further, he suggests that the appropriateness of individual vis-a-vis group decision making in most situations can be determined by what's needed for implementing the decision.

1. If the value of the decision is independent of implementation, group processes are unnecessary.
2. If the value of the decision will depend on implementation by others, group processes are likely to prove more effective if the "requirements" have been built into the group or groups participating in the decision-making process.

Another way of saying this is that the best decision in the world, poorly implemented, is a poor decision. If the people who are to carry out your decision don't understand it or aren't committed to it, the implementation is likely to be ineffective.

The model I have in mind to illustrate the point demonstrates, I believe, that a company must have both individual and group processes to reach quality decisions. It also illustrates, I believe, the inherent fallacies in the myths we have been discussing. Let me put these as sort of "rules":

Managers will make business decisions unaffected by emotions.
The individual is the exclusive building block of the human organization.
Groups cannot make decisions.

Now let's invent a company, simpler than most real-life organizations but complex enough to illustrate the point. Our mythical company's technology is based on ferrous and nonferrous metals, and until recently everything it has touched has turned to dollars. Its growth has been rapid but has slowed down in the past few years, and capital requirements are beginning to hurt a bit.

This is a functional organization (but I find a product model has similar problems). It has a president, two executive vice presidents, and vice presidents of production, engineering, sales and marketing, and research and development. The company prides itself on its clear lines of authority and responsibility, and while it has the usual liaison and advisory committees, it expects its individual executives and managers to be decision makers in the best interest of the company. Let's go a little further and say that the "rules" stated above are clearly understood to be the management philosophy of the company.

There are no incompetent people in our model. You, the president, have decided that priorities must be placed on research and development projects in order to place the weight of the company's talents and capital funds behind those which are most promising. This is an excellent decision on your part, and is so viewed at every level of the organization. The value of the decision, however, depends on its implementation and it is here that "individual unemotional decisions only" becomes a myth. Don't misunderstand me: your decision *was* good, but you've convinced your organization that groups can't make decisions and let's say they absolutely refuse to use group processes. If this *were* the case, an intelligent decision couldn't be implemented. You don't believe me?

Well, let's just look at our R&D (Research and Development) organization and the chain of command from project to president. Our R&D organization has six project directors, each of whom has five projects under way and at different stages of maturity. Three of these project directors report to a director of R&D for ferrous metals and three to a director of R&D for nonferrous metals. Fifteen projects are ferrous and fifteen are nonferrous. As it should be, each research project is a love affair in so far as the researchers are concerned.

The two directors report to the vice president for research and development, who reports to one of the two executive vice presidents who, in turn, reports to you, the president. Remember, purely rational decisions are made by individuals uncluttered by emotion and you've made yours. Okay, *make it work!*

You can play with this model for years—verticalize it, diagonalize it, do anything you like—but you can't make it work on purely an individual decision-making basis. Nor can you banish emotions by magic. Let me be absolutely clear. It won't work either by simply naming people to committees or forming task forces at every level. Unless mutual trust, mutual support, open communications and the other vital requirements are present in these committees, teams, task forces or groups, they will indeed be nothing more than a collection of differences with no chance of resolution. The result is almost certain to be simply more confusion, inefficiency and lack of implementation.

For example, suppose you bring your officers together to "help you make a decision." The vice president for R&D mentions several projects he believes most promising. Unfortunately, the marketing vice president disagrees, at least in part, based on his knowledge of the market and his commitment to more "practical" projects. However, he doesn't want to joust openly with science, so he smoothly beclouds the issue with statistics. The engineering vice president knows that even if Projects A, B and C can be brought to the commercial development stage, scale-up presents some insoluble problems; but he's still smarting under your charge (made last week) of "overconservation" so he figures to let you learn the hard way. The production vice president knows that Project B will take operating skills not now on the payroll, but doesn't say so because you and his associates might think he wasn't cost conscious. And so on for days. To further complicate matters, the vice president for R&D suspects that his two directors disagree with him as to which projects are most promising and knows they secretly disagree with each other because each comes to him separately with arguments which boost his own and downgrade the other's projects. Needless to say, the same thing is happening elsewhere in every function of your company.

Mind you, the entire organization agrees with your "initiating" decision and each man is sincerely trying to implement it. In the end, you, the president, will probably have to make some arbitrary decisions based on pure guts and instinct, but the quality of these is questionable even in your mind and the response of the organization is certain to be defensive and unsatisfying.

All right. Suppose I've convinced you, at least intellectually, that some decisions *need* group processes and that these don't occur naturally but must be built over a period of time. How do we build them and how do we find the time to build them while still carrying on the work of the organization?

I don't know how Non-Linear[7] does it, but our very limited experimentation suggests that with good planning these processes can occur simultaneously once the leader has become committed to change.

The degree of change possible depends very much on the organizational level of the leader (how much of the organization he influences and is responsible for) and the attitude of his superiors (is he permitted to make the necessary changes?) The next several processes are complex and theoretically simultaneous.

For example, suppose we take natural work groups (including leaders) or form them where they don't exist and begin to meet to devise unique, high-goal team objectives which seem likely to contribute to the success of our own and the larger organization. The objectives seek to combine the special skills of the individual members in support of powerful interdependent purposes. (Incidentally, "work groups" can and should exist at all levels of the organization, . . . top to bottom.)

We will find, of course, that we disagree on common purposes and that we cannot achieve them unless we work through our differences openly, in an atmosphere of mutual trust, mutual support, and open, authentic, face-to-face communication. We're not accustomed to working openly with differences nor are we used to being open with each other so we will have to work on this deliberately and self-consciously. One way we can do this is to stop the process periodically and take simply anonymous data on how each of us (including the leader) perceives the levels of mutual trust, mutual support, etc., to be at any time. Similarly, we can take data on such things as our understanding of and commitment to team objectives. These data can be used by the group to further the process.

As the levels of trust, support, communication, and commitment rise, the group will be in the process of learning self-control. As its ability grows, we will be (hopefully) simultaneously removing as many of the controls (largely paperwork) as possible. We will be simplifying procedures and building "whole-team jobs."

The diminution of paperwork controls and the simplification of procedures begin to provide the time necessary for both building the team and doing the work. Both individual and group decision-making processes become more efficient as the rising level of commitment takes the place of more and more external controls.

In time only important decisions will need to be worked through by the whole group, and because of mutual trust there will be much delegation of individual responsibility—not only by leaders to members, but also by members to leaders and to each other.

Assuming that groups like these are being developed at every level throughout the total organization, other things begin to happen. As the levels of trust, support, communication, and commitment begin to rise in the total organization, they begin to affect the relationships between and among groups. Some people become members of overlapping groups both laterally and vertically and perform "linking pin" functions between and among interdependent work groups.

The formal organization structure simplifies. Communication blocks begin to disappear. Since less time is spent in "controlling" one another, more time is available for problem solving. Individuals become more effective in their contributions and in time work groups will need to concern themselves only with maintaining their effectiveness in terms of group variables and dealing with important interdependent decisions.

The "building block" groups, the individual leaders and members, and the total organization will find themselves more flexible, more dynamic, more able to deal with emergencies and more innovative in performing solid contributive work with a minimum of complicating interferences.

Theoretical? Yes: We don't have any total or even any large segment of our organization operating in such a manner. We do, however, have organizations moving in that direction, and the probability that no organization will ever perform perfectly and completely by these principles doesn't make the theory less useful. (In its technological processes, Union Carbide has never achieved absolute zero or a perfect vacuum, but we've made a lot of technological and financial progress by using these theories.)

The price of specialization is interdependence. The systematic knowledge is available to enable us to build effective (not perfect!) interdependent organizations. I suggest we build them.[8]

Early in 1965, Mr. Jones was on the threshold of being given additional responsibilities outside those of managing the OD department. He felt that this new assignment would require that some of the OD managing responsibility should be passed on to one of the members of the group and that this man should be considered a possible successor to himself if he were moved. (See Exhibit 2 pp. 389-393 for biographical data on members of OD in 1965.) In attempting to decide which of his men should be given these responsibilities, Mr. Jones asked his group to make recommendations, as he had done on previous occasions with regard to other matters. During the last two or three years, in fact, the OD group itself has been more involved in making decisions that were once made by individuals in the group. In a memorandum of June 24, 1965, Mr. Jones asked each member of the group to respond to the following question:

Assume you had an opportunity to nominate a successor to the present general manager, Organization Department, and bearing in mind both the relationships within the group and with the rest of the Corporation, whom would you choose?

In July 1965 Mr. Jones was promoted to a new assignment in the corporation, and the man who had received the most votes (a substantial majority) was officially appointed general manager of the organization development department.

Exhibit 2
UNION CARBIDE CORPORATION'S ORGANIZATION
DEVELOPMENT DEPARTMENT (A)
Biographical Sketches of OD Department Staff[9]

JOHN PAUL JONES, MANAGER

John Paul Jones is General Manager of Organization Development for Union Carbide Corporation in New York.

Mr. Jones joined the industrial relations function of the Corporation's Chemicals Division in 1941. He became Plant Manager of Industrial Relations in 1951, Divisional Negotiator the following year, Labor Relations Coordinator for the Corporation in 1956, and Assistant General Manager—Industrial Relations in 1957. He assumed his present position in 1959. His function provides internal consultative services on management personnel problems, including those of organization, compensation, training, and development.

Mr. Jones is a member of the Research Advisory Council of the Foundation for Research on Human Behavior.

GEORGE H. MURRAY, JR.

George H. Murray, Jr., is a member of the Organization Development Department of Union Carbide Corporation in New York and operates as a consultant to the corporation at large. Mr. Murray, a native of Rhode Island, was graduated from Georgia Institute of Technology with a B.S. in Industrial Engineering.

His industrial experience includes a short stint as a designer in the research laboratory of the Oak Ridge Gaseous Diffusion Plant in 1946. In 1948, he subsequently became a staff industrial engineer to the Director in the start-up of the Oak Ridge National Laboratory. Concurrent with this, Mr. Murray taught Industrial Engineering and Management courses at the extension division of the University of Tennessee. He was appointed Personnel Manager of the Oak Ridge National Laboratory in 1953. In 1956, he moved to Cleveland, Ohio, to help start the new Union Carbide Research Center. His initial responsibilities were focused on the personnel function and developed into concern for the over-all administration of the Research Center. Mr. Murray was transferred to New York to participate in forming the Organization Development Department in 1959 and served as consultant and salary administrator for the General Departments and staffs of Union Carbide Corporation before concentrating on general corporate-wide consulting.

CONSTANTINE S. DADAKIS

Educational data: Graduate of Massachusetts Institute of Technology. Majored in Business Administration—Industrial Engineering.

Occupational data: Joined Union Carbide in 1934 as an Engineer at the Linde Apparatus Factory in Newark. Served there until 1948 in various capacities including Chief Inspector and Assistant General Foreman. Transferred to the Factory Manager's Department of Linde in New York in 1948 as an Associate Engineer. In 1956, transferred to the Industrial Relations Department of Union Carbide as Exempt Salary Administrator for the General Departments. On June 1, 1959, became Manager of Salary Administration for the Corporation. As Manager of Salary Administration, duties are to:

1. Coordinate and guide the exempt salary program of the Corporation.
2. Undertake or participate in salary surveys and investigations.
3. Recommend budgets for annual merit and promotion increases.
4. Study, develop, and propose policies and procedures to improve the salary administration practices of the Corporation.

GLENN E. RIGGS, JR.

Glenn E. Riggs, Jr., is a Consultant in the Organization Development Department of Union Carbide Corporation in New York.

Prior to his employment with Union Carbide, Mr. Riggs attended Columbia College (A.B. 1953) and served in U.S. Navy as a destroyer officer for three years.

Mr. Riggs joined the Corporation's New York Personnel Department in 1957 and worked in the areas of recruiting and placement and benefit plan administration. He joined the Organization Development Department in 1960. The department provides internal consultative services on management personnel problems, including those of organization, compensation, training and development.

PAUL A. VAN TASSEL

Education
B.S.—Science and Mathematics, Hilldale College, Hilldale, Michigan
M.S.—Industrial Education, University of Michigan

Experience
15 years—Teacher and Vocational Guidance Counselor, Monroe, Michigan
5 years—Consultant, State Board of Vocational Education,

San Antonio, Texas
Consultant, Texas Engineering Extension Service, A & M
College, College Station, Texas
11 years—Training Director, Union Carbide Chemicals Company
Training Coordinator, Union Carbide Chemicals Company
Consultant, Union Carbide Corporation

JOHN CAMERON McDONALD

John Cameron McDonald. Born in Ontario, Canada. Graduated in Chemical Engineering from the University of Toronto in 1946 after a year in the Canadian Navy.

Joined the Bakelite Company Canada Limited in 1947 as a production engineer. Worked in various production supervision jobs until 1955 when appointed Production Superintendent. In 1957, started up a small Development and Technical service group. In 1960, took over Market Research and Sales Development.

In 1962, moved to Toronto as Manager, Personnel Administration, in the Industrial Relations Department, a new position concerned with job evaluation and salary administration, university recruiting, and personnel research. The latter function concerned research and recommendations on such matters as the most effective approach to management development, training, performance appraisals, etc.

Joined the Organization Development Department in August 1965.

G. K. FRANKLIN

Work History:

1947   Shipping Clerk, Delco Remy Division, General Motors, Dayton, Ohio
1948   Truck Driver, Southeastern Kentucky Coal Fields
1948–52   Naval Air Corps, Naval Academy
1952–53   Technician, Jet Engine Test Department, Westinghouse Gas Turbine Division
1953–63   Various personnel/industrial relations department Satellite Division. Last position there before joining O.D. department: Manager, personnel development.

Education:

Naval Academy and various business management and accounting courses and seminars.

Community and Civic Experiences:

Wide range of committee and boards of directors experience at city and state levels.

TOM WOOD

Education

A.B.   University of Rochester
M.B.A.   (1939) Wharton. Personnel Administration Major

Experience

1 year —Accountant, Standard Oil Company
6 years—Personnel research, Procter and Gamble
2 years—U.S. Army
4 years—Administrative staff, University of Rochester
1 year —Business management of large church
4 years—Personnel consulting

UNION CARBIDE CORPORATION'S ORGANIZATION DEVELOPMENT DEPARTMENT (B)

"We're being asked to participate in more and more projects, such as the Kanawha Valley engineering study," commented the general manager of Union Carbide Corporation's organization development department in late 1965, "and we simply do not have the staff to do the jobs that we are being asked to do."

The Kanawha Valley Engineering Study

In early 1963, the organization development department at Union Carbide Corporation's corporate headquarters in New York City was asked to make a presentation outlining a plan of action to a committee of Kanawha Valley engineering and operating executives, preliminary to the committee's selection of professional consultants in organization problems.[10]

This committee was formed in the fall of 1962 to study the over-all problems of Union Carbide's unwieldy, overlapping engineering organizations in the

Exhibit 1

UNION CARBIDE CORPORATION'S ORGANIZATION DEVELOP-
MENT DEPARTMENT (B)

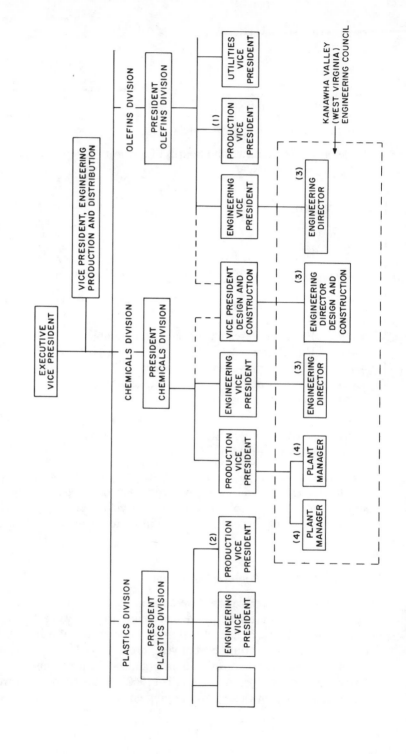

giant chemicals, plastics, and olefins divisions in South Charleston in the Kanawha Valley of West Virginia. There were five separate engineering departments at this time. (See Exhibit 1 p. 394 for a chart showing the executives and operating units involved in the study.) At Kanawha Valley, there was a complex of problems involving duplication of effort, poor communications, poor coordination between engineering specialties, and a general lack of cooperation not only between engineering specialties but also between the engineering and production units within the individual divisions and plants. The situation appeared to have developed over the years as a result of rapid growth and of moves designed to coordinate some of the activities of what were historically strongly decentralized, autonomous divisions. Because of the somewhat circuitous reporting relationships, actual organizational unity existed several levels above the divisions at corporate headquarters. As cognizant corporate executives became more aware of the problem, they began exerting various pressures down the chain of command to get something done about it. It was as a result of these general urgings that the Kanawha Valley engineering and operating committee was formed.

This committee comprised three engineering directors and two plant managers. At the outset they readily recognized the necessity for improving performance in many areas. One of their early moves was to consider seeking the assistance of professional consultants.

They asked several leading management consulting firms to make presentations. The organization development department (OD) at corporate headquarters also was asked to make a presentation.

At this time, the members of the OD department, which had only been formed in November 1959, could not offer an internal "client" list as evidence of their capabilities, nor could they offer the kinds of back-up resources often available in large consulting firms. They, however, did offer to work directly for the committee itself and be bound by the committee's decisions on reporting and other communications, up and down, and on the extent of involvement of those outside the committee. The day following their presentation, on April 3, 1963, the staff of OD was officially notified that the department had been chosen for the job.

The OD project leader for this assignment began meeting with the committee regularly. From his very first meeting with the committee, he became an integral member of it. An early task to be accomplished was to develop the committee into a cohesive work group, for, according to the OD project leader, there were a number of old barriers that, if not removed, were certain to limit severely the accomplishments of the committee. As an illustration, he described one aspect of this problem—the lack of communication between production and engineering in the individual divisions and operating units—as follows:

Over a period of thirty or more years some tremendous walls had been built up among these people; suspicion and mistrust characterized many of the relationships. There was little or no swapping of people. You must remember that the production units had built up their own engineering staffs within the walls of their own production units. One of the sharpest issues to come into focus, as a result of gathering data in an organized way, was the conflict between the production point of view and the engineering point of view. For instance, the engineering point of view, appropriately loaded with accompanying feelings and attitudes, was roughly as follows: "When we finish a project—design a new facility, a new piece of equipment, develop or improve a process—we take it down to them (production), and we get stopped at the gate. These people inside the plant say 'Throw it over to us, and good-bye.' We never get to see how it works or what's wrong with it if it doesn't work. We get no feedback. We are just cut off."

The production viewpoint was something like this: "Those guys up there[11] in engineering bring the thing down here; they heave it over the fence and leave it. We have to fix it and make it work ourselves. They live up on the hill in an ivory-tower atmosphere; it's a beautiful campus-like place, plush; we live down here in this dirty, old, unpleasant, outmoded plant."

The OD project leader recalled an early meeting at which these two conflicting points of view were inhibiting the committee's progress. During the discussion at this meeting, he began unobtrusively drawing on the blackboard a castle on a high hill and an old industrial plant in the valley. As the discussion proceeded, he began slowly and casually drawing a block wall between the two buildings, one block at a time. At one point in the discussion—after the wall had reached considerable proportions—all discussion stopped rather abruptly. The members were all staring at the blackboard. One of them finally said "Yeah, that's it," or something to that effect. Members of the committee gradually moved to focus on the barriers to communication and understanding between the production and the engineering groups and among one another personally.

Shortly after the OD project leader became a regular member, the committee changed its designation to "engineering council." The council formally stated its operating principles in a progress report dated June 1964.

One was that the best results could be obtained "by self-appraisal of operations and by self-determination of changes to be effected." The members of the council realized they would have to learn to work more effectively together to obtain results.

Another principle was that "successful improvement in the form of reorganization and changes in working systems depended heavily on the individual commitment of the members of these organizations and that this commitment required the participation of everyone." They hoped "to tap the novel ideas, unique information, and support for new concepts which are distributed widely at all levels of the organization."

"As a result of these ideas, the (engineering) directors and plant managers who were initially a loosely organized committee formed themselves into an action-oriented engineering council. They received divisional and corporate officer support and encouragement to pursue improvements with a charter which included the obligation to make policy, to develop and enunciate basic ground rules, and to provide distinct and aggressive leadership as a group."

In the same report, the council gave the following as its reasons for selecting internal consulting assistance:

A choice between outside management-consulting firms and internal corporate consulting help was resolved in favor of the internal help primarily because of the orientation of the internal group which had supported true self-examination. Additionally, the internal group had a built-in knowledge of much of the complexity and history of the organization which would have required extensive effort and time by an outsider to acquire. The internal group was also considered to be more flexible and able to commit more effort over a longer period of time for study, work and follow-up activities. Consideration was also given to lower out-of-pocket costs and lack of risk of proprietary information.

The council planned to sharpen its identification of areas for improvement by tapping the experience and knowledge of people in all parts and at all levels of the organization. Therefore, the Organization Development (OD) department was commissioned to conduct these interviews, starting with the corporate and divisional officers most directly concerned. This starting point was selected because it was clear that the viewpoints and expectations of these officer groups had and will continue to have a significant effect on the successful operation of the line-engineering groups.

Significant differences of viewpoint as well as general concepts, ideas, and suggestions were solicited. There was also the implication that continued involvement of these people to obtain their unique contributions was highly desirable.

From early April to mid-May 1963, members of OD interviewed corporate and divisional officers and the individual council members. After the OD staff had consolidated the results of these interviews, the OD project leader began meeting with executives at various levels of the corporate and divisional officer organizations to validate the findings of the staff and to feed back to these executives the major differences in executive viewpoints on the over-all problems in the Kanawha Valley engineering situation.

The council then proceeded to plan the task of gathering information and ideas from the various subordinate work groups in the Kanawha Valley organizations. After considerable discussion, members of the council decided that everyone should be interviewed ". . . in order to obtain a good understanding of the complex interplay of ideas and concerns and to maximize the sense and reality of participation.[12]" They also decided because of the large numbers of people involved—over 900—that, first, they would hold a week of orientation meetings for groups of 50, organized by department, where they would not only review what had taken place to date but also ask for suggestions and recommendations concerning key problem areas. Then, they would hold interviews with smaller groups of eight to ten people, generally of the same organizational level, selected from the larger 50-man groups. These interviews took place between late May and early June 1963, and the results were pooled by OD staff people, who extracted what they termed "central issues."

A report on one of their early data-consolidation efforts was widely distributed in abbreviated form. It contained a summary of the survey of opinions from the following groups:

(1) All engineering personnel in engineering functions at Valley sites.
(2) Operations and maintenance personnel from both operating plants.
(3) Personnel from other functions of the two divisions (chemicals and olefins), including research and development, accounting, purchasing etc.

The results, for the purposes of this summary, were presented in four major sections: *Management of People; Organization; Methods and Procedures;* and *General Management and Philosophies and Attitudes.* The report referred to the summary of the results as a mixture of comments and suggestions that appeared to the interviewers to represent important areas of concern to the general engineering population of the Valley. The body of this summary report is given below:

A.   MANAGEMENT OF PEOPLE

1. There is a need for much greater interchange or movement of people between existing departments.
2. The administration of salaries is poorly understood and is regarded as lacking equity—both in the sense of internal departmental relationships (compression) and broadly across departmental and company lines.
3. Engineers in all groups need programs for helping them update their technical competence. This area involves both specific technologies, such as those represented by a number of our specialists (for example, distillations, compressors, mass transfer, and computers), and the broader industry-wide technologies.
4. Many senior men, including a wide number of specialists, are underutilized.
5. There is a strong desire for practical "people development" programs.

6. Engineers believe that increased attendance at professional meetings would help them make a greater contribution to the job.
7. There is a need for greater freedom to make decisions at all levels.
8. Individuals and groups need much more rapid and candid feedback on their performance.
9. Engineers would like to be exposed to the reasons underlying important technical, business, and organization decisions.
10. All engineers should participate much more in setting goals in areas which they influence.
11. Engineers need to know more of the problem before contributing professional advice or answers and should have better feedback on how this counsel or data was used.
12. Managers should encourage getting bad news as well as favorable information.
13. Managers should not avoid discussing sensitive issues with individuals and groups.
14. Individuals, especially at lower levels, need greater opportunity to present their ideas fully.
15. There is a degree of concern about performing red-tape work which engineers believe can be minimized.
16. The criteria used to appraise individual performance seem, in general, to be more mechanical and less professional.
17. Communications among the engineering departments and plant works engineering groups range from fair to poor.
18. Engineers suggest more information-sharing meetings.
19. Wider publication of organization charts would help save considerable time in locating critical skills, know-how, and data.
20. More general knowledge of progress and problems in project activities would significantly help engineers in their individual and group performance.
21. The valley needs something on the order of a "Special Skills Inventory"—much wider information for everyone on the breadth and scope of engineering resources available.
22. Many groups still do not have sufficient understanding of the purpose and methods of the Chemicals Division's Business-Team operation.
23. Greater individual commitment and contributions would result from fuller communication of corporate and division business plans and problems and procedures. Engineers suggest more educational programs.
24. The Valley organizations need more skill in problem resolution and less resort to arbitrations.

25. Need to publish much more data on project timetables and progress.
26. Need wider circulation of inside technical reports and outside technical journals.
27. Supervisors tend to need more background in communications technique prior to assignment of supervisory responsibilities.
28. Distribute design manuals more widely.
29. There are indications that communications at the Officer level are sometimes incomplete, especially in terms of joint planning for manpower on multiple or large projects.
30. Broader information about business and engineering objectives of Plastics, Chemicals, and Olefins Divisions would help the Valley engineering groups improve their effectiveness.
31. Specific communications between engineering groups and maintenance and operating groups on new facilities are poor and result in excessive delays and costs.

B.   ORGANIZATION

1. Distribution of type and size of engineering assignments between the works engineering groups and the central engineering departments is inefficient.
2. The organization of works engineering groups tends to inhibit growth opportunities of engineers. There are limits to challenging assignments.
3. The utilization of engineering specialities in all groups is significantly limited by formal organization, especially between plant and technical center groups.
4. Organization of instrument engineering inhibits needed coordination ranging from initial concepts of instrumentation and control through application of engineering to plant instrument maintenance.
5. The present organization does not provide for the kind of engineering research that engineers believe is desirable. Need to establish such a group.
6. General facilities planning should be centralized.
7. Utilities engineering, although recently reorganized, is still poorly coordinated.
8. The organization of computer services does not permit full utilization of this technology.
9. Can the business-team concept of organization be applied to the business of engineering?
10. Are there compelling reasons for maintaining the full separation of Chemicals and Olefins engineering organizations?

C. METHODS AND PROCEDURES

1. General purchasing methods and practices act to reduce effectiveness of engineering efforts.
2. The present methods of planning and scheduling are inefficient. They lack coordination—techniques are out of date.
3. The total engineering effort needs wide participation in formulating standards and methods and more uniform application.
4. Engineering projects which involve more than one organization need much better central coordination.
5. Much greater use should be made of outside contractors.
6. Project management procedures neglect to involve all potentially interested individuals and groups at the beginning. Eventual contributions by everyone are less effective.
7. More joint project endeavors which formally involve more than one department will help improve interdepartmental working relationships.
8. There is unnecessary rigidity in the budgeting systems involved in each department to the extent that it hinders good working relationships between departments.
9. Over-all workload fluctuations are not utilized by current planning, scheduling, and project coordination procedures.
10. The lack of uniform drafting standards causes some delays and tends to hinder cooperative efforts between departments.
11. The lack of uniform design standards and criteria causes significant delays and contributes to more costly designs in terms of difficulty both for construction groups and operating people.
12. There is duplication of effort involved in the preparations and submission procedures for capital investment authorizations.

D. GENERAL MANAGEMENT AND PHILOSOPHIES AND ATTITUDES

1. General management attitudes toward and understanding and support of certain engineering specialties such as Instrument Engineering appear to be poor.
2. Local and vice president levels of management indicate a degree of departmental independence, pride, loyalty and defensiveness which directly affects over-all performance.
3. The top levels of management of Chemicals and Olefins Divisions including the council have not set goals and objectives which are common to all groups in the Valley.

4. There seems to be a reluctance to analyze and evaluate the ideas and methods of companies outside the corporation.

5. Better coordination of objectives and programs by Chemicals and Olefins management would provide a better framework for improved operation in the Valley.

6. There are indications that unreasonable time schedules get adopted because of lack of complete understanding of situations existing in the conduct of projects in the Valley. The results of some of these schedules are significantly increased costs of initial installation and ultimate operating costs.

7. Attitudes of corporate and division management regarding lowest initial investment versus long-term maintenance and operating costs appear to vary considerably from one part of the organization to another.

8. Each department seems to have a "charter" established and maintained by management which is highly independent of the others. No interlocking.

9. The isolation of the technical center from plants is a glaring problem.

10. There is an erroneous impression held by management that increased personal pressure produces increased effectiveness.

The council explained that another important objective of the OD department's data-consolidation meetings was to determine who "owned" or ought to own the various problems identified in the interviews.

After the interview results were reviewed and consolidated, the OD groups met with the 50-man groups for "feedback" purposes and for validation of their syntheses and problem definitions. This phase was completed by mid-August 1963.

During the month of September, the council made formal reports to various division and corporate officers concerning the project's progress. Included were a summary of the results of the survey, a listing of the major areas of opportunities for improvement, and the plans and methods developed by the council for generating change. During the last half of September and the first half of October, the council spent considerable time analyzing the problem areas in greater detail and developing specific reorganization proposals. These proposals were reviewed with the division vice presidents of engineering and production on October 10, 1963. For the next two months the council concentrated on refining the proposals and methods of approach.

On December 2, 1963, information meetings of the council and all engineering groups were held to communicate the details of the various proposals and tentative plans. The council then began to meet with "task groups" to discuss the task-group assignments, organizational problems, and task-group methods. These task-groups comprised individuals who "owned" a particular problem; earlier meetings had helped to identify those individuals to whom the particular problem "belonged."

The OD project leader recalled another incident occurring early in 1964 that was representative of a different kind of barrier to progress and one that temporarily threatened the very existence of the council and its project. Because of the council's decision to gather data and ideas from a wide variety of sources and because of the self-determined commitment to feed back the information and ideas to those who contributed them, progress in the early stages appeared to be extremely slow, especially to certain executives at headquarters. At one point, one of these key executives attempted to speed up the process. The OD project leader was convinced of the man's sincere interest in helping the project along, but somehow the "message" was received by the council as pressure to disband the council and start taking action that would show some results in organizational change.

At first, the council's attitude was to throw in the towel, according to the OD project leader, but after thorough discussion among themselves, the members of the council decided to resist efforts to force premature action. They therefore went to New York to attempt to persuade cognizant headquarters executives of the dangers inherent in failing to follow through as planned. They explained that, if the rug were pulled out from under them now, the organizations would be far more seriously damaged because of the commitments already made. Since, with headquarters approval, everyone had been encouraged to get involved in trying to solve the various problems, any change in these commitments would seriously affect organizational development efforts for years to come. The council members were able to make their point, and pressures to have some immediate action quickly subsided.

This episode, said the OD project leader, tended to cause the headquarters people to withdraw somewhat from participation in the reorganization activities in the Kanawha Valley. The OD project leader felt this withdrawal was unfortunate from an over-all standpoint, though it did not seriously prevent the council members from achieving their general objectives.

Beginning early in 1964, the council and task groups began to make more apparent progress. The council added one new task group to the original number and met with the groups as required to help resolve overlap problems. Actual progress made up to mid-1964 was summarized in the council's June report of that year. Below are excerpts from that report:

IV. ORGANIZATION CONSOLIDATION AND IMPROVEMENTS

The basic and most important change has been the decision of the engineering departments in the Kanawha Valley to operate as a unified engineering organization. This does not involve formal changes in divisional affiliation, but it represents a change in attitudes and relationships which is a prerequisite to all the specific moves that are now accomplished or in progress.

The question of divisional affiliations and of the need for maintaining divisional engineering departments at the technical center has received serious consideration by engineering officers of the Chemicals and Olefins Divisions. Analysis of the many functions of these groups shows that a rather good classification can be made based on the degree to which activities are "business centered" or "technology centered." In general, the highly business-centered activities relate directly to divisional problems of operation and planning and must be controlled directly and flexibly by division managements. The highly technology-centered activities, in contrast, are not particularly influenced by the divisional origin of the problems dealt with; in a number of areas, such activities have been consolidated for years past under the administration of one or another of the engineering departments.

Some of the engineering department functions, of course, represent mixtures of the above characteristics. On the whole, a surprisingly large proportion of the work done by the engineering departments is either wholly or strongly business oriented, and for this reason it has been concluded that the recognition and continuation of divisional affiliations is desirable. At the same time, it has been recognized that some existing disadvantages must be overcome. These relate principally to duplication of effort in technical areas and to poor coordination of effort. It is considered that the plans that have been developed for unified operation and for consolidation of technical activities will very largely eliminate these difficulties. Furthermore, the attitudes that have been engendered will promote further change or evolution in the future as the environment changes.

The specific individual changes planned or already in effect up to the present time are briefly described in the ensuing paragraphs:

1. *Plant Engineering Function.* Effective June 15, 1964, the works engineering departments of the South Charleston and Institute Plants were consolidated with the engineering groups at the technical center. Administratively, they become part of the chemicals division engineering department. At the outset, approximately 130 people are affected. During succeeding months, refinements of functions and reassignments of people will be made.

Primary objectives are the improvement of the engineering service to the plants and the improved utilization of personnel. This consolidation provides greater flexibility and broader assignments of both project and specialized engineering people in the plant and technical center engineering groups. It is intended to reduce time and cost and to improve quality of engineering. An important objective is to improve the methods for selecting projects on which to use plant engineering forces.

2. *Instrumentation Function.* Effective June 15, instrument engineering work is

consolidated within the olefins division engineering department. Eleven people from the chemicals division engineering department will be transferred. As a consequence, this new group, known as controls systems engineering, and the special instrumentation department are under the same engineering administration. They are continuing studies to develop full integration of instrumentation activity with the consequent realignment and reassignment of people and groups and possible reorientation and/or elimination of some activities. . . .

3. *Utilities and Utilities Distribution Functions.* On June 1, ten people in the design and construction department concerned with the engineering of utilities units and utilities distribution facilities will be consolidated within the olefins division engineering department. This is a final step in a series of moves which started ten years ago to eliminate duplication and diffusion of effort in this area. This consolidated utilities group has as its goal the total upgrading of utilities systems and the coordination of all efforts in this area.

V. IMPORTANT ACHIEVEMENTS OTHER THAN ORGANIZATION CONSOLIDATIONS

Although the reorganizations and consolidations underway will be important contributions to improved performance, the fundamental achievement which will contribute most to effective engineering is the development of improved interdepartmental and intergroup working relationships. Sizeable barriers to communication and understanding among departments and groups have been minimized or eliminated. Consequently, more information of all kinds is shared. The whole process has been one of increasing interdependence and mutual support and assistance of groups based on understanding and trust.

Another consequence of this effort is that the council and the departments and groups are recognizing and reacting more quickly to business and organizational situations calling for change (i.e., consolidation of effort, new methods and new criteria to meet competition pressures).

Of particular concern to the council were the differences in attitude and misunderstandings which had grown up over the years among various groups within the company. The council has established a strong trend in the direction of mutual respect and support between the groups by first developing relationships among the plant managers and directors. As a result, subordinate members of these groups were required to work together on the solutions of problems, with consequent achievement of genuine understanding and respect. The basic need for a close, effective working relationship was understood by most of the people in these groups and the council recognized that its major task was to lead the way, to demonstrate the practical ways of demolishing the barriers.

Concrete illustrations of the changing work environment include:

1. JOINT WORK LOAD AND MANPOWER PLANNING SYSTEM. This system, proposed by the council and under development by a planning board made up of responsible managers, will provide master project and work load schedules, information leading to

assignment of work to groups having the necessary skills, and means to realign manpower to meet project load and to provide opportunity for broader experience for personnel.

2. PROJECT MANAGEMENT AND COST CONTROL.   One of the natural evolutions of joint study and planning efforts by the council and engineering groups is the current development of joint coordination of engineering and construction projects. The purpose of this effort is to provide more direct accountability, faster and cheaper construction, and quicker response in normal operating situations and special situations.

3. USE OF THE TASK GROUP OR TEAM APPROACH.   Although the idea of the task group approach to problem solving has occurred several times in this summary, it is important enough as a concept and operating technique to emphasize again here.

Carrying through the basic concept which the council developed for its own operation, most of the complex and pressing problems have been attacked by the task groups made up of people from various groups at all levels of the organization. This approach has produced some unusual results. It has also built an ever-increasing store of vital understanding and skill in team operation.

Many of the hidden complications within the proposed organization changes were either discovered or much more clearly identified and understood.

Significantly better solutions were obtained for a number of problems because of the novel and important insights obtained.

The spread of knowledge and understanding throughout the whole organization of both technical and organizational problems has increased significantly by the use of task groups. Each group, on whatever problem, has involved many other people at all levels.

Interest and participation in joint efforts to innovate and to upgrade operations, systems and procedures continues to expand.

4. INTERNAL DEPARTMENTAL IMPROVEMENTS.   A number of internal programs in each of the functional departments were triggered or stimulated by the study. In many cases, the basic techniques of the study were carried over into the internal programs or activities. These programs, although not highly publicized, have had significant effect on the morale of personnel with resulting lower costs and increased efficiencies. Better understanding of company policies and increased interest in improving the corporate position became apparent.

VI.   THE FUTURE

The council views the present status as the conclusion of the initial phase of a continuing improvement program. Problems that will be tackled immediately include further relocation of personnel; reassignments; further consolidations or elimination of certain functions; more direct responsibility for the administration of projects; and the development of modern cost control techniques. The council intends to increase its effectiveness as a quick reacting group, directing its efforts to engineering and project matters and to support and contribute to the wider management group dealing with all Kanawha Valley organizational, operational, and manpower problems.

Shortly after the release of the June 1964 report, the council met with corporate and divisional officers to review the study in more detail. One of the conclusions reached as a result of this meeting, held on July 30, 1964, was that the council should concentrate on consolidating improvements in organization and work systems before extending the study further. Their November 24, 1964, report carried the results of these efforts in several different areas.

On December 31, 1964, the council prepared and distributed a single-page memorandum which carried the following quotation from the minutes of a meeting held on December 14:

> The Kanawha Valley engineering council discussed with the operating committee the progress they had made toward improving and consolidating the engineering activities in the Kanawha Valley. A number of changes have been made including consolidation of the works engineering departments at each plant into the chemicals engineering department and realigning of duplicate activities into one organization. The council felt that as a result of these consolidation steps more work was being accomplished with the same people, communications were better, and over-all performance had improved. Each member of the council is strongly committed to the objectives they have established. The problems that the council is approaching now are: (1) how to act as one body, (2) how to manage projects more effectively, and (3) how to develop an effective organizational relationship with the plastics engineering, UCI (Union Carbide International) engineering, and the Texas City works engineering departments.

This memorandum ended with the following paragraph:

> We will continue our efforts to improve our engineering performance along these lines with your cooperation and participation.

Although the council remained active in continuing the work already underway, the organization development department gradually withdrew from the project. By late 1965, OD considered the project consultation formally terminated.

The Future of OD

By this time, OD had serviced a number of other internal "clients" and had a backlog of requests for its services, which was beginning to cause the new general manager of organization development considerable concern.[13] These requests were so numerous that he knew the department could not fill them. Furthermore, he did not believe this department necessarily *should* be expanded to provide such services from corporate headquarters. Instead, he was considering various approaches to providing the OD type of consulting services throughout the corporation by using division personnel. But, because he was not convinced that all personnel managers could make good OD consultants, he did not consider that an organizational chart change designating personnel managers as OD counselors throughout the company would solve the problem. He was concerned, moreover, by two other complicating aspects of any such plan. First, he was aware that, although top management support of OD's work was not openly used, the fact that OD reported directly to top corporate management had undoubtedly produced certain effects. Such effects would not be present when a consultant was simply appointed within a division. Second, he wondered about the effects of a consultant working in his "own back yard," for a division consultant would clearly not experience the relative detachment enjoyed by a headquarters-based consultant.

Finally, the new general manager was not too sure that the necessary qualifications for success as an OD consultant were clearly known or easily identifiable in a possible candidate for such a position. Thus, even if a plan were developed to service the 74,000–employee corporation, recruitment decisions would be very difficult whether the candidates came from inside or outside the corporation.

NOTES

1. Reproduced by permission of the Harvard Case Clearing House, Soldiers Field Road, Boston, Massachusetts.
2. Douglas McGregor, Professor of Industrial Management, Massachusetts Institute of Technology; Rensis Likert, Director, Institute for Social Research, University of Michigan; and Mason Haire, Professor of Psychology, Institute of Industrial Relations, University of California.
3. J. P. Jones, "Evolving Principles of Modern Management," a report, dated September 23, 1959, on a seminar that was conducted by the Foundation for Research on Human Behavior in Aspen, Colorado, from July 12–July 18, 1959, p. ii. Reproduced by permission of the author.
4. John Paul Jones, "People—The Independent Variable," a paper presented at the Businessman's Symposium on Organization and Practice, conducted by the Foundation for Research on Human Behavior in Ann Arbor, Michigan, on December 19 and 20, 1960, and published in a collection of the symposium papers *Organization Theory in Industrial Practice*, edited by Mason Haire (New York: John Wiley & Sons, Inc., 1962), pp. 48–51. Excerpts from this paper are reproduced by permission of the author and the publisher.
5. John Paul Jones, "The Management of Human Effort—A New Concept in Action," a speech delivered to the American Management Association Fall Personnel Conference, September 25, 1961. Excerpts from the speech are reproduced by permission of the author.
6. American Management Association, *A Look at Personnel Through the President's Eye*, Management Bulletin No. 66 (New York: The Association,

Personnel Division, 1965), pp. 13–14. This bulletin was adapted from the Presidents' Professional Association (now called The Presidents Association) Special Study No. 15, *Improving Performance in the Personnel Department*, published in 1963 by the PPA. The original study was based on a series of interviews with company presidents and chairmen of the board and also with a number of prominent personnel executives. Excerpts from this paper are reproduced by permission of the author and the American Management Association.

7. Mr. Jones referred to a company on the West Coast that had been experimenting with applications of behavioral sciences in the management of the company.

8. John Paul Jones, "How Should We Manage—By Myth, Magic or Knowledge?," a speech delivered before the American Management Association Midwinter Personnel Conference in February 1964. The excerpts quoted from the speech are reproduced by permission of the author.

9. The biographical summaries on all but Mr. Wood are reproduced as provided by each department member. Mr. Wood's was prepared from notes of an interview with him.

10. See the Union Carbide Corporation's Organization Development Department (A) case for the company background and for the history of the organization development department.

11. The engineering groups were situated on a hill overlooking the Kanawha Valley, where the production operations were located.

12. From the council's June 1964 summary report of the study.

13. A new general manager had been appointed in July 1965, when Mr. Jones was given a special assignment position working for Union Carbide's top corporate executives. See Union Carbide Corporation's Organization Development Department (A) case.

Chapter 19

Cases On Applications
Of Management By Objectives

THE Union Carbide Chemicals Division case on its introduction and operation of an MBO program was selected primarily because it was launched long enough ago to be able to assess its operation over time. It was initiated in 1960 by the top officers of the division and the president, Mr. Edgar E. Fogle, played a leading role in its launch. It had the advantage—or disadvantage, depending upon one's viewpoint—of having the assistance of a reputable consulting firm help with its installation. The first case describes the philosophy underlying the program and details the policies and procedures adopted to start the program. The second case offers, through interviews with various employees (whose names are disguised), their administration of, and reactions to, the MBO program in 1964. Following this is an up-date briefly describing the status of the program some 15 years after its beginning. Included in this up-date by your author is an analysis of the causes of the status of the program 15 years after its initiation.

UNION CARBIDE CORPORATION'S CHEMICALS DIVISION (A)

Union Carbide Corporation was founded in 1917 by the consolidation of four companies, Linde Air Products Company, National Carbon Company, Prest-O-Lite Company, and Union Carbide Company. By 1964, Union Carbide had become one of the largest corporations in the United States with sales in excess of $1,878,000,000. It had grown from the original four companies into a corporation with 15 major divisions, the principal business activities of which were in chemicals, consumer products (Prestone and Ever-Ready brand names), food products, nuclear materials, metals, plastics, and carbon products. Union Carbide, with headquarters in New York City, employed 72,000 people in plants throughout the world.

410

Chemicals Division

The chemicals division was one of the largest divisions of the corporation, accounting for close to 35% of the corporation's total sales. Major products of this division included chemical intermediates, monomers, petroleum, plastic, fiber, and specialty chemical industries. The chemicals division operated several plants and bulk storage facilities. Sales offices and warehouses were located throughout the United States.

Although the entire corporation had a history of outstanding employee relations, the chemicals division had been particularly successful in this area. Little time had been lost because of work stoppages or strikes. Relatively few of the division's plants were unionized in spite of the existence of strong unions in the industry. The chemical plants in the Kanawha valley of West Virginia, which employed 16,000 people, were believed to represent one of the largest nonunion industrial complexes in the world.

Morale at the management level was considered to be very high. Management turnover was known to be comparatively low, and the division was known to have a high proportion of long-term employees. Fringe benefits and wage scales were above the national average for similar size firms. The chemicals division, and Union Carbide Corporation as a whole, had a reputation as a good place to work.

The Initial Examination

In 1960, the officers of the chemicals division began a concentrated examination of the internal operations of their organization. The president of the division, Mr. Edgar E. Fogle, stated that this effort was not initiated by poor performance but resulted from "a conviction that the very best efforts of any human organization, or of the individual member himself, are always susceptible to improvement if given unusual attention and constructive critical examination." The decision to begin a self-examination of the division's organization and management philosophy gained impetus from the work of the corporation's organization development department in experimentally applying the principles of Douglas McGregor's "Theory Y." See Exhibit 1 p. 419 for partial organization chart.

This investigation indicated to management that more attention to the development of management skills might be worthwhile. Mr. Fogle summarized the preliminary conclusions of this study as follows:

First, we need to produce a greater number of competent, creative, growing individuals and managers than we have ever had if we are to take fullest advantage of the growth and profitability opportunities available to us. It would appear, from an analysis of our future business and of the general economic climate and conditions under which we must operate, that we will never again have working for us, to our advantage, so many favorable conditions as we have enjoyed for the last three decades. The competition for scientific personnel, the demand for new chemical products, the maturity of the industry and our position in it have produced conditions unlike those that contributed to past successes. If we are to get a greater level of performance out of ourselves, individually and as an organization, than has been our habit.

Second, the conditions that have determined the way in which we have managed our businesses in the past have changed radically within the last 15 years. These conditions are an outgrowth of changes that began right after the war. One change is in the nature of the work force as to education and skills. We are rapidly approaching the point where the majority of employees in any business are either college trained professionals or highly trained, technically skilled high school graduates. The general size and complexity of business organizations and their increasing technical and scientific emphasis require revised systems and methods. Old systems designed to create control in large complex organizations have, in effect, stifled creativity and innovation and have created the "organization man."

Third, the last 15 years have produced a tremendous amount of research, discovery, and invention in the field of the physical sciences, and similar efforts have been applied in the social sciences. Recent work in the field of human motivation and performance and in organizational behavior has produced findings that have given us a new insight into how people really work and how managers should manage to allow the greatest possible creativity and innovation toward the accomplishment of organizational goals.

Dr. Carl Rogers, of the University of Chicago, puts it this way: "In a time when knowledge, constructive and destructive, is advancing by the most incredible leaps and bounds into a fantastic atomic age, genuinely creative adaption seems to represent the only possibility that man can keep abreast of the kaleidoscopic change in his world. . . . A generally passive and culture-bound people cannot cope with the multiplying issues and problems. Unless individuals, groups, and nations can imagine, construct, and creatively revise new ways of relating to these complex changes, the lights will go out. . . . Not only individual maladjustment and group tensions, but international annihilation will be the price we pay for a lack of creativity."

Dr. McGregor, of MIT, says, "Management by direction and control—whether implemented with the hard, the soft, or the firm-but-fair approach—fails under today's conditions to provide effective motivation of human effort toward organizational objectives. It fails because direction and control are useless methods of motivating people whose physiological and safety needs are reasonably satisfied and whose social, egoistic, and self-fulfillment needs are predominant."

Chemicals Division's Marketing Department Experiment

This initial examination led the chemicals division management to consider a tentative program based upon a philosophy of management generally described a "management by objectives." Before being convinced that their proposed program would fit the division's needs, however, management decided to experiment with their tentative conclusions in the division's marketing department. The marketing department experiment began in June 1960, under the general direction of the department's vice president. An outside consulting firm, Barrington Associates, was employed to work directly with the vice president. Barrington was asked to explain the purpose and the principles of this program to all the marketing department managers. The Barrington consultants also were responsible for helping the managers in explaining the program to their subordinates and for getting everyone to begin operating according to the procedures tentatively established by the chemicals division management and Barrington Associates.

The marketing department experiment served to demonstrate the areas of strength and weakness in the original program. Based on the experience gained from the test, several modifications were made. By August 1961, Mr. Fogle and the marketing department people themselves concluded that the experiment had been successful and that the program had resulted in observable individual and organizational growth.

The Principles of the Chemicals Division's Management-by-Objectives Program

The management-by-objectives program that was adopted in final form in the marketing department was based on five basic principles. The first was that the prime objective of the company was growth, defined as improved economic performance. The second was that growth for the company was dependent on growth of individuals in the company. The third principle was that individual growth could not be commanded but must result from self-development. Underlying this principle was the belief that people grow, improve themselves, work harder, and work better to the degree that they are committed to what they are doing and are capable of changing their actions to produce this growth. The fourth principle of the philosophy was that the manager's chief responsibility was the establishment of a climate in which individuals could grow and would want to improve their economic performance. Therefore, since a manager had this responsibility, the fifth principle was that managerial performance was measured by the degree to which a manager's subordinates grew. (In application, however, managerial performance was actually judged on the basis of achievement of business objectives.)

The Mechanics of the Management-by-Objectives Program

It was found that several areas of agreement between the superior and the subordinate had to be achieved if these principles were to be successful in actual practice. The mechanics of the adopted program, therefore, were largely concerned with establishing mutual agreement and commitment between the superior and subordinate. This agreement and commitment were sought at a number of steps, or stages, in the management-by-objectives program.

Appraisal of performance was generally considered to be an informal and continuing process. However, under the new program in the chemicals marketing department, the individual was expected to write a formal appraisal of his own performance at least once a year. More often than not, a quarterly written review of performance was made. A performance appraisal included:

a)   An evaluation of performance against objectives in terms of the agreed-upon standards of performance.

b)   A statement of the degree of personal growth over the appraisal period.

c)   The development needs that the individual felt were necessary, what he planned to do to fulfill these needs, and what he wanted his superior to do to help him.

Performance appraisals were jointly reviewed by superior and subordinate. Any deviation from goals, whether the targets were exceeded or not attained, had to be discussed. Both individuals sought to better understand the reasons for the results achieved. While considerable time was spent on review, the appraisal conference provided the basis for the next year's objectives program. (Theoretically, a good deal of effort was to be made to utilize the understanding of areas of strength and weakness achieved from the review to build a better plan for the future.)

Thus, after the appraisal review session, next year's objectives and standards of performance were formulated. Although this process was cyclical and involved a series of stages, efforts were made to make this program as flexible as possible.

A middle manager in the chemicals division, who commented on the company's belief that the program should be adopted to fit the particular needs of the situation, said:

One of the difficulties in regard to the setting of objectives stems from the fact that, in most cases, we started this "Management examination process" by defining people's generic duties and responsibilities and recognize that what we want to accomplish—what we have to accomplish—is set for us by the market place and other factors which are constantly changing. As our problems and our objectives change, we may be required to provide ourselves with, and use, additional duties and responsibilities to accomplish these objectives.

The objectives of the company, of a division, or of any group, both long term and short term, really determine what duties and responsibilities must be performed by any particular position at a given time. The objectives of the enterprise determine the structure of the organization and what positions must be established to achieve these objectives. It is possible that a man in any one year may have outstanding performance against objectives and actually need to perform duties and carry out responsibilities that do not appear in a generic job description. The market place, the particular economic conditions under which we operate, dictate what we should or should not do, not a man's generic job description.

A written report of each subordinate's performance was submitted by the superior to the next higher level of management each year. This report contained the subordinate's own written appraisal, as well as the superior's comments on how well he believed the objectives were achieved. An employee's salary level and chances for promotion were largely determined by his performance relative to his objectives and the personal growth the employee achieved as determined by the nature of the objectives he had accomplished. Consideration was given to the difficulty or magnitude of the objective undertaken. Accomplishing the objective was not necessarily a measure of success, especially if the objective was considered to be a relatively easy one.

Implementation of the Management-by-Objectives Program

Management by objectives first became an established operating procedure in the marketing department, where the experiment had been conducted earlier. It was this experiment that convinced Mr. Fogle of the merit of extending this program to the entire division. The degree of Mr. Fogle's enthusiasm and dedication to this philosophy was suggested in a discussion with the division managers in which Mr. Fogle stated:

I am sure you can all recognize that this system of managing is, of necessity, a more demanding system than the traditional authoritarianism. Under authoritarianism the individual performer's sense of responsibility is constantly watered down by superior management doing his job for him, or by establishing restrictive rules under which the individual is to perform. The subordinate can always say under this arrangement that his superior didn't give him the tools to do the job, and, furthermore, had set unreasonable objectives or too high a standard of performance. Authoritarianism tends to produce dependency. We want independent individuals working toward interlocking objectives.

Under this system we should begin to get some fine examples of exceptional performance. As a matter of fact, we should begin to get improved performance out of individuals whom we thought were incapable of growth.

It will be said by some of you, and has been said already by some of us, that the application of this managerial concept takes too much time away from, quote, getting our jobs done, unquote. That statement often highlights our greatest difficulty. We have frequently overlooked the fact that we have not defined "our jobs." I'm not talking now about a job description. I'm talking about defining our managerial responsibilities in terms of long-range objectives and clearly defining the job of a manager. In the process of developing a better understanding of our jobs under this concept, we may generate a considerable amount of paper which will have objectives, policies, standards of performance, and similar things written out. We are not interested in generating paper for its own sake. We are interested in getting a better understanding of what produces improved performance. To the degree these papers produce this understanding, I'm for them. The paper production is only a means toward an end. It is difficult to discuss and come to agreement about a concept such as this without putting it in writing. The thoughts embodied in our Declaration of Independence were widely and commonly held; but, without their having been written down, one wonders if agreement could have been achieved. Many years ago, John Milton wrote, "When there is much desire to learn, there, of necessity, will be much arguing, much writing, many opinions; for opinion in good men is but knowledge in the making."

I have not prepared this talk just to have made one more. This should be the beginning of a process of change. It is a process of change which is within the power of every one in this room to initiate and carry out. We, as individuals, do not have to wait for anyone else to start. I say this recognizing that in some cases, perhaps many, it describes what you are now doing. You already have this concept. In other cases, I am sure, it does not describe your present approach to your managerial duties. If the latter is your situation, we shall attempt to provide all the help you may need to put these principles into practice and thus grow in your own job by increasing your effectiveness as a manager. Those who have been using these concepts will be encouraged and helped to sharpen and improve them in the solution of business problems. This is not a one-shot proposition. It will take effort, determination, and time on your part. It will require careful critical examination of your managerial actions to determine whether they are contributing to the growth of your subordinates—growth measured in terms of improved results in working toward clearly established objectives. We are seeking improvements in management which will result in improved economic performance. With this concept, we can do something concrete, organized, and purposeful about our growth and the development of better managers for the jobs ahead. This is not something we will do by taking time out for two weeks of seminars. We will do it on the job as we go about our daily tasks. It is truly training on the job—self-development in the art of self-control and improvement—the important job of securing maximum growth on the part of subordinates. This is our intention. . . .

Now, you may ask: What do I propose to do personally to help in this process? I assure you I will watch my own managerial performance to see that it is such as to produce a growth climate for all my associates. I will sit down with each of them and work out clearly their areas of responsibility—areas in which they will be free to perform. Much of this has already been done—it needs only to be spelled out clearly. Then, individual objectives need to be set and agreed upon. I will do everything in my power to think and act in terms of improving individual performance—my own and others—and the total economic performance of the business. I shall watch closely the managerial performance of all our people as they work toward objectives established in accordance with this managerial concept. . . . I believe that most people in an organization are capable of growth and really desire it. I do not believe that only the uncommon man is capable of growing. The desire for growth and the ability to achieve it exists for all of our people whatever may be their training or background. We need only to create the proper climate for it to flower into extraordinary performance.

If this talk sounds like a call to arms, I hope you realize that is exactly what I am trying to make it. This is only the beginning of what I believe can be a wonderfully rewarding and productive effort for all of us. I guess I'm just as competitive as the next man—perhaps a little more so. I would like my performance to be better than anyone else in the corporation or in the United States who is performing the same job. I would like you, as managers, and all of us as a company to perform at a level significantly better than any division of the corporation or any company in our industry. I believe that the ideas we have outlined here will help, if practiced fully, to produce that kind of performance. I pledge *to you* all the support and effort I am able to give in working with you toward these goals.

Some wise man once said that nothing of any importance had happened in man's long history unless someone or a group became excited about something. I am really excited about this managerial concept and the future of our company *and hope you will join me in that excitement.*

Mr. Fogle made the above comments in August of 1961. Since 1960, key department managers were being continuously exposed to the management-by-objectives philosophy and were kept current on the status of the experiment in the marketing department. During 1960 and 1961, managers were asked at several meetings to consider the implications of this concept. In addition, literature discussing new ideas of human motivation and performance, authored by such well-known behavioral scientists as Dr. Carl R. Rogers and Dr. Douglas McGregor, was regularly distributed. The foundation for acceptance of the new principles was being slowly established over a two-year period. Careful attention was given to the avoidance of a feeling that a revolutionary new technique was being quickly forced upon the organization. Considerable effort was made towards encouraging self-acceptance and personal enthusiasm for the new ideas.

Even after Mr. Fogle's explicit statement of his commitment to the management-by-objectives program, directives for its use were avoided. One marketing manager stated that he believed the concept was received enthusiastically in the marketing department because of three reasons:

First, the program was not forced upon us. We felt that we were being asked to express our views and play a part in deciding on the merits of the program. More importantly, we were being asked to solicit the opinions of our subordinates on these ideas. Everybody was part of the same team.

The next reason for quick acceptance was that top management's dedication to these ideas was infectious. They began establishing objectives and really tried to conduct themselves in accordance with the principles of the program. This attitude on their part was quite effective in getting us in the lower management ranks to try the system. When they demonstrated their willingness to manage by this concept, some of the uncertainty and skepticism we had about management by objectives was removed.

The third reason why this manager thought this program took hold so quickly was that assistance in implementing the program was furnished to division management. He pointed out that the services of Barrington Associates were offered to any manager who wanted to use them to explain the program and its mechanics. The manager explained:

Competent people from Barrington visited any location and spent two or three days getting the system started. Employees were asked to drop their everyday business activities and devote their full attention to implementation of the program. These meetings were usually devoted to an explanation of the principles and mechanics of the objectives concept, asking and answering questions, establishing position analyses, and to starting a list of objectives for the coming year. The Barrington people visited most of the division's sales and marketing departments before the end of 1961.

The marketing manager concluded:

We all knew that the company was spending a lot of money and effort in getting this program to us. Therefore, I think that all of us were willing to try to understand the program and use it. I guess I can summarize by saying that the company provided the proper environment and that the management-by-objectives program really sold itself.

UNION CARBIDE CORPORATION'S CHEMICALS DIVISION (B)

The management-by-objectives program in the marketing department of the chemicals division of Union Carbide Corporation had been started in June 1960.[2] In December 1964, the case writer thought it would be worthwhile to learn how the program was being implemented after three years' experience with it. Several interviews were arranged with divisional personnel.

This case contains excerpts from interviews with a technical representative, a field sales manager, and a division distribution manager.[3]

The Technical Representative

Mr. Peter Walker had been graduated in 1958 from a large midwestern university with a degree in chemical engineering. After spending two years in the Army, he joined the chemicals division as a sales trainee. He was promoted to the field sales force in 1962, and he had been in the same territory ever since.

Case Writer: Mr. Walker, have you been participating in the "objectives" program?

Mr. Walker: Yes. I began as soon as I finished the sales training program.

Case Writer: How do you go about deciding what your objectives should be?

Mr. Walker: By several different ways. First, I know a good deal about what I can reasonably sell to each of my customers. This can be thought of as my

Exhibit 1

UNION CARBIDE CORPORATION'S CHEMICALS DIVISION (A)

PARTIAL ORGANIZATION CHART (1961)

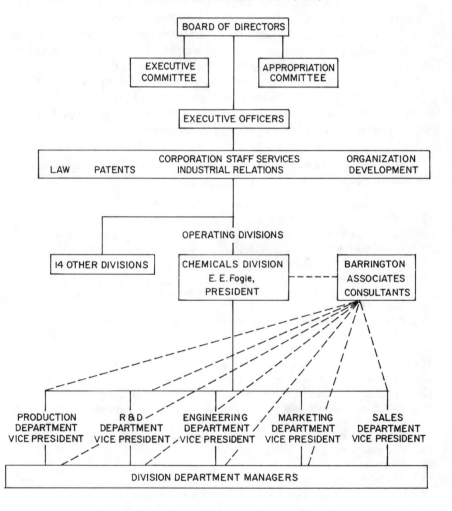

personal customer sales consideration. I arrive at this by historical results, future customer needs, competitive activity, etc. However, I also aim to better the previous year's performance, if at all possible.

Next, top management has goals they want to achieve, such as sales volume, new product and/or new market development, and profit targets. These goals are usually transmitted to me from my boss, and we try to incorporate them into my plans. The company has certain expectations of me and my territory. Nevertheless, I am free to determine, in part with my boss, the best way to achieve these expectations. I know the general direction the company wants to move in, and how far they expect to go in a year. I then do all I can as one salesman to get in step and help the company reach its destination.

Case Writer: How well have you done on this year's objectives?

Mr. Walker: I can show you because I've just finished working on the review of my performance. Here is a copy of the definition of my job, together with my objectives for 1962 and my self-appraisal review letter.

The Technical Representative

His primary function is to sell our product. He should provide or be provided with the following information.

1. Knowledge of costs which are controllable by him.
2. Relative profitability of our products.
3. Technical and sales training.
4. Knowledge of services available to him.
5. Ways and costs of distribution.
6. Manufacturing capabilities.
7. Competitive information—both local and national.
8. Market potential.
9. Proper methods of communication (who, what, when, why).
10. Knowledge that he should be self-reliant in his decisions—degree of his taking risks.
11. Knowledge of his sales responsibilities.
12. Understanding of all company policies.
13. Company background and economics.
14. Understanding personal responsibility for helping formulate policies and procedures.
15. Objectives and standards of performance to help in performing present job.
16. Knowledge of each customer's business.
17. Technical education.
18. Availability of supervisor.
19. Useful information obtained by all levels of management.

1962 OBJECTIVES FOR PETER WALKER,
Technical Representative

A. Business Objectives

Background

This territory covers the states of Maryland and West Virginia and includes approximately 275 accounts which have been active in the past three years. 1961 total volume will be about $2.5 million, with some 40% coming from four major accounts. Approximately 200 accounts will have made one or more purchases from us by the end of the year. Principal volume chemicals in this territory are acetone, methanol, and ethylene glycol going primarily to the paint industry centered in the city of Pleasantville.

1961 sales goal had been set at $2.25 million. This figure will be exceeded by approximately $250,000 due to unanticipated purchases of acetone by Quick-Kote Company for use at newly completed facilities. This "windfall" volume totaled approximately $350,000. Volume with *other* customers will fall approximately $100,000 short of 1961 target, primarily due to the price weakness since midyear in methanol and a consequent loss to competitors of substantial market share in the vinyl industry.

1962 Sales Goal

The territory should be able to produce a twelve-month volume of approximately $2,750,000 next year; this is our sales target. (Not included in this case is an analysis of planned sales by account which usually accompanies the objectives plan.)

There is a possibility that additional production capacity will be on stream at American Coating Company by the end of the third quarter. If this is so, the total volume goal for this territory should then be augmented by an additional quarter of a million dollars, to total $3.0 million in 1962. This upward revision should be determined by July 1.

B. Implementing Objectives

General comment

There have been no changes of major significance during 1961 in the nature or potential of the list of accounts and prospects constituting this territory. Other than general industry trends, there has been only one change in the local competitive situation which would require any significant modification of selling programs in the territory.

The Fluid Chemical Company recently acquired a major distributor headquartered in Baltimore, who will be operating effectively in their behalf by the beginning of 1962. This reseller has ten salesmen covering the western part of Maryland and the northern part of West Virginia. The company has its own fleet for daily delivery service, and ample facilities for both bulk and package deliveries.

Personal operating goals

In 1962, there are 15 basic problems which will have to be solved in this territory to help assure the most profitable attainment of the volume objectives stated above. Their solutions are stated here as implementing objectives, with appropriate standards of performance.

1. To obtain a broader base of customers for methanol and ethylene glycol for the purpose of spreading our competitive risk in the paint industry.
    This objective will have been met when initial methanol or ethylene glycol orders are booked from five accounts in the territory not sold in 1961.
2. To improve our franchise with the "big four" customers (Quick-Kote Co., Jones & Locker Co., Allison Industries, Sure-Stitch Co.) in this area, so that continuing competitive efforts do not diminish our share of the total business of these important customers.
3. To improve my personal business relationships with those prospects in the area included in the group of approximately 75 companies which purchased nothing from us in the past three years.
    This objective will have been met when I have been able to perform some gratuitous service for, or to arrange cordial social contacts with, fifteen executives in at least ten of these companies who have a voice in purchasing decisions.
4. To improve the frequency with which I am able to make in-person contact with the bulk of our customers, specifically those not included in the territories' "big four."
    This objective will have been met if I have developed and am following a suitably revised basic travel plan by July 1.
5. To develop additional increments of volume with old, and also prospective new, customers in the medium-size company category.
    This objective will have been accomplished if:
    a) 1962 total volume goals are met and
    b) such customers account for an additional 5% of total
    dollar income, i.e., 65% of sales.
6. To improve our ability to project annual and monthly territorial volume requirements for production planning purposes.
7. To protect the company against potential volume losses in methanol anticipated because of the present price weakness.
    This objective will have been met if, by April 1, 1962, the marketing research group have initiated a thorough study of the formulations which are being purchased by the vinyl industry as an alternative to methanol, including price, packaging, and delivery and convenience-of-use aspects.
8. To strengthen our position with Quick-Kote, and that entire industry, by providing a complete promotional program tied in with our preeminent position as the developer and principal marketer of acetone.
    This objective will have been met if:
    a) the advertising group delivers a total promotional package by no later than May 15,

b) the company succeeds in getting it used for a fall promotional program by at least four of the seven major companies in this industry.

c) if this territory delivers at least one additional company of the required minimum of seven major participants.

9. To improve the ratio of the more profitable "growth" chemicals sales to "basic" chemicals sales in this territory.

This objective will have been met when the percentage of total sales dollars accounted for by "growth" chemicals has been increased from 65% to 70%.

10. To protect our relationship with New Process Gas Co. in the long range, so that we will continue to enjoy our present share position with them when their new production capacity becomes operative in 1962 and 1963.

This objective will have been met when the company is able to work out a satisfactory defensive-sales program with this customer in the face of evidence of increasing reciprocity pressures on the part of two principal competitors.

11. To hold down direct costs of selling which are under my control with the end of contributing to optimum territorial profit.

This objective will have been met if the year-end average of monthly expenses reported does not exceed the median range of those for territories of comparable type, volume, and geographical size.

12. To determine whether it is desirable to acquire additional resellers in the northern part of West Virginia, in view of the steady growth in numbers of new, smaller end-user prospects for some of our specialty products.

This objective will have been met if, by April 1, I am able to obtain a clear-cut policy on the appointment of resellers, together with an adequate understanding of the economics supporting this policy.

13. To gain a comprehensive knowledge of natural gas industry which, while not the territory's dominant industry potential in terms of pounds, represents the highest profit potential, by industry, in the territory.

14. To master a thorough knowledge of all uses for ethylene glycol, the product for which there is the third largest number of individual customers in this territory.

This objective will have been met if, by October 1, I have completed an intensive program of indoctrination at the Technical Service Laboratory of not less than three full days' duration.

15. To improve my knowledge of the actual pound potential of this territory which is available to compete for (as opposed to calculated total consumption data, including captive production).

This objective will have been met when useable data has been obtained from the market research group on a minimum of three products: acetone, methanol, and ethylene glycol.

1962 PERFORMANCE APPRAISAL

Written by Peter Walker, Technical Representative

Business Objectives

My 1962 sales were $2.90 million dollars. This represents a 5.5% increase over my sales target. This increase is largely because American Coating Co. was on stream by the end of November. In June, I noted that we could expect this development. American Coating will be buying at the million-dollar level as predicted in my 1962 objectives.

Although I did exceed plan, my four major accounts did not buy quite up to expectations. The "big four" only accounted for 33% of my business. I believe that our loss at these accounts was largely due to increased competitive activities. The new distributor of Fluid Chemical has been particularly aggressive and he has a competitive advantage in being able to make deliveries much quicker than we can. This is one area that we will have to pay particular attention to in 1963. I must also explain that we were not able to develop any useful Technical Service Laboratory Projects for these customers as planned. Here again, I must review this possibility for 1963 with everyone concerned.

I think I have done a good job in accomplishing my IOs (implementing objectives). Of the 15 problem areas that I centered my personal operating goals around, I consider that I have achieved 8 fully and 5 in part. I shall review each one in order.

1. In the past year I obtained a methanol or ethylene glycol sale at seven accounts we had never sold. This was largely due to my personal efforts, as well as the company efforts through advertising and promotion. I consider that we have materially enhanced our position in the paint industry in my territory.
2. As mentioned above, I was not able to improve our position with the "big four." This problem will require an improved distribution ability. I plan to review this with our distribution department.
3. I consider that I was successful in establishing good personal relationships with at least 25 executives of accounts where we have not had business. This objective was accomplished primarily through my new membership in the National Paint, Varnish and Lacquer Association. In fact, through this contact I think I was able to achieve the first bulk shipments to the Smith Paint Co. and Union Industries.
4. A travel plan was established in April. Since then I have increased my call frequency from 4 accounts per day to an average of 5 1/2 accounts per day.
5. The objective for increasing business outside of my big four was met. Now 67% of my sales are from medium-sized accounts or new accounts. I obtained new bulk business from 9 accounts we had never sold before.
6. I was able to increase my contracts. However, as you know, Allison Industries canceled one big contract on MEK because we would not be competitive on price. Approximately 86% of my total volume is under contract.
7. The price weakness in methanol never developed. Thus, there was no need to make any reformulations.
8. As you know by now, our advertising and promotional efforts in the industrial finishes industry were well accepted by the trade. Quick-Kote was pleased with our efforts and rewarded us with additional purchases of acetone. I think that this is something we should try in other industries.
9. The objective of improving my sales of growth chemicals has been achieved, I think. However, the definition of a "growth" chemical may be misleading. I would say that at least 70% of my sales meet this definition, but I would like to clarify this during my formal appraisal review.

10. New Process Company did come on with new production capacity. However, we
     did not get the new business. Reciprocal Chemical got the initial fill because they
     buy over one half of New Process's production. More new capacity is planned for
     1963 and I have some specific ideas on what it will take for us to get this business. I
     will make this situation part of my objectives for 1963.
11. I cannot fully evaluate how well I did on my direct selling expenses as I do not
     know what the other salesmen did. I can point out, however, that my total year's
     expense account is about 6% lower than 1961.
12. John Lambert of the distributor sales group and I made an extensive study of the
     reseller situation. As a result, it was decided to appoint a new reseller in northern
     West Virginia. Already our sales in this area are picking up.
13. I am especially proud of my performance on the natural gas objective. As you
     know, with the help of the Technical Service Laboratory we undertook some
     corrosion studies of diethylene glycol. This study opened the door at several new
     accounts where we are just beginning to sell in significant quantities.
14. I never was able to spend the three days at the laboratory studying all the uses of
     ethylene glycol. On the other hand, I have reviewed all the literature we offer on
     this product. This can be demonstrated by my first sale of this product to the
     tobacco industry.
15. The market research group has furnished me with detailed information on
     acetone, methanol, and ethylene glycol. I have been able to use this data to
     pinpoint new potential. In fact, I have even helped them to improve their
     knowledge of these products' users in my territory.

I think I have done a good job. My total dollar sales have increased, and I have met
most of my implementing objectives. I feel satisfied that I am a better salesman than I
was last year.

However, there are several areas where problems persist. I have mentioned many of
these above while reviewing my performance. These problems will be a major part of
my 1963 objectives. I'm looking forward to the help and advice of everyone concerned
in further improving the sales in my territory and my own ability as a salesman.

The District Sales Manager

Mr. David Jefferson had been with the division for eight years. Recently he
was promoted from a salesman to sales manager of the Charlotte district. As
sales manager, Mr. Jefferson was responsible for both selling and
administrative duties in his district.

Case Writer: Mr. Jefferson, could you give me some idea of one of your major
objectives for 1964?

Mr. Jefferson: Yes. A big objective of mine was to sell $5,000,000 (of chemicals) to
the major accounts in this district for which I'm personally responsible. This plan
represents a 15 per cent increase over last year's sales.

Case Writer: How are you doing?

Mr. Jefferson: Let me show you this chart. (Mr. Jefferson removes a graph from his briefcase which showed his actual sales plotted against his plan.) You can see that I have sold $4,985,000 as of December 15.

Case Writer: Are you going to make $5,000,000?

Mr. Jefferson: Yes. I'm quite sure I will. I expect I'll probably exceed my plan by one or two hundred thousand dollars when all the figures are in for 1964.

Case Writer: Will you receive a pay increase because you achieved your objective?

Mr. Jefferson: Yes. I hope so!

Case Writer: If you had set your objective for sales of $7,000,000 would your sales be higher than $4,985,000 now?

Mr. Jefferson: No. We try to set objectives that are challenging, but also realistic. I suppose I could possibly increase my sales to $7,000,000, but only at the expense of long-term benefits. My job is not just to sell as much as I can today, but to maximize the long-range sales to my customers. This means that I have to do a lot of missionary selling to discover my customers' needs and how Carbide can best fill these needs. I have other objectives for these considerations (missionary selling) which are also very important to my evaluation.

Case Writer: Why didn't you set your objectives at $4,000,000 and be a real hero? Would you have received a whopping increase for exceeding your target by so much?

Mr. Jefferson: No. This system (management by objectives) doesn't work that way. You are not automatically rewarded for achieving your goals. My superior considers the degree of difficulty of my objectives when he evaluates me as well as how well I did relative to my plans. A sales goal of $4,000,000 would not have been challenging.

The Manager of Distribution—Chemicals Division

Mr. Fletcher Adams had been with the chemicals division for 30 years. He had worked his way up in the organization from plant engineer. The manager of distribution was responsible for overseeing distribution activities in a shipping terminal and had functional responsibility for distribution in a number of nearby plants.

Case Writer: I believe I understand how the objectives are established at the beginning of the year and how they are reviewed formally in December. Mr. Adams, could you tell me something about how the objectives concept works throughout the year?

Mr. Adams: Yes. I think so. You must recognize that there is a continuing need for review of performance and establishing objectives. Two meetings a year are not enough to manage an organization and develop your people. Often during the year it is necessary to establish new goals or modify old ones. You know this only by reviewing the progress of each of your subordinates.

Case Writer: You are saying that the objectives program is a continuous activity and cannot only be considered once or twice a year?

Mr. Adams: Exactly. If we operated only on the objectives we established at the beginning of the year we would be unable to adjust to changing needs. The objectives concept is more than a formal program: it is a way of managing that can be used throughout the year.

Case Writer: Can you give me an example of how you use this concept throughout the year?

Mr. Adams: Yes. I believe I can. Let me show you this series of correspondences I have had with Bruce Houser, the manager of our Newark distribution function. I've known Bruce ever since I've been with the company. I consider him to be a good manager, but during part of this year there were several areas of his performance that I thought needed improvement. These letters explain the situation and the way in which it was handled.

August 10, 1964

Mr. B. L. Houser
Union Carbide Corporation
Chemicals Division
Newark, N.J.

Dear Bruce,

This letter will confirm the areas of discussion and mutual agreement during my visit on July 30, 1964, regarding the operation of the Newark Plant Distribution Department.

a) We agreed that Mr. D. J. Howe, foreman, would be delegated more responsibility in the operation of the distribution facilities and, particularly, that you would promptly turn over to him for handling correspondence of the operations which are delegated to him. You are going to establish a procedure for following up on this correspondence and the "losing" of delegated correspondence will stop immediately. Also, we expect a reduction in the reported "loss" of mail to and from the Newark plant.

b) We agreed that you would continue to grant Mr. John Davis full responsibility for the new storage for acetone at Newark. As much as possible you will confine your activity in this project to a consulting basis. Mr. Davis has exhibited an ability to handle the project and he should be fully utilized.

c) Immediately upon return from his vacation you are going to take every opportunity to train Mr. Douglas Weiner in the performing of customer delivery notification. To assist you in this program, Mr. D. S. Cox will arrange for Mr. Weiner to visit the Region Office and receive a concentrated program on delivery-notification procedures. I expect to see Mr. Weiner performing delivery notification by the first of September 1964.

d) You agreed to expedite further required training of Mr. J. Kaiser to qualify him as a warehouse leadman. If he is not now capable of this training, he never will be. I am of the opinion he requires only your assigning him the responsibility to measure up to the job.

e) On or before Mr. Kaiser is moved from warehouseman to leadman, you will be posting the warehouseman job for bid and fill it with the next qualified for training and senior individual in the department.

f) You are going to continue your recently acquired practice of jobbing out your facilities repair work such as painting, cleaning, etc. Your serviceman and mechanic should be utilized in these positions of the jobs for which they are specifically trained, e.g., supervision of installation, piping, vacuum testing, electrical circuit testing, etc.

g) We had considerable discussion over the amount of premium overtime incurred by clerical help at Newark. Mr. H. J. Frank and I have reviewed the amount of clerical work required and it is agreed that some overtime, possibly 10–12 hours per month per man, is required at Newark and any other similar type operation. We cannot overlook the fact that our office people have been delegated added work. Unfortunately, the office at Newark has assumed a habitual pattern in excess of the time required. As discussed with you, on numerous occasions there is not enough added work to justify permanent-type help and we have repeatedly suggested you investigate the use of Manpower, Kelly Girl, etc., for periodic help.

You were shown that almost twice as much time could be secured for the premium time now being paid. Mr. Frank supplied you with the Newark Manpower phone number and the name of the manager. Please get this project in motion promptly.

As pointed out to you, I am not being critical of the work you do, except that you are doing too much yourself and leaving too little time for proper management of the department. You simply must delegate more of the work you are doing yourself.

I will be watching your progress with the items discussed above, and if I can be of any help on a consulting basis, please feel free to contact me.

Best regards

Fletcher Adams,
Manager of Distribution

September 30, 1964

Mr. B. L. Houser
Union Carbide Corporation
Chemicals Division
Newark, N.J.

Dear Bruce,

Please refer to my personal letter to you dated August 10, 1964, regarding operation of the Newark Distribution Department.

At this time I would like an item-by-item written report from you on your progress with the areas discussed in my letter.

Your reply by October 15, 1964, would be appreciated.

Very truly yours,

Fletcher Adams,
Manager of Distribution

(The following letter was hand written.)

October 13, 1964

Mr. Fletcher Adams
Manager of Distribution
New York, N.Y.

Dear Mr. Adams,

During your plant visit on July 30, 1964, a number of subjects were discussed. This will relate my progress to date, item by item.

Mr. Howe clearly understands he must assume more responsibility in the operation of the Newark Plant's distribution department. I have informed him that all correspondence relative to operations would be delegated to him; when a reply was needed, a due date would be indicated; and I would expect an answer by that date. I also informed him that my desk calendar would be marked for follow-up accordingly. I explained to him our reputation for "lost mail" was the poorest in the company and it simply could no longer be tolerated. In fairness, I must admit Mr. Howe is showing considerably more interest in distribution operations.

Mr. Davis has been given the full responsibility of the new storage facilities at Newark and, believe me, he is doing a truly fine job. Admittedly he is prone to be somewhat too easy with contractors and suppliers, but I'm certain he is beginning to realize you simply must establish an almost impossible due date in order to obtain results. I find it very gratifying to not have the research and ordering of necessary materials.

Mr. Weiner, as you know, visited the region office recently and he was impressed with the manner in which he was accepted by the Region Office personnel. Since then, he has begun a formal program of customer-delivery notification. His work with Dupont and Interchemical has been particularly successful. I'm sure he benefited greatly by his visit and he now knows the many ramifications that can come up during a customer-delivery notification. I'm certain that he can handle the notification service.

Under date of September 1, 1964, Mr. Kaiser was upgraded to a warehouse leadman. Previous to this change, the job of warehouseman was posted on the bulletin board, and, to my agreeable surprise, the man whom I wanted in the job was the only signature. As you know, Mr. Albert Zuchini was awarded the job. He has proven to be all that we expected and, in the not too distant future, will be capable of being upgraded himself.

We will continue to job out the type of work not normally performed by our warehouse personnel. Only this week we had a painting contractor paint the acetone storage unit. Mr. Davis has made arrangements with the South Side Iron Works to fabricate the steel supports for the Propylene Glycol storage tanks.

Immediately after your visit, I presented the hourly overtime record you had Mr. Frank prepare. I informed both men in the office that only essential and needed overtime would be granted and, before any overtime, Mr. Howe or myself should be consulted so that *we* could make the decision as to its necessity. You can note our improved record on this matter in our monthly reports. Needless to say, there was a little "sulking" at first, but the attitude is greatly improved as of today.

I have not contacted the Manpower people as I told you over the phone, as, until I have another desk at which I can set someone to work, I don't think it a good idea. As you know, our annual budget request included a desk, and, when received, I will contact the necessary people and arrange for this kind of help. In this manner we can have someone trained before the next vacation period.

You may be assured that I will make every effort to be a better manager and, again, always feel free to "bang me over the ears" when you think I'm not doing the job right.

Yours very truly,

Bruce Houser,
Newark Plant Distribution
Department Manager

October 20, 1964

Mr. B. L. Houser
Chemicals Division
Newark, N.J.

Dear Bruce,

Thanks for your letter of October 13, describing your progress on items we discussed during my July 30 visit. I have had the opportunity to carefully analyze your progress and think that the groundwork accomplished is good. You will need to continue with adequate follow-up of your initial efforts.

I am sure your discussion with D. J. Howe is bearing fruit. Dan has the experience and the capability, and there is no reason why he should be leaning on you like a green trainee. Please be sure that he continues to bear his share of the responsibility in the operation of the department.

Recognizing that there have been many problems associated with the acetone storage facilities at Newark, it still seems to me that we should be further along towards completion of this job. John Davis appears to have plenty of ability, but is a little short on initiative and drive. Our prime objective with him should be a faster pace consistent with department requirements.

I am pleased to see that you have Doug Weiner performing customer-delivery notification and I am sure that he will do a good job for you. Please promote this arrangement.

We have noticed payroll tickets placing Mr. Kaiser in the warehouse leadman classification. How is he working out?

I cannot help but point out to you that your initial fear regarding the bidding on jobs was unfounded and that in the case of Mr. Zuchini you have the man you wanted. Most of these job assignments can be successfully accomplished with a little groundwork and a straightforward appeal to the people involved.

I am pleased that you are jobbing out the maintenance work and advise that you continue to do so.

Mr. Frank and I have both noted the diminishing of office overtime at Newark. At the same time we fail to note any problem with receiving of reports on time in this office. I would say there appears to be adequate proof that previous overtime experienced was mainly unnecessary. On the other hand, you must be fair in the evaluation of necessary overtime and use it if temporary help cannot be obtained.

Please continue to follow up on the changes you have implemented. The progress you are making is most satisfactory. You and I will be reviewing your formal yearly objectives during the latter part of December. At that time we will also want to review your progress on these items we have been discussing in this letter.

Very truly yours,

Fletcher Adams
Manager of Distribution

UNION CARBIDE CORPORATION CHEMICALS DIVISION MBO PROGRAM UP-DATE

Although responses of certain individual managers do not agree, the spokesmen of three of the four Chemicals Division plants claim that some form of Management-by-Objectives style program is in operation at their units. Of the four plants surveyed, only two were members of the Chemicals division at the time of the launch of the original MBO program in 1960. Two of the four plants were added to the division about 4 years after the launch. As of 1972, neither of these two had formal programs, but one of them had installed a program similar to MBO by 1976. The actual evolution of the program is best characterized by the realities of plant operations during the years 1960–1971 as described by an unnamed plant management employee in response to a questionnaire survey. Below is his excellent chronicle of the events during this period having a bearing on the growth and development of such programs in his plant.

UNION CARBIDE CORPORATION

A SUMMARY OF PLANT IMPROVEMENT AND CHANGE PROCESS

A. *Background*

Improvement and change efforts have been emphasized as an important part of the plant's operation since its startup. Prior to the 1960's no formal system existed. The generation of projects and achievement was left to the individual initiative of managers and supervisory personnel at all organizational levels. Without question significant improvements were achieved even though no mechanism existed for measuring the total results and comparing the results from year to year.

In the early 1960's a formal Objectives program, encompassing all facets of plant operation, was implemented. Each department documented specific objectives at the beginning of each year and submitted them to their respective Assistant Plant Managers. With this program each year started out with very specific good intentions, but the absence of a built-in follow-up effort resulted in less achievement than would have been experienced otherwise.

In 1964 the Corporation-wide OIP (Assume Operations Improvement Program) was introduced at one plant and the previous broad Objectives program was abandoned. Reactions to the new OIP program were mixed. Some viewed the program favorably as a useful tool in accelerating the realization of improvement. Others reacted negatively, viewing the introduction of the program as criticism of past improvement performance and resenting the fact that it focused only on cost reduction and excluded all other areas of improvement. Nonetheless, the cost reduction achievement experienced during the first two years was impressive. Over $6,000,000 per year recurring savings were reported each of the first two years and most every one agreed that this level of achievement far exceeded the performance level of past years.

In early 1964 intensive union activity began and in July of 1966 the plant hourly personnel were organized as a bargaining unit. During the following two years considerable conflict existed between management and the bargaining unit. A considerable amount of time was devoted to grievances and labor relations. Time and effort were diverted from improvement projects and OIP achievements declined sharply. On July 1, 1968, the plant experienced a work stoppage and salary personnel operated the plant efficiently on a status-quo basis for seven months. Essentially improvement and change activity ceased during this period and the climate for change reached a historical low point.

B. *How the Current Improvement and Change Process was Established*

Shortly after the work stoppage ended in January, 1969, plant management reached the conclusion that a deliberate and systematic effort was mandatory to reestablish a climate of commitment to and enthusiasm for improvement and change. A management consulting firm, which has considerable experience in this area, was retained to help guide the effort. The basic assumptions and principles underlying the renewed improvement and change process are:

1. The process must start with the Plant Managers Department.
2. Planning and achievement should be focused initially on a relatively small number of challenging objectives.
3. The initial objectives should be ones the Managers Department are ready and want to work on.
4. These objectives should be accomplished through a series of mutually-supporting work projects involving a cross section of plant personnel.

5. Expanded capability and enthusiasm for improvement and change can be accomplished through well guided task projects that achieve direct results.
6. Work projects should be designed to accomplish the tasks themselves as well as to advance both individual and organizational development.
7. Written assignments to launch these projects should be developed collaboratively with the established line organization and the inter-departmental task groups assigned.
8. Disciplined work planning and review processes should be developed and institutionalized. Sustained effort and commitment of the members of top management are critically important to accomplish this.
9. Successes on initial tasks should serve to create the confidence and ability to undertake more challenging succeeding ones.
10. Ultimately the effort should expand to involve all levels of the managerial, technical, and supervisory groups and perhaps even the hourly work force.

The initial steps in establishing the process were a series of informal discussions between the consultant and each member of the Plant Managers Department. These discussions took place over a period of several months and were aimed at determining what plantwide problem areas each manager considered most important and which ones they were ready and willing to tackle. Some time before mid year 1969 the managers got together several times and hammered out a list of plant goals for the balance of the year. These goals were largely based on the items identified during the previous manager/consultant discussions.

One goal, to minimize periodic excessive emissions from the powerhouse stacks, was singled out for immediate attention. A task group was assigned to the project which developed a clear definition of its assignment and a work plan. Responsibility for this project was assigned to one of the Plant Managers.

Late in 1969 the Plant Managers Department held a series of meetings to examine in depth the progress made during the year. While considerable tangible progress had resulted from the Clear Stacks Task Group effort, progress on most of the other goals was found to be disappointing. The most significant factors identified as being responsible for the lack of progress were:

1. Individual responsibility for each goal was not assigned at the Plant Managers level. Everyone assumed someone else was carrying the ball when in fact this was not always the case.
2. Manpower resources were not assigned to the goals as a means of achieving them.

3.   Follow-up on progress was inadequate.

Drawing upon the experience gained during the previous nine months, the Managers Department developed plans for 1970. Plant goals were reestablished and responsibility for each one was assigned to one of the Managers. Task Forces were assigned to work on specific goals. Clear definitions of task force assignments were formulated, and work plans including time tables, individual team member assignments, and follow-up check points were developed. Individual departmental objectives were developed and published and the Plant Managers Department scheduled periodic meetings for providing follow-up on the process. The plant organization responded exceptionally well and highly impressive progress was made on many of the goals. One weakness identified around mid-1970 was the inability to relate individual departmental objectives and the plant goals. There was no effective means of determining how or to what extent departmental objectives supported plant goals. Realization of this problem resulted in establishment of a task force to develop an integrated management by objectives system for the plant.

By the end of 1970 a total of 27 task groups were established. Of these, 8 have successfully completed their assignments, 10 are still in process, and 9 have had their missions changed to provide ongoing periodic checkups, reviews or services.

Of some 490 managerial, technical, and supervisory employees, 102 or about 20 per cent have been directly involved as members of task groups. The majority of the remaining exempt and many of the non-exempt have been involved in task group activities through interviews and questionnaires.

As results of the undertaking have become visible, requests have been increasing from exempt employees not yet involved that they be included in future task groups.

The effort has given the participants at all levels in the organization a unique opportunity to work with others whom they ordinarily have little contact with. Overall company matters have assumed greater importance. Individual departmental affairs are no longer their exclusive concern. Top managers have better bases for appraising the potentials of individuals.

Critically important to the success of the undertaking were the development, understanding, and carrying through of the basic principles mentioned earlier. Regular strategy sessions, planning sessions, and review sessions of the Managers Department have been essential; also the assignment of one of the members of the Managers Department in liaison with each task group. We have also learned about the importance of creating written assignments and written work plans, and how to do so.

We have learned that this is hard work, but extremely rewarding in terms of personal satisfaction, in our development as individual managers, and for the organization as a whole.

Finally, during the past year one of our own managers, under the guidance of the consultant retained to guide our efforts, has developed the capability to serve as our own in-house resource consultant, thereby enabling us to become self-sufficient in maintaining this process.

CONCLUSIONS

The reader can readily see that such programs do not grow and take nurture in vacua. Strikes occur diverting management energies from other less critical activities. Personnel turnover, internal (promotions, transfers, etc.) as well as external, affects the growth of such programs. As an example of the possible effects of turnover, note below the succession of presidents of the Chemicals Division from program launch until 1971:

During the launch period: E. Edgar Fogle
            1964: Paul L. Alspaugh
            1966: Donald B. Benedict
            1967: Charles M. Blair
            1968: W. M. Anderson
            1969: R. D. Bower

Most proponents of Management-by-Objectives insist that the installation will take somewhere between 3 and 10 years of consistent support from top and middle management. With major marketing, finance, and labor problems facing top management, it is unreasonable to expect six different presidents over a 10 year period to provide this consistent support. Much of the time of the short tenures above was likely spent in familiarization activities and realigning the management teams to suit their approaches to the job.

From these cases, it becomes clear that the establishment of an MBO Program is a complex and difficult task which will likely require several times longer than typically expected and certainly cannot be launched with a batch of forms with a cover memo from a manager and nurtured to full growth by a team of consultants.

NOTES

1. This case series reproduced by permission of the Harvard Case Clearing House, Soldiers Field Road, Boston, Massachusetts.
2. See the Union Carbide Corporation's Chemicals Division (A) case for description of the company, the Chemicals Division, and the conception and installation of the management-by-objectives program.
3. Names of individuals, figures, and locations have been disguised.

Chapter 20

Case of a Company Attempting
To Apply a Variety of Modern
Human Relations Theories

MOST human resource management program launches which either appear to have initial success or are based on values, theories and teachings of behavioral scientists will attract a lot of attention. Removing a demoralized incentive system or allowing a special worker motivation-leader style program to die is hardly done with the same fanfare as its installation. The "case" presented by Professor Erwin L. Malone on the following pages is somewhat of an exception. This may have been partly because the company's "experiments" involved the entire company and when the experiment began to fail, the entire company was threatened.

Because Non-Linear Systems, Inc. had a significant share of their market, major changes in their performance would be readily noted by business and industry media. And since the heralding was still underway through second-hand versions of their great experiment—in management training sessions, behavioral science professors' classroom handouts and the like—any significant change in company performance would be news. During the reorganization of the company in response to the experiment's failure, one terminated vice-president was busily looking for an authorship grant to support his writing of a book about how wonderful the results of the approach had been!

Below begins Malone's excellent objective report and analysis of the Non-Linear Systems, Inc.[1] bold experiment. In my opinion, it is one of the most instructive pieces to be found in the behavioral science literature.

THE NON-LINEAR SYSTEMS EXPERIMENT IN PARTICIPATIVE MANAGEMENT

I. INTRODUCTION

The human relations theory of management states that man's psychological needs are at least as important as his physiological needs. This theory holds that employee satisfaction and increased productivity and creativity are obtained under conditions where employees have high security and maximum opportunities for self-direction and self-control.

Non-Linear Systems, Inc., of Del Mar, California, went to unusual lengths to apply human relations concepts to a functioning business. The experiment drew the attention of scientists, writers, educators, engineers, consultants, and representatives of governments and industries from all parts of the world, although most of the evaluative reporting of the experiment was incomplete or simply erroneous. This paper reports many details of the experiment for the first time and throws new light on its outcome.

II. THE COMPANY'S HISTORY

Non-Linear Systems, Inc. (which hereafter will be designated as NLS) was established in Del Mar, California, in 1952 and incorporated in California in 1953. Its entire corporate stock was held by Andrew F. Kay, president, and his family until recently, when some distribution to employees was made. The company principally manufactures a complete line of digital electrical measuring instruments, ranging in price from $500 to over $20,000 per unit, which are also tailored to specific requirements of such customers as U.S. governmental agencies, universities, and, through subcontractors, utilities, petroleum, chemical, textile, and other industries. The company grew from an initial five employees in 1952 to a high of 340 (75 percent of them male) in the 1960s; it now employs one-third that number. Dun and Bradstreet rated the company as a $6 million enterprise. For years NLS was the leader in an industry where it and six competitors took 95 percent of the available business and some 50 others shared the remaining 5 percent.

The company had been in business for 8 years and was firmly established in its field before the experiment in "participative management" was initiated in 1960–61. There never had been unionization in any department of the company. The experiment was completely voluntary on the part of the company. It was set up by a liberal-minded president whose early life observations of the critical impact of working policies and conditions on his parents, himself, and others generated an insatiable interest in methods to better human relations in industry and develop each individual's potential to the full. The experiment was instituted after years of deliberation and long conferences with professional scientists and industrialists who professed similar interests and after many months of discussion with employees and with their full consent.

III. ELEMENTS OF THE PARTICIPATIVE MANAGEMENT EXPERIMENT

The general theory of the Non-Linear Systems experiment drew on the writings of behavioral scientists, most of whom were identified with the human relations approach. These included Peter F. Drucker, Douglas McGregor, and A. H. Maslow.[2] The view of human nature and worker motivation drawn from these writers included the following points:

1. Work is as natural as play or rest, and if made a source of satisfaction it will be performed willingly and voluntarily.
2. In the service of objectives to which he is committed, man requires little or no external direction or control. He will exercise self-direction and self-control. The degree of his self-control will depend upon the degree to which he is committed to these objectives.
3. Commitment to objectives is a function of rewards associated with their achievement, these rewards being those which go to satisfy man's physiological, psychological, safety, social, ego, and self-actualization needs.
4. Many humans not only are ready to accept responsibility, they seek to shoulder it. Avoidance of responsibility, lack of ambition, and emphasis on security are not inherent human characteristics.
5. The powers of imagination, ingenuity, and creativity are more widely distributed throughout the population than most executives admit. They simply await the proper time, place, stimulus, and atmosphere of receptivity to pour forth.
6. Under the conditions of modern industrial life, man's intellectual potentialities are only partially realized.

To apply these beliefs to the day-to-day operations of a business required that they be translated into specific objectives and then into changes in the structure and procedures of the firm. These changes were as follows:

WAGES.   Human relations theory states that wages can satisfy human needs for security, safety, and status, but that hourly and piecework wages are not needed to evoke employee effort. To eliminate the punishment-reward psychology of hourly wages, toward the end of 1960 all hourly rated employees (who were already being paid higher-than-average area wages of $1.90 an hour, or $75 a week) were advanced $0.60 an hour and placed on a straight salary of $100 a week. Thereafter no deductions were made for arriving late, for leaving early, for cleanup or wash-up time in any amount, or for fatigue or coffee breaks taken at the employee's convenience. No records were kept of these or of any other work absences.

Not long after the new salary scale was put into effect, older employees requested the president of NLS to start new employees at the rate of $85 a week instead of at the $100 a week rate and that salary scale was adopted, with the increase to $100 a week coming after a probationary period of flexible length. There never was a specific plan other than this for merit or length-of-service increases; such increases were proposed by managers of departments and acquiesced in by the president; they were few in number and moderate in amount. Salaries of technicians, draftsmen, and other employees were advanced in 1960–61 wherever revision was deemed desirable in order to keep their remuneration reasonably commensurate with the increases given hourly rated employees.

ORGANIZATION. Human relations theory, with its emphasis on self-direction, argues for making the staff an advisory rather than an authoritarian administrative body. Prior to the experiment, NLS operated with a traditional "vertical" organization: a board of directors; president; vice-presidents; managers for production, sales, accounting, inspection, quality, purchasing, engineering, and shipping; engineers; superintendents; technicians; draftsmen; foremen; inspectors; assemblers; shippers; and miscellaneous workers. In the experiment, although the corporate-level structure remained the same, the organization structure shown on charts distributed throughout the plant was vastly different. In the new setup there were three "zones":

Zone 1: trustee management. This consisted of the four members of the board of directors of the company, including Andrew F. Kay, chairman of the board. Responsibilities: to determine the basic policies and the basic course of the business.

Zone 2: general management. This was an eight-member Executive Council consisting of seven members chosen by the president, plus the president himself. The council was to establish operating policies; plan, coordinate, and control the business as a whole; and appraise results. The seven members held titles indicating prime interest in certain areas of operation: vice-president—innovation; vice-president—productivity; vice-president—physical and financial resources; vice-president—profitability; vice-president—manager performance and development; vice-president—marketing; vice-president—legal council and public responsibility. (Note that in the organization charts the office of president was eliminated: the president was a member of the Executive Council and that was the level at which he functioned.) The Executive Council was to operate as a unit, never directing or controlling. Decisions were to be advisory, by mutual consent of the members present at any meeting.

Zone 3: departmental management. At this level were the 30 department units, also called project teams. Each consisted of three to 12 employees, including the department manager. They were to "manage the business of their departments for the objectives defined and authorized by the Executive Council." Department unit managers had been chosen by the president with the aid of the former works manager who became an Executive Council vice-president. Department managers were responsible for day-to-day methods, operations, and procedures in their units. Typical of these numerous department units were: project team (designing and developing company products); industrial engineering; materials; fabrications (assembling instruments from parts supplied to these units in kits coming from the warehouse); instrument assembly (nonkit assembly); systems; distribution (receiving and filling customers' orders and also invoicing outgoing material); plant facilities; personnel services; sales promotion; regional sales (numerous such units, each responsible for sales in a specified territory.)

Executive Council meetings were held daily for a period, then weekly. Managers of project and production teams met daily or as needed. Managers of other departments met irregularly.

PRODUCTION SETUP.   Prior to the time of change, two assembly lines produced two basic models of digital voltmeters. Relatively slight changes or additions adapted these two basic models to specific needs of individual customers. These assembly lines were discontinued in 1960–61. They were replaced by departmental units of three to 12 people, each in a separate room, each headed by a manager, each responsible for creating completed instruments from parts brought to it from the stockroom. Each group assembled, calibrated, inspected, packed its instruments, usually making five to 10 instruments at a time. Each group worked at its own pace, making its own decisions as to whether each man would make a complete instrument from start to finish or whether the group would operate on an assembly-line basis with each person contributing certain operations to the line. Each group worked out its own internal problems of tardiness, absences, jealousies, breaks, and grievances; only in rare instances did such problems reach the Executive Council. Groups made their own rules of procedure. If they kept any records it was because they chose to do so. Records were not required.

The manager of a group was well qualified from his previous work experience to lead the group, but he was not a "boss" or a disciplinarian. Since the members of his group had the authority to do about what they wished, when, as, and how they wished, his job was one of consultation, direction, and advice at this lowest level. The group (unit) managers reported to the Executive Council as a whole, not to any individual member.

Indoctrination programs. At the start of the experiment, every effort was made to acquaint each member of the organization, individually, with the new policy of the company and to inform one department after another of the potential benefits as the details of operation were described. The president personally addressed employees en masse, in groups, and individually, answering all questions freely and accepting suggestions.

The Executive Council was lectured to by many of the very prominent persons in the field of human and industrial relations, among whom were James V. Clark, Richard E. Farson, Abraham H. Maslow, Vance Packard, Carl Rogers, Robert Tannenbaum, and Frances Torbert.

A Los Angeles personnel-testing service interviewed every employee in the company in behalf of the program. Industrial relations counselors were retained on a permanent consulting basis to counsel employees, interview new applicants, and help indoctrinate them when they became employees of the company.

Training procedures. Each new employee was first thoroughly informed as to the company's policies and operations. He then received an on-the-job training of some length. Thereafter, any employee, male or female, could have almost any type of job training he or she desired, inside or outside the plant. Courses of study taken outside the company premises were paid for in full by the company upon their completion.

Time clocks. Punching a time clock is held to be degrading by most people who work in factories. They feel it implies mistrust. Time clocks were eliminated from all departments of the plant.

Record keeping. Douglas McGregor had stated that keeping performance records would vitiate the principle of self-control,[3] inasmuch as records could be used by management to control a subordinate and as a check on his performance. So far as production and personnel records were concerned, NLS became a company that operated essentially on a "put nothing in writing" basis. Because of this, statistical data of almost every sort are lacking; the data cited hereafter are from the personal knowledge, recollection, and papers of the board of directors, of Andrew F. Kay in his capacity as an Executive Council member, other members of the Executive Council, and company employees who were intimately in touch with operations from 1960 to 1965.

ACCOUNTING. The Accounting Department as a unit was eliminated. Accountants were dispersed to purchasing, shipping, and personnel where separate books were kept, balances being reported to the treasurer at intervals.

INSPECTION. The Inspection Department, as such, was eliminated. Each separate production unit was made responsible for the quality of its work, the members of each unit deciding how and when the inspection, or inspections, would be made on the product the unit made.

IV. TERMINATION OF THE EXPERIMENT

For 5 years those who visited the plant at Del Mar, to witness firsthand this pioneering test of a new theory, came, saw, and departed unaware of any serious defects in the firm's operations. Although critical kinds of quantitative information were not furnished to these visitors, they generally concluded that the experiment was proceeding smoothly and could be expected to continue indefinitely. Yet early in 1965, NLS introduced modifications so extensive and extreme as to signify the end of the experiment in participative management. These included the following:

1. "Line" organization procedures were reestablished at the top levels.
2. Direct supervision was provided.
3. Specific duties and responsibilities were assigned.
4. Standards of performance and quality were reestablished.
5. Authority was delegated commensurate with responsibility.
6. Records were reinstituted and maintained.
7. Remuneration was related to effort.
8. Factory department units were accorded a large measure of autonomy to schedule work within their units in the fashion they wished. In this respect the department units function reasonably closely to the manner in which they operated during the years of the experiment. The state of the firm at that point was as follows:

1. Sales volume was not measuring up to expectations; and, for the actual volume of sales, administrative and sales costs were heavy.
2. Organization restlessness had been developing at management levels.
3. Productivity as a whole remained unchanged.
4. Employee layoffs began in 1963. Other layoffs occurred in 1964 and 1965.
5. Competition in the industry was multiplying.
6. The sales force resisted efforts to decrease sales costs.
7. The company was finding itself becoming progressively less profitable the longer it continued with participative management. The question was

arising: how long would the company be able to afford the luxury of pursuing a theory of operation which bid fair to bring about its demise?

V. WHY DID THE EXPERIMENT FAIL?

The numerous reports published during the experiment generally fail to prepare the reader for the failure acknowledged by the company's turnabout in 1965. This section quotes some of these and also refers to opinions of behavioral scientists (some of whom were employed by NLS to counsel the firm and its employees) as these were made during the experiment and afterward. It also presents evaluations of these statements and explanations.

Business Conditions

It has been said that the firm made overoptimistic predictions of sales, leading to excessive increases in personnel in sales, advertising, development, engineering, and in other outlays. Thus, when the error was realized (in 1965) the firm was forced to jettison all but the most essential programs and tighten cost controls in every possible way.

Actually, in the period from 1953 to 1960 the company had experienced a phenomenal rate of growth, with sales doubling year after year. It cannot be said, now or then, that such a trend would not have continued. The management did anticipate that the sales mix might change from the 90 percent government and indirect-government sales of 1960 to the 60 percent which it became in 1965, and so it provided both a larger sales force and additional employees to take care of far greater sales.

Sales volume did increase each year from 1960 to 1963, but the rate of increase diminished. Late in 1963 and again in 1965 sales dropped sharply. At these times orthodox management would have reduced plant employment in line with the incoming order rate, but such an action would have been in conflict with the goals of job and personal security. Layoffs were not given the degree of serious consideration that was warranted until long after the problem of diminishing sales first arose, although the costs of retaining this manpower reserve were tremendous and were depleting the firm's treasury. Even when layoffs did occur, the higher-salaried engineering and research personnel were shifted to lower-rated production jobs without the usual downward salary adjustment, in the belief that this would keep them available when improved conditions warranted their services.

Organization and Autonomy

The form of organization adopted under the experiment in participative management left many former administrators restless and frustrated because they no longer had specific operating responsibilities. The Executive Council comprised seven vice-presidents plus the company president. The seven vice-presidents formerly had been vigorously active in the midst of daily problems and were more or less expert in their individual specialties. Under participative management these men were practically immobilized as "sideline consultants." Their duties were not well defined. New organization charts every 6 months or so often changed their designations, for example, to "vice-presidents function virtually as assistant presidents," but without outlining specific duties or authority. In council meetings they were always in danger of being overwhelmed by the brilliant, mercurial thinking of President Kay, whose ability to originate new ideas on the spur of the moment, or to change direction, was astounding. It also was disconcerting. It is difficult to see how this group could be other than restless and frustrated.

Department managers were heads of units engaged in production, sales, design, development, personnel, plant facilities, order distribution, etc. They managed their departments as well as they could. When technical problems arose and they went to the Executive Council for advice perhaps only one, or, at the most, two council members had the proficiency in the specific matters to be able to advise. When these men were not available, others could not make decisions that would be meaningful. So either the department managers made up their own minds or frustration developed as the problems remained unsolved. And since the questions had been asked verbally—nothing needed to be put in writing—there were no permanent records for future take-up at subsequent council meetings.

Each department manager oversaw the work of employees in his department, to whom he was adviser, coordinator, consultant. With a modicum of experience behind them, numerous of these managers had need of the guidance and training they normally would have received had they worked directly under individually responsible supervisors. Under participative management they were chiefly on their own. Many found it disquieting to have to seek aid from the Executive Council as a whole. And no matter how well experienced, young men in subordinate positions appear to want some measure of authoritative direction—someone else to help shoulder some of their problems.

Wages, Production, and Productivity

After the end of the experiment, a number of NLS executives told the author that the wage increase from $76 to $100 per week was a substantial burden on the company. Yet, during the experiment, reports such as these were common in the press: "Man-hours devoted to building each instrument have been cut in half—enabling Non-Linear to offer the highest pay in the community."[4]

"Production man-hours have been sliced in half, while production is 30% higher than it ever has been."[5] "Within six months productivity began to rise. It's now averaging 50% more for each of the 350 employees."[6] "Productivity in man-hours per instrument has steadily improved. Today it is 30% better than at any period in the company's history."[7]

Actually, no production records were kept from 1960 to 1965 which would show whether productivity increased or decreased. President Kay and the members of the Executive Council who were interviewed in July 1965 were in complete agreement with the statement that "on some items there may have been a productivity increase, but on other items there may have been a productivity decrease. In the plant as a whole, there probably was no change in productivity." It is very probable that productivity (the output per individual in any given time) remained the same at the $100 per week salary as it was at the $76 per week wage, since there appears to have been no decrease in the man-hours required per instrument assembled. (Note: the 31–32 percent increase in direct labor cost increased the sales cost less than 5 percent.)

Quite a different matter is that of increased production (the output of the factory in any given time). In 1963 the output from the factory was in the neighborhood of 30 percent more than it was in 1960. But the number of employees rose from 240 to 340, an increase of 42 percent over the same period. (The NLS officers agree with the figures given here.) Even allowing for a greater number of models of more intricate design, there is no indication of NLS ever having increased its plant efficiency during the entire run of the experiment.

Layoffs

At least one outside consultant to NLS has told the author that, if the company had possessed greater financial resources, standard instruments could have been stocked in a warehouse during periods when sales were low and employee layoffs avoided.

From 1952, when the company first began to operate, to 1960, when the experiment started, models of digital computers were sufficiently similar so that they could be made on two assembly lines. By 1965 specifications were more individualistic and more complicated—so much so that with 200 different models (counting adaptations) made annually, there could be no certainty that any instrument put into inventory would move out within six months or over. Models obsolesce quickly. Though the principle of inventory buildup during slack periods would supplement the participative management theory, it hardly can apply at NLS where a total of perhaps 10 instruments would have comprised a maximum salable inventory. Working capital was sufficient for NLS's needs, and total assets were well in line with sales. It was not due to lack of working capital that no appreciable inventory of instruments was carried.

Sales-Force Behavior and Competition

Over the period of the experiment (and since), there was an increase in the number and vigor of competitors, many of them offering reduced prices. To increase a company's sales in such a market, the company must provide something extra in the way of design, operation, adaptability, quality, service or delivery. Beginning in 1960 NLS anticipated this by the creation of an expanded research and development staff and an augmented sales force covering the nation, and was quite successful in retaining its leadership with a major share of the market.

The company had employed sales representatives from 1953 to 1959. During 1960, 19 sales offices were opened throughout the country, and, in keeping with the human relations emphasis on security of income, staffed by salaried salesmen. Each district office was given a flat yearly sum to cover salaries, expenses for travel and entertainment, the purchase of new cars every 2 years, and office expenses. Each district office ran its own affairs, had its own bank account, paid its own bills, and sent the paid receipts to the home office. Sales reports and salesmen's expense books were not required.

Sales increased, but unfortunately the increased sales volume was not commensurate with the increased sales costs, and there were great differences in the ratios of costs to sales among districts with similar potential. In 1964 an attempt was made to lower sales costs by requesting each sales district to service its own customers rather than have servicemen sent out from the home office. A number of salesmen—some competent to service and others not—refused to service instruments, although the practice was not unusual in the industry. Instead of welcoming this opportunity to be of service to their customers, many salesmen took it as a lowering of their status and quit the company. In 1965, after the experiment's end, salaried salesmen were replaced by commission sales agents. This constituted a major policy change.

Product Quality

The quality of work was acceptable. What at one time had been thought to be a work-quality problem, which plagued the company for many months, was discovered to be caused by damage in transit at a particular transfer point; when shipments were routed around this point, the problem was solved. Yet, because no company records were kept from 1960 to 1965, there is no statistical basis for published reports like these, which could only have been based on general impressions or wishful thinking: "Customer complaints fell 70%."[8] "Complaints from customers have dropped 90%."[9] "The number of complaints from the field: these are now 70% fewer than they were three years ago."[10] "Improvements in quality steadily reduced the number of complaints from the field. Though the business doubled in the four years after the assembly lines were dismantled, the number of complaints diminished by over 70% during that time."[11]

Job Satisfaction

Employee satisfaction with a job at NLS depended on the employee's position. Shop workers at the factory level obtained higher wages, greater autonomy and a voice in the production process, extensive opportunities to increase competence through training at company expense, and the numerous psychological benefits which undoubtedly followed from these. For them, NLS was a good place to work, and there was always a long list of applicants waiting to be hired. Employees brought in their relatives: 18 percent were related in 1965. Absenteeism was 2.8 percent in 1960 and 2.5 percent in 1965, and labor turnover was 4–5 percent in both years, about normal for manufacturing plants in the Del Mar area. Morale was high and grievances were few.

At the lower management level, department managers, many of them engineers and technicians, experienced a drop in morale during the course of the experiment. These technically skilled employees had often remained working at the plant long after quitting time. Toward the end they departed promptly after putting in an 8–hour day, and their offices were deserted on Saturdays, Sundays, and holidays as never before. Despite "ideal" working conditions and high salaries, 13 of the 30 department managers who were with the company in 1962 were not with NLS in 1965: the company ran out of work for three specialists, two had personality problems, one became discouraged, one resented the company's sales policy, one was permitted to resign because of inability to produce sales, four left for better jobs, and one went with a product division that NLS disposed of to another company.

For the seven executives who, with President Kay, made up the Executive Council, the experiment seems to have been highly unsatisfactory. The Executive Council did not prove to be effective in working out, or even in raising policy differences, and the seven subordinate executives felt that participative management had restricted rather than widened their horizons. They made constant, rather unsuccessful, attempts to define specific duties for their individual members.

Initially, three of the seven had favored the plan, two had cooperated even though unconvinced of its merit, and three had cooperated while privately believing that it could not succeed. During the 5 years of the experiment, one

new member was added, and one was dismissed and then later rehired. After
the end of the experiment in 1965 three were given long advance notice of
employment termination, a fourth left of his own volition after refusing a
salary reduction, and death overtook two.

Creativity

It had been hoped that participative management would encourage latent
powers of imagination and creativity and uncover incipient managerial ability
and provide the proper medium for its development. While it is difficult to
conceptualize and measure these qualities, there is no evidence of an unusual
development of human potential. During the 5 years of the experiment, many
men were helped by the training and instruction they received, and many
enlarged their work skills. But only two gave indications of greatness, and in 5
years any plant with 300 or more employees should expect to find two men of
well-above-average caliber.

In addition, NLS was far from being an ordinary plant. Factory workers
had at least a full high school education and were well trained, well adjusted,
multitested, and highly screened by professional personnel experts who were
generally sympathetic to the goals and methods of the human relations
movement. Such a group may well be unique. But its accomplishments cannot
be shown to have been especially high under participative management,
whether accomplishment is measured by average performance or by the
development of unusually productive individuals.

Profitability

When NLS initiated participative management in 1960, it looked forward to
increasing the prosperity and well-being of everyone concerned. No thought
may have been given to raising profits above the 1959–60 level reached prior to
the experiment, but it hardly could have been expected that profits, which had
increased yearly from 1953 to 1960, would begin in 1961 to spiral downward
until the losses sustained compelled abandonment of the experiment in 1965.
In retrospect, it is surprising now to read: "We feel we are well launched on an
exciting experiment that ultimately will not only pay off in larger profits for
the company, but will also contribute in some small measure toward the betterment of our industrial society."[12] "The company's unique experiment has
attracted considerable national attention from management specialists,
production people, and educators. Company morale has been examined by
many outsiders and termed sky-high—and company profits have climbed
too—even though the electronics industry as a whole has suffered a major
price let-down."[13] "The program, under way now for five years, is beginning to

show gains that sharpen NLS's competitive edge. . . . A. H. Maslow, Brandeis University psychologist, believes NLS's experiment shows the way to the future."[14]

In contrast to these hopeful statements, all made more than halfway through the experiment, we have the much more recent remark by a behavioral scientist who had been employed on the NLS experiment since its inception: "I think we know now that Human Relations don't have a lot to do with profit and productivity."[15]

VI. AFTERMATH: WHAT DID THE EXPERIMENT SHOW?

In 1965 NLS retreated, in the face of overwhelming financial pressure, to the relatively conventional management methods described in Section IV above. The results are described by a long-time director with considerable business experience: "Both management and factory workers appear not dissatisfied with these changes. The company probably avoided bankruptcy by abandoning the experiment and returning to orthodox methods of management; it is now operating with a small profit and expanding into other, but related, fields."[16] Beyond this, the question remains of what the NLS experiment shows about the validity of the human relations and participative management approaches. Some of those who are familiar with the NLS experiment have suggested that much of the outcome was due to the unique personality of the president, Andrew F. Kay, and that a less powerful and less experimentally oriented individual might have produced results much more favorable to these theories. Of course, only an individual of Mr. Kay's unusual qualifications and position would have considered risking a thriving, multimillion-dollar business to test a theory previously untested on anything like this scale, and, in any case, we need to make the most of such a large and costly experiment, no matter how imperfect its design. In that spirit, the following conclusions are offered as being reasonably supported by the evidence.

1. The removal of the high-level NLS executives from their individual responsibilities for planning, directing, and controlling specific areas of operations was not successful. Whatever Kay may have done to make their problems more difficult, there is little reason to believe that these individuals could have achieved high productivity and job satisfaction within the rules of the experiment, regardless of who was president. It remains to be seen whether any individuals organized as a collective of advisers can perform successfully and, if so, what sorts of persons and training programs are required.

2. Quite similar conclusions apply to the lower levels of management, where productivity and job satisfaction dropped as a result of the experiment.

These department managers wanted and needed more direction than the Executive Council was able to give, either collectively or as individuals. It remains to be seen whether any individuals could have performed the department manager functions productively and with satisfaction and, if so, how such individuals should be selected and trained.

3. At the level of the shop floor, job satisfactions increased, but there was no marked welling up of energy and creativity, much less a productivity improvement sufficient to overcome the loss of productivity at the executive levels, and none should be expected.

4. Over all, the sort of thoroughgoing adoption of human relations theories tried at NLS may be possible only while a firm enjoys an unusually profitable, protected market and has owners who are willing to accept unusually high frustrations and negligible or negative future returns. Smaller, more limited applications of a vastly modified participative management-human relations approach may continue to be considered in frameworks which retain effective supervision and rewards. But in a competitive market a company must receive from its employees enough in return to offset the extra costs of higher wages, additional benefits, lower work standards, better work conditions, and less efficient operations. If it does not, it soon will cease to exist.

NOTES

1. Reproduced with permission from *The Journal of Business of the University of Chicago*, Vol. 48, No. 1, January 1975, pp. 52–64. Erwin L. Malone is Professor of Administration and Management Studies, Bloomfield College, Bloomfield, New Jersey; and management and marketing consultant, Rice & Malone, Maplewood, New Jersey.

   The author spent 2 weeks at Non-Linear Systems shortly after the termination of the experiment in 1965. There, at the invitation of the company, he interviewed directors, officers, managers, and operative employees and was given free access to all correspondence, records, and employees in and out of the plant. Since then, he has been in frequent contact with important actors in and observers of the experiment.

2. Peter F. Drucker, *The Practice of Management* (New York: Harper & Row, 1954), pp. 125–36; Douglas McGregor, *The Human Side of Enterprise* (New York: McGraw-Hill Book Co., 1960), pp. 33–48; A. H. Maslow, "A Theory of Human Motivation," *Psychological Review* 50, no. 4, July, 1943, pp. 370–96.

3. McGregor, p. 160.

4. Vance Packard, "A Chance for Everyone to Grow," *Readers Digest*, November, 1963, p. 115.

5. "No-Assembly-Line Plan Gets Nothing But Results," *Steel*, May 25, 1964, p. 90.

6. "Non-Conformity at Non-Linear," *Quality Assurance*, August, 1964, p. 28.

7. Arthur H. Kuriloff, "An Experiment in Management—Putting Theory Y to the Test," *Personnel*, November-December, 1963, p. 14.

8. "When Workers Manage Themselves," *Business Week*, March 20, 1965, p. 94.

9. Packard.

10. Kuriloff.

11. Arthur H. Kuriloff, *Reality in Management* (New York: McGraw-Hill Book Co., 1966), p. 44.

12. Kuriloff, "An Experiment in Management," p. 17.

13. See number 6.

14. See number 8.

15. Richard Farson, quoted in "Where Being Nice to People Didn't Work," *Business Week*, January 20, 1973, p. 94.

16. Ludwig Weindling, management consultant, L. Weindling & Co., Rancho Santa Fe, California, and director, Non-Linear Systems, in letter to the author, April, 1974.

CONCLUSIONS AND PROJECTIONS

PART VII represents an attempt to see the future of management theory and prescriptions over the next 20 years. Most projections in the literature are for rapid and significant changes in the way organizations will be managed. These projections appear to be mostly wish-fulfillment on the parts of the prognosticators. The evidence simply does not support radical departures from the present management practices, as can be seen from data given in the chapter. The direction of predicted changes in the literature appears to be supported somewhat by trend analyses, but the rate of these projected changes certainly is not.

The most significant wish-fulfillment-oriented change I would hope for would be that managers gain the ability to evaluate management theory which should naturally be followed up by an increase in their reliance on their common sense and reasoning powers. But the evidence still suggests that, although this may happen, it will also take place more gradually than I would hope for. The final chapter taken as a whole is, nonetheless, an appeal to the manager or student reader to begin to increase the use of these faculties.

Chapter 21

Management Theories and Prescriptions in the Future

THE safest, rarest, and usually the most accurate prediction about the future developments in any applied field of human relations endeavor is simply that not much is likely to happen, and this has to be the best assessment at this writing of management's future over the next 20 years. In their updated study of Muncie, Indiana, which was first studied in 1929 and later in 1937 as a typical American community by sociologists Robert and Helen Lynd, Theodore Caplow and his team of sociologists conclude that not much has changed: "We have not been able to find any trace of the disintegration of traditional social values described by observers who rely on their own intuitions."[1] ". . . almost all the social forces shaping life in modern-day Muncie were already present in 1924. It amounts to a startling message about the nation: that American life has not changed very much in 50 years."[2]

Given the momentum of large institutions which tend to set patterns for all but very small institutions, little can be done to alter substantially the behavior and performance of only one of the system's interdependent elements such as management. Organizations follow a law similar to this: the bigger the moving object—supertanker, government, aircraft, or corporation—the greater the turning circle. This law guarantees that the U.S. Federal government, General Motors and Ohio State University will change very little over the next couple of decades. Only catastrophic causes such as nuclear war between or major revolution within industrialized nations are forces strong enough to cause major changes in the managements of these organizations. The reasons that other forces lack the power to overcome apparent management inertia are many.

On the academic "micro" level this prediction makes sense. The vast majority of management theorists, consultants, and researchers virtually ignore many of management practitioners' real and well-publicized problems.

455

There are no useful definitive theories of any consequence on the causes and cures of industrial conflict, absenteeism, grievances, or the shortage of competent managers. The problem of helping employees to learn to tolerate the inevitable boredom portion of *most* jobs is likewise left untouched by behavioral scientists. (The behavioral scientists' value that boredom is "bad" in and of itself regardless of its ultimate benefits to society in the form of inexpensive penicillin and washing machines probably accounts for this neglect.) The study of *proxemics* whose preliminary findings suggest that serious consequences for human behavior result from various dimensions of worker density is all but ignored by management theorists, in spite of the fact that most of them appear very much concerned with what would appear to be the problems of managing human resources. Their favorite journals deal mostly with a narrow scope of research on human behavior and prescriptions for those who must manage it. A U.S. Academy of Management poll reported on members' rankings of 19 journals. They considered academic stature, contribution to knowledge, usefulness in teaching and usefulness for research. Five of the top eight publications are exclusively behavioral science journals and three devote the majority of their space to the behavioral sciences.[3] Of the remaining 11 journals, all but three are either exclusively concerned with behavioral science or dominated by such concerns. Only three journals not dominated by behavioral science—*Business Horizons, Harvard Business Review*, and Michigan State University's *Business Topics*—appear on the list.

From most of these journals it is evident that the academic researcher continues to research the introductory psychology class or the sophomores in management classes, strongly suggesting that his or her erroneous view of management and the natures of subordinates will be perpetuated. The latest issue of the *Academy of Management Journal* at this writing carries an article by James M. McFillen with the enticing title of "Supervisory Power as an Influence in Supervisor-Subordinate Relations."[4] The article starts with the standard references to related experimental efforts. Further on the description of the "methodology" reveals that the subjects were ninety male undergraduate business students who performed for the experiment for *four three-minute periods* and completed a questionnaire for $2.00 plus some academic credit! A search for the original researches cited early in the article as warranting the testing of McFillen's hypothesis reveals further such opportunistic sampling. Six of the seven researches cited use the following as subjects:[5]

1. 60 introductory psychology students at Stanford University.
2. 40 male volunteers from a Dartmouth College introductory psychology course.
3. 10 male undergraduates at the University of California at Los Angeles.

4. 21 male undergraduates at the University of California at Los Angeles.
5. 48 male university freshmen.
6. 200 management undergraduate students.

The seventh study is an analysis of a questionnaire administered to 184 supervisors from five different companies.[6] The continuation of the 'publish-or-perish' syndrome coupled with such myopic views limiting the scope of management research will prevent any significant break-throughs in management theory which might produce meaningful management behavioral change. The management theorists themselves and their editors believe differently. In an article entitled "Management and the New Humanism," the editor of *Administrative Management* predicted, in 1970, drastic changes during the decade: "A profound change in the way management deals with people will become evident in the 1970's."[7] The directions of this profound change he stated as follows: "Management . . . will be more the art of motivating open-ended creativity . . . jobs . . . will be designed more around people's talents and the things they like to do . . . work will be performed less out of duty and more for self-satisfaction."[8]

I can grant that these were the directions of tiny incremental changes, but the profundity was missing. Such predictions spring more from the self-referenced hopes and desires of behavioral scientists than from any real analysis of the forces operating on managers and their environments. And the "rapid-change" predictions for management are not limited to the human relations arena. In their article "The Coming of the New Management," William H. Gruber and John S. Niles predicted great changes in management due to the uses of operations research, systems analysis, computerized information systems, and other management science techniques. They used case examples of business performance improvements which they ascribed, with appropriate reservations, to the use of such techniques. Their prime case example in the banking industry was the North Carolina National Bank. From *Business Week* and other sources the authors gave the main reasons this bank has performed so well. In 1967 the bank introduced a computerized system which provided performance data on 25 profit centers by the third day of each month with below par figures underlined in black. The bank also "pioneered" a system which gives top management profitability by service lines giving top management guidance for determining the bank's funds mix. What the bank appears to have done is to have made a little better use of their computer than was typical at the time. Analyses of profit center performance certainly did not begin with computers and the determination of profitability by product line is hardly an invention of MIS or operations research experts. Their article is sprinkled with predictions of rapid change: ". . . there will be a significant shift toward a Future Firm level (their term for a company using the systems analyses, MIS, operations research, etc.) of management competence during the interval from 1974–1980 . . . We also project a *rapid* movement of firms from the Prior Firm (antique) classification into a Present Firm classification . . . There are several reasons for this forecast of *extraordinary* improvement.[9] (Italics and parenthetical phrases added)

Again, as with predicted changes in the management of human effort, the changes in managements' uses of management science have been in small increments and most of these have been in the use of computers to do more of what managers had been doing all along the hard way, such as general recordkeeping, logistics problem-solving, cost analyses, profitability on various dimensions, etc.

There are evidences from the social sciences themselves, although seldom noted, which portend a very slow rate of change for management. From sociology and anthropology we learned some time ago that society is a semistationary integrated unit and that the introduction of a new element affects other elements. Many elements in the society or culture must be changed to accommodate the new elements and this reordering process is an extremely slow one.[10] From social psychology we have learned that perception is functionally selective and that beliefs and culturally acquired attitudes about leaders and followers play a significant role in determining the nature of this selectivity and tend to determine the meaning of these perceptions. We have learned that the data available to an individual which is contradictory to his or her beliefs and attitutdes will not likely be fully perceived and will be assimilated in such a way that the basic beliefs are not changed. He or she will often simply pay lip service to the new approach, but will not have to make real behavioral changes.[11]

The Ohio State University Studies in the 1950's indicated that human relations training (with role-playing, group discussion, etc.) had no measurable effect on plant behavior after return to work. "The results clearly indicated that the foreman is more responsive to the day-to-day climate in which he operates than to any special course of training he may have been given."[12]

Even the prognosticator in the fields of non-social science and technology, which, incidentally, have probably produced most of the significant changes in human behavior, gets carried away when he addresses the future. Arthur B. Bronwell, in his 1970 preface to *Science and Technology in the World of the Future*, succumbed to the temptation to predict rather rapid direct changes in human behavior. Unmindful of the simple fact that almost all of science and technology's influence has been indirect—interchangeable parts, vaccines which have doubled life expectancies in a couple of decades, the "bomb," and the "pill"—he ignored the fundamental causes of change in human behavior. He made such questionable predictions as this:

Long before the year A.D. 2000, I believe that all the academic disciplines will have developed means of grappling with this fourth dimension of philosophical, speculative, imaginative projectivism, not with certainties. In the process *they will have created the interdisciplinary forums and institutionalisms for the interplay of ideas in the much larger auras of philosophical adventure, lifting man's creative potentials far beyond those possible today.*[13] (Italics added)

The paradox in this forecast is that Bronwell had spent 13 pages explaining that great contributions from science in the past have typically gone unnoticed for long periods. He cites Goddard's 37 years of rocket development and its much later space exploration consequences, and Frank Lloyd Wright's contributions to architectural philosophy which he claims were ignominiously renounced by his profession for decades. The curious aspect of his forecast is that he clearly recognizes that our intellectual disciplines are out of touch with the realities and problems of our times. He fails to note that at the time of his writing in 1970 they were, for the most part, quite out of touch with each other as well. In 1949, I predicted in a term paper as a naive clinical psychology graduate student, that the main hope for dealing effectively with the psychoses and severe neuroses would come "soon" from the psychologists, biochemists, psychiatrists, pharmacologists and endocrinologists getting together. Almost thirty years later, most still keep their distances. In arriving at my prediction, I failed to note how very long it took some of the biologists and chemists, and the geographers and political scientists to get together.

Bronwell's collection of forecasts seems to prove that science and technology experts have some of the same blind spots which afflict the behavioral scientists. Few of them seem willing or interested in dealing with the economic, political, and professional variables which inevitably affect the development and applications of most scientific or technological innovations. Robert A. Nelson and Paul W. Shuldiner in their article in the book blithely ignored operational economics and politics, and then predicted that only sonic booms would temporarily hinder the growth of supersonic air transportation. They also predicted that long before the year 2000, interplanetary travel would be well underway.[14] Since their 1970 predictions we have witnessed cancellations and reductions in these directions based almost entirely on political and economic grounds.

REGRESSIVE INFLUENCES

Fully as heretical as predicting little change is the notion that in some ways management practice may be regressing over the next couple decades. In the area of first-line supervisory development, managements have probably been moving backwards. Many of the middle and upper management development efforts since the 1950's have been at the expense of first-line supervisory training. An analysis of 4,266 articles from 1950–1970 from five journals[15] which typically cover topics pertaining to supervisory and management development revealed a drastic loss of interest in first-line supervisory training. Below are summary statistics from this analysis[16]:

TABLE 21-1
Changes in Literature Coverage of Training Topics 1950-1969

Year	% Supervisory Training	% Management Training	% Operative Training	% Training and Development (Totals)
1950	13	4	3	20
1953	16	11	5	32
1956	15	12	3	30
1959	12	12	3	27
1962	5	13	3	21
1965	3	12	2	17
1968	2	7	3	12
1969	1	10	2	13

A follow-up sampling in 1977 indicated no significant change in the 1969 ratios. Although no research has been done on changes in training departments' budget allocations, my acquaintance with changes in a dozen or so companies' training activities over the years leads me to be convinced that actual training activity ratios follow the literature ratios. And a poll I conducted in an industrial area in Southeastern Ohio tends to confirm this. Of the 153 supervisors polled who attended a program sponsored by the International Management Council in 1973, 101 claimed to have had *no* formal training of any kind during the previous 12 months. Only 30 had had more than six hours of formal training during this period.

The virtual elimination of regular first-line supervisory training in many firms seems to me to be throwing the baby out with the bathwater. The role of the foreman is certainly more complex today than 30 years ago. The work technologies are more complex, motivation of employees more difficult because of affluence, welfare, and changing values about work, and regulations governing supervisory behavior have been increasing exponentially. Failure to provide training support coupled with other reductions in the attractiveness of the first-line supervisory job may account for the steady increase over the years of promotion rejection rates in the firms I am familiar with. One personnel manager claimed that about half of the promotions to supervision offered today are rejected in his company.

I expect managements to eventually respond to this problem by restoring some of the attractiveness to the job. One of the ways they will do this will probably be through providing more support through training. In the meantime, I consider this problem as representing a regressive phenomenon.

Another example of regression, in my opinion, is the middle-managers' loss of confidence in the value of the rather extensive training program packages they have been forced to accept. Many middle-managers have been in the arena long enough to be able to observe personally the extreme faddism in this area. Their acquiescent responses to faddism seem to be regressive. They merely tolerate whatever new training content or program is introduced.

Another regressive trend which has been underway for at least a decade and is likely to continue is managements' withdrawal from efforts at economic education. Their response to the public's increasing overestimation of profit rates (about 700% at this writing) has been less than it was in the early 1950's when this phenomenon was first measured. Their increasing reluctance to speak out on controversial issues of all kinds must be considered regressive also. Our Occupational Safety and Health administrators' searches without warrants or reasons violated managements' rights under the fourth amendment for years before anyone challenged them. And the successful challenge came, not from the sophisticated halls of major American corporations headquarters, but from small Texas and Idaho entrepreneurs.[17] There is little evidence of major challenges by the management community to general governmental encroachments on their environments. And I see nothing on the horizon which suggests any changes in managements' efforts to alter the attitudes of their employees regarding the roles their institutions play in producing jobs and in otherwise benefitting society.

POSITIVE TRENDS

Although small and sometimes unsophisticated, many managements are realizing that it has been possible for years to run operations in such a way that their employees do not feel the need for a union. Union membership in the U.S. remained at about a quarter of the non-farm labor force for about 25 years, and now appears to be dropping slightly. Union representation decertification election results are also moving in managements' favor. In 1968 unions won slightly over 60 percent of these elections compared to only 25% in 1979. This suggests that the knowledge which was available 50 years ago in the many companies which have remained non-union through all the major unionization drives over the years has spread. In addition, it perhaps suggests a beginning of the end of the "I give up" posture which began with the management-born predictions at the passing of the Wagner Act in 1933 that "the unions will be running the country in 5 years." Managements got little help from the behavioral scientist in how to avoid unions, however. The slight pendulum swing away from unionization has come about from operations decentralization, managements doing better the things they had been doing all along, and from unions' failures to take into account changes in the workforce. Through decentralization managements inherited former farmers as employees. They tend to have stronger work ethics and less need for interdependence. Management doing a better job of handling grievances and maintaining rationalized wage and benefit policies have also contributed. Increasing worker affluence and increasing numbers of women and minorities in the U.S. workforce went relatively unnoticed for years by union organizing strategists, if their campaign promises are indicative, and this partly accounts for the lack of membership growth.

It can be expected that overall, little further change will take place in the union/non-union ratio in the U.S. over the next 15–20 years. This is because the additional efforts underway now to campaign against unionization are being partly offset by some contract agreements at "mother" plants which call for the company to refrain from campaigning against unionization at new decentralized plants. And unions can be expected to wake up in a few years to their need to learn how to attract different clienteles to further offset managements' increasing success in unionization elections.

MANAGEMENT MYTHS AND THEIR PERPETUATION

Although there are hints that at the forefront of the art of the practice of management many popular theories about management are losing ground, the overall behavior of managers in general will probably be to perpetuate many more myths. Unfortunately, when one hears an occasional manager rejecting as ineffective such techniques as sensitivity training, he often hears that another fad has replaced it. At this writing, the newest fad-in-the-making on the horizon is Neurolinguistic Programming or NLP as its founders call it. By the time this book reaches the market, managers will be throwing away company funds on this panacea which is guaranteed to make their people better managers, salesmen, engineers, negotiators, buyers, or whatever.

According to an NPL mailer advertising workshops in New York, Tallahassee, Milwaukee, Cincinnati and Ann Arbor, "NPL is a unique model, with techniques that produce exquisitely refined levels of communication and understanding." The flyer also claimed that its record of success ". . . has led to a world-wide demand for training in these concepts and techniques." These "concepts and techniques" turn out to be an elaborate system of notation about how people perceive and organize sensory impressions and how these perceptions lead to a response. Once the student of NLP learns how to "read" people through analyses of how their sensory modes operate, it is a simple matter of then learning how to get what you want out of them—hard work, a sales order, or a concession in negotiations. NPL's co-gurus Richard Bander and John Grinder recently began to franchise their trademark. They train, supervise and certify the franchise-holder for a percentage of the profits. NPL claims a "respectable" academic base from linguistics, body language and communications systems theory. There have been no follow-up studies on NPL's effectiveness, however, even though it has been practiced since 1975. And, as with other behavioral science based fads, it assumes that permanent behavior of the total organism can be reprogrammed in a few training sessions. Its perpetuation will depend upon the tales and testimonials of its success and in a relatively short time we will have another management myth in the making. After NPL has swept through major American corporations, governmental training agencies will install it as standard training fare. Testimonials from industry will make them feel backward if they don't. Shortly thereafter, church organizations will follow, since such a breakthrough can't help but make preachers better at their work. The only major U.S. institution which is likely to avoid wasting its money on NPL or other behavioral science fads is organized labor. Perhaps this is because union leaders would have to justify such expenditures to their memberships. Can you picture a bunch of teamsters or steelworkers authorizing their unions to spend some of their dues money for sensitivity training or transactional analysis for union field representatives or for regional officers? This is possibly because the kind of proof union members would demand of the effectiveness of the training is just not available.

The Nature of Myths

A typical definition of a myth in a standard dictionary would likely refer to a tale having a supernatural frame of reference which serves to sanctify some concept, technique, institution or natural phenomenon. The "tales" in our frame of reference would be the theories, "principles," and techniques on how to manage effectively. The "supernatural frame of reference" would be the awesome intelligence and wisdom of behavioral and management scientists. They are our Zeus who gave birth to Athena (and others) through his cranium, our Argus, whose hundred eyes were transplanted, and our Athena who transformed Arachne into a spider. If management is to eventually become a professionalized occupation, one of its goals must be to avoid the perpetuation of the following myths:

MYTHS ON ORGANIZATIONAL THEORY—Knowledge and application of modern organizational theory is *essential* to effective management. All managers should be trained in modern organization theory so that they can restructure their companies to be consistent with the modern principles of organization which research has shown will improve overall company effectiveness.

—Our antiquated bureaucratic organizational structures must undergo radical change to become organic structures if we are to survive rapid changes in our society already under way. Management must be made aware of the advantages of the organic structure so that changes from the bureaucratic structures can be facilitated.

MYTHS ABOUT THE MANAGEMENT OF CHANGE—The leader has enough power to effectively manage change provided his change model is appropriate for his situation. Behavioral science consultants can determine the appropriate change model for any given management situation.

—Organizational development (OD) has proven its effectiveness in facilitating change. Companies should establish OD departments or hire OD consultants if successful organizational changes are to be made.

—Attitudes of those whose behavior must be changed must first be dealt with. Once attitudes have changed, behavioral change will follow. Managers should practice the use of known effective techniques for changing attitudes before they attempt changes in the behavior of their subordinates.

MYTHS ABOUT MOTIVATION TO WORK—Money no longer motivates. The behavioral approach, because it is rooted in social science and because it concentrates on establishing proper conditions in which human effort can be effective, is the appropriate motivational approach.

—Improved morale through increased job satisfaction leads to improved performance.

—Knowledge of and application of Maslow's need hierarchy is essential to effective management. All managers should be trained in the various techniques discovered through research on Maslow's need hierarchy model. Company personnel policies should be adjusted to be consistent with the model.

—Although only a theory when McGregor first proposed it in the early 1950's, research has shown Theory Y to be the ideal management style. Training in Theory Y concepts and techniques should be a part of all managers' training.

—All employees want to participate in making decisions which affect them or their organization. If they are given this opportunity, they will be committed to their work and therefore perform better.

—The only solutions to the devastating productivity losses through boredom are job enrichment and job enlargement. Once installed, these programs raise worker morale and improve productivity and product quality.

—The only really effective management approach is "Management by Objectives," since it is consistent with modern management motivational principles and can be installed without great difficulty.

—Everyone is potentially very creative and would be motivated to realize their full capabilities if it were not for the stifling factors in their work environment such as tight controls, lack of encouragement, and too much direction from superiors.

—Conflict between individuals, groups and organizational units is invariably dysfunctional and leads to low motivation and poor performance. This is often due to the insensitivities on the part of the managers and these can be corrected by various organizational development techniques.

MYTHS ABOUT MANAGEMENT SCIENCE—The scientific approach to decision-making when learned and adopted by managers vastly improves the quality and timeliness of their decisions. Managers should be trained in such techniques so that their decision-making reflects what management science has contributed to the field.

—The formation of operations research departments represents the quickest way for managements to provide modern scientific approaches to decision-making in their organizations.

MYTHS ABOUT MANAGEMENT INFORMATION SYSTEMS—Management information systems specialists, because of their unique training, are best suited to develop the general information system needed by management in a modern organization.

—The kinds of information required by top management for the effective discharge of their duties can be made available to them through general information systems. Such systems provide easy access to information necessary for forecasting, planning and effective day-to-day managing.

MYTHS ABOUT COMMUNICATIONS—The causes of many organizational problems today are largely caused by faulty communications techniques. The training of managers in the complexity of the *processes* of communications will go far in alleviating these difficulties.

—The training of managers in the importance and techniques of effective listening, interpersonal, intra-group and intergroup communications will result in significant improvements in communications behavior, thus drastically reducing problems resulting from poor communications.

THE UNIVERSALITY AND PROFESSIONALITY MYTHS—Basic management principles are universal; they are relatively unaffected by such variables as technology, culture, political environments, etc.

—Since management has achieved professional status with a common body of knowledge, all present and future managers should be exposed to this knowledge.

THE KEYS TO MYTH REDUCTION FOR THE FUTURE

There are two *theoretical* approaches to the reduction of myths in management: (1) restore the confidence of managers in their common sense born of their native intelligence and their experiences, and (2) convince managers to force the theorists and researchers to relate their work directly to the real life problems facing managers. The reader should note the term "theoretical" carefully. It is used simply because the obstacles to convincing managers thusly are as formidable as those which have prevented managers from making profound changes in their styles as a result of the reading of an article or attending a training program. Still, the main hope for the professionalization of the occupation is, from my viewpoint, the straight-forward exposé by managers of theories supported by questionable or lack of evidence. The motivation to expose them must spring from the recognition that these theories are mainly the result of self-referenced desires of the theorists and the obvious gullibility of the practitioners. And I must add with considerable reluctance that from a scientific standpoint, we know very little about the elimination of gullibility.

NOTES

1. *Time*, October 16, 1978, p. 106.
2. *Ibid.*, p. 108.
3. They are in ranked order as follows: *The Administrative Science Quarterly, Journal of Applied Psychology, Organizational Behavior and Human Performance, Academy of Management Journal, Human Relations, Personnel Psychology, Industrial Relations,* and *The Journal of Applied Behavioral Science.* Source: Letter to Academy of Management members, August, 1978.
4. James M. McFillen, "Supervisory Power as an Influence in Supervisor-Subordinate Relations," *Academy of Management Journal,* Vol. 21, No. 3 (September, 1978), pp. 419–433.
5. M. Rothbart, "Effects of Motivation, Equity, and Compliance on the Use of Reward and Punishment," *Journal of Personality and Social Psychology,* Vol. 9 (1968), pp. 353–362; J. T. Lanzetta and T. E. Hannah, "Reinforcing Behavior of Naive Trainers," *Journal of Personality and Social Psychology,* Vol. II (1969), pp. 245–252; A. W. Kruglanski, "Attributing Trustworthiness in Supervisory-Worker Relations," *Journal of Experimental Social Psychology,* Vol. 6 (1970), pp. 214–232, (Samples nos. 3 and 4 were used in the Kruglanski article); D. Kipnis and A. J. Cosenting, "Use of Leadership Powers in Industry," *Journal of Applied*

Psychology, Vol. 53 (1969), pp. 460–466; B. Goodstadt and D. Kipnis, "Situational Influences on the Use of Power," *Journal of Applied Psychology*, Vol. 54 (1970), pp. 201–207.

6. G. F. Farris and F. G. Lin, "Effects of Performance on Leadership, Cohesiveness, Influence, Satisfaction, and Subsequent Performance," *Journal of Applied Psychology*, Vol. 53 (1969), pp. 490–497.

7. Walter A. Kleinschrod, "Management and the New Humanism," *Administrative Management*, Vol. 31 (January, 1970), pp. 24–25.

8. *Ibid.*, p. 25.

9. William H. Gruber and John S. Niles, "The Coming of the New Management," *Organizational Dynamics*, Spring 1974, p. 73.

10. William F. Ogburn and Meyer F. Nimkoff, *Sociology*, (New York, N.Y.: Houghton-Mifflin Company, 1946), pp. 880–882.

11. David Krech and Richard S. Crutchfield, *Theory and Problems of Social Psychology*, (New York, N.Y.: McGraw-Hill, 1948), pp. 190–192.

12. Edwin A. Fleishman, Edwin F. Harris, and Harold E. Burtt, *Leadership and Supervision in Industry: An Evaluation of Supervisory Training Programs*, Monograph No. 33, (Columbus, Ohio, Bureau of Educational Research, Ohio State University, 1955), p. 94.

13. Arthur B. Bronwell, *Science and Technology in the World of the Future*, (New York, N.Y.: John Wiley and Sons, 1970), p. xv.

14. *Ibid.*, pp. 95–125.

15. *Training and Development Journal, Personnel, Personnel Journal, Personnel Administration*, and *Personnel Management Abstracts*.

16. James A. Lee and John E. Stinson, "The Deemphasis of Supervisory Training," *Training and Development Journal*, February, 1975, p. 39.

17. James Kilpatrick, "One Small Kick in OSHA's Rear," *Athens Messenger*, January, 1977.

NAME INDEX

A

Adam, Everett E., 147fn
Adams, J. S., 128, 147fn
Aiken, E. G., 119fn
Alderfer, Clayton P., 73fn
Alexander the Great, 233
Alexander, Tom, 173, 192fn
Alford, L. P., 146fn
Alvarez, D., 231fn
Andreski, Stanislav, 6, 8, 9, 11, 21fn, 101, 103fn, 107, 120fn
Antonetti, J., 299fn
Argyle, Michael, 54, 59fn
Argyris, Chris, 63, 266, 267, 276fn, 300fn
Aristotle, 41, 72, 73fn
Aronson, Elliot, 119fn
Atkinson, J. W., 62, 74, 78, 85, 86, 87, 88, 89fn, 90fn, 103fn, 106, 107
Aver, E., 32

B

Babbage, Charles, 25
Bander, Richard, 463
Bardeen, J. P., 171fn
Barnard, Chester, 227, 231fn, 232fn
Barnes, Louis B., 236, 254fn
Barnlund, Dean C., 163, 171fn
Barth, Carl, 35, 40fn, 300fn
Bass, Bernard, 228, 230, 232fn
Bauer, Alice, 237, 254fn
Bauer, Raymond, 237, 254fn
Baxter, J. C., 310fn
Beach, Dale S., 218fn
Beer, M., 73fn
Behling, Orlando, X, 100, 103fn, 113, 114, 115, 118, 120fn
Bendix, Reinhard, 217fn
Bennis, Warren, X, 63, 192fn. 199, 200, 218fn, 255fn, 275fn, 276fn
Berelson, Bernard, 109, 110, 120fn, 156, 170fn, 174, 255fn
Berg, P. O., 241, 254fn
Berger, Phillip K., 89fn
Berlew, David, 79, 89fn

Biderman, Albert D., 170fn
Blackett, P. M. S., 38
Blake, Robert R., 170fn
Blanchard, Kenneth, 102fn, 254fn
Blum, Milton L., 39fn
Bowers, David G., 254fn
Bradburn, N. M., 89fn
Bradford, 79
Brayfield, A. H., 94, 95, 96, 102fn, 104
Bronwell, A. B., 459, 467fn
Brooker, W. M. A., 312, 315fn
Brown, Philip J., 218fn
Brussell, E. E., 314fn
Burtt, H. E., 231fn, 467fn
Butterfield, Alexander, 219
Byrd, R. E., 300fn
Byrne, Donn, 58fn
Byron, 251

C

Caesar, Julius, 221
Cammann, Cortlandt, 148fn
Campbell, John P., 242, 254fn
Caplow, Theodore, 455
Capwell, D. F., 102fn
Carey, Alex, X, 6, 44, 47, 48, 54, 55, 58fn, 59fn
Carlson, Robert, 168-169, 171fn
Carroll, S. J., 281, 282, 299fn, 300fn
Carter, L., 230fn
Cartwright, Dorwin, 173, 191fn, 192fn
Castro, Fidel, 189
Cato, 25, 278
Cecil, Earl A., 193fn
Chamberlain, J., 148fn
Champoux, Joseph E., 102fn
Chase, Stuart, 43, 45, 46, 58fn
Chemers, Martin M., 225, 231fn
Chertkoff, Jerome M., 193fn
Chesser, R. J., 300fn
Christ, 251
Clark, J. V., 70, 73fn
Cleveland, Harlan, 219, 230fn
Cleveland, President, 28
Conrad, Simon, 32

SUBJECT INDEX

480